The Best Bed &

England • Scotland

1996

Sigourney Welles

Jill Darbey

Joanna Mortimer

The finest Bed & Breakfast accommodation in the

British Isles

from the Hebrides to Belgravia

Country Houses, Town Houses, City Apartments, Manor
Houses, Village Cottages, Farmhouses, Castles.

U.K.H.M. Publishing. London, U.K.

1

© U.K.H.M. Publishing Ltd. 1996

U.K.H.M. Publishing Ltd.

P.O. Box 2070,

London W12 8QW

England.

The publishers have made every reasonable effort to ensure that the accommodation mentioned in this guide are as stated, however the Publishers cannot accept liability for any inaccuracies, errors or omissions that may occur.

U.K. ISBN 0-907500-53-6

Front Cover: The Grange. Fort William. Scotland.

Typeset by U.K.H.M. Publishing Ltd.London.

Printed by Mandarin Offset Ltd. Hong Kong.

Hatpins. Old Bosham.

St. Peters House. Spexhall.

Contents

Higher House. West Bagborough.

Foreword

Bed & Breakfast has suddenly become the fashionable way to travel. The secret has escaped & thousands of people are discovering for themselves that it is possible to combine high quality accommodation with friendly, personal attention at very reasonable prices. The New York Times said about us that "...after an unannounced inspection of rooms booked through The Worldwide Bed & Breakfast Association it is clear that the standards of comfort & cleanliness are exemplary ...at least as good as in a five star hotel & in most cases, better, reflecting the difference between sensitive hosts taking pride in their homes & itinerant hotel staff doing as little as they can get away with..."

Discerning travellers are turning away from the impersonal hotels with the expensive little refridgerators & microwave breakfasts in each room. How much nicer to have a real English breakfast to begin the day, enough to keep you going until evening. Many of our houses will provide dinner too - often the hostess will be a Cordon Bleu cook & the price will be within your range. We try to provide the best accommodation possible within a wide range of prices, some as little as £12.00 per person per night, whilst others will be up to £55.00 per person per night. The choice is yours, but you can be certain that each will be the best available in that particular area of the country at that price.

Our inspectors are out & about visiting our homes to ensure that standards are maintained. We encourage everyone to use the recommendations & complaints page at the back of the book. Let us know your opinion of the accommodation or inform us of any delightful homes you may have come across & would like to recommend for future inclusion.

In order to avoid the classification trap, which we feel is invidious, we encourage you to read about each home, what they offer & their respective price range, so that you find the one that best suits your expectations. Our hosts in turn offer hospitality in their own unique style, so each home naturally retains its individuality & interest. We have found this to be a very successful recipe which has often led to firm friendships with invitations being extended to visit each other again.

Bed & Breakfast really is a marvellous way to travel, meeting a delightful cross section of fellow travellers with whom to exchange information & maybe the address of ...that lovely little place which was discovered by chance and which serves the most delicious dinner or... the best route to take to a particular farmhouse but make sure you get there by 5 o'clock so that you're in time to watch the evening milking...

This is the fun & real pleasure that is part of Bed & Breakfasting. Once you've tried it you will be a dedicated Best Bed & Breakfaster.

How to use this Guide

To get the full benefits of staying at our Bed & Breakfast homes it is important to appreciate how they differ from hotels, so both hosts & guests know what to expect.

Arrival & Departure

These times are more important to a family than to hotel desk clerks, so your time of arrival (E.T.A.) is vital information when making a reservation either with the home directly or with one of our agencies. This becomes even more important to your reception if you intend travelling overnight & will be arriving in the early morning. So please have this information & your flight number ready when you book your rooms. Under most circumstances the usual check-in time is 6 p.m., & you will be expected to check out by 10a.m. on the morning of departure. These arrangements do vary from home to home so the secret to an enjoyable visit is to let your hosts know as much about your plans as possible & they will do their best to meet your requirements.

Other personal requests

There are a few other details that you should let your hosts know when planning your Bed & Breakfast trip that will make everyone much happier during your visit.

* Do you smoke? Would you prefer to be in a non-smoking home?

* Do you suffer from any allergies? Some families have cats, dogs, birds & other pets in the house.

* Can you make it up a flight of stairs? Would you prefer the ground floor?

* Do you have any special dietary requirements? Will you be staying for dinner?

* Do you prefer a private bathroom or are you prepared to share facilities?

* Do you prefer a shower instead of a bath?

* The ages of any children travelling

In all these cases let your host know what you need & the details can be arranged before you arrive rather than presenting a problem when you are shown to your rooms.

Prices

The prices quoted throughout the guide are the *minimum* per person per night. These prices will increase during the busy seasons. You should always confirm the prevailing rate when you make a reservation.

Facilities

The bathroom & toilet facilities effect the prices. Sharing is the cheapest, private is a little more costly & en-suite carries a premium.

Descriptions

Rooms are described as follows: Single = 1 bed (often quite small); Double = 1 large bed (sometimes King or Queen size); Twin = 2 separate single beds; Four-poster = a King or Queen size bed with a canopy above supported by four corner posts.

Bathrooms & toilets are described as follows: Shared = these facilities are shared with some other guests or perhaps the hosts; Private = for your use only, however they may occasionally be in an adjacent room; En-suite = private facilities within your bedroom suite.

Widbrook Grange. Widbrook.

Making a Reservation

Once you have chosen where you want to stay, have all the following information ready & your reservation will go smoothly without having to run & find more travel documents or ask someone else what they think you should do. Here is a brief check list of what you will probably be asked & examples to illustrate answers:

* Dates & number of nights .... August 14-19 (6 nights).
* Estimated time of arrival at the home ....7 p.m. (evening) & flight number.
* Type & number of rooms.... 1 Double & 2 Singles.
* Toilet & Bathroom facilities ...1 Double en-suite) & 2 singles (shared)
* Smoking or Non-smoking?
* Any allergies?
* Special dietary requests?
* Children in the party & their ages?
* Any other preferences .... Is a shower preferred to a bath?
* Maximum budget per person per night based on all the above details.

London Reservations
There is a two night minimum stay at our London Homes

These can only be made through one of the Worldwide Bed & Breakfast Agencies. A list appears overleaf & they can be contacted by phone or fax.

All reservations must be confirmed with advance payments which are non-refundable in the event of cancellation & you simply pay the balances due after you arrive at the home. The advance payment can be made with the major credit & charge cards or by cheque. Cash is the preferred method of paying the balance & always in pounds sterling.

The advance payments confirm each night of your visit - **not just the first one.** When arriving at a later date or departing at an earlier date than those confirmed, the guest will be liable to pay only the appropriate proportion of the stated balance that is due, For example, staying three nights out of four booked means paying 3/4 of the stated balance due. A minimum of 2 nights will always apply.

Outside London

We encourage you to make use of the information in this guide & contact the homes directly. The hosts may require varying amounts of advance payments & may or may not accept credit & charge cards.

If you wish one of the agencies to make the reservations for you there will be a standard booking fee of £15 (or currency equivalent) for each location confirmed & the entire cost must be paid in advance. This full payment can be charged to a major credit card or paid by cheque. The confirmed prices shall be those prevailing on the dates required ... as previously mentioned, *the prices shown in this guide are the minimum & will increase during the busy seasons.*

Alterations

If you wish to alter or change a previously confirmed booking through one of the agencies there will be a further fee of £15 per alteration.

Cancellations

All advance payments for London are non-refundable.

All booking fees Outside London are non-refundable.

Notice of cancellation must be given as soon as possible & the following suggested rates shall apply **outside London only**

50 days notice - Full refund.

30-49 days notice - 80% refund.

10-29 days notice - 50% refund

0-9 days notice - No refund.

The Worldwide Bed & Breakfast Agencies reserve the right to alter your accommodation should it be necessary & will inform you of any alteration as soon as possible.

The Discount Offer

This offer is made to people who have bought this book & wish to make reservations for Bed & Breakfast in London through one of our participating agencies listed below.

The offer only applies to a minimum stay of three consecutive nights at one of our London homes between the following January 1. 1996 & April 15. 1996 then from September 15 .1996 to December 1. 1996. Only one discount per booking is allowed. Call the reservation office to make your booking in the normal way & tell the clerk that you have bought the book & wish to have the discount. After a couple of questions the discount will be deducted from the advance payment required to confirm the reservation.

Participating Agencies

In the U.K. call:

Tel: 0181 742 9123 (24 Hrs.)

Fax: 0181 749 7084

Outside the U.K. call:

Tel: 44 181 742 9123 (24 Hrs.)

Fax: 44 181 749 7084

In the U.S call: Toll Free 800 852 2632

Look for this symbol

Counties map

Each county has been assigned a page number where a more detailed map can be found. These maps include principal towns, major roads & the location of each Bed & Breakfast establishment.

WESTERN ISLES

SUTHERLAND

ROSS-SHIRE

HIGHLAND

ISLE of SKYE **559**

INVERNESS **554**

ABERDEENSHIRE **536**

GRAMPIAN

SCOTLAND
533

PERTHSHIRE **561**

536

TAYSIDE

ARGYLL

CENTRAL

FIFESHIRE **552**

Edinburgh **543**

LOTHIAN **559**

Berwickshire **541**

DUMBARTON **543**
LANARKSHIRE
AYRESHIRE **539**
STRATHCLYDE

SELKIRK
PEEBLES **568**
ROXBURGHSHIRE
BORDER

NORTHUMBERLAND

DUMFRIES & **541**
GALLOWAY

TYNE AND WEAR
340

CUMBRIA
120

DURHAM   CLEVELAND

North Sea

YORKSHIRE

LANCASHIRE
301

HUMBERSIDE **497**

Irish Sea

MERSEYSIDE

MANCHESTER

ENGLAND

CHESHIRE **87**

CLWYD **578**

GWYNEDD

591

DERBYSHIRE
&
STAFFORD-
SHIRE **378**

155

NOTT-
INGHAM
&
LEICESTER-
SHIRE

309

LINCOLNSHIRE
317

NORFOLK
324

SHROP-
SHIRE

608
POWYS

WARWICK-
SHIRE **455**

CAMBRIDGE-
SHIRE
& NORTHAMPTON-
SHIRE **78**

SUFFOLK
413

HEREFORD
&
WORCESTER **265**

WALES
582 **576**
DYFED

226

GWENT **586**

GLOUCESTER
SHIRE

OXFORD
SHIRE **357**

BEDFORDSHIRE,
BERKSHIRE,
BUCKINGHAMSHIRE,
&
HERTFORDSHIRE **66**

ESSEX
219

584
GLAMORGAN

AVON **34**

WILTSHIRE
476

LONDON
18

SURREY **423**

KENT
279

HAMPSHIRE
251

SUSSEX
433

SOMERSET
393

DORSET
204

DEVON
169

CORNWALL **96**

English Channel

Regions

To assist tourists with information during their travels, counties have been grouped together under Regional Tourist Boards that co-ordinate the various efforts of each county.

The British Tourist Authority has designated these areas in consultation with the English, Scottish & Wales Tourist Boards & we have largely adopted these areas for use in this guide

Counties are listed alphabetically throughout our guide & then have a sub heading indicating which Tourist Region they belong to.

ENGLAND
Cumbria
County of Cumbria
Northumbria.
Counties of Cleveland, Durham, Northumberland, Tyne & Wear.
North West
Counties of Cheshire, Greater Manchester, Lancashire, Merseyside, High Peaks of Derbyshire.
Yorkshire & Humberside
Counties of North Yorkshire, South Yorkshire, West Yorkshire, Humberside.
Heart of England
Counties of Gloucestershire, Herefordshire & Worcestershire, Shropshire, Staffordshire, Warwickshire, West Midlands.
East Midlands
Counties of Derbyshire, Leicestershire, Lincolnshire, Northamptonshire, Nottinghamshire.
East Anglia
Counties of Cambridgeshire, Essex, Norfolk, Suffolk.
West Country
Counties of Avon, Cornwall, Devon, Dorset (parts of), Somerset, Wiltshire, Isles of Scilly.
Southern
Counties of Hampshire, Dorset (East & North), Isle of Wight.
South East
Counties of East Sussex,Kent, Surrey West Sussex.

SCOTLAND
The subdivisions of Scottish Regions in this guide differ slightly from the current Marketing Regions of the Scottish Tourist Board.

The Borders, Dumfries & Galloway
Districts & counties of Scottish Borders, Dumfries & Galloway.
Lothian & Strathclyde
City of Edinburgh, Forth Valley, East Lothian, Kirkaldy, St. Andrews & North-East Fife, Greater Glasgow, Clyde Valley, Ayrshire & Clyde Coast, Burns Country.
Argyll & The Isles
Districts & counties of Oban & Mull, Mid Argyll, Kintyre & Islay, Dunoon, Cowal, Rothesay & Isle of Bute, Isle of Arran.
Perthshire, Loch Lommond & The Trossachs.
Districts & counties of Perthshire, Loch Lomond, Stirling & Trossachs.
The Grampians
Districts & counties of Banff & Buchan, Moray, Gordon, Angus, City of Aberdeen, Kincardine & Deeside, City of Dundee.
The Highlands & Islands
Districts & counties of Shetland, Orkney, Caithness, Sutherland, Ross & Cromarty, Western Isles, South West Ross & Isle of Skye, Inverness, Loch Ness & Nairn, Aviemore & Spey Valley, Fort William & Lochaber.

WALES
The regions are defined as follows:
North Wales
Counties of Clwyd & Gwynedd (northern)
Mid Wales
Counties of Gwynedd (southern), Dyfed (northern) & Powys (northern)
South Wales
Counties of Gwent, West, South & Mid Glamorgan, Dyfed (southern) & Powys (southern).

The photographs appearing in the Introductions & Gazeteers are by courtesy of the appropriate Tourist Board for each county or W.W.B.B.A.

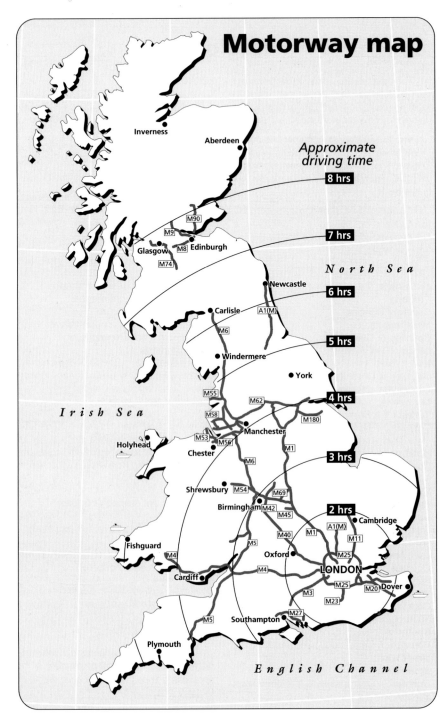

Motorway map

Approximate driving time

8 hrs
7 hrs
6 hrs
5 hrs
4 hrs
3 hrs
2 hrs

North Sea

Irish Sea

English Channel

Inverness
Aberdeen
M90
M9
M8 Edinburgh
Glasgow
M74
Newcastle
Carlisle
A1(M)
M6
Windermere
York
M55
M62
M58
M180
M53
Manchester
Holyhead
M56
Chester
M1
M6
Shrewsbury
M54
M69
Birmingham
M42
M45
Cambridge
A1(M)
M40
M1
M11
M5
M25
Fishguard
M4
Oxford
LONDON
Cardiff
M4
M25
M3
M20 Dover
M23
M5
Southampton
M27
Plymouth

General Information

To help overseas visitors with planning their trip to Britain, we have compiled the next few pages explaining the basic requirements & customs you will find here.

Before you arrive

Documents you will have to obtain before you arrive;

Valid passports & visas. Citizens of Commonwealth countries or the U.S.A. don't need visas to enter the U.K.

Bring your local Driving Licence.

Medical Insurance.

This is strongly recommended although visitors will be able to receive free emergency treatment. If you have to stay in hospital in the U.K. you will be asked to pay unless you are a citizen of European Community Countries.

Restrictions on arrival

Immigration procedures can be lengthy & bothersome, be prepared for questions like:

a) where are you staying in the U.K.?

b) do you have a round trip ticket?

c) how long do you intend to stay?

d) how much money are you bringing in with you?

e) do you have a credit card?

Do not bring any animals with you as they are subject to 6 months quarantine & there are severe penalties for bringing in pets without appropriate licences. Do not bring any firearms, prohibited drugs or carry these things for anyone else. If you are in doubt about items in your possession, declare them by entering the Red Channel at Customs & seek the advice of an officer.

After you have arrived

You can bring in as much currency as you like. You can change your own currency or travellers cheques at many places at varying rates.

Airports tend to be the most expensive places to change money & the 'Bureau de Change" are often closed at nights. So bring enough Sterling to last you at least 2 or 3 days. Banks often charge commission for changing money. Some Cashcard machines (or A.T.M.'s) will dispense local currency using your charge card, if they are affiliated systems, & don't charge commissions to your account.

Major credit cards/charge cards are widely accepted & you may only need to carry small amounts of cash for "pocket money".

Driving

Don't forget to drive on the Left... especially the first time you get into a car... at the airport car hire parking lot... or from the front of a railway station... or straight after breakfast... old habits are hard to shake off. If you need to know the rules, get a copy of the Highway Code. You must wear a seat belt & so must any other front seat passenger. The speed limits are clearly shown in most areas - generally 30 mph. in residential areas (48 kph) & 70 mph on motorways (113 kph.). Traffic lights are at the side of the road & not hanging overhead. Car hire is relatively expensive in the U.K. & it is often a good idea to arrange this before you arrive. Mileage charges, V.A.T. (Sales Tax) & insurance are usually charged extra & you will need to be over 21 to hire a car in the U.K. Petrol (gas) is also relatively expensive & you may find petrol stations hard to find or closed at night in rural areas... so fill up often. Driving in London is not a recommended experience for newcomers & parking is also a very complex arrangement which can become a nightmare if the car gets "clamped" (immobilised) or towed away.

General Information

Buses & Coaches

If you are not driving & only want to travel 5-10 miles there are good bus services within most towns & cities, however, rural routes have seriously declined over the last few years. There are regular & fast coach services between the major towns which are very popular - so book ahead to be sure of a seat.

Trains

There is an extensive railway system throughout the U.K. which serves the major towns on a fast & frequent basis. British Rail is a relatively expensive service & like most railway systems subject to delays.

However, if you plan to do lots of rail travel the best deal is to buy a Britrail Pass before you leave home (you can't buy these once in the U.K.)

Tubes (Subways)

London is the only city with an extensive subway system although some other towns do have "Metro" trains of linked under & overground systems.

The "tube" is a very popular means of getting around London, but it can get very crowded & unpleasant at "rush hours". It is often the preferred way to get into London from say Heathrow airport in the early morning, when there are long delays on the roads that hold up both buses & taxis with increasingly expensive rides into the city centre, £25 is not unusual for this cab fare, compared with a few pounds on the "tube". The "tube" in London is operated by London Transport which also operates the London bus service ... the famous red buses. They sell tickets which allow you to travel all over London on tubes, buses & trains at very good rates, called Travelcards... a transfer system. Ask your local travel agent about these & other travel passes throughout the U.K.

Telephones

-When calling the U.K. from abroad always drop the 0 from the area code. In the U.K. the only free calls are the operator - 100, enquiries - 192 (international 153), emergencies - 999.

You may use your calling card to call home which is billed to your account or call collect, ask the operator to "reverse charge" the call. The famous red telephone kiosks are slowly being replaced with new glass booths & they differ in that the old boxes only take 10 & 50 pence pieces & don't give any change, whereas the new ones take many combinations of coins & do give change. Phonecards are becoming more popular as the number of boxes that only accept these cards increases. Cards can be bought at Post Offices & many newsagents & shops.

Doctors/Chemists

All local police stations have lists of chemists & doctors should you need one, at night, for instance.

Voltage

The standard voltage throughout the country is 240v AC.50Hz. If you bring small electrical appliances with you, a converter will be required.

Tipping

Is not obligatory anywhere but a general guide if you wish to leave a tip for service is between 10%-15%.

Pubs

Most open between 11 a.m. & 11 p.m. every day.
You must be over 18 years old to buy & drink alcohol in pubs .

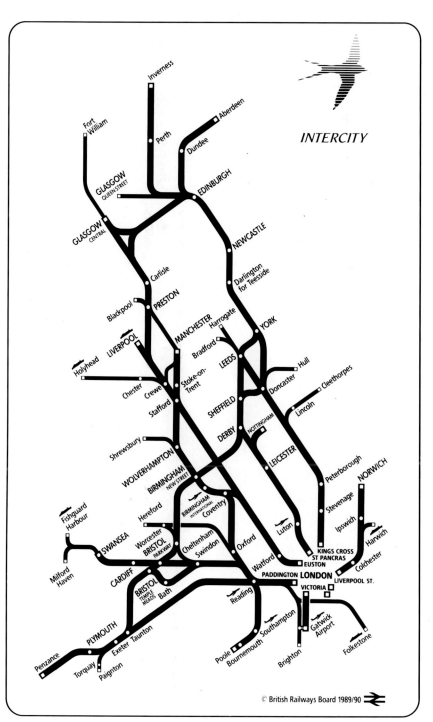

INTERCITY

© British Railways Board 1989/90

LONDON MAP

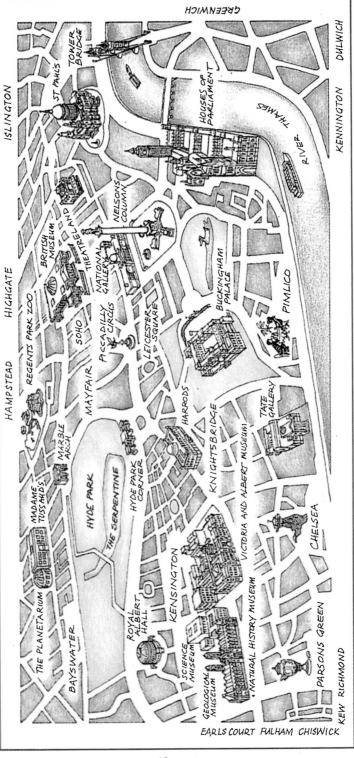

UNDERGROUND

91/1258

	Nearest Tube / Description	rate from £ per person	children taken	evening meals	animals taken
Home No. 03 W.W.B.B.A. London Tel: 0181-742-9123 (24hrs.) Fax: 0181-749-7084 U.S. Toll Free 800-852-2632	Nearest Tube: Parsons Green. Located less than two minutes walk from the underground, in a quiet & leafy street in Parsons Green. A comfortable Victorian terraced house which is delightfully furnished & decorated to a high standard. The charming hosts offer two twin-bedded rooms, 1 with access to own garden, both have en-suite bathroom, colour T.V. & hairdryer. The enjoyment of your stay is the first consideration of the hosts. Only 20 minutes from Piccadilly, Knightsbridge & Buckingham Palace.	£25.00	N	N	N
Home No. 07 W.W.B.B.A. London Tel: 0181-742-9123 (24hrs.) Fax: 0181-749-7084 U.S. Toll Free 800-852-2632	Nearest Tube: Turnham Green. Located in the leafy suburb of Chiswick - a conservation area - close to the tube station & within easy reach of Heathrow & central London. This large Victorian family residence, has many antiques, & offers 1 double bedded guest room situated on the first floor with private bathroom. Tastefully furnished with all the comforts of home, including colour T.V. & tea/coffee-making facilities. A full English breakfast is served.	£25.00	Y	N	N
Home No. 11 W.W.B.B.A. London Tel: 0181-742-9123 (24hrs.) Fax: 0181-749-7084 U.S. Toll Free 800-852-2632	Nearest Tube: Barons Court. A very pretty town house on 3 floors in a private square, only two minutes walk from the underground & less than 7 minutes to Harrods. The charming hostess offers a most attractive newly decorated twin & single room. Ideal for parties of 3. A comfortable lounge for guests use with antiques, china & many books. A cosy kitchen/dining room where breakfast is served & a pretty garden. The house is on a direct underground line from Heathrow.	£25.00	N	N	N
Home No. 15 W.W.B.B.A. London Tel: 0181-742-9123 (24hrs.) Fax: 0181-749-7084 U.S. Toll Free 800-852-2632	Nearest Tube: Parsons Green. Situated in fashionable Parsons Green & located only minutes from the tube. This friendly host offers 1 comfortable twin bedded room with private shower & 1 single bedded room. Ideal for parties of three. A continental breakfast is served. An excellent base from which to go sight-seeing around London. Many varied restaurants & interesting antique shops close by.	£25.00	Y	N	N
Home No. 18 W.W.B.B.A. London Tel: 0181-742-9123 (24hrs.) Fax: 0181-749-7084 U.S. Toll Free 800-852-2632	Nearest Tube: High St. Ken. A beautiful house, furnished with many interesting paintings & situated in the heart of Kensington. The charming host offers 1 light & airy, twin bedded room with a good private bathroom. There is also another, equally attractive twin bedded room, across the hall, which is ideal for a third or fourth member of the party. Each bedroom is well-furnished & a T.V. is available. Only a short walk from the High Street with its many shops & restaurants & within easy reach of Kensington Palace & gardens, Knightsbridge & the museums.	£28.00	N	N	N

London

			rate from £ per person	children taken	evening meals	animals taken

Home No. 19
W.W.B.B.A.
London
Tel: 0181-742-9123 (24hrs.)
Fax: 0181-749-7084
U.S. Toll Free
800-852-2632

Nearest Tube: Parsons Green
Located in the quiet Parsons Green area of Fulham. This superb house offers accommodation in 1 king-size bedded room with private facilities & 2 double rooms with shared bathroom. Each room is beautifully decorated & comfortably furnished. This is an ideal home for visitors to London. Buckingham Palace & Knightsbridge are only 15 minutes away by tube.

£25.00 — N — N — N

Home No. 20
W.W.B.B.A.
London
Tel: 0181-742-9123 (24hrs.)
Fax: 0181-749-7084
U.S. Toll Free
800-852-2632

Nearest Tube: Camden Town
A Regency terraced house set in a quiet leafy street very close to Regents Park. A beautiful double or twin room with walk-in wardrobe & an adjoining bathroom complete with shower. 1 small but attractive double room looking into a conservatory & garden. Ideal for parties of 2 or more. 3 mins. from underground & 15 mins. from Knightsbridge. From here guests can easily walk to Regent Street & Piccadilly. Several excellent restaurants are nearby.

£30.00 — Y — N — N

(no smoking symbol)

Home No. 22
W.W.B.B.A.
London
Tel: 0181-742-9123 (24hrs.)
Fax: 0181-749-7084
U.S. Toll Free
800-852-2632

Nearest Tube: Notting Hill Gate
A delightful cottage in the heart of Bayswater offering self-catering accommodation in 2 twin-bedded rooms, which are prettily decorated to reflect the cottage atmosphere. An attractive living room, most comfortably furnished with spacious dining area. A fully fitted kitchen. Ideal for a family or two couples. Well appointed for visiting all the sights of London.

£25.00 — Y — N — N

Home No. 26
W.W.B.B.A.
London
Tel: 0181-742-9123 (24hrs.)
Fax: 0181-749-7084
U.S. Toll Free
800-852-2632

Nearest Tube: Holland Park
A lovely modern townhouse set in a private & quiet garden square, which has been stylishly decorated, & offers 3 delightful guest rooms. Each room has private or en-suite bathroom, colour T.V. & tea/coffee facilities. Pretty garden views. Convenient for all that London has to offer, this home has the added bonus of private parking, enabling you to leave your car & explore at a leisurely pace. Many shops & restaurants, & pretty Holland Park are close by. Easy access to Heathrow, Harrods & the West End.

£30.00 — Y — N — N

Home No. 29
W.W.B.B.A.
London
Tel: 0181-742-9123 (24hrs)
Fax: 0181-749-7084
U.S. Toll Free
800-852-2632

Nearest Tube: East Putney
Located in the residential area of Putney, this is a lovely Victorian house set in a quiet street - yet only 20 mins. to central London by tube. The charming & helpful host offers 2 beautiful guest rooms, 1 a spacious double/twin & the other a double overlooking the rear garden; ideal for parties of 2 or more. Guests have their own private bathroom. A delicious & varied breakfast is served. Many good local pubs & restaurants.

£27.00 — Y — N — N

London

Home No. 33 **W.W.B.B.A.** **London** **Tel: 0181-742-9123 (24hrs.)** **Fax: 0181-749-7084** **U.S. Toll Free** **800-852-2632**	Nearest Tube: Holland Park A lovely home centrally situated in Holland Park offering 2 very attractive rooms. 1 a Kingsize double with en-suite jacuzzi, power shower & cable T.V., & 1 double/twin with en-suite bathroom & power shower. Each room is furnished with comfort in mind, fresh flowers & overhead fans etc.. The Gathering Room is an elegant & yet comfortable room with large fireplace, overlooks the patio where breakfast can be served in summer. Easy access to Knightsbridge, West End & Oxford. Heathrow Airbus stops nearby.	£35.00	Y	Y	N
Home No. 34 **W.W.B.B.A.** **London** **Tel: 0181-742-9123 (24hrs.)** **Fax: 01810749-7084** **U.S. Toll Free** **800-8952-2632**	Nearest Tube: Earls Court A beautifully furnished apartment situated in a peaceful square, yet only a few minutes walk from the tube station. The charming host offers 1 very attractive double/twin bedded room, tastefully furnished with many interesting pictures & curios. A private bathroom is just a few steps away. This is a delightful base from which to explore London, with easy access to Chelsea, Knightsbridge, South Kensington & the museums, & Victoria. Many good restaurants locally. Children over 12 years.	£30.00	Y	N	N
Home No. 39 **W.W.B.B.A.** **London** **Tel: 0181-742-9123 (24hrs.)** **Fax: 0181-749-7084** **U.S. Toll Free** **800-852-2632**	Nearest Tube: Earls Court A superb home, designer decorated & furnished to the highest standard with antiques throughout. 2 double & 1 twin bedded rooms. Each beautiful bedroom is large & airy with a lovely bathroom en-suite, T.V. & tea/coffee facilities. A large dining room. A delightful garden where breakfast can be served if the weather is good. Guests have their own private entrance. Only 10 mins. to Harrods. Children over 12 years. *see PHOTO over*	£38.00	Y	N	N
Home No. 40 **W.W.B.B.A.** **London** **Tel: 0181-742-9123 (24hrs.)** **Fax: 0181-749-7084** **U.S. Toll Free** **800-852-2632**	Nearest Tube: Gunnersbury A large Victorian residence, with garden, only a few minutes walk from the tube station, with easy access to Heathrow, central London, Richmond & beautiful Kew Gardens. The charming host offers 2 spacious guest rooms suitable for doubles or twins & ideal for families. Each room has an en-suite bathroom, T.V., tea/coffee-making facilities & are decorated in natural tones with stripped pine. Children are especially welcome.	£25.00	Y	N	N
Home No. 42 **W.W.B.B.A.** **London** **Tel: 0181-742-9123 (24hrs.)** **Fax: 0181-749-7084** **U.S. Toll Free** **800-852-2632**	Nearest Tube: Parsons Green A large Victorian house, situated in a quiet street, only 5 mins walk from the station. Pleasantly furnished & decorated, there is a comfortable twin bedded room, located on the 1st floor which overlooks the rear garden. A private bathroom is just a few steps away. There is also a double room available on the top floor for another member of the party. Parsons Green is an attractive area with many excellent shops & restaurants, & has good access to central London. Children welcome.	£25.00	Y	N	N

Home No. 39. London.

	rate from £ per person	children taken	evening meals	animals taken
Home No. 45 **W.W.B.B.A.** **London** **Tel: 0181-742-9123 (24hrs.)** **Fax: 0181-749-7084** **U.S. Toll Free** **800-852-2632** Nearest Tube: Barons Court A charming flat on the 4th floor of a mansion block, with a lift. Beautifully decorated with antiques & china. Offering a prettily decorated twin room & a large single room. Guests have their own bathroom. A comfortable sitting room where guests can relax. A large continental breakfast is served. Excellent transport facilities close by providing easy access to many London attractions. Only 10 mins. from Harrods. For parking info, please call host in advance. Children over 10.	£25.00	N	N	N
Home No. 47 **W.W.B.B.A.** **London** **Tel: 0181-742-9123 (24hrs.)** **Fax: 0181-749-7084** **U.S. Toll Free** **800-852-2632** Nearest Tube: Knightsbridge Set in a splendid location only a few minutes walk from Harrods, this elegant Victorian townhouse offers every comfort combined with superb hospitality. 2 delightful rooms which are tastefully furnished. Each has T.V. & an excellent en-suite or private bathroom with power shower. A lovely conservatory is also available for guests use. Knightsbridge is an exclusive area with many good restaurants & chic stores, & is an ideal base from which to explore London. The V & A, Hyde Park & the West End are within easy reach.	£33.00 (no smoking)	N	N	N
Home No. 48 **W.W.B.B.A.** **London** **Tel: 0181-742-9123 (24hrs.)** **Fax: 0181-749-7084** **U.S. Toll Free** **800-852-2632** Nearest Tube: Parsons Green A beautifully decorated, very stylish early Victorian house, situated in leafy Parsons Green & only 10 mins. from Harrods. The charming host offers 3 attractive twin rooms & 1 double room, all with en-suite showers & furnished to the highest standards of comfort. Guests are welcomed with a glass of sherry. A country house breakfast is served. This is a no smoking house.	£30.00 (no smoking)	N	N	N
Home No. 52 **W.W.B.B.A.** **London** **Tel: 0181-742-9123 (24hrs.)** **Fax: 0181-749-7084** **U.S. Toll Free** **800-852-2632** Nearest Tube: Earls Court A spacious 2nd floor apartment set in a lovely property built around the 1900s'. It is beautifully decorated, with many interesting prints & artifacts. There is a charming dining area where breakfast is served. The friendly hosts offer 1 spacious double bedded room, overlooking a peaceful rear garden. It has an excellent en-suite shower room, T.V. & tea/coffee-making facilities. A lovely home, only a 7 min walk from South Kensington & the museums. Many good local restaurants.	£30.00	Y	N	N
Home No. 56 **W.W.B.B.A.** **London** **Tel: 0181-742-9123 (24hrs.)** **Fax: 0181-749-7084** **U.S. Toll Free** **800-852-2632** Nearest Tube: Hammersmith A lovely house, pleasantly situated in leafy Brook Green mid-way between Hammersmith & Kensington. Offering a spacious & comfortably furnished double bedded room with private bathroom & tea/coffee making facilities. There is also an attractive single room available, ideal for a third member of the party. Each room overlooks the rear garden. A pretty lounge with T.V. in which guests may choose to relax. An ideal base, with good access to Heathrow & central London.	£27.00 (no smoking)	Y	N	N

London

		rate from £ per person	children taken	evening meals	animals taken
Home No. 57 **W.W.B.B.A.** **London** **Tel: 0181-742-9123 (24hrs.)** **Fax: 0181-749-7084** **U.S. Toll Free** **800-852-2632**	Nearest Tube: Queensway A beautiful mews house, peacefully situated in the heart of Bayswater, only a 3 min stroll from Hyde Park. This friendly host offers 2 very stylish double bedded rooms, each with en-suite facilities & T.V. (Located on the 1st floor with access via a spiral staircase.) 1 of the rooms has French doors which open out onto a small roof terrace. A superb location, ideal for exploring London & within easy reach of Knightsbridge, Kensington & Mayfair. Many good local restaurants.	£30.00	N	N	N
Home No. 60 **W.W.B.B.A.** **London** **Tel: 0181-742-9123 (24hrs.)** **Fax: 0181-749-7084** **U.S. Toll Free** **800-852-2632**	Nearest Tube: High St. Ken. A beautifully appointed home located in a quiet cul-de-sac, close to Kensington Palace. A lift will take you to the 2nd floor accommodation. A delightful, spacious double room with brass bed, T.V., tea/coffee-making facilities & biscuits are also provided. A delicious varied breakfast is also served. Knightsbridge, Kensington & Hyde park are all just a short walk from here.	£30.00	N	N	N
Home No. 62 **W.W.B.B.A.** **London** **Tel: 0181-742-9123 (24hrs.)** **Fax: 0181-749-7084** **U.S. Toll Free** **800-852-2632**	Nearest Tube: Chalk Farm An exquisitely furnished interior designed Victorian home, comfortable & extremely attractive. The charming hosts who really make you feel at home, offer 1 beautiful twin bedded room with private bathroom & 1 super double & single which share a bathroom. Each room has a colour T.V. & fans. Ideally located close to Regents Park & only 5 mins. from the tube, this is a perfect base from which to explore London & its attractions; ideal for theatreland, shops etc.	£30.00	Y	N	N
Home No. 66 **W.W.B.B.A.** **London** **Tel: 0181-742-9123 (24hrs.)** **Fax: 0181-749-7084** **U.S. Toll Free** **800-852-2632**	Nearest Tube: Earls Court A spacious apartment located at garden level offering attractive accommodation in 1 double bedded room with en-suite facilities & T.V. The friendly host (an interior designer) has tastefully furnished & pleasantly decorated this apartment with many interesting paintings. Guests may relax in the garden which is accessible from their room. Situated only a few minutes walk from the underground station, this home is within easy reach of museums, galleries, shops & theatres.	£27.00	N	N	N
Home No. 67 **W.W.B.B.A.** **London** **Tel: 0181-742-9123** **(24hrs.)** **Fax: 0181-749-7084** **U.S. Toll Free** **800-852-2632**	Nearest Tube: Notting Hill Gate An attractive Victorian maisonette, set in the heart of Notting Hill. The friendly host offers 1 light, airy & comfortable double bedded room with en-suite bathroom. A Continental breakfast is served in the tastefully furnished dining area which overlooks a pretty garden. Situated only a stones throw away from the renowned Portobello Road with its many antique shops & 'world famous' market; this is the ideal place from which to explore London. Many good local pubs & restaurants.	£30.00	N	N	N

Home No. 75 . London.

London

		rate from £ per person	children taken	evening meals	animals taken

Home No. 70 **W.W.B.B.A.** **London** **Tel: 0181-742-9123 (24hrs.)** **Fax: 0181-749-7084** **U.S. Toll Free** **800-852-2632**	Nearest Tube: Earls Court A lovely home with a traditional family atmosphere situated in Kensington. The very friendly & helpful hosts offer 1 ground floor double bedded room with an adjacent private shower room & 1 double/twin bedded room located on the 1st floor, with private bathroom. There are also 2 single rooms available for a 3rd or 4th member of a party. Delicious breakfasts are served in the attractive kitchen/dining area with Aga. Easy access to Heathrow, Knightsbridge, & the museums.	£27.00 🚭	Y	N	N
Home No. 75 **W.W.B.B.A.** **London** **Tel: 0181-742-9123 (24hrs.)** **Fax: 0181-749-7084** **U.S. Toll Free** **800-852-2632**	Nearest Tube: Southfields This is a most charming house in Wimbledon, only five minutes walk from the All England Tennis Club. A very pretty twin room & a single which share the same bathroom suite. Quiet & luxurious. It is like being in the heart of the country with pretty gardens & trees all around. The hostess will provide dinner if ordered in advance & will collect from the station whenever possible. *see PHOTO over*	£26.00	N	N	N
Home No. 76 **W.W.B.B.A.** **London** **Tel: 0181-742-9123 (24hrs.)** **Fax: 0181-749-7084** **U.S. Toll Free** **800-852-2632**	Nearest Tube: Earls Court One very nice double or twin room with en-suite bath & shower, 1 large double with private bath & shower & 1 double for 1 or 2 other members of the party. All 3 rooms have colour T.V. & have been attractively decorated & furnished by this most helpful host. There's a lovely tiled patio for breakfast or tea. Very close to all the best places for shopping & sight-seeing, walking distance to excellent restaurants.	£25.00 🚭	N	N	N
Home No. 77 **W.W.B.B.A.** **London** **Tel: 0181-742-9123 (24hrs.)** **Fax: 0181-749-7084** **U.S. Toll Free** **800-852-2632**	Nearest Tube:Clapham Jt.(B.R.) A large Edwardian house built for Earl Spencer backing onto a private park. Breakfast may be served in the dining room or large conservatory. There is 1 double en-suite room, 1 family room en-suite, 1 twin bedded room with private facilities, also, 1 double room with shared bathroom. Plenty of car parking space. There are two cats & a friendly dog. A charming & most friendly host. Smoking permitted on the ground floor. *see PHOTO over*	£25.00	N	N	N
Home No. 78 **W.W.B.B.A.** **London** **Tel: 0181-742-9123 (24hrs.)** **Fax: 0181-749-7084** **U.S. Toll Free** **800-852-2632**	Nearest Tube: Parsons Green This is an impressive Victorian house with pretty garden, overlooking a common with nearby public tennis court. Excellent restaurants & shops closeby & only 6 mins to the tube. The charming host is an author, with a friendly cat & dog. There are 2 attractive bedrooms, each with a double bed, T.V. & hairdryer & adjacent private facilities. (1 with bath & the other a shower.) Gluten-free diet served by arrangement.	£27.00 🚭	N	N	N

Home No. 77 . London.

London

		rate from £ per person	children taken	evening meals	animals taken
Home No. 79 **W.W.B.B.A.** **London** **Tel: 0181-742-9123 (24hrs.)** **Fax: 0181-749-7084** **U.S. Toll Free** **800-852-2632**	Nearest Tube: East Putney An elegant Victorian house with a pretty garden located in the residential area of Putney. The charming hosts offer 2 stylishly decorated guest rooms, located on the 2nd floor. An attractive & spacious twin room with a lovely private bathroom & one large, sunny double bedroom with shower room en-suite. Each room has colour T.V. Only 25 minutes to Windsor Castle on the train or central London by tube. River trips to Greenwich, Hampton Court & Kew go from Putney Bridge just 10 minutes walk away.	£25.00 (no smoking)	Y	N	N
Home No. 81 **W.W.B.B.A.** **London** **Tel: 0181-742-9123 (24hrs.)** **Fax: 0181-749-7084** **U.S. Toll Free** **800-852-2632**	Nearest Tube: Fulham Broadway Situated in Fulham, with many good restaurants, pubs & antique shops nearby. This is an attractive Victorian house, standing in a quiet street. The friendly hosts offer 1 spacious double/twin bedded room with an exquisite en-suite bathroom & another lovely, light & airy twin bedded room with a beautiful private bathroom adjacent. Each bedroom is well-furnished & has T.V. & tea/coffee-making facilities. Very good access to central London & the sights by bus or tube.	£25.00	Y	N	N
Home No. 99 **W.W.B.B.A.** **London** **Tel: 0181-742-9123 (24hrs.)** **Fax: 0181-749-7084** **U.S. Toll Free** **800-852-2632**	Nearest Tube: Knightsbridge A fine Victorian house standing in an elegant tree-lined street. The well-travelled hosts offer 1 beautifully furnished double bedded room with an excellent en-suite bathroom. A full English breakfast is served in the attractive dining room furnished with antiques. Many good restaurants in the area. An ideal location from which to explore London's many attractions.	£33.00 (no smoking)	N	N	N
Home No. 100 **W.W.B.B.A.** **London** **Tel: 0181-742-9123 (24hrs.)** **Fax: 0181-749-7084** **U.S. Toll Free** **800-852-2632**	Nearest Tube: Gloucester Rd. This is a very pleasant, large, well decorated apartment in the much sought after area of Kensington. The accommodation comprises a large en-suite double room with tea/coffee-making facilities. Ideal for sight-seeing, this home is just a 5 min stroll from the V & A & is within easy reach of West End theatres, Chelsea, Knightsbridge, Sloane Square & Piccadilly.	£33.00 (no smoking)	N	N	N
Home No. 118 **W.W.B.B.A.** **London** **Tel: 0181-742-9123 (24hrs.)** **Fax: 0181-749-7084** **U.S. Toll Free** **800-852-2632**	Nearest Tube: Sloane Square Located in the Royal Borough of Kensington & Chelsea, close to the famous Physic Gardens, with easy access to all the sights & sounds of London. A beautifully furnished home, offering 1 spacious double bedded room with private bathroom. A Continental breakfast is served by your friendly host, who will make your stay in Chelsea most enjoyable.	£31.00 (no smoking)	N	N	N

Avon

Avon
(West Country)

Avon emerged as a county in 1974 as a result of the rearrangement of the boundaries of Gloucestershire, Wiltshire & Somerset, but its newness is only on the surface, for the county holds a wealth of tradition & history. Getting to Avon is easy, whether by road, rail or air. The M5 runs the length of the county & rail services are fast & direct, a journey of just over an hour from Bristol to London. Bristol Airport not only serves travellers from other parts of Britain but also provides a direct link with Europe.

The county is centred on Bristol & Bath & stretches north & south of the River Avon from which it takes its name. To the west of Bristol between the Severn River & the Cotswolds, are the quiet pastoral lowlands around Thornbury, an ancient town with a castle. The great landmark of this area is the magnificent Severn Bridge forming the Southern approach to Wales.

The Cotswolds, like the Mendips to the south, are officially designated as being of outstanding natural beauty, famous for their honey-coloured limestone villages. This area is particularly rich in stately homes. A tour of Badminton House, Dodington House, Dyrham

Dyrham House

Park & Horton Court will reveal a mixture of architecture ranging from the grand Classical tradition to the small Cotswold Manor house. Chipping Sodbury is the principal town of this area & its buildings, a rich mixture of Georgian brick & Cotswold stone, reflect its position between Wold & Dale. All along the Cotswold escarpment are superb views across the valley to the Severn & the hills beyond. Tog Hill is a famous viewpoint.

Between the Avon Valley & the county's southern border is the manmade lakeland of Chew Valley & Blagdon. Here are splendid opportunities for fishing, sailing, picnicking & bird watching in the shadow of the majestic Mendip Hills.

Bath is one of the most loved historic cities in England. It owes its existence to the hot springs which bubble up five hundred thousand gallons of water a day at a temperature of some 120° F. According to legend, King Bladud appreciated the healing qualities of the waters & established his capital here, calling it Aquae Sulis. He built an elaborate healing & entertainment centre around the springs including reservoirs, baths & hypercaust rooms.

The Roman Baths, not uncovered until modern times, are on the lowest of three levels. Above them came the mediaeval city & on the top layer at modern street level is the elegant Georgian Pump Room.

Edward was crowned the first King of all England in 973, in the Saxon Abbey which stood on the site of the present fifteenth century abbey. This building, in the graceful perpendicular style with elegant fan vaulting, is sometimes called the "lantern of the West", on account of its vast clerestories & large areas of glass.

Avon

During the Middle Ages the town prospered through Royal patronage & the development of the wool industry. Bath became a city of weavers, the leading industrial town in the West of England.

The 18th century gave us the superb Georgian architecture which is the city's glory. John Wood, an ambitious young architect laid out Queen Anne's Square in the grand Palladian style, & went on to produce his masterpiece, the Royal Crescent. His scheme for the city was continued by his son & a number of other fine architects, using the beautiful Bath stone. Bath was a centre of fashion, with Beau Nash the leader of a glittering society

In 1497 John & Sebastian Cabot sailed from the Bristol quayside to the land they called Ameryke, in honour of the King's agent in Bristol, Richard Ameryke. Bristol's involvement in the colonisation of the New World & the trade in sugar, tobacco & slaves that followed, made her the second city in the kingdom in the 18th century. John Cabot is commemorated by the Cabot Tower on grassy Brandon Hill - a fine vantage point from which to view the city. On the old docks below are the Bristol Industrial Museum & the SS Great Britain, Brunel's famous iron ship. Another achievement of this master engineer, the Clifton Suspension Bridge, spans Bristol's renowned beauty spot, the Clifton Gorge. For a glimpse of Bristol's elegant past, stroll through Clifton with its stately terraces & spacious Downs.

A short walk from the busy city centre & modern shopping area, the visitor in search of history will find cobbled King Street with its merchant seamens almhouses & The Theatre Royal, the oldest theatre in continuous use in England, & also Llandoger Trow, an ancient inn associated with Treasure Island & Robinson Crusoe.

Roman Baths; Bath.

Avon

Avon Gazeteer

Areas of Outstanding Natural Beauty
The Cotswolds & the Mendip Hills

Historic Houses & Castles

Badminton House - Badminton
Built in the reign of Charles II. Huge parkland where Horse Trials are held each year. Home of the Duke of Beaufort.

Clevedon Court - Clevedon
14th century manor house, 13th century hall, 12th century tower. Lovely garden with rare trees & shrubs. This is where Thackerey wrote much of 'Vanity Fair'.

Dodington House - Chipping Sodbury
Perfect 18th century house with superb staircase. Landscape by Capability Brown.

Dyrham Park - Between Bristol & Bath
17th century house - fine panelled rooms, Dutch paintings, furniture.

Horton Court - Horton
Cotswold manor house altered & restored in 19th century.

No. 1 Royal Crescent - Bath
An unaltered Georgian house built 1767.

Red Lodge - Bristol
16th century house - period furniture & panelling.

St. Vincent's Priory - Bristol
Gothic revival house, built over caves which were sanctuary for Christians.

Blaise Castle House - Henbury Nr. Bristol
18th century house - now folk museum, extensive woodlands.

Priory Park College - Bath
18th century Georgian mansion, now Roman Catholic school.

Claverton Manor - Nr. Bath
Greek revival house - furnished with 17th, 18th, 19th century American originals.

St Catherine's Court - Nr. Bath
Small Tudor house - associations with Henry VIII & Elizabeth I.

Cathedrals & Churches

Bristol Cathedral
Mediaeval. Eastern halfnave Victorian. . Chapterhouse richly ornamented.

Bristol (St Mary Radcliffe)
Iron screen, 3 fonts" fairest parish church in all England".

Bristol (St. Stephens')
Perpendicular - monuments, magnificent tower.

Backwell (St. Andrew)
12th to 17th century, 15th century tower, repaired 17th century. 15th century tomb & chancel, 16th century screen, 18th century brass chandelier.

Bath Abbey
Perpendicular - monastic church, 15th century foundation. Nave finished 17th century, restorations in 1674.

Iron Acton (St. James the Less)
Perpendicular - 15th century memorial cross. 19th century mosaic floors, Laudian alter rails, Jacobean pulpit, effigies.

Wrington (All Souls)
15th century aisles & nave; font, stone pulpit, notable screens.

Yate (St. Mary)
Splendid perpendicular tower.

Museums & Galleries

American Museum in Britain - Claverton Nr. Bath
American decorative arts 17th to 19th century displayed in series of furnished rooms & galleries of special exhibits. Paintings, furniture, glass wood & metal work, textiles, folk sculpture, etc.

Holburne of Menstrie Museum - Bath
Old Master paintings, silver, glass, porcelain, furniture & miniatures in 18th century building. Work of 20th century craftworkers.

Victoria Art Gallery - Bath
Paintings, prints, drawings, glass, ceramics, watches, coins, etc. Bygones - permanent & temporary exhibitions. Geology collections.

Roman Museum - Bath
Material from remains of extensive Roman baths & other Roman sites.

Museum of Costume - Bath
Collection of fashion from 17th century to present day.

St. Nicholas Church & City Museum - Bristol
Mediaeval antiquities relating to local

Avon

history, Church plate & vestments. Altarpiece by Hogarth.

City of Bristol Museum - Bristol
Egyptology, archaeology, ethnography, geology. Bristol ships.

Bristol Industrial Museum - Bristol
Collections of transport items of land, sea & air. Many unique items.

City of Bristol Art Gallery - Bristol
Permanent & loan collections of paintings, English & Oriental ceramics.

Chatterton House - Bristol
Birth place of boy poet.
Historic Monuments

Kings Weston Roman Villa - Lawrence Weston
3rd & 4th centuries - mosaics of villa - some walls.

Hinton Priory - Hinton Charterhouse
13th century - ruins of Carthusian priory.

Temple Church - Bristol
14th & 15th century ruins.

Stoney Littleton Barrow - Nr. Bath
Neolithic burial chamber - restoration work 1858.

Roman Baths - Bath

Other things to see & do

Clifton Zoological Gardens - Bristol
Flourishing zoo with many exhibits - beautiful gardens.

Clifton Suspension Bridge - Bristol
Designed by Isambard Kingdom Brunel, opened in 1864. Viewpoint & picnic spot Camera Obscura.

The Pump Room - Bath
18th century neo-classical interior. Spa water can be drunk here overlooking the famous hot springs.

Clifton Suspension Bridge. Bristol.

AVON

Map reference

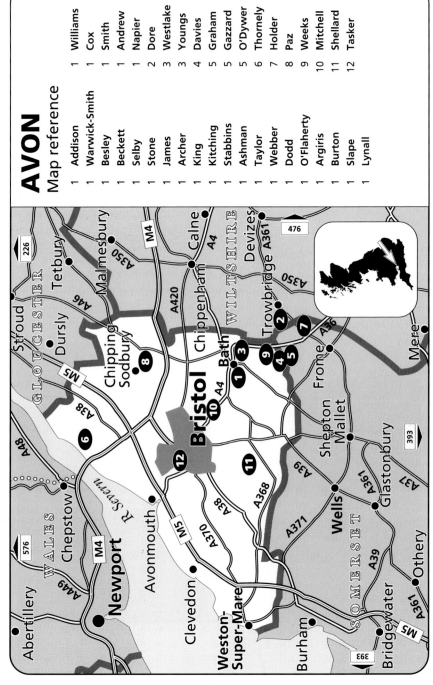

1	Addison
1	Warwick-Smith
1	Besley
1	Beckett
1	Selby
1	Stone
1	James
1	Archer
1	King
1	Kitching
1	Stabbins
1	Ashman
1	Taylor
1	Webber
1	Dodd
1	O'Flaherty
1	Argiris
1	Burton
1	Slape
1	Lynall

1	Williams
1	Cox
1	Smith
1	Andrew
1	Napier
2	Dore
3	Westlake
3	Youngs
4	Davies
5	Graham
5	Gazzard
5	O'Dywer
6	Thornely
7	Holder
8	Paz
9	Weeks
10	Mitchell
11	Shellard
12	Tasker

Cranleigh. Bath.

Avon

		rate from £ per person	children taken	evening meals	animals taken
Mrs I. Lynall **Circus Mansions** **36 Brock Street** **Bath** **BA1 2LJ** **Tel: (01225) 336462** **Open: ALL YEAR (Excl. Xmas)** **Map Ref No. 01**	Nearest Road: A.4 Circus Mansions is an elegant house situated in the Circus, in the heart of this Georgian city. The theatre, museums & antique centres, as well as shops & restaurants, are a few mins' walk away. Circus Mansions offers spacious, comfortably furnished rooms, with private facilities, T.V., tea/coffee-making facilities & central heating in all rooms. There is a charming breakfast room. Children over 3 yrs welcome.	£25.00	Y	N	N
Marion Dodd **Brocks** **32 Brock Street** **Bath BA1 2LN** **Tel: (01225) 338374** **Fax (01225) 334245** **Open: ALL YEAR** **Map Ref No. 01**	Nearest Road: A.4 Brocks is a beautiful Georgian town house situated between the Circus and Royal Crescent. Very close to the historic Roman Baths, Assembly Rooms, etc. This really is a wonderful part of Bath. This historic house has all modern conveniences. Most rooms have private facilities. The aim here is to offer guests the highest standards, and personal attention. A delightful base from which to explore beautiful Bath. CREDIT CARD VISA M'CARD	£22.00	Y	N	N
Mrs Jill Smith **Marlborough House** **Marlborough Lane** **Bath BA1 2NQ** **Tel:(01225) 318175** **Fax (01225) 466127** **Open: ALL YEAR** **Map Ref No. 01**	Nearest Road: A.4 Marlborough House has recently been extensively renovated, & retains many of its Victorian features. Situated 5 mins' level walk from the centre of Bath, the Theatre Royal & the Roman Baths, & only 2 mins from the Royal Crescent & Victoria Park. Spacious double/twin bedrooms with T.V., tea/coffee facilities & hairdryers. 2 with a 4-poster bed. All are en-suite. Also, single rooms. A non-smoking house with private parking. Discounts available when staying 3 nights or more. CREDIT CARD VISA M'CARD AMEX	£20.00	Y	N	N
Chrissie Besley **The Old Red House** **37 Newbridge Road** **Bath** **BA1 3HE** **Tel: (01225) 330464** **Open: ALL YEAR** **Map Ref No. 01**	Nearest Road: A.4 This charming Victorian Gingerbread House is colourful, comfortable & warm; full of unexpected touches & intriguing little curiosities. Its leaded & stained glass windows are now double-glazed to ensure a peaceful stay. The extensive breakfast menu, a delight in itself, is served in a sunny conservatory. Parking. Special rates for 3 or more nights. Dinner available at a local riverside pub. Brochure on request. Children over 5 yrs.	£20.00 🚭 *see PHOTO over* CREDIT CARD VISA M'CARD AMEX	Y	N	Y
Arthur & Christine Webber **Cranleigh** **159 Newbridge Hill** **Bath** **BA1 3PX** **Tel: (01225) 310197** **Fax 01225 423143** **Open: ALL YEAR** **Map Ref No. 01**	Nearest Road: A.431 Situated in a quiet residential area, this comfortable Victorian house has great character, with exceptionally spacious, stylishly decorated bedrooms. All are en-suite, & most have lovely views across the Avon Valley. Breakfast includes such choices as fresh-fruit salad & scrambled eggs with smoked salmon. There is private parking & easy access to the heart of Bath. Around their home, the Webbers have many interesting items from their own travels, & they keep a wealth of information to help you make the most of your stay. Children over 4.	£25.00 🚭 *see PHOTO over* CREDIT CARD VISA M'CARD	Y	N	N

The Old Red House. Bath.

Gainsborough Hotel. Bath.

Avon

		rate from £ per person	children taken	evening meals	animals taken

Richard Warwick **Gainsborough Hotel** **Weston Lane** **Bath BA1 4AB** **Tel: (01225) 311380** **Fax 01225 447411** **Open: ALL YEAR** **Map Ref No. 01**	Nearest Road: A.4 The Gainsborough is a large country-house hotel, comfortably furnished & set in its own grounds near the Botanical Gardens & Victoria Park. Offering 16 attractive en-suite bedrooms, each with colour T.V., direct-dial telephone, tea/coffee-making facilities & hairdryer. The dining room & small cocktail bar overlook the lawns, where guests often relax during the summer on the sun terrace. Private parking available.	£27.00 *see PHOTO over* CREDIT CARD VISA M'CARD AMEX	Y	Y	N
Derek & Maria Beckett **Cedar Lodge** **13 Lambridge** **London Rd** **Bath** **BA1 6BJ** **Tel: (01225) 423468** **Open: ALL YEAR** **Map Ref No. 01**	Nearest Road: A.4, A.46 Conveniently located, this beautiful detached Georgian house offers period elegance combined with home comforts. 3 individually designed bedrooms, 1 with a 4-poster, 1 with a half-tester & 1 twin-bedded. All with en-suite/private bathrooms, colour T.V. & central heating. Guests may relax in the lovely garden, or by the fire in the comfortable drawing room. A choice of breakfasts, served with home-made preserves. Excursions planned. Private, locked car park.	£20.00 (no smoking)	Y	N	N
Margaret Addison **Bailbrook Lodge Hotel** **35/37 London Road West** **Bath BA1 7HZ** **Tel: (01225) 859090** **Fax 01225 859090** **Open: ALL YEAR** **Map Ref No. 01**	Nearest Road: A.4 Bailbrook Lodge is an imposing Georgian house located 1 mile east of Bath. There is a choice of 12 elegantly furnished en-suite bedrooms (some 4-posters), all with T.V. & hospitality tray. Evening meals with traditional English cuisine are provided. The lounge bar & dining room overlook the garden. Bailbrook Lodge is an ideal base for exploring Bath & touring the beautiful surrounding countryside. Ample car-parking.	£25.00 *see PHOTO over* CREDIT CARD VISA M'CARD AMEX	Y	Y	N
Derek & Marjorie Dore **Arnolds Court** **Wingfield** **Bath** **BA14 9LB** **Tel: (01225) 752025** **Open: APR - OCT** **Map Ref No. 02**	Nearest Road: A.36, A.366 This delightful Edwardian country house is set in 5 acres of attractive grounds, & offers comfortable accommodation in gracious surroundings amid a relaxed & friendly atmosphere. 3 double/twin bedrooms, 2 en-suite, each with colour T.V. & tea/coffee-making facilities. Guests are free to relax in the sitting room or in the garden around the outdoor swimming pool. Ideally situated for visiting Bath, Longleat, Stonehenge, Salisbury & Wells.	£20.00 (no smoking)	N	N	N
Leslie & Traudle Graham **Monmouth Lodge** **Norton St. Philip** **Bath** **BA3 6LH** **Tel: (01373) 834367** **Open: ALL YEAR** **Map Ref No. 05**	Nearest Road: A.36, B.3110 Monmouth Lodge is situated in an acre of attractive gardens looking onto the Somerset hills surrounding this historic village. 3 attractively furnished, ground-floor en-suite bedrooms, each with colour T.V. & tea/coffee-making facilities. Guests may relax in the comfortable sitting room or enjoy the garden with views beyond. 10 mins' drive from Bath, this is an ideal base from which to explore the many interesting sites nearby. Secluded parking. Meals in a 13th-century pub within a short walking distance.	£24.00	Y	N	N

Bailbrook Lodge. Bath.

The Old School House. Bathford.

Avon

		rate from £ per person	children taken	evening meals	animals taken

Sonia & Rodney Stone **The Old School House** **Church Street, Bathford** **Bath BA1 7RR** **Tel: (01225) 859593** **Fax 01225 859590** **Open: ALL YEAR** **Map Ref No. 01**	Nearest Road: A.4, M.4. Built in 1837, The Old School House is situated within a conservation area, with beautiful views over the Avon Valley & its wooded hillsides, & yet only 3 miles from the Georgian city of Bath. Offering a charming country-home atmosphere, with log fires on chilly evenings. 2 of the 4 double/ twin rooms are on the ground floor. All have en-suite bathrooms, 'phone, colour T.V., tea/coffee, hairdryer & trouser press. An entirely no-smoking establishment. Children over 8 yrs.	£30.00 *see PHOTO over* CREDIT CARD VISA M'CARD	Y	Y	N
Geoff & Avril Kitching **Wentworth House** **106 Bloomfield Road** **Bath** **BA2 2AP** **Tel: (01225) 339193** **Fax 01225 310460** **Open: ALL YEAR** **Map Ref No. 01**	Nearest Road: A.367 Stay 3 nights or more & receive a complimentary bottle of bubbly in your room & a 10% discount at this imposing Victorian Bath stone mansion (1887) standing in secluded grounds with stunning views of the valley. Situated in a quiet part of the city with a large, car park in the grounds & within walking distance of the city, Abbey & Roman Baths. All 18 rooms, with private facilities, are individual with a high standard of comfort. A licensed bar lounge. An outdoor swimming pool, golf & walks close by. Lots of information on Bath, the area & Somerset.	£23.00 CREDIT CARD VISA M'CARD	Y	Y	N
Anthony & Nicole O'Flaherty **Oldfields Guest House** **102 Wells Road** **Bath BA2 3AL** **Tel: (01225) 317984** **Fax 01225 444471** **Open: ALL YEAR** **Map Ref No. 01**	Nearest Road: A.367 A Victorian house built in Bath stone & overlooking the city towards Kelson Round Hill. 14 delightful rooms with T.V. & tea/coffee-making facilities. 7 with a bath/shower en-suite. Each room has recently been restored & completely refurbished. The character remains, however, & the Victorian elegance has been lightened by fresh Laura Ashley wallpapers & fabrics. Anthony & Nicole provide plenty of books & newspapers, & ... Mozart at breakfast. Parking available.	£24.00 CREDIT CARD VISA M'CARD	Y	N	Y
Mrs Nicky Stabbins **The Hollies** **Hatfield Road, Wellsway** **Bath BA2 2BD** **Tel: (01225) 313366** **Open: ALL YEAR (Excl.** **Xmas & New Year)** **Map Ref No. 01**	Nearest Road: A. 367 The Hollies is a lovely old Victorian, Grade II listed house situated within walking distance of the city. With just 3 pretty guest rooms, personal attention and hospitality are assured. Each room has en-suite or private facilities, colour T.V., beverage-making facilities, hairdryer & radio/alarm clock. A wide breakfast menu is served. Private parking is available. Rooms overlook the secluded garden of apple trees, herbs & roses. The Hollies is a charming home, ideal for exploring Bath.	£19.00	Y	N	N
Mrs M. Ashman-Marr **Haydon House** **9 Bloomfield Park** **Bath BA2 2BY** **Tel/Fax: (01225) 444919** **Fax 01225 427351** **Open: ALL YEAR** **Map Ref No. 01**	Nearest Road: A.367 A true oasis of tranquility, this secluded, elegantly furnished Edwardian townhouse is situated in a quiet residential area with easy parking, not far from the city centre. Every conceivable comfort is offered in the 5 tastefully decorated en-suite bedrooms. Guests can enjoy a welcoming cup of tea in the beautifully appointed antique-filled sitting room, with sunshine filtering through the vine-clad pergola, & innovative breakfasts are stylishly served to a background of gentle classical music.	£25.00 *see PHOTO over* CREDIT CARD VISA M'CARD AMEX	Y	N	N

Haydon House. Bath.

Bloomfield House. Bath.

Meadowland. Bath.

	rate from £ per person	children taken	evening meals	animals taken

Catherine Andrew **Meadowland** **36 Bloomfield Park** **Bath BA2 2BX** **Tel: (01225) 311079** **Fax 01452 505606** **Open: ALL YEAR** **Map Ref No. 01**	Nearest Road: A.367 Set in its own quiet secluded grounds, Meadowland offers the highest standards in beautifully appointed en-suite accommodation. There is a comfortable residents' lounge, with an interesting selection of books & magazines, & an imaginative breakfast is served in the charming dining room. Private parking & lovely gardens surround this elegant non-smoking house. A peaceful retreat for the discerning traveller. *see PHOTO over* CREDIT CARD VISA M'CARD	£26.00	Y	N	N
David & Davina James **Highways House** **143 Wells Road** **Bath BA2 3AL** **Tel: (01225) 421238** **Fax 01225 481169** **Open: ALL YEAR (Excl. Xmas)** **Map Ref No. 01**	Nearest Road: A.367 An elegant, Victorian, family-run home offering superior accommodation in 7 rooms (including 1 twin room on the ground floor) with private facilities, colour T.V. & tea/coffee makers. A tastefully decorated home, with a lovely guest lounge. Full English breakfast is served. Located only 10 mins from the city centre. A perfect base from which to tour the Cotswolds, Stonehenge, Salisbury & Wells. Children over 5 please. Parking. *see PHOTO over* CREDIT CARD VISA M'CARD	£24.00	Y	N	N
John & Sue Burton **Badminton Villa** **10 Upper Oldfield Park** **Bath BA2 3JZ** **Tel: (01225) 426347** **Fax 01225 420393** **Open: ALL YEAR** **Map Ref No. 01**	Nearest Road: A.367 John & Sue welcome you to the friendly & relaxed atmosphere of Badminton Villa, with its magnificent views of Bath. Conveniently situated in a quiet road just a 10-min walk from the city centre. The attractive bedrooms are all en-suite & have colour T.V. & tea/coffee facilities. Badminton Villa, with a private car park, is the perfect location for visitors to Bath or for exploring the beautiful West Country. Children over 5 yrs. CREDIT CARD VISA M'CARD	£25.00	Y	N	N
Bridget & Malcolm Cox **Bloomfield House** **146 Bloomfield Rd** **Bath** **BA2 2AS** **Tel: (01225) 420105** **Fax 01225 481958** **Open: ALL YEAR** **Map Ref No. 01**	Nearest Road: A.367 An elegant Georgian country house in a sylvan setting with stunning views over the city. Antique furniture, French crystal chandeliers, silver-service breakfast & open fires. All rooms have an en-suite bath/shower, direct-dial telephone, colour T.V. & canopied or 4-poster beds. Also, the lavish principal bedroom of the Mayor & Mayoress of Bath (1902/3). Bloomfield House offers the finest, the friendliest, the best. A car park. A 2-bed, self-contained family flat also available. *see PHOTO over* CREDIT CARD VISA M'CARD	£25.00	N	N	N
Jenny King **Oakleigh House** **19 Upper Oldfield Park** **Bath BA2 3JX** **Tel: (01225) 315698** **Fax 01225 448223** **Open: ALL YEAR** **Map Ref No. 01**	Nearest Road: A.367 Your comfort is assured at Oakleigh House, quietly situated only 10 mins from the city centre. Oakleigh combines Victorian elegance with today's comforts to make your stay that extra bit special. All rooms are attractively furnished & have an en-suite bath/shower & w.c., hair-dryers, colour T.V., clock radios and tea/coffee-making facilities. A private car park. Oakleigh is an ideal base for beautiful Bath and beyond. CREDIT CARD VISA M'CARD	£24.00	N	N	N

Highways House.   Bath.

Eagle House. Bathford.

Avon

		rate from £ per person	children taken	evening meals	animals taken
Jane & Brian Taylor **Dorian House** **One Upper Oldfield Park** **Bath BA2 3JX** **Tel: (01225) 426336** **Fax 01225 444699** **Open: ALL YEAR** **Map Ref No. 01**	Nearest Road: A.367 A warm welcome and an aura of nostalgic luxury await every guest at this gracious Victorian house. Accommodation is in 8 charming bedrooms, all en-suite, are fully appointed, with tea/coffee trays, hairdryers, telephones and colour T.V.. There is a lounge & a small licensed bar, and a Full English breakfast menu is served. Parking available, and only a 10-minute stroll to the city centre. Dorian House is ideal for a relaxing break.	£29.00 *see PHOTO over* CREDIT CARD VISA M'CARD AMEX	Y	N	N
David & Kathleen Slape **Leighton House** **139 Wells Road** **Bath** **BA2 3AL** **Tel: (01225) 314769** **Fax 01225 443079** **Open: ALL YEAR** **Map Ref No. 01**	Nearest Road: A.367 Enjoy a true haven of friendliness at this delightful Victorian home, built in the 1870s & set in award-winning gardens with views over the city & surrounding hills. There are 8 elegant & spacious bedrooms, all tastefully furnished & decorated. Each has an en-suite bathroom, & is well equipped with colour T.V., radio, 'phone, hairdryer, hospitality tray & many extras. There is an excellent & wide choice of breakfasts to set you up for the day. Special breaks available. Ample car parking, & 10 mins' stroll from Bath's centre.	£30.00 *see PHOTO over* CREDIT CARD VISA M'CARD	Y	N	N
John & Rosamund Napier **Eagle House** **Church Street** **Bathford** **Bath BA1 7RS** **Tel/Fax: (01225) 859946** **Open: ALL YEAR** **Map Ref No. 01**	Nearest Road: A.363, A.4 Eagle House is a fine Georgian Grade II listed house set in 2 acres of garden in the heart of picturesque Bathford. There are 8 comfortable, en-suite bedrooms with 'phone, T.V. & tea/coffee-making facilities, plus spacious public rooms - the drawing room has a 16-ft ceiling, as well as views over the garden down the valley. The house is elegant, yet the atmosphere is informal, & all are welcome. There is also a lovely cottage for 4.	£26.00 *see PHOTO over* CREDIT CARD VISA M'CARD	Y	N	Y
Christopher & Juliet Davies **Green Lane House** **1 Green Lane** **Hinton Charterhouse** **Bath** **BA3 6BL** **Tel: (01225) 723631** **Open: ALL YEAR** **Map Ref No. 04**	Nearest Road: A.36, B.3110 Pretty, comfortably furnished, 18th-century stone house in a quiet location, near the centre of a conservation village, in beautiful, wooded countryside. Tastefully combining original features, including exposed beams & working fireplaces, with the comforts of modern living. 4 double/twin bedrooms (2 en-suite), tea/coffee makers, guest lounge, dining room, parking, 4-course English breakfast & a friendly personal service. Convenient for Bath, Bristol, Cotswolds, Wells, Glastonbury, Longleat, Stonehenge, etc.	£18.00 CREDIT CARD VISA M'CARD AMEX	Y	N	Y
Mrs Joan Youngs **Lindisfarne** **41a Warminster Road** **Bathampton** **Bath BA2 6XJ** **Tel: (01225) 466342** **Open: DEC - OCT** **Map Ref No. 03**	Nearest Road: A.36 Situated just 1 1/2 miles from the city centre. Lindisfarne is a lovely home offering comfortable en-suite accommodation with colour T.V. & refreshment facilities. Many good eating venues within walking distance. A large private car park & a frequent bus service to Bath centre. The perfect place from which to explore this beautiful city. A warm welcome & personal attention guaranteed by the resident owners.	£17.50	Y	N	Y

Leighton House. Bath.

Dorian House. Bath.

Villa Magdala Hotel. Bath.

Avon

			rate from £ per person	children taken	evening meals	animals taken

Brian & Audrey Archer **Bath Tasburgh Hotel** **Warminster Road** **Bath** **BA2 6SH** **Tel: (01225) 425096** **Fax 01225 463842** **Open: ALL YEAR** **Map Ref No. 01**	Nearest Road: A.4, A.36 Built in 1890 as a mansion for a photographer to the Royal Family, the Tasburgh is set in 7 acres of lovely gardens & grounds - with canal frontage & breathtaking views - near the city centre. The house, retaining many original features, offers 14 tastefully furnished rooms (designer fabrics & Laura Ashley), with en-suite bathrooms, 'phones, radio/alarms, tea/coffee facilities & T.V.. Victorian elegance & charming decor prevails. English/wholefood breakfasts, & ample parking. Brian & Audrey provide many extras, & personal care.	£27.00 *see PHOTO over* CREDIT CARD VISA M'CARD AMEX	Y	N	N
Mrs Shelley Weeks **Wheelbrook Mill** **Laverton** **Bath** **BA3 6QY** **Tel: (01373) 830263** **Open: ALL YEAR** **Map Ref No. 09**	Nearest Road: A.36 A warm welcome, log fires on chilly nights & good food await you in this picturesque mill, nestling in a quiet valley & overlooking the brook, fields & woodland, 15 mins from Bath. The pretty, en-suite, oak-beamed bedrooms are centrally heated, furnished with antique pine & Laura Ashley Linens, & have all facilities. A large garden & a cosy sitting room with log fire, books, games & magazines, in a very relaxed, family atmosphere.	£24.00 (no smoking)	Y	Y	Y
David & Sue Selby **Brompton House** **St. Johns Road** **Bath BA2 6PT** **Tel: (01225) 420972** **Fax 01225 420505** **Open: ALL YEAR (Excl.** **Xmas & New Year)** **Map Ref No. 01**	Nearest Road: A.4, A.36 Brompton House is beautifully situated in the secluded surroundings of a prize-winning garden. A Georgian rectory built in 1777, it has been converted & extended with exquisite care & attractive furnishings, & is a few mins' walk from the city centre. The business is family owned & family-run, with the wish to offer every comfort & service to all guests. All rooms are en-suite, & equipped with colour T.V., a direct-dial 'phone & tea/coffee-making facilities. A car park within the grounds. Children over 5 yrs.	£27.50 (no smoking) *see PHOTO over* CREDIT CARD VISA M'CARD AMEX	Y	N	N
Mrs Ann Thornely **Eastcote Cottage** **Knapp Road East** **Thornbury** **Bristol BS12 2HJ** **Tel: (01454) 413106** **Open: ALL YEAR (Excl. Xmas)** **Map Ref No. 06**	Nearest Road: M.4, M.5, A.38 Eastcote is a charming 200-year-old stone house located in a lovely rural setting, with splendid views across open countryside. Guests have a choice of 4 comfortable bedrooms with modern amenities. A colour-T.V. lounge is available for guests' use. Conveniently situated for the M.4/M.5 interchange for the Cotswolds, with Bristol, Bath, Cheltenham & the Wye Valley easily accessible. Private parking available.	£19.00	Y	N	N
Alison Williams **Villa Magdala Hotel** **Henrietta Road** **Bath BA2 6LX** **Tel: (01225) 466329** **Fax 01225 483207** **Open: ALL YEAR** **Map Ref No. 01**	Nearest Road: A.4, A.36 A detached Victorian town-house hotel set in its own grounds, the Villa Magdala is situated in a quiet residential road only a 5-min. level walk away from the city centre. All 17 bedrooms have en-suite bathrooms, 'phones, radio/alarms, T.V.s & tea/coffee-making facilities, while many overlook the Henrietta Gardens. The hotel offers ample private parking, & is an ideal base for discovering Bath & its many attractions.	£28.00 *see PHOTO over* CREDIT CARD VISA M'CARD	Y	N	N

Brompton House. Bath.

The Tasburgh Bath. Bath.

Monkshill. Monkton Combe.

Avon

		rate from £ per person	children taken	evening meals	animals taken
Shirley O'Dwyer **Bath Lodge** **Warminster Road** **Norton St. Philip** **Bath BA3 6NH** Tel:(01225) 723040/723737 **Open: ALL YEAR** Map Ref No. 05	Nearest Road: A.36 Bath Lodge is a superbly converted, Heritage Grade II listed, former gatehouse to Farleigh Castle. The alterations & landscaping have been completed within the last few years. All of the rooms are beautifully located & have many castellated features within them. Private balconies from 3 of the rooms overlook the natural gardens & adjacent deer forest. Situated just 7 miles south of Bath on the A.36.	£37.50 🚭 *see PHOTO over* CREDIT CARD M'CARD	N	N	N
Mrs Muriel Mitchell & **Mrs Sarah Leighton** **Brunel's Tunnel House** **Hotel** **High Street, Saltford** **Bristol BS18 3BQ** Tel: (01225) 873873 Fax 01225 874875 **Open: ALL YEAR (Excl. Xmas)** Map Ref No. 10	Nearest Road: A.4 A fine listed Georgian building once owned by Isambard Kingdom Brunel, situated in picturesque Saltford, only minutes away from Bath & Bristol. A tasteful decor, with antique furniture, creates a comfortable relaxed atmosphere. All of the attractive bedrooms are en-suite, coordinated & individual, with telephone, colour T.V., radio & hospitality tray. Ample private parking. An efficient, courteous, friendly service from the resident owners. Come & enjoy the personal hospitality once offered only to Brunel's privileged guests.	£24.00 CREDIT CARD VISA M'CARD AMEX	Y	Y	N
Mr & Mrs M. Westlake **Monkshill** **Shaft Road** **Monkton Combe** **Bath** **BA2 7HL** Tel: (01225) 833028 Fax 01225 833028 **Open: ALL YEAR** Map Ref No. 03	Nearest Road: A.3062 This distinguished Edwardian house is set in its own beautiful gardens, on an English-country hilltop commanding spectacular countryside views, & yet lies only 5 mins from the centre of Bath. Take a lovely stroll through the small mediaeval village of Monkton Combe, at the valley's base, & return to tea amid the elegant antiques, fireplace & grand piano that complement the drawing room. The bedrooms, containing a host of amenities, are elegant, with colourful flowing drapes, charming brass beds, bath/shower & fine views over the gardens & valley below.	£25.00 *see PHOTO over* CREDIT CARD VISA M'CARD AMEX	Y	N	N
Gill & Terry Gazzard **The Plaine** **Norton St. Philip** **Bath BA3 6LE** Tel: (01373) 834723 Fax 01373 834101 **Open: ALL YEAR** Map Ref No. 05	Nearest Road: A.36 The Plaine is a delightful listed building, dating from the 16th century & situated in the heart of an historic conservation village. There are 3 beautiful en-suite rooms, all with 4-poster beds. Opposite is the famous George Inn - one of the oldest hostelries in England. Delicious breakfasts are prepared with local produce and free-range eggs. A convenient location for Bath, Wells, Longleat and the Cotswolds. Parking.	£21.00 🚭 *see PHOTO over* CREDIT CARD VISA M'CARD AMEX	Y	N	N

When booking your accommodation please mention
The Best Bed & Breakfast

Bath Lodge. Norton St. Philip.

The Plaine. Norton St. Philip.

	rate from £ per person	children taken	evening meals	animals taken
Jayne & Oliver Holder **Irondale House** **67 High Street** **Rode** **Bath BA3 6PB** **Tel/Fax: (01373) 830730** **Open: ALL YEAR (Excl. Xmas)** **Map Ref No. 07** Nearest Road: A.36 A warm welcome is extended by Jane & Oliver to their late-18th-century home, set in a quiet rural village within a lovely walled garden, 10 miles south of Bath. The bedrooms are decorated to the highest standard, with colour T.V. & hairdryers. An excellent breakfast is provided in the attractive dining room, & guests can relax in the comfortable drawing room. Ideal for touring the West Country. Bath, Wells, Salisbury, Stourhead & Longleat are all within reach. Children over 12.	£22.50 *see PHOTO over* CREDIT CARD VISA M'CARD	Y	Y	N
John & Daphne Paz **Dornden Guest House** **15 Church Lane** **Old Sodbury** **Bristol BS17 6NB** **Tel: (01454) 313325** **Fax 01454 312263** **Open: ALL YEAR (Excl. Xmas & New Year)** **Map Ref No. 08** Nearest Road: A.432 Dornden, built of local Cotswold stone, stands in a beautiful garden enjoying the peace of the countryside & magnificent views to the west. There are 9 attractive rooms, 5 en-suite, overlooking the garden and the open country beyond. Delicious meals are prepared, using home-grown produce (where possible) and free-range eggs. There is also a grass tennis court available to guests. A delightful home, with a warm, friendly atmosphere, ideal for exploring the beautiful West Country.	£24.50	Y	Y	Y
Ruth Shellard **Overbrook** **Stowey Bottom** **Bishop Sutton** **Bristol** **BS18 4TN** **Tel: (01275) 332648** **Open: ALL YEAR** **Map Ref No. 11** Nearest Road: A.368 Overbrook is a charming house, tastefully furnished, with a lovely garden by a brook. Situated in a quiet & peaceful lane, with a little ford by the gate, Overbrook can offer 1 twin-bedded en-suite room & 1 double bedroom with private shower & W.C.. Both rooms have colour T.V.. There is a comfortable sunny sitting room, with French windows leading into the garden, for guests' use. Bath, Wells, Bristol & Cheddar Gorge are within easy reach, & superb trout fishing on Chew Lake is only 5 mins away.	£17.50 (no smoking)	Y	Y	N
Mrs Philippa Tasker **Downs Edge** **Saville Rd, Stoke Bishop** **Bristol BS9 1JD** **Tel: (0117) 9683264** **Mobile 0585 866463** **Open: ALL YEAR** **Map Ref No. 12** Nearest Road: A.4018 Downs Edge occupies a superb position on the very edge of Bristol's famous Downs - an open park of 450 acres. Set in beautiful gardens, close to the spectacular Avon Gorge with its views across the Bristol Channel, it is conveniently located for the city centre, though it also enjoys a countryside location. Breakfast in elegant surroundings from a delicious & extensive menu. Car parking in the grounds.	£27.50 CREDIT CARD VISA M'CARD	Y	Y	N

When booking your accommodation please mention
The Best Bed & Breakfast

Irondale House. Rode.

Beds:Berks:Bucks:Herts.

Bedfordshire
(Thames & Chilterns)

The county of Bedfordshire is an area of great natural beauty from the Dunstable Downs in the south to the great River Ouse in the north, along with many country parks & historic houses & gardens.

Two famous wildlife parks are to be found, at Woburn &Whipsnade. The Woburn Wild Animal Kingdom is Britain's largest drive-through safari park, with entrance to an exciting leisure park all included in one admission ticket.

Whipsnade Zoo came into existence in the 1930's as a country retreat for the animals of London Zoo, but is now very much a zoo in its own right & renowned for conservation work.

Woburn Abbey, home of the Dukes of Bedford for three centuries, is often described as one of England's finest showplaces. Rebuilt in the 8th century the Abbey houses an important art collection & is surrounded by a magnificent 3,000 acre deer park.

John Bunyan drew on local Bedfordshire features when writing the Pilgrims Progress, & the ruins of Houghton House, his "House Beautiful" still remain.

Buckinghamshire
(Thames & Chilterns)

Buckinghamshire can be divided into two distinct geographical regions: The high Chilterns with their majestic beechwoods & the Vale of Aylesbury chosen by many over the centuries as a beautiful & accessible place to build their historical homes.

The beechwoods of the Chilterns to the south of the county are crisscrossed with quiet lanes & footpaths., Ancient towns & villages like Amersham & Chesham lie tucked away in the

Rose gardens;St.Albans. Herts.

folds of the hills & a prehistoric track; the Ichnield Way winds on its 85 mile journey through the countryside.

The Rothschild family chose the Vale of Aylesbury to create several impressive homes, & Waddesdon House & Ascott House are both open to the public. Benjamin Disraeli lived at Hughenden Manor, & Florence Nightingale, "the Lady with the Lamp", at Claydon House. Sir Francis Dashwood, the 18th century eccentric founded the bizarre Hellfire Club, which met in the man-made caves near West Wycombe House.

Berkshire
(Thames & Chilterns)

Berkshire is a compact county but one of great variety & beauty.

In the East is Windsor where the largest inhabited castle in the world stands in its majestic hilltop setting. Nine centuries of English monarchy have lived here, & it is home to the present Queen. The surrounding parkland, enormous yards, vast interior & splendour of the State Apartments make a trip to Windsor Castle an unforgettable experience.

To the West are the gently rolling Berkshire Downs where many a champion racehorse has been trained.

Beds:Berks:Bucks:Herts.

To the north of the county, the River Thames dominates the landscape - an opportunity for a river-bank stroll & a drink at a country pub.

In the south is the Kennet & Avon Canal, a peaceful waterway with horse-drawn barges.

Historically, Berkshire has occupied an important place due to its strategic position commanding roads to & from Oxford & the north, & Bath & the west. Roundheads & Cavaliers clashed twice near Newbury during the 17th century English Civil Wars. Their battles are colourfully recreated by historic societies like the Sealed Knot.

The Tudor period brought great wealth from wool-weaving. Merchants built wonderful houses & some built churches but curiously, there is no cathedral in Berkshire.

Hertfordshire
(Thames & Chilterns)

Old & new exist side by side in Hertfordshire. This attractive county includes historic sites, like the unique Roman theatre in St. Albans, as well as new additions to the landscape such as England's first Garden City at Letchworth.

The countryside varies from the chalk hills & rolling downlands of the Chilterns to rivers, lakes, canals & pretty villages. The county remains largely rural despite many large towns & cities. The Grand Union Canal, built at the end of the 18th century to link the Midlands to London, passes through some glorious scenery, particularly at Cassiobury Park in Watford.

Verulamium was a newly-built town of the Roman Empire. It was the first name of Alban, himself a Roman, who became the first Christian to be martyred for his faith in England. The great Abbey church was built by the Normans around his original church, & it was re-established under the Rule of St. Benedict & named St. Albans some 600 years after his death.

Tussauds Exhibition. Windsor. Berks.

Beds:Berks:Bucks:Herts.

Bedfordshire
Gazeteer
Area of outstanding natural beauty.
Dunstable Downs, Ivinghoe Beacon.

Historic Houses
Woburn Abbey - house & gardens, extensive art collection, deer park, antiques centre.
Luton Hoo - the Wernher collection of Old Masters, tapestries, furniture, ivories & porcelain, unique collection of Russian Faberge jewellry. Parkland landscaped by Capability Brown.

Other Things to see & do
Woburn Wildlife Park
Whipsnade Zoo-Whipsnade
Old Warden - the village houses a collection of working vintage aeroplanes with flying displays each month from April to October.

Berkshire
Gazeteer
Areas of outstanding natural beauty.
North West Downs.

Historic Houses & Castles
Windsor Castle - Royal Residence at Windsor
State apartments, house, historic treasures. The Cloisters, Windsor Chapel. Mediaeval house.
Basildon Park - Nr. Pangbourne
Overlooking the Thames. 18th century Bath stone building, massive portico & linked pavilions. Painted ceiling in Octagon Room, gilded pier glasses. Garden & wooded walks.
Cliveden - Nr. Taplow
Once the home of Nancy Astor.

Churches
Lambourn (St. Michael & All Saints)
Norman with 15th century chapel. 16th century brasses, glass & tombs.
Padworth (St. John the Baptist)
12th century Norman with plastered exterior, remains of wall paintings, 18th century monuments.

Warfield (St. Michael & All Angels)
14th century decorated style. 15th century wood screen & loft.
Henry Reitlinger Bequest - Maidenhead
Chinese, Italian, Persian & European pottery, paintings, sculpture.

Museums
Newbury Museum - Newbury
Natural History & Archaeology -
Paleolithic to Saxon & Mediaeval times.
Household Cavalry Museum - Windsor

Other Things to see & do
Racing - at Newbury, Ascot & Windsor
Highlight of the racing year is the Royal Meeting at Ascot each June, attended by the Queen & other members of the Royal Family.
Antiques - Hungerford is a famous centre for antiques.
Windsor Safari Park.

Buckinghamshire
Gazeteer
Area of outstanding natural beauty.
Burnham Beeches - 70 acres of unspoilt woodlands, inspiration to poet Thomas Gray.

Historic Houses
Waddesdon Manor & Ascott House - homes of the Rothschilds.
Chalfont St. Giles - cottage home of great English poet John Milton.
Old Jordans & the Meeting House - 17th century buildings associated with William Penn, the founder of Pennsylvania & with the Society of Friends, often called the Quakers.

Things to see & do
Buckinghamshire Railway Centre - at Quainton
Vintage steam train rides & largest private railway collection in Britain.
Chalfont Shire Horse Centre -
home of the gentle giants of the horse world.

Beds:Berks:Bucks:Herts.

Hertfordshire

Gazeteer

Areas of outstanding natural beauty.
Parts of the Chilterns.

Historic Houses & Castles

Hatfield House - Hatfield
Home of the Marquess of Salisbury.
Jacobean House & Tudor Palace -
childhood home of Queen Elizabeth I.
Knebworth House - Knebworth
Family home of the Lyttons. 16th century
house transformed into Victorian High
Gothic. Furniture, portraits. Formal
gardens & unique Gertrude Jekyll herb
garden.
Shaw's Corner - Ayot St. Lawrence
Home of George Bernard Shaw.

Cathedrals & Churches

St. Albans Cathedral - St. Albans
9th century foundation, murals, painted
roof over choir, 15th century reredos,
stone rood screen.

Stanstead St. Abbots (St. James)12th
century nave, 13th century chancel, 15th
century tower & porch, 16th century
North chapel, 18th century box pews
& 3-decker pulpit.
Watford (St. Mary)
13 - 15th century. Essex chapel.
Tuscan arcade. Morryson tombs

Museums

**Rhodes Memorial Museum &
Commonwealth Centre** - at Bishop
Stortford
Zoological Museum - Tring
Gardens
Gardens of the Rose - Chiswell Green
Nr. St Albans
Showgrounds of the Royal National Rose
Society
Capel Manor
Extensive grounds of horticultural
college.
Many fine trees, including the largest
copper beech in the country.

Bledlow Village; Bucks.

BEDS/BUCKS
BERKSHIRE
HERTS

Map reference

1 Miles
2 Lochrie
3 Power
4 Lemin
5 Wilson
6 Cooper
7 Ryder
8 Cook
9 Steeds
10 Thornely
11 Jackson
12 Barker
13 Must
14 Butler
15 French
16 Codd
17 Pollock-Hill
18 McAlpine
19 Knowles
20 Baldwin
21 Shand
22 Walker

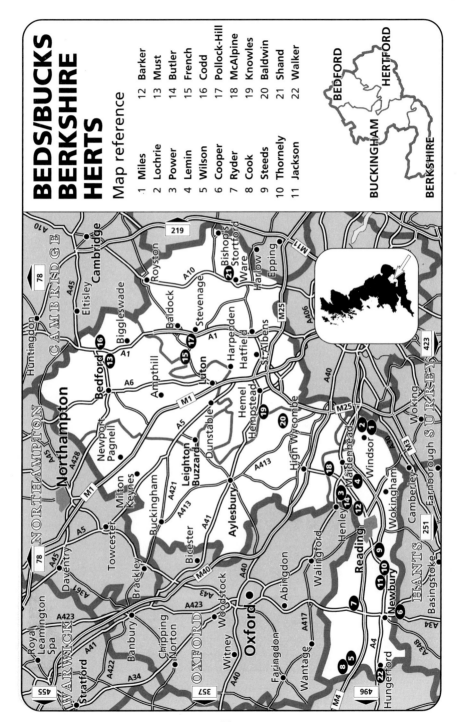

Berkshire

		rate from £ per person	children taken	evening meals	animals taken
John & Sieglinde Miles **Ennis Lodge Guest** **House** **Winkfield Road** **Ascot SL5 7EX** **Tel/Fax: (01344) 21009** **Open: ALL YEAR** **Map Ref No. 01**	Nearest Road: A.329, A.30 Ennis Lodge is situated in central Ascot, adjacent to the racecourse. There are 4 tastefully furnished twin-bedded rooms & 1 single, each en-suite with colour T.V., tea/coffee-making facilities, trouser press, hairdryer & radio alarm. Conveniently located within walking distance of the mainline station. London only 45 mins by rail. Also within easy reach of Windsor, Heathrow Airport, M.3, M.4 & M.25. Single room supplement.	£20.50 🚭 CREDIT CARD VISA M'CARD	Y	N	Y
Marjie Lochrie **Lyndrick Guest House** **The Avenue** **Ascot SL5 7ND** **Tel: (01344) 883520** **Fax 01344 891243** **Open: ALL YEAR** **Map Ref No. 02**	Nearest Road: A.30, M.4 'Lyndrick' is a 5-bedroom Victorian house located in a quiet tree-lined avenue. All bedrooms have colour T.V., tea/coffee, hairdryer, trouser press & face cloths, & most are en-suite. Breakfast is served in a pleasant conservatory. Windsor is 10 mins away, Ascot racecourse is 2 mins & Wentworth golf course is 10 mins. London (Waterloo) is 45 mins by train, Heathrow Airport 25 mins. Easy access to M.4, M.3, M.25, & A.30.	£20.00 🚭 CREDIT CARD VISA M'CARD	Y	N	Y
Mike & Elsebeth Walker **Marshgate Cottage** **Hotel** **Marsh Lane** **Hungerford RG17 0QX** **Tel: (01488) 682307** **Fax 01488 685475** **Open: ALL YEAR** **Map Ref No. 22**	Nearest Road: A.4, A.338 Marshgate Cottage is a friendly, family-run hotel at the edge of Hungerford. Tucked at the end of a quiet country lane, it backs onto the Kennet & Avon Canal & Freemen's Marsh with trout streams & wildlife. 9 very attractive guest bedrooms. Most are at ground level & are en-suite, all are furnished to a high standard & are well-equipped. Excellent meals served in the courtyard restaurant. An ideal touring base for southern England. Oxford, Salisbury, the Cotswolds, Windsor & Bath are all within an hour's drive.	£19.75 CREDIT CARD VISA M'CARD AMEX	Y	Y	N
Mrs Mary Wilson **Fishers Farm** **Shefford Woodlands** **Hungerford RG17 7AB** **Tel: (01488) 648466** **Fax 01488 648706** **Open: ALL YEAR** **Map Ref No. 05**	Nearest Road: A.338, M.4 Jt.14 A traditional farmhouse on a working arable & livestock farm with all modern comforts & a beautiful large garden in a secluded & peaceful location, yet only 1 mile from Jt. 14 of the M.4 motorway. Accommodation is in 3 large bedrooms with en-suite/private bathrooms. An ideal base for exploring southern England, & within easy reach of Heathrow & Gatwick Airports. A heated indoor swimming pool. Excellent cooking using many home-grown ingredients.	£20.00	Y	Y	Y
Michael & Joanna Power **Woodpecker Cottage** **Warren Row** **Maidenhead RG10 8QS** **Tel: (01628) 822772** **Fax 01628 822125** **Open: ALL YEAR** **Map Ref No. 03**	Nearest Road: A.4 Idyllic woodland setting at edge of rural village, & yet M.4, M.40, Oxford, Heathrow & Windsor within easy reach. Henley-on-Thames 5 miles. Peaceful house in large pretty garden with croquet lawns. 2 large ground-floor rooms, 1 double with en-suite shower & W.C., & 1 twin with private bathroom. Both have T.V. & radio, tea/coffee-making facilities, hairdryers, etc. Children over 8 years welcome. Breakfast includes delicious home-made bread & jams.	£20.00 🚭	Y	N	N

Lodge Down. Lambourn.

Berkshire

	rate from £ per person	children taken	evening meals	animals taken

Bar Barbour & Sue Lemin **Beehive Manor** **Cox Green Lane** **Maidenhead** **SL6 3ET** **Tel: (01628) 20980** **Open: ALL YEAR** **Map Ref No. 04**	Nearest Road: A.404 (M) Beehive Manor offers all the charm & country-house atmosphere of a Tudor home set in a traditional English garden. Yet, amongst the massive oak beams, latticed windows & linenfold panelling are also all the comforts of the 20th century. Within its wisteria-clad walls, 3 superb bedrooms are available to guests, as well as a sunny drawing & a delightful dining room. London is just 35 mins away by train. Children over 12.	£28.00	Y	N	N
John & Sally Cook **Lodge Down** **Lambourn** **Newbury RG16 7BJ** **Tel: (01672) 540304** **Fax 01672 540304** **Open: ALL YEAR** **Map Ref No. 08**	Nearest Road: B.4000, M.4 A warm welcome is assured at Lodge Down, a country house with superb accommodation & en-suite bathrooms, set in lovely grounds. Excellent & varied dining in surrounding villages. Easy access to the M.4 motorway at Jts 14 & 15. 1 hour or less for Heathrow (60 miles), Bath (43 miles) & Oxford (26 miles). This location provides a central base for excursions to Stonehenge, Salisbury & the Cotswolds, etc., or an easy drive to Heathrow & London.	£20.00	Y	N	N
		see PHOTO over			
Jonathan & Diana Ryder **Langley Hall Farm** **World's End** **Beedon** **Newbury RG20 8SD** **Tel: (01635) 248222** **Fax 01635 247007** **Open: ALL YEAR** **Map Ref No. 07**	Nearest Road: M.4, A.34 Large, early-Victorian manor farmhouse situated in 600 acres of unspoilt Berkshire countryside, with far-reaching, glorious views. Working farm, with livestock. Every comfort is offered in spacious, attractive bedrooms with colour T.V. & tea/coffee-making facilities. Delicious farmhouse breakfast served in large dining room. This is an excellent base for visiting Oxford, Bath, Stratford & London. Within easy reach of Heathrow. A warm & friendly welcome is guaranteed at Langley Hall, a delightful home. Excellent local pubs.	£18.50	Y	N	N
Sarah Cooper **Adbury Holt House** **Burghclere** **Newbury** **RG20 9BW** **Tel: (01635) 42846** **Open: ALL YEAR** **Map Ref No. 06**	Nearest Road: A.34, M.3, M.4 A delightful, secluded Victorian mansion set in its own grounds of 12 acres: of particular interest to gardening enthusiasts, for there are over 100 varieties of trees & many unusual shrubs & plants. The accommodation is very attractive, in 5 lovely, well-appointed bedrooms, 4 with own bathroom, & each with radio, T.V., & tea/coffee-making facilities. Pets welcome by arrangement. Parking. Non-smokers preferred.	£19.50	Y	N	Y
Mrs Jane Steeds **Highwoods** **Burghfield Common** **Reading RG7 3BG** **Tel: (01734) 832320** **Fax 01734 831070** **Open: ALL YEAR (Excl. Xmas)** **Map Ref No. 09**	Nearest Road: A.4, M.4 A friendly & relaxing atmosphere at this fine Victorian country house set in 4 acres of attractive grounds, with unspoilt, far-reaching views. Offering 2 spacious, comfortable, attractively furnished rooms (1 en-suite) with all modern amenities, including T.V.. Guests are welcome to use the garden & hard tennis court. Also, a gallery specialising in English watercolours & prints. Easy access to London, Heathrow Airport, Windsor, Oxford & Bath. Non-smokers preferred.	£19.50	Y	N	N

Berkshire

		rate from £ per person	children taken	evening meals	animals taken
Mrs Jill Thornely **Bridge Cottage** **Station Road** **Woolhampton** **Reading** **RG7 5SF** **Tel: (01734) 713138** **Open: ALL YEAR (Excl. Xmas)** **Map Ref No. 10**	Nearest Road: A.4, M.4, M.3 A warm welcome awaits the visitor to this delightful 300-year-old riverside cottage, offering 5 bedrooms with beamed ceilings, including a twin-bedded room with en-suite facilities. Breakfast is served in a lovely conservatory overlooking the River Kennet, where old narrow boats pass by. It is surrounded by lovely countryside. Close by is the local pub which serves excellent home-cooked suppers. London 1 hour away. Ideal for Heathrow & rail/air connections to Reading & London, etc.	£19.50	Y	N	N
Mrs Auriol Jackson **Hunts Cottage** **Midgham Green** **Reading** **RG7 5TT** **Tel: (01734) 712540** **Open: ALL YEAR (Excl. Xmas)** **Map Ref No. 11**	Nearest Road: A.4 Built around 1620, Hunts Cottage is a listed, timber-framed house with masses of exposed beams & a pair of inglenook fireplaces. There are 3 guest rooms: a twin with en-suite bath, a double - with a full-tester, oak, 4-poster bed & private bath - & a single. All have a colour T.V. & tea-making equipment. Guests are welcome to use the sitting room, the outdoor heated pool & the large garden. Children over 12.	£22.50	Y	N	N
Mrs Carel Barker **The Hermitage** **63 London Road** **Twyford** **RG10 9EJ** **Tel: (01734) 340004** **Fax 01734 340004** **Open: ALL YEAR (Excl. Xmas)** **Map Ref No. 12**	Nearest Road: A.4, M.4, M.40 A large, elegant Victorian house with unique Victorian additions. A central village location. An ideal base for exploring the Thames Valley (including Henley, Oxford & Windsor). Convenient for Heathrow. A short walk to the mainline station (London 40 mins). A choice of 5 bedrooms (3 en-suite, including 2 in the recently converted coach house), all with colour T.V. & tea/coffee-making facilities. A spacious dining room overlooking a large established garden, which guests are welcome to use. Children over 10.	£20.00	Y	N	N
Mrs Elisabeth Butler **Martens House** **Willow Lane** **Wargrave** **RG10 8LH** **Tel: (01734) 403707** **Open: ALL YEAR** **Map Ref No. 14**	Nearest Road: A.321 This a comfortable, friendly Edwardian house, with lawns down to the Thames & views across meadowland. There are 2 spacious & attractive twin bedrooms, 1 en-suite & 1 with private bath. There are also tea/coffee-making facilities. Wargrave has several places to eat, & 3 miles away is Henley-on-Thames, known for its Royal Regatta & Festival. Easy access to the M.4, M.40, M.25 & Heathrow.	£20.00	Y	N	Y

When booking your accommodation please mention
The Best Bed & Breakfast

Bedfordshire & Buckinghamshire

		rate from £ per person	children taken	evening meals	animals taken
Mrs Janet Must **Church Farm** **41 High Street** **Roxton MK44 3EB** **Tel: (01234) 870234** **Fax 01234 871576** **Open: ALL YEAR** **Map Ref No. 13**	Nearest Road: A.1, A.428 Church Farm is a lovely 17th-century farmhouse with Georgian frontage, set in a secluded village. Furnished with a pleasant mixture of family antiques, the comfortable guest accommodation has its own staircase & bathroom, with tea/coffee-making facilities in the rooms. Breakfast is served in the beamed dining room, & a lounge is available with open fire & colour T.V.. Whether on business or on a short break, a warm welcome awaits you.	£16.00	Y	N	Y
Mrs Margaret Codd **Highfield Farm** **Great North Road** **Sandy SG19 2AQ** **Tel: (01767) 682332** **Open: ALL YEAR** **Map Ref No. 16**	Nearest Road: A.1 A tranquil & very welcoming house with comfort, warmth & a friendly atmosphere in a lovely setting on an arable farm. 6 attractive bedrooms, 4 en-suite, including 3 ground-floor rooms in tastefully converted stables. Highfield Farm is set back off the A.1, giving peaceful seclusion & yet easy access to London, Cambridge, Bedford, the Shuttleworth Collection, the R.S.P.B. & the east-coast ports. Ample parking. Most guests return.	£16.00	Y	N	Y

Buckinghamshire

		rate from £ per person	children taken	evening meals	animals taken
The Country House **Bisham Road** **Marlow SL7 1RP** **Tel: (01628) 890606** **Fax 01628 890983** **Open: ALL YEAR** **Map Ref No. 18**	Nearest Road: A.404 The Country House is a small private hotel, established in 1987 in a carefully restored Edwardian building. Individually furnished rooms offer a full range of facilities, & personal care & attention to detail are a feature. Set in beautiful gardens, overlooking farmland & woods, & yet only 200 yds' walk to Marlow suspension bridge & the High Street, with a wide range of restaurants & shops. An ideal base for touring.	£41.00 CREDIT CARD VISA M'CARD AMEX	Y	N	N

Hertfordshire

		rate from £ per person	children taken	evening meals	animals taken
Mrs Alison Knowles **Broadway Farm** **Berkhamsted HP4 2RR** **Tel: (01442) 866541** **Fax 01442 866541** **Open: ALL YEAR** **Map Ref No. 19**	Nearest Road: A.4251 A warm welcome is guaranteed at Broadway, a working arable farm with its own fishing lake. There are 3 comfortable en-suite rooms in a recently converted building adjacent to the farmhouse. Each has tea/coffee-making facilities & colour T.V.. Everything for the leisure or business guest: the relaxation of farm life in an attractive rural setting, yet easy access to London, airports, motorways & mainline rail services.	£19.00	Y	N	N
Mrs Lesley Baldwin **Venus Hill Farm** **Venus Hill, Bovingdon** **Hemel Hempstead HP3 0PG** **Tel: (01442) 833396** **Fax 01442 833209** **Open: MAR - OCT** **Map Ref No. 20**	Nearest Road: A.41, M.25, M.1 A delightful 350-year-old converted farmhouse, with 2 acres of garden, a heated outdoor swimming pool & tennis court. Set in open countryside, this is an ideal spot for a quiet relaxing holiday, or for visiting Windsor Castle, Hatfield House, Woburn Abbey, St. Albans Abbey & many other interesting places. Heathrow & London are also easily accessible. Guests will receive a warm welcome, with comfortable accommodation. 3 bedrooms with modern amenities, tea/coffee makers & T.V..	£20.00	Y	N	N

Homewood. Knebworth.

Hertfordshire

		rate from £ per person	children taken	evening meals	animals taken
Lady Rosemary French **Little Offley** **Great Offley** **Hitchin SG5 3BU** **Tel: (01462) 768243** **Fax 01462 768243** **Open: ALL YEAR** **Map Ref No. 15**	Nearest Road: A.505 Little Offley is a beautiful 17th-century house set in 800 acres of farmland in the Chiltern Hills. Quiet, warm & comfortable, the accommodation comprises 3 attractively furnished double bedrooms, 2 with a private bathroom. A swimming pool & croquet lawn are available in summer. Dinner by prior arrangement only. Little Offley makes an ideal base for visiting Harefield House, Luton Hoo, Woburn Abbey, Whipsnade Zoo & Cambridge, & London is just 30 mins by train.	£30.00 CREDIT CARD VISA M'CARD	N	Y	N
Mrs Samantha Pollock-Hill **Homewood** **Park Lane** **Knebworth** **Stevenage** **SG3 6PP** **Tel: (01438) 812105** **Open: ALL YEAR** **Map Ref No. 17**	Nearest Road: A.1 M Offering friendly, gracious living at a very reasonable price. Homewood is a classic blend of comfort & style: an Edwardian country house which is also a well-equipped family home. Homewood has been used as a location for period drama by the B.B.C., & is often sought out by admirers of its designer, the distinguished architect Edwin Lutyens. You will be treated as a member of the family, or your privacy will be respected - whichever you prefer. Additional meals can easily be arranged, including dinner. 2 lovely bedrooms, each with private bathroom.	£35.00 *see PHOTO over*	Y	Y	N
Mrs Angela C. Shand **Timber Hall** **Cold Christmas** **Ware SG12 7SN** **Tel: (01920) 466086** **Fax 01920 462739** **Open: ALL YEAR** **Map Ref No. 21**	Nearest Road: A.10 Timber Hall is an old farmhouse of great character & comfort, situated in the Rib Valley & looking out over open countryside. An hour from London, & rather less from Cambridge, it offers quiet accommodation in 4 elegantly furnished bedrooms, with lovely walks from the house & several golf courses close by. Meals are served in the old family hall, & there is a spacious drawing room opening onto a large garden.	£17.50	Y	Y	Y

When booking your accommodation please mention
The Best Bed & Breakfast

Cambridge & Northants

Cambridgeshire
(East Anglia)

A county very different from any other, this is flat, mysterious, low-lying Fenland crisscrossed by a network of waterways both natural & man-made.

The Fens were once waterlogged, misty marshes but today the rich black peat is drained & grows carrots, sugar beet, celery & the best asparagus in the world.

Drive north across the Fens & slowly you become aware of a great presence dominating the horizon. Ely cathedral, the "ship of the Fens", sails closer. The cathedral is a masterpiece with its graceful form & delicate tracery towers. Begun before the Domesday Book was written, it took the work of a full century before it was ready to have the timbered roof raised up. Norman stonemasons worked with great skill & the majestic nave is glorious in its simplicity. Their work was crowned by the addition of the Octagon in the 14th century. Despite the ravages of the Reformation, the lovely Lady Chapel survives as one of the finest examples of decorated architecture in Britain with its exquisitely fine stone carving.

To the south, the Fens give way to rolling chalk hills & fields of barley, wheat & rye, & Cambridge. Punts gliding through the broad river, between smooth, lawned banks, under willow trees, past college buildings as extravagant as wedding cakes. The names of the colleges resound through the ages - Peterhouse, Corpus Christi, Kings, Queens, Trinity, Emmanuel. A city of learning & progress, & a city of great tradition where cows graze in open spaces, just 500 yards from the market square.

Northamptonshire
(East Midlands)

Northamptonshire has many features to attract & interest the visitor, from the town of Brackley in the south with its charming buildings of mellow stone, to ancient Rockingham Forest in the north. There are lovely churches, splendid historic houses & peaceful waterways.

The Waterways Museum at Stoke Bruerne makes a popular outing, with boat trips available on the Grand Union Canal beside the museum. Horse-racing at Towcester & motor-racing at Silverstone draws the crowds, but there are quieter pleasures in visits to Canons Ashby, or to Sulgrave Manor, home of George Washington's ancestors.

In the pleasantly wooded Rockingham Forest area are delightful villages, one of which is Ashton with its thatched cottages, the scene of the World Conker Championships each October. Mary Queen of Scots was executed at Fotheringay, in the castle of which only the mound remains.

Rockingham Castle has a solid Norman gateway & an Elizabethan hall; Deene Park has family connections with the Earl of Cardigan who led the Charge of the Light Brigade & Kirby Hall is a dramatic Elizabethan ruin.

The county is noted for its parish churches, with fine Saxon examples at Brixworth & at Earl's Barton, as well as the round Church of the Holy Sepulchre in the county town itself.

Northampton has a fine tradition of shoemaking, so it is hardly surprising that boots & shoes & other leather-goods take pride of place in the town';s museums. The town has one of the country's biggest market squares, an historic Royal Theatre & a mighty Wurlitzer Organ to dance to at Turner's Musical Merry-go-round ! !

Cambridge & Northants

Cambridgeshire Gazeteer

Areas of outstanding natural beauty
The Nene Valley

Historic Houses & Castles

Anglesy Abbey - Nr. Cambridge
Origins in the reign of Henry I. Was redesigned into Elizabethan Manor by Fokes family. Houses the Fairhaven collection of Art treasures - stands in 100 acres of Ground.

Hinchingbrooke House - Huntingdon
13th century nunnery converted mid-16th century into Tudor house. Later additions in 17th & 19th centuries.

King's School - Ely
12th & 14th centuries - original stonework & vaulting in the undercroft, original timbering 14th century gateway & monastic barn.

Kimbolton Castle - Kimbolton
Tudor Manor house - has associations with Katherine of Aragon. Remodelled by Vanbrugh 1700's - gatehouse by Robert Adam.

Longthorpe Tower - Nr. Peterborough
13th & 14th century fortification - rare wall paintings.

Peckover House - Wisbech
18th century domestic architecture - charming Victorian garden.

University of Cambridge Colleges

Peterhouse	1284
Clare	1326
Pembroke	1347
Gonville & Caius	1348
Trinity Hall	1350
Corpus Christi	1352
King's	1441
Queen's	1448
St. Catherine's	1473
Jesus	1496
Christ's	1505
St. John's	1511
Magadalene	1542
Trinity	1546
Emmanuel	1584
Sidney Sussex	1596
Downing	1800

Wimpole Hall - Nr. Cambridge
18th & 19th century - beautiful staterooms - aristocratic house.

Cathedrals & Churches

Alconbury (St. Peter & St. Paul)
13th century chancel & 15th century roof. Broach spire.

Babraham (St. Peter)
13th century tower - 17th century monument.

Ely Cathedral
Rich arcading - west front incomplete. Remarkable interior with Octagon - unique in Gothic architecture.

Great Paxton (Holy Trinity)
12th century.

Harlton (Blessed Virgin Mary)
Perpendicular - decorated transition. 17th century monuments

Hildersham (Holy Trinity)
13th century - effigies, brasses & glass.

Lanwade (St. Nicholas)
15th century - mediaeval fittings

Peterborough Cathedral
Great Norman church fine example - little altered. Painted wooden roof to nave - remarkable west front - Galilee Porch & spires later additions.

Ramsey (St. Thomas of Canterbury)
12th century arcades - perpendicular nave. Late Norman chancel with Angevin vault.

St. Neots (St. Mary)
15th century

Sutton (St. Andrew)
14th century

Trumpington (St. Mary & St. Nicholas)
14th century. Framed brass of 1289 of Sir Roger de Trumpington.

Westley Waterless (St. Mary the Less)
Decorated. 14th century brass of Sir John & Lady Creke.

Wimpole (St. Andrew)
14th century rebuilt 1749 - splendid heraldic glass.

Yaxley (St. Peter)
15th century chancel screen, wall paintings, fine steeple.

Museums & Galleries

Cromwell Museum - Huntingdon
Exhibiting portraits, documents, etc. of the Cromwellian period.

Fitzwilliam Museum - Cambridge
Gallery of masters, old & modern, ceramics, applied arts, prints & drawing, mediaeval manuscripts, music & art library.

Cambridge & Northants

Scott Polar Research Institute - Cambridge
Relics of expeditions & the equipment used. Current scientific work in Arctic & Antarctic.

University Archives - Cambridge
13th century manuscripts, Charters, Statutes, Royal letters & mandates. Wide variety of records of the University.

University Museum of Archaeology & Anthropology - Cambridge
Collections illustrative of Stone Age in Europe, Africa & Asia.
Britain prehistoric to mediaeval times. Prehistoric America.

Ethnographic material from South-east Asia, Africa & America.

University Museum of Classical Archaeology - Cambridge
Casts of Greek & Roman Sculpture - representative collection.

Whipple Museum of the History of Science - Cambridge16th, 17th & 18th century scientific instruments - historic collection.

Other Things to see & do

Nene Valley Railway
Steam railway with locomotives & carriages from many countries.

Caius College; Cambridge.

Cambridge & Northants

Northamptonshire Gazeteer

Historic Houses & Castles

Althorp - Nr. Northampton
Family home of the Princess of Wales, with fine pictures & porcelain.

Boughton House - Nr. Kettering
Furniture, tapestries & pictures in late 17th century building modelled on Versailles, in beautiful parkland.

Canons Ashby House - Nr. Daventry
Small 16th century manor house with gardens & church.

Deene Park - Nr. Corby
Family home for over 4 centuries, surrounded by park, extensive gardens & lake.

Holdenby House - Nr. Northampton
Gardens include part of Elizabethan garden, with original entrance arches, terraces & ponds. Falconry centre. Rare breeds.

Kirby Hall - Nr. Corby
Large Elizabethan mansion with fine gardens.

Lamport Hall - Nr. Northampton
17th & 18th century house with paintings, furniture & china. One of the first garden rockeries in Britain. Programme of concerts & other special events.

Rockingham Castle - Rockingham, Nr. Market Harborough
Norman gateway & walls surrounding mainly Elizabethan house, with pictures & Rockingham china. Extensive gardens with 16th century yew hedge.

Rushton Triangular Lodge - Nr. Kettering
Symbolic of the Trinity, with 3 sides, 3 floors, trefoil windows.

Sulgrave Manor - Nr. Banbury
Early English Manor, home of George Washington's ancestors.

Museums

Abington Museum - Northampton
Domestic & social life collections in former manor house.

Museum of Leathercraft - Northampton
History of leather use, with Queen Victoria's saddle, & Samuel Pepys' wallet.

Waterways Museum - Stoke Bruerne Nr. Towcester
200 years of canal & waterway life, displayed beside the Grand Union Canal.

Cathedrals & Churches

Brixworth Church - Nr. Northampton
One of the finest Anglo-Saxon churches in the country, mostly 7th century.

Earls Barton Church - Nr. Northampton
Fine Anglo-Saxon tower & Norman arch & arcading.

Church of the Holy Sepulchre - Northampton
Largest & best preserved of four remaining round churches in England, dating from 1100.

Other Things to see & do

Billing Aquadrome - Nr. Northampton
Boating, fishing, swimming & amusements.

Wicksteed Park - Kettering
Large playground & variety of amusements for families.

Lilford Park - Nr. Oundle
Birds & farm animals in parkland setting where many special events are held.

Rushton Triangular Lodge.

CAMBRIDGESHIRE & NORTHAMPTONSHIRE

Map reference

0 Peek
1 Greening
1 Axhorn
2 Nix
3 Scott
4 Bailey
5 Elbourn
6 Hindley
7 Clarke
8 Faulkner
9 Barlow

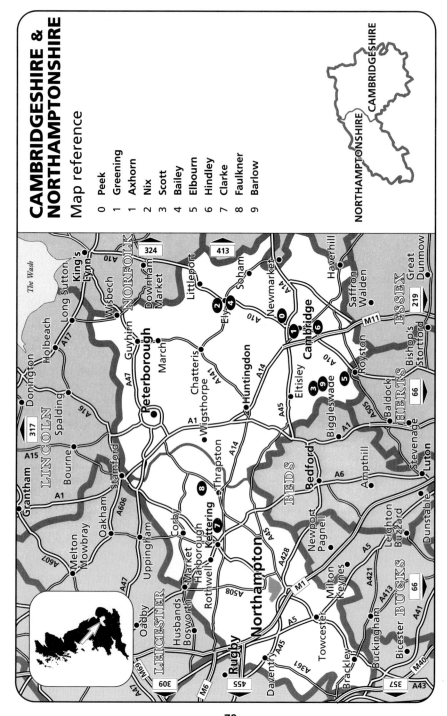

Cambridgeshire

		rate from £ per person	children taken	evening meals	animals taken
Peter & Maggie Scott **Church Farm** **Gransden Road, Caxton** **Cambridge CB3 8PL** **Tel: (01954) 719543** **Fax 01954 718999** **Open: ALL YEAR** **Map Ref No. 03**	Nearest Road: A.1198 This elegant & spacious listed farmhouse, which retains original 16th- & 17th-century features with 19th-century additions, is set in over 3 acres of rural peace. A wealth of oak beams, antiques, English watercolours, open log fires, comfortable beds & imaginative country-house cooking make for a relaxing stay. Ely Cathedral, Wimpole Hall, Kings College Chapel, Audley End & the Fitzwilliam Museum are all within easy reach.	£24.50	Y	Y	N
Pamela Axhorn **Kirkwood House** **172 Chesterton Road** **Cambridge CB4 1DA** **Tel: (01223) 313874** **Open: FEB - DEC** **Map Ref No. 01**	Nearest Road: M.11, A.10 This Edwardian townhouse offers 4 comfortable designer decorated bedrooms, each equipped with hospitality tray & colour T.V.. 2 rooms are en-suite. A delicious breakfast is served from pretty English china & gleaming silver amid antique furniture. Situated close to the River Cam & a short walk from the city centre & its colleges. Children over 7 yrs.	£24.00	Y	N	N
Mrs Jane Greening **7 Water Street** **Cambridge** **CB4 1NZ** **Tel: (01223) 355550** **Open: ALL YEAR** **Map Ref No. 01**	Nearest Road: A.14 A warm welcome & a friendly atmosphere await you at this lovely mediaeval coaching house overlooking the River Cam. Accommodation is in a choice of 3 charming rooms, with tea/coffee-making facilities & views across the delightful walled garden. A colour T.V. lounge is available for guests' use. A pleasant walk along the tow path leads to the many historic sights in Cambridge. Children over 12 yrs.	£19.00	Y	N	N
Sally Peck **Berry House** **High Street** **Waterbeach** **Cambridge CB5 9JU** **Tel: (01223) 860702** **Fax 01223 860702** **Open: ALL YEAR** **Map Ref No. 00**	Nearest Road: A.10, A.14 Berry House is a Grade II listed building built around 1820. The garden still contains a number of fruit trees from the original orchards. The elegant bedrooms have mahogany double beds, Edwardian & Georgian furniture & modern en-suite facilities, including powerful Victorian-style showers. Tea/coffee-making facilities, radio/alarms & electric blankets are provided in the rooms, which have a warm, period, cottage style. A beautiful home, perfect for visiting both Cambridge & Ely, or for exploring this county.	£25.00	Y	Y	N
Mrs Hilary Nix **Hill House Farm** **9 Main Street** **Coveney** **Ely** **CB6 2DJ** **Tel: (01353) 778369** **Open: ALL YEAR** **Map Ref No. 02**	Nearest Road: A.142, A.10 A warm welcome awaits you at this spacious Victorian farmhouse, situated in the quiet village of Coveney, 3 miles west of the cathedral city of Ely. Open views of the surrounding countryside & easy access to Cambridge, Newmarket & Huntingdon. It is ideally placed for touring Cambridgeshire, Norfolk & Suffolk. Wicken Fen & Welney wildfowl refuge are nearby. 3 tastefully furnished bedrooms, 1 twin & 2 double en-suite rooms, 1 ground floor. All have their own entrance, T.V., clock/radio & tea/coffee facilities. A lounge & garden for guests' use. Children over 12.	£19.00	Y	N	N

		rate from £ per person	children taken	evening meals	animals taken
Mr & Mrs Derek Bailey **Springfields** **Ely Road** **Little Thetford** **Ely CB6 3HJ** **Tel: (01353) 663637** **Fax 01353 663130** **Open: JAN - NOV** **Map Ref No. 04**	Nearest Road: A.10 Located in a quiet area, yet only 2 miles from the historic Ely Cathedral & city centre. Springfields is a lovely home set in an acre of beautiful garden. Offering 3 delightful bedrooms, 1 en-suite. All rooms have modern amenities, tea/coffee makers & T.V.. A Full English breakfast is served. A warm & friendly welcome awaits you at Springfields, where the accent is on hospitality. Stay a while, & smell the roses. Springfields is a perfect base from which to explore the changeless beauty of the Fens.	£20.00	N	N	N
Olga & David Hindley **Purlins** **12 High Street** **Little Shelford CB2 5ES** **Tel: (01223) 842643** **Fax (01223) 842643** **Open: FEB - DEC** **Map Ref No. 06**	Nearest Road: A.10, M.11 Lovely, individually designed family home, with 2 acres of parkland, situated in a quiet, pretty village on the Cam, 4 miles south of Cambridge. An ideal centre for Colleges, Audley End House, the Imperial War Museum & bird watching. There are 3 well-appointed double bedrooms (2 ground-floor), all with en-suite bathrooms, colour T.V. & tea/coffee facilities. Varied breakfasts (special diets by arrangement). Restaurants nearby. Children over 8 welcome.	£21.00	Y	N	N
Bernice & John Elbourn **Chiswick House** **Chiswick End** **Meldreth** **Royston SG8 6LZ** **Tel: (01763) 260242** **Open: ALL YEAR** **Map Ref No. 05**	Nearest Road: A.10 A beautiful timber-framed farmhouse dating from the 16th century. The royal crest of King James I is found above the fireplace, suggesting this was his hunting lodge in the early 1600s. Jacobean panelling, oak beams & open fireplaces create a wonderful atmosphere. 6 en-suite rooms, with tea/coffee-making facilities. T.V. is available. Many excellent inns nearby. An ideal base for touring Cambridge, Suffolk & Hertfordshire.	£20.00 *see PHOTO over*	Y	N	Y
Mrs Sue Barlow **Model Farm** **Little Gransden** **Sandy** **SG19 3EA** **Tel: (01767) 677361** **Open: ALL YEAR** **Map Ref No. 09**	Nearest Road: A.1198 A warm & friendly welcome awaits visitors to this traditional 1870s farmhouse situated on a working family farm. The farmhouse, providing comfortable accommodation & lovely views, is set in open countryside between the villages of Little Gransden & Longstowe. Guests are welcome to walk around the farm & garden. Cambridge can be reached in 20 mins via the B.1046 which takes the motorist on a picturesque drive through villages. A delightful home.	£14.00	Y	N	Y

When booking your accommodation please mention
The Best Bed & Breakfast

Chiswick House. Royston

Northamptonshire

		rate from £ per person	children taken	evening meals	animals taken
Mrs Audrey Clarke **Dairy Farm** **Cranford St. Andrew** **Kettering** **NN14 4AQ** **Tel: (01536) 330273** **Open: ALL YEAR** **Map Ref No. 07**	Nearest Road: A.14, A.604 Situated in an idyllic Northamptonshire village, Dairy Farm is a charming 17th-century farmhouse, featuring oak beams & inglenook fireplaces. There are 4 very comfortable bedrooms, each with en-suite/private bathroom. Families are well catered for. There is a delightful garden, containing an ancient circular dovecote, for guests to enjoy in a relaxed & friendly atmosphere. Delicious meals, using farmhouse produce.	£20.00	Y	Y	N
Margaret Faulkner **The Maltings** **Main Street** **Aldwincle** **Oundle NN14 3EP** **Tel: (01832) 720233** **Fax 01832 720326** **Open: ALL YEAR** **Map Ref No. 08**	Nearest Road: A.1, A.605, A.14 There is a warm & friendly welcome with personal attention at this former 16th century maltings - the Faulkner family home for 25 years. A lovely stone house & charming conversion of a small granary, all bordering a plant lover's garden, in a quiet village setting. Exposed beams, inglenooks & antique furniture complete this period home. 3 cosy bedrooms - all with bathrooms - 24-hour heating & good eating places nearby. Children over 10 please. Local attractions: Burghley House, Rockingham Castle & Rutland Water.	£21.50 CREDIT CARD VISA M'CARD	Y	N	N

All the establishments mentioned in this guide are members of
The Worldwide Bed & Breakfast Association

**All the establishments mentioned in this guide
are members of the
Worldwide Bed & Breakfast Association.**

**If you have any comments regarding your
accommodation please send them to us
using the form at the back of the book.
We value your comments.**

Cheshire & Merseyside

Cheshire & Merseyside (North West)

Cheshire is located between the Peak District & the mountains of North Wales & is easily accessible from three major motorways. It has much to attract long visits but is also an ideal stopping-off point for travellers to the Lake District & Scotland, or to North Wales or Ireland. There is good access eastwards to York & the east coast & to the south to Stratford-upon-Avon & to London.

Cheshire can boast seven magnificent stately homes, the most visited zoo outside London, four of Europe's largest Garden Centres & many popular venues which feature distinctive Cheshire themes such as silk, salt, cheese, antiques & country crafts.

The Cheshire plain with Chester, its fine county town, & its pretty villages, rises up to Alderley Edge in the east from where there are panoramic views, & then climbs dramatically to meet the heights of the Peaks.

To the west is the coastline of the Wirral Peninsula with miles of sandy beaches & dunes &, of course, Liverpool.

The countryside shelters very beautiful houses. Little Moreton Hall near Congleton, is one of the most perfect imaginable. It is a black & white "magpie" house & not one of its walls is perpendicular, yet it has withstood time & weather for nearly four centuries, standing on the waterside gazing at its own reflection.

Tatton Hall is large & imposing & is splendidly furnished with many fine objects on display. The park & gardens are a delight & especially renowned for the azaleas & rhododendrons. In complete contrast is the enormous radio telescope at Jodrell Bank where visitors can be introduced to planetary astronomy in the planetarium.

Chester is a joy; a walk through its streets is like walking through living history. The old city is encircled by city walls enclosing arcaded streets with handsome black & white galleried buildings that blend well with modern life. There are many excellent shops along these "Rows". Chester Cathedral is a fine building of monastic foundation, with a peaceful cloister & outstanding wood carving in the choir stalls. Boat rides can be taken along the River Dee which flows through the city.

Manchester has first rate shopping, restaurants, sporting facilities, theatres & many museums ranging from an excellent costume museum to the fascinating Museum of Science & Industry.

Little Moreton Hall.

Liverpool grew from a tiny fishing village on the northern shores of the Mersey River, receiving its charter from King John in 1207. Commercial & slave trading with the West Indies led to massive expansion in the 17th & 18th centuries. The Liverpool of today owes much to the introduction of the steam ship in the mid 1900s, which enabled thousands of Irish to emigrate when the potatoe famine was at its height in Ireland. This is a city with a reputation for patronage of art, music & sport.

Cheshire & Merseyside

Cheshire & Merseyside Gazeteer

Area of outstanding natural beauty
Part of the Peaks National Park

Houses & Castles

Addington Hall - Macclesfield
15th century Elizabethan Black & White half timbered house.

Bishop Lloyd's House - Chester
17th century half timbered house (restored). Fine carvings. Has associations with Yale University & New Haven, USA.

Chorley Old Hall - Alderley Edge
14th century hall with 16th century Elizabethan wing.

Forfold Hall - Nantwich
17th century Jacobean country house, with fine panelling.

Gawsworth Hall - Macclesfield
Fine Tudor Half timbered Manor House. Tilting ground. Pictures, furniture, sculptures, etc.

Lyme Park - Disley
Elizabethan with Palladian exterior by Leoni. Gibbons carvings. Beautiful park with herd of red deer.

Peover Hall - Over Peover, Knutsford
16th century- stables of Tudor period; has the famous magpie ceiling.

Tatton Park - Knutsford
Beautifully decorated & furnished Georgian House with a fine collection of glass, china & paintings including Van Dyke & Canaletto. Landscaping by Humphrey Repton.

Little Moreton Hall - Nr. Congleton
15th century timbered, moated house with 16th century wall-paintings.

Cathedrals & Churches

Acton (St. Mary)
13th century with stone seating around walls. 17th century effigies.

Bunbury (St. Boniface)
14th century collegiate church - alabaster effigy.

Congleton (St. Peter)
18th century - box pews, brass candelabrum, 18th century glass.

Chester Cathedral - Chester
Subjected to restoration by Victorians - 14th century choir stalls.

Malpas (St. Oswalds)
15th century - fine screens, some old stalls, two family chapels.

Mobberley (St. Wilfred)
Mediaeval - 15th century Rood Screen, wall paintings, very old glass.

Shotwick (St. Michael)
Twin nave - box pews, 14th century quatre - foil lights, 3 deck pulpit.

Winwick (St. Oswald)
14th century - splendid roof. Pugin chancel.

Wrenbury (St. Margaret)
16th century - west gallery, monuments & hatchments. Box pews.

Liverpool Cathedral - the Anglican Cathedral was completed in 1980 after 76 years of work. It is of massive proportions, the largest in the British Isles, but containing much delicate & detailed work.

Museums & Galleries

Grosvenor Museum - Chester
Art, folk history, natural history, Roman antiquities including a special display of information about the Roman army.

Chester Heritage Centre - Chester
Interesting exhibition of the architectural heritage of Chester.

Cheshire Military Museum - Chester
The three local Regiments are commemorated here.

King Charles Tower - Chester
Chester at the time of the Civil War illustrated by dioramas.

Museum & Art Gallery - Warrington
Anthropology, geology, ethnology, botany & natural history. Pottery, porcelain, glass, collection of early English watercolours.

West Park Museum & Art Gallery - Macclesfield
Egyptian collection, oil paintings, watercolours, sketches by Landseer & Tunnicliffe.

Norton Priory Museum - Runcorn
Remains of excavated mediaeval priory. Also wildlife display.

Quarry Bank Mill - Styal
The Mill is a fine example of industrial building & houses an exhibition of the cotton industry: the various offices retain

Cheshire & Merseyside

their original furnishing, & the turbine room has the transmission systems & two turbines of 1903.

Nether Alderley Mill - Nether Alderley
15th century corn mill which was still used in 1929. Now restored.

The Albert Dock & Maritime Museum - Liverpool
Housing the Liverpool Tate Gallery, the Tate of the North.

Walker Art Gallery - Liverpool

Jodrell Bank - radio telescope & planetarium.

Historic Monuments

Chester Castle - Chester
Huge square tower remaining.

Roman Amphitheatre - Chester
12th legion site - half excavated.

Beeston Castle - Beeston
Remains of a 13th century fort.

Sandbach Crosses - Sandbach
Carved stone crosses dating from 9th century.

Gardens

Arley Hall - Northwich
Walled Gardens, topiary, shrub roses, herbaceous borders, azaleas & rhododendrons.

Cholmondeley Castle Gardens - Malpas
Gardens, lake, farm with rare breeds. Ancient chapel in park.

Ness Gardens - S. Wirral
Beautiful trees & shrubs, terraces, herbaceous borders, rose collection & herb garden.

Tatton Park - Knutsford.
Framed for azaleas & rhododendrons, an Italian terraced garden.
A Japanese water garden, an orangery & a fernery.

Mersey Estuary & Ferry.

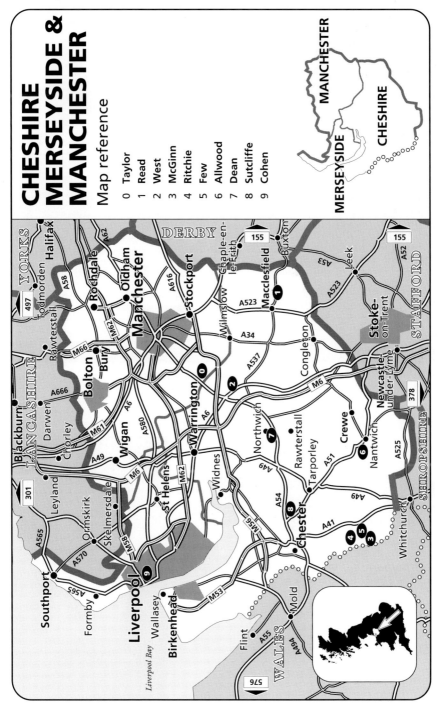

CHESHIRE MERSEYSIDE & MANCHESTER

Map reference

0 Taylor
1 Read
2 West
3 McGinn
4 Ritchie
5 Few
6 Allwood
7 Dean
8 Sutcliffe
9 Cohen

MANCHESTER

MERSEYSIDE

CHESHIRE

Broughton House. Threapwood.

Cheshire

	rate from £ per person	children taken	evening meals	animals taken
David Taylor **Ash Farm Country Guest House** **Little Bollington** **Altrincham** **WA14 4TJ** **Tel: (0161) 9299290** **Open: ALL YEAR (Excl. Xmas)** **Map Ref No. 00**	Nearest Road: A.56 Set in beautiful N.T. countryside, David & Janice have renovated this 18th-century farmhouse to a very high standard. Bedrooms are en-suite & have many features to delight the discerning traveller. The residents' lounge & dining area is furnished with an antique oak dining suite & open log fire & is the setting for excellent farmhouse food. Located only 5 mins' walk to Dunham Deer Park; 2 miles from M.56 & less than 6 miles to the M.6. Manchester Airport is only 10 mins away. Easy access to Manchester city centre & Chester.	£24.00 CREDIT CARD VISA M'CARD AMEX	N	Y	N
Pauline & Stephen West **The Longview Hotel &** **Restaurant** **55 Manchester Road** **Knutsford WA16 0LX** **Tel: (01565) 632119** **Fax 01565 652402** **Open: ALL YEAR** **Map Ref No. 02**	Nearest Road: M.6, A.50 Set in this pleasant Cheshire market town overlooking the common is this lovely hotel, furnished with antiques that reflect the elegance of this Victorian building. Care has been taken to retain its character, while also providing all comforts for the discerning traveller. All 23 en-suite bedrooms are prettily decorated, giving them that cared-for feeling which is echoed throughout the hotel. You are assured of a warm friendly welcome as soon as you step into reception.	£30.00 *see PHOTO over* CREDIT CARD VISA M'CARD AMEX	Y	Y	Y
Mrs Anne Read **Hardingland Farm** **Macclesfield Forest** **Macclesfield SK11 0ND** **Tel: (01625) 425759** **Open: MAR - NOV** **Map Ref No. 01**	Nearest Road: A.537 Enjoy yourself in this early-Georgian farmhouse, lovingly restored & furnished with antiques. In a beautiful position in the Peak National Park, with superb views over the Cheshire Plain. Relax in the delightful lounge, & enjoy delicious meals prepared by Anne, who is renowned for her cooking. There are 3 bedrooms, 2 en-suite & all individually decorated. Ideally situated for the Peak District & Cheshire.	£18.00	N	Y	N
Valerie & John McGinn **Broughton House** **Threapwood** **Malpas** **SY14 7AN** **Tel: (01948) 770610** **Fax 01948 770610** **Open: ALL YEAR** **Map Ref No. 03**	Nearest Road: A.41 A friendly welcome to a warm & comfortable home, part of the elegant Georgian stables built for a former 17th-century mansion. Breakfasts are served in the conservatory overlooking parkland & the Welsh hills. Luxurious bedrooms, some with king-size 4-poster beds, have T.V.s & are all en-suite & ground-floor. A large garden, with croquet & tennis. 1 hour from Manchester & convenient for Chester & North Wales. Many charming pubs & restaurants in the area that serve dinner. Children over 10.	£23.00 *see PHOTO over* CREDIT CARD VISA	Y	N	N
Kathie & Neil Ritchie **Tilston Lodge** **Tilston** **Malpas** **SY14 7DR** **Tel/Fax: (01829) 250223** **Open: ALL YEAR** **Map Ref No. 04**	Nearest Road: A.41 A warm welcome is assured at this glorious Victorian country house. Peacefully situated on the fringe of a pretty conservation village, & surrounded by 16 acres of gardens & pasture, Tilston Lodge is the ideal place to relax. All rooms are exceptionally spacious & well-furnished with antiques. The en-suite bedrooms have either 4-poster or twin beds & are generously equipped to ensure guests have a comfortable stay. An ideal base for exploring Chester & North Wales.	£25.00	Y	N	N

Longview Hotel. Knutsford.

Cheshire & Merseyside

		rate from £ per person	children taken	evening meals	animals taken
Mrs Anthea Few **Laurel Farm** **Chorlton Lane** **Malpas SY14 7ES** **Tel: (01948) 860291** **Fax 01948 860291** **Open: ALL YEAR** **Map Ref No. 05**	Nearest Road: A.41 A delightful 19th-century farmhouse with well-appointed en-suite bedrooms, all with lovely views over rolling countryside to the Welsh hills. A relaxed & comfortable atmosphere, in a real home. Guests may use the private-annexe suite all day, & it is perfect for parties of up to 5. A ground-floor room (with shower) is suitable for the less able. Excellent base for visiting this beautiful area, which boasts a wealth of interesting places to visit & superb sports facilities. Children over 12.	£24.00	Y	Y	Y
Michael & Sandra Allwood **Burland Farm** **Wrexham Road, Burland** **Nantwich CW5 8ND** **Tel: (01270) 524210** **Open: ALL YEAR (Excl.** **Xmas & New Year)** **Map Ref No. 06**	Nearest Road: A.534, M.6 This charming, centrally heated Victorian farmhouse is furnished with antiques & set in a lovely garden. The delightful sitting room is available to guests throughout the day, as are the 3 luxurious, en-suite, individually decorated bedrooms with colour T.V. & hot-drink facilities. Excellent breakfasts served in the dining room. Near Bridgemere Garden World & Stapeley Water Gardens. Easy access to Chester & potteries.	£20.00 *see PHOTO over*	N	N	Y
Barbara Ann Dean **Ayrshire Guest House** **31 Winnington Lane** **Winnington** **Northwich CW8 4DE** **Tel: (01606) 74871** **Open: ALL YEAR** **Map Ref No. 07**	Nearest Road: A.533, A.49 A charming turn-of-the-century house, offering warmth, comfort & a friendly relaxed atmosphere. All of the 7 bedrooms, 4 of which are en-suite, are tastefully decorated, & have tea/coffee-making facilities & T.V. A lounge, with colour T.V., is also available throughout the day, & a generous breakfast is served in the pleasant dining room. Conveniently situated for the many attractions of Cheshire & the North West.	£15.00	Y	N	Y
Mr & Mrs Sutcliffe **Roughlow Farm** **Chapel Lane, Willington** **Tarporley CW6 0PG** **Tel/Fax: (01829) 751199** **Mobile 0973 432145** **Open: ALL YEAR** **Map Ref No. 08**	Nearest Road: A.51, A.54 An 18th-century sandstone farmhouse in an outstanding position, with magnificent views to Shropshire & Wales. A friendly family home very elegantly furnished. 3 comfortable bedrooms (all en-suite), 1 with its own sitting room. Attractive garden with a cobbled courtyard. Tennis court. Dinner by prior arrangement (min. 4 persons). A superb home in a peaceful, rural situation, only 15 mins east of Chester. Ideal for exploring Cheshire, the Potteries & N. Wales. Children over 6.	£20.00	Y	Y	N

Merseyside

		rate from £ per person	children taken	evening meals	animals taken
Anna & David Cohen **Anna's, 65 Dudlow Lane** **Calderstones** **Liverpool L18 2EY** **Tel: (0151) 7223708** **Fax 0151 7228699** **Open: ALL YEAR (Excl.** **Xmas & New Year)** **Map Ref No. 09**	Nearest Road: A.562, M.62 Anna's is a comfortable family home where every effort is made to ensure that visitors become one of the family. Eating well is of the utmost importance here, & guests may bring their own wine if they choose. Accommodation is in 4 rooms, all with modern amenities, radio & tea/coffee-making facilities. A resident T.V. lounge is also available, as is the garden. Anna's is right in the heart of 'Beatle land'. Penny Lane & Strawberry Fields are moments away.	£16.50	Y	N	Y

Burland Farm. Nantwich.

Cornwall

Cornwall
(West Country)

Cornwall is an ancient Celtic land, a narrow granite peninsula with a magnificent coastline of over 300 miles & wild stretches of moorland.

The north coast, washed by Atlantic breakers, has firm golden sands & soaring cliffs. The magnificent beaches at Bude offer excellent surfing & a few miles to the south you can visit the picturesque harbour at Boscastle & the cliff-top castle at Tintagel with its legends of King Arthur. Newquay, with its beaches stretching for over seven miles, sheltered coves & modern hotels & shops, is the premier resort on Cornwall's Atlantic coast. St. Ives, another surfing resort, has great charm which has attracted artists for so long & is an ideal place from which to explore the Land's End peninsula.

The south coast is a complete contrast - wooded estuaries, sheltered coves, little fishing ports, & popular resorts. Penzance, with its warmth & vivid colours, is an all-the-year-round resort & has wonderful views across the bay to St. Michael's Mount. Here are excellent facilities for sailing & deep-sea fishing, as there are at Falmouth & Fowey with their superb harbours. Mevagissey, Polperro & Looe are fine examples of traditional Cornish fishing villages.

In the far west of Cornwall, you can hear about a fascinating legend: the lost land of Lyonesse - a whole country that was drowned by the sea. The legend goes that the waters cover a rich & fertile country, which had 140 parish churches. The Anglo-Saxon Chronicle records two great storms within a hundred years, which drowned many towns & innumerate people. Submerged forests are known to lie around these coasts - & in Mount's Bay beech trees have been found with the nuts still hanging on the branches, so suddenly were they swamped.

Today, St Michael's Isles of Scilly are said t... remains of the vanished land. St. Michael's Mount, with its tiny fishing village & dramatic castle, can be visited on foot at low tide or by boat at high water. The Isles of Scilly, 28 miles beyond Land's End, have five inhabited islands, including Tresco with its sub-tropical gardens. Day trips to the numerous uninhabited islands are a special feature of a Scilly holiday.

Inland Cornwall also has its attractions. To the east of Bodmin, the county town, are the open uplands of Bodmin Moor, with the county's highest peaks at Rough Tor & Brown Willy. "Jamaica Inn", immortalised in the novel by Daphne du Maurier, stands on the lonely road across the moor, & "Frenchman's Creek" is on a hidden inlet of the Helford River.

There is a seemingly endless number & variety of Cornish villages in estuaries, wooded, pastoral or moorland settings, & here customs & traditions are maintained. In Helston the famous "Fleury Dance" is still performed, & at the ancient port of Padstow, May Day celebrating involves decorating the houses with green boughs & parading the Hobby Horse through the street to the tune of St. George's Song.

Helford Creek

Cornwall

Areas of outstanding natural beauty.
Almost the entire county.

Historic Houses & Castles

Anthony House - Torpoint
18th century - beautiful & quite unspoiled
Queen Anne house, excellent panelling &
fine period furnishings.

Cotehele House - Calstock
15th & 16th century house, still contains
the original furniture, tapestry, armour,
etc.

Ebbingford Manor - Bude
12th century Cornish manor house, with
walled garden.

Godolphin House - Helston
Tudor - 17th century colonnaded front.

Lanhydrock - Bodmin
17th century - splendid plaster ceilings,
picture gallery with family portraits 17th/
20th centuries.

Mount Edgcumbe House - Plymouth
Tudor style mansion - restored after
destruction in 1949. Hepplewhite furniture
& portrait by Joshua Reynolds.

St. Michael's Mount - Penzance
Mediaeval castle & 17th century with 18th
& 19th century additions.

Pencarrow House & Gardens - Bodmin
18th century Georgian Mansion -
collection of paintings, china & furniture -
mile long drive through fine woodlands &
gardens.

Old Post Office - Tintagel
14th century manor house in miniature -
large hall used as Post Office for a period,
hence the name.

Trewithen - Probus Nr. Truro
Early Georgian house with lovely
gardens.

Trerice - St. Newlyn East
16th century Elizabethan house, small
with elaborate facade. Excellent
fireplaces, plaster ceilings, miniature
gallery & minstrels' gallery.

Cathedral & Churches

Altarnun (St. Nonna)
15th century, Norman font, 16th century
bench ends, fine rood screen.

Bisland (St. Protus & St. Hyacinth)
15th century granite tower - carved wagon
roofs, slate floor. Georgian wine - glass
pulpit, fine screen.

Kilkhampton (St. James)
16th century with fine Norman doorway,
arcades & wagon roofs.

Laneast (St. Michael or St. Sedwell)
13th century, 15th century enlargement,
16th century pulpit, some painted glass.

Lanteglos-by-Fowley (St. Willow)
14th century, refashioned 15th century,
13th century font, 15th century brasses &
altar tomb, 16th century bench ends.

Launcells (St. Andrew)
Interior unrestored - old plaster & ancient
roofs remaining, fine Norman font with
17th century cover, box pews, pulpit,
reredos, 3 sided alter rails.

Probus (St. Probus & St. Gren)
16th century tower, splendid arcades,
three great East windows.

St. Keverne (St. Keverne)
Fine tower & spire. Wall painting in 15th
century interior.

St. Neot (St. Neot)
Decorated tower - 16th century exterior,
buttressed & double-aisled. Many
windows of mediaeval glass renewed in
19th century.

Museums & Galleries

Museum of Witchcraft - Boscastle
Relating to witches, implements &
customs.

Military Museum - Bodmin
History of Duke of Cornwall's Light
Infantry.

Public Library & Museum - Cambourne
Collections of mineralogy, archaeology,
local antiquities & history.

Cornish Museum - East Looe
Collection of relics relating to witchcraft
customs & superstitions. Folk life &
culture of district.

Helston Borough Museum - Helston
Folk life & culture of area around Lizard.

Museum of Nautical Art - Penzance
Exhibition of salvaged gold & silver
treasures from underwater wreck of
1700's.

Museum of Smuggling - Polperro
Activities of smugglers, past & present.

Cornwall

Penlee House Museum - Penlee, Penzance
Archaeology & local history & tin mining exhibits.
Barbara Hepworth Museum - St. Ives
Sculpture, letters, documents, photographs, etc., exhibited in house where Barbara Hepworth lived.
Old Mariners Church - St. Ives
St. Ives Society of Artists hold exhibitions here.
County Museum & Art Gallery - Truro
Ceramics, art local history & antiquities, Cornish mineralogy.

Historic Monuments

Cromwell's Castle - Tresco (Scilly Isles)
17th century castle.
King Charles' Fort - Tresco (Scilly Isles)
16th century fort.
Old Blockhouse - Tresco (Scilly Isles)
16th century coastal battery.
Harry's Wall - St. Mary's (Scilly Isles)
Tudor Coastal battery
Ballowall Barrow - St. Just
Prehistoric barrow.
Pendennis Castle - Falmouth
Fort from time of Henry VII.

Restormel Castle - Lostwithiel
13th century ruins.
St. Mawes Castle - St. Mawes
16th century fortified castle.
Tintagel Castle - Tintagel
Mediaeval ruin on wild coast, King Arthur's legendary castle.

Things to see & do

Camel trail - Padstow to Bodmin
12 miles of recreation path along scenic route, suitable for walkers, cyclists & horse-riders.
Tresco Abbey Gardens - Tresco
Collection of sub-tropical flora
Trethorne Leisure Farm - Launceston
Visitors are encouraged to feed & stroke the farm animals
Seal sanctuary - Gweek Nr. Helston
Seals, exhibition hall, nature walk, aquarium, seal hospital, donkey paddock.
Dobwalls Theme Park - Nr. Liskeard
2 miles of scenically dramatic miniature railway based on the American railroad.
Padstow tropical bird gardens - Padstow
Mynack Theatre - Porthcurno

Lands End.

95

CORNWALL

Map reference

1	Smith	19	Hilder
2	Lock	19	Hopkins
3	Thompson	20	Mercer
3	Purslow	20	Lee
4	Knight	21	Taylor
4	Ruff	22	Wooldridge
4	Sibley	23	Tuckett
6	Walker	23	Spring
7	Tremayne	24	Rowe
8	Ford	25	Epperson
9	Stanley	26	Studley
10	Griffin	27	Nancarrow
11	Colwill	28	Mason
12	Low	28	Sykes
13	Norman	28	Batty
14	Owens	29	Henderson
15	Wynn	30	Rayner
16	Mackenzie	30	Charlick
17	Martin	31	Crowther
18	Shepherd	32	Dymond
19	Stacey	34	Walker

Whitehay. Withiel.

Cornwall

		rate from £ per person	children taken	evening meals	animals taken

	Nearest Road: A.30, B.3268	£19.00	Y	N	N
...**)*, ***4405** **Open: ALL YEAR (Excl.** **Xmas & New Year)** **Map Ref No. 01**	An historic, listed Georgian farmhouse which adjoins N.T. Lanhydrock, with its stately home, glorious gardens and miles of country walks. You are guaranteed a warm welcome here, and delicious home-cooking in generous quantities! You can enjoy relaxing in the pretty bedrooms (one with a 4-poster) and in the wood-panelled lounge. Search out Cornwall's rugged cliffs and sandy coves from a very central location.	(no smoking)			
Ian & Felicity Lock **Whitehay** **Withiel** **Bodmin** **PL30 5NQ** **Tel: (01208) 831237** **Open: ALL YEAR** **Map Ref No. 02**	Nearest Road: A.30 Whitehay is really special. Totally private, & surrounded by its own land of fields, orchard, woodland & river. A lovely Cornish home with a wonderfully welcoming atmosphere. Antiques, Persian carpets, log fires, fresh flowers. 2 quiet & delightful double bedrooms, furnished with English chintzes & fine furniture, offering guests a high standard of comfort. Both rooms have private bathrooms, colour T.V. & tea/coffee facilities. Children over 12 years welcome.	£30.00 *see PHOTO over*	Y	N	N
Mrs Eileen Purslow **Orchard Lodge** **Gunpool Lane** **Boscastle PL35 0AT** **Tel: (01840) 250418** **Open: APR - JAN** **Map Ref No. 03**	Nearest Road: A.39, B.3266 Orchard Lodge, set in its own attractive gardens, is a large, delightful base for a relaxing holiday. Offering 6 very pleasant guest rooms, decorated & furnished to a high standard, with modern facilities. A delicious Full English or Continental breakfast is served in the pretty dining room, with pine furnishings, which overlooks the garden. Ample parking. An ideal base for touring Cornwall. A warm & friendly welcome awaits you.	£16.00	N	N	N
Brenda & Brian Thompson **St. Christopher's Hotel** **High Street** **Boscastle** **PL35 0BD** **Tel: (01840) 250412** **Open: MAR - OCT** **Map Ref No. 03**	Nearest Road: A.39 A superb Georgian house retaining its original character while providing excellent, comfortable accommodation in 9 charming rooms, 8 en-suite & all with modern facilities. Here, the welcome & standards are marvellous. The lovely harbour village is unspoilt. There is a wealth of history all around, with plenty of interesting places to visit. Meals are well-prepared, delicious & personally supervised. An excellent touring base.	£17.00 CREDIT CARD VISA M'CARD	N	Y	Y
Mrs Muriel Knight **Manor Farm** **Crackington Haven** **Bude** **EX23 0JW** **Tel: (01840) 230304** **Open: ALL YEAR** **Map Ref No. 04**	Nearest Road: A.39 A really super 11th-century manor house, retaining all its former charm & elegance. Mentioned in the 1086 Domesday book, it belonged to the Earl of Mortain, half-brother to William the Conqueror. Delightfully located in a beautiful & secluded position, & surrounded by both attractive gardens & 40 acres of farmland. Guest rooms have private facilities. There is a games room for guests' use. Dining at Manor Farm is considered the highlight of the day. Only 1 mile from the beach. Non-smokers only. West Country winner of the Best B&B award.	£28.00 *see PHOTO over*	N	Y	N

Manor Farm. Crackington Haven

Cornwall

		rate from £ per person	children taken	evening meals	animals taken
Mrs Lorraine Ruff **Nancemellan** **Crackington Haven** **Bude EX23 0NN** **Tel/Fax: (01840) 230283** **Open: ALL YEAR (Excl.** **Xmas & New Year)** **Map Ref No. 04**	Nearest Road: A.39 A beautiful Grade II listed Victorian country home set in 9 acres of grounds with stunning views towards the sea. The 3 guest rooms are delightfully furnished, all with en-suite or private bathrooms, colour T.V. & tea/coffee-making facilities. The atmosphere is warm & informal, & open log fires make for a cosy winter stay. Breakfast is taken in the large family kitchen. A charming home from which to explore beautiful Cornwall.	£20.00 see PHOTO over	N	N	N
Brian & Lin Sibley **Cliff Hotel** **Maer Down Road** **Crooklets Beach** **Bude EX23 8NG** **Tel/Fax: (01288) 353110** **Open: APR - OCT** **Map Ref No. 04**	Nearest Road: A.39 A small, quiet family hotel with an indoor swimming pool, all-weather tennis court & bowls. All rooms are en-suite & have colour T.V.s, telephone, radio & drinks. The hotel is located adjacent to cliff walks, a designated Area of Outstanding Natural Beauty. 200 yds west: Crooklets beach, 200 yds south: a golf course, 200 yds east: Maer Lake Reserve, where peregrines hunt. The excellent cuisine is freshly cooked & includes local fish, French & traditional.	£21.50 CREDIT CARD VISA M'CARD	Y	Y	Y
Mrs Jill Walker **Arrowan Common Farm** **Coverack** **TR12 6SH** **Tel: (01326) 280328** **Mobile 0378 934678** **Open: ALL YEAR** **Map Ref No. 06**	Nearest Road: A.3083, B.3293 A 150-year-old traditional Cornish farmhouse, recently updated but retaining its original character. This peaceful home is furnished with antiques, & has a beamed lounge with a granite fireplace & wood burner. A pretty sun lounge is also available, with vines & lemon trees. 5 attractive bedrooms: each is comfortable & has tea/coffee-making facilities, & most enjoy views across the gardens & fields to the sea. A delightful home, where all the joys of the farm can be expected, yet with none of the drawbacks.	£19.50	Y	N	N
Mr & Mrs T. P. Tremayne **'The Home' Country** **House Hotel, Penjerrick** **Falmouth TR11 5EE** **Tel: (01326) 250427** **Fax 01326 250143** **Open: Easter - OCT** **Map Ref No. 07**	Nearest Road: A.39 A quiet & charming country house, with views over Maenporth & Falmouth Bay. Accommodation is in 17 rooms, each with a private/en-suite bath/shower. All have tea/coffee-making facilities. A colour T.V. lounge & bar are provided, & guests may relax in the beautiful sheltered garden. A golf course & boating facilities nearby. A friendly host, who prepares delicious meals using local produce. Special diets by arrangement. Children over 6.	£20.00	Y	Y	Y
Mrs Judy Ford **Treviades Barton** **High Cross** **Constantine** **Falmouth TR11 5RG** **Te/Fax: (01326) 340524** **Open: ALL YEAR** **Map Ref No. 08**	Nearest Road: A.39 This charming, 16th-century, listed farmhouse stands in beautiful gardens close to the Helford River. Offering 3 comfortable double bedrooms with radio & tea/coffee makers; 2 with en-suite facilities. Guests stay in a family atmosphere. A wide range of relaxing or energetic holiday opportunities available throughout the year. Evening meals by arrangement. A delightful home & an ideal base for touring Cornwall,	£18.00 CREDIT CARD VISA M'CARD	Y	Y	Y

Nancemellan. Crackington Haven.

Coombe Farm. Widegates

Cornwall

Mrs Valerie Griffin Wheatley Farm Maxworthy Launceston PL15 8LY Tel/Fax: (01566) 781232 Open: APR - SEPT Map Ref No. 10	Nearest Road: A.39, A.30 You will be made very welcome at Wheatley, a spacious farmhouse, built by the Duke of Bedford in 1871, which stands in landscaped gardens on a working farm in the peaceful Cornish countryside. 4 luxurious & charming en-suite bedrooms, 1 with 4-poster, each with T.V. & tea/coffee-making facilities. A tantalising & varied dinner menu. Log fires. A games room (and a secret one for children!). Pony rides. A spectacular coastline nearby.	£		
Mrs Agnes Colwill Sutton Farm Boyton Launceston PL15 9RN Tel: (01409) 271269 Open: APR - OCT Map Ref No. 11	Nearest Road: B.3254 A delightful 300-acre working farm. Accommodation is in 3 bedrooms, with 2 shared bathrooms. There is an attractive lounge with colour T.V.. Delicious Full English breakfasts are served. T.V. snacks on request. Families are well catered for. A cot/high chair available. Guests are made very welcome, & can relax in the beautiful garden. Sutton Farm is an ideal base for visiting the moors & many resorts.	£13.00	Y N Y
Mr & Mrs Peter Stanley Landewednack House Church Cove The Lizard TR12 7PQ Tel: (01326) 290909 Fax 01326 290909 Open: ALL YEAR Map Ref No. 09	Nearest Road: A.3083 An elegant Grade II listed Georgian country house, idyllically positioned overlooking the sea, offering absolute peace & comfort. Delightful sea-view bedrooms, furnished with antiques; 4-poster & half-tester beds with private bathrooms (1 with jacuzzi). Relax in front of log fires, laze in the secluded walled garden, play boules or croquet or just step onto the Heritage coastal footpath of the outstandingly beautiful Lizard Peninsula. A delightful home at England's most southerly point.	£29.00 CREDIT CARD VISA M'CARD	Y Y N
Alexander & Sally Low Coombe Farm Widegates Looe PL13 1QN Tel: (01503) 240223 Fax 01503 240223 Open: MAR - OCT Map Ref No. 12	Nearest Road: B.3253, A.38 A lovely country house, beautifully furnished with antiques, set in 10 acres of lawns, meadows, woods, streams & ponds, with superb views down a wooded valley to the sea. The atmosphere is delightful, with open log fires, a candlelit dining room (in which to enjoy delicious home-cooking) & an informal, licensed bar. An old barn has been converted for indoor games, including snooker & table tennis. Also a croquet lawn, a heated outdoor swimming pool & many birds & animals, including peacocks & horses. All rooms en-suite.	£18.00 *see PHOTO over*	Y Y N
Pat & Bryan Norman Fieldhead Hotel Portuan Road Looe PL13 2DR Tel: (01503) 262689 Fax 01503 264114 Open: FEB - DEC Map Ref No. 13	Nearest Road: A.38 A delightful hotel with a fine reputation: guests return year after year. Set in its own grounds, with panoramic views of the sea, & within 200 yds of the beach. 14 most attractive & comfortable rooms, with en-suite facilities. All have radio, T.V. & tea/coffee makers. An attractive residents' lounge, games room, a heated outdoor pool & lovely garden. The area is wonderful for all sports - riding, walking, fishing, sailing, golfing - & the beaches are great. The Norman family make all visitors most welcome. Children over 5 yrs.	£28.00 CREDIT CARD VISA M'CARD AMEX	Y Y N

Allhays Country House. Looe.

Cornwall

Name & Address	Description	rate from £ per person	children taken	evening meals	animals taken
Brian & Lynda Spring **Allhays Country House** **Talland Bay** **Looe PL13 2JB** **Tel: (01503) 272434** **Fax 01503 272929** **Open: ALL YEAR (Excl. Xmas)** **Map Ref No. 23**	Nearest Road: A.387 Overlooking the beautiful smugglers cove of Talland Bay. House guests enjoy all the warmth & comfort of a family home, complete with magnificent fireplaces & log fires. All 7 bedrooms have satellite-link colour T.V., telephone & tea/coffee makers. Most are en-suite, including 2 ground-floor rooms. Enjoy award-winning food & wine in the candlelit dining room, or amidst the beautiful 'outdoor' surroundings of the Victorian-style conservatory. Children over 10 yrs.	£28.00 *see PHOTO over* CREDIT CARD VISA M'CARD AMEX	Y	Y	Y
Barry & Jane Wynn **Harescombe Lodge** **Watergate** **Looe PL13 2NE** **Tel: (01503) 263158** **Open: ALL YEAR** **Map Ref No. 15**	Nearest Road: A.387 Once the shooting lodge of the Trelawne Estate, Harescombe Lodge is situated twixt Looe & Polperro, in the picturesque hamlet of Watergate, overlooking the West Looe River. An idyllic location with interesting walks & wildlife. Peaceful surroundings will appeal to the discerning visitor to south-east Cornwall. There are 3 very attractive en-suite bedrooms.	£17.00	N	Y	N
Mrs Diana Owens **Mevagissey House** **Vicarage Hill** **Mevagissey PL26 6SZ** **Tel: (01726) 842427** **Fax 01726 842427** **Open: MAR - OCT** **Map Ref No. 14**	Nearest Road: A.390, B.3273 An elegant Georgian rectory standing in 4 acres of woodland, overlooking the beautiful woodland & valley leading to the harbour & sea beyond. Here, guests can unwind & relax in pleasant, comfortable surroundings. 6 rooms, 4 en-suite, all with modern amenities, T.V. & tea/coffee-making facilities. Snacks, morning coffee & Cornish cream teas are available on request. Evening meals are also served. Close by are fishing, beaches & golf courses. Children over 7.	£19.00 CREDIT CARD VISA M'CARD	Y	Y	N
Mac & Jennie Mackenzie **Trenance Lodge** **Restaurant** **83 Trenance Road** **Newquay TR7 2HW** **Tel: (01637) 876702** **Fax 01637 872034** **Open: ALL YEAR** **Map Ref No. 16**	Nearest Road: A.3075 An attractive house standing in its own grounds, overlooking lakes & gardens of Trenance Valley leading to the Gannel Estuary. The restaurant has a reputation for serving the finest fresh local food in elegant surroundings. Adjoining the restaurant is a spacious, relaxing bar lounge. There are 5 comfortable bedrooms, en-suite, with colour T.V., radio & tea/coffee facilities. An excellent base for touring this beautiful & historic region, with a warm welcome assured.	£22.00 CREDIT CARD VISA M'CARD	N	Y	N
Michael & Pat Walker **The Old Mill Country House** **Little Petherick** **Padstow PL27 7QT** **Tel: (01841) 540388** **Open: MAR - OCT** **Map Ref No. 34**	Nearest Road: A.39, A.389 This delightful, 16th-century, converted corn mill, complete with water wheel, stands in its own grounds at the head of Little Petherick Creek. The bedrooms are furnished with antiques, & each has either an en-suite or private bathroom & tea/coffee-making facilities. Licensed, with a colour T.V. available for the guests' use. There is also a terraced sun garden. A varied supper menu is available & all meals are traditionally cooked, & offer very good value.	£23.50 *see PHOTO over* CREDIT CARD VISA M'CARD AMEX	N	Y	Y

The Old Mill. Little Petherick.

Nanscawen House. Par.

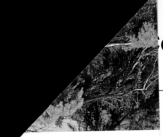

	rate from £ per person	children taken	evening meals	animals taken

	Nearest Road: A.390	£17.00	Y	N	N

Nanscawen is a delightful country house set in an idyllic location. It stands in 5 acres of grounds & gardens in a nature-conservation area. Guests have a choice of 3 luxury en-suite rooms with spa baths. The elegantly furnished drawing room leads into the conservatory, where breakfast is enjoyed. Many good restaurants within easy reach. An ideal base for touring all of Cornwall. Guests may like to use the heated swimming pool & whirlpool hot tub. Children over 12 yrs.

see PHOTO over

CREDIT CARD
VISA
M'CARD

Open ALL YEAR (Excl. **Xmas & Boxing Day)**
Map Ref No. 17

Cliff Paul & Barry Sheppard
Prospect House
1 Church Rd
Penryn TR10 8DA
Tel/Fax: (01326) 373198
Open: ALL YEAR
Map Ref No. 18

Nearest Road: A.39, B.3292 | £23.50 | Y | Y | Y

Prospect House is a gentleman's residence built in around 1830 for a local ship owner. On the edge of busy little Penryn, it is ideally situated for access to Cornwall's beauty spots, beaches, gardens, walks, N.T. properties & English Heritage monuments; but when a quiet day at home is needed, there is the walled rose garden in summer & log fires in winter. There are 3 double/twin bedrooms, all en-suite, & the house is furnished throughout with antiques. Children over 12 yrs.

see PHOTO over

CREDIT CARD
VISA
M'CARD

Trish & Richard Hilder
Carnson House
East Terrace
Penzance
TR18 2TD
Tel: (01736) 65589
Open: ALL YEAR
Map Ref No. 19

Nearest Road: A.30 | £15.00 | Y | Y | N

Carnson offers you a Cornish welcome & a friendly atmosphere. 8 modern bedrooms, with heating, colour T.V. & tea/coffee makers. Some en-suite. Licensed, with a pleasant lounge. Enjoying one of Penzance's most central positions close to the railway & bus stations. Coach & boat trips, car hire & bus tours are available all year round, & can be arranged by the hotel. Add international recommendations for food, & it all makes for a happy & memorable visit. Children over 12.

CREDIT CARD
VISA
M'CARD
AMEX

John & Cherry Hopkins
Woodstock Guest House
29 Morrab Road
Penzance TR18 4EZ
Tel: (01736) 69049
Fax 01736 69049
Open: ALL YEAR
Map Ref No. 19

Nearest Road: A.30 | £11.00 | Y | N | Y

A warm, friendly welcome awaits you at Woodstock. The sub-tropical Morrab Gardens are at the rear of the house, & close to all amenities. Offering 7 charming & comfortable bedrooms, all with modern facilities, including T.V. & tea/coffee makers. 2 rooms are en-suite (1 ground floor). A comfortable T.V. lounge. An attractive dining-room, with an extensive breakfast menu. An ideal base for exploring Mounts Bay & the Land's End peninsula.

CREDIT CARD
VISA
M'CARD
AMEX

Mr & Mrs R. J. Lee
Boscean Country Hotel
Boswedden Road
St. Just-in-Penwith
Penzance TR19 7QP
Tel/Fax: (01736) 788748
Open: APR - OCT
Map Ref No. 20

Nearest Road: A.30, A.3071 | £20.00 | Y | Y | Y

A warm & hospitable welcome awaits you at Boscean, a beautiful country house standing in 3 acres of walled grounds overlooking the sea & open countryside. 12 en-suite bedrooms, all with tea/coffee facilities. Guest lounge & bar. Delicious meals made with fresh, local or home-grown produce. Situated in an area of natural charm & beauty. An ideal place for touring the many interesting places in the Land's End peninsula.

CREDIT CARD
VISA
M'CARD

Prospect House. Penryn.

Cornwall

		rate from £ per person	children taken	evening meals	animals taken
M. J. & C. J. Mercer **Roseudian** **Crippas Hill** **St. Just** **Penzance TR19 7RE** **Tel: (01736) 788556** **Open: MAR - OCT** **Map Ref No. 20**	Nearest Road: B.3306, A.30 A small guest house in a quiet rural setting. An ideal centre for exploring the Land's End area. A traditional Cornish cottage, now comfortably modernised, standing in a 3/4-acre terraced garden for guests to enjoy. 3 attractive en-suite rooms, with tea/coffee-making facilities, delicious home-cooked meals, using seasonal garden produce, a lounge, with T.V., & the warmest of welcomes all ensure a friendly, relaxed stay. Children over 5. Dogs by prior arrangement.	£17.00	Y	Y	Y
Mrs Christine Taylor **Ednovean Farm** **Perranuthnoe** **Penzance TR20 9LZ** **Tel: (01736) 711883** **Open: ALL YEAR** **Map Ref No. 21**	Nearest Road: A.394 A small working farm nestling above the peaceful village of Perranuthnoe, with stunning views over Mounts Bay & St. Michael's Mount. A unique 17th-century barn, lovingly renovated, offering guests 3 elegant, country-style bedrooms, en-suite & charmingly decorated with fresh flowers, pretty chintz & stylish linen. Stroll across the fields to the village pub, beach, cliff-top paths & secluded coves. Perfect peace! Children over 10.	£20.00	Y	N	Y
Mr & Mrs K. Wooldridge **Beach Dunes Hotel** **Ramoth Way** **Perranporth TR6 0BY** **Tel: (01872) 572263** **Fax 01872 573824** **Open: JAN - OCT incl.** **Map Ref No. 22**	Nearest Road: A.30, B.3285 A small friendly hotel pleasantly situated in almost an acre of grounds amidst the sand dunes adjoining the golf course, & overlooking Perran Bay with its 3 miles of golden sands & Atlantic beach. 9 en-suite bedrooms, each with tea/coffee, T.V./radio & private 'phone. Excellent food is freshly prepared. Facilities include an indoor pool, a squash court, a cosy bar & a residents' lounge. An excellent touring centre. Children over 4 yrs. CREDIT CARD VISA M'CARD AMEX	£24.50	Y	Y	Y
Lynne & Anthony Tuckett **Trenderway Farm** **Pelynt** **Polperro** **PL13 2LY** **Tel: (01503) 272214** **Open: ALL YEAR (Excl. Xmas)** **Map Ref No. 23**	Nearest Road: A.387 Built in the late 16th century, this mixed working farm is set in peaceful, beautiful countryside at the head of the Polperro Valley. Bedrooms here are truly superb, with bathrooms as big as some hotel bedrooms, & are decorated with the flair of a professional interior designer. A hearty farmhouse breakfast is served in the sunny conservatory, using local produce. Although an evening meal is not provided, an excellent range of nearby restaurants can be recommended.	£26.00	N	N	N
Eric & Meryl Rowe **Landaviddy Manor** **Landaviddy Lane** **Polperro** **PL13 2RT** **Tel: (01503) 272210** **Open: FEB - OCT** **Map Ref No. 24**	Nearest Road: A.38 A beautiful, licensed, 18th-century, small manor house built of traditional Cornish stone. Situated in lovely grounds on a hillside above the picturesque fishing village of Polperro, commanding charming views of the bay & surrounding N.T. countryside. Retaining its former character while incorporating modern comforts. All rooms are individually furnished, with T.V. & tea/coffee. Many are en-suite, & include 4-poster or Victorian bedrooms. Excellent restaurants within 10 mins' walk. Children over 10. *see PHOTO over* CREDIT CARD VISA M'CARD	£22.00	Y	N	N

Landaviddy Manor. Polperro.

Cornwall

		rate from £ per person	children taken	evening meals	animals taken
...well, Illogan ...edruth TR16 4QZ Tel: (01209) 842256 Fax 01209 843744 Open: ALL YEAR Map Ref No. 26	Nearest Road: A.30 Aviary Court stands in 2 1/2 acres of ground on the edge of Illogan Woods. This part 300-year-old house offers guests a choice of 6 comfortable bedrooms, all with en-suite facilities, overlooking the gardens. Each has radio, colour T.V., tea/coffee-making facilities & 'phone. The comfortable lounge has a bar &, in winter, a log fire. The restaurant serves delicious food with a selection of wine. Children over 3 yrs welcome.	£27.00 CREDIT CARD VISA M'CARD AMEX	Y	Y	N
Cdr. & Mrs S. Epperson Anchorage House Nettles Corner Tregrahan St. Austell PL25 3RH Tel: (01726) 814071 Open: ALL YEAR Map Ref No. 25	Nearest Road: A.390 Every attention has been paid to the smallest detail in this beautiful antique-filled home. The 3 sunny, en-suite bedrooms are furnished to a high standard, with every convenience, including large comfortable beds & a 4-poster. Guests comment on the warm hospitality, special touches & superb cooking. Perfectly situated for visiting Cornwall's historic treasures, plantsmen's gardens, Carlyon Bay beach & golf (at a reduced price). Private parking, & a flower-filled garden to enjoy.	£21.00 🚭 see PHOTO over	N	Y	N
Judith Nancarrow Poltarrow Farm St. Mewan St. Austell PL26 7DR Tel: (01726) 67111 Open: ALL YEAR Map Ref No. 27	Nearest Road: A.390 Set in 45 acres of pastoral farmland, this wisteria-clad farmhouse holds a commanding position, with views across rolling pastures. 5 attractively furnished & individually decorated bedrooms with en-suite/private bathroom, T.V. & tea/coffee. The dining room offers traditional farmhouse fare, with a Full English breakfast made using fresh local produce & served in generous Cornish portions. The sitting room is comfortable, & has a quiet atmosphere, & a log fire for chilly evenings. Close to south coast of Cornwall, yet centrally situated between Plymouth & Penzance.	£19.00 CREDIT CARD VISA M'CARD	Y	Y	N
Moira & Wally Batty The Grey Mullet 2 Bunkers Hill St. Ives TR26 1LJ Tel: (01736) 796635 Open: ALL YEAR Map Ref No. 28	Nearest Road: A.3074 The Grey Mullet, an 18th-century, Grade II listed building with oak beams & exposed granite walls, is situated in the old fishing & artists' quarters of St. Ives, & is a 2-min walk from the Tate Gallery. Visitors are given a warm welcome in comfortable & homely surroundings. Some of the 7 bedrooms are en-suite, & all have colour T.V. & tea/coffee-making facilities. Vegetarian & low-calorie diets catered for. A delightful home.	£17.00	Y	N	N
Diana & Derek Mason Kandahar 11 The Warren St. Ives TR26 2EA Tel: (01736) 796183 Open: ALL YEAR (Excl. Xmas & New Year) Map Ref No. 28	Nearest Road: A.3074 Kandahar has a unique water's-edge location, lapped by the Atlantic & overlooking the harbour. The town centre, beaches, coach & railway station are all within 150 yds. All of the 5 comfortable rooms have superb sea views, colour T.V., tea/coffee-making facilities & full central heating. There are 2 en-suite bedrooms. English & vegetarian breakfasts served. There are many restaurants close by. A charming home & the perfect spot for a relaxing break.	£16.00	Y	N	N

Anchorage House. Boscundle.

Trebrea Lodge. Trenale.

Cornwall

		rate from £ per person	children taken	evening meals	animals taken
Irene & John Sykes **The Old Vicarage Hotel** **Parc-an-Creet** **St. Ives TR26 2ET** **Tel: (01736) 796124** **Open: APR - OCT** **Map Ref No. 28**	Nearest Road: A.30 The Old Vicarage Hotel, set in its own wooded grounds, secluded & peaceful, on the edge of the moorlands to the west of St. Ives. Offering 8 bedrooms, 6 with a private bath/shower, some with colour T.V.. All rooms have tea/coffee makers. Families well catered for. A delightful large garden for guests to relax in, & a safe recreation area for children. Convenient for beach & places of interest.	£18.00 CREDIT CARD VISA M'CARD AMEX	Y	N	Y
John & Christina Rayner **The Old Borough House** **Bossiney Road** **Bossiney** **Tintagel PL34 0AY** **Tel: (01840) 770475** **Open: ALL YEAR** **Map Ref No. 30**	Nearest Road: A.39, B.3263 A delightful 17th-century Cornish stone house, formerly the home of J. B. Priestley. It is located between Tintagel & Boscastle in an Area of Outstanding Natural Beauty with N.T. property nearby. The 6 comfortable bedrooms, (3 en-suite/private) have modern amenities & tea/coffee makers. A colour-T.V. lounge & garden are also available for guests. Close by are safe bathing coves, caves & coastal walks. Delicious food & wine available. Children over 4 years.	£15.50	Y	Y	N
John Charlick & **Sean Devlin** **Trebrea Lodge, Trenale** **Tintagel PL34 0HR** **Tel: (01840) 770410** **Fax 01840 770092** **Open: FEB - DEC** **Map Ref No. 30**	Nearest Road: A.395 This lovely Grade II listed Georgian house, set in 4 1/2 acres of wooded hillside, has outstanding views of the north Cornish coast. The land was originally granted by the Black Prince to the Bray family, who lived here for 600 years. The beautiful bedrooms are individually decorated with antique furniture, & all have en-suite bathrooms. High-quality home cooking, log fires & a relaxed atmosphere. A truely delightful home. Unsuitable for young children.	£35.00 *see PHOTO over* CREDIT CARD VISA M'CARD	Y	Y	Y
Elizabeth Henderson **Bissick Old Mill** **Ladock** **Truro TR2 4PG** **Tel: (01726) 882557** **Open: ALL YEAR (Excl.** **Xmas & New Year)** **Map Ref No. 29**	Nearest Road: A.30, A.390 Bissick Old Mill, formerly a working corn mill, is conveniently situated in the village of Ladock (10 mins' drive from Truro), & provides exceptional standards of comfort, cuisine & hospitality. Its central position makes it an ideal base from which to visit all areas of Cornwall, whether it be on business or purely for pleasure. A chef proprietor (mostly English/French dishes). A residential licence. Children over 10.	£27.00 CREDIT CARD VISA M'CARD	Y	Y	Y
Mrs Alison Y. Crowther **Treworga Farmhouse** **Treworga** **Ruan High Lanes** **Truro** **TR2 5NP** **Tel: (01872) 501423** **Open: ALL YEAR (Excl. Xmas)** **Map Ref No. 31**	Nearest Road: A.3078 A charming Grade II listed farmhouse. Local legend ascribes the site to a castle in the Middle Ages. Today, it has many old beams, & includes a fascinating barrel-vaulted plaster ceiling, c.1570. Recently renovated to include all modern comforts; there are super double rooms with private facilities, tea/coffee, etc. A pretty garden, with barn, studio & old roundhouse. Situated in the lovely scenery of the St. Just-in-Roseland peninsula, & close to beaches, coves, sailing, wonderful coastal walks, the River Fal & Trelissick Gardens (N.T.). Off the A.3078 to St. Mawes. Children over 10 yrs.	£19.00	Y	Y	Y

Cornwall

		rate from £ per person	children taken	evening meals	animals taken
Ernie & Bridget Dymond **Trevispian-Vean Farm** **Guest House** **Trevispian-Vean** **St. Erme** **Truro TR4 9BL** **Tel: (01872) 79514** **Open: APR - OCT** **Map Ref No. 32**	Nearest Road: A.3076 A delightful farmhouse, dating back over 300 years, offering a very warm welcome & good accommodation in 12 pleasant, comfortable guest rooms, 9 en-suite. Situated only 7 miles from the coast, & surrounded by beautiful countryside, it is a perfect base for everyone. Families will particularly enjoy it here, as children can look around the farm, & there are plenty of places to visit & things to do. There's even a donkey for the children.	£17.00	Y	Y	N

All the establishments mentioned in this guide

are members of

The Worldwide Bed & Breakfast Association

When booking your accommodation please mention
The Best Bed & Breakfast

Cumbria

Cumbria

The Lake District National Park is deservedly famous for its magnificent scenery. Here, England's highest mountains & rugged fells surround shimmering lakes & green valleys. But there is more to Cumbria than the beauty of the Lake District. It also has a splendid coastline, easily accessible from the main lakeland centres, as well as a border region where the Pennines, the backbone of England, reach their highest point, towering over the Eden valley.

Formation of the dramatic Lakeland scenery began in the Caledonian period when earth movements raised & folded the already ancient rocks, submerging the whole mass underseas & covering it with limestone. During the ice age great glaciers ground out the lake beds & dales of todays landscape. There is tremendous variety, from the craggy outcrops of the Borrowdale Volcanics with Skiddaw at 3054 feet, to the gentle dales, the open moorlands & the lakes themselves. Each lake is distinctive, some with steep mountain sides sliding straight to the water's edge, others more open with sloping wooded hillsides. Ellerwater, the enchanting "lake of swans" is surrounded by reed & willows at the foot of Langdale. The charm of Ullswater inspired Wordsworth's famous poem "Daffodils". Whilst many lakes are deliberately left undisturbed for those seeking peace, there are others - notably Windermere - where a variety of water sports can be enjoyed. The changeable weather of the mountainous region can produce a sudden transformation in the character of a tranquil lake, raising choppy waves across the darkened surface to break along the shoreline. It is all part of the fascination of Lakeland.

Fell walking is the best way to appreciate the full beauty of the area. There are gentle walks along the dales, & the tops of the ridges are accessible to walkers with suitable footwear & an eye to the weather.

Ponytrekking is another popular way to explore the countryside & there are many centres catering even for inexperienced riders.

There are steamboats on lakes such as Coniston & Ullswater, where you can appreciate the scenery. On Windermere there are a variety of boats for hire, & facilities for water-skiing.

Traditional crafts & skills are on display widely. Craft centres at Keswick, Ambleside & Grasmere, & the annual exhibition of the Guild of Lakeland Craftsmen held in Windermere from mid-July to early September represent the widest variety of craft artistry.

Fairs & festivals flourish in Lakeland. The famous Appleby Horse Fair, held in June is the largest fair of its kind in the world & attracts a huge gypsy gathering. Traditional agriculture shows, sheep dog trials & local sporting events abound. The Grasmere Sports, held each August include gruelling fell races, Cumberland & Westmoreland wrestling, hound trails & pole-leaping.

The traditional custom of "Rush-bearing" when the earth floors of the churches were strewn with rushes still survives as a procession in Ambleside & Grasmere & many other villages in the summer months

The coast of Cumbria stretches from the estuaries of Grange-over-Sands & Burrow-in-Furness by way of the beautiful beaches between Bootle & Cardurnock, to the mouth of the Solway Firth. The coastal areas, especially the estuaries, are excellent for bird-watching. The sand dunes north of the Esk are famous for the colony of black-headed gulls which can be visited by arrangement, & the colony of seabirds at St. Bees Head is the largest in Britain.

Cumbria

Cumbria
Gazeteer
Area of outstanding natural beauty.
The Lake District National Park.

House & Castles
Carlisle Castle - Carlisle
12th century. Massive Norman keep - half-moon battery - ramparts, portcullis & gatehouse.
Brough Castle - Kirby Stephen
13th century - on site of Roman Station between York & Carlisle.
Dacre Castle - Penrith
14th century - massive pele tower.
Sizergh Castle - Kendal
14th century - pele tower - 15th century great hall. English & French furniture, silver & china - Jacobean relics. 18th century gardens.
Belle Island - Boweness-on-Windermere
18th century - interior by Adams Brothers, portraits by Romney.
Swarthmoor Hall - Ulverston
Elizabethan house, mullioned windows, oak staircase, panelled rooms. Home of George Fox - birthplace of Quakerism - belongs to Society of Friends.
Lorton Hall - Cockermouth
15th century pele tower, priest holes, oak panelling, Jacobean furniture.
Muncaster Castle - Ravenglass
14th century with 15th & 19th century additions - site of Roman tower.
Rusland Hall - Ulveston
Georgian mansion with period panelling, sculpture, furniture, paintings.
Levens Hall - Kendal
Elizabethan - very fine panelling & plasterwork - famous topiary garden.
Hill Top - Sawrey
17th century farmhouse home of Beatrix Potter - contains her furniture, china & some of original drawings for her children's books.
Dove Cottage - Town End, Grasmere
William Wordsworth's cottage - still contains his furnishing & his personal effects as in his lifetime.
Brantwood
The Coniston home of John Ruskin, said to be the most beautifully situated house in the Lake District. Exhibition, gardens, bookshops & tearooms.

Cathedrals & Churches
Carlisle Cathedral - Carlisle
1130. 15th century choir stalls with painted backs - carved misericords, 16th century screen, painted roof.
Cartmel Priory (St. Mary Virgin)
15th century stalls, 17th century screen, large east window, curious central tower.
Lanercost Priory (St. Mary Magdalene)
12th century - Augustinian - north aisle now forms Parish church.
Greystoke (St. Andrew)
14th/15th century. 19th century misericords. Lovely glass in chancel.
Brougham (St. Wilfred)
15th century carved altarpiece.
Furness Abbey
12th century monastery beautiful setting. Shap Abbey
12th century with 16th century tower.

Museums & Galleries
Abbot Hall - Kendal
18th century, Georgian house with period furniture, porcelain, silver, pictures, etc. Also contains modern galleries with contemporary paintings, sculptures & ceramics. Changing exhibitions on show.
Carlisle Museum & Art Gallery - Carlisle
Archaeological & natural history collections. National centre of studies of Roman Britain. Art gallery principally exhibiting paintings & porcelain.
Hawkshead Courthouse - Kendal
Exhibition of domestic & working life housed in mediaeval building.
Helena Thompson Museum - Workington
displays Victorian family life & objects of the period.
Lakeland Motor Museum - Holker Hall - Grange-over-Sands
Exhibits cars, bicycles, tricycles, motor cycles, etc., & model cars.
Millom Folk Museum - St. George's Road, Millom
Reconstructions of drift in iron ore mine, miner's cottage kitchen, blacksmith's forge & agricultural relics.
Ravenglass Railway Museum - Ravenglass
History of railways relics, models, etc.

Cumbria

Wordsworth Museum - Town End, Grasmere
Personal effects, first editions, manuscripts, & general exhibits from the time of William Wordsworth.
Border Regiment Museum - The Castle, Carlisle.
Collection of uniforms, weapons, trophies, documents, medals from 1702, to the present time.
Whitehaven Museum - Whitehaven
History & development of area show in geology, paleontology, archaeology, natural history, etc. Interesting maritime past.
Fitz Park Museum & Art Gallery - Keswick.

Collection of manuscripts - Wordsworth, Walpole, Coleridge, Southey.
The Beatrix Potter Gallery - Hawkshead

Things to see & do

Fell Walking - there is good walking throughout Cumbria, but check weather reports, clothing & footwear before tackling the heights.
Pony-trekking - opportunities for novice & experienced riders.
Watersports - Windermere is the ideal centre for sailing, waterskiing, windsurfing, scuba-diving.
Golf - championship course to the north at Silloth.

Grasmere.

CUMBRIA

Map reference

1	Seedhouse	24	Knowles
2	Hart	25	Bryant
3	Rhone	26	Lowe
4	Wilkinson	27	Langcake
5	Cervetti	28	Graham
6	Hood	28	Davenport
7	Butcher	29	Appleton
8	Stobbart	30	White
9	Edwards	31	Weightman
10	Sisson	32	Whittam
11	Staff	33	Tully
12	Hodge	34	Hart
13	Murray	35	Greenhalgh
14	Tylor	35	Holcroft
15	Wilkinson	35	Tyson
16	Danson	35	Lawless
17	Clark	35	Butterworth
18	Savasi	35	Fielding
19	Hatch	35	Cox
19	Davies	35	Garside
20	Brind	35	Fishman
21	Midwinter	35	Sanderson
22	Wightman	35	Naylor
23	Kettle	36	Smith
		37	Kirby

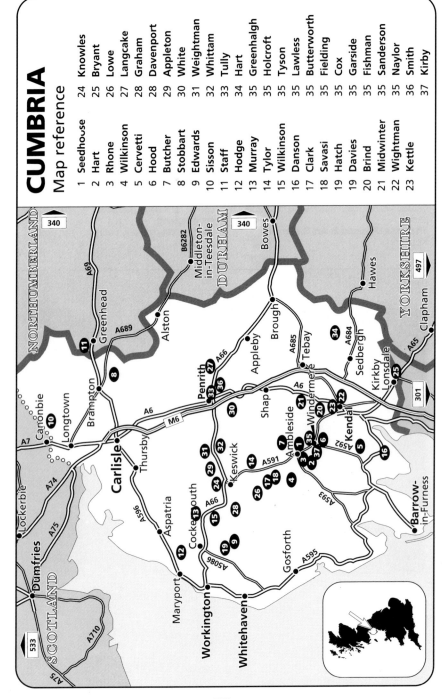

120

Laurel Villa. Ambleside.

Riverside Lodge Country House. Rothay Bridge.

		rate from £ per person	children taken	evening meals	animals taken
Brian Seedhouse **Laurel Villa** **Lake Road** **Ambleside** **LA22 0DB** **Tel: (015394) 33240** **Open: ALL YEAR** **Map Ref No. 01**	Nearest Road: A.591 Visited by Beatrix Potter, this charming Victorian residence, now sympathetically restored & refurbished to a very high standard, offers 8 particularly comfortable en-suite bedrooms; 2 of which boast 4-poster beds whilst some at the rear have splendid views over the village & surrounding fells. A residents' lounge in which to relax & an attractive dining room. Major outdoor activities are catered for nearby, including watersports, pony trekking &, of course, fell walking. Car park. *see PHOTO over* CREDIT CARD VISA M'CARD	£30.00	N	Y	N
Mr & Mrs Alan Rhone **Riverside Lodge** **Rothay Road** **Rothay Bridge** **Ambleside LA22 0EH** **Tel: (015394) 34208** **Open: ALL YEAR** **Map Ref No. 03**	Nearest Road: A.591 Riverside Lodge is an early-Georgian house superbly situated in a unique riverside setting, just a short walk from both the centre of Ambleside & Lake Windermere. The house has been refurbished to a high standard & exudes character & charm, with beamed ceilings. 5 tasteful modern holiday cottages within the grounds for those who wish to cater for themselves. A beautiful home, ideal for touring the surrounding countryside. *see PHOTO over* CREDIT CARD VISA M'CARD	£20.00	N	N	N
Robert & Helen Kirby **Buckle Yeat Guest House** **Sawrey, Hawkshead** **Ambleside LA22 0LF** **Tel: (015394) 36538** **Tel/Fax 015394 36446** **Open: ALL YEAR** **Map Ref No. 37**	Nearest Road: B.5285, A.592 Buckle Yeat is famous for its connections with Beatrix Potter. Although over 200 years old, it has been sympathetically & tastefully refurbished. There is a large lounge with log fire & an attractive dining room which also serves morning coffee & afternoon teas. 7 comfortable en-suite bedrooms. Many good local pubs & restaurants offer excellent meals. An ideal position for touring Lakeland with walks, fishing & birdwatching all nearby. CREDIT CARD VISA M'CARD	£20.00	Y	N	Y
Peter & Anne Hart **Bracken Fell** **Outgate** **Ambleside** **LA22 0NH** **Tel: (015394) 36289** **Open: ALL YEAR** **Map Ref No. 02**	Nearest Road: B.5286, A.591 Bracken Fell is situated in beautiful open countryside in the picturesque hamlet of Outgate. Located between Ambleside & Hawkshead, this makes an ideal base for exploring the Lake District. 7 comfortable rooms, all with tea/coffee-making facilities & outstanding views. Each has either en-suite or private facilities. There is also a comfortable lounge & dining room. All major outdoor activities are catered for nearby, including sailing, fishing, windsurfing & pony trekking.	£19.50	Y	N	N
Philip & Jane Butcher **Rowanfield Country House** **Kirkstone Road** **Ambleside** **LA22 9ET** **Tel: (015394) 33686** **Open: FEB - DEC** **Map Ref No. 07**	Nearest Road: A.591 Set in quiet countryside 3/4 of a mile outside Ambleside, with fabulous lake & mountain views. A beautiful period house, with Laura Ashley-style decor. A warm welcome assured, & a homely atmosphere. All bedrooms are en-suite, & individually & tastefully furnished. Central heating, tea/coffee-making facilities, colour T.V., radio/alarm & hairdryer in all rooms. A top professional chef/patron creates exciting evening meals from the finest fresh produce. Unlicensed, but own wine welcome. Children over 5 yrs. *see PHOTO over* CREDIT CARD VISA M'CARD	£25.00	Y	Y	Y

Rowanfield Country House. Ambleside.

Fairfield Country House Hotel. Bowness–on–Windermere.

	rate from £ per person	children taken	evening meals	animals taken
Mrs M. Wilkinson **Long House** **Great Langdale** **Ambleside** **LA22 9JS** **Tel: (015394) 37222** **Open: FEB - NOV** **Map Ref No. 04**	Nearest Road: B.5343 A 17th-century Lakeland cottage enjoying a peaceful position near the foot of Langdale Pikes, with superb open views. 2 acres of orchard & garden. Beamed ceilings, stained glass windows & original slate floors. Pretty en-suite bedrooms, full of character & very individual. Enclosed parking. Ideal walking country, & centrally placed for the motorist. Home cooking, with quality food a speciality. Children over 10 yrs.	£22.00 🚭 CREDIT CARD VISA M'CARD	N	Y	N
John & Ann Taylor **Woodland Crag** **How Head Lane** **Grasmere** **Ambleside LA22 9SG** **Tel: (015394) 35351** **Open: ALL YEAR** **Map Ref No. 14**	Nearest Road: A.591 A warm welcome & an informal atmosphere are found in this delightful house, situated on the edge of Grasmere near Dove Cottage. Secluded but with easy access to all facilities, the accommodation has tastefully decorated bedrooms, all with individual character & wonderful views of the lake, fells or garden. Ideal for walking, & centrally placed for the motorist. Enclosed parking. Totally non-smoking.	£24.00 🚭	N	N	N
Mrs Evelyn Cervetti **'Lightwood Farmhouse'** **Cartmel Fell** **Bowland Bridge** **LA11 6NP** **Tel: (015395) 31454** **Open: FEB - DEC** **Map Ref No. 05**	Nearest Road: A.592 Lightwood is a 17th-century farmhouse built in approx. 1650. It possesses all modern amenities whilst retaining the charm of original oak beams & staircase. 2 acres of lovely gardens, with streams running through. Individually decorated rooms, with countryside views. 7 bedrooms have en-suite bathrooms. Cosy lounge with T.V. & log fire. Charming dining room facing the early morning sun. 2 miles southern end of Lake Windermere. Good English breakfast, with free-range eggs.	£23.00 CREDIT CARD VISA M'CARD	Y	N	N
Ray & Barbara Hood **Fairfield Country House** **Hotel** **Brantfell Rd** **Bowness-on-Windermere** **LA23 3AE** **Tel/Fax: (015394) 46565** **Open: ALL YEAR** **Map Ref No. 06**	Nearest Road: A.591 Fairfield is a small, friendly, 200-year-old lakeland hotel found in a peaceful garden setting, 200 metres from Bowness village, 400 metres from the shores of Lake Windermere & at the end of the Dales Way (an 81-mile walk from Ilkley to Bowness). The Beatrix Potter Exhibition is within easy walking distance. Well-appointed & tastefully furnished bedrooms all have a colour T.V., a welcome tray & private showers/bathrooms. Breakfasts are a speciality. Leisure facilities.	£24.00 🚭 *see PHOTO over* CREDIT CARD VISA M'CARD	Y	N	N
Iain & Jackie Garside **Fayrer Garden House** **Lyth Valley Road** **Bowness-on-Windermere** **LA23 3JP** **Tel: (015394) 88195** **Fax 015394 45986** **Open: ALL YEAR** **Map Ref No. 35**	Nearest Road: A.5074 Iain & Jackie welcome you to their beautiful Lakeland home, peacefully set in 5 acres of landscaped gardens & overlooking the lake & mountains. Delightful decor & tastefully furnished, spacious en-suite rooms with modern amenities. Some 4-poster rooms & jacuzzis. Convenient for the golf club, sailing, restaurants, etc. Free use of the local leisure brochure. A free colour brochure available. An ideal spot for a relaxing break or for exploring Cumbria & the Lake Disrtict.	£25.00 *see PHOTO over* CREDIT CARD VISA M'CARD AMEX	Y	Y	Y

Fayrer Garden House. Bowness-on-Windermere.

Pickett Howe. Brackenthwaite.

Bessiestown Farm.   Catlowdy.

Cumbria

	rate from £ per person	children taken	evening meals	animals taken
Mrs Sheila Stobbart 'Hullerbank' Talkin Brampton CA8 1LB Tel: (016977) 46668 Open: ALL YEAR (Excl. Xmas & New Year) Map Ref No. 08	Nearest Road: A.69, M.6 A Georgian farmhouse, dated 1635 - 1751, standing in its own grounds near the picturesque village of Talkin, 2 1/2 miles from Brampton. Superb walking country, central for visiting Hadrian's Wall, the Lake District & the borders. A warm, friendly, relaxed atmosphere awaits. 3 comfortable bedrooms, with private facilities, electric underblankets & tea makers. A comfortable T.V. lounge, & dining room with excellent home cooking, including home-produced lamb & fresh produce. Children over 12 welcome. CREDIT CARD VISA M'CARD	£19.50	Y	Y	N
David & Dani Edwards Pickett Howe Buttermere Valley CA13 9UY Tel: (01900) 85444 Fax 01900 85209 Open: MAR - NOV Map Ref No. 09	Nearest Road: B.5292, A.66 A Lord-Inglewood-award winner, this 17th-century longhouse offers caring, friendly & relaxing hospitality. Peacefully set in 15 acres amidst stunning mountain scenery, its slate floors, oak beams & mullioned windows are enhanced by quality furnishings & antiques. 4 fully en-suite bedrooms, with whirlpool baths, hot-drinks trays, 'phones, clock/radios, Victorian brass & iron bedsteads. Renowned creative cooking (meat & vegetarian), & outstanding breakfast menu. Children over 10. *see PHOTO over* CREDIT CARD VISA M'CARD	£35.00	Y	Y	N
Jack & Margaret Sisson Bessiestown Farm Catlowdy Longtown Carlisle CA6 5QP Tel/Fax: (01228) 577219 Open: ALL YEAR Map Ref No. 10	Nearest Road: B.6318, A.7 An award-winning farm, overlooking the Scottish borders, where a friendly, relaxing atmosphere is assured. Accommodation is in 4 pretty, en-suite rooms with radio, T.V. & tea/coffee-making facilities. Delicious home cooking. A residential drinks licence. Guests may also use the indoor, heated pool (May - Sept). An excellent base for touring or a stop-off to/from Scotland & N. Ireland. Smoking restricted to the bar/lounge. *see PHOTO over* CREDIT CARD VISA M'CARD	£19.50	Y	Y	N
Brian & Pauline Staff 'Holmhead' Licensed Guest House Hadrian's Wall Greenhead Carlisle CA6 7HY Tel/Fax: (016977) 47402 Open: ALL YEAR Map Ref No. 11	Nearest Road: A.69, B.6318 Standing in 300 acres of grounds, with Hadrian's Wall below, Holmhead, a 150-year-old traditional farmhouse, is an excellent base for visiting an area full of Roman history. 4 charming en-suite bedrooms with modern amenities. The longest breakfast menu in the world. All meals prepared with fresh produce. Guests dine together at a candlelit table. Birdswald, the highest remains of the Wall & the Roman Army Museum are close by. The host is a qualified tour guide & expert on Hadrian's Wall. Licensed. *see PHOTO over* CREDIT CARD VISA M'CARD	£22.50	Y	Y	N
Pauline & Bob Hodge Sundawn Carlisle Road, Bridekirk Cockermouth CA13 0PA Tel: (01900) 822384 Open: ALL YEAR (Excl. Xmas) Map Ref No. 12	Nearest Road: A.595 Bob & Pauline offer you a warm & friendly welcome. The emphasis here is on comfort, relaxation, personal service & imaginative home cooking. From the sunlounge, view the panorama of the Lakeland Fells & the historic market town of Cockermouth, birthplace of William Wordsworth. Offering 4 tastefully decorated rooms, 2 en-suite, all with modern amenities & tea/coffee makers.	£15.00	Y	Y	Y

Holmhead. Greenhead.

New House Farm. Lorton.

Cumbria

		rate from £ per person	children taken	evening meals	animals taken
Enid Davies **Low Hall Guest House** **Brandlin Gill** **Cockermouth CA13 0RE** **Tel: (01900) 826654** **Open: MAR - NOV** **Map Ref No. 19**	Nearest Road: A.66 Tea by the fire, birthday bouquets & celebration champagne welcome you to Low Hall. A friendly atmosphere fills every room in this 17th-century farmhouse, commanding uninterrupted views of lake, stream & fell. The oak-beamed dining room sets the scene for your evening meal, with the very best of country cooking using fresh local produce. (Rate includes dinner.) A rural retreat & excellent value for money. Children over 10. CREDIT CARD VISA M'CARD	£40.00	Y	Y	N
John & Hazel Hatch **New House Farm** **Lorton** **Cockermouth** **CA13 9UU** **Tel: (01900) 85404** **Open: ALL YEAR** **Map Ref No. 19**	Nearest Road: A.66, B.5289 John & Hazel Hatch live in what must surely be one of the best settings for a country guest house. New House Farm is surrounded by Lakeland fells, & has its own fields, woods, streams & ponds. The award-winning house is a traditional Lakeland stone house, dating back to 1650 but brought into the 20th century by careful restoration. There are 3 very charming en-suite bedrooms available. Children over 12 years welcome. *see PHOTO over*	£30.00	Y	Y	Y
Eric & Joan Murray **Lakeside** **Bassenthwaite Lake** **Cockermouth** **CA13 9YD** **Tel: (017687) 76358** **Open: JAN - NOV** **Map Ref No. 13**	Nearest Road: A.66 An elegant country house offering friendly & relaxing hospitality, with superb views across Bassenthwaite Lake to Skiddaw & the surrounding fells. Keswick is only a short drive away. Also, the peaceful western fells & lakes of Buttermere & Crummock Water. 8 tastefully furnished bedrooms, 7 en-suite, each with T.V., & tea/coffee. Oak floors & a panelled hall. A pleasant lounge in which to relax, & delicious home cooking - 5-course evening meal & wine if required. *see PHOTO over*	£20.00	Y	Y	N
Fred & Hazel Wilkinson **Riggs Cottage** **Routenbeck** **Bassenthwaite Lake** **Cockermouth** **CA13 9YN** **Tel: (017687) 76580** **Fax 017687 76580** **Open: ALL YEAR** **Map Ref No. 15**	Nearest Road: A.66 Riggs Cottage is a super 17th-century cottage of great character & charm, with many exposed oak beams, a log-burning inglenook fireplace & period furniture. The accommodation, in 3 rooms, is comfortable, & tastefully furnished with modern amenities. The cosy lounge is available throughout the day. In the nicely furnished dining room, tasty home-cooked meals are served, using only the best ingredients. Oven-fresh bread & home-made preserves are a speciality. Situated 'off the beaten track', this is an ideal base for a Lakeland holiday. Children over 5 yrs. *see PHOTO over*	£19.00	Y	Y	N
Joe & Anne Danson **Greenacres** **Lindale** **Grange-over-Sands** **LA11 6LP** **Tel: (015395) 34578** **Open: JAN - NOV** **Map Ref No. 16**	Nearest Road: A.590 Greenacres is a charming 19th-century cottage ideally located for exploring the lakes & dales. Situated in the National Park, in the small village of Lindale at the foot of the beautiful Winster Valley, where you can walk in unspoilt countryside. All bedrooms are luxury en-suite. There is a lovely lounge & conservatory, & cosy dining room where excellent home-cooking is served. Friendly & relaxed atmosphere. CREDIT CARD VISA M'CARD	£24.50	Y	Y	N

Lakeside. Bassenthwaite.

Riggs Cottage. Bassenthwaite Lake

Banerigg House. Grasmere.

Cumbria

		rate from £ per person	children taken	evening meals	animals taken
Angela & Martin Clark **Banerigg Guest House** **Lake Road** **Grasmere** **LA22 9PW** **Tel: (015394) 35204** **Open: ALL YEAR** **Map Ref No. 17**	Nearest Road: A.591 Delightfully situated overlooking Grasmere Lake is this small, friendly guest house. The informal hospitality & relaxing atmosphere make this a super base for a holiday. All 6 comfortable rooms have modern amenities. A pleasant lounge with a cosy log fire. Delicious, plentiful home-cooking is served daily. Ideally located for fell walking, sailing, canoeing & fishing. Angela & Martin ensure that guests have a memorable Lakeland holiday. Evening meals for group bookings only.	£17.50 🚭 *see PHOTO over*	Y	N	N
Mr & Mrs Attilio Savasi **Oak Bank Hotel** **Broadgate** **Grasmere LA22 9TA** **Tel: (015394) 35217** **Tel/Fax 015394 35685** **Open: FEB - DEC** **Map Ref No. 18**	Nearest Road: A.591 The Oak Bank Hotel is a little gem one stumbles upon all too rarely, with a new conservatory dining room overlooking the garden, by which the river Rothay flows. An award-winning hotel for Cordon Bleu cuisine, hospitality & comfort. Log fires in the lounge/bar & delightful Victorian-style bedrooms complete this restful, owner-run hotel. The Oak Bank Hotel is the perfect spot for a relaxing break or for touring the Lake District.	£27.00 CREDIT CARD VISA M'CARD	Y	Y	Y
Paul & Honor Brind **Burrow Hall Country** **Guest House** **Plantation Bridge** **Kendal LA8 9JR** **Tel: (01539) 821711** **Open: ALL YEAR** **Map Ref No. 20**	Nearest Road: A.591 This delightful guest house, situated on the A.591 between Kendal & Windermere, was built in 1648. The 'olde worlde' charm of oak beams & log fire is maintained in the principal guest lounge. There is an extensive breakfast menu, & 4-course dinner (with accompanying wine list), followed by coffee & mints. All-round enjoyment is ensured here. Burrow Hall is a lovely home, & is ideally situated for exploring Cumbria.	£22.50 CREDIT CARD VISA M'CARD	N	Y	N
Alison & Philip Midwinter **Low Jock Scar** **Selside** **Kendal LA8 9LE** **Tel: (01539) 823259** **Fax 01539 823645** **Open: MAR - OCT incl.** **Map Ref No. 21**	Nearest Road: A.6 A charming country guest house. A relaxing & friendly atmosphere with genuine warmth. In an idyllic setting with 6 acres of garden & woodland, it is a peaceful base from which to explore the Lakes & Yorkshire Dales. 5 comfortable bedrooms (3 en-suite, 2 on the ground floor) & a lounge well-stocked with books & maps. Excellent freshly prepared dinners - vegetarians catered for. Residential licence.	£20.00 🚭 *see PHOTO over*	N	Y	Y
Eileen & Brian Kettle **Holmfield** **41 Kendal Green** **Kendal LA9 5PP** **Tel: (01539) 720790** **Fax 01539 720790** **Open: ALL YEAR** **Map Ref No. 23**	Nearest Road: A.591, M.6 Superbly located, detached Edwardian house set in 1 acre of quiet gardens with croquet lawn, swimming pool & panoramic views. Spacious bathrooms adjacent to 3 lovely bedrooms (1 4-poster; 1 twin), with views, tea/coffee facilities, radio, T.V., etc. Elegant lounge & dining room, superb views, central heating, log fires. Walking distance from Kendal's many amenities & excellent restaurants. Renowned hospitality. Private parking. Children over 12.	£19.00 🚭	Y	N	N

Low Jock Scar. Selside

Cumbria

			rate from £ per person	children taken	evening meals	animals taken
Mrs Ada Wightman **The Glen** **Oxenholme** **Kendal** **LA9 7RF** **Tel: (01539) 726386** **Open: MAR - NOV** **Map Ref No. 22**	Nearest Road: M.6, A.65 A large detached house standing in its own grounds. Offering 3 rooms, all with private facilities & modern amenities including radio, colour T.V. & tea/coffee-making facilities. A delicious Full English breakfast is served, & there is a lounge for guests to relax in. Situated only minutes from Oxenholme railway station, 'The Glen' is an excellent base for touring the idyllic Lake District. Children over 12 years welcome.		£18.00	Y	Y	N
Eileen & David Davenport **Greystones** **Ambleside Road** **Keswick** **CA12 4DP** **Tel: (017687) 73108** **Open: FEB - NOV** **Map Ref No. 28**	Nearest Road: A.66, A.591 Greystones is a comfortable traditional Lakeland house where David & Eileen aim to create a friendly atmosphere for a happy, relaxed holiday. All bedrooms have private facilities, & most have excellent fell views. Imaginative home-made meals are served, using the best-quality fresh produce available. Situated in a quiet area of Keswick on Derwentwater, Greystones is only a short distance from the town centre, fells & lakeshore. Children over 8 yrs.		£22.50 🚭 CREDIT CARD VISA M'CARD	Y	Y	N
John & Ruth Knowles **Blease Farm** **Blease Road** **Threlkeld** **Keswick CA12 4SF** **Tel/Fax: (017687) 79087** **Open: ALL YEAR (Excl. Xmas)** **Map Ref No. 24**	Nearest Road: A.66 A recently refurbished 250-year-old Cumbrian farmhouse on the south-facing slopes of Blencathra with stunning views towards Helvellyn & a warm welcome. Rooms are comfortably furnished, en-suite, & have T.V. & tea-making facilities. Quality evening meals a speciality. Guests are encouraged to use the sun room & large sitting room with log fire. Over 200 walks & drives listed for guests'. Children over 12.		£24.00 🚭	N	Y	N
Alan & Sheila Appleton **Scales Farm** **Threlkeld** **Keswick** **CA12 4SY** **Tel: (017687) 79660** **Open: ALL YEAR** **Map Ref No. 29**	Nearest Road: A.66 Wonderful open views & a friendly personal welcome await you at Scales Farm, a sensitively modernised, 17th-century farmhouse. All 5 en-suite, centrally heated bedrooms have colour T.V., tea/coffee makers & fridge, providing luxurious accommodation to the highest standards. Guests have access to their rooms through a separate entrance at all times. Private car parking. An ideal location from which to visit all areas of the Lake District.		£21.00	Y	N	Y
Alan & Shirley Lowe & **Family** **Dale Head Hall** **Lake Thirlmere** **Keswick CA12 4TN** **Tel: (017687) 72478** **Fax 017687 71070** **Open: ALL YEAR** **Map Ref No. 26**	Nearest Road: A.591, A.66 Lose yourself in the ancient woodlands & mature gardens of an Elizabethan country manor, set serenely on the shores of Lake Thirlmere. Delicious dinners prepared by mother & daughter, using fresh produce from the Victorian kitchen garden, served with fine wines in the oak-beamed dining room. 9 individually decorated bedrooms, some with 4-posters, each with bath/shower rooms. Together with the lounge & bar, there are unspoilt views across lawns, lakes & fells.		£30.50 *see PHOTO over* CREDIT CARD VISA M'CARD	Y	Y	N

Dale Head Hall. Lake Thirlmere

	rate from £ per person	children taken	evening meals	animals taken
Ron & Pauline Graham **Thornleigh** 23 Bank Street Keswick CA12 5JZ Tel: (017687) 72863 Open: ALL YEAR Map Ref No. 28 Nearest Road: A.591, A.66 A traditional Lakeland stone building situated in Keswick town. All en-suite bedrooms have views of the magnificent mountains & fells, making Thornleigh an idyllic base for walking or touring the Northern Lakes. The attractive bedrooms have T.V. & tea/coffee-making facilities. The charming hosts offer a warm welcome & delicious Full English breakfast to all guests, old & new. CREDIT CARD VISA M'CARD	£20.00	N	N	N
Ian Bryant & Jocelyn Ruffle **Hipping Hall** Cowan Bridge Kirkby Lonsdale LA6 2JJ Tel: (015242) 71187 Fax 015242 72452 Open: MAR - NOV Map Ref No. 25 Nearest Road: A.65 Hipping Hall is a 17th-century country house set in 4 acres of walled gardens on the edge of the Yorkshire Dales National Park, 3 miles from pretty Kirkby Lonsdale & only half an hour from Windermere. The 7 bedrooms (all en-suite) & 2 apartments are attractively furnished & fully equipped. Guests dine together in the beautiful Great Hall with a Minstrel's Gallery. All dishes are freshly prepared by Jos Ruffle from home & local produce. Children over 12. *see PHOTO over* CREDIT CARD VISA M'CARD	£39.50	Y	Y	Y
Ros Sanders **Hornby Hall** Brougham Penrith CA10 2AR Tel: (01768) 891114 Fax 01768 88248 Open: ALL YEAR (Excl. Xmas) Map Ref No. 27 Nearest Road: A.66 Hornby Hall is a 16th-century farmhouse situated in quiet countryside near the River Eamont. There are 7 tastefully furnished & comfortable guest rooms, with beverage facilities. 2 are en-suite. Dinner is served in the original sandstone-floored dining hall. Advance bookings are essential, as only the freshest local ingredients are used. Special diets catered for. Licensed. An ideal base for touring the Lake District, Dales, North Pennines & Hadrian's Wall. CREDIT CARD VISA M'CARD	£19.00	Y	Y	N
Mrs Lesley White **Beckfoot Country House** **Hotel, Helton** Penrith CA10 2QB Tel: (01931) 713241 Fax 01931 713391 Open: MAR - NOV Map Ref No. 30 Nearest Road: M.6 A fine old residence featuring a half-panelled hall, staircase & attractive panelled dining room. Set in 3 acres of grounds in the delightful Lake District, it is a quiet, peaceful retreat for a holiday base, & is within easy reach of the many pleasure spots in the area. Offering 6 rooms, all with private shower/bathroom & tea/coffee-making facilities. A dining room, drawing & reading room. This is a delightful base for a touring holiday.	£24.00	Y	Y	Y
Brian & May Smith **Hill Top House** Morland Penrith CA10 3AX Tel: (01931) 714561 Open: ALL YEAR Map Ref No. 36 Nearest Road: A.6, M.6 Far from the madding crowd but within easy reach of Lakeland, Scotland & the Yorkshire Dales, Hill Top House stands in an elevated position in the ancient, picturesque & peaceful village of Morland. Brian & May will give you a warm welcome to their friendly Georgian house & secluded garden. 3 rooms, 2 en-suite & a single with private bathroom. You can dine with your hosts or walk to the village inn. Come & relax at this beautiful home.	£19.00	Y	Y	N

Hipping Hall. Kirkby Lonsdale

Cross Keys Hotel. Sedbergh.

Cumbria

	Nearest Road	rate from £ per person	children taken	evening meals	animals taken
Christine Weightman **Near Howe Farm Hotel** **Mungrisdale** **Penrith CA11 0SH** **Tel: (017687) 79678** **Fax 017687 79678** **Open: MAR - NOV** **Map Ref No. 31**	Nearest Road: A.66 A comfortable traditional Cumbrian family house, where guests receive a warm, friendly welcome. Standing in 300 acres of rolling moorland, it offers 7 nice bedrooms (most with en-suite facilities), a T.V. lounge, a games room & a smaller lounge with a well-stocked bar & log fire. In the pleasant dining room, freshly prepared meals are served, using local produce when possible. Close by are golf, fishing, pony trekking, boating & walking.	£18.00	Y	Y	Y
Mrs Marjorie Whittam **Netherdene Guest House** **Troutbeck** **Penrith** **CA11 0SJ** **Tel: (017684) 83475** **Open: ALL YEAR** **Map Ref No. 32**	Nearest Road: A.66, M.6 A traditional Lakeland house set in its own grounds, with extensive mountain views. Offering a warm welcome & personal attention. Accommodation is in 5 attractively furnished bedrooms, all en-suite, each with central heating, colour T.V. & tea/coffee-making facilities. A cosy lounge with log fire & T.V. is available throughout the day, & a dining room with excellent home cooking. Private parking. An ideal location from which to explore the Lake District. Children over 7 yrs.	£16.50	Y	Y	N
Mrs Carole Tully **Brandelhow Guest House** **1 Portland Place** **Penrith CA11 7QN** **Tel: (01768) 864470** **Open: ALL YEAR** **Map Ref No. 33**	Nearest Road: M.6, A.6, A.66 Brandelhow is a very pleasant Victorian house situated in the lovely market town of Penrith. Accommodation is in 5 tastefully decorated, bright & comfortable rooms, all with modern amenities, central heating, colour T.V. & tea/coffee-making facilities. Penrith is an ideal base for touring the Lake District & enjoying the usual outdoor sporting activities. A warm & friendly welcome is assured.	£15.00	Y	N	N
Frank & Lesley Hart **Cross Keys Hotel** **Cautley** **Sedbergh** **LA10 5NE** **Tel: (015396) 20284** **Open: MAR - DEC** **Map Ref No. 34**	Nearest Road: M.6, A.683 Delightful, tiny 400-year-old National Trust inn & old coaching stop. Magnificent mountain views & homely, very traditional, comfortable & relaxing atmosphere. Beautifully cooked food to individual tastes, all home-made & served with guests' own wine. No corkage charged. Home-baked bread, biscuits, jams & marmalades. Log fires, antiques, books, maps & guides. No T.V.s anywhere. Cooking & walking holidays by arrangement. Horseback tours available.	£25.00 🚭 *see PHOTO over*	Y	Y	N
Anthony & Aurea **Greenhalgh** **The Archway** **13 College Road** **Windermere** **LA23 1BU** **Tel: (015394) 45613** **Open: ALL YEAR** **Map Ref No. 35**	Nearest Road: A.591 Impeccable small Victorian guest house, quietly situated a stone's throw from Windermere village centre, yet with marvellous, open mountain views. Beautifully furnished throughout: antiques, interesting paintings & prints, good books, fresh flowers. Accommodation is in 5 individually decorated bedrooms, all en-suite, all with telephone, colour T.V., tea/coffee trays & Victorian patchwork quilts. Renowned for gourmet home-cooking using fresh local produce. Home-baked bread. Excellent wine list. No smoking.	£22.00 🚭 *see PHOTO over* CREDIT CARD VISA M'CARD AMEX	N	Y	N

The Archway. Windermere.

Beaumont Hotel. Windermere.

Cumbria

		rate from £ per person	children taken	evening meals	animals taken
Sheila & Joe Lawless **Green Gables** **37 Broad Street** **Windermere** **LA23 2AB** **Tel: (015394) 43886** **Open: ALL YEAR (Excl.** **Xmas & New Year)** **Map Ref No. 35**	Nearest Road: A.591, A.592 Green Gables is a pleasant, family-run Victorian guest house located in the centre of Windermere. The shops, restaurants, bus & railway stations close by make it a good base for touring the area. Accommodation is in 8 cosy bedrooms, some non-smoking, 3 with private facilities, all with colour T.V., tea/coffee makers & hair dryers. A comfortable T.V. lounge is also available. Golf can be arranged at Windermere & Kendal. The perfect location for a Lakeland holiday.	£14.00	Y	N	N
Frances & Brian Holcroft **Lynwood Guest House** **Broad Street** **Windermere** **LA23 2AB** **Tel: (015394) 42550** **Fax 015394 42550** **Open: ALL YEAR** **Map Ref No. 35**	Nearest Road: A.591 A Victorian, Lakeland stone house built in 1865, offering 9 comfortable & centrally heated bedrooms, each with en-suite bathrooms, all with modern amenities including colour T.V. & tea/coffee-making facilities. Guests may relax in the T.V. lounge available throughout the day. Centrally located, only 150 yards from village shops & restaurants, & only 5 mins from the bus & railway station. The host is a Lakeland tour guide, & is happy to assist in planning your stay.	£14.00	Y	N	N
Malcolm Cox & Kathy Naylor **The Beaumont Hotel** **Holly Road** **Windermere** **LA23 2AF** **Tel: (015394) 47075** **Open: FEB - DEC** **Map Ref No. 35**	Nearest Road: A.591 This elegant Victorian house hotel combines all the grace & charm of its time with all the comforts of today. Ideal for Windermere & Bowness, & perfect for touring the lakes. 10 attractive, en-suite bedrooms, with tea-making facilities, T.V. & hairdryers. Two 4-poster bedrooms available for special occasions, & a 'Romantic Presentation' of wine, chocolates, fruit & flowers may be ordered. The standards are high, breakfasts are hearty & the hospitality is warm & sincere. Private parking. Comfort with a touch of class. *see PHOTO over* CREDIT CARD VISA M'CARD AMEX	£22.00	Y	N	N
Neil & Carol Cox **Kirkwood** **Prince's Road** **Windermere LA23 2DD** **Tel: (015394) 43907** **Open: ALL YEAR** **Map Ref No. 35**	Nearest Road: A.591 Kirkwood occupies a quiet spot between Windermere and Bowness, offering guests a warm and friendly atmosphere with an individual, personal service. The 7 rooms are large, & all are en-suite. Some have 4-poster beds, all have T.V. and tea/coffee facilities. Your hosts will be pleased to help plan tours or walks, with maps provided. Drying facilities. Packed lunches available. CREDIT CARD VISA M'CARD	£19.00	Y	N	Y
Mr & Mrs I Fishman **Fir Trees Guest House** **Lake Road** **Windermere** **LA23 2EQ** **Tel/Fax: (015394) 42272** **Open: ALL YEAR** **Map Ref No. 35**	Nearest Road: A.591 Fir Trees is a handsome Victorian guest house of considerable charm & character, & is furnished with antiques throughout. Just 7 guest bedrooms, all lovely & spacious, with private bath or shower rooms, providing a truly home-like atmosphere. Fir Trees is well situated, within easy walking distance of Windermere, Bowness or the lake. Simply scrumptious breakfasts. But most of all, old-fashioned hospitality. Excellent value. *see PHOTO over* CREDIT CARD VISA M'CARD AMEX	£19.50	Y	N	N

Fir Trees. Windermere.

Hawksmoor Guest House.   Windermere.

Cumbria

		rate from £ per person	children taken	evening meals	animals taken
Barbara & Bob Tyson **Hawksmoor** **Lake Road** **Windermere** **LA23 2EQ** **Tel: (015394) 42110** **Fax 015394 42110** **Open: FEB - NOV** **Map Ref No. 35**	Nearest Road: A.591 Hawksmoor is situated halfway between the centres of Windermere & Bowness, just 10 mins' walk from the lake. Standing in lovely grounds, this creeper-clad house has 10 charming rooms, all en-suite & with garden views; some, also, with 4-poster beds & some strictly no smoking. A comfortable residents' lounge with T.V., & a garden for guests' enjoyment. Residential licence. Boating, golf, tennis, swimming, fishing & pony trekking all nearby. Phone for availability before booking. Children over 6. CREDIT CARD VISA M'CARD	£21.00 *see PHOTO over*	Y	Y	N
Alan & Dorothy Fielding **Rosemount** **Lake Road** **Windermere** **LA23 2EQ** **Tel: (015394) 43739** **Fax 015394 43739** **Open: ALL YEAR** **Map Ref No. 35**	Nearest Road: A.591 The Fieldings have built up a reputation over many years for offering warm & caring hospitality in their beautiful Victorian guest house which is just a short walk from Lake Windermere. 8 tastefully furnished bedrooms, including 2 singles, all with private facilities. Delicious traditional breakfasts (or a refreshing fruit alternative). Their local knowledge is freely given when planning your daily sightseeing & onward travel, with personal advice on local restaurants too. Excellent value & exclusively for non-smokers. CREDIT CARD VISA M'CARD AMEX	£18.00	Y	N	N
Jackie & Frank Sanderson **Blenheim Lodge Hotel** **Brantfell Road** **Bowness-on-Windermere** **Windermere LA23 3AE** **Tel/Fax: (015394) 43440** **Open: ALL YEAR** **Map Ref No. 35**	Nearest Road: A.592 A beautiful Lakeland guest house, overlooking Lake Windermere, offering peace & quiet & yet close to the Lake & shops. Jaqueline Sanderson is an expert in traditional English cuisine, & guests' admiration for the food has resulted in their own award-winning cookbook. Fresh local produce. A delightful home & the perfect place for a Lakeland holiday. Please 'phone for booking. Children over 6 yrs welcome. CREDIT CARD VISA M'CARD AMEX	£22.00	Y	Y	N
Brenda Butterworth **Orrest Head House** **Kendal Road** **Windermere** **LA23 IJG** **Tel: (015394) 44315** **Open: FEB - DEC** **Map Ref No. 35**	Nearest Road: A.591 A traditional Lakeland-style house, partly 17th-century, standing in 3 acres of garden. This lovely old house offers 5 rooms: each en-suite, all with tea/coffee-making facilities & T.V.. Located above Windermere village, with distant views towards the Lake & mountains beyond. Guests can relax in the resident's lounge with log fires, or in the tranquil garden with its lovely surroundings. Very convenient for the railway station & bus terminal. Ample parking. Children over 6 yrs.	£19.50 *see PHOTO over*	Y	N	N

When booking your accommodation please mention
The Best Bed & Breakfast

Orrest Head House. Windermere.

Derby & Staffs

Derbyshire
(East Midlands)

A county with everything but the sea, this was Lord Byron's opinion of Derbyshire, & the special beauty of the Peak District was recognised by its designation as Britain's first National Park.

Purple heather moors surround craggy limestone outcrops & green hills drop to sheltered meadows or to deep gorges & tumbling rivers.

Derbyshire's lovely dales have delightful names too - Dove Dale, Monk's Dale, Raven's Dale, Water-cum-Jolly-Dale, & they are perfect for walking. The more adventurous can take up the challenge of the Pennine Way, a 270 mile pathway from Edale to the Scottish border.

The grit rock faces offer good climbing, particularly at High Tor above the River Derwent, & underground there are extensive & spectacular caverns. There are show caves at the Heights of Abraham, which you reach by cable-car, & at Castleton, source of the rare Blue John mineral, & at Pole's Cavern in Buxton where there are remarkable stalactites & stalagmites.

Buxton's splendid Crescent reflects the town's spa heritage, & the Opera House is host to an International Festival each summer.

The waters at Matlock too were prized for their curative properties & a great Hydro was built there in the last century, to give treatment to the hundreds of people who came to "take the waters".

Bakewell is a lovely small town with a fascinating market, some fine buildings & the genuine Bakewell Pudding, (known elsewhere as Bakewell tart).

Well-dressing is a custom carried on throughout the summer in the villages & towns. It is a thanksgiving for the water, that predates the arrival of Christianity in Britain. Flower-petals, leaves, moss & bark are pressed in

Haddon Hall; Derby.

Derby & Staffs

intricate designs into frames of wet clay & erected over the wells, where they stay damp & fresh for days.

The mining of lead & the prosperity of the farms brought great wealth to the landowning families who were able to employ the finest of architects & craftsmen to design & build their great houses. Haddon Hall is a perfectly preserved 12th century manor house with with terraced gardens of roses & old-fashioned flowers. 17th century Chatsworth, the "Palace of the Peak", houses a splendid collection of paintings, drawings, furniture & books, & stands in gardens with elaborate fountains.

Staffordshire
(Heart of England)

Staffordshire is a contrast of town & county. Miles of moorland & dramatic landscapes lie to the north of the country, & to the south is the Vale of Trent & the greenery of Cannock Chase. But the name of Staffordshire invokes that of the Potteries, the area around Stoke-on-Trent where the world-renowned ceramics are made.

The factories that produce the Royal Doulton, Minton, Spode & Coalport china will arrange tours for visitors, & there is a purpose-built visitor centre at Barlaston displaying the famous Wedgwood tradition.

The Gladstone Pottery Museum is set in a huge Victorian potbank, & the award-winning City museum in Stoke-on-Trent has a remarkable ceramics collection.

There is lovely scenery to be found where the moorlands of Staffordshire meet the crags & valleys of the Peak District National Park. From the wild & windy valleys of The Roaches (from the French 'roche') you can look across the county to Cheshire & Wales. Drivers can take high moorland roads that are marked out as scenic routes.

The valleys of the Dove & Manifold are beautiful limestone dales & ideal for walking or for cycling. Sir Izzak Walton, author of 'The Compleat Angler', drew his inspiration, & his trout, from the waters here.

The valley of the River Churnet is both pretty & peaceful, being largely inaccessible to cars. The Caldon Canal, with its colourful narrowboats, follows the course of the river & there are canalside pubs, picnic areas, boat rides & woodland trails to enjoy. The river runs through the grounds of mock-Gothic Alton Towers, now a leisure park.

The Vale of Trent is largely rural with small market towns, villages, river & canals.

Cannock Chase covers 20 square miles of heath & woodland & is the home of the largest herd of fallow deer in England. Shugborough Hall stands in the Chase. The ancestral home of Lord Lichfeld, it also houses the Staffordshire County Museum & a farm for rare breeds including the famous Tamworth Pig.

Burton-on-Trent is known as the home of the British brewery industry & there are two museums in the town devoted to the history of beer.

Lichfield is a small & picturesque city with a cathedral which dates from the 12th century & has three graceful spires known as the 'Ladies of the Vale'. Dr. Samuel Johnson was born in the city & his house is now a museum dedicated to his life & work.

One of the Vale's villages retains its mediaeval tradition by performing the Abbot's Bromley Horn Dance every September.

Derby & Staffs

Derbyshire

Gazeteer

Areas of outstanding natural beauty.
Peak National Park. The Dales.

Houses & Castles

Chatsworth - Bakewell
17th century, built for 1st. Duke of Devonshire. Furniture, paintings & drawings, books, etc. Fine gardens & parklands.
Haddon Hall - Bakewell
Mediaeval manor house - complete. Terraced rose gardens.
Hardwick Hall - Nr. Chesterfield
16th century - said to be more glass than wall. Fine furniture, tapestries & furnishings. Herb garden.
Kedlestone Hall - Derby
18th century - built on site of 12th century Manor house. Work of Robert Adam - has world famous marble hall. Old Master paintings. 11th century church nearby.
Melbourne Hall - Nr. Derby
12th century origins - restored by Sir John Coke. Fine collection of pictures & works of art. Magnificent gardens & famous wrought iron pagoda.
Sudbury Hall - Sudbury
Has examples of work of the greatest craftsmen of the period-Grinling Gibbons,Pierce and Laguerre.
Winster Market House   Nr. Matlock
17th century stone built market house.

Cathedrals & Churches

Chesterfield (St. Mary & All Saints)
13th & 14th centuries.
4 chapels, polygonal apse, mediaeval screens, Jacobean pulpit.
Derby (All Saints)
Perpendicular tower - classical style - 17th century plate, 18th century screen.
Melbourne (St. Michael & St. Mary)
Norman with two west towers & crossing tower.
Splendid plate, 18th century screen.
Normbury (St. Mary & St. Barloke)
14th century - perpendicular tower.
Wood carving & brasses.
Wirksworth (St. Mary)
13th century, restored & enlarged.

Staffordshire

Gazeteer

Houses & Castles

Ancient High House - Stafford
16th century - largest timber-framed town house in England.
Shugborough - Nr. Stafford
Ancestral home of the Earl of Lichfield. Mansion house, paintings, silver, ceramics, furniture. County Museum. Rare Breeds Farm.
Moseley Old Hall - Nr. Wolverhampton
Elizabethan house formerly half-timbered.
Stafford Castle
Large & well-preserved Norman castle in grounds with castle trail.
Tamworth Castle
Norman motte & bailey castle with later additions. Museum.

Cathedrals & Churches

Croxden Abbey
12th century foundation Cistercian abbey. Ruins of 13th century church.
Ingestre (St. Mary the Virgin)
A rare Wren church built in1676.
Lichfield Cathedral
Unique triple-spired 12th century cathedral.
Tamworth (St. Editha's)
Founded 963, rebuilt 14th century. Unusual double spiral staircase.
Tutbury (St. Mary's)
Norman church with impressive West front.

Museums & Galleries

City Museum & Art Gallery - Stoke-on-Trent
Modern award-winning museum.
Ceramics, decorative arts, etc.
Dr. Johnson Birthplace Museum - Lichfield
Gladstone Pottery Museum - Longton
Izaak Walton Cottage & Museum - Shallowfield, Nr. Stafford
National Brewery Museum & the Bass Museum of Brewing-both in Stoke-on-Trent
Stafford Art Gallery & Craft Shop - Stafford
Major gallery for the visual arts & centre for quality craftsmanship.

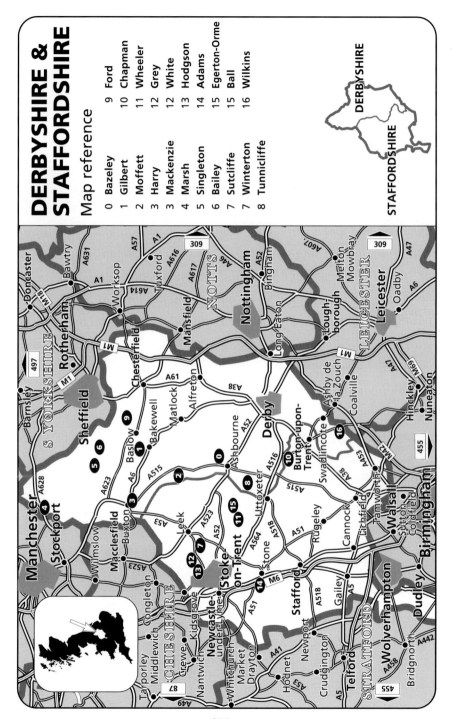

DERBYSHIRE & STAFFORDSHIRE

Map reference

0 Bazeley	9 Ford
1 Gilbert	10 Chapman
2 Moffett	11 Wheeler
3 Harry	12 Grey
3 Mackenzie	12 White
4 Marsh	13 Hodgson
5 Singleton	14 Adams
6 Bailey	15 Egerton-Orme
7 Sutcliffe	15 Ball
7 Winterton	16 Wilkins
8 Tunnicliffe	

DERBYSHIRE

STAFFORDSHIRE

The Beeches Farmhouse. Waldley.

Derbyshire

		rate from £ per person	children taken	evening meals	animals taken
Penny & Mark Bazeley **Biggin Mill Farm** **Biggin By Hulland** **Ashbourne DE6 3FN** Tel: (01335) 370414 Fax 01335 370414 Open: ALL YEAR Map Ref No. 00	Nearest Road: A.517 A stone farmhouse of charm & character (dated 1757) with walls 2 feet thick. A 3-acre hideaway with mature woods, ducks & a stream in the rural Derbyshire Dales. A truly restful experience offering every quality facility, with interior design throughout & antiques. 2 double bedrooms (en-suite/spa bathroom), a cosy guest lounge, books & a log burner, honour bar, breakfast room & extensive breakfast menu. Superb walks from the grounds. Country pubs nearby. *see PHOTO over* CREDIT CARD VISA M'CARD AMEX	£37.50	N	N	N
Barbara Ann Tunnicliffe **The Beeches Farmhouse** **Waldley** **Doveridge** **Ashbourne DE6 5LR** Tel/Fax: (01889) 590288 Open: ALL YEAR Map Ref No. 08	Nearest Road: A.50 A delightful 18th-century farmhouse situated in the Derbyshire Dales. 10 elegant en-suite bedrooms, each well-appointed & furnished to a high standard. Enjoy dining in the award-winning, oak-beamed, licensed restaurant - after exploring the Derbyshire countryside, or the thrills of Alton Towers. Children will love feeding the many animals on this 160-acre working dairy farm. A charming home within easy reach of a wealth of places of interest. *see PHOTO over* CREDIT CARD VISA M'CARD AMEX	£23.00	Y	Y	N
Mrs Sheila Gilbert **Castle Cliffe Private Hotel** **Monsal Head** **Bakewell DE45 1NL** Tel: (01629) 640258 Open: ALL YEAR Map Ref No. 01	Nearest Road: A.6 You can be sure of a warm, friendly welcome & personal service in this elegant country house. Built in 1886, overlooking beautiful Monsal Dale & its famous viaduct, with superb views from its 9 bedrooms. 4 are en-suite & all have tea/coffee makers. There are open fires in the lounge & bar where you can relax after one of Sheila's delicious meals cooked using local produce & regional British recipes. It is an ideal base for visits to the Peak National Park & nearby Chatsworth House. CREDIT CARD VISA M'CARD	£22.00	Y	Y	N
Mary Mackenzie **Staden Grange** **Staden Lane** **Buxton** **SK17 9RZ** Tel: (01298) 24965 Fax 01298 72067 Open: ALL YEAR Map Ref No. 03	Nearest Road: A.515 A pleasant, spacious country house set in 25 acres & enjoying splendid uninterrupted views over open farmland. Attractive & comfortable en-suite rooms, 1 with 4-poster, each with satellite T.V., radio, 'phone & tea/coffee makers. The 'Foxlow Restaurant' offers excellent cuisine, & menus change daily. Lovely lounge & cocktail bar with T.V., also a large garden. Riding & shooting, masseuse, sauna, sunbed, jacuzzi & a golf course nearby. Only 2 miles from Buxton, & ideal for touring, walking & riding in this scenic region. CREDIT CARD VISA M'CARD AMEX	£25.00	Y	Y	Y
John & Linda Harry **Coningsby** **6 Macclesfield Road** **Buxton** **SK17 9AH** Tel: (01298) 26735 Open: FEB - NOV Map Ref No. 03	Nearest Road: A.515 John & Linda's home, 'Coningsby', is a beautifully restored, detached Victorian house surrounded by a delightful garden in a conservation area close to the Pavilion Gardens. Guests are assured of a warm welcome, excellent accommodation, an extremely high standard of cleanliness, good home-cooked food & reasonably priced wine. An ideal centre for a holiday, & within easy reach of the Peak District National Park & many other places of interest. Brochure on request.	£20.00	N	Y	N

Biggin Mill Farm. Biggin By Hulland.

Derbyshire

	rate from £ per person	children taken	evening meals	animals taken
James & Maria Moffett **Biggin Hall** **Biggin-by-Hartington** **Buxton SK17 0DH** **Tel: (01298) 84451** **Fax 01298 84681** **Open: ALL YEAR** **Map Ref No. 02**	Nearest Road: A.515 A delightful 17th-century stone house, completely restored & keeping all the character of its origins, with massive oak beams. 15 comfortable rooms, all charmingly furnished, 1 with a 4-poster bed, all with en-suite facilities & modern amenities. Guests have the choice of 2 sitting rooms, 1 with a log fire, 1 with colour T.V. & library, & there is a lovely garden. The house is beautifully furnished, with many antiques. Evening meals are available. Non-smoking areas. Children over 12.	£20.00 *see PHOTO over* CREDIT CARD VISA M'CARD	Y	Y	Y
Mr & Mrs A. C. Singleton **Underleigh House** **Edale Road Hope** **Castleton S30 2RF** **Tel/Fax: (01433) 621372** **Open: ALL YEAR** **Map Ref No. 05**	Nearest Road: A.625 A 19th-century farmhouse-style home in a superb, secluded hillside position, with beautiful countryside views, in the heart of the National Park. Each of the 6 en-suite rooms are furnished to the highest standard, with many extras, & each has a resident teddy bear! Renowned for hearty breakfasts & gourmet house-party dinners prepared by the owner/chef. Ideally situated for walking or exploring the area by car.	£22.00 CREDIT CARD VISA M'CARD	N	Y	N
Mrs Margaret Ford **Horsleygate Hall** **Horsleygate Lane** **Holmesfield** **Chesterfield S18 5WD** **Tel: (0114) 2890333** **Open: ALL YEAR** **Map Ref No. 09**	Nearest Road: A.621 Lying on the eastern side of the Peak Park, Horsleygate Hall is an informal country house, set amongst large, secluded grounds. The accommodation is country-style, comfortable & attractive, with excellent views of the surrounding countryside from all rooms. The Hall, in the peaceful & rural Cadwell Valley (a special landscape & conservation area), is well placed for walking, riding & exploring Derbyshire. Chatsworth House & Bakewell nearby.	£18.00 🚭	Y	N	N
Peter Marsh **The Wind in the Willows** **Derbyshire Level** **Off Sheffield Road** **Glossop** **SK13 9PT** **Tel: (01457) 868001** **Fax 01457 853354** **Open: ALL YEAR** **Map Ref No. 04**	Nearest Road: A.57, M.67 An early-Victorian house with 5 acres of land, The Wind in the Willows is a haven of tranquility set amidst unspoilt views of the Peak District National Park & the Pennine Hills. Providing an escape from the pressures of modern-day life in the atmosphere & surroundings of a bygone era. Wealth of oak-panelling, with traditional furnishings & open fires. Bedrooms are well-equipped & are en-suite. With an emphasis upon friendliness, relaxation & first-class home-cooking, your hosts pay unobtrusive but close attention to ensure your stay is memorable. Children over 10.	£34.00 CREDIT CARD VISA M'CARD AMEX	Y	Y	N
Mrs Clemency Wilkins **The Old Hall** **Netherseal** **Swadlincote DE12 8DF** **Tel: (01283) 760258** **Fax 01283 762991** **Open: ALL YEAR** **Map Ref No. 16**	Nearest Road: A.444 A Grade II listed manor house situated in 18 acres of private gardens & woodland, overlooking a lake. The house, built originally as a monastery, dates from 1644, & despite all modern conveniences retains its unique character & original features. Many of the rooms are panelled, & all are decorated in a country-house style. 3 attractive, well-equipped bedrooms with en-suite/private facilities. Traditional English food is served by arrangement, using fresh & local produce.	£22.00 🚭	N	Y	Y

Biggin Hall.   Biggin by Hartington.

Derbyshire & Staffordshire

		rate from £ per person	children taken	evening meals	animals taken
Mary Bailey **Carr Head Farm** **Hathersage** **Sheffield** **S30 1BR** **Tel: (01433) 650383** **Fax 01433 650383** **Open: ALL YEAR** **Map Ref No. 06**	Nearest Road: A.625 In a most peaceful setting high on the hillside above the village of Hathersage, an unusual farmhouse dating back to 1650, full of character & friendly charm. Surrounded by beautiful mature gardens, all rooms have magnificent unspoilt views. 2 spacious & superbly furnished en-suite bedrooms, 1 with 4-poster. Oak-beamed dining room with many interesting features & an elegant drawing room. Decorated throughout in period style. Traditional & varied breakfast is served, & the village offers a wide choice of eating places. The village has Charlotte Bronte connections.	£22.00 (no smoking)	N	N	N

Staffordshire

		rate from £ per person	children taken	evening meals	animals taken
Mr & Mrs J. Chapman **The Mill House** **Cornmill Lane, Tutbury** **Burton-on-Trent** **DE13 9HA** **Tel:(01283) 813300/813634** **Open: ALL YEAR (Excl. Xmas)** **Map Ref No. 10**	Nearest Road: A.50 A corn mill has occupied this site since the Domesday Book. Situated in open countryside, 1/2 mile from the village, the Georgian mill & adjoining red-brick mill house are easy to find. The 3 spacious bedrooms are beautifully furnished & en-suite, with colour T.V. & tea-making facilities. Delicious breakfasts are served in the inglenook breakfast room. Conveniently placed for N.T. properties, Kedleston, Calke & Sudbury.	£20.00 (no smoking)	Y	N	N
Mrs Elizabeth Winterton **Brook House Farm** **Brook House Lane** **Cheddleton** **Leek ST13 7DF** **Tel: (01538) 360296** **Open: ALL YEAR** **Map Ref No. 07**	Nearest Road: A.520 Brookhouse is a dairy farm in a picturesque valley 1/2 a mile from the A.520, down a private lane. Many pleasant walks locally; convenient for the Peak District, pottery museums and Alton Towers. Comfortable rooms in the farmhouse, and 2 spacious family rooms with patio doors in a tastefully converted annex. All en-suite & centrally heated, with tea/coffee facilities. Good farmhouse food served in a conservatory with magnificent views. A warm welcome assured.	£16.00	Y	Y	N
William & Elaine Sutcliffe **Choir Cottage & House** **Ostlers Lane** **Cheddleton** **Leek** **ST13 7HS** **Tel: (01538) 360561** **Open: ALL YEAR** **Map Ref No. 07**	Nearest Road: A.520 This is no ordinary B&B: you won't be staying in someone else's home but in 'Choir Cottage', a 350-year-old stone cottage adjacent to the proprietors' own home. Just 2 bedrooms, each with 4-poster beds, 1 king-size & 1 on the ground floor with a private patio. The decor & furnishings are to a high standard, with en-suite facilities, c/h, colour T.V., etc., & provide complete independence & privacy. Quiet location, convenient for Alton Towers, the Potteries & the Peak District. Childen over 5 yrs.	£23.00 (no smoking) *see PHOTO over*	Y	N	N

When booking your accommodation please mention
The Best Bed & Breakfast

Choir Cottage. Cheddleton

Staffordshire

		rate from £ per person	children taken	evening meals	animals taken
Mrs Maggie Wheeler **Old Furnace Farm** **Greendale** **Oakamoor** **Stoke-on-Trent** **ST10 3AP** **Tel: (01538) 702442** **Open: ALL YEAR** **Map Ref No. 11**	Nearest Road: A.52 The farm is situated in an idyllic position, overlooking the Dimmingsdale Valley. The Victorian farmhouse, which has been tastefully renovated & furnished in keeping with the period, offers quality accommodation & friendly service. There are 2 bedrooms, each an with en-suite bathroom, & colour T.V.. Full central heating, & log fire in visitors' lounge. An ideal location for Alton Towers (2 miles), potteries (12 miles), rambling, or just simply relaxing.	£20.00	Y	N	N
Mrs M. Egerton-Orme **Bank House** **Farley Lane** **Oakamoor** **Stoke-on-Trent** **ST10 3BD** **Tel/Fax: (01538) 702810** **Open: ALL YEAR** **Map Ref No. 15**	Nearest Road: A.52, A.50 A handsome house, overlooking the picturesque Churnet Valley. This elegantly furnished home provides superb en-suite accommodation. All rooms are extremely well-equipped. The aim at Bank House is to create a relaxed & friendly 'house party' ambience for guests, & the facilities are all that one might expect from a friend's country house that has all the comforts of a quality hotel. Excellent 4-course evening meals served. Wonderful centre for touring this region.	£25.00 CREDIT CARD VISA M'CARD	Y	Y	Y
Mrs I. Grey **The Old Vicarage** **Leek Road, Endon** **Stoke-on-Trent** **ST9 9BH** **Tel: (01782) 503686** **Open: ALL YEAR** **Map Ref No. 12**	Nearest Road: A.53 A friendly atmosphere is found at this delightful 70-year-old former vicarage. It is situated in a quiet spot in the village of Endon, between the Staffordshire moorlands & Stoke-on-Trent. Accommodation is in 3 rooms, all with modern amenities, T.V. & tea/coffee-making facilities. There is also a colour-T.V. lounge. This makes a good base from which to visit the world-famous potteries, the wonderful countryside & museums.	£15.00	Y	N	N
Mrs Anne Hodgson **The Hollies** **Clay Lake, Endon** **Stoke-on-Trent ST9 9DD** **Tel: (01782) 503252** **Open: ALL YEAR** **Map Ref No. 13**	Nearest Road: A.53, B.5051 A delightful Victorian family house, built in 1872, quietly situated off the B.5051 at Endon. There are 5 spacious, comfortable rooms, with en-suite or private facilities. All have colour T.V. & tea/ coffee makers. A large secluded garden, with ample parking. On the edge of a lovely stretch of countryside, yet just 5 miles from the city & 14 miles from Alton Towers. Sorry, no smoking.	£17.00	Y	N	Y
Mrs Barbara White **Micklea Farm** **Micklea Lane, Longsdon** **Stoke-on-Trent** **ST9 9QA** **Tel: (01538) 385006** **Fax 01538 382882** **Open: ALL YEAR** **Map Ref No. 12**	Nearest Road: A.53 Micklea Farm is an 18th-century cottage set in a lovely quiet garden. There are 2 twin & 2 single rooms, with cots available. There is also a charming sitting room for guests, with an open fire & colour T.V.. Evening meals are available, using home-grown garden produce & home baking. A choice of English or Continental breakfast; also, packed lunches. Conveniently situated for the potteries, Alton Towers & the Peak District, it is the perfect base for a relaxing break.	£16.00	Y	Y	N

Manor House Farm.   Prestwood.

Staffordshire

		rate from £ per person	children taken	evening meals	animals taken
Mrs G. Adams **The Boat House** **Newcastle Road** **Stone** **ST15 8LD** **Tel: (01785) 815389** **Open:** ALL YEAR (Excl. Xmas) **Map Ref No. 14**	Nearest Road: M.6, A.34 A friendly, relaxed atmosphere awaits you at this renovated 18th-century former inn, set in delightful gardens alongside the Trent & Mersey Canal. Traditionally furnished, it offers accommodation in 3 comfortable rooms, 1 with private bathroom, & each with T.V. & tea/coffee-making facilities. This is an ideal base for visiting Wedgwood & the potteries, the Peak District & Alton Towers. Easy access to the M.6. Children over 7 yrs.	£18.00	Y	N	N
Mr C. M. Ball **Manor House Farm** **Prestwood** **Denstone** **Uttoxeter ST14 5DD** **Tel: (01889) 590415** **Fax 01335 342198** **Open:** ALL YEAR (Excl. Xmas) **Map Ref No. 15**	Nearest Road: A.50, A.52 A beautiful Grade II listed farmhouse, set amid rolling hills & rivers. 3 bedrooms, each with modern amenities, 2 with en-suite or private bathroom. 1 room with 4-poster bed. Tastefully furnished with antiques, & retaining many traditional features, including an oak-panelled breakfast room. Guests may relax in the extensive gardens, with grass tennis court, & the Victorian summer house. Ideal for visiting Alton Towers, the Peak District or the Potteries.	£18.00 *see PHOTO over*	Y	N	N

All the establishments mentioned in this guide are members of
The Worldwide Bed & Breakfast Association

When booking your accommodation please mention
The Best Bed & Breakfast

Devon

Devon
(West Country)

Here is a county of tremendous variety. Two glorious & contrasting coastlines with miles of sandy beaches, sheltered coves & rugged cliffs. There are friendly resorts & quiet villages of cob & thatch, two historic cities, & a host of country towns & tiny hamlets as well as the wild open spaces of two national parks.

From the grandeur of Hartland Point east to Foreland Point where Exmoor reaches the sea, the north Devon coast is incomparable. At Westward Ho!, Croyde & Woolacombe the rolling surf washes the golden beaches & out to sea stands beautiful Lundy Island, ideal for bird watching, climbing & walking. The tiny village of Clovelly with its cobbled street tumbles down the cliffside to the sea. Ilfracombe is a friendly resort town & the twin towns of Lynton & Lynmouth are joined by a cliff railway.

The south coast is a colourful mixture of soaring red sandstone cliffs dropping to sheltered sandy coves & the palm trees of the English Riviera. This is one of England's great holiday coasts with a string of popular resorts; Seaton, Sidmouth, Budleigh Salterton, Exmouth, Dawlish, Teignmouth & the trio of Torquay, Paignton & Brixham that make up Torbay. To the south, beyond Berry Head are Dartmouth, rich in navy tradition, & Salcombe, a premiere sailing centre in the deep inlet of the Kingsbridge estuary. Plymouth is a happy blend of holiday resort, tourist centre, historic & modern city, & the meeting-point for the wonderful old sailing vessels for the Tall Ships Race.

Inland the magnificent wilderness of Dartmoor National Park offers miles of sweeping moorland, granite tors, clear streams & wooded valleys, ancient stone circles & clapper bridges. The tors, as the Dartmoor peaks, are called are easily climbed & the views from the tops are superb. Widecombe-in-the-Moor, with its imposing church tower, & much photographed Buckland-in-the-Moor are only two of Dartmoor's lovely villages.

The Exmoor National Park straddles the Devon/Somerset border. It is a land of wild heather moorland above deep wooded valleys & sparkling streams, the home of red deer, soaring buzzards & of legendary Lorna Doone from R.D. Blackmore's novel. The south west peninsula coastal path follows the whole of the Exmoor coastline affording dramatic scenery & spectacular views, notably from Countisbury Hill.

The seafaring traditions of Devon are well-known. Sir Walter Raleigh set sail from Plymouth to Carolina in 1584; Sir Francis Drake began his circumnavigation of the world at Plymouth in the "Golden Hind" & fought the Spanish Armada off Plymouth Sound. The Pilgrim Fathers sailed from here & it was to here that Sir Francis Chichester returned having sailed around the world in 1967.

Exeter's maritime tradition is commemorated in an excellent museum located in converted riverside warehouses but the city's chief glory is the magnificent 13th century cathedral of St. Mary & St. Peter, built in an unusual decorated Gothic style, with its west front covered in statues.

The River Dart near Dittisham.

Devon

Devon
Gazeteer

Areas of outstanding natural beauty.
North, South, East Devon.

Houses & Castles

Arlington Court - Barnstaple
Regency house, collection of shell, pewter & model ships.

Bickleigh Castle - Nr. Tiverton
Thatched Jacobean wing. Great Hall & armoury. Early Norman chapel, gardens & moat.

Buckland Abbey - Nr. Plymouth
13th century Cistercian monastery - 16th century alterations. Home of Drake - contains his relics & folk gallery.

Bradley Manor - Newton Abbot
15th century Manor house with perpendicular chapel.

Cadhay - Ottery St. Mary
16th century Elizabethan Manor house.

Castle Drogo - Nr.Chagford
Designed by Lutyens - built of granite, standing over 900 feet above the gorge of the Teign river.

Chambercombe Manor - Illfracombe
14th-15th century Manor house.

Castle Hill - Nr. Barnstaple
18th century Palladian mansion - fine furniture of period, pictures, porcelain & tapestries.

Hayes Barton - Nr. Otterton
16th century plaster & thatch house. Birthplace of Walter Raleigh.

Oldway - Paignton
19th century house having rooms designed to be replicas of rooms at the Palace of Versailles.

Powederham Castle - Nr. Exeter
14th century mediaeval castle much damaged in Civil War. Altered in 18th & 19th centuries. Fine music room by Wyatt.

Saltram House - Plymouth
Some remnants of Tudor house built into George II house, with two rooms by Robert Adam. Excellent plasterwork & woodwork.

Shute Barton - Nr. Axminster
14th century battlemented Manor house with Tudor & Elizabethan additions.

Tiverton Castle - Nr. Tiverton
Fortress of Henry I. Chapel of St. Francis. Gallery of Joan of Arc.

Torre Abbey Mansion - Torquay
Abbey ruins, tithe barn. Mansion house with paintings & furniture.

Cathedrals & Churches

Atherington (St. Mary)
Perpendicular style - mediaeval effigies & glass, original rood loft. Fine screens, 15th century bench ends.

Ashton (St. John the Baptist)
15th century - mediaeval screens, glass & wall paintings. Elizabethan pulpit with canopy, 17th century altar railing.

Bere Ferrers (St. Andrew)
14th century rebuilding - 14th century glass, 16th century benches, Norman font.

Bridford (St. Thomas a Becket)
Perpendicular style - mediaeval glass & woodwork. Excellent rood screen c.1530.

Cullompton (St. Andrew)
15th century perpendicular - Jacobean west gallery - fan tracery in roof, exterior carvings.

Exeter Cathedral
13th century decorated - Norman towers. Interior tierceron ribbed vault (Gothic) carved corbels & bosses, moulded piers & arches. Original pulpitum c.1320. Choir stalls with earliest misericords in England c.1260.

Haccombe (St. Blaize)
13th century effigies, 14th century glass, 17th century brasses, 19th century screen, pulpit & reredos.

Kentisbeare (St. Mary)
Perpendicular style - checkered tower. 16th century rood screen.

Ottery St. Mary (St. Mary)
13th century, 14th century clock, fan vaulted roof, tomb with canopy, minstrel's gallery, gilded wooded eagle. 18th century pulpit.

Parracombe (St. Petrock)
Unrestored Georgian - 16th century benches, mostly perpendicular, early English chancel.

Sutcombe (St. Andrew)
15th century - some part Norman. 16th century bench ends, restored rood screen, mediaeval glass & floor tiles.

Swimbrige (St. James)
14th century tower & spire - mediaeval stone pulpit, 15th century rood screen, font cover of Renaissance period.

Devon

Tawstock (St. Peter)
14th century, Italian plasterwork ceiling, mediaeval glass, Renaissance memorial pew, Bath monument.
Buckfast Abbey
Living Benedictine monastery, built on mediaeval foundation. Famous for works of art in church, modern stained glass, tonic wine & bee-keeping.

Museums & Galleries

Bideford Museum - Bideford
Geology, maps, prints, shipwright's tools, North Devon pottery.
Burton Art Gallery - Bideford
Hubert Coop collection of paintings etc.
Butterwalk Museum - Dartmouth
17th century row of half timbered buildings, nautical museum. 140 model ships.
Newcomen Engine House - Nr. Butterwalk Museum
Original Newcomen atmospheric/pressure steam engine c.1725.
Royal Albert Memorial Museum Art Gallery - Exeter
Collections of English watercolours, paintings, glass & ceramics, local silver, natural history & anthropology.
Rougemont House Museum - Exeter
Collections of archaeology & local history. Costume & lace collection
Guildhall - Exeter
Mediaeval structure with Tudor frontage - City regalia & silver.
Exeter Maritime Museum - Exeter
Largest collection in the world of working boats, afloat, ashore & under cover.
The Steam & Countryside Museum - Exmouth
Very large working layout - hundreds of exhibits.
Including Victorian farmhouse - farmyard pets for children.
Shebbear - North Devon
Alcott Farm Museum with unique collections of agricultural implements & photographs, etc.
The Elizabethan House - Totnes
Period costumes & furnishings, tools, toys, domestic articles, etc.
The Elizabethan House - Plymouth
16th century house with period furnishings.

City Museum & Art Gallery - Plymouth
Collections of pictures & porcelain, English & Italian drawing. Reynolds' family portraits, early printed books, ship models.
Cookworthy Museum - Kingsbridge
Story of china clay. Local history, shipbuilding tools, rural life.
Honiton & Allhallows Public Museum - Honiton
Collection of Honiton lace, implements etc. Complete Devon Kitchen.
Lyn & Exmoor Museum - Lynton
Life & history of Exmoor.
Torquay & Natural History Society Museum - Torquay
Collection illustrating Kent's Cavern & other caves - natural history & folkculture.

Historic Monuments

Okehampton Castle - Okehampton
11th -14th century chapel, keep & hall.
Totnes Castle - Totnes
13th - 14th century ruins of Castle.
Blackbury Castle - Southleigh
Hill fort - well preserved.
Dartmouth Castle - Dartmouth
15th century castle - coastal defence.
Lydford Castle - Lydford
12th century stone keep built upon site of Saxon fortress town.
Hound Tor - Manaton
Ruins of mediaeval hamlet.

Other things to see & do

The Big Sheep - Abbotsham
Sheep-milking parlour, with gallery, dairy & production rooms. Exhibition & play area.
Dartington Crystal - Torrington
Watch skilled craftworkers make lead crystalware. Glass centre & exhibition.
Dartmoor Wildlife Park - Sparkwell Nr. Plymouth
Over 100 species, including tigers, lions, bears, deer, birds of prey & waterfowl.
The Devon Guild of Craftsmen - Riverside Mill, Bovey Tracey
Series of quality exhibitions throughout the year.
Paignton Zoological & Botanical Gardens - Paignton
Third largest zoo in England. Botanical gardens, tropical house, "The Ark" family activity centre.

DEVON

Map reference

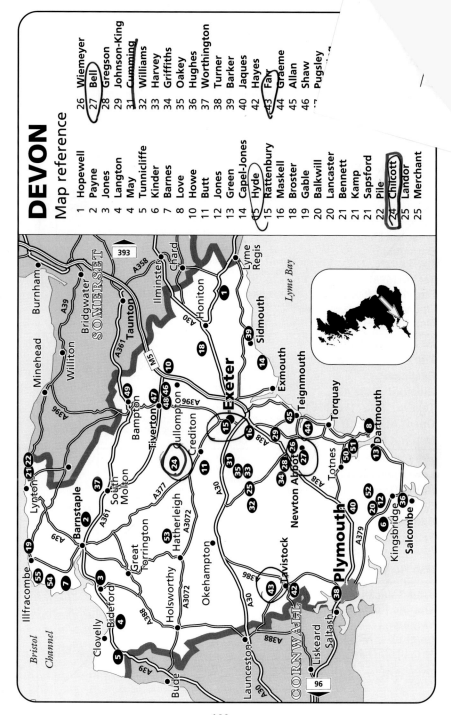

1	Hopewell
2	Payne
3	Jones
3	Langton
4	May
5	Tunnicliffe
6	Kinder
7	Barnes
8	Love
10	Howe
11	Butt
12	Jones
13	Green
14	Capel-Jones
15	Hyde
15	Rattenbury
16	Maskell
18	Broster
19	Gable
20	Balkwill
20	Lancaster
21	Bennett
21	Kamp
21	Sapsford
22	Pile
24	Chilcott
25	Landor
25	Merchant

26	Wiemeyer
27	Bell
28	Gregson
29	Johnson-King
31	Cumming
32	Williams
33	Harvey
34	Griffiths
35	Oakey
36	Hughes
37	Worthington
38	Turner
39	Barker
40	Jaques
42	Hayes
43	Fair
44	Graeme
45	Allan
46	Shaw
	Pugsley

Devon

		rate from £ per person	children taken	evening meals	animals taken
Mrs Helga Hopewell **Lambley Brook** **Springhead Lane** **Kilmington** **Axminster EX13 7SS** **Tel: (01297) 35033** **Open: FEB - DEC** **Map Ref No. 01**	Nearest Road: A.35 A warm & friendly atmosphere is found at this delightful, secluded, 19th-century, converted cottage, standing in its own grounds, & surrounded by open countryside & woodland, on the outskirts of this picturesque village. Offering comfortable & spacious accommodation in 3 pleasant bedrooms, with tea/coffee trays & lovely views. An idyllic retreat for nature lovers. Cosy, elegant lounge, with colour T.V., & for the more energetic, bicycles & packed lunches. Children over 10 please.	£18.00	Y	N	N
Jackie & Antony Payne **Huxtable Farm** **West Buckland** **Barnstaple** **EX32 0SR** **Tel: (01598) 760254** **Fax 01598 760254** **Open: ALL YEAR (Excl. Xmas)** **Map Ref No. 02**	Nearest Road: A.361 Relax in this mediaeval longhouse & listed barn, carefully restored & furnished with antiques. This secluded sheep farm, with pygmy goats & poultry (2 miles from M.5 link road) is ideally situated for Exmoor, North Devon coast & Tarka Trail. Offering 6 rooms, 5 with en-suite facilities & 1 with private facilities, T.V. & tea/coffee makers. Enjoy 4-course candlelit dinners made using farm/local produce served with complementary glass of home-made wine. Award-winning cook. Games, fitness & sauna room. Children welcome.	£22.00	Y	Y	N
Mr & Mrs C. B. Jones **The Pines at Eastleigh** **Eastleigh** **Bideford EX39 4PA** **Tel/Fax: (01271) 860561** **Open: ALL YEAR** **Map Ref No. 03**	Nearest Road: A.39 A warm welcome awaits you at this Georgian home set in 7 acres with glorious views over Bideford to the sea at Lundy Island & Hartland Point. 7 pretty bedrooms (6 en-suite) have colour T.V., tea/coffee-making facilities & full central heating. Enjoy beautifully prepared food or a quiet drink; or, when the shutters are closed, curl up in front of log fires. Golf, riding & watersports available. A delightful home.	£18.00 CREDIT CARD VISA M'CARD	Y	Y	Y
Mrs Caroline May **Lower Waytown** **Horns Cross** **Bideford** **EX39 5DN** **Tel: (01237) 451787** **Open: EASTER - OCT** **Map Ref No. 04**	Nearest Road: A.39 This beautifully converted barn & roundhouse have created a delightful, spacious & comfortable home offering superb accommodation. Extensive grounds with ponds & ornamental waterfowl, & a coastal footpath nearby. The en-suite bedrooms, 2 double (1 ground floor) & 1 twin-bedded, are tastefully furnished, & each has central heating, colour T.V., hairdryers & tea/coffee-making facilities. The unique, round, beamed sitting room adjoins the spacious dining room, where excellent breakfasts are served. Children over 12.	£20.00	Y	N	N
Jean & Jack Langton **The Old Rectory** **Parkham** **Bideford EX39 5PL** **Tel: (01237) 451443** **Open: ALL YEAR (Excl. Xmas & New Year)** **Map Ref No. 04**	Nearest Road: A.39 Charming, delightfully furnished country house. Log fires, unique ambience & superb cuisine. 3 en-suite/private-facility bedrooms, very prettily decorated & furnished with every comfort in mind. Dine with your hosts, & enjoy good wine with your excellent evening meal, which, using fresh local produce, is home-cooked by Jean to the highest of standards. Set in an Area of Outstanding Natural Beauty, it is ideally situated for the coast, picturesque Clovelly & Exmoor. Children over 12.	£35.00 *see PHOTO over*	Y	Y	N

The Old Rectory. Parkham.

		rate from £ per person	children taken	evening meals	animals taken
Petre Josephine Tunnicliffe **Henaford Manor Farm** **Welcombe** **Bideford** **EX39 6HE** **Tel: (01288) 331252** **Open: ALL YEAR** **Map Ref No. 05**	Nearest Road: A.39 Henaford Manor is a 13th-century farmhouse, set in 226 acres, retaining many traditional features, including beamed ceilings & large fireplaces. 3 tastefully furnished bedrooms, 1 en-suite, all with modern amenities, including 'phone, radio, T.V. & tea/coffee facilities. Guests can relax in the spacious garden or lounge, available throughout the day. Excellent meals, & guests may bring their own wine. Within 3 miles of Devon's Atlantic coast, where there are several beaches & small coves, including Clovelly & Tintagel.	£17.50	Y	Y	Y
Mrs Jean Barnes **Denham Farm** **North Buckland** **Braunton EX33 1HY** **Tel: (01271) 890297** **Fax 01271 890297** **Open: ALL YEAR** (Excl. Xmas) **Map Ref No. 07**	Nearest Road: A.361 Denham is a beautiful country house situated in the heart of the countryside, with 160 acres of its own farmland. Only a short drive away are superb beaches, breathtaking scenery & lovely coastal walks. Situated only 3 miles from a championship golf course, this delightful house offers 10 en-suite bedrooms with colour T.V. & tea/coffee-making facilities. The inglenook fireplace & bread oven are a part of the character of this country home, built in the 1700s.	£22.50 CREDIT CARD VISA M'CARD	Y	Y	N
Col. & Mrs Stephen Love **Southdown Farm** **Brixham** **TQ5 0AJ** **Tel: (01803) 857991** **Fax 01803 857991** **Open: MAY - SEPT** **Map Ref No. 08**	Nearest Road: A.3022 A large, secluded Georgian farmhouse with panoramic views over farmland to the sea 1/2 a mile away. 2 attractive rooms, each with an en-suite/private bathroom. Outdoor pool, sauna & tennis court. Evening meals with advance notice. Historic links locally with the U.S.A.; & situated near the beautiful River Dart, Dartmoor & Torbay, with access to the coastal path on foot from the house. B.H.S.-approved riding stables on the farm, with a qualified instructor & all facilities.	£23.00	Y	Y	N

When booking your accommodation please mention The Best Bed & Breakfast

All the establishments mentioned in this guide are members of the Worldwide Bed & Breakfast Association.

If you have any comments regarding your accommodation please send them to us using the form at the back of the book. We value your comments.

The New Inn. Coleford.

Devon

		rate from £ per person	children taken	evening meals	animals taken
Paul & Irene Butt **The New Inn** **Coleford** **Crediton EX17 5BZ** **Tel: 01363 84242** **Fax 01363 85044** **Open: ALL YEAR** **Map Ref No. 11**	Nearest Road: A.377 The New Inn is a 13th-century thatched inn nestling in a quiet valley by the side of a brook. Accommodation in this attractive property includes 3 en-suite bedrooms with 'phone, T.V. & tea/coffee-making facilities. There is also an extensive menu, using fresh local produce whenever possible. Local amenities include several golf courses, fishing, horse riding & sport & leisure facilities. Easy access to Dartmoor, Exmoor & the north & south Devon coasts. *see PHOTO over* CREDIT CARD VISA M'CARD AMEX	£26.00	Y	Y	N
Mrs Jacki Howe **Millhayes** **Kentisbeare** **Cullompton EX15 2AF** **Tel: (01884) 266412** **Fax 01884 266412** **Open: ALL YEAR** **Map Ref No. 10**	Nearest Road: A.373 Millhayes is a delightfully located country mill in a peaceful, secluded setting with tastefully decorated rooms. There are 4 attractive bedrooms, 2 with en-suite facilities. A delicious Aga-cooked breakfast is served in the elegant dining room. A 2-acre lake for coarse fishing & a tennis court are for guests' use. Evening meals are recommended in the excellent local pub. Dartmoor & Exmoor are within easy reach, as are many N.T. properties & the North & South coasts. *see PHOTO over*	£21.00	Y	N	N
Robert & Brenda Green **Boringdon House** **1 Church Road** **Dartmouth** **TQ6 9HQ** **Tel: (01803) 832235** **Open: MAR - DEC** **Map Ref No. 13**	Nearest Road: A.3122, A.379 Boringdon is a lovely, welcoming Georgian house in a quiet part of Dartmouth, lying within a large, secluded leafy garden & looking down to the town & river, & sea beyond. Courtyard parking. Only a short, 10-min walk through picturesque lanes down to the historic town. 3 spacious en-suite bedrooms, attractively furnished with Laura Ashley drapes. Comfortable & relaxing, with colour T.V., & tea/coffee facilities.	£22.50	N	N	N
David & Jennie Capel-Jones **Thorn Mill Farm** **Frogmore Road** **East Budleigh** **EX9 7BB** **Tel: (01395) 444088** **Open: ALL YEAR (Excl. Xmas)** **Map Ref No. 14**	Nearest Road: A.3052 A warm welcome awaits you at this 16th-century family home with beamed lounge & inglenook fireplace in a classic Devon village. The house faces south over the River Otter Valley, with footpaths to coastal paths. Close to Bicton Gardens & N.T. properties, in a designated Area of Outstanding Natural Beauty. 1 double en-suite, 1 twin & 2 singles, all with colour T.V., radio & hospitality trays. Evening family dining by prior arrangement. Children over 8 yrs welcome.	£19.00	Y	N	N

When booking your accommodation please mention
The Best Bed & Breakfast

Millhayes. Kentisbeare.

Lower Grimpstonleigh. East Allington.

Devon

		rate from £ per person	children taken	evening meals	animals taken
Mrs Joy Jones **Lower Grimpstonleigh** **East Allington** **TQ9 7QH** **Tel: (01548) 521258** **Fax 01548 521329** **Open: ALL YEAR** **Map Ref No. 12**	Nearest Road: A.381 Idyllic rural retreat situated at the end of quiet Devon lane just 4 miles from Kingsbridge. Old stone house in courtyard-garden setting, with ancient thatched barn. Spacious & very comfortably furnished bedrooms, with exposed roof timbers & en-suite bath/shower. Colour T.V., tea/coffee facilities, hairdryers & bathrobes provided. Breakfast, with choice of menus, served in splendid farmhouse kitchen or courtyard garden (weather permitting). Golf, sailing, riding & beaches all within easy reach.	£25.00 *see PHOTO over*	N	Y	N
Michael & Kay Rattenbury **The Edwardian** **30 & 32 Heavitree Road** **Exeter EX1 2LQ** **Tel: (01392) 76102/54699** **Fax 01392 76102/54699** **Open: ALL YEAR (Excl. Xmas)** **Map Ref No. 15**	Nearest Road: M.5, A.30, A.38 Elegant Edwardian townhouses near Roman walls, cathedral, indoor swimming pool & city centre. Friendly hosts. Most rooms en-suite, with antique bedsteads & original Lloyd Loom furniture. Also, romantic 4-poster room & ground-floor room. Spa bath. All rooms have direct-dial telephones, colour T.V.s & hospitality trays. Large car park opposite. Choice of good restaurants nearby. Wonderful West Country touring base. Discounts for stays of 3 days or longer.	£22.00 CREDIT CARD VISA M'CARD AMEX	Y	N	Y
Richard & Sue Hyde **Raffles** **11 Blackall Road** **Exeter EX4 4HD** **Tel: (01392) 70200** **Open: ALL YEAR** **Map Ref No. 15**	Nearest Road: M.5 Raffles is a delightful Victorian hotel situated minutes from the heart of one of England's cathedral cities, & elegantly furnished throughout with antique furniture. The accommodation is in 7 spacious bedrooms, all with en-suite bathrooms, colour T.V., tea/coffee facilities & central heating. Emphasis is placed on your comfort & care, with excellent home cooking & fine wines.	£19.00 CREDIT CARD VISA M'CARD AMEX	Y	Y	Y
Mr & Mrs J. Maskell **Bridford Guest House** **Bridford** **Exeter** **EX6 7HS** **Tel: (01647) 252563** **Open: Easter - New Year** **Map Ref No. 16**	Nearest Road: B.3212, B.3193 A warm welcome awaits you at this 350-yr-old guest house situated on Dartmoor. Accommodation includes 5 comfortable & tastefully decorated bedrooms, 2 en-suite, each with tea/coffee facilities. The lounge, with granite fireplace & woodburner, has colour T.V.. Plentiful home-cooking includes vegetarian preferences. An ideal base for Dartmoor rambles. Horse-riding & golf are within 10 mins. Exeter & the M.5 8 miles. Coastal resorts within easy reach.	£14.00	Y	Y	Y
Gordon Broster **Colestocks House Hotel** **Payhembury Road** **Feniton** **Honiton EX14 0JR** **Tel: (01404) 850633** **Fax 01404 850901** **Open: MAR - OCT** **Map Ref No. 18**	Nearest Road: A.30 Pink-washed & newly re-thatched, a lovely 16th-century, Grade II listed country house set in 2 acres of gardens. Tranquil rural situation, & well placed for touring the West Country. All rooms have en-suite bath/shower, colour T.V. & tea-making facilities. Many antiques, 1 4-poster, 1 canopied brass bed & 2 half testers. Log fires in the huge inglenook fireplace. Excellent restaurant, all home-cooking. Wines personally chosen & imported by the proprietor. Children over 10 years. Reductions for 2 nights or more.	£27.50 *see PHOTO over* CREDIT CARD VISA M'CARD	Y	Y	Y

Colestocks House.   Honiton.

Devon

		rate from £ per person	children taken	evening meals	animals taken
Roy & Barbara Gable **Varley House** **Chambercombe Park** **Ilfracombe EX34 9QW** **Tel: (01271) 863927** **Fax 01271 863927** **Open: MAR - OCT** **Map Ref No. 19**	Nearest Road: A.399 A spacious Victorian character house on the outskirts of Ilfracombe, having both sea & country views. The aim is quality, comfort, courtesy & care, with a personal touch. Accommodation is in 9 attractive rooms, all fully en-suite & with colour T.V. & tea/coffee-making facilities. The house is elegantly furnished & the food served is imaginative & plentiful. An excellent base for exploring this lovely area.	£20.50 CREDIT CARD VISA M'CARD AMEX	Y	Y	Y
John & Jill Balkwill **Court Barton Farmhouse** **Aveton Gifford** **Kingsbridge** **TQ7 4LE** **Tel: (01548) 550312** **Open: ALL YEAR (Excl. Xmas)** **Map Ref No. 20**	Nearest Road: A.379 An absolutely delightful 16th-century, listed manor farmhouse situated on a 40-acre farm. Accommodation is in 7 comfortable bedrooms, 6 with en-suite facilities. A comfortable, well-furnished T.V. lounge with lots of books. Delicious country breakfasts are served in the sunny breakfast room. Full central heating & log fires in cooler weather. Close to moorland & beaches. Ideal for walking, sailing, fishing & birdwatching.	£18.00	Y	N	N
Mrs Christine Lancaster **Helliers Farm** **Ashford** **Aveton Gifford** **Kingsbridge TQ7 4ND** **Tel/Fax: (01548) 550689** **Open: ALL YEAR (Excl. Xmas)** **Map Ref No. 20**	Nearest Road: A.379 Set in the heart of South Hams countryside, this recently modernised farmhouse offers accommodation in 4 pleasant bedrooms with tea/coffee-making facilities. Also, a spacious dining room, where good farmhouse breakfasts are served, a comfortable lounge, with T.V., & a games room. Close to the beaches, moors, golf courses, N.T. walks & the city of Plymouth. A non-smoking establishment.	£16.00	Y	N	N
David & Georgiana Kinder **Trebles Cottage Hotel** **Kingston** **Kingsbridge** **TQ7 4PT** **Tel/Fax: (01548) 810268** **Mobile 0589 769991** **Open: ALL YEAR** **Map Ref No. 06**	Nearest Road: A.379, B.3392 Originally a family cottage (built in 1801), & now a small hotel set in secluded grounds on the edge of an attractive, unspoilt village. 5 bedrooms, all en-suite & tastefully & individually furnished, with colour T.V., radio/alarm, tea/coffee makers & hair dryers. A small cocktail bar complements the excellent restaurant. Lovely coastal walks, a picturesque beach & golf nearby. David & Georgiana offer a warm welcome, personal service & a high standard of comfort & good food. Special Xmas packages available. Children over 12 yrs.	£23.00 CREDIT CARD VISA M'CARD AMEX	Y	Y	Y
June & Adrian Kamp **Southcliffe** **Lee Road** **Lynton EX35 6BS** **Tel: (01598) 753328** **Fax 01598 753328** **Open: MAR - OCT** **Map Ref No. 21**	Nearest Road: A.39 A charming private hotel of the Victorian era. Modernised throughout, yet retaining many original features, such as the natural pitch-pine staircase & doors. Beautifully appointed bedrooms, all with private bathrooms, colour T.V. & beverage makers. June & Adrian Kamp have been at Southcliffe since 1978, & have a reputation for good food, comfort, cleanliness & value for money. Children over 8 welcome.	£20.00 CREDIT CARD VISA M'CARD AMEX	Y	Y	N

Devon

	rate from £ per person	children taken	evening meals	animals taken
Ben & Jane Bennett **Victoria Lodge** **Lee Road** **Lynton** **EX35 6BS** **Tel: (01598) 753203** **Fax 01598 753203** **Open: FEB - DEC** **Map Ref No. 21**	Nearest Road: A.39 A warm & friendly welcome awaits you at Victoria Lodge. Relax in elegant, comfortable surroundings, & enjoy the friendly hospitality & food that is a gourmet's delight. This gracious house provides charming period features, but with all modern conveniences. All 10 bedrooms are en-suite, with colour T.V., radio, hair dryer & tea/coffee, & are decorated to a very high standard. 2 4-poster bedrooms. Conveniently located for exploring Exmoor & the picturesque coastline. Excellent value for money.	£18.00 CREDIT CARD VISA M'CARD	Y	Y	N
Mrs Bryony Sapsford **Longmead House Hotel** **9 Longmead** **Lynton** **EX35 6DQ** **Tel: (01598) 752523** **Open: MAR - OCT** **Map Ref No. 21**	Nearest Road: A.39 A haven for good home-cooking, with that little extra flair which makes many guests return. Bryony & Brian offer a warm welcome to their home, & encourage a relaxed, friendly atmosphere. The 8 bedrooms are all individual, comfortable & attractive; 5 are en-suite. Set in a large garden with ample parking, & close to the Valley of Rocks, Longmead provides an ideal base from which to discover Exmoor.	£17.00	Y	Y	Y
Rosemary & Susan Pile **Coombe Farm** **Countisbury** **Lynton** **EX35 6NF** **Tel: (01598) 741236** **Open: MAR - NOV** **Map Ref No. 22**	Nearest Road: A.39 Coombe is a 365-acre, hill-sheep farm, with an early-17th-century farmhouse set betwixt Lynmouth & the legendary Doone Valley. The coast path runs through the farm at Desolate. All within the spectacular Exmoor National Park. There are 2 doubles, en-suite, 1 twin & 2 family. All have hot-drink facilities, shaver points, & bath & hand towels. Central heating. Delicious home-cooked meals, using local produce served in the beamed dining room (residential licence). A lounge with woodburner fire & colour T.V..	£16.75	Y	N	N
Stephen & Dawn Chilcott **Wigham** **Morchard Bishop** **EX17 6RJ** **Tel: (01363) 877350** **Fax 01363 877350** **Open: ALL YEAR** **Map Ref No. 24**	Nearest Road: A.377 Wigham is a 16th-century Devon longhouse, with a 30-acre farm which provides fresh fruit, vegetables & dairy produce for imaginative meals. Accommodation is in 5 double rooms, including a 4-poster suite. All with colour T.V. & video & full private bathroom. There are 2 sitting rooms in which guests may relax & a snooker lounge & outdoor heated pool for pleasure. Licensed. Stabling - livery by arrangement. Children over 8.	£27.50 *see PHOTO over* CREDIT CARD VISA M'CARD AMEX	Y	Y	N
Stephen & Phyllis Landor **Cross Tree House** **Cross Street** **Moretonhampstead** **TQ13 8NL** **Tel: (01647) 440726** **Open: MAR - DEC** **Map Ref No. 25**	Nearest Road: A.382 Cross Tree House is a tastefully restored, listed Queen Anne house located on the village edge in Dartmoor National Park. Offering guests every comfort. There are 3 large, comfortable & attractive, south-facing bedrooms, 2 with en-suite & 1 with private bathroom/shower room. Good English & Cordon Bleu cuisine is served. A delightful walled garden for relaxation. This is excellent base for walks & for touring Devon.	£18.00	Y	Y	Y

Wigham. Morchard Bishop.

Gate House. North Bovey.

		rate from £ per person	children taken	evening meals	animals taken
Mrs Trudie Merchant **Great Sloncombe Farm** **Moretonhampstead** **TQ13 8QF** **Tel: (01647) 440595** **Open: ALL YEAR** **Map Ref No. 25**	Nearest Road: A.382 Great Sloncombe Farm is a listed, granite-&-cob-built, 13th-century farmhouse. Set in a peaceful Dartmoor valley, the rambling house has a magical atmosphere, & is furnished with oak & pine, antique china & interesting old photographs. The 3 warm & pleasant bedrooms are all en-suite, with every facility included. Delicious breakfasts, with home-made bread & plentiful Devonshire suppers, are served. Children over 8 years.	£19.00	Y	Y	Y
John & Sheila Williams **Gate House** **North Bovey** **Moretonhampstead** **TQ13 8RB** **Tel/Fax: (01647) 440479** **Open: ALL YEAR** **Map Ref No. 32**	Nearest Road: A.30, A.382 A listed mediaeval thatched house, with beamed ceilings, granite fireplace & bread oven. All bedrooms have en-suite/private bathrooms, colour T.V. & tea/coffee-making facilities. There is a secluded garden, a swimming pool & delightful views. North Bovey is a classic Dartmoor village with a green surrounded by thatched cottages. 2 miles from Moretonhampstead. There are lovely walks on Dartmoor, & golf & riding nearby. Children over 15 years.	£24.00 *see PHOTO over*	Y	Y	Y
Mrs Judith Harvey **Budleigh Farm** **Moretonhampstead** **TQ13 8SB** **Tel: (01647) 440835** **Fax 01647 440436** **Open: MAR - NOV** **Map Ref No. 33**	Nearest Road: A.382, A.38 Budleigh, a delightful old thatched farmhouse, nestles in a wooded valley in the Dartmoor National Park half a mile from Moretonhampstead. All bedrooms have tea/coffee-making facilities & handbasins. Small apartments, with every comfort, are available out of season, making stays a real treat. Board games, paperbacks & magazines, maps & books are available. A delightful garden, with an outdoor swimming pool, croquet & barbecue, make this the perfect touring base.	£15.00	Y	N	N
Gillian & David Oakey **Great Doccombe Farm** **Doccombe** **Moretonhampstead** **TQ13 8SS** **Tel: (01647) 440694** **Open: ALL YEAR** **Map Ref No. 35**	Nearest Road: A.30 Great Doccombe Farm is situated in the pretty hamlet of Doccombe, within the Dartmoor National Park, on the B.3212 from Exeter. An ideal base for walking in the Teign Valley & nearby moors, with golf, riding & fishing nearby. This lovely 16th-century granite farmhouse is surrounded by gardens & fields. The bedrooms (1 ground-floor) are all en-suite, & have shower, T.V. & tea/coffee facilities. Traditional English breakfast served.	£16.00	Y	N	N
Hazel & Nigel Bell **Sampsons Farm** **Restaurant** **Preston** **Newton Abbot TQ12 3PP** **Tel: (01626) 54913** **Fax 01626 54913** **Open: ALL YEAR** **Map Ref No. 27**	Nearest Road: A.38, A.380 A super, relaxed, family atmosphere is found at this traditional thatched Devon longhouse. This Grade II listed building, of historical importance, retains much of its original charm & character, with oak beams, panelling & inglenook fireplaces. All rooms have modern amenities, & there are 4-poster & en-suite rooms available. A delicious breakfast is served, & an extensive a la carte & table d'hote menu is offered in the evening. A view of Dartmoor from the windows. Short distance from coast. Riding, fishing, golf nearby.	£16.00 *see PHOTO over* CREDIT CARD VISA M'CARD AMEX	Y	Y	Y

Sampsons Farm Restaurant. Newton Abbot

Penpark. Bickington.

Devon

	rate from £ per person	children taken	evening meals	animals taken
Klaus & Janice Wiemeyer **The Thatched Cottage** **Restaurant** **9 Crossley Moor Road** **Kingsteignton** **Newton Abbot TQ12 3LE** **Tel: (01626) 65650** **Open: ALL YEAR** **Map Ref No. 26**	Nearest Road: A.380 A beautiful 400-year-old, Grade II listed, thatched longhouse where old oak beams & a large open fireplace lend a cosy & welcoming atmosphere. Accommodation is in 4 attractive bedrooms, all with colour T.V. & tea/coffee-making facilities. A full English breakfast is served. Character bar & restaurant, where table d'hote & a la carte menus are available each evening. A pretty garden for guests' use. An excellent base for touring, with a warm welcome assured. 🚭 CREDIT CARD VISA M'CARD AMEX	£16.00	Y	Y	N
Mrs Madeleine Gregson **Penpark** **Bickington** **Newton Abbot TQ12 6LH** **Tel: (01626) 821314** **Fax 01626 821101** **Open: ALL YEAR** **Map Ref No. 28**	Nearest Road: A.38 In the Dartmoor National Park, with secluded, beautiful woodland gardens, tennis court & glorious panoramic views, Penpark is an elegant, charming country house, a gem of its period, designed by the famous architect Clough Williams Ellis. Your lovely, spacious double/twin room has a balcony, sofa, chairs, colour T.V., tea/coffee facilities & handbasin. Adjoining is a single room & bathroom. A warm welcome awaits you. 🚭 *see PHOTO over*	£20.00	Y	N	N
Peter & Patricia Johnson-King **Oakfield** **Exeter Road, Chudleigh** **Newton Abbot TQ13 0DD** **Tel/Fax: (01626) 852194** **Open: APR - OCT** **Map Ref No. 29**	Nearest Road: A.38 This lovely old family home, beautifully furnished with antiques, & surrounded by 20 acres of delightfully landscaped gardens, orchards & paddocks, with glorious views of the Devon countryside, offers perfect peace & tranquility. Peter & Patricia treat their guests as friends, & emphasise comfort, relaxation & excellent food. 3 very attractive en-suite bedrooms. Guests may also enjoy the drawing room, billiards room, library & heated swimming pool. 🚭 *see PHOTO over*	£30.00	N	Y	N
Mrs Mary Cuming **Wooston Farm** **Moretonhampstead** **Newton Abbot** **TQ13 8QA** **Tel/Fax: (01647) 440367** **Open: ALL YEAR (Excl. Xmas)** **Map Ref No. 31**	Nearest Road: B.3212, A.30 Wooston, once part of the Manor House Estate owned by Lord Hambledon, is situated high above the Teign Valley in the Dartmoor National Park, with views over open moorland, & plenty of walks nearby. The farmhouse, located on a working farm, is surrounded by a delightful garden. Good home-cooking & cosy log fires in season await you. 3 comfortable rooms, 2 with en-suite, 1 with 4-poster & all with colour T.V. & tea/coffee-making facilities. Children over 8 yrs.	£18.00	Y	Y	N
Mrs Pauline Griffiths **Lower Elsford Cottage** **Bovey Tracey** **Newton Abbot** **TQ13 9NY** **Tel: (01647) 277408** **Open: ALL YEAR** **Map Ref No. 34**	Nearest Road: A.38, A.382 A 17th-century stone cottage in a magical woodland setting, with spectacular views over glorious countryside in an Area of Outstanding Natural Beauty. Complete peace and quiet, every home comfort, central heating. 1 double room, with en-suite facilities, & 1 single room with h&c. Both south-facing. Situated within the Dartmoor National Park, & ideal for touring, riding, golf, fishing and walking. Children over 8 welcome. 🚭	£17.00	Y	N	Y

Oakfield. Chudleigh.

Devon

		rate from £ per person	children taken	evening meals	animals taken
John & Daphne Turner **Westways** **706 Budshead Road** **Crownhill** **Plymouth** **PL6 5DY** **Tel/Fax: (01752) 776617** **Open: ALL YEAR** **Map Ref No. 38**	Nearest Road: A.38 Situated approx. 3 1/2 miles from Plymouth city centre, this attractive detached house offers pleasant accommodation in 3 well-furnished rooms, with tea/coffee-making facilities. Excellent breakfasts served in the elegant dining room. Guests may relax & plan their excursions in the comfortable sitting room, & there is also a small T.V. room. A homely & friendly base for visitors wishing to make the most of the many attractions in the area, & for touring beautiful Devon.	£16.00 CREDIT CARD VISA M'CARD	N	N	N
Mrs P. J. Hughes **Maryknowle** **Malborough** **Salcombe** **TQ7 3DB** **Tel: (01548) 842159** **Open: ALL YEAR** **Map Ref No. 36**	Nearest Road: A.38 Maryknowle is a lovely 400-year-old south-facing farmhouse situated in a peaceful & secluded valley only 1 mile from Salcombe. This delightful home is very well-furnished & comfortable. It offers 3 attractive guest rooms, each with a private bathroom. There is a lovely mature walled garden with an adjoining courtyard & pergola. It is an ideal base from which to explore the coast & the many attractions of Devon.	£16.00	Y	Y	Y
Tom Hart & Brent **Barker** **Broad Oak** **Sid Road** **Sidmouth** **EX10 8QP** **Tel: (01395) 513713** **Open: ALL YEAR** **Map Ref No. 39**	Nearest Road: A.3052, M.5 Broad Oak was built in 1830 as a gentleman's residence. Lovingly restored by its present owners, it offers all modern facilities, whilst retaining its Victorian charm. 3 delightful, well-appointed guest rooms. Breakfasts are generous, & are served in the attractive dining room. Set in delightful gardens, which overlook The Byes & the River Sid, Broad Oak, though in a peaceful location, is only a 5-min stroll from the Esplanade & town centre, & is an ideal base for touring.	£20.00	N	N	N
Allan & Bunny Jaques **Coombe House** **North Huish** **South Brent** **TQ10 9NJ** **Tel: (01548) 821277** **Fax 01548 821277** **Open: ALL YEAR (Excl. Xmas)** **Map Ref No. 40**	Nearest Road: A.38 A Georgian house set in a tranquil & beautiful valley. 3 en-suite bedrooms - 1 single, with private bathroom. All rooms have a tea/coffee tray & overlook the garden. Breakfast is served in the elegant dining room, & there is a separate guest lounge. Washing, drying & ironing facilities & a payphone are available to guests. Many eating places nearby. The coast, Dartmoor, Kingsbridge, Totnes, Plymouth & Exeter are all within easy reach. In the grounds are 4 attractive barn conversions for self-catering holidays.	£18.50	Y	N	N

When booking your accommodation please mention
The Best Bed & Breakfast

All the establishments mentioned in this guide are members of the Worldwide Bed & Breakfast Association.

If you have any comments regarding your accommodation please send them to us using the form at the back of the book. We value your comments.

Devon

Mr & Mrs C. Worthington **Court Hall** **The Square** **North Molton** **South Molton EX36 3HP** **Tel: (01598) 740224** **Open: APR - OCT** **Map Ref No. 37**	Nearest Road: A.361 Court Hall is set in an 18th-century park overloo the moor & wooded valley. Exceptionally qui offers a relaxed 'country house' atmosphere comfort & delicious food, including vegeta.... from the garden & eggs from Charles & Sally's own Bantams. A tennis court & swimming pool available in the walled, secret garden. Within easy reach of the moors, the coast & many beautiful gardens. A delightful home.				
Martin Hayes, Suki & **Nick Hardesty** **Colcharton** **Gulworthy** **Tavistock PL19 8HU** **Tel: (01822) 613047** **Open: ALL YEAR** **Map Ref No. 42**	Nearest Road: A.390 A warm welcome & an informal family atmosphere await you at this charming, listed, 16th-century farmhouse, located in a quiet valley within easy reach of the moors. 3 pleasant bedrooms (including a family room), with modern amenities & tea/coffee makers. This makes a good base for touring both Devon & Cornwall. A short drive away are Tavistock, Plymouth, Cotehele House, Lydford Gorge & the historic part of Morwelham.	£17.00	Y	N	Y
Gill & Andrew Farr **Moorland Hall Hotel** **Brentor Road** **Mary Tavy** **Tavistock PL19 9PY** **Tel: (01822) 810466** **Open: ALL YEAR** **Map Ref No. 43**	Nearest Road: A.386 Moorland Hall is a Victorian country-house hotel, with some parts over 200 yrs old. It stands within 5 acres of gardens & paddocks, with direct access to the Dartmoor National Park. 7 en-suite bedrooms with T.V., tea/coffee making, etc., & 2 rooms have 4-poster beds. Excellent menu changes daily & includes vegetarian dishes. The coasts of Devon & Cornwall are within easy reach, & it is a good base for touring & walking.	£30.00 CREDIT CARD VISA M'CARD	Y	Y	Y
Mrs Jennifer Graeme **Fonthill** **Torquay Road** **Shaldon** **Teignmouth TQ14 0AX** **Tel: (01626) 872344** **Fax 01626 872344** **Open: ALL YEAR** **Map Ref No. 44**	Nearest Road: A.381, B.3199 Visitors are warmly welcomed to this lovely Georgian house, for a peaceful holiday in charming & very comfortable accommodation. Fonthill stands in 20 acres of beautiful gardens, woodland & fields on the edge of Shaldon, a pretty village on the South Devon coast. 3 delightful rooms, with en-suite/private bathrooms & every comfort. The lovely garden is for guests' enjoyment, & there is also a tennis court in the grounds. Several sandy beaches nearby, & an 18-hole golf course.	£23.00 *see PHOTO over*	Y	N	N

All the establishments mentioned in this guide
are members of
The Worldwide Bed & Breakfast Association

Fonthill. Shaldon

Thomas Luny House. Teignmouth.

Devon

		rate from £ per person	children taken	evening meals	animals taken
Alison & John Allan **Thomas Luny House** **Teign Street** **Teignmouth** **TQ14 8EG** **Tel: (01626) 772976** **Open: FEB - DEC** **Map Ref No. 45**	Nearest Road: A.381 A Grade II listed Georgian house, built by the marine artist Thomas Luny. Tucked away in the old quarter of Teignmouth, it forms a quiet oasis surrounded by its own high walls. Each superb, en-suite bedroom is individual in style. Alison & John place great emphasis on the fact that this is their home, & they spare no effort in preparing the delicious dinners & attending to their guests' general well-being. Licensed. Children over 12.	£27.50 *see PHOTO over*	Y	Y	N
Mrs Jenny Shaw **Poole Farm** **Ash Thomas** **Tiverton EX16 4NS** **Tel: (01884) 820201** **Open: ALL YEAR** **Map Ref No. 46**	Nearest Road: M.5, A.361 An attractive old farmhouse, recently renovated, with 18 acres & a pretty garden. Set in a peaceful hamlet, Poole Farm has 2 comfortable, en-suite bedrooms, with colour T.V., tea tray & full central heating. There are plenty of good places to eat nearby, but evening meals can usually be provided by prior arrangement. It is an ideal touring base or stop-over en-route.	£20.00	Y	N	Y
Mrs Barbara Pugsley **Hornhill** **Exeter Hill** **Tiverton** **EX16 4PL** **Tel: (01884) 253352** **Open: ALL YEAR** **Map Ref No. 47**	Nearest Road: A.361, M.5 Hornhill, originally a coaching inn, has panoramic views over the beautiful Exe valley. Set in a large garden & surrounded by farmland. The charming hosts offer guests comfort, warmth, delicious home-cooking & a happy atmosphere. The house, furnished with antiques, has 3 attractive bedrooms (1 with a Victorian 4-poster), each with private bathroom, T.V. & tea/coffee facilities. 1 is suitable for the partially disabled. Guests are invited to relax in the elegant drawing room, with plenty of books & a log fire on chilly evenings.	£17.50 *see PHOTO over*	N	Y	N
Mrs Ruth Hill-King **Little Holwell** **Collipriest** **Tiverton EX16 4PT** **Tel: (01884) 258741** **Fax 01884 258741** **Open: ALL YEAR (Excl. Xmas)** **Map Ref No. 48**	Nearest Road: M.5, A.361 Little Holwell is a delightful 'olde worlde' farmhouse, standing in beautiful Devon countryside & surrounded by rolling hills & woodland. This 13th-century home has many oak beams, an inglenook fireplace & a spiral staircase. 3 attractive rooms, 1 en-suite & each with tea/coffee-making facilities. A lounge is also available. Home-made bread, & a welcome cup of tea awaits you. Good for touring, as Tiverton, Exeter, Exmouth & Torbay are within easy reach. Phone for directions.	£15.00 CREDIT CARD VISA M'CARD	Y	Y	N
Mrs Diane Burnell **The Old Mill Guest House** **Shillingford** **Tiverton EX16 9BW** **Tel: (01398) 331064** **Open: ALL YEAR** **Map Ref No. 49**	Nearest Road: B.3227 Set in a pretty riverside 'edge of village' location, The Old Mill, a former water-powered corn mill, offers superb accommodation in self-contained suites. Suite 1 is suitable for 2 - 4 persons, while Suite 2 offers 1/2 family bedrooms. Each has private or en-suite bathrooms, colour T.V. & tea/coffee-making facilities. A beautiful garden & 4 large patios provide ample relaxation areas. Shooting, fishing & horse-riding breaks available. Restaurant licence. Children over 5 yrs.	£22.00	Y	Y	N

Hornhill. Tiverton.

The Old Forge at Totnes. Totnes.

Devon

		rate from £ per person	children taken	evening meals	animals taken
Jeannie & Peter Allnutt **The Old Forge at Totnes** **Seymour Place** **Totnes** **TQ9 5AY** **Tel: (01803) 862174** **Open: ALL YEAR** **Map Ref No. 50**	Nearest Road: A.381, A.384 The Old Forge at Totnes is a delightfully converted, working, 600-year-old smithy. This family-run hotel, located in the centre of Totnes, offers visitors 10 comfortable, well-equipped bedrooms, most en-suite, all with radio, T.V. & tea/coffee-making facilities. A cottage suite is also available for families. There is also a pleasant walled garden for guests' use, where delicious cream teas are served. The Old Forge is ideally located for touring the Torbay coast & Dartmoor. Golf breaks a speciality. Licensed.	£22.00 🚭 *see PHOTO over* CREDIT CARD VISA M'CARD	Y	N	N
John & Elizabeth Watts **The Red Slipper** **Stoke Gabriel** **Totnes TQ9 6RU** **Tel: (01803) 782315** **Fax 01803 782315** **Open: Mid MAR - OCT** **Map Ref No. 51**	Nearest Road: A.385 A small, friendly establishment appointed to a high standard, located in the centre of one of Devon's picturesque & peaceful villages on the River Dart, where there are launching facilities. There are 4 attractive & well-equipped en-suite rooms. The restaurant & tea garden are available for residents & non-residents all day. Mrs Watts uses her skill & imagination to produce appetising meals, including cream teas, from high-quality local produce.	£20.00	Y	Y	Y
Mrs Helen Worth **Orchard House** **Horner** **Halwell** **Totnes TQ9 7LB** **Tel: (01548) 821448** **Open: MAR - OCT** **Map Ref No. 52**	Nearest Road: A.381 Tucked away in a rural hamlet of the South Hams, between Totnes & Kingsbridge, Orchard House nestles within an old cider orchard. It offers superb accommodation: all bedrooms are en-suite with colour T.V., radio, tea/coffee-making facilities & beautiful furnishings. Breakfasts are ample, with cereals, juice, yoghurts & grapefruit, followed by a cooked platter with toast & croissants. Also, guests' own sitting & dining room, with a log fire. Large garden & private parking.	£20.00 *see PHOTO over*	Y	N	N
Jenny Howell **North Barwick** **Iddesleigh** **Winkleigh** **EX19 8BP** **Tel: (01837) 83902** **Open: ALL YEAR** **Map Ref No. 53**	Nearest Road: A.30 North Barwick is a 16th-century thatched Devon long house. Originally the main farmhouse for the hamlet of Barwick, it has commanding views of beautiful countryside, & affords tasteful accommodation in 3 attractive bedrooms, each with an en-suite/private bathroom & tea/coffee-making facilities, & some with colour T.V. This, when accompanied by delicious breakfasts & fine cuisine, makes North Barwick an ideal place to stay. Very convenient for Dartmoor, Exmoor & the wonderful coast.	£25.00 🚭 CREDIT CARD VISA	N	Y	N

When booking your accommodation please mention
The Best Bed & Breakfast

Orchard House. Halwell.

		rate from £ per person	children taken	evening meals	animals taken
Jean & Charles Boorman **'Sandunes'** **Beach Road** **Woolacombe** **EX34 7BT** **Tel: (01271) 870661** **Open: MAR - OCT** **Map Ref No. 54**	Nearest Road: A.361 'Sandunes' is a very pleasant, most comfortable modern guest house where you are assured of a friendly welcome, a relaxed atmosphere & courteous service. Conveniently located for Woolacombe Sands & the village. The comfortable accommodation is in 7 en-suite bedrooms, many with lovely sea views. The well appointed guest lounge & sun patio have marvellous panoramic views out to sea. This is an ideal base for touring, with sandy beaches, Illfracombe, Lynton, Lynmouth & Exmoor within easy reach.	£16.00	N	Y	N
Mr & Mrs V. W. Bassett **Sunnycliffe Hotel** **Chapel Hill** **Mortehoe** **Woolacombe EX34 7EB** **Tel/Fax: (01271) 870597** **Open: FEB - NOV** **Map Ref No. 55**	Nearest Road: A.361 This small hotel, with the ambience of quiet luxury, has 8 en-suite bedrooms, all with sea views, colour T.V. & tea-making facilities. Delightfully situated above the golden cove of Combesgate, this is a lovely base from which to explore Devon. You will be in the skilful hands of the highly qualified proprietor chef. A hint of this & a touch of that gives the mainly traditional English food that special something.	£25.00	N	Y	N

All the establishments mentioned in this guide are members of
The Worldwide Bed & Breakfast Association

When booking your accommodation please mention
The Best Bed & Breakfast

**All the establishments mentioned in this guide
are members of the
Worldwide Bed & Breakfast Association.**

**If you have any comments regarding your
accommodation please send them to us
using the form at the back of the book.
We value your comments.**

Dorset

Dorset
(West Country)

The unspoilt nature of this gem of a county is emphasised by the designation of virtually all of the coast & much of the inland country as an Area of Outstanding Natural Beauty. Along the coast from Christchurch to Lyme Regis there are a fascinating variety of sandy beaches, towering cliffs & single banks, whilst inland is a rich mixture of downland, lonely heaths, fertile valleys, historic houses & lovely villages of thatch & mellow stone buildings.

Thomas Hardy was born here & took the Dorset countryside as a background for many of his novels. Few writers can have stamped their identity on a county more than Hardy on Dorset, forever to be known as the "Hardy Country". Fortunately most of the area that he so lovingly described remains unchanged, including Egdon Heath & the county town of Dorchester, famous as Casterbridge.

In the midst of the rolling chalk hills which stretch along the Storr Valley lies picturesque Cerne Abbas, with its late mediaeval houses & cottages & the ruins of a Benedictine Abbey. At Godmanstone is the tiny thatched "Smiths Arms" claiming to be the smallest pub in England.

The north of the county is pastoral with lovely views over broad Blackmoor Vale. Here is the ancient hilltop town of Shaftesbury, with cobbled Gold Hill, one of the most photographed streets in the country.

Coastal Dorset is spectacular. Poole harbour is an enormous, almost circular bay, an exciting mixture of 20th century activity, ships of many nations & beautiful building of the 15th, 18th & early 19th centuries.

Westwards lies the popular resort of Swanage, where the sandy beach & sheltered bay are excellent for swimming. From here to Weymouth is a marvellous stretch of coast with scenic wonders like Lulworth Cove & the arch of Durdle Door.

Chesil Beach is an extraordinary bank of graded pebbles, as perilous to shipping today as it was 1,000 years ago. It is separated from the mainland by a sheltered lagoon known as the Fleet. From here a range of giant cliffs rises to 617 feet at Golden Gap & stretches westwards to Lyme Regis, beloved by Jane Austen who wrote "Persuasion" whilst living here.

Dorset has many interesting archaeological features. Near Dorchester is Maiden Castle, huge earthwork fortifications on a site first inhabited 6,000 years ago. The Badbury rings wind round a wooded hilltop near Wimborne Minster; legend has it that King Arthur's soul, in the form of a raven, inhabited this "dread" wood. The giant of Cerne Abbas is a figure of a man 180 feet high carved into the chalk hillside. Long associated with fertility there is still speculation about the figures' origins, one theory suggesting it is a Romano-British depiction of Hercules. A Roman amphitheatre can be seen at Dorchester, & today's road still follows the Roman route to Weymouth.

Corfe Castle.

Dorset

Dorset
Gazeteer

Areas of outstanding natural beauty.
The Entire County.

Houses & Castles

Athelthampton
Mediaeval house - one of the finest in all England. Formal gardens.

Barneston Manor - Nr. Church Knowle
13th - 16th century stone built manor house.

Forde Abbey - Nr. Chard
12th century Cistercian monastery - noted Mortlake tapestries.

Manor House - Sandford Orcas
Mansion of Tudor period, furnished with period furniture, antiques, silver, china, glass, paintings.

Hardy's Cottage - Higher Bockampton
Birthplace of Thomas Hardy, author (1840-1928).

Milton Abbey - Nr. Blandford
18th century Georgian house built on original site of 15th century abbey.

Purse Caundle Manor - Purse Caundle
Mediaeval Manor - furnished in style of period.

Parnham House - Beaminster
Tudor Manor - some later work by Nash. Leaded windows & heraldic plasterwork. Home of John Makepeace & the International School for Craftsmen in Wood. House, gardens & workshops.

Sherborne Castle - Sherborne
16th century mansion - continuously occupied by Digby family.

No. 3 Trinity Street - Weymouth
Tudor cottages now converted into one house, furnished 17th century.

Smedmore - Kimmeridge
18th century manor.

Wolfeton House - Dorchester
Mediaeval & Elizabethan Manor. Fine stone work, great stair. 17th century furniture - Jacobean ceilings & fireplaces.

Cathedrals & Churches

Bere Regis (St. John the Baptist)
12th century foundation - enlarged in 13th & 15th centuries.
Timber roof & nave, fine arcades. 16th century seating.

Blandford (St. Peter & St. Paul)
18th century - ashlar - Georgian design. Galleries, pulpit, box pews, font & mayoral seat.

Bradford Abbas (St. Mary)
14th century - parapets & pinnacled tower, panelled roof. 15th century bench ends, stone rood screen. 17th century pulpit.

Cerne Abbas (St. Mary)
13th century - rebuilt 15th & 16th centuries, 14th century wall paintings, 15th century tower, stone screen, pulpit possibly 11th century.

Chalbury (dedication unknown)
13th century origin - 14th century east windows, timber bellcote. Plastered walls, box pews, 3-decker pulpit, west gallery.

Christchurch (Christ Church)
Norman nave - ribbed plaster vaulting - perpendicular spire. Tudor renaissance Salisbury chantry - screen with Tree of Jesse: notable misericord seats.

Milton Abbey (Sts. Mary, Michael, Sampson & Branwaleder)
14th century pulpitum & sedilla, 15th century reredos & canopy, 16th century monument, Milton effigies 1775.

Sherborne (St. Mary)
Largely Norman but some Saxon remains - excellent fan vaulting, of nave & choir. 12th & 13th century effigies - 15th century painted glass.

Studland (St. Nicholas)
12th century - best Norman church in the country. 12th century font, 13th century east windows.

Whitchurch Canonicorum (St. Candida & Holy Cross)
12th & 13th century. 12th century font, relics of patroness in 13th century shrine, 15th century painted glass, 15th century tower.

Wimbourne Minster (St. Cuthberga)
12th century central tower & arcade, otherwise 13th-15th century. Former collegiate church. Georgian glass, some Jacobean stalls & screen. Monuments & famed clock of 14th century.

Yetminster (St. Andrew)
13th century chancel - 15th century rebuilt with embattled parapets. 16th century brasses & seating.

Dorset

Museums & Galleries

Abbey Ruins - Shaftesbury
Relics excavated from Benedictine Nunnery founded by Alfred the Great.

Russell-Cotes Art Gallery & Museum - Bournemouth
17th-20th century oil paintings, watercolours, sculptures, ceramics, miniatures, etc.

Rothesay Museum - Bournemouth
English porcelain, 17th century furniture, collection of early Italian paintings, arms & armour, ethnography, etc.

Bournemouth Natural Science Society's Museum
Archaeology & local natural history.

Brewery Farm Museum - Milton Abbas
Brewing & village bygones from Dorset.

Dorset County Museum - Dorchester
Geology, natural history, pre-history. Thomas Hardy memorabilia

Philpot Museum - Lyme Regis
Old documents & prints, fossils, lace & old fire engine.

Guildhall Museum - Poole
Social & civic life of Poole during 18th & 19th centuries displayed in two-storey Georgian market house.

Scapolen's Court - Poole
14th century house of local merchant exhibiting local & archaeological history of town, also industrial archaeology.

Sherborne Museum - Sherborne
Local history & geology - abbey of AD 705, Sherborne missal AD 1400, 18th century local silk industry.

Gallery 24 - Shaftesbury
Art exhibitions - paintings, pottery, etc.

Red House Museum & Art Gallery - Christchurch
Natural history & antiques of the region. Georgian house with herb garden.

Priest's House Museum - Wimbourne Minster
Tudor building in garden exhibiting local archaeology & history.

Other things to see & do

Abbotsbury Swannery - Abbotsbury
Unique colony of Swans established by monks in the 14th century. 16th century duck decoy, reed walk, information centre.

Dorset Rare Breeds Centre - Park Farm, Gillingham

Poole Potteries - the Quay, Poole

Sea Life Centre - Weymouth
Variety of displays, including Ocean Tunnel, sharks, living "touch" pools.

West Bay.

DORSET
Map reference

1 Smith
1 DuFaur
1 Edwards
2 O'Rourke
3 Davies
4 Diment
6 Vear
7 Walker
8 Rowse
9 Smith
10 Hipwell
11 Tomblin
12 Haggett
13 Barraclough
14 Willis
15 Walford
16 Lake
17 Collier
18 Bradley-Watson
20 Ingleton
21 Eley

22 Partridge
23 Hookham-Bassett
24 Newson-Smith
25 Wingate-Saul
26 Norman
27 Gregory
28 Turnbull
29 Spender

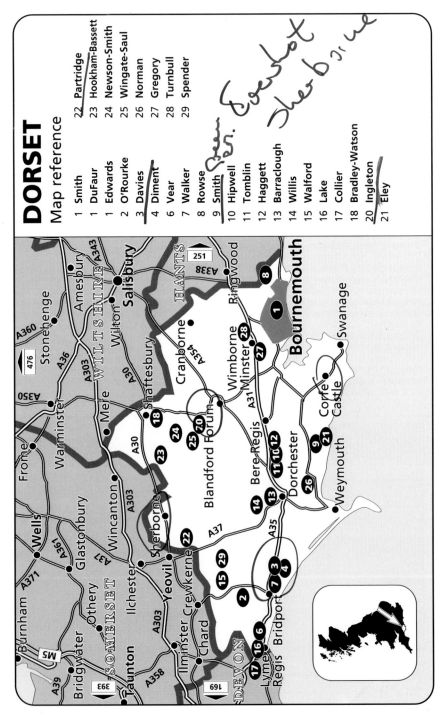

204

Dorset

	Nearest Road	rate from £ per person	children taken	evening meals	animals taken
Michael J. O'Rourke **The Lodge** **Beaminster** **DT8 3BL** **Tel: (01308) 863468** **Open: ALL YEAR** **Map Ref No. 02**	Nearest Road: A.3066 The Lodge is a fine Grade II listed Georgian house on the edge of the charming town of Beaminster. The interior is particularly interesting, retaining all the original features. There are 5 attractive en-suite/private bedrooms. The kitchen provides good English home-cooking, most of the ingredients coming from the kitchen garden. There are 2 all-weather tennis courts & a swimming pool for your enjoyment. A friendly welcome awaits you from your host Michael O'Rourke.	£28.00 *see PHOTO over* CREDIT CARD VISA M'CARD	Y	Y	Y
Alan & Jackie Edwards **Gervis Court Hotel** **38 Gervis Road** **East Cliff** **Bournemouth BH1 3DH** **Tel/Fax: (01202) 556871** **Open: ALL YEAR** **Map Ref No. 01**	Nearest Road: A.335 Gervis Court is a family-run, licensed hotel, set among the pines on the fashionable East Cliff, 2 mins from the cliff top, cliff lift & sea. Each bedroom is tastefully furnished with comfort in mind, & has modern amenities, including T.V. & tea/coffee-making facilities. Many are en-suite & situated on the ground floor. An ideal place to visit the beautiful Dorset countryside, yet only a short walk to the theatres, cinemas, pier & gardens - & the town centre, with its fashionable shops.	£17.00 CREDIT CARD VISA M'CARD	Y	N	N
Jo & Bill Smith **Silver Trees** **57 Wimborne Road** **Bournemouth** **BH3 7AL** **Tel/Fax: (01202) 556040** **Open: ALL YEAR** **Map Ref No. 01**	Nearest Road: A.347 A charming Victorian house standing in its own wooded grounds, with sweeping lawns, colourful flowers & shrubs. Offering comfortable accommodation in 5 en-suite bedrooms with colour T.V.. Breakfast is cooked to order in the elegant dining room overlooking the garden. Early morning tea & refreshments are available on request & served in your room, or in the lounge. Ideally located for visiting the New Forest & Dorset.	£20.00 CREDIT CARD VISA M'CARD AMEX	Y	N	N
Colin & Jean Du Faur **Sandhurst Private Hotel** **16 Southern Road** **Southbourne** **Bournemouth BH6 3SR** **Tel: (01202) 423748** **Open: ALL YEAR** **Map Ref No. 01**	Nearest Road: A.35 Guests' comfort is a priority at this friendly, welcoming hotel. There's a choice of 8 comfortable rooms. 5 of these large rooms (incl. a ground-floor one) have private facilities. All have colour T.V. & tea/coffee makers. Good home-cooked breakfasts, & evening meals available. Situated 2 mins from the beach in a quiet suburb of Bournemouth. An ideal centre for touring, with Christchurch, Beaulieu, the New Forest, Salisbury & Dorchester a short drive. Private parking.	£16.00 🚭	Y	Y	N
Ann & Dan Walker MHCIMA **Britmead House** **West Bay Road** **Bridport** **DT6 4EG** **Tel: (01308) 422941** **Open: ALL YEAR** **Map Ref No. 07**	Nearest Road: A.35 A friendly welcome in a relaxed & comfortable atmosphere. Renowned for good food, a high standard of facilities, personal service & attention to detail. Situated between Bridport, the fishing harbour of West Bay, Chesil Beach & the Dorset Coastal Path. 7 individually decorated bedrooms, 6 en-suite, 1 on the ground floor, all with T.V., tea facilities & hairdryer. A south-facing lounge & dining room overlook the garden & open countryside. Optional dinner, incorporating local fish & produce. Licensed. Parking.	£19.00 CREDIT CARD VISA M'CARD AMEX	Y	Y	Y

The Lodge. Beaminster.

Dorset

		rate from £ per person	children taken	evening meals	animals taken
Sydney Davies **Innsacre Farmhouse** **Shipton Gorge** **Bridport DT6 4LJ** Tel: (01308) 456137 Fax 01308 456137 Open: ALL YEAR (Excl. Xmas) Map Ref No. 03	Nearest Road: A.35 Innsacre is a 17th-century converted farmhouse plus barns, hidden midway between Lyme Regis & Dorchester, 3 miles from the sea & N.T. coastal path. A magical & peaceful setting, south-facing, with 10 acres of spinneys, steep hillsides, orchards & lawns. All rooms are en-suite, with either antique French or cottage-style beds; log fires, beams & delicious breakfasts. An easy atmosphere - always welcoming, personally run.	£29.00 CREDIT CARD VISA M'CARD	Y	N	Y
Mrs Sue Diment **Rudge Farm** **Chilcombe** **Bridport DT6 4NF** Tel: (01308) 482630 Fax 01308 482635 Open: ALL YEAR Map Ref No. 04	Nearest Road: A.35 Rudge Farm is peacefully situated on a gentle south-facing slope overlooking the beautiful Bride Valley, just over 2 miles from the sea. After a day spent exploring the lovely West Dorset countryside, relax in this comfortable Victorian farmhouse & enjoy dinner prepared mainly from fresh local produce. All rooms are en-suite, with T.V., tea tray & far-reaching views, & are attractively furnished.	£20.00	N	Y	N
Anne & Vernon Vear **Newlands House** **Stonebarrow Lane** **Charmouth** **DT6 6RA** Tel: (01297) 560212 Open: MAR - OCT Map Ref No. 06	Nearest Road: A.35 A house of character set in about 2 acres of garden & orchard on the eastern fringe of Charmouth village. Offering good food & wines, comfort & an ambience of quiet relaxation. There is no smoking, except in the bar lounge. Ample car parking. Newlands House is surrounded by an Area of Outstanding Natural Beauty, & is perfect either for walking & or as a centre for touring. Children over 6 yrs.	£23.00	Y	Y	N
Michael & Jane Rowse **Monks Revel** **Winkton** **Christchurch BH23 7AR** Tel: (01202) 479430 Fax 01202 479430 Open: ALL YEAR Map Ref No. 08	Nearest Road: B.3347 An enchanting Georgian house with grounds down to the River Avon. Luxury en-suite bedrooms, a delightful drawing room with comfortable sofas (log fires in Winter) & French windows to a sun terrace overlooking the river. An attractive dining room; delicious, individually prepared table d'hote meals, or pre-ordered local game & seafood specialities. Close to the picturesque harbour, unspoilt beaches & New Forest.	£25.00 CREDIT CARD VISA M'CARD	N	Y	N
Anthea & Michael Hipwell **The Old Vicarage** **Affpuddle** **Dorchester DT2 7HH** Tel: (01305) 848315 Open: ALL YEAR (Excl. Xmas & New Year) Map Ref No. 10	Nearest Road: A.35, B.3390 The Old Vicarage is a traditional country house standing in a large mature garden in the charming Piddle Valley, at the heart of the Dorset countryside. Accommodation is in 3 comfortable and attractively furnished rooms, each with private bathroom; & all facilities are at hand, at your request. Your hosts will be pleased to help with advice on the numerous places of interest and places to dine. Children over 6 years.	£20.00	Y	N	N

Dorset

		rate from £ per person	children taken	evening meals	animals taken
Marian Tomblin **Lower Lewell Farmhouse** **West Stafford** **Dorchester DT2 8AP** **Tel: (01305) 267169** **Open: ALL YEAR** **Map Ref No. 11**	Nearest Road: A.35, A.352 Lower Lewell Farmhouse dates from the 17th century, & is situated in the delightful Frome Valley in the midst of Thomas Hardy country. Indeed, the house is reputed to be the Talbothays Dairy portrayed in Hardy's novel 'Tess of the D'Urbervilles'. 3 bedrooms are available, equipped with tea/coffee-making facilities, & a Full English breakfast is served. There is a sitting room with colour T.V.. A delightful touring centre.	£16.00	Y	N	N
Mrs D. M. Haggett **Vartrees House** **Moreton** **Dorchester** **DT2 8BE** **Tel: (01305) 852704** **Open: ALL YEAR** **Map Ref No. 12**	Nearest Road: B.3390 off A.35 Peaceful & secluded character country house set in 3 acres of picturesque woodland gardens. Built by Hermann Lea, friend of Thomas Hardy. Accommodation throughout is spacious & comfortable. Tea/coffee makers in all 3 rooms, 1 en-suite. T.V. lounge. Situated near the pretty village of Moreton, with its renowned church & burial place of Lawrence of Arabia. Coast 4 miles. Station 1/4 of mile. Excellent local pubs. Children over 10 yrs welcome.	£16.00	Y	N	Y
Charles & Jennie Smith **Manor House** **Winfrith Newburgh** **Dorchester DT2 8JR** **Tel: (01305) 852988** **Fax 01305 854988** **Open: ALL YEAR** **Map Ref No. 09**	Nearest Road: A.352 This much-loved manor house with large walled garden is near Lulworth Cove, a spectacular coast path & Hardy Country. A Jacobean staircase ascends to the Green Room with a large double bed, 18th-century panelling & an en-suite bathroom with roll-top bath. The Victorian Room has twin brass beds with a private shower room adjacent. Both have T.V., tea facilities & antique furniture. Self-contained wing available. 2 nearby pubs serve evening meals. Minimum stay 2 nights.	£20.00	Y	N	N
Nicky Willis **Lamperts Cottage** **Sydling St. Nicholas** **Cerne Abbas** **Dorchester DT2 9NU** **Tel: (01300) 341659** **Fax 01300 341699** **Open: ALL YEAR** **Map Ref No. 14**	Nearest Road: A.37 Lamperts Cottage is a charming 16th-century thatched cottage standing in fields, with streams running front & back, on the outskirts of the village. Beautiful roses climb around the windows & door. Accommodation is in 3 very comfortable guest bedrooms, each equipped with tea/coffee-making facilities. Full English breakfast, or Continental if preferred. Lamperts Cottage is an ideal base for a relaxing break or for visiting Dorset's many beauty spots.	£18.00	N	N	N
Diana Lake **Rashwood Lodge** **Clappentail Lane** **Lyme Regis DT7 3LZ** **Tel: (01297) 445700** **Open: FEB - NOV** **Map Ref No. 16**	Nearest Road: A.3052 Rashwood Lodge is an unusual octagonal house, located on the western hillside with views over Lyme Bay. Just a short walk away is the coastal footpath & Ware Cliff, famed for its part in 'The French Lieutenant's Woman'. The attractive bedrooms have their own facilities, & a south-facing aspect which overlooks a large & colourful garden set in peaceful surroundings. Golf course 1 mile. A charming home.	£17.00	Y	N	N

Dorset

		rate from £ per person	children taken	evening meals	animals taken
Mrs Chris Walford **Rectory House** **Fore Street** **Evershot DT2 0JW** **Tel: (01935) 83273** **Fax 01935 83273** **Open: JAN - NOV** **Map Ref No. 15**	Nearest Road: A.37 Rectory House is an 18th-century listed building set in the picturesque village of Evershot. There are 6 delightfully appointed bedrooms with en-suite bathrooms, colour T.V. & tea/coffee-making facilities. Superb home-cooking of traditional & exotic dishes. Delicious breakfasts include freshly baked bread & locally made sausages. Melbury Estate adjoins the village, with beautiful walks & scenery. Ideally located for visiting Bath, Bournemouth & Lyme Regis.	£28.00 *see PHOTO over* CREDIT CARD VISA M'CARD	N	Y	N
Tony & Vicky Norman **The Red House** **Sidmouth Road** **Lyme Regis** **DT7 3ES** **Tel: (01297) 442055** **Fax 01297 442055** **Open: MAR - NOV** **Map Ref No. 16**	Nearest Road: A.3052 This distinguished house, set in mature grounds, enjoys spectacular coastal views, & yet is only a short walk to the centre of Lyme Regis. The 3 en-suite bedrooms (1 for family use; 2 are especially spacious) are furnished with every comfort, including tea/coffee makers, colour T.V., clock-radio, desk, armchairs, a drink refrigerator, central heating & electric heaters. Fresh flowers & magazines are among the little extras. Breakfast can be taken on the garden balcony. Private parking. Children over 8 years.	£18.00	Y	N	N
Ian & Betty Collier **Amherst Lodge Farm** **Uplyme** **Lyme Regis** **DT7 3XH** **Tel: (01297) 442773** **Open: MAR - OCT** **Map Ref No. 17**	Nearest Road: A.35 Originally a Devon long house, converted in the 20s in 'the grand manner', Amherst Lodge Farm lies in a wooded valley with trout lakes, Jacob sheep & an abundance of wildlife. The River Lyme runs through the old established & informal garden extending to 2 acres of maples, rhododendrons & orchard. There are 3 bedrooms, all with en-suite bathrooms, colour T.V. & tea/coffee-making facilities. Children over 10 yrs.	£20.00	Y	N	N

When booking your accommodation please mention
The Best Bed & Breakfast

Rectory House.   Evershot.

Dorset

	rate from £ per person	children taken	evening meals	animals taken
Mrs Joyce Norman **Dingle Dell** **Church Lane** **Osmington DT3 6EW** Tel: (01305) 832378 Fax 01305 832378 Open: MAR - OCT Map Ref No. 26	Nearest Road: A.353 Dingle Dell is situated on the edge of the village of Osmington, in its own charming garden, with roses covering the mellow stone walls. 2 spacious & comfortable bedrooms (1 en-suite), furnished to the highest of standards, & with each overlooking the garden & countryside. Both rooms have colour T.V. & tea/coffee facilities. A generous English breakfast is served. Dingle Dell provides a truly peaceful spot to rest & relax, & is also a convenient base from which to explore Dorset.	£19.00	N	N	N
Richard & Tavy Bradley-Watson **Melbury Mill** **Melbury Abbas** **Shaftesbury SP7 0DB** Tel: (01747) 852163 Open: ALL YEAR Map Ref No. 18	Nearest Road: A.350 Mr & Mrs Bradley-Watson offer a warm welcome at this old working mill, set in 9 acres of meadows & overlooking a mill pond abounding with waterfowl. All bedrooms are large & have en-suite facilities. Located just south of Shaftesbury, famous for its Gold Hill, it is in picturesque Thomas Hardy countryside. Ideal for walkers, with N.T. downland & the properties of Stourhead & Kingston Lacy close by. 3-course dinners are provided using fresh local produce.	£18.00	Y	Y	N
Ann & Jack Partridge **Manor Farmhouse** **High Street** **Yetminster** **Sherborne DT9 6LF** Tel: (01935) 872247 Open: ALL YEAR (Excl. Xmas) Map Ref No. 22	Nearest Road: A.37 This 17th-century farmhouse, with oak panelling, beams & inglenook fireplaces, offers every comfort to the discerning visitor. 4 bedrooms, all with private facilities & modern amenities, including T.V. & tea/coffee makers. Delicious meals served, made from traditional recipes & using fresh local produce. The village described as the best 17th-century stone-built village in the south of England. An excellent centre for visiting Sherborne, Glastonbury, New Forest & Hardy's Dorset.	£25.00 *see PHOTO over* CREDIT CARD VISA M'CARD	N	Y	N
J. Ingleton **Fiddleford Millhouse** **Fiddleford** **Sturminster Newton** **DT10 2BX** Tel: (01258) 472786 Open: ALL YEAR Map Ref No. 20	Nearest Road: A.357 An idyllically situated, Grade I listed 16th-century farm/manor house of great architectural interest overlooking the River Stour in peacefully secluded countryside. This is a beautifully furnished & decorated family home. 3 large bedrooms, 1 with a 16th-century moulded plaster ceiling & en-suite bathroom, the other 2 sharing a bathroom. All have tea-making facilities & T.V.. A beautiful garden with a sitting area. 2 pubs within walking distance. Country pursuits available locally.	£17.50	N	N	N
Mary Ann & Peter Newson-Smith **Lovells Court, Marnhull** **Sturminster Newton** **DT10 1JJ** Tel: (01258) 820652 Fax 01258 820487 Open: ALL YEAR Map Ref No. 24	Nearest Road: A.30, A.303 Lovells Court is a rambling old house of character, set in the delightful countryside of Thomas Hardy, & with fine views across the Blackmore Vale. The market town of Sturminster Newton & the Abbeys of Sherborne & Milton Abbas are nearby. An excellent base for enjoying rural Dorset & its many N.T. properties. 3 en-suite rooms & 1 with private bathroom, all with colour T.V., radio & tea-making facilities. There are 2 excellent village inns for food all year round.	£22.00	Y	N	N

Manor Farmhouse. Yetminster.

	rate from £ per person	children taken	evening meals	animals taken
Jill & Ken Hookham-Bassett **Stourcastle Lodge** **Gough's Close** **Sturminster Newton** **DT10 1BU** **Tel: (01258) 472320** **Fax 01258 473381** **Open: ALL YEAR** **Map Ref No. 23** Nearest Road: A.357 Stourcastle Lodge is a family-run business, offering a very high standard of accommodation, with personal service & excellent cuisine. A superb breakfast is served in the attractive dining room. Each of the elegant bedrooms is south-facing & overlook the delightful garden, which is stocked full of herbaceous & perennial borders. Stourcastle Lodge is a beautiful home, & an ideal base for exploring Dorset & its many attractions.	£21.00 *see PHOTO over* CREDIT CARD VISA M'CARD	Y	Y	N
Charles & Sally Wingate-Saul **Holebrook Farm** **Lydlinch** **Sturminster Newton** **DT10 2JB** **Tel: (01258) 817348** **Open: ALL YEAR** **Map Ref No. 25** Nearest Road: A.357 Holebrook Farm is a family-run mixed farm located in the heart of Hardy Country. Accommodation is in the Georgian stone farmhouse or the delightfully converted stables with own sitting room, colour T.V., shower room & kitchen. Breakfast is served in the lovely old farmhouse kitchen with its flagstone floors, original fireplace & bread oven. A small swimming pool & games room, with darts, pool table & table tennis, are available for guests' use. Clay shooting can also be arranged.	£21.00	Y	Y	N
Tony & Mary Eley **Gatton House** **West Lulworth** **Wareham BH20 5RU** **Tel: (01929) 400252** **Fax 01929 400252** **Open: MAR - OCT** **Map Ref No. 21** Nearest Road: A.352 Spectacularly positioned, quiet & comfortable, this small hotel is set amongst the Purbeck Hills, yet only a strolling distance from famous Lulworth Cove. Lovely lounge areas, a breakfast room & attractive bedrooms. Outside, the terrace provides a perfect venue for morning coffee or afternoon tea. Ideal location for walking or touring Dorset's beauty spots. Within easy reach of Bournemouth, Poole, Swanage, Dorchester & Weymouth.	£20.50 CREDIT CARD VISA M'CARD	Y	N	Y
Mrs Margaret Gregory **Ashton Lodge** **10 Oakley Hill** **Wimborne BH21 1QH** **Tel: (01202) 883423** **Fax 01202 886180** **Open: ALL YEAR** **Map Ref No. 27** Nearest Road: A.31 A detached family residence with a relaxed family atmosphere. The dining room overlooks an attractively-laid-out garden. Full English breakfast is a speciality. 2 of the 4 bedrooms have en-suite facilities, & all have colour T.V., tea/coffee-making facilities & hairdryers. Ironing facilities are available on request, & packed lunches can be arranged with prior notice. Conveniently placed for the coast, New Forest & cross channel ferries.	£17.50	Y	N	N
John & Sara Turnbull **Thornhill** **Holt** **Wimborne** **BH21 7DJ** **Tel: (01202) 889434** **Open: ALL YEAR** **Map Ref No. 28** Nearest Road: A.31 Visitors are warmly welcomed to this large, thatched family house located in rural surroundings 3 1/2 miles from Wimborne. Large garden. Hard tennis court available. Double, twin & single rooms. 1 private bathroom, & another which may be shared. Sitting room with colour T.V. & coffee/tea-making & laundry facilities. Plenty of good local pubs. Well situated for exploring the coast, New Forest & Salisbury area.	£18.00	N	N	N

Stourcastle Lodge. Sturminster Newton.

Dorset

	rate from £ per person	children taken	evening meals	animals taken
Peter & Jane Spender **Halstock Mill** **Halstock** **Yeovil** **BA22 9SJ** **Tel: (01935) 891278** **Open: ALL YEAR (Excl. Xmas)** **Map Ref No. 29**	Nearest Road: A.37 At the end of a 1/2-mile private lane is 17th-century Halstock Mill. The 400 acres of pastureland surrounding it ensure a peaceful, relaxing stay. Accommodation is in 4 spacious en-suite bedrooms with colour T.V. & tea/coffee makers. The beamed drawing room has an inglenook log fire. Jane offers a superb 4-course dinner, prepared with home/local produce. An ideal base for touring Dorset, Somerset & Devon.	£22.00 *see PHOTO over* CREDIT CARD VISA M'CARD AMEX	Y	Y	Y

All the establishments mentioned in this guide

are members of

The Worldwide Bed & Breakfast Association

When booking your accommodation please mention
The Best Bed & Breakfast

Halstock Mill. Halstock.

Essex

Essex
(East Anglia)

Essex is a county of commerce, busy roads & busier towns, container ports & motorways, yet it is also a landscape of mudflats & marshes, of meadows & leafy lanes, villages & duckponds. Half timbered buildings & thatched & clapboard cottages stand among rolling hills topped by orange brick windmills.

The coast on the east, now the haunt of wildfowl, sea-birds, sailors & fishermen has seen the arrival of Saxons, Romans, Danes, Vikings & Normans. The names of their settlements remain - Wivenhoe, Layer-de-la-Haye, Colchester & Saffron Walden - the original Saxon name was Walden, but the Saffron was added when the crocus used for dyes & flavouring was grown here in the 15th century.

The seaside resorts of Southend & Clacton are bright & cheery, much-loved by families for safe beaches. Harbours here are great favourites with anglers & yachtsmen.

Inland lie the watermeadows & windmills, willows & cool green water which shaped the life & work of John Constable, one of the greatest landscape painters. Scenes are instantly recognisable today as you walk from Dedham to Flatford Mill with the swift River Stour flowing by.

Colchester is England's oldest recorded town, once the Roman capital of Britain trading in corn & cattle, slaves & pearls. Roman remains are still to be seen & their original street plan is the basis of much of modern Colchester. A great feast is held here annually to celebrate the famous oyster - the "Colchester native".

South Essex, though sliced through by the M.25 motorway is still a place of woodland & little rivers. The ancient trees of Epping Forest, hunting ground for generations of monarchs, spread 6,000 acres of leafy glades & heathland into the London suburbs.

Flatford Mill.

Essex

Essex
Gazeteer

Areas of outstanding natural beauty.
Dedham Vale (part), Epping Forest.

Houses & Castles

Audely End House - Saffron Walden
1603 - Jacobean mansion on site of
Benedictine Abbey. State rooms & Hall.
Castle House - Dedham
Home of the late Sir A. Munnings.
President R.A. Paintings & other works.
Hedingham Castle - Castle Hedingham
Norman keep & Tudor bridge.
Layer Marney Tower - Nr. Colchester
1520 Tudor brick house. 8 storey gate
tower. Formal yew hedges & lawns.
Payecock's - Coggeshall
1500 - richly ornamented - merchant's
house - National Trust.
St. Osyth's Priory - St. Osyth
Was Augustinian Abbey for 400 years until
dissolution in 1537, 13th-18th century
buildings. 13th century chapel. Wonderful
gatehouse containing works of art
including ceramics & Chinese Jade.
Spains Hall - Finchingfield
Elizabethan Manor incorporating parts of
earlier timber structure. Paintings,
furniture & tapestries.

Cathedrals & Churches

Brightlingsea (All Saints)
15th century tower - some mediaeval
painting fragments. Brasses.
Castle Hedingham (St. Nicholas)
12th century doorways, 14th century rood
screen, 15th century stalls, 16th century
hammer beams, altar tomb.
Copford (St. Michael & All Angels)
12th century wall paints. Continuous
vaulted nave & chancel
.**Finchingfield** (St. John the Baptist)
Norman workmanship. 16th century tomb
-18th centuary tower & cupola.
Layer Marney (St. Mary)
Tudor brickwork, Renaissance
monuments, mediaeval screens, wall
paintings.
Little Maplestead (St. John the Baptist)
14th century, one of the five round

churches in England, having hexagonal
nave, circular aisle, 14th century arcade.
Newport (St. Mary the Virgin)
13th century. Interesting 13th century
altar (portable) with top which becomes
reredos when opened. 15th century
chancel screen. Pre-Reformation Lectern.
Some old glass.

Museums & Galleries

Dutch Cottage Museum - Canvey Island
17th century thatched cottage of octagonal
Dutch design. Exhibition of models of
shipping used on the Thames through the
ages.
Ingatestone Hall - Ingatestone
Documents & pictures of Essex.
The Castle - Colchester
Norman Keep now exhibiting
archeological material from Essex &
especially Roman Colchester.
Southchurch Hall - Southend-on-Sea
14th century moated & timber framed
manor house - Tudor wing, furnished as
meiaeval manor.
Thurrock - Grays
Prehistoric, Romano-British & pagan
Saxon archaeology.

Other things to see & do

Colchester Oyster Fishery - Colchester
Tour showing cultivating, harvesting,
grading & packing of oysters. Talk, tour
& sample.

Burnham on Crouch.

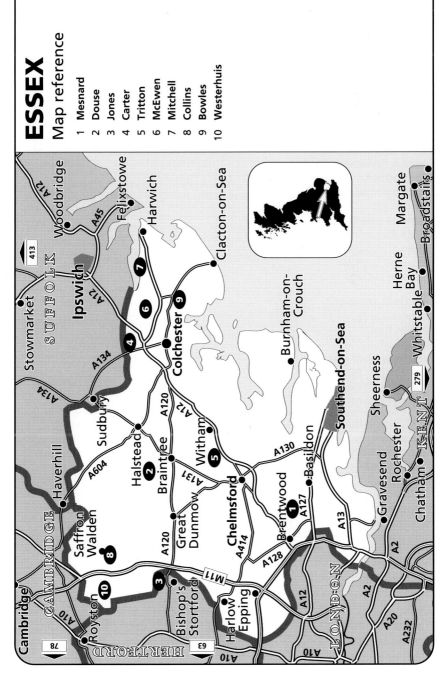

ESSEX

Map reference

1 Mesnard
2 Douse
3 Jones
4 Carter
5 Tritton
6 McEwen
7 Mitchell
8 Collins
9 Bowles
10 Westerhuis

		rate from £ per person	children taken	evening meals	animals taken
Mrs Margaret Mesnard **Oakwood House** **126 Norsey Road** **Billericay CM11 1BH** **Tel/Fax: (01277) 655865** **Open: ALL YEAR (Excl. Xmas & New Year)** **Map Ref No. 01**	Nearest Road: A.129 A detached Tudor-style house with a large rear garden backing onto Norsey Woods Nature Reserve. Accommodation is offered in a choice of 3 en-suite bedrooms or 1 single room with private bathroom. Each room is equipped with a tea/coffee-making facilities & colour T.V.. Guests may relax in their own T.V. lounge, or in the conservatory overlooking the garden. An ideal location for visiting London. Children over 5 yrs.	£20.00	Y	N	N
Peter & Rosemary Jones **The Cottage** **71 Birchanger Lane** **Birchanger** **Bishops Stortford** **CM23 5QA** **Tel/Fax: (01279) 812349** **Open: ALL YEAR** **Map Ref No. 03**	Nearest Road: A.120, M.11 Situated within a quiet village, this charming 17th-century listed house offers 8 very comfortable en-suite bedrooms, all with colour T.V. & tea/coffee makers. Oak-panelled reception rooms with log burners, & a conservatory/dining room looking onto mature gardens. A convenient base for trips to Cambridge, London & East Anglia, & within easy reach of Stansted Airport & Bishops Stortford. Private parking available. A delightful home, ideal for a relaxing short break. CREDIT CARD VISA M'CARD	£22.50	Y	Y	N
Mrs Delia Douse **Spicers Farm** **Rotten End** **Wethersfield** **Braintree CM7 4AL** **Tel: (01371) 851021** **Open: ALL YEAR** **Map Ref No. 02**	Nearest Road: A.120 Rotten End is a quiet, secluded hamlet in an area designated of special landscape value. The attractive farmhouse is well-situated & offers 3 charming & comfortable en-suite bedrooms with colour T.V., tea/coffee-making facilities, clock/radio & lovely views. Enjoy a delicious breakfast in the sunny conservatory overlooking the large garden. Conveniently situated for Harwich, Stansted & Cambridge.	£15.00	Y	N	N
Mrs Linda Tritton **The Wick** **Terling Hall Road** **Hatfield Peverel** **Chelmsford CM3 2EZ** **Tel: (01245) 380705** **Open: ALL YEAR** **Map Ref No. 05**	Nearest Road: A.12 Grade II listed, 16th-century farmhouse in a pleasant rural setting. A large garden, with duck ponds and stream. Accommodation is in 2 attractive & comfortable bedrooms, 1 single, 1 twin, with private guest bathroom. A cosy drawing room with log fire, books, games, T.V., video. Delicious home-cooked meals are served in the dining room or large pine kitchen. Easy access to London and east-coast ports.	£19.00	Y	Y	N
Col. & Mrs Jeremy Carter **Round Hill House** **Church Road** **Boxted** **Colchester CO4 5ST** **Tel/Fax: (01206) 272392** **Open: ALL YEAR** **Map Ref No. 04**	Nearest Road: A.134 Round Hill House is an attractive, comfortable house with beautiful views & a delightful garden set in Constable country overlooking the Dedham Vale, with tennis & coarse fishing available on the premises. On the doorstep is rural East Anglia with its mediaeval villages, great churches & antique shops. Also, music festivals, art galleries, great houses & beautiful gardens. Walking, racing at Newmarket, golf, riding, trout fishing & safe beaches are all within easy distance.	£18.00	Y	Y	Y

	rate from £ per person	children taken	evening meals	animals taken
Helen Bowles **Hockley Place, Frating** **Colchester CO7 7HF** **Tel: (01206) 251703** **Fax 01206 251578** **Open: ALL YEAR (Excl.** **Xmas & New Year)** **Map Ref No. 09** Nearest Road: A.133 Hockley Place, built in the Lutyens style, has 3 en-suite, attractive & well-appointed bedrooms with T.V. & tea/coffee facilities. (Extra-long beds.) An excellent 5-course dinner is served in the beamed dining room. Ideally situated for the Harwich ferry, Beth Chatto's gardens, Colchester's Norman castle & Constable country. The gymnasium & heated outdoor swimming pool are also available to guests. Licensed. Children over 12. (No Smoking) CREDIT CARD VISA M'CARD	£28.00	Y	Y	N
Mr & Mrs C. McEwen **Aldhams** **Bromley Road, Lawford** **Manningtree CO11 2NE** **Tel: (01206) 393210** **Fax 01255 870722** **Open:ALL YEAR (Excl. Xmas)** **Map Ref No. 06** Nearest Road: A.120, A.137 Set in 3 acres of grounds, Aldhams is a fine example of a converted Queen Anne farmhouse. The charming hosts offer 3 elegantly furnished bedrooms, each with radio, tea/coffee-making facilities & colour T.V., 2 with en-suite bathroom. A Full English or Continental breakfast is served. Vegetarians catered for. Within easy reach of Colchester (Britain's oldest recorded town), Norwich, London & Constable country. (No Smoking)	£18.00	Y	N	N
Mrs H. P. Mitchell **New Farm House** **Spinnel's Lane** **Wix** **Manningtree CO11 2UJ** **Tel: (01255) 870365** **Fax 01255 870837** **Open: ALL YEAR** **Map Ref No. 07** Nearest Road: A.120 Modern farmhouse set in picturesque garden welcomes visitors with its friendly atmosphere. The location offers proximity to Constable Country, Colchester & Ipswich, & is within 10 min's drive of Harwich Port. 12 bedrooms, all with colour T.V., radio, tea & coffee. Option of en-suite facilities. 2 guests' lounges, including snack-making facilities. Menu for breakfast, with choice of farmhouse, Continental, etc. Children very welcome: cots, etc., & play area with equipment & space for general activities. Residential licence. CREDIT CARD VISA M'CARD	£18.50	Y	Y	Y
Arthur & Susan Collins **The Stow** **Great Sampford** **Saffron Walden** **CB10 2RG** **Tel: (01799) 586354** **Open: ALL YEAR (Excl. Xmas)** **Map Ref No. 08** Nearest Road: B.1053, A.184 The Stow is a lovely 16th-century farmhouse, situated in the centre of the delightfully attractive village of Great Sampford. The house itself is a real treat, featuring beamed ceilings, buttoned chairs, Persian rugs, patchwork & embroidered cushions. The kitchen is pinewood, & delicious meals are prepared on the large Aga cooker. Accommodation is in 3 rooms, with modern amenities & tea/coffee-making facilities. Also, a residents' colour T.V. lounge, & a super garden.	£25.00	Y	Y	Y
Mrs Tineke Westerhuis **Rockells Farm** **Duddenhoe End** **Saffron Walden** **CB11 4UY** **Tel: (01763) 838053** **Open: ALL YEAR** **Map Ref No. 10** Nearest Road: A.11.M, B.1039 Rockells is an arable farm in a beautiful corner of Essex. The Georgian house has a large garden with a 3-acre lake for private fishing. All 3 rooms have private facilities. 1 room is on the ground floor. On the farm are several footpaths. Beautiful villages in the area. Within easy reach are Audley End House, Duxford Air Museum & Cambridge. London is approx. 1 hour by car or train. Stansted Airport 30 mins by car.	£18.00	Y	N	N

Gloucestershire

Gloucestershire
(Heart of England)

The landscape is so varied the people speak not of one Gloucestershire but of three - Cotswold, Vale & Forest. The rounded hills of the Cotswolds sweep & fold in graceful compositions to form a soft & beautiful landscape in which nestle many pretty villages. To the east there are wonderful views of the Vale of Berkeley & Severn, & across to the dark wooded slopes of the Forest of Dean on the Welsh borders.

Hill Forts, ancient trackways & long barrows of neolithic peoples can be explored, & remains of many villas from late Roman times can be seen. A local saying "Scratch Gloucester & find Rome" reveals the lasting influence of the Roman presence. Three major roads mark the path of invasion & settlement. Akeman street leads to London, Ermine street & the Fosse Way to the north east. A stretch of Roman road with its original surface can be seen at Blackpool Bridge in the Forest of Dean, & Cirencester's museum reflects its status as the second most important Roman city in the country.

Offa's Dyke, 80 miles of bank & ditch on the Welsh border was the work of the Anglo-Saxons of Mercia who invaded in the wake of the Romans. Cotswold means "hills of the sheepcotes" in the Anglo-Saxon tongue, & much of the heritage of the area has its roots in the wealth created by the wool industry here.

Fine Norman churches such as those at Tewkesbury & Bishops Cleeve were overshadowed by the development of the perpendicular style of building made possible by the growing prosperity. Handsome 15th century church towers crown many wool towns & villages as at Northleach, Chipping Camden & Cirencester, & Gloucester has a splendid 14th century cathedral. Detailing on church buildings gives recognition to the source of the wealth-cloth-workers shears are depicted on the north west buttresses of Grantham church tower & couchant rams decorate church buttresses at Compton Bedale.

Wool & cloth weaving dominated life here in the 14th & 15th centuries with most families dependent on the industry. The cottage craft of weaving was gradually overtaken by larger looms & water power. A water mill can be seen in the beautiful village of Lower Slaughter & the cottages of Arlington Row in Bibury were a weaving factory.

The Cotswold weaving industry gave way to the growing force of the Lancashire mills but a few centres survive. At Witney you can still buy the locally made blankets for which the town is famous.

From the 16th century the wealthy gentry built parks & mansions. Amongst the most notable are the Jacobean Manor house at Stanway & the contrasting Palladian style mansion at Barnsley Park. Elizabethan timber frame buildings can be seen at Didbrook, Dymock & Deerhurst but houses in the local mellow golden limestone are more common, with Chipping Camden providing excellent examples.

Cheltenham was only a village when, in 1716 a local farmer noticed a flock of pigeons pecking at grains of salt around a saline spring in his fields. He began to bottle & sell the water & in 1784 his son-in-law, Henry Skillicorne, built a pump room & the place received the name of Cheltenham Spa. Physicians published treatises on the healing qualities of the waters, visitors began to flock there & Cheltenham grew in style & elegance.

Gloucestershire

Gloucestershire Gazeteer

Areas of outstanding natural beauty
The Cotswolds, Malvern Hills & the Wye Valley

Houses & Castles

Ashleworth Court - Ashleworth
15th century limestone Manor house. Stone newel staircase.

Berkeley Castle - Berkeley
12th century castle - still occupied by the Berkeley family. Magnificent collections of furniture, paintings, tapestries & carved timber work. Lovely terraced gardens & deer park.

Chavenage - Tetbury
Elizabethan Cotswold Manor house, Cromwellian associations.

Clearwell Castle - Nr. Coleford
A Georgian neo-Gothic house said to be oldest in Britain, recently restored.

Court House - Painswick
Cotswold Manor house - has original court room & bedchamber of Charles I. Splendid panelling & antique furniture.

Kelmscott Manor - Nr. Lechlade
16th century country house - 17th century additions. Examples of work of William Morris, Rosetti & Burne-Jones.

Owlpen Manor - Nr. Dursley
Historic group of traditional Cotswold stone buildings. Tudor Manor house with church, barn, court house & a grist mill. Holds a rare set of 17th century painted cloth wall hangings.

Snowshill Manor - Broadway
Tudor house with 17th century facade. Unique collection of musical instruments & clocks, toys, etc. Formal garden.

Sudeley Castle - Winchcombe
12th century - home of Katherine Parr, is rich in historical associations, contains art treasures & relics of bygone days.

Cathedrals & Churches

Gloucester Cathedral
Birthplace of Perpendicular style in 14th century. Fan vaulting, east windows commemorate Battle of Crecy - Norman Chapter House.

Prinknash Abbey - Gloucester
14th & 16th century - Benedictine Abbey.

Tewkesbury Abbey - Tewkesbury
Dates back to Norman times, contains Romanesque & Gothic styles. 14th century monuments.

Bishops Cleeve (St. Michael & All Saints)
12th century with 17th century gallery.Magnificent Norman West front & south porch.Decorated chancel. Fine window.

Bledington (St.Leonards)
15th century glass in this perpendicular church--Norman bellcote.Early English east window.

Buckland (St. Michael)
13th century nave arcades. 17th century oak panelling, 15th century glass.

Cirencester (St. John the Baptist)
A magnificent church - remarkable exterior, 3 storey porch, 2 storey oriel windows, traceries & pinnacles. Wine-glass pulpit c.1450. 15th century glass in east window, monuments in Lady chapel.

Hailes Abbey - Winchcombe
14th century wall paintings, 15th century tiles, glass & screen, 17th century pulpit. Elizabethan benches.

Newland (All Saints)
13th century, restored 18th century. Pinnacled west tower; effigies.

Museums & Galleries

Bishop Hooper's Lodgings - Gloucester
3 Tudor timber frame buildings - museum of domestic life & agriculture in Gloucester since 1500.

Bourton Motor Museum - Bourton-on-the-Water
Collection of cars & motor cycles - also vintage advertising.

Cheltenham Art Gallery - Cheltenham
Gallery of Dutch paintings, collection of oils, watercolours, pottery, porcelain, English & Chinese; furniture.

City Wall & Bastion - Gloucester
Roman & mediaeval city defences in an underground exhibition room.

Stroud Museum - Cirencester
Depicts earlier settlements in the area & has a very fine collection of Roman antiquities.

Gloucestershire

Lower Slaughter.

Historic Monuments

Chedworth Roman Villa - Yanworth
Remains of Romano-British villa.
Belas Knap Long Barrow - Charlton Abbots
Neolithic burial ground - three burial chambers with external entrances.
Hailes Abbey - Stanway
Ruins of beautiful mediaeval abbey built by son of King John, 1246.
Witcombe Roman Villa - Nr. Birdlip
Large Roman villa - Hypocaust & mosaic pavements preserved.
Hetty Pegler's Tump - Uley
Long Barrow - fairly complete, chamber is 120 feet long.

Ashleworth Tithe Barn - Ashleworth
15th century tithe barn - 120 feet long - stone built, interesting roof timbering.
Odda's Chapel - Deerhurst
Rare Saxon chapel dating back to 1056.

Other things to see & do

Cheltenham International Festival of Music & Literature - Annual event.
Cotswolds Farm Park - dozens of rare breeds of farm animals
The Three Choirs Festival - music festival staged in alternating years at Gloucester, Hereford & Worcester Cathedrals.
Slimbridge - Peter Scott's Wildfowl Trust.

GLOUCESTERSHIRE

Map reference

1	Royce
2	Farley
2	Minchin
2	Ellis
3	Adams
3	Wright
3	Bolton
4	Gisby
6	Milton
6	Berg
6	Stone
6	Medforth
7	Enstone
8	Beauvoisin
9	Burrough
10	Woolford
11	Loving
12	Wilson
12	Carey-Wilson
13	Brown
15	Cassidy
16	Alexander
17	Gomm
18	Parsons
19	Fletcher
20	Beddows
21	Reid
22	Helm
23	Alderson
24	Dean
25	Anderson
26	Thompson
28	Wells
29	Blatchley
30	Peacock
31	Keyte
31	Allen
32	Herford
33	Hassell
33	Brunsdon
37	Tremellen
39	Saunders

		rate from £ per person	children taken	evening meals	animals taken
Michael & Annette Royce **Kings Head Inn &** **Restaurant** **The Green** **Bledington OX7 6HD** **Tel/Fax: (01608) 658365** **Open: ALL YEAR** **Map Ref No. 01**	Nearest Road: B.4450 Facing the village green complete with brook & ducks (all known locally by name) stands the 15th-century Kings Head Inn. Ideally situated in the heart of the Cotswolds, the Kings Head retains the olde worlde charm of bygone years, with original old beams, an inglenook fireplace, pews & settles. 12 charming rooms with full facilities, T.V. & 'phone. An inventive personal cuisine with an excellent reputation & value. Golf, fishing & horseriding all nearby. CREDIT CARD VISA M'CARD	£30.00	Y	Y	N
Graham & Diana Ellis **Coombe House** **Rissington Road** **Bourton-on-the-Water** **GL54 2DT** **Tel: (01451) 821966** **Fax 01451 810477** **Open: ALL YEAR** **Map Ref No. 02**	Nearest Road: A.429, A.424 This quiet Cotswold home offers gentle elegance, a garden with unusual plants, & an easy riverside walk to the renowned village centre. The 7 pretty, thoughtfully equipped bedrooms have en-suite facilities. A delightful small drawing room. Heaps of assistance. Ample parking. Begin the day with a delicious English/Continental breakfast, then meander through the beautiful Cotswolds. Within easy reach of Hidcote, Barnsley, Oxford, Blenheim, Stratford & Warwick. CREDIT CARD VISA M'CARD AMEX	£26.00	Y	N	N
Sean & Sylvia Farley **Rooftrees** **Rissington Road** **Bourton-on-the-Water** **GL54 2EB** **Tel: (01451) 821943** **Open: ALL YEAR** **Map Ref No. 02**	Nearest Road: A.429, A.424 Warmth, comfort & hospitality are offered in the relaxed atmosphere of this detached Cotswold stone guest house, situated on the edge of the famous village of Bourton-on-the-Water. Offering 3 en-suite bedrooms, 2 with 4-poster beds & 2 on the ground floor. Traditional English home-cooking, using fresh produce. An enjoyable stay is assured here while visiting the Cotswolds. Evening meals by arrangement. CREDIT CARD VISA M'CARD	£19.00	Y	Y	N
Mrs J. Bolton **Clapton Manor** **Clapton-on-the-Hill** **Bourton-on-the-Water** **GL54 2LG** **Tel: (01451) 810202** **Open: ALL YEAR** **Map Ref No. 03**	Nearest Road: A.40 Clapton Manor is a 17th-century house situated at the top of a secluded village with stunning views across the Windrush Valley. Period furniture & large inglenook fireplaces lend an atmosphere of informal comfort. 2 bedrooms, 1 with a private bathroom & the other with a bathroom en-suite. Dinner & breakfast are served either in the dining room or, weather permitting, on the terrace. Within easy reach of Oxford, Cheltenham & Stratford.	£20.00	Y	Y	N
Mrs J. M. Wright **Farncombe** **Clapton-on-the-Hill** **Bourton-on-the-Water** **GL54 2LG** **Tel: (01451) 820120** **Fax 01451 820120** **Open: ALL YEAR** **Map Ref No. 03**	Nearest Road: A.429, A.40 Come & share the peace, tranquility & superb views of Farncombe, & eat, drink & sleep - smoke-free - 700ft above sea level & only 2 miles from Bourton-on-the-Water. 2 attractive doubles, with showers, & 1 twin en-suite. A spacious dining room, with tea/coffee-making facilities, & a comfortable T.V. lounge. There is a large selection of tourist information, maps & books & current menus for your choice when eating out. Numerous walks & drives, with easy access to all attractions & places of interest.	£18.00	N	N	N

Gloucestershire

		rate from £ per person	children taken	evening meals	animals taken
Mrs Helen Adams **Upper Farm** **Clapton-on-the-Hill** **Bourton-on-the-Water** **GL54 2LG** **Tel: (01451) 820453** **Open: MAR - NOV** **Map Ref No. 03**	Nearest Road: A.40, A.429 If peace & tranquility is what you require, then this charming undiscovered village 2 miles from Bourton is certainly the spot. Clapton enjoys one of the finest Cotswold views from its hill position. Here, you will find Upper Farm, with its 17th-century stone farmhouse lovingly restored & yet retaining a wealth of original charm. Delightful accommodation, commanding views & personal attention are complemented with fresh farmhouse fayre. Children over 6 yrs.	£16.00 (non-smoking)	Y	N	N
Mrs Elizabeth Beauvoisin **The Old Rectory** **Church Street, Willersey** **Broadway WR12 7PN** **Tel: (01386) 853729** **Fax 01386 858061** **Open: ALL YEAR** **Map Ref No. 08**	Nearest Road: A.44 Hidden at the end of a lane, opposite the 11th-century church, this old Georgian rectory, built of Cotswold stone, is very quiet & comfortable. Superb en-suite, spacious rooms, 4-posters. In winter, a roaring log fire greets you at breakfast, in the elegant dining room, & in summer the walled garden, with its 300-year-old Mulberry tree, offers tranquility. T.V. & all amenities. Only 300 yards to the 13th-century Bell Inn, serving excellent meals. Good walking/touring country.	£25.00 (non-smoking) CREDIT CARD VISA M'CARD	Y	N	N
Sybil Gisby **College House** **Chapel Street** **Broadwell GL56 0TW** **Tel: (01451) 832351** **Open: ALL YEAR (Excl. Xmas & New Year)** **Map Ref No. 04**	Nearest Road: A.429 Hidden in an enchanting & unspoilt Cotswold village, College House offers the most luxurious accommodation in lovely bedrooms with en-suite facilities. Exposed beams & ancient flagstone floors, & mullioned windows with hand-painted shutters. A tranquil sitting room, with a massive stone fireplace. Every comfort is provided, & Mrs Gisby enjoys spending time with her guests. This is the ideal base for a relaxing break.	£21.00	N	Y	N
Jane & Michael Medforth **Lypiatt House** **Lypiatt Road** **Cheltenham GL50 2QW** **Tel: (01242) 224994** **Fax 01242 224996** **Open: ALL YEAR** **Map Ref No. 06**	Nearest Road: A.40 Lypiatt House is situated 5 mins' walk from the attractive area of Montpelier. It was built towards the end of the last century, & is set in its own grounds. There is an elegant drawing room & charming conservatory, & each of the 10 comfortable bedrooms has its own private bathroom, direct-dial telephone, T.V. & other amenities. The emphasis is on comfort, relaxation & a friendly personal service.	£27.50 CREDIT CARD VISA M'CARD AMEX	Y	N	N
Stephanie & St. John Milton **Milton House Hotel** **12 Royal Parade** **Bayshill Road** **Cheltenham GL50 3AY** **Tel: (01242) 582601** **Fax 01242 222326** **Open: ALL YEAR** **Map Ref No. 06**	Nearest Road: A.40, M.5 Milton House stands in a quiet tree-lined avenue of elegant Regency homes. Situated just a 4-min stroll from the imposing promenade, restaurants & the Imperial Gardens. Guests have a choice of 8 en-suite, individually styled & decorated bedrooms, all with colour T.V., 'phone & tea/coffee makers. A choice of healthy & generously proportioned breakfasts is available, together with the morning papers. There is also a pretty sun lounge with bar & T.V.. An ideal base from which to explore the lovely Cotswolds.	£25.00 *see PHOTO over* CREDIT CARD VISA M'CARD AMEX	Y	N	N

Milton House Hotel. Cheltenham.

Gloucestershire

		rate from £ per person	children taken	evening meals	animals taken
John & Marian Enstone **Cleeve Hill Hotel** **Cleeve Hill** **Cheltenham** **GL52 3PR** **Tel: (01242) 672052** **Open: ALL YEAR** **Map Ref No. 07**	Nearest Road: M.5, B.4632 Situated in an Area of Outstanding Natural Beauty, Cleeve Hill has the friendly, relaxed atmosphere of a family home. All bedrooms have superb views, some to the Malvern Hills, & all are en-suite & equipped to the highest standards with 'phone, T.V., radio/alarm & beverage facilities. The excellent breakfasts are generous, & provide the perfect start to the day. Located in the heart of the Cotswolds, it is ideally placed for visiting Bath, Oxford, Stratford, Warwick. Children over 8. *see PHOTO over* CREDIT CARD VISA M'CARD AMEX	£30.00	Y	N	N
Jurgen & Annette Berg **Hollington House Hotel** **115 Hales Road** **Cheltenham GL52 6ST** **Tel: (01242) 256652** **Fax 01242 570280** **Open: ALL YEAR** **Map Ref No. 06**	Nearest Road: A.40, A.435 An elegant Victorian house, easy to find off the London Road/A.40, with a large garden, croquet lawn & ample parking. Spacious bedrooms, with en-suite facilities, tea/coffee trays & colour T.V.. Good food for breakfast & dinner, with a choice of menu. A pleasant, relaxed atmosphere, with proprietors' personal attention, & a comfortable lounge with a bar. The perfect location, within easy driving distance of Oxford, Bath, Stratford-upon-Avon & the beautiful Cotswolds. CREDIT CARD VISA M'CARD AMEX	£25.00	Y	Y	N
Mera & Bev Stone **Charlton House** **18 Greenhills Road** **Charlton Kings** **Cheltenham GL53 9EB** **Tel/Fax: (01242) 238997** **Open: ALL YEAR** **Map Ref No. 06**	Nearest Road: A.435 Charlton House is a friendly, family-run guest house located in a good residential area of Cheltenham with views of the Cotswold Hills. This comfortable home is fully double-glazed & centrally heated, with good-quality fitments & furnishings throughout. Excellent home-cooking. Your special dietary requirements provided for by a trained nutritionist. Reductions for extended stays. Ample off-road parking.	£20.00	Y	Y	N
Michael & Pamela Minchin **The Ridge** **Whiteshoots Hill** **Bourton-on-the-Water** **Cheltenham GL54 2LE** **Tel: (01451) 820660** **Open: ALL YEAR** **Map Ref No. 02**	Nearest Road: A.429, A.40 The Ridge stands in 2 acres of beautiful secluded grounds just 1 mile from the centre of Bourton-on-the-Water. A large country house with 5 individually decorated, centrally heated bedrooms, most with en-suite facilities. 1 is on the ground floor. This house provides an extremely pleasant & comfortable base for touring the Cotswolds. A delicious Full English breakfast is served. Good restaurants & pubs nearby serve excellent evening meals. Children over 6 years welcome.	£16.00	Y	N	N
Jenny & David Burrough **Windrush Farm** **Bourton-on-the-Water** **Cheltenham GL54 3BY** **Tel: (01451) 820419** **Fax 01451 820419** **Open: MAR - DEC** **Map Ref No. 09**	Nearest Road: A.436 This 150-acre farm is situated in the heart of the glorious Cotswolds, renowned for its beauty & interest. The traditional, stone-mullioned farmhouse has a lovely garden & commands superb views, & yet is only 2 miles from Bourton. The guest rooms are tastefully furnished, & comprise 1 twin-bedded & 1 double room, with en-suite bathrooms & beverage-making facilities. A delicious English breakfast is served. Jenny & David enjoy helping to plan your day.	£18.00	N	N	N

Cleeve Hill Hotel. Cleeve Hill.

Westward. Sudeley.

Gloucestershire

		rate from £ per person	children taken	evening meals	animals taken
Susan Woolford **Cotteswold House** **Market Place, Northleach** **Cheltenham GL54 3EG** **Tel: (01451) 860493** **Open: ALL YEAR (Excl. Xmas Day)** **Map Ref No. 10**	Nearest Road: A.40, A.429 This is a fine listed Cotswold stone house, & having been carefully renovated to a high standard, it shows some architectural features of note. The bedrooms, of individual character, are comfortably furnished. Private facilities are available at most times. Northleach is a quiet town of historical interest & an ideal base from which to tour the beautiful Cotswolds. Within easy reach of Bath, Stratford-upon-Avon etc.	£18.50	Y	N	N
Pauline Loving **Northfield B & B** **Cirencester Road** **Northleach** **Cheltenham GL54 3JL** **Tel: (01451) 860427** **Open: ALL YEAR** **Map Ref No. 11**	Nearest Road: A.429, A.40 Northfield is a detached family house in the country, with large gardens, & own garden produce to complement home-cooking. Close to all local services in the small market town of Northleach. Accommodation is in 3 very comfortable en-suite bedrooms. It is an excellent centre for visiting many lovely Cotswold villages. Also easily reached by car are Cheltenham, Oxford, Cirencester & Stratford-upon-Avon.	£18.00	Y	Y	N
Mrs Susie Wilson **Westward** **Sudeley** **Winchcombe** **Cheltenham GL54 5JB** **Tel: (01242) 604372** **Fax 01242 604372** **Open: ALL YEAR** **Map Ref No. 12**	Nearest Road: A.40, A.46 The Wilson families share this beautiful Georgian house on the scarp of the Cotswolds above Sudeley Castle, sitting within its own 600-acre estate with spectacular views to the Malverns. The heart of the Cotswolds is very close, with Broadway, Oxford & Stratford within easy reach. The Wilsons combine good food - Susie trained at Prue Leith's - with elegance & comfort in a relaxed family home. There are 2 attractively furnished en-suite rooms available. *see PHOTO over* CREDIT CARD VISA M'CARD	£29.00	Y	Y	Y
Nick & Jean Brown **The Malt House** **Broad Campden** **Chipping Campden** **GL55 6UU** **Tel: (01386) 840295** **Fax 01386 841334** **Open: ALL YEAR** **Map Ref No. 13**	Nearest Road: A.44, A.429 Nick & Jean Brown have achieved a blend of relaxed & yet professional service, welcoming guests as part of an extended house party. This 17th-century former malting house is set in extensive gardens, with orchard & croquet lawn. Public rooms are furnished with antiques. Bedrooms are en-suite & individually decorated, with T.V., tea/coffee & hairdryers, & overlook the gardens. The Windrush Suite has an 18th-century 4-poster bed, & family & private garden suites are available. The accomplished chef serves a table d'hote evening meal using ingredients from the kitchen gardens. English breakfasts equally good. *see PHOTO over* CREDIT CARD VISA M'CARD	£35.00	Y	Y	Y

When booking your accommodation please mention
The Best Bed & Breakfast

The Malt House. Broad Campden.

Shawswell Country House. Rendcomb.

Winstone Glebe. Winstone.

Gloucestershire

		rate from £ per person	children taken	evening meals	animals taken

Ian & Mary Cassidy **Waterton Garden Cottage** **Ampney Crucis** **Cirencester** **GL7 5RX** Tel: **(01285) 851303** Open: **ALL YEAR (Excl. Xmas)** **Map Ref No. 15**	Nearest Road: A.417 Situated in the heart of the Cotswolds, Waterton Garden Cottage, part of a late-Victorian stable block, has been sympathetically converted, & retains many original features. A high standard of comfort, & an ambience which would match many small country houses, are to be found. All bedrooms are en-suite & one can expect fine cuisine & attention to detail without unnecessary formality. Every effort is made to ensure that your stay is both memorable & enjoyable.	£25.00	N	Y	N
David & Muriel Gomm **Shawswell Country House** **Rendcomb** **Cirencester GL7 7HD** Tel: **(01285) 831779** Open: **FEB - NOV** **Map Ref No. 17**	Nearest Road: A.435 A glorious hillside location, offering peace & tranquility. Set in 25 acres overlooking the Churn Valley. A lovely 17th-century house, which has been lovingly restored, & it boasts a wealth of beams, cosy inglenooks & 5 superb en-suite bedrooms. A 4-poster also. The emphasis is on personal service, high standards & imaginative home cooking. Ideally situated in the heart of the Cotswolds, with excellent facilities for walking, cycling, riding, golf & touring. Children over 10.	£22.50 *see PHOTO over*	Y	N	N
Shaun & Susanna Parsons **Winstone Glebe** **Winstone** **Cirencester** **GL7 7JU** Tel: **(01285) 821451** Fax 01285 821451 Open: **ALL YEAR** **Map Ref No. 18**	Nearest Road: A.417 A small Georgian rectory overlooking a Saxon church in a Domesday-listed village, enjoying spectacular rural views. Ideal for exploring Cotswold market towns, with their mediaeval churches, antique shops & rich local history. 3 delightful rooms, with private/en-suite bathroom. Being an Area of Outstanding Natural Beauty, there are many well-signposted walks. The more energetic can borrow a bicycle & explore , or just enjoy warm hospitality & good food produced by Susanna, who was a professional cook.	£22.00 *see PHOTO over* CREDIT CARD VISA M'CARD	Y	Y	Y
Mr & Mrs R. Fletcher **Tudor Farmhouse Hotel** **High Street, Clearwell** **Coleford GL16 8JS** Tel: **(01594) 833046** Fax 01594 837093 Open: **ALL YEAR** **Map Ref No. 19**	Nearest Road: A.466 Situated in the charming village between the Forest of Dean & the beautiful Wye Valley, this 13th-century farmhouse features oak beams & original wall panelling, as well as an historic spiral staircase. Accommodation comprises 9 rooms, including 4-poster bedrooms, all en-suite with colour T.V., 'phone & tea/coffee-making facilities. Facilities include a cocktail bar, a conservatory & a candlelit dining room.	£25.00 *see PHOTO over* CREDIT CARD VISA M'CARD AMEX	Y	Y	Y
Mrs Carol Alexander **The Old School House** **Whittles Lane** **Frampton-on-Severn** **Gloucester GL2 7EB** Tel: **(01452) 740457** Open: **ALL YEAR** **Map Ref No. 16**	Nearest Road: A.38 The Old School House is situated in a quiet backwater in the picturesque village of Frampton-on-Severn, which is steeped in history & boasts the longest village green in England. 2 attractive bedrooms, 1 en-suite & 1 with a private bathroom. Each has tea/coffee-making facilities. A comfortable sitting room with T.V. for guests' use, & also a pretty garden. Charming hosts with a number of friendly pet dogs. An ideal base for a relaxing break, with many places of interest nearby.	£20.00	Y	N	Y

Tudor Farmhouse. Clearwell.

Hunters Lodge. Minchinhampton.

Gloucestershire

		rate from £ per person	children taken	evening meals	animals taken
Mrs Elizabeth Beddows **New House Farm** **Barrel Lane** **Longhope** **GL17 0LS** **Tel: (01452) 830484** **Open: ALL YEAR** **Map Ref No. 20**	Nearest Road: A.40, M.50 Clive & Betty Beddows give you a warm welcome to their Georgian farmhouse, set in 80 acres of farmland, with many lovely walks. Each of the lovely bedrooms have private or en-suite bathrooms, radio/alarms, satellite T.V., electric blankets & tea/coffee-making facilities. Full English breakfast & hearty evening meals are all home-cooked, with a selection of wines from the small but well-stocked bar.	£17.00	Y	Y	Y
Sheila & James Reid **Edale House** **Folly Road, Parkend** **Lydney GL15 4JF** **Tel: (01594) 562835** **Fax 01594 564488** **Open: FEB - DEC** **Map Ref No. 21**	Nearest Road: A.48, B.4234 Edale House is a fine Georgian residence facing the cricket green in the village of Parkend in the heart of the Royal Forest of Dean. Once the home of local G.P. Bill Tandy, author of 'A Doctor in the Forest', the house has been tastefully restored to provide comfortable & attractive en-suite accommodation with every facility for guests. Enjoy delicious dinners prepared by your hosts, previously chef/proprietors of a well-known local restaurant. Children over 12.	£17.50 CREDIT CARD VISA M'CARD	Y	Y	Y
Margaret Helm **Hunters Lodge** **Dr Brown's Road** **Minchinhampton** **GL6 9BT** **Tel: (01453) 883588** **Fax 01453 731449** **Open: ALL YEAR (Excl. Xmas)** **Map Ref No. 22**	Nearest Road: A.419, A.46 A friendly and helpful welcome is assured for guests at this beautifully furnished Cotswold stone country house situated adjoining 600 acres of N.T. common land and golf course. Central heating throughout. All of the pretty bedrooms have colour T.V., tea/coffee facilities and private or en-suite bathrooms. A visitors' lounge, with colour T.V., adjoins a delightful conservatory overlooking a large garden. An ideal centre for Bath, Cheltenham, Cirencester and the Cotswolds. Mrs Helm is a registered tourist guide.	£19.00 *see PHOTO over*	Y	N	Y
David & Caroline Anderson **Gunn Mill House** **Lower Spout Lane** **Mitcheldean GL17 0EA** **Tel: (01594) 827577** **Fax 01594 827577** **Open: ALL YEAR** **Map Ref No. 25**	Nearest Road: A.4136, A.48 Bounded by its mill stream & the Forest of Dean, the Andersons' Georgian country home stands in 5 acres of gardens & meadows. Refurbished to a high standard, the galleried sitting room & large en-suite bedrooms (2 doubles, 1 twin/family suite) are filled with antiques & collectables from around the world. Share your hosts' love of good food, including some ethnic fare, homemade breads & jams. Vegetarians catered for. Liquor licence. Overseas visitors especially welcomed.	£19.50 *see PHOTO over*	Y	Y	Y
Mrs Elizabeth Alderson **Townend Cottage &** **Coach House, High Street** **Moreton-in-Marsh** **GL56 0AD** **Tel: (01608) 650846/651621** **Open: MAR - JAN incl.** **Map Ref No. 23**	Nearest Road: A.429, A.44 This delightful Cotswold stone cottage & its coach house, situated on the edge of Moreton, provide a warm welcome & comfortable accommodation, with an excellent breakfast. All 4 bedrooms have their own character, with heating, colour T.V., tea/coffee facilities & an en-suite or adjoining bathroom. A licensed restaurant & tea garden operates during the daytime (except Mon. & Wed.), & guests may reserve an evening meal in advance, or enjoy Moreton's many restaurants & pubs.	£16.00	Y	N	N

Gunn Mill House. Mitcheldean.

Orchard House. Kilcot.

Gloucestershire

		rate from £ per person	children taken	evening meals	animals taken
Mr & Mrs B. L. Dean **Treetops Guest House** **London Road** **Moreton-in-Marsh** **GL56 0HE** **Tel: (01608) 651036** **Open: ALL YEAR** **Map Ref No. 24**	Nearest Road: A.44 A beautiful family home offering traditional Bed & Breakfast. 6 attractive bedrooms, all with a bathroom en-suite, & 2 of which are on the ground floor and thus suitable for disabled persons or wheelchair users. All rooms have T.V., radio and tea/coffee facilities. Cots and high chairs available. Delightful secluded gardens to relax in. Ideally situated for exploring the Cotswolds. A warm and homely atmosphere awaits you here. CREDIT CARD VISA M'CARD	£20.00	Y	Y	Y
Mrs Anne Thompson **Orchard House** **Aston Ingham Road** **Kilcot** **Newent** **GL18 1NP** **Tel: (01989) 720417** **Open: ALL YEAR** **Map Ref No. 26**	Nearest Road: M.50, B.4222 This beautiful, Tudor-style country house is completely surrounded by 5 acres of well-tended lawns, paddocks & woodland trails. A relaxed & friendly atmosphere with every modern comfort & delicious food - traditional & vegetarian. The elegant & finely furnished rooms include 4 attractive double bedrooms overlooking the gardens, an original beamed T.V. lounge, with log fires in winter, & a spacious dining room. A residential licence. Well located for visiting the Wye Valley, the Cotswolds & the Malverns. *see PHOTO over* CREDIT CARD VISA M'CARD	£19.50	N	Y	N
Mrs Barbara Blatchley **Thorne** **Friday Street** **Painswick** **GL6 6QJ** **Tel: (01452) 812476** **Open: APR - OCT** **Map Ref No. 29**	Nearest Road: A.46 A Grade II listed Tudor cloth-merchants house located in the centre of Painswick. 2 original Market Hall pillars in situ. A perfect example of Cotswold secular architecture. 2 twin bedrooms, each with own shower & toilet. Central heating, tea making & T.V. in each room. A wonderful walking area, including the Cotswold Way. Within easy reach of many tourist attractions including Bath, Stratford, Slimbridge & Berkeley Castle. *see PHOTO over*	£18.00	N	N	N
Mrs Joan Wells **Painswick Mill** **Kingsmill Lane** **Painswick** **GL6 6SA** **Tel: (01452) 812245** **Open: ALL YEAR** **Map Ref No. 28**	Nearest Road: A.46 A beautiful Grade II listed Cotswold stone mill, dating from 1634, is set in 4 acres of lawn & natural garden - traversed by 2 streams, & with a water garden. 2 beamed bedrooms (1 en-suite, the other private) with tea/coffee facilities & T.V.. A lounge, garden & hard tennis court available to guests. Painswick, the Queen of the Cotswolds, is a good base for touring & walking. Superb local pubs & restaurants serve delicious meals. Unsuitable for young children & the disabled.	£25.00	Y	N	N

When booking your accommodation please mention
The Best Bed & Breakfast

Thorne. Painswick.

Cinderhill House. St. Briavels.

Gloucestershire

		rate from £ per person	children taken	evening meals	animals taken
Gillie Peacock **Cinderhill House** **St. Briavels** **GL15 6RH** **Tel: (01594) 530393** **Fax 01594 530098** **Open: ALL YEAR** **Map Ref No. 30**	Nearest Road: A.466 A pretty, 14th-century house tucked into the hill below the castle in St. Briavels, with magnificent views across the Wye Valley to the Brecon Beacons & Black Mountains. A comfortable, lovingly restored & tastefully furnished house with 5 bedrooms (& 2 4-posters), 4 with a private or en-suite bathroom. The host is a professional cook, & takes delight in ensuring that all meals are well cooked using local produce. 3 self-catering cottages, 1 specifically for the disabled. Licensed.	£24.00 *see PHOTO over*	Y	Y	N
Tony & Valerie Keyte **The Limes** **Tewkesbury Road** **Stow-on-the-Wold** **GL54 1EN** **Tel: (01451) 830034** **Open: ALL YEAR** **Map Ref No. 31**	Nearest Road: A.424 A large family house offering excellent accommodation, with 4 rooms, 1 with a 4-poster. All have modern facilities (including T.V., radio & tea/coffee facilities), 2 are en-suite & 1 has a private bathroom. Situated only 4 mins' walk from the centre of town, it overlooks the countryside in a quiet area. A large, attractive garden, with an ornamental pool & waterfall. A choice of good English breakfasts. From here, Bourton-on-the-Water, Broadway, Burford, Chipping Campden & Moreton-in-Marsh are just a short drive away.	£16.00	Y	N	Y
Mr & Mrs B. Allen **Bretton House** **Fosseway** **Stow-on-the-Wold** **GL54 1JU** **Tel: (01451) 830388** **Open: ALL YEAR (Excl. Xmas)** **Map Ref No. 31**	Nearest Road: A.429 Bretton House is an elegant Edwardian residence, tastefully furnished to high standards, combining good cooking with comfort & a friendly atmosphere. Set in the heart of the Cotswolds, with glorious views, there is 1 twin room & 2, 4-poster double rooms, all with en-suite bathrooms, colour T.V. & tea/coffee-making facilities. Centrally situated for exploring all of the Cotswolds, making the ideal setting for restful breaks. Set in its own grounds of 2 acres, just a few mins' walk from Stow.	£21.00	N	Y	Y
Queenie Mary Hassell **Burleigh Cottage** **Burleigh** **Minchinhampton** **Stroud GL5 2PW** **Tel: (01453) 884703** **Open: ALL YEAR** **Map Ref No. 33**	Nearest Road: A.419 Situated on 600 acres of Minchinhampton Common (designated as an Area of Outstanding Natural Beauty), Burleigh Cottage offers 2 attractively decorated rooms with en-suite bathrooms, tea/coffee-making facilities, T.V. & beautiful views. Ideal for walking, horse riding, golf or mere relaxation; or for wandering around the many tranquil villages nearby or stopping for refreshment in the delightful tea shops.	£18.00	N	N	N
Sheila & Garth Brunsdon **Hope Cottage Guest House** **Box** **Stroud GL6 9HD** **Tel: (01453) 832076** **Open: FEB - NOV** **Map Ref No. 33**	Nearest Road: A.46, A.419 For peace & tranquility, this charming, undiscovered village 10 miles from Cirencester is unrivalled. Box is in an Area of Outstanding Natural Beauty enjoying glorious Cotswold views. Here, you can savour the charm of this delightful country house, set in 3 acres of landscaped gardens & with a heated pool. Comfortable en-suite rooms, all with colour T.V. & hospitality tray. Sumptuous traditional English breakfasts. The perfect base for exploring this fascinating region.	£17.50 *see PHOTO over*	Y	N	N

Hope Cottage. Box.

Gloucestershire

		rate from £ per person	children taken	evening meals	animals taken
Janet & Tim Tremellen **Tavern House** **Willesley** **Tetbury** **GL8 8QU** **Tel: (01666) 880444** **Fax 01666 880254** **Open: ALL YEAR** **Map Ref No. 37**	Nearest Road: A.433 A Grade II listed, part-17th-century, former staging post, Tavern House has been sympathetically refurbished to provide an exceptionally high standard of accommodation. All rooms have bath & shower en-suite, direct-dial telephones, T.V., etc. Delightful, secluded, walled gardens in which to relax. Ideally situated for Westonbirt Arboretum, & convenient for Bath, Cheltenham & Gloucester. A genuine country-house atmosphere, & an excellent base from which to explore the Cotswolds. Charming inns offering dinner close-by. Children over 10.	£27.50 *see PHOTO over* CREDIT CARD VISA M'CARD	Y	N	N
H. W. Herford **Upper Court** **Kemerton** **Tewkesbury GL20 7HY** **Tel: (01386) 725351** **Fax 01386 725472** **Open: APR - OCT** **Map Ref No. 32**	Nearest Road: A.438 A fine Georgian Cotswold manor near Cheltenham, with an idyllic lake-side setting & 15-acre garden. The delightful home of antique collectors Bill & Diana Herford, who welcome you to enjoy tennis, swimming, croquet, riding, fly-fishing & boating, or tour the Cotswolds. The bedrooms are beautifully decorated, & all are en-suite, 4-posters or twin-bedded; also, charming cottages available (s/c). Fine food & wine; open fires; house parties welcome.	£25.00 CREDIT CARD VISA M'CARD AMEX	Y	Y	Y
Mrs J. G. Saunders **Great House** **Castle Street** **Winchcombe GL54 5JA** **Tel: (01242) 602490** **Open: ALL YEAR** **Map Ref No. 39**	Nearest Road: A.46, B.4632 A superb Jacobean house offering comfortable accommodation with modern facilities. A warm welcome awaits the visitor here. It is only half a mile's walking distance to Sudeley Castle, in the heart of the Cotswolds. There are 2 rooms available with T.V., & 1 with a 4-poster bed. There is also a garden for guests' use. The Great House is an ideal touring centre. Children over 4 years.	£18.00	Y	N	N

WORLDWIDE BED & BREAKFAST ASSOCIATION

When booking your accommodation please mention
The Best Bed & Breakfast

Tavern House. Willesley.

Hampshire

Hampshire (Southern)

Hampshire is located in the centre of the south coast of England & is blessed with much beautiful & unspoilt countryside. Wide open vistas of rich downland contrast with deep wood-lands. Rivers & sparkling streams run through tranquil valleys passing nest-ling villages. There is a splendid coast-line with seaside resorts & harbours, the cathedral city of Winchester & the "jewel" of Hampshire, the Isle of Wight.

The north of the county is known as the Hampshire Borders. Part of this countryside was immortalised by Richard Adams & the rabbits of 'Water-ship Down'. Beacon Hill is a notable hill-top landmark. From its slopes some of the earliest aeroplane flights were made by De Haviland in 1909. Pleas-ure trips & tow-path walks can be taken along the restored Basingstoke Canal.

The New Forest is probably the area most frequented by visitors. It is a landscape of great character with thatched cottages, glades & streams & a romantic beauty. There are herds of deer & the New Forest ponies wander at will. To the N.W. of Beaulieu are some of the most idyllic parts of the old forest, with fewer villages & many little streams that flow into the Avon. Lyndhurst, the "capital" of the New Forest offers a range of shops & has a contentious 19th century church con-structed in scarlet brickwork banded with yellow, unusual ornamental deco-ration, & stained glass windows by William Morris.

The Roman city of Winchester became the capital city of Saxon Wessex & is today the capital of Hamp-shire. It is famous for its beautiful mediaeval cathedral, built during the reign of William the Conquerer & his notorious son Rufus. It contains the great Winchester Bible.

William completed the famous Domesday Book in the city, & Richard Coeur de Lion was crowned in the cathedral in 1194.

Portsmouth & Southampton are major ports & historic maritime cities with a wealth of castles, forts & Naval attractions from battleships to museums.

The channel of the Solent guarded by Martello towers, holds not only Southampton but numerous yachting centres, such as Hamble, Lymington & Bucklers Hard where the ships for Admiral Lord Nelson's fleet were built.

The River Test.

The Isle of Wight

The Isle of Wight lies across the sheltered waters of the Solent, & is easily reached by car or passenger ferry. The chalk stacks of the Needles & the multi-coloured sand at Alum Bay are among the best known of the is-land's natural attractions & there are many excellent beaches & other bays to enjoy. Cowes is a famous interna-tional sailing centre with a large num-ber of yachting events throughout the summer. Ventnor, the most southerly resort is known as the "Madeira of England" & has an exotic botanic gar-den. Inland is an excellent network of footpaths & trails & many castles, manors & stately homes.

Hampshire

Hampshire
Gazeteer
Areas of outstanding natural beauty.
East & South Hampshire, North Wessex
Downs & Chichester Harbour.

Houses & Castles
Avington Park - Winchester
16th century red brick house, enlarged in
17th century by the addition of two wings
& a classical portico. Stateroom, ballroom
with wonderful ceiling. Red drawing room,
library, etc.

Beaulieu Abbey & Palace House -
Beaulieu
12th century Cistercian abbey - the
original gatehouse of abbey converted to
palace house 1538. Houses historic car
museum.

Breamore House - Breamore
16th century Elizabethan Manor House,
tapestries, furniture, paintings. Also
museum.

Jane Austen's Home - Chawston
Personal effects of the famous writer.

Broadlands - Romsey
16th century - park & garden created by
Capability Brown. Home of the Earl
Mountbatten of Burma.

Mottisfont Abbey - Nr. Romsey
12th century Augustinian Priory until
Dissolution. Painting by Rex Whistler
trompe l'oeil in Gothic manner.

Stratfield Saye House - Reading
17th century house presented to the Duke
of Wellington 1817. Now contains his
possessions - also wild fowl sanctuary.

Sandham Memorial Chapel - Sandham,
Nr. Newbury
Paintings by Stanley Spencer cover the
walls.

The Vyne - Sherbourne St. John
16th century red brick chapel with
Renaissance glass & rare linenfold
panelling. Alterations made in 1654 -
classical portico. Palladian staircase
dates form 1760.

West Green House - Hartley Wintney
18th century red brick house set in a
walled garden.

Appuldurcombe House - Wroxall, Isle of
Wight
The only house in the 'Grand Manner' on
the island. Beautiful English baroque east
facade. House now an empty shell
standing in fine park.

Osbourne House - East Cowes, Isle of
Wight
Queen Victoria's seaside residence.

Carisbrooke Castle - Isle of Wight
Oldest parts 12th century, but there was a
wooden castle on the mound before that.
Museum in castle.

Cathedrals & Churches
Winchester Cathedral
Largest Gothic church in Europe. Norman
& perpendicular styles, three sets of
mediaeval paintings, marble font c.1180.
Stalls c.1320 with 60 misericords.
Extensive mediaeval tiled floor.

Breamore (St. Mary) - Breamore
10th century Saxon. Double splayed
windows, stone rood.

East Meon (All Saints)
15th century rebuilding of Norman fabric.
Tournai marble front.

Idsworth (St. Hubert)
16th century chapel - 18th century bell
turret. 14th century paintings in chancel.

Pamber (dedication unknown)
Early English - Norman central tower, 15th
central pews, wooden effigy of knight
c.1270.

Romsey (St. Mary & St. Ethelfleda)
Norman - 13th century effigy of a lady -
Saxon rood & carving of crucifixion, 16th
century painted reredos.

Silchester (St. Mary)
Norman, perpendicular, 14th century effigy
of a lady, 15th century screen, Early
English chancel with painted patterns on
south window splays, Jacobean pulpit with
domed canopy.

Winchester (St. Cross)
12th century. Original chapel to Hospital.
Style changing from Norman at east to
decorated at west. Tiles, glass,
wall painting.

HAMPSHIRE

Map reference

0	Mason	15	Blatter
1	Whitaker	15	Thomson
2	Mallam	16	Sanderson
3	Kendall	17	Matthews
4	Buckley	18	Pennefather
5	Taylor	19	Baigent
6	Tose	20	Taylor
7	Cadman	21	Nixon
8	Duckworth	22	Hughes
9	Harris	23	Humphryes
10	Ratcliffe	24	Dugdale
11	Skelton	25	Chivers
12	Watling	26	Talbot
13	Poulter	27	Parker
14	Barnfield	28	Ford
15	Cutmore	29	Lalonde
15	Gallagher	30	Mutton

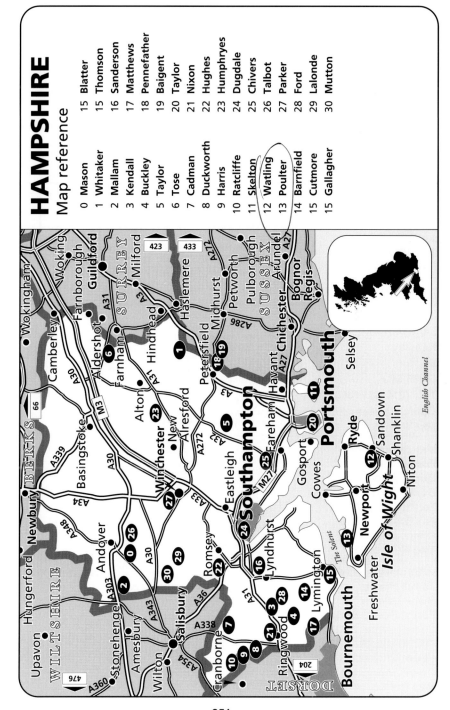

251

	rate from £ per person	children taken	evening meals	animals taken

Richard & Patricia Mason
Malt Cottage
Upper Clatford
Andover SP11 7QL
Tel: (01264) 323469
Fax 01264 334100
Open: ALL YEAR
Map Ref No. 00

Nearest Road: A.303
Walk around the beautiful 6-acre garden with chalk stream & lakes, or sit by the fire in the beamed sitting room. Malt Cottage, an ideal stop en-route from London/Heathrow to the West Country, is situated in a picturesque village with many thatched cottages. 3 attractive bedrooms with en-suite/private facilities. There are many places to visit locally, including Stonehenge, Salisbury & Winchester. A delightful home.

£18.50 | Y | N | N

see PHOTO over

Mrs Carolyn Mallam
Broadwater
Amport
Andover SP11 8AY
Tel: (01264) 772240
Fax 01264 772240
Open: ALL YEAR
Map Ref No. 02

Nearest Road: A.303
Broadwater is a 17th-century, listed, thatched cottage situated in a peaceful unspoilt village just off the A.303. It is an ideal base for sightseeing in Hampshire, with easy access to the West Country & London. The cottage offers 2 delightful, twin-bedded rooms, both with en-suite facilities. A private & very comfortable sitting room, with an inglenook & a private dining room, together with home cooking, are all available. Colour T.V..

£20.00 | Y | Y | N

Jeremy & Philippa Whitaker
Land of Nod
Headley
Bordon
GU35 8SJ
Tel: (01428) 713609
Open: ALL YEAR (Excl. Xmas)
Map Ref No. 01

Nearest Road: A.3
A large neo-Georgian house set in 7 acres of garden in the centre of 100 acres of a private woodland estate. Offering 2 twin-bedded rooms with private or en-suite bathroom, T.V. & tea/coffee-making facilities. 1 hour from London, Heathrow, Gatwick & Portsmouth, & within easy reach of some of the finest gardens & historic houses in the south of England, it is the perfect spot for a relaxing break. A car is essential for maximum enjoyment. Children over 12.

£25.00 | Y | Y | N

Mrs Jane Kendall
Forest Thatch
Burley Street
Burley BH24 4DD
Tel: (01425) 403391
Fax 01425 403243
Open: JAN - NOV
Map Ref No. 03

Nearest Road: A.31
Forest Thatch, a 17th-century, Grade II listed thatch cottage set in an olde English garden in the heart of the New Forest. Oak-beamed bedrooms & dining room evoke an atmosphere of times past. Luxury accommodation in double, en-suite, twin bedrooms, where fresh flowers greet your entrance. Tea/coffee making. Colour T.V.. Country walks & rides abound.   Ideally placed for Winchester & Salisbury.

£18.00 | Y | N | Y

🚭

P. Buckley & W. Witt
Tothill House
Black Lane
Forest Road, Burley
Christchurch BH23 8DZ
Tel: (01425) 674414
Fax 01425 672235
Open: JAN - NOV
Map Ref No. 04

Nearest Road: A.35
An Edwardian country house set in 12 acres of woodland. An Area of Outstanding Natural Beauty noted for its flora & fauna. Only 5 mins from Burley village, a popular New Forest tourist attraction. Offering good food & 3 attractive en-suite rooms, individually decorated, with T.V. & tea-making facilities. Very secluded, with peace & tranquility. Local sporting & recreational activities, & a variety of places to visit. Children over 16 yrs welcome. The perfect spot for a relaxing break.

£25.00 | Y | N | N

🚭

Malt Cottage. Upper Clatford.

Rudge House. Crondall.

Hampshire

		rate from £ per person	children taken	evening meals	animals taken

Rosemary Taylor **Moortown Farm** **Soberton** **Droxford** **SO32 3QU** **Tel: (01489) 877256** **Open: ALL YEAR** **Map Ref No. 05**	Nearest Road: A.32, B.2150 A friendly atmosphere is found at Moortown in the heart of the Meon Valley, an Area of Outstanding Natural Beauty, crossed by both the Wayfarers Walk & Southdowns Way. 2 rooms, each with en-suite/private bathroom & radio, T.V. & tea-making facilities. Situated in a peaceful village within easy reach of many places of historical interest such as Winchester, home of King Arthur's Round Table, Portsmouth, with the Mary Rose & Nelson's Flagship, Chichester & the New Forest. Parking.	£17.50	Y	N	N
Nigel & Sandra Tose **Rudge House** **Itchel Lane** **Crondall** **Farnham GU10 5PR** **Tel: (01252) 850450** **Fax 01252 850829** **Open: JAN - Mid DEC** **Map Ref No. 06**	Nearest Road: M.3, A.287 Elegant, spacious family home, dating from the 1850s, featuring a 4-acre garden with tennis court & croquet lawn. Edging an historic village, the house is quiet & secluded, bordering farmland, yet within 45 mins of Heathrow, Gatwick & London. Windsor, Ascot, Winchester & Oxford highly accessible. Extremely comfortable accommodation, offering en-suite/private facilities & pump showers, plus T.V. lounge & tea/coffee makers. Evening meal & packed lunches by arrangement. Children over 12 yrs.	£25.00 *see PHOTO over*	Y	Y	N
Mrs G. Cadman **Cottage Crest** **Castle Hill, Woodgreen** **Fordingbridge SP6 2AX** **Tel: (01725) 512009** **Open: ALL YEAR** **Map Ref No. 07**	Nearest Road: A.338 Woodgreen is a typical New Forest village, with cottages surrounded by thick hedges to keep out the cattle & ponies. Cottage Crest is a Victorian drover's cottage set high in its own 4 acres, & enjoying superb views of the River Avon & valley below. Bedrooms are spacious & decorated to a very high standard. All have a private bathroom/ shower & w.c.. Children over 10 yrs welcome.	£19.00 *see PHOTO over*	Y	N	N
Mr & Mrs G. Duckworth **Weir Cottage** **Bickton** **Fordingbridge** **SP6 2HA** **Tel: (01425) 655813** **Open: ALL YEAR** **Map Ref No. 08**	Nearest Road: A.338 Bickton is a tiny hamlet on the River Avon half a mile from the New Forest & 30 mins from Salisbury, Bournemouth & Southampton. 200-year-old Weir Cottage offers 2 comfortable double rooms, each with a private bathroom. Enjoy attractive views as you breakfast in the splendid, upstairs, beamed living room overlooking the river as it flows under the mill. The Garden Room, with colour T.V., leads out into the secluded terraced garden. 2 pianos available on request. Children over 8 yrs.	£19.50	Y	Y	N
Mrs Jean Harris **Colt Green** **North End** **Damerham** **Fordingbridge** **SP6 3HA** **Tel: (01725) 518240** **Open: MAR - NOV** **Map Ref No. 09**	Nearest Road: A.354, A.336 You might look out on full-blown orange poppies from your bedroom window, or drifts of daffodils & bluebells, or roses. Across the river, a meadow, with cows, calves & buttercups. Colt Green was built in this lovely spot by our parents for their pleasure & comfort. Carefully modernised, it has 3 rooms, with en-suite shower or private bathroom, antique furniture, log fires. Easily reached from London for a quiet weekend, & perfect for exploring the New Forest & Wessex. Children over 6 yrs.	£18.00	Y	Y	Y

Cottage Crest. Woodgreen.

Hampshire

		rate from £ per person	children taken	evening meals	animals taken
Mrs P. A. Ratcliffe **Hendley House** **Rockbourne** **Fordingbridge SP6 3NA** **Tel: (01725) 518303** Fax 01725 518546 **Open: FEB - NOV** **Map Ref No. 10**	Nearest Road: A.338, A.354 Beautiful, south-facing, 16th-century Grade II listed house, with later addition, situated on the edge of the village & overlooking a water meadow & farmland. Accommodation is in 2 charming bedrooms, 1 twin with en-suite shower, etc., & 1 double with private bathroom, in a very relaxing family home with oak beams & log fires. A spacious garden, with a heated swimming pool. Children over 10 years welcome.	£23.00	Y	N	N
Mrs Geraldine Watling **The Grange** **Alverstone** **Sandown** **Isle of Wight PO36 0EZ** **Tel: (01983) 403729** **Open: FEB - NOV** **Map Ref No. 12**	Nearest Road: A.3056, A.3055 Enjoy a peaceful stay at The Grange. Set in a large garden beneath the Downs, it is ideally situated for all aspects of the island. A nature trail passes through the village, & there are sandy beaches just 2 miles away. The 7 tastefully furnished bedrooms have en-suite facilities, the house is centrally heated & there is a comfortable lounge with a log fire. Traditional English breakfast is served to start the day, & there is an excellent, varied menu for evening meals.	£18.50	Y	Y	N
Mrs Sylvia Poulter **Quinces** **Cranmore Avenue** **Yarmouth** **Isle of Wight PO41 OXS** **Tel: (01983) 760080** **Open: ALL YEAR** **Map Ref No. 13**	Nearest Road: A.3054 An attractive modern house, centrally heated throughout, peacefully set between a vineyard & a dairy farm on a private road 2 miles from Yarmouth. 2 delightful bedrooms, with tea/coffee-making facilities. Also available to guests is a comfortable living room with colour T.V. & log fires in season. The Poulters offer an ideal base for exploring the lovely & varied countryside & coastline of the West Wight, as well as the option of wildlife holidays tailored to your interests.	£16.00	Y	N	Y
Tony Barnfield **The Nurse's Cottage** **Station Road** **Sway** **Lymington SO41 6BA** **Tel: (01590) 683402** Fax 01590 683402 **Open: XMAS - Mid NOV** **Map Ref No. 14**	Nearest Road: A.337 "Wining & dining can be one of the great pleasures in life", says Tony Barnfield, who has transformed the former District Nurse's cottage in this New Forest village into an award-winning licensed guest house. Guests are welcomed with afternoon tea, & the overnight rate includes a 3-course dinner from an extensive menu backed by a selection of over 70 wines from around the world. 3 en-suite, ground-floor bedrooms with many 'creature comforts' incl. fresh fruit, flowers, local bottled water, Beaulieu Chocolates & T.V., etc. CREDIT CARD VISA M'CARD AMEX	£40.00	Y	Y	Y
Jennifer & Peter Cutmore **Wheatsheaf House** **Gosport Street** **Lymington** **SO41 9BG** **Tel: (01590) 679208** **Open: ALL YEAR** **Map Ref No. 15**	Nearest Road: A.337 A beautifully appointed early-17th-century former tavern, Wheatsheaf House is close to the centre of this charming Georgian market town, & only 3 mins' walk from the historic town quay. Tea/coffee is available on request in a choice of 3 large comfortable rooms with either en-suite or private facilities. Ideally placed for sailing, the New Forest & for touring the whole region. You are assured of a warm welcome. Self-catering accommodation also available.	£22.50	Y	N	Y

Hampshire

	rate from £ per person	children taken	evening meals	animals taken
Mrs Wendy M. Gallagher **Albany House** **3 Highfield** **Lymington** **SO41 9GB** Tel: (01590) 671900 Open: ALL YEAR (Excl. Xmas) Map Ref No. 15	Nearest Road: A.337 This fine Regency house, built in 1842, provides a warm welcoming atmosphere in a traditionally furnished home. There are views over the town of Solent & the Isle of Wight. 3 very comfortably furnished bedrooms, each with en-suite facilities, colour T.V. & tea/coffee makers. Delicious meals are served in the elegant dining room using freshly prepared ingredients. In season, shellfish & New Forest game will be provided.	£19.50	Y	Y	Y
Mrs Ann Blatter **14 Captains Row** **Lymington** **SO41 9RP** Tel: (01590) 671937 Open: ALL YEAR Map Ref No. 15	Nearest Road: M.27 Built in 1790, this is a delightful Georgian property where the congenial host offers superb accommodation in 3 charming & elegantly furnished bedrooms, with private facilities. Each is well equipped, & has tea/coffee-making facilities. Guests may relax in the very pretty garden, an outstanding feature of this property. Ideally situated for touring.	£16.00 🚭	Y	N	N
Mrs P. A. Thomson **St. Mary's Lodge** **Captains Row** **Lymington** **SO41 9RR** Tel: (01590) 678576 Fax 01590 678576 Open: ALL YEAR Map Ref No. 15	Nearest Road: A.337 A superbly furnished, gracious Georgian house, Grade II listed, in a splendid position with lovely views over the Lymington River, Solent & Isle of Wight beyond. Close to the Old Town quay & marinas. Excellent restaurants & pubs, & Lymington town with its famous Saturday market & good shops. 4 bedrooms, each with an en-suite/private bathroom. The New Forest, walks, cycling, golf, riding, a ferry to I.o.W., within 5 mins' walk. Enviable comfort for a memorable stay.	£22.00	Y	N	Y
Paul & Jackie Sanderson **Knightwood Lodge Hotel** **Southampton Road** **Lyndhurst SO43 7BU** Tel: (01703) 282502 Fax 01703 283730 Open: ALL YEAR Map Ref No. 16	Nearest Road: A.35 Situated on the edge of Lyndhurst, & overlooking the New Forest, is Knightwood Lodge. Originally built as a guest house in the 1920s, it has been carefully modernised, yet retains its original character. Providing an ideal base for exploring the forest & surrounding area, including Beaulieu Motor Museum. 15 well-equipped, en-suite bedrooms. Indoor leisure centre. Cosy bar. Holiday cottage available.	£27.50 CREDIT CARD VISA M'CARD AMEX	Y	Y	N
Mrs Daphne Matthews **Yew Tree Farm** **Bashley Common Road** **New Milton** **BH25 5SH** Tel: (01425) 611041 Open: ALL YEAR Map Ref No. 17	Nearest Road: A.35 Yew Tree Farm offers 2 lovely, spacious bed-sitting rooms, marvellously comfortable, with double or twin beds & each with their own bathrooms, in a traditional, cosy thatched farmhouse on the edge of the New Forest. Extensive breakfasts (taken in bedroom) & home-made dinners (if ordered in advance), using top-quality produce. Private entrance & ample parking. Very easily located about 1 mile off the A.35 road on the B.3058 road.	£25.00 🚭	N	Y	N

Hampshire

		rate from £ per person	children taken	evening meals	animals taken
Cdr. & Mrs W. Pennefather **Westmark House** **Westmark, Sheet** **Petersfield GU31 5AT** **Tel: (01730) 263863** **Open: ALL YEAR (Excl. Xmas/New Year's Eve)** **Map Ref No. 18**	Nearest Road: A.3, A.272 Westmark House is a spacious & elegant country house of Georgian origins, standing in 2 acres of mature grounds, with tennis court & heated swimming pool. It has fine southerly views, & is ideal for exploring Hampshire. Chichester & Goodwood are nearby for theatre, cathedral & racing, & Cowdray Park for polo. Excellent pubs & restaurants are within a few miles. Portsmouth 18 miles. London 50 miles. Evening meals by prior arrangement. Children over 8 years welcome.	£22.00	Y	Y	N
Mrs G. W. Baigent **Trotton Farm** **Trotton, Rogate** **Petersfield GU31 5EN** **Tel: (01730) 813618** **Fax 01730 816093** **Open: ALL YEAR** **Map Ref No. 19**	Nearest Road: A.272 This charming home, set in 200 acres of farmland, offers comfortable accommodation in 2 twin-bedded rooms & 1 double-bedded room each with en-suite shower & modern amenities, including tea/coffee-making facilities. Residents' lounge is available throughout the day. Games room & pretty garden for guests' relaxation. Ideally situated for visiting many local, historical & sporting attractions, & 1 hour from Gatwick & Heathrow.	£17.50	Y	N	Y
David & Diane Skelton **Cockle Warren Hotel** **36 Seafront, Hayling Island** **Portsmouth PO11 9HL** **Tel: (01705) 464961** **Tel/Fax 01705 464838** **Open: ALL YEAR** **Map Ref No. 11**	Nearest Road: A. 27.M, A.3 A delightful seafront cottage hotel with tile hanging, white picket fencing & a smuggler's tunnel running beneath the large garden. Lovely en-suite bedrooms facing out to sea or overlooking the swimming pool, all with colour T.V., phones, etc., some with 4-poster & Victorian beds. Enjoy French & English country cooking with home-made bread & French wine, & relax by the open log fire to the sound of the sea just a few yards away. National award winners. Children over 12.	£26.00 *see PHOTO over* CREDIT CARD VISA M'CARD AMEX	Y	Y	Y
Dr A. & Mrs C. Taylor **11 Clarence Parade** **Southsea** **Portsmouth PO5 3NU** **Tel: (01705) 736510** **Fax 01705 874844** **Open: ALL YEAR** **Map Ref No. 20**	Nearest Road: M.27 This elegant, Georgian-style house overlooks Southsea Common, with magnificent views across the Solent & the Isle of Wight. Convenient for Continental Ferry Port, Isle of Wight ferries & ancient ships. Parking in front of house. 3 large, beautifully decorated & comfortable bedrooms, 2 en-suite & 1 private, all with T.V., coffee/tea, etc. The seafront, tennis courts, shops & restaurants within a few mins' walk. A warm welcome awaits you here. German spoken. Children over 12.	£20.00	Y	N	N
Mrs Yvonne Nixon **The Nest** **10 Middle Lane** **Off School Lane** **Ringwood BH24 1LE** **Tel/fax: (01425) 476724** **Mobile 0589 854505** **Open: ALL YEAR** **Map Ref No. 21**	Nearest Road: A.31, B.3347 Charming Victorian house situated in a quiet residential lane 5 mins' walk to Ringwood centre, a New Forest market town with many restaurants & inns. This former schoolmaster's residence, offers excellent-value, character accommodation in pretty, well-equipped 'Laura Ashley'-style bedrooms. Convenient location with off-road parking. Close to Bournemouth, Poole, Portsmouth, Salisbury & Southampton. Breakfast is served in the delightful, sunny 'Garden Room' surrounded by an unusual collection of old potties!	£16.00	Y	N	N

Cockle Warren Cottage Hotel.   Hayling Island.

Hampshire

		rate from £ per person	children taken	evening meals	animals taken
Robin & Mary Ford **Holmans** **Bisterne Close** **Burley** **Ringwood BH24 4AZ** **Tel: (01425) 402307** **Open: ALL YEAR** **Map Ref No. 28**	Nearest Road: A.35, A.31 Holmans is a charming country house in the heart of the New Forest, set in 4 acres with stabling available for guests' own horses. Superb walking, horse riding & carriage driving, with a golf course nearby. A warm, friendly welcome is assured. A tastefully furnished twin en-suite, or a double & twin with a bathroom adjoining. Tea/coffee-making facilities, radio, hairdryer. C.T.V. in the lounge (with an adjoining orangery), & log fires in winter.	£20.00	Y	N	Y
Mrs R. Lalonde **Michelmersh House** **Michelmersh** **Romsey** **SO51 0NS** **Tel: (01794) 368644** **Open: JAN - NOV** **Map Ref No. 29**	Nearest Road: A.31, A.33 Michelmersh House is a late-Georgian farmhouse set in 4 acres of grounds in the pretty village of Michelmersh. It stands on high ground, overlooking the famous River Test Valley, in a quiet position, with a tennis court & a pool. 2 very charming rooms (1 double & 1 twin) with private bathrooms. Full English or Continental breakfast served. A delightful home, ideal for exploring Hampshire & south Wiltshire, & with many good pubs & restaurants nearby. Children over 8.	£17.50	Y	N	N
Anthea Hughes **Spursholt House** **Salisbury Rd** **Romsey SO51 6DJ** **Tel: (01794) 512229** **Fax 01794 523142** **Open: ALL YEAR** **Map Ref No. 22**	Nearest Road: A.27 Spursholt House dates from the 17th century, with Victorian extensions for Lord Palmerston. The gardens extend to 2 acres, with paved terraces, a topiary, a parterre & roses. Rooms are furnished with antiques, & bedrooms are spacious & panelled, with large beds. The sitting room, available at all times, is super, with knole sofas, T.V. & telephone at hand. Coffee/tea facilities. Excellent touring area, equidistant from Winchester, Salisbury & New Forest.	£20.00	Y	N	Y
Laraine & Adam Humphryes **Belmont House** **Gilbert Street** **Ropley SO24 0BY** **Tel: (01962) 772344** **Open: ALL YEAR (Excl.** **Xmas & Easter)** **Map Ref No. 23**	Nearest Road: A.31 Belmont, dating back to the 19th century, is situated on a quiet country lane, & set in an acre of beautiful garden, with rural views from the house. Offering 1 attractively furnished bedroom with private facilities, T.V. & tea/coffee makers. A short walk to the village with an ancient church, shop & 3 pubs. Within easy reach of Petersfield, Salisbury & Winchester by car. Appox. 1 hour from London airports.	£18.00	N	N	N
Mr & Mrs V. M. Dugdale **Hunters Lodge Hotel** **25 Landguard Road** **Shirley** **Southampton SO15 5DL** **Tel: (01703) 227919** **Fax 01703 230913** **Open: ALL YEAR** **Map Ref No. 24**	Nearest Road: M.3, M.27 A friendly welcome will ensure that you start to relax as soon as you arrive at Hunters Lodge. A conveniently situated hotel, with easy access to the city centre, University & ferry ports. The well-appointed & very comfortable bedrooms are equipped with tea/coffee-making facilities, & many are en-suite. The cosy lounge bar, with open floor fire in winter, creates a warm, friendly atmosphere in which to relax. Southampton is an ideal centre for touring, & is within easy reach of the New Forest, Salisbury & Winchester.	£23.50 CREDIT CARD VISA M'CARD AMEX	Y	Y	Y

Hampshire

		rate from £ per person	children taken	evening meals	animals taken
Philip & Janet Mutton **Yew Tree House** **Broughton** **Stockbridge** **SO20 8AA** **Tel: (01794) 301227** **Open: ALL YEAR** **Map Ref No. 30**	Nearest Road: A.30 Experience the delights of traditional English gracious living in this Grade II listed Georgian home, where Charles Dickens is said to have stayed. The house, set in a beautiful walled garden, is exquisitely furnished with antiques, & every consideration is made for the comfort of your stay, including good home cooking. Broughton is a picturesque, award-winning village situated midway between Winchester & Salisbury.	£19.00	Y	Y	N
Mrs Y. M. Chivers **Montrose** **Solomons Lane** **Shirrell Heath** **Wickham** **SO3 2HU** **Tel: (01329) 833345** **Open: ALL YEAR** **Map Ref No. 25**	Nearest Road: B.2177, A.32 Montrose offers accommodation of a high standard in tasteful surroundings. 3 delightful bedrooms, 1 en-suite. Comfort & personal attention has helped to build a superb reputation. Situated in the Meon Valley between the historical villages of Wickham & Bishops Waltham, & yet close to the M.27, M.3 & continental ferry ports, thus providing an ideal base for exploring the towns of Winchester, Portsmouth & Southampton, & the lovely Hampshire countryside & coastline.	£22.00	N	N	N
James & Jean Talbot **Church Farm** **Barton Stacey** **Winchester SO21 3RR** **Tel: (01962) 760268** **Fax 01962 760268** **Open: ALL YEAR** **Map Ref No. 26**	Nearest Road: A.34, A.303 Church Farm is a 15th-century tithe barn with Georgian & modern additions. It features an adjacent coach house & groom's cottage, recently converted, where guests may be totally self-contained, or be welcomed to the log-fired family drawing room & dine on locally produced fresh food. 7 beautiful bedrooms for guests, most with en-suite, T.V., tea/coffee-making facilities. Horses are kept. Swimming pool & croquet. Tennis court. CREDIT CARD VISA M'CARD AMEX	£22.00	Y	Y	Y
John & Judy Parker **East View** **16 Clifton Hill** **Winchester SO22 5BL** **Tel: (01962) 862986** **Fax 01962 862986** **Open: ALL YEAR** **Map Ref No. 27**	Nearest Road: A.272, A.34 This Victorian townhouse is set in its own secluded, landscaped garden, & yet is only 5 mins from the city centre. East View has splendid views over the city & cathedral to the South Downs beyond. There are 3 attractive bedrooms, each with en-suite/private facilities, T.V., radio, tea/coffee trays. Elegant sitting room & dining room furnished with antiques. In summer, breakfast is served in the conservatory. Private car park. CREDIT CARD VISA M'CARD	£22.50	N	N	N

When booking your accommodation please mention
The Best Bed & Breakfast

Hereford & Worcester

Hereford & Worcester
(Heart of England)

Hereford is a beautiful ancient city standing on the banks of the River Wye, almost a crossing point between England & Wales. It is a market centre for the Marches, the border area which has a very particular history of its own.

Hereford Cathedral has a massive sandstone tower & is a fitting venue for the Three Choirs festival which dates from 1727, taking place yearly in one or the other of the three great cathedrals of Hereford, Worcester & Gloucester.

The county is fortunate in having many well preserved historic buildings. Charming "black & white" villages abound here, romantically set in a soft green landscape.

The Royal Forest of Dean spreads its oak & beech trees over 22,000 acres. When people first made their homes in the woodlands it was vaster still. There are rich deposits of coal & iron mined for centuries by the foresters, & the trees have always been felled for charcoal. Ancient courts still exist where forest dwellers can & do claim their rights to use the forest's resources.

The landscape alters dramatically as the land rises to merge with the great Black Mountain range at heights of over 2,600 feet. It is not possible to take cars everywhere but a narrow mountain road, Gospel Pass, takes traffic from Hay-on-Wye to Llanthony with superb views of the upper Wye Valley.

The Pre-Cambrian Malvern Hills form a natural boundary between Herefordshire & Worcestershire & from the highest view points you can see over 14 counties. At their feet nestle pretty little villages such as Eastonor with its 19th century castle in revived Norman style that looks quite mediaeval amongst the parklands & gardens.

There are, in fact, five Malverns. The largest predictably known as Great Malvern was a fashionable 19th century spa & is noted for the purity of the water which is bottled & sold countrywide.

The Priory at Malvern is rich in 15th century stained glass & has a fine collection of mediaeval tiles made locally. William Langland, the 14th century author of "Piers Ploughman", was educated at the Priory & is said to have been sleeping on the Malvern Hills when he had the visionary experience which led to the creation of the poem. Sir Edward Elgar was born, lived & worked here & his "Dream of Gerontius" had its first performance in Hereford Cathedral in 1902.

In Worcestershire another glorious cathedral, with what remains of its monastic buildings, founded in the 11th century, stands beside the River Severn. College Close in Worcester is a lovely group of buildings carefully preserved & very English in character.

The Severn appears to be a very lazy waterway but flood waters can reach astonshing heights, & the "Severn Bore" is a famous phenomenon.

A cruise along the river is a pleasant way to spend a day seeing villages & churches from a different perspective, possibly visiting a riverside inn. To the south of the county lie the undulating Vales of Evesham & Broadway - described as the show village of England.

The Malvern Hills.

Hereford & Worcester

Hereford & Worcester Gazeteer

Areas of outstanding natural beauty.
The Malvern Hills, The Cotswolds, The Wye Valley.

Historic Houses & Castles

Berrington Hall - Leominster
18th century - painted & plastered ceilings. Landscape by Capability Brown.

Brilley - Cwmmau Farmhouse - Whitney-on-Wye
17th century timber-framed & stone tiled farmhouse.

Burton Court - Eardisland
14th century great hall. Exhibition of European & Oriental costume & curios. Model fairground.

Croft Castle - Nr. Leominster
Castle on the Welsh border - inhabited by Croft family for 900 years.

Dinmore Manor - Nr. Hereford
14th century chapel & cloister.

Eastnor Castle - Nr. Ledbury
19th century - Castellated, containing pictures & armour. Arboretum.

Eye Manor - Leominster
17th century Carolean Manor house - excellent plasterwork, paintings, costumes, books, secret passage. Collection of dolls.

Hanbury Hall - Nr. Droitwich
18th century red brick house - only two rooms & painted ceilings on exhibition.

Harvington Hall - Kidderminster
Tudor Manor house with moat, priest's hiding places.

The Greyfriars - Worcester
15th century timber-framed building adjoins Franciscan Priory.

Hellen's - Much Marcle
13th century manorial house of brick & stone. Contains the Great hall with stone table - bedroom of Queen Mary. Much of the original furnishings remain.

Kentchurch Court - Hereford
14th century fortified border Manor house. Paintings & Carvings by Grinling Gibbons.

Moccas Court - Moccas
18th century - designed by Adam - Parklands by Capability Brown - under restoration.

Pembridge Castle - Welsh Newton
17th century moated castle.

Sutton Court - Mordiford
Palladian mansion by Wyatt, watercolours, embroideries, china.

Cathedrals & Churches

Amestry (St. John the Baptist & St.Alkmund)
16th century rood screen.

Abbey Dore (St. Mary & Holy Trinity)
17th century glass & great oak screen - early English architecture.

Brinsop (St. George)
14th century, screen & glass, alabaster reredos, windows in memory of Wordsworth, carved Norman tympanum.

Bredon (St. Giles)
12th century - central tower & spire. Mediaeval heraldic tiles, tombs & early glass.

Brockhampton (St. Eadburgh)
1902. Central tower & thatched roof.

Castle Frome (St. Michael & All Angles)
12th century carved font, 17th century effigies in alabaster.

Chaddesley Corbett (St. Cassian)
14th century monuments, 12th century font.

Elmley (St. Mary)
12th century & 15th century font, tower, gargoyles, mediaeval.

Great Witley (St. Michael)
Baroque - Plasterwork, painted ceiling, painted glass, very fine example.

Hereford (All Saints)
13th-14th centuries, spire, splendid choir stalls, chained library.

Hereford Cathedral
Small cathedral.
Fine central tower c.1325, splendid porch, brasses, early English Lady Chapel with lancet windows. Red sandstone.

Kilpeck (St. Mary & St. David)
Romanesque style - mediaeval windows - fine carvings.

Leominster (St. Peter & St. Paul)
12th century doorway, fine Norman arches, decorated windows.

Much Marcle (St. Bartholomew)
13th century. 14th & 17th century monuments.

HEREFORD & WORCESTER

Map reference

0 Cutler
1 Smith
2 Allen
3 Lee
4 Jancey
5 Price
6 Fothergill
7 Gelderen
7 Williams
8 Blunt
9 Young
10 Conolly
11 Meekings
12 Page
14 Dean
15 Stringer
16 Mason
17 Williams
18 Keel
19 Lloyd
20 Addison

Herefordshire

			rate from £ per person	children taken	evening meals	animals taken
Hildegard & Graham Cutler **Lower House** **Adforton** **SY7 0NF** **Tel: (01568) 770223** **Open: ALL YEAR** **Map Ref No. 00**	Nearest Road: A.4110, A.4113 Lower House originates from the early 17th century, & its 2 1/2 acres of gardens are set in peaceful, unspoilt countryside. 2 double & 2 twin rooms with en-suite facilities. First-class dinners are served in the elegant dining room, which features exposed beams, antiques & an inglenook fireplace. There is excellent walking from the house in the Wigmore Rolls. Children over 10 welcome. Unlicensed, but guests may bring their own wine. A self-catering granary also available.	£23.00 *see PHOTO over*	Y	Y	N
Mr & Mrs E. W. Smith **Dormington Court** **Dormington** **Hereford** **HR1 4DA** **Tel: (01432) 850370** **Fax 01432 850370** **Open: ALL YEAR** **Map Ref No. 01**	Nearest Road: A.438 Dormington Court is a beautiful Grade II listed part-Georgian/Elizabethan manor farm house, with oak beams, a Jacobean staircase, inglenooks & antiques. Spacious bedrooms, mostly en-suite, with colour T.V., tea/coffee-making facilities, hairdryers & lovely country views. There are 2 acres of attractive grounds, a tree-lined drive & a sun terrace. Surrounded by apple orchards & hop fields. The perfect base to visit & enjoy castles, cathedrals, hills & valleys in the surrounding area.	£25.00 CREDIT CARD VISA M'CARD	N	N	Y
Mrs Rosemary Price **Dinedor Court** **Dinedor** **Hereford** **HR2 6LG** **Tel: (01432) 870481** **Open: MAR - NOV** **Map Ref No. 05**	Nearest Road: A.49 Dinedor Court is a listed 16th-century rambling farmhouse furnished with beautiful antiques. Set in a large garden overlooking pretty cider orchards & the River Wye. There are 2 very attractive & comfortable guest bedrooms, 1 a double & the other twin-bedded, each with tea/coffee-making facilities. With beautiful views & peaceful & relaxing surroundings, it is the ideal base for a relaxing break. Within easy reach of Hereford.	£17.00	Y	N	Y
Mrs Gladys W. Lee **Cwm Craig Farm** **Little Dewchurch** **Hereford** **HR2 6PS** **Tel: (01432) 840250** **Open: ALL YEAR** **Map Ref No. 03**	Nearest Road: A.49 Spacious Georgian farmhouse, surrounded by superb unspoilt countryside. Situated between the Cathedral city of Hereford & Ross-on-Wye, & just a few mins' drive from the Wye Valley. Ideal base for touring the Forest of Dean. All 3 bedrooms have modern amenities, shaver points & tea/coffee facilities. 1 is en-suite. There is a lounge & separated dining room, both with colour T.V.. A full English breakfast is served.	£16.00	Y	N	N
Mr & Mrs M. & W. Jancey **Bredwardine Hall** **Bredwardine** **Hereford** **HR3 6DB** **Tel: (01981) 500596** **Open: MAR - OCT** **Map Ref No. 04**	Nearest Road: A.438 A charming 19th-century manor house with immense character and literary interest, standing in secluded, wooded gardens & providing elegant and well-appointed accommodation. 4 delightful bedrooms; spacious en-suite bathrooms; full central heating; tea/coffee facilities; colour T.V.s; ample parking. Excellent food and wine; a relaxed, friendly atmosphere; personal service. Set in the tranquil Wye Valley, near Hay-on-Wye and its world-famous bookshops.	£23.00	N	Y	N

Lower House. Adforton.

Herefordshire

rate from £ per person
children taken
evening meals
animals taken

		rate from £ per person	children taken	evening meals	animals taken
Roger & Judy Young **Priors Court** **Aylton** **Ledbury HR8 2QE** **Tel: (01531) 670748** **Fax 01531 670860** **Open: ALL YEAR** **Map Ref No. 09**	Nearest Road: A.438 Priors Court is a Tudor farmhouse, originally a cider mill, whose origins date back to the Domesday Book. Set in the rolling Herefordshire countryside, in its own peaceful farmland, it also has 2 acres of delightful gardens with a stream & a lake. Each comfortable, beamed bedroom has T.V., tea/coffee facilities & private bathroom. Ideal for walks in the Malverns, Cotswolds or Welsh hills, & for fishing in the River Wye. Cheltenham, Stratford & Bath within easy reach.	£18.00	Y	N	N
Peter & Jane Conolly **The Hills Farm** **Leysters** **Leominster** **HR6 0HP** **Tel: (01568) 750205** **Open: FEB - NOV** **Map Ref No.10**	Nearest Road: A.4112 Magnificent views & a splendid welcome await you at this 15th-century farmhouse on the edge of the village of Leysters betwixt Ludlow & Leominster. Delightful en-suite bedrooms have colour T.V.s & beverage-making facilities. 3 are in charming barn conversions offering complete seclusion. Scrumptious dinners, traditional or vegetarian, are available in the individually tabled dining room - the dairy in days gone by - which is unlicensed, so bring your own wine. CREDIT CARD VISA M'CARD	£20.00	N	Y	Y
Catherine & Marguerite **Fothergill** **Highfield, Newtown** **Ivington Road** **Leominster HR6 8QD** **Tel: (01568) 613216** **Open: ALL YEAR** **Map Ref No. 06**	Nearest Road: A.44, A.49 Twins Catherine & Marguerite are eager to make you feel welcome & at home in their elegant Edwardian house, set in a rural tranquil location. You will be very comfortable in any of the 3 attractive bedrooms all with a bathroom (1 being en-suite). There is a large garden & a T.V. lounge with a crackling fire, & the home-made food is absolutely delicious. Residential licence. An ideal base for exploring this scenic region.	£18.50	N	Y	N
Mike & Anne Allen **Broxwood Court** **Broxwood** **Leominster** **HR6 9JJ** **Tel: (01544) 340245** **Fax 01544 340573** **Open: ALL YEAR (Excl. Feb)** **Map Ref No. 02**	Nearest Road: A.44, A.4112 Broxwood Court occupies a commanding position, with superb views of the Black Mountains & surrounding countryside. The garden, with its sweeping lawns, magnificent trees & lake, offers a unique atmosphere of peace & tranquility. Pure white & coloured peacocks roam the grounds. The delightful bedrooms have either en-suite or private bathrooms. Anne is an excellent Cordon Bleu cook, & meals include produce from the extensive organic kitchen garden. Ideal for exploring this beautiful area. Children over 10. **see PHOTO over** CREDIT CARD VISA M'CARD	£35.00	Y	Y	Y
Peggy & Geoff Williams **Sunnymount Hotel** **Ryefield Road** **Ross-on-Wye** **HR9 5LU** **Tel: (01989) 563880** **Open: ALL YEAR** **Map Ref No. 07**	Nearest Road: M.50, A.40 Quietly situated on the edge of the town, this attractive Edwardian house is warm & inviting. Offering 6 well-appointed bedrooms, with en-suite/private bathroom, all with tea/coffee facilities. The sitting rooms (1 with colour T.V.) & dining room overlook the pretty garden. A wide choice of breakfasts using home & local produce freshly prepared for each meal. English/French cooking. Licensed. Ample private parking. An ideal base from which to explore this fascinating area. CREDIT CARD VISA M'CARD AMEX	£23.50	Y	Y	N

Broxwood Court. Broxwood.

Herefordshire & Worcestershire

Val & Tony Blunt **Woodlea Hotel** **Symonds Yat West** **Ross-on-Wye** **HR9 6BL** **Tel: (01600) 890206** **Fax 01600 890206** **Open: Mid FEB - DEC** **Map Ref No. 08**	Nearest Road: A.40 A delightful, family-owned Victorian guest house set amid glorious scenery, with wonderful valley views. The house has a privileged position, & overlooks the famous Wye Rapids. 9 rooms, with modern amenities, telephone & radio. Most rooms have en-suite facilities. A T.V. lounge, reading lounge & a lounge bar where guests can relax with a drink. In the spacious dining room, imaginative & delicious meals are served, accompanied by wine from the well-stocked cellar.	£22.00 CREDIT CARD VISA M'CARD	Y	Y	Y
Renate van Gelderen **Edde Cross House** **Edde Cross Street** **Ross-on-Wye** **HR9 7BZ** **Tel: (01989) 565088** **Open: FEB - NOV** **Map Ref No. 07**	Nearest Road: A.40 Edde Cross House, once the home of Sybil the Dame of Sark, is a Georgian town house of great charm & character overlooking the river. Offering 3 beautifully decorated & comfortable furnished bedrooms, each with en-suite/private bathroom, tea/coffee makers, colour T.V. & hairdryer. Extensive breakfast menu, including vegetarian. This is an ideal base from which to explore the Wye Valley & Forest of Dean. Children over 10.	£21.00	Y	N	N

Worcestershire

Mrs Barbara Meekings **Leasow House** **Laverton Meadows** **Broadway** **WR12 7NA** **Tel: (01386) 584526** **Fax 01386 584596** **Open: ALL YEAR** **Map Ref No. 11**	Nearest Road: A.46, B.4632 Leasow is a charming 17th-century Cotswold stone farmhouse. Recently renovated, it offers 7 delightful spacious bedrooms, with shower/bath en-suite, T.V. & tea/coffee facilities. Set in the peaceful tranquility of the open countryside, it is only 2 1/2 miles from Broadway village with wonderful panoramic views of the Cotswold escarpment. Ideal for the Cotswolds & the Vale of Evesham. A warm welcome, friendly hosts & superb accommodation ensure a memorable stay.	£25.00 *see PHOTO over* CREDIT CARD VISA M'CARD AMEX	Y	N	Y
Frances & Jim Page **Crofton Lodge** **80 New Road** **Bromsgrove B60 2LA** **Tel: (01527) 874136** **Open: ALL YEAR (Excl. Xmas)** **Map Ref No. 12**	Nearest Road: A.38 Crofton Lodge is an attractive Victorian town house, with a walled garden, built in 1880. 1 double, 1 twin & 1 single room, with the usual coffee/tea-making facilities, are available together with a sitting room, with colour T.V., for guests' use. Stratford, Worcester & Birmingham are within half an hour, & the Cotswolds, Malvern Hills, Shropshire & Herefordshire are within an hour's drive. Leaflet available. Children over 6.	£16.50	Y	N	N

Leasow House. Broadway.

Church Farm. Oddingley.

Worcestershire

	rate from £ per person	children taken	evening meals	animals taken
Mrs Anne Dean **Church Farm** **Oddingley** **Droitwich** **WR9 7NE** **Tel/Fax: (01905) 772387** **Open: ALL YEAR** **Map Ref No. 14**	Nearest Road: M.5 Jt. 6 A secluded, attractive house set in 230 acres of grounds. 3 tastefully furnished & comfortable en-suite bedrooms, each with T.V., radio & tea/coffee-making facilities. Excellent breakfasts & delicious evening meals are available. Vegetarian cuisine by arrangement. Guests may relax in the pleasant lounge or pretty gardens with tennis court. Conveniently situated, with easy access to the M.5 & the Midlands. Bristol 1 hour.	£27.50 *see PHOTO over*	Y	Y	N
Sue Stringer **Cowleigh Park Farm** **Cowleigh Road** **Malvern** **WR13 5HJ** **Tel: (01684) 566750** **Open: ALL YEAR** **Map Ref No. 15**	Nearest Road: A.449, B.4219 Cowleigh Park Farm is a delightful, Grade II listed timber farmhouse. This beautifully restored home is peacefully situated at the foot of the Malvern Hills, creating a tranquil setting for a relaxing & friendly stay. Period furnishings throughout, & a choice of 3 comfortable rooms, all with en-suite shower rooms or private bathroom & colour T.V.. Guests are welcome to use the attractive gardens. Plenty of secure parking within the grounds.	£21.00	N	Y	Y
Judith & Jon Williams **Wyche Keep** **22 Wyche Road** **Malvern** **WR14 4EG** **Tel: (01684) 567018** **Fax 01684 561676** **Open: ALL YEAR** **Map Ref No. 17**	Nearest Road: B.4218 Wyche Keep is a unique arts-&-crafts castle-style house, perched high on the Malvern Hills, built by the family of Sir Stanley Baldwin, Prime Minister, to enjoy the spectacular 60-mile views. 3 elegant double suites, incl. a 4-poster. Dinner is served in a 'house party' atmosphere. Traditional English home-cooking a speciality. From a magical garden, enjoy inspirational walks. The home of internationally acclaimed Mediaeval/Tudor journeys & garden tours with a historian host.	£20.00 *see PHOTO over*	N	Y	N
Jenny Mason **The Steps** **6 High Street** **Feckenham** **Redditch** **B96 6HS** **Tel: (01527) 892678** **Open: ALL YEAR** **Map Ref No. 16**	Nearest Road: A.441 The Steps is conveniently situated in the high street of one of the prettiest villages in Worcestershire nestling on the site of King John's hunting ground. This lovely Georgian house has been carefully improved & restored to give a high degree of comfort in a relaxed & homely atmosphere. The sitting room boasts antique furniture, colour T.V. & open fire. The elegant dining room is furnished with family heirlooms, & the bedrooms are all equally tastefully furnished.	£18.00	Y	Y	Y
Jane Keel **Hunthouse Farm** **Frith Common** **Tenbury Wells** **WR15 8JY** **Tel: (01299) 832277** **Open: ALL YEAR (Excl. Xmas)** **Map Ref No. 18**	Nearest Road: A.456, A.443 Relax and enjoy comfort, peace and hospitality in this beautiful, 16th-century, timbered farmhouse ideally situated on a 180-acre arable/sheep farm, commanding memorable views. The 3 comfortable bedrooms are all en-suite, with tea-making facilities. There is a colour television in the guests' sitting room, where guests are welcomed with tea and home-made cake. Excellent local eating houses. Children over 8 please.	£17.00	Y	N	N

Wyche Keep. Malvern.

Worcestershire

		rate from £ per person	children taken	evening meals	animals taken
Mrs Val Lloyd **40 Britannia Square** **Worcester** **WR1 3DN** **Tel: (01905) 611920** **Fax 01905 27152** **Open: ALL YEAR** **Map Ref No. 19**	Nearest Road: A.449, A.38 A lovely Regency house in a quiet conservation square near the city centre. Spacious, comfortable bedrooms with en-suite bathrooms, tea/coffee facilities & colour T.V.. Decorated with period furnishings to a very high standard & featured in design magazines. A gourmet English breakfast is served in the elegant dining room. Easy walking distance to the cathedral, Royal Worcester Porcelain, racecourse, county cricket gound, theatre & shopping. A pretty garden where guests may relax. An ideal base for touring.	£25.00	Y	N	N
Mrs Ann Addison **Old Parsonage Farm** **Hanley Castle** **Worcester** **WR8 0BU** **Tel: (01684) 310124** **Open: Mid JAN - Mid DEC** **Map Ref No. 20**	Nearest Road: A.38, M.5, M.50 Old Parsonage Farm is a fine, mellow-brick, 18th-century country residence enjoying beautiful views of the Malvern Hills. The house has been sympathetically modernised, whilst retaining such period details as an inglenook fireplace & a bread oven. All the bedrooms have private facilities, & the owners, Tony & Ann, specialise in good food & interesting wines. Ann is an accomplished cook, producing imaginative dishes of a high standard, whilst Tony is a wine importer with about 100 different wines in stock. A lovely place to relax & recharge the batteries.	£20.50	N	Y	Y

All the establishments mentioned in this guide are members of
The Worldwide Bed & Breakfast Association

When booking your accommodation please mention
The Best Bed & Breakfast

Kent

Kent
(South East)

Kent is best known as "the garden of England". At its heart is a tranquil landscape of apple & cherry orchards, hop-fields & oast-houses, but there are also empty downs, chalk sea-cliffs, rich marshlands, sea ports, castles & the glory of Canterbury Cathedral.

The dramatic chalk ridgeway of the North Downs links the White Cliffs of Dover with the north of the county which extends into the edge of London. It was a trade route in ancient times following the high downs above the Weald, dense forest in those days. It can be followed today & it offers broad views of the now agricultural Weald.

The pilgrims who flocked to Canterbury in the 12th-15th centuries, (colourfully portrayed in Chaucer's Canterbury Tales), probably used the path of the Roman Watling Street rather than the high ridgeway.

Canterbury was the cradle of Christianity in southern England & is by tradition the seat of the Primate of All England. This site, on the River Stour, has been settled since the earliest times & became a Saxon stonghold under King Ethelbert of Kent. He established a church here, but it was in Norman times that the first great building work was carried out, to be continued in stages until the 15th century. The result is a blending of styles with early Norman work, a later Norman choir, a vaulted nave in Gothic style & a great tower of Tudor design. Thomas Becket was murdered on the steps of the Cathedral in 1170. The town retains much of its mediaeval character with half-timbered weavers' cottages, old churches & the twin towers of the west gate.

Two main styles of building give the villages of Kent their special character. The Kentish yeoman's house was the home of the wealthier farmers & is found throughout the county. It is a timber-frame building with white lath & plaster walls & a hipped roof of red tiles. Rather more modest in style is a small weatherboard house, usually painted white or cream. Rolvenden & Groombridge have the typical charm of a Kentish village whilst Tunbridge Wells is an attractive town, with a paved parade known as the Pantiles & excellent antique shops.

There are grand houses & castles throughout the county. Leeds Castle stands in a lake & dates back to the 9th century. It has beautifully landscaped parkland. Knowle House is an impressive Jacobean & Tudor Manor House with rough ragstone walls, & acres of deer-park & woodland.

Kent is easily accessible from the Channel Ports, Gatwick Airport & London.

Ightham Mote

Kent

Kent
Gazeteer

Areas of outstanding natural beauty.
Kent Downs.

Historic Houses & Castles

Aylesford, The Friars - Nr. Maidstone
13th century Friary & shrine of Our Lady,
(much restored), 14th century cloisters -
original.

Allington Castle -Nr. Maidstone
13th century. One time home of Tudor
poet Thomas Wyatt. Restored early 20th
century. Icons & Renaissance paintings.

Black Charles - Nr. Sevenoaks
14th century Hall house - Tudor fireplaces,
beautiful panelling.

Boughton Monchelsea Place - Nr.
Maidstone
Elizabethan Manor House - grey stone
battlements - 18th century landscaped
park, wonderful views of Weald of Kent.

Chartwell - Westerham
Home of Sir Winston Churchill.
Chiddingstone Castle - Nr. Edenbridge
18th century Gothic revival building
encasing old remains of original Manor
House - Royal Stuart & Jacobite
collection.
 Ancient Egyptian collection - Japanese
netsuke, etc.

Eyehorne Manor - Hollingbourne
15th century Manor house with 17th
century additions.

Cobham Hall - Cobham
16th century house - Gothic &
Renaissance - Wyatt interior. Now school
for girls.

Fairfield - Eastry, Sandwich
13th-14th centuries - moated castle. Was
home of Anne Boleyn. Beautiful gardens
with unique collection of classical statuary.

Knole - Sevenoaks
15th century - splendid Jacobean interior -
17th & 18th century furniture. One of the
largest private houses in England.

Leeds Castle- Nr. Maidstone
Built in middle of the lake, it was the home
of the mediaeval Queens of England.

Lullingstone Castle - Eynsford
14th century mansion house - frequented
by Henry VIII & Queen Anne.
Still occupied by descendants of the
original owners

Long Barn - Sevenoaks
14th century house - said to be home of
William Caxton. Restored by Edwin
Lutyens; 16th century barn added to
enlarge house. Galleried hall - fine
beaming & fireplaces. Lovely gardens
created by Sir Harold Nicholson & his wife
Vita Sackville-West.

Owletts - Cobham
Carolean house of red brick with
plasterwork ceiling & fine staircase.

Owl House - Lamberhurst
16th century cottage, tile hung; said to be
home of wool smuggler. Charming
gardens.

Penshurst Place - Tonbridge
14th century house with mediaeval Great
Hall perfectly preserved.English Gothic.
Birthplace of Elizabethan poet, Sir Philip
Sidney
Fine staterooms, splendid picture gallery,
famous toy museum. Tudor gardens &
orchards.

Saltwood Castle - Nr. Hythe
Mediaeval - very fine castle & is privately
occupied. Was lived in by Sir Ralph de
Broc, murderer of Thomas a Becket.

Squerreys Court - Westerham
Manor house of William & Mary period,
with furniture, paintings & tapestries of
time. Connections with General Wolfe.

Stoneacre - Otham
15th century yeoman's half-timbered
house.

Cathedrals & Churches

Brook (St. Mary)
11th century paintings in this unaltered
early Norman church.

Brookland (St. Augustine)
13th century & some later part. Crown-
post roofs, detached wooden belfry with
conical cap. 12th century lead font.

Canterbury Cathedral
12th century wall paintings, 12th & 13th
century stained glass. Very fine Norman
crypt. Early perpendicular nave &
cloisters which have heraldic bosses.
Wonderful central tower.

Charing (St. Peter & St. Paul)
13th & 15th century interior with 15th
century tower. 17th century restoration.

Kent

Cobham (St. Mary)
16th century carved & painted tombs - unequalled collection of brasses in county.
Elham (St. Mary the Virgin)
Norman wall with 13th century arcades, perpendicular clerestory. Restored by Eden.
Lullingstone (St. Botolph)
14th century mainly - 16th century wood screen. Painted glass monuments.
Newington-on-the-Street (St. Mary the Virgin)
13th & 14th century - fine tower. 13th century tomb. Wall paintings.
Rochester Cathedral
Norman facade & nave, otherwise early English.
12th century west door. 14th century doorway to Chapter room.
Stone (St. Mary)
13th century - decorated - paintings, 15th century brass, 16th century tomb.
Woodchurch (All Saints)
13th century, having late Norman font & priest's brass of 1320. Arcades alternating octagonal & rounded columns. Triple lancets with banded marble shafting at east end.

Museums & Galleries

Royal Museums - Canterbury
Archaeological, geological, mineralogical exhibits, natural history, pottery & porcelain. Engravings, prints & pictures.
Westgate - Canterbury
Museum of armour, etc. in 14th century gatehouse of city.
Dartford District Museum - Dartford
Roman, Saxon & natural history.
Deal Museum - Deal
Prehistoric & historic antiquities.
Dicken's House Museum - Broadstairs
Personalia of Dickens; prints, costume & Victoriana.
Down House - Downe
The home of Charles Darwin for 40 years, now his memorial & museum.
Dover Museum - Dover
Roman pottery, ceramics, coins, zoology, geology, local history, etc.
Faversham Heritage Society - Faversham
1000 years of history & heritage.
Folkestone Museum & Art Gallery - Folkestone
Archeology, local history & sciences.

Herne Bay Museum - Herne Bay
Stone, Bronze & Early Iron Age specimens. Roman material from Reculver excavations. Items of local & Kentish interest.
Museum & Art Gallery - Maidstone
16th century manor house exhibiting natural history & archaeolgical collections. Costume Gallery, bygones, ceramics, 17th century works by Dutch & Italian painters. Regimental museum

Historic Monuments

Eynsford Castle - Eynsford
12th century castle remains.
Rochester Castle - Rochester
Storied keep - 1126-39
Roman Fort & Anglo-Saxon Church - Reculver
Excavated remains of 3rd century fort & Saxon church.
Little Kit's Coty House - Aylesford
Ruins of burial chambers from 2 long barrows.
Lullingstone Roman Villa - Lullingstone
Roman farmstead excavations.
Roman Fort & Town - Richborough
Roman 'Rutupiae' & fort
Tonbridge Castle - Tonbridge
12th century curtain walls, shell of keep & 14th century gatehouse.
Dover Castle - Dover
Keep built by Henry II in 1180. Outer curtain built 13th century.

Gardens

Chilham Castle Gardens - Nr. Canterbury
25 acre gardens of Jacobean house, laid out by Tradescant.
Lake garden, fine trees & birds of prey. Jousting & mediaeval banquets.
Great Comp Gardens - Nr. Borough Green
Outstanding 7 acre garden with old brick walls.
Owl House Gardens - Lamberhurst
16th century smugglers cottage with beautiful gardens of roses, daffodils & rhododendrons.
Sissinghurst Castle Gardens - Sissinghurst
Famous gardens created by Vita Sackville-West around the remains of an Elizabethan mansion.

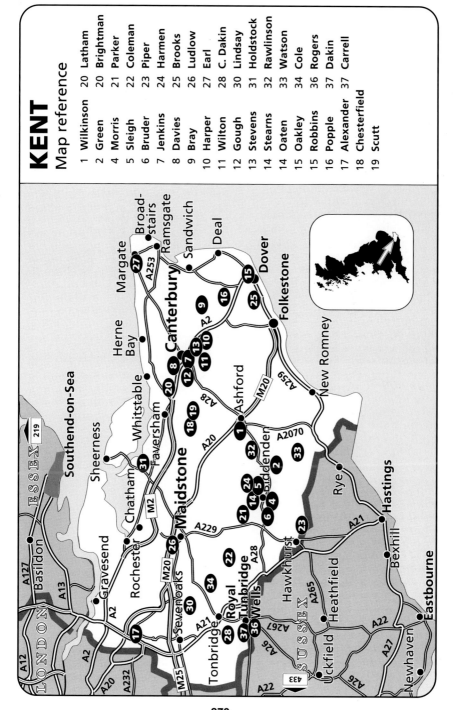

KENT
Map reference

1 Wilkinson	20 Latham
2 Green	20 Brightman
4 Morris	21 Parker
5 Sleigh	22 Coleman
6 Bruder	23 Piper
7 Jenkins	24 Harmen
8 Davies	25 Brooks
9 Bray	26 Ludlow
10 Harper	27 Earl
11 Wilton	28 C. Dakin
12 Gough	30 Lindsay
13 Stevens	31 Holdstock
14 Stearns	32 Rawlinson
14 Oaten	33 Watson
15 Oakley	34 Cole
15 Robbins	36 Rogers
16 Popple	37 Dakin
17 Alexander	37 Carrell
18 Chesterfield	
19 Scutt	

279

Hales Place. High Halden.

Kent

	rate from £ per person	children taken	evening meals	animals taken
Charles & Denise Wilkinson **Worten House** **Great Chart** **Ashford TN23 3BU** **Tel: (01233) 622944** **Open: ALL YEAR** **Map Ref No. 01** Nearest Road: A.20.M, A.28 A beautiful 18th-century farmhouse set in a large garden in the heart of the Kent countryside. Offering 2 very comfortable twin-bedded rooms, each with tea/coffee-making facilities. Denise & Charles Wilkinson & their family assure the visitor of a warm welcome. Plenty of parking space. Within easy reach of Dover, ferry ports & Channel Tunnel. Dinner by arrangement.	£20.00	Y	Y	N
Roger & Ellen Green **Hales Place** **High Halden** **Ashford** **TN26 3JQ** **Tel: (01233) 850219** **Fax 01233 850716** **Open: ALL YEAR** **Map Ref No. 02** Nearest Road: A.28, M.20 Hales Place is a Kent hall house with a colourful history, but is now a comfortable home set in an area of natural beauty. It is surrounded by 11 acres of gardens & paddocks, with 2 wildlife ponds. The prolific kitchen garden provides fresh fruit & vegetables for the table. Preserves & chutneys are home-made, & the bread is freshly baked on the Aga. There are 3 delightful bedrooms, with en-suite/private facilities. Situated in the heart of Kent, Hales Place makes the ideal touring base. Children over 4 yrs.	£21.50 *see PHOTO over* CREDIT CARD VISA M'CARD	Y	Y	N
Mrs Susan Morris **Tudor Cottage** **25 High Street** **Biddenden** **Ashford TN27 8AL** **Tel: (01580) 291913** **Open: MAR - OCT** **Map Ref No. 04** Nearest Road: A.262 Tudor Cottage is a beautiful 15th-century house in the centre of the charming & historic village of Biddenden, with 2 good restaurants nearby. Accommodation is in 3 delightful double bedrooms, 2 en-suite, 1 with private facilities, each well-equipped with colour T.V. & tea/coffee. Children over 10 years are welcome. Tudor Cottage is a perfect location from which to explore beautiful Kent & East Sussex.	£19.00	Y	N	N
Sue & John Bruder **Crit Hall** **Cranbrook Road** **Benenden TN17 4EU** **Tel: (01580) 240609** **Fax 01580 241743** **Open: Mid JAN - Mid DEC** **Map Ref No. 06** Nearest Road: A.229 Crit Hall is an elegant Georgian house in a peaceful country setting with panoramic Wealdon views. A very warm welcome awaits guests. There are lovely double & twin-bedded rooms, with either an en-suite or a private bathroom. All facilities, r/c T.V., etc. Imaginative dinners/breakfasts served, with local produce a feature. Fully licensed. Excellent base for touring Kent & East Sussex. Near many N.T. properties, including Sissinghurst. Children over 10 yrs.	£24.00 *see PHOTO over* CREDIT CARD VISA M'CARD	Y	Y	N
Sara & Bill Sleigh **River Hall Coach House** **Biddenden** **TN27 8JE** **Tel: (01580) 291565** **Fax 01580 292137** **Open: Mid JAN - Mid DEC** **Map Ref No. 05** Nearest Road: A.262, A.274 A very well-appointed country house with 15th-century origins, in a remarkably peaceful rural setting, ideally based for touring Kent & East Sussex; including nearby Sissinghurst. Elegantly furnished with fine antiques throughout; a drawing room & conservatory exclusively for guests, & there are large well-appointed en-suite bedrooms. All facilities, including r/c T.V.. An imaginative cuisine featuring local produce. Dinner available by arrangement. Children over 12 most welcome. A pretty garden with a stream.	£25.00	Y	Y	N

Crit Hall. Benenden.

Thanington Hotel. Canterbury.

Kent

		rate from £ per person	children taken	evening meals	animals taken
David & Jill Jenkins **Thanington Hotel** **140 Wincheap** **Canterbury** **CT1 3RY** **Tel: (01227) 453227** **Fax 01227 453225** **Open: ALL YEAR** **Map Ref No. 07**	Nearest Road: A.28 A lovely Georgian (1810) house with pretty walled garden & private courtyard car parking. Only a min's stroll from the cathedral & the city centre. 30 mins' drive to Dover, Ramsgate & the Channel Tunnel. 10 pretty en-suite bedrooms & a lounge, swimming pool, snooker room & bar. An elegant dining room where a varied breakfast menu is served. Enjoy the quiet, friendly ambience, together with the comfort & superior facilities found in this B & B hotel. Each evening, sample the cuisine of Canterbury's excellent restaurants. *see PHOTO over* CREDIT CARD VISA M'CARD AMEX	£28.00	Y	N	Y
Ann & John Davies **Magnolia House** **36 St Dunstan's Terrace** **Canterbury CT2 8AX** **Tel/Fax: (01227) 765121** **Mobile 0585 595970** **Open: ALL YEAR** **Map Ref No. 08**	Nearest Road: A.2, M.2 Magnolia House is a charming, detached late-Georgian house situated in a quiet, residential street a 10-min walk from the city centre. The bedrooms are individually coordinated to a high standard, & have every facility for an enjoyable stay. A varied breakfast menu is served in the dining room overlooking the attractive walled garden, where you are welcome to relax after a busy day's sightseeing. Evening meals available Nov-Feb. Children over 12. *see PHOTO over* CREDIT CARD VISA M'CARD AMEX	£27.50	Y	Y	N
Richard & Rosemary Bray **Ratling House** **Ratling, Aylesham** **Canterbury CT3 3HL** **Tel: (01304) 842200** **Open: APR - OCT** **Map Ref No. 09**	Nearest Road: A.2 A comfortable 18th-century country house in a quiet rural setting near the A.2. Off the B.2046 approx. 1 mile east of Adisham, & 1 mile north of Aylesham. Centrally heated double bedrooms, 1 with en-suite facilities, T.V., etc., 2 with adjacent bathroom. Large gardens of 2 acres. Ample private parking. Convenient for Channel ports & Tunnel. Dover & Canterbury 9 miles.	£20.00	N	N	N
Hilary Harper **East Bridge Country Hotel** **Bridge Hill, Bridge** **Canterbury CT4 5AS** **Tel: (01227) 830808** **Fax 01227 832181** **Open: ALL YEAR** **Map Ref No. 10**	Nearest Road: A.2, M.2 A friendly, elegant & comfortable Georgian house in a pretty village. 15 mins from the sea ports of Dover & Folkestone. Overlooking open countryside of outstanding beauty, the house offers accommodation in 8 comfortable rooms, 4 en-suite, all with modern amenities, T.V. & tea/coffee-making facilities. Ideal for walking, riding, fishing. Close to Kent's historic castles. Tasty English breakfasts. A licensed restaurant available to residents & non-residents. CREDIT CARD VISA M'CARD	£20.00	Y	Y	N
Sheila Wilton **Walnut Tree Farm** **Lynsore Bottom** **Upper Hardres** **Canterbury** **CT4 6EG** **Tel: (01227) 709375** **Open: ALL YEAR (Excl. Xmas)** **Map Ref No. 11**	Nearest Road: A.2 Set in 6 acres of its own land, this delightful 14th-century thatched farmhouse offers peace & tranquility in unspoilt countryside. Accommodation offered for family or for friends wishing to share, in 2 double adjacent bedrooms, with shower rooms en-suite, or double en-suite, or in dormer of cottage. Tea/coffee in all rooms. Good farmhouse breakfast, home-made bread, marmalade, preserves & fresh eggs. Swimming pool. Ideal base for walking, bird watching, & en-route to Continent. Excellent pub food 2 miles away.	£20.00	Y	N	N

Magnolia House. Canterbury.

Iffin Farmhouse. Canterbury.

Kent

		rate from £ per person	children taken	evening meals	animals taken
Colin & Rosemary Stevens **Iffin Farmhouse** **Iffin Lane** **Canterbury CT4 7BE** **Tel: (01227) 462776** **Fax 01227 462776** **Open: ALL YEAR** **Map Ref No. 13**	Nearest Road: M.2, A.2 A warm welcome awaits you in this old 18th-century farmhouse, renovated to a very high standard. 3 large double bedrooms, each with views to the garden & orchards, colour T.V., tea/coffee, & 2 with en-suite bathroom. Enjoy a full English breakfast, served in a lovely dining room. Super dinners available by prior arrangment. Set in 10 acres of gardens, paddocks & orchards, Iffin Farmhouse (only 6 mins' drive from historic Canterbury) is a delightful spot for touring Kent. *see PHOTO over*	£18.00	Y	Y	N
Mrs Diana Gough **The Willows** **Howfield Lane** **Chartham Hatch** **Canterbury CT4 7HG** **Tel/Fax: (01227) 738442** **Open: ALL YEAR** **Map Ref No. 12**	Nearest Road: A.28 Dr & Mrs Gough welcome you to The Willows. Spoil yourselves in the comfort of their home, furnished with family antiques, where you can relax in a peaceful atmosphere. Situated in a quiet country lane, just 2 miles from Canterbury Cathedral & only 20 mins from Dover & the Channel ports. A traditional English breakfast is served in the conservatory, overlooking a garden for real enthusiasts. Ample parking. Evening meals by arrangement.	£20.00	Y	Y	N
James & Pat Stearns **Sissinghurst Castle Farm** **Cranbrook** **TN17 2AB** **Tel: (01580) 712885** **Open: ALL YEAR** **Map Ref No. 14**	Nearest Road: A.262 This elegant Victorian farmhouse is delightfully situated next to Sissinghurst Castle Gardens. All rooms are spacious & attractively furnished, with tranquil, beautiful views. 1 bedroom has en-suite facilities & 1 a private shower, all with tea/coffee-making facilities. A guests' sitting room. There is a beautiful garden with croquet set. Children over 8 welcome. The perfect spot to stay for visiting many historic properties.	£21.00	Y	N	N
Heather & Kenneth Parker **Maplehurst Mill** **Mill Lane, Frittenden** **Cranbrook TN17 2DT** **Tel: (01580) 852203** **Fax 01580 852203** **Open: ALL YEAR** **Map Ref No. 21**	Nearest Road: A.229 Maplehurst Mill is a beautiful water mill, attached to a mediaeval mill house & standing in 11 acres of landscaped gardens. 3 attractively furnished guest rooms (incl. 1 4-poster), with en-suite/private bathroom, T.V., etc. Each has views over the water & the surrounding countryside. Breakfast & candlelit dinner are served in the mediaeval miller's house, in a beautiful beamed dining room with inglenook, antiques & silver. A warm welcome awaits you. Children over 12. CREDIT CARD VISA M'CARD	£28.00	N	Y	N
Bridget & Robin Oaten **Hancocks Farmhouse** **Tilsden Lane** **Cranbrook** **TN17 3PH** **Tel: (01580) 714645** **Open: ALL YEAR** **Map Ref No. 14**	Nearest Road: A.229, A. 262 Extended in the late 16th century, Hancocks Farmhouse is now a lovely Grade II listed building, surrounded by farmland on the edge of the Wealden town of Cranbrook. Comfortably furnished with antiques, the accommodation is in 3 beautifully decorated bedrooms, 1 with a 4-poster, each with an en-suite/private bathroom, T.V., radio & tea/coffee-making facilities. Dinner here is delicious, & all the bread, rolls, cakes & jams are home-made. A lounge is available, & guests may also relax in the pretty country garden. *see PHOTO over* CREDIT CARD VISA M'CARD	£25.00	N	Y	Y

Hancocks Farmhouse. Cranbrook.

Kent

		rate from £ per person	children taken	evening meals	animals taken
Chris & Lea Oakley **Wallett's Court** **West Cliffe, St. Margarets** **Dover CT15 6EW** **Tel: (01304) 852424** **Fax 01304 853430** **Open: ALL YEAR** **Map Ref No. 15**	Nearest Road: A.258, A.2 A wonderful 17th-century manor house, home of William Pitt the Younger, situated in countryside above the White Cliffs of Dover. 10 delightful bedrooms, all en-suite. Oak beams & inglenook fireplaces. A true 17th-century atmosphere. Home-made produce for breakfast, & Saturday is 'Gourmet Evening' in the restaurant. Kingsdown Golf Course close by. A very warm welcome awaits all visitors to this lovely house.	£27.50 CREDIT CARD VISA M'CARD AMEX	Y	Y	N
Diana Brooks **Rose Hill Farm** **Mill Lane** **West Hougham** **Dover** **CT15 7BD** **Tel: (01304) 240609** **Open: ALL YEAR** **Map Ref No. 25**	Nearest Road: A.20 Following a successful feature in the guide at Lucy's, Hythe, the Brookses are now at a lovely 17th-century listed farmhouse with antique furniture, beams, log fires & charming en-suite bedrooms; 2 lovely cottages. A 1 1/2 acre garden with heated swimming pool, croquet lawn & lovely garden views - Dover Castle in the distance. Less than 10 mins' drive to Dover Port & the Channel Tunnel. Excellent dinners by prior arrangement. A quiet & idyllic setting, & an ideal base for visiting the many places of historic interest in Kent.	£19.00	Y	N	N
Barry & Lyn Popple **Sunshine Cottage** **The Green** **Shepherdswell** **Dover CT15 7LQ** **Tel: (01304) 831359** **Open: ALL YEAR** **Map Ref No. 16**	Nearest Road: A.2 A 17th-century, Grade II listed cottage, overlooking Shepherdswell village green, with a wealth of beams, an inglenook fireplace & 2 lounges. Tastefully furnished, & with a homely atmosphere. 6 attractive bedrooms. A pretty garden & courtyard available to guests. Good home-cooking & home-made preserves. Good food also available at a nearby pub. Shepherdswell is situated halfway between Canterbury & Dover, 25 mins from the Channel Tunnel. BR station 5 mins' walk away.	£25.00	Y	Y	N
Mr & Mrs L. Robbins **Dell Guest House** **233 Folkestone Road** **Dover** **CT17 9SL** **Tel: (01304) 202422** **Open: ALL YEAR** **Map Ref No. 15**	Nearest Road: A.20, B.2011 A friendly welcome is extended to all guests, together with comfort & cleanliness, at this pleasant Victorian house. Offering 5 bedrooms with modern facilities. A colour-T.V. lounge is also available. The Robbinses serve an English breakfast from 7 a.m.; before then, it's Continental, so that those catching the early-morning cross-channel ferries can get a good early start. Conveniently located close to the docks & station. Parking.	£16.00	Y	N	N
Mrs Sarah Alexander **Home Farm** **Riverside** **Eynsford DA4 0AE** **Tel: (01322) 866193** **Fax 01322 868600** **Open: MAR - NOV** **Map Ref No. 17**	Nearest Road: A.225 Situated in a picturesque village within an Area of Outstanding Natural Beauty. This 18th-century farmhouse, set on a dairy/arable farm, offers 3 attractively furnished, en-suite bedrooms. Ideal for London, Gatwick & the Channel ports. Only 2 miles from the M.25/M.20 junction. Leeds Castle, Brands Hatch & many National Trust properties within easy reach. There are many places to eat in the village. Children over 10 yrs.	£19.50	Y	N	N

Kent

Mrs Susan Chesterfield **Frith Farm House** Otterden Faversham ME13 0DD Tel: (01795) 890701 Fax 01795 890009 Open: ALL YEAR Map Ref No. 18	Nearest Road: A.2, A.20, M.2 A warm welcome awaits guests at this restored Georgian farmhouse, surrounded by lovely cherry trees. It stands in an Area of Outstanding Natural Beauty. Accommodation is in a choice of 3 comfortable en-suite rooms with radio, T.V. & tea/coffee-making facilities. This makes a pleasant base from which to tour the whole of Kent. Leeds Castle, Rochester, Chilam & Canterbury are nearby. Children over 10 years only.	£23.50 🚭 *see PHOTO over*	N	Y	N
Annette & Alan Brightman **The Granary** Plumford Lane Ospringe Faversham ME13 0DS Tel: (01795) 538416 Fax 01795 538416 Open: ALL YEAR Map Ref No. 20	Nearest Road: A.2 Set deep in apple-orchard country, The Granary - recently part of a working farm - has been tastefully & beautifully converted to provide an interesting & spacious home. All rooms are delightfully furnished to a high standard, whilst retaining a rustic charm. 3 charming bedrooms, each with an en-suite/private bathroom. The guests' own lounge, with a balcony, overlooks the surrounding countryside. Well situated for local pubs offering excellent food. An ideal location for touring historic Kent.	£19.00 CREDIT CARD VISA M'CARD	Y	N	N
Mrs Corrine Scutt **Leaveland Court** Leaveland Faversham ME13 0NP Tel: (01233) 740596 Open: FEB - NOV Map Ref No. 19	Nearest Road: A.251 Guests are warmly welcomed to this enchanting 15th-century timbered farmhouse, & its delightful gardens with heated swimming pool. Situated in a quiet rural setting, between 13th-century Leaveland church & woodlands, & surrounded by a 300-acre downland farm. All rooms are en-suite facilities, T.V. & tea/coffee tray. Conveniently placed only 5 mins from M.2 & Faversham, 20 mins Canterbury & 30 mins Channel ports.	£20.00 🚭 CREDIT CARD VISA M'CARD	Y	N	Y
Prudence Latham **Tenterden House** 209 The Street Boughton Faversham ME13 9BL Tel: (01227) 751593 Open: ALL YEAR Map Ref No. 20	Nearest Road: A.2, M.2 Tenterden House is a listed Tudor building in the village of Boughton, which is 6 miles from Canterbury & 1 mile from the M.2. The old gardener's cottage has been renovated to provide a bathroom & 2 bedrooms (1 double & 1 twin), h&c, T.V. & tea/coffee facilities. Full English breakfast is served in the main house. Restaurants & pubs within walking distance, as is Boughton Golf Course. An ideal centre for walking, touring, bird-watching & reaching all Channel Ports.	£17.50	Y	N	N
Mrs S. Coleman **Crowbourne Farmhouse** Goudhurst TN17 1ET Tel: (01580) 211226 Open: ALL YEAR Map Ref No. 22	Nearest Road: A.262 Crowbourne is a delightful 17th-century farmhouse peacefully situated in a 125-acre fruit & sheep farm, with glorious views just outside the charming village of Goudhurst. Accommodation is in 3 lovely, comfortable rooms with bath (1 en-suite), & sitting room with T.V. & tea/coffee-making facilities. Delicious evening meals, using local produce, by arrangement only. Ideal for visiting Kent castles, especially Sissinghurst. Golf, fishing & sailing nearby. Gatwick 1 hour.	£20.00 🚭	Y	Y	N

Frith Farm House. Otterden.

Swale Cottage. Penshurst.

Kent

		rate from £ per person	children taken	evening meals	animals taken

Mrs Rosemary Piper **Conghurst Farm** **Conghurst Lane** **Hawkhurst TN18 4RW** **Tel: (01580) 753331** **Fax 01580 754579** **Open: FEB - NOV** **Map Ref No. 23**	Nearest Road: A.268 Set in peaceful, totally unspoilt countryside, Conghurst Farm offers a perfect spot for a restful holiday. Within easy reach of all the marvellous houses & gardens that this part of the country has to offer. Accommodation is in 3 very comfortable bedrooms, with en-suite/private bathrooms. There is a drawing room, a separate T.V. room &, in the summer, a delightful garden for guests to enjoy. An ideal base from which to explore Kent.	£20.00	N	Y	N
Mrs Jane Harman **Vine Farm** **Waterman Quarter** **Headcorn TN27 9JJ** **Tel: (01622) 890203** **Fax 01622 891819** **Open: ALL YEAR** **Map Ref No. 24**	Nearest Road: A.274, M.20 Vine Farm is an enchanting, 16th-century, listed farmhouse lying in a glorious rural situation & surrounded by farmland & livestock, ponds & gardens (Jane Harman is a keen gardener). All rooms are attractively furnished with antiques. Guests have their own sitting room, & there are 3 charming en-suite bedrooms. Centrally situated, close to Leeds & Sissinghurst Castles, ideal for visiting many famous houses, gardens & historic sites. London 1 hour by train. Children over 12. **CREDIT CARD** VISA M'CARD	£19.50	Y	Y	N
Mrs Ann Earl **The Greswolde Hotel** **20 Surrey Road** **Cliftonville** **Margate CT9 2LA** **Tel: (01843) 223956** **Open: ALL YEAR** **Map Ref No. 27**	Nearest Road: M.2, A.299 The Greswolde is a 6-bedroomed Victorian hotel retaining much of its original character & charm. All rooms have en-suite facilities, with colour T.V. & tea makers. A quiet, relaxing lounge/reading room. Located 100 yds from the promenade, & close to championship indoor & outdoor bowling greens. Many golf courses within easy reach. Pubs & eating places are nearby. Ideal for touring, with Channel ports close by. Children over 8. **CREDIT CARD** VISA M'CARD	£18.00	Y	N	Y
Cynthia Dakin **Swale Cottage** **Off Poundsbridge Lane** **Penshurst** **TN11 8AH** **Tel/Fax: (01892) 870738** **Open: ALL YEAR** **Map Ref No. 28**	Nearest Road: A.26, B.2176 Swale Cottage is a charmingly converted listed Grade II Kentish barn in a glorious country setting, overlooking a mediaeval manor house with lake & gardens. 3 spacious & en-suite, beamed bedrooms with colour T.V. (4-poster, double & twin). Award winning Swale Cottage is situated 1/2 mile south-east of the mediaeval village of Penshurst (off the B.2176) with inns, tea shops, an antique shop & Penshurst Place with a Tudor garden. Near to Hever & Chartwell. Gatwick 30 mins' drive. London 40 mins by train. *see PHOTO over*	£24.00	Y	N	Y
Mrs Jo Lindsay N.D.D. A.T.D. **Jordans** **Sheet Hill** **Plaxtol** **Sevenoaks** **TN15 0PU** **Tel: (01732) 810379** **Open: ALL YEAR** **Map Ref No. 30**	Nearest Road: M.25, A.227 Beautiful, picture-postcard, 15th-century Tudor house (awarded a 'Historic Building of Kent' plaque) in the picturesque village of Plaxtol, among orchards & parkland. It is beautifully furnished, & has leaded windows, inglenook fireplaces, oak beams & an enchanting old English garden with rambler roses & espalier trees. Within easy reach are Ightham Mote, Leeds & Hever Castle, Penshurst, Chartwell & Knole. 3 lovely rooms, with en-suite/private facilities. London 35 mins by train, & easy access to airports. Children over 12. *see PHOTO over*	£24.00	N	N	N

Jordans. Plaxtol.

Kent

		rate from £ per person	children taken	evening meals	animals taken

Mrs A. J. Holdstock **Hempstead House** **London Road** **Bapchild** **Sittingbourne ME9 9PP** Tel: **(01795) 428020** Fax 01795 428020 **Open: ALL YEAR** **Map Ref No. 31**	Nearest Road: A.2 Hempstead House is a private Victorian country house situated on the main A.2 between Sittingbourne & Canterbury, & set well back in 3 acres of beautifully landscaped gardens. All major towns in the area are easily accessible, as are the coastal ports. 7 superb en-suite bedrooms, with dressing areas, tea/coffee-making & T.V.. All food is home-cooked using vegetables from the garden & local meat & fish. All guests are welcomed as friends, & encouraged to enjoy the house as much as their hosts do.	£31.00 🚭 CREDIT CARD VISA M'CARD AMEX	Y	Y	Y
Maureen & Alan Rawlinson **Brattle House** **Watermill Bridges** **Tenterden** **TN30 6UL** Tel: **(01580) 763565** **Open: ALL YEAR** **Map Ref No. 32**	Nearest Road: A.28 A handsome 17th century Georgian farmhouse, surrounded by 11 acres of garden meadow & woodland in rolling countryside. Breakfast in the conservatory, relax in the low-beamed sitting room, dine by candlelight in the elegant dining room (furnished with antiques) & retire to 1 of 3 luxury en-suite bedrooms. Cooking is imaginative & of a high standard, using fresh produce. Sissinghurst, Gt Dixter are close by. Gatwick 70 mins. Heathrow 85 mins. Children over 12.	£26.50 🚭 *see PHOTO over*	N	Y	N
Mr & Mrs Ian Watson **Wittersham Court** **Wittersham** **Tenterden TN30 7EA** Tel: **(01797) 270425** **Open: ALL YEAR (Excl.** **Xmas & New Year)** **Map Ref No. 33**	Nearest Road: A.28, B.2082 Wittersham Court is a Grade II listed period house, tastefully furnished & set in an acre of peaceful garden on the famous Isle of Oxney, midway between Tenterden & Rye. 3 attractive bedrooms, each with an en-suite/private bathroom. Excellent evening meals available. There are many beautiful gardens & castles in the area to visit, as well as Romney Marsh with its lovely churches. Only 45 mins from Dover & Folkestone. Single supplement.	£28.00 CREDIT CARD VISA M'CARD	N	Y	N
Shirley & Vernon Cole **Goldhill Mill** **Golden Green** **Tonbridge TN11 0BA** Tel: **(01732) 851626** Fax 01732 851881 **Open: ALL YEAR (Excl.** **Mid JUL - SEPT)** **Map Ref No. 34**	Nearest Road: A.26 Goldhill Mill, as mentioned in The Doomsday Book, was a working water mill for 850 years. Peacefully set in 20 acres, the beautiful old mill house has been lovingly restored, & affords superb accommodation enhanced by high-quality decor & antique furniture. 3 attractive, well-equipped, en-suite double bedrooms (1 with romantic 4-poster, 2 with jacuzzi bath). Breakfast is served in the farmhouse kitchen with Tudor beams. An idyllic setting, with gracious living & a relaxed atmosphere. Children over 12.	£33.75 🚭 CREDIT CARD VISA M'CARD	Y	N	N
Richard & Sue Rogers **Ashtree Cottage** **Eden Road** **Tunbridge Wells TN1 1TS** Tel: **(01892) 541317** **Open: ALL YEAR (Excl.** **Xmas & New Year)** **Map Ref No. 36**	Nearest Road: A.21, M.25 Ashtree Cottage is situated in a quiet private road just above the famous Pantiles, & is within a few minutes' walk of the high street & station. There are 2 charming & attractively furnished bedrooms with en-suite bathrooms, radio, T.V., tea/coffee-making facilities & plenty of tourist information. There is an excellent choice of restaurants & country pubs nearby, & many places of interest are within easy reach.	£20.00 🚭	Y	N	N

Brattle House. Tenterden.

The Old Parsonage. Tunbridge Wells.

Kent

	rate from £ per person	children taken	evening meals	animals taken
Tony & Mary Dakin **The Old Parsonage** **Church Lane** **Frant** **Tunbridge Wells** **TN3 9DX** **Tel: (01892) 750773** **Fax 01892 750773** **Open: ALL YEAR** **Map Ref No. 37**	Nearest Road: A.267 Peacefully situated by the church in pretty Frant village (with 2 pubs & restaurant nearby), The Old Parsonage provides superior accommodation echoing the gracious living enjoyed here nearly 200 yrs ago by the local Lord. This fine Georgian house has excellent en-suite bedrooms, elegant, antique-furnished reception rooms & a spacious conservatory & ballustraded terrace, where guests can relax with afternoon tea, overlooking the secluded walled garden. A short drive to 15 historic houses & castles. Gatwick 40 mins, Heathrow 70 mins, London 40 mins by train.	£26.00 *see PHOTO over* CREDIT CARD VISA M'CARD	Y	N	Y
Mrs Carolyn Carrell **Rowden House Farm** **Frant** **Tunbridge Wells** **TN3 9HS** **Tel: (01892) 750259** **Open: APR - OCT** **Map Ref No. 37**	Nearest Road: A.267 A delightful Elizabethan house, listed as of architectural interest, standing in 20 acres, with sheep, horses, dogs & chickens. Surrounded by the beautiful, rolling, wooded countryside of Sussex, it is perfectly placed for visiting the stately homes & towns of Kent & Sussex. Accommodation is in 1 twin-bedded room, with private bathroom, & 2 singles with wash basins. All have tea/coffee-making facilities. An attractive drawing room, with colour T.V.. Gatwick 1 hour, London 1 1/4 hours. Children over 10 welcome.	£20.00	Y	N	N
Judy Ludlow **Woodgate** **Birling Road** **Leybourne** **West Malling ME19 5HT** **Tel: (01732) 843201** **Open: ALL YEAR** **Map Ref No. 26**	Nearest Road: M.20 This is a very pretty 17th-century cottage, situated in a rural location & yet within easy reach of the M.20. Set in 4 acres of woodland garden, with tropical bird aviaries. Unusual chickens wander freely during daylight hours. Rooms are tastefully & distinctively decorated, with antiques collected during the years spent living overseas. Meals (available with prior notice) are a speciality, & are unusual & interesting. A delightful home.	£19.00	Y	Y	Y

When booking your accommodation please mention
The Best Bed & Breakfast

Lancashire

Lancashire
(North West)

Lancashire can prove a surprisingly beautiful county. Despite its industrial history of cotton production, there is magnificent scenery & there are many fine towns & villages. Connections with the Crown & the clashes of the Houses of Lancaster & York have left a rich heritage of buildings with a variety of architecture. There are old stone cottages & farmhouses, as well as manor houses from many centuries.

For lovers of the countryside, Lancashire has the sweeping hills of Bowland, the lovely Ribble Valley, the moors of Rossendale & one mountain, mysterious Pendle Hill.

The Royal Forest of Bowland is a forest without trees, which has provided rich hunting grounds over the centuries. An old windswept pass runs over the heights of Salter Fell & High Cross Fell from Slaidburn, where the Inn, the "Hark to Bounty", was named after the noisiest hound in the squire's pack & used to be the courtroom where strict forest laws were enforced.

Further south, the Trough of Bowland provides an easier route through the hills, & here is the beautiful village of Abbeystead in Wynesdale where monks once farmed the land. The church has stained glass windows portraying shepherds & their flocks & there are pegs in the porch where shepherds hung their crooks.

Below the dramatic hills of Bowland, the green valley of the Ribble climbs from Preston to the Yorkshire Dales. Hangridge Fell, where the tales of witches are almost as numerous as those of Pendle Hill, lies at the beginning of the valley.

Pendle Hill can be reached from the pretty village of Downham which has Tudor, Jacobean & Georgian houses, village stocks & an old inn. Old Pendle rises abruptly to 1831 feet & is a strange land formation. It is shrouded in legend & stories of witchcraft.

Between Pendle Hill & the moors of Rossendale are the textile towns of Nelson, Colne, Burnley, Accrington & Blackburn. The textile industry was well established in Tudor times & the towns grew up as markets for the trading of the cloth woven in the Piece Halls.

The moors which descend to the very edges of the textile towns are wild & beautiful & have many prehistoric tumuli & earthworks. Through the towns & the countryside, winds the Liverpool & Leeds canal, providing an excellent towpath route to see the area.

Lancaster is an historic city boasting the largest castle in England, dating back to Norman times.

Lancashire's coastal resorts are legendary, & Blackpool is Queen of them all with her miles of Illuminations & millions of visitors.

Downham Village.

Lancashire

Lancashire Gazeteer

Areas of outstanding natural beauty.
The Forest of Bowland, Parts of Arnside & Silverdale.

Historic Houses & Castles

Rufford Old Hall - Rufford
15th century screen in half-timbered hall of note. Collection of relics of Lancashire life.

Chingle Hall - Nr. Preston
13th century - small manor house with moat. Rose gardens. Haunted!

Astley Hall - Chorley
Elizabethan house reconstructed in 17th century. Houses pictures, tapestries, pottery & furniture.

Gawthorpe Hall - Padiham
17th century manor house with 19th century restoration. Moulded ceilings & some fine panelling. A collection of lace & embroidery.

Bramall Hall - Bramall
Fine example of half-timbered (black & white) manor house built in 14th century & added to in Elizabethan times. Fine grounds.

Lancaster Castle - Lancaster
Largest of English castles - dates back to Norman era.

Astley Hall - Chorley
16th century half-timbered grouped around central court. Rebuilt in the Jacobean manner with long gallery. Unique furniture.

Hoghton Tower - Nr. Preston
16th century - fortified hill-top mansion - magnificent banquet hall. Dramatic building - walled gardens & rose gardens.

Thurnham Hall - Lancaster
13th century origins. 16th century additions & 19th century facade. Beautiful plasterwork of Elizabethan period. Jacobean staircase.

Cathedrals & Churches

Lancaster (St. Mary)
15th century with 18th century tower. Restored chapel - fine stalls.

Whalley (St. Mary)
13th century with 15th century tower, clerestory & aisle windows. Fine wood carving of 15th century canopied stalls.

Halsall (St. Cuthbert)
14th century chancel, 15th century perpendicular spire. 14th century tomb. Original doors, brasses & effigies. 19th century restoration.

Tarleton (St. Mary)
18th century part 19th century.

Great Mitton (All Hallows)
15th century rood screen, 16th century font cover, 17th century pulpit.

Museums & Galleries

Blackburn Museum - Blackburn
Extensive collections relating to local history archeology, ceramics, geology & natural history. One of the finest collection of coins & fine collection of mediaeval illuminated manuscripts & early printed books.

Bury Museum & Art Gallery - Bury
Houses fine Victorian oil & watercolours. Turner, Constable, Landseer, de Wint

City Gallery - Manchester
Pre-Raphaelites, Old Masters, Impressionists, modern painters all represented in this fine gallery; also silver & pottery collections.

Higher Mill Museum - Helmshaw
One of the oldest wool textile finishing mills left in Lancashire. Spinning wheels, Hargreave's Spinning Jenny, several of Arkwrights machines, 20 foot water wheel.

Townley Hall Art Gallery & Museum, & Museum of Local Crafts & Industries - Burnley

LANCASHIRE

Map reference

1 Rothwell
2 Lawrence
3 Butler
5 Ireland
6 Townend
7 Smith

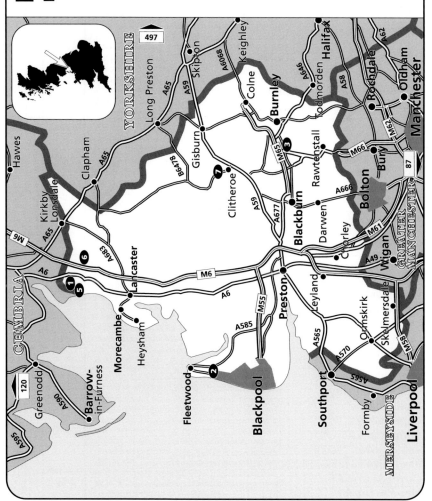

Lancashire

		rate from £ per person	children taken	evening meals	animals taken
Mr & Mrs M. Lawrence **Burlees Hotel** **40 Knowle Avenue** **North Shore** **Blackpool FY2 9TQ** **Tel: (01253) 354535** **Open: FEB - NOV** **Map Ref No. 02**	Nearest Road: A.586 Traditionally built as a guest house, Burlees provides quality accommodation with 9 well-equipped, comfortable, en-suite bedrooms. A guest lounge & separate bar ensure a relaxed atmosphere. Excellent breakfast & dinner menus offer variety & choice. Families welcome, & baby sitting is provided. Ideal location for inland exploration of Lancashire, combined with the excitement of Britain's premier fun resort.	£20.00 CREDIT CARD VISA M'CARD	Y	Y	N
Mrs M. Butler **Eaves Barn Farm** **Hapton** **Burnley** **BB12 7LP** **Tel: (01282) 771591** **Open: ALL YEAR** **Map Ref No. 03**	Nearest Road: M.65, A.679 Eaves Barn Farm is a mixed working farm situated in a semi-rural location. The award-winning accommodation comprises a spacious cottage, with 3 bedrooms, attached to the main house, furnished to a high standard & offering superb facilities, & fronted by attractive gardens. Breakfast is served in the conservatory. Delicious evening meals, with home-made preserves a speciality. Easy access to all Lancashire's tourist attractions & places of historic interest. Convenient for Manchester Airport. Children over 10.	£20.00	Y	Y	N
Mrs S. A. Rothwell **The Bower** **Yealand Road** **Yealand Conyers** **Carnforth** **LA5 9SF** **Tel: (01524) 734585** **Open: ALL YEAR** **Map Ref No. 01**	Nearest Road: A.6, M.6 A beautiful, small Georgian country house, set in an Area of Outstanding Natural Beauty. Superb walks right from the door, including to Leighton Moss RSPB reserve. 2 lovely bedrooms, 1 with a double & single bed & en-suite bathroom, & 1 with double bed & private bathroom. Both have T.V., clock radio, hairdryer & tea/coffee facilities. Delicious home-cooked, 4-course dinners. Perfect for exploring the Lake District & Yorkshire Dales. 10 mins from M.6. Very peaceful & ideal for stop-overs to or from Scotland. Children over 12 yrs.	£23.00	Y	Y	Y
Mrs Adelaide Ireland **Thwaite End Farm** **Bolton-le-Sands** **Carnforth LA5 9TN** **Tel: (01524) 732551** **Open: ALL YEAR** **Map Ref No. 05**	Nearest Road: A.6 Guests will find a comfortable, friendly atmosphere in this delightful 17th-century farmhouse. Situated on a small sheep & beef-rearing farm of 52 acres, it is conveniently located between Carnforth & Bolton-le-Sands. Offering 3 pleasant rooms, 2 with en-suite facilities & all with T.V. & tea/coffee-making facilities. 2 comfortable lounges, one with colour T.V.. Hot drinks & biscuits are served. Breakfast is served in the attractive dining room.	£20.00	N	N	N
Mrs Sally Townend **New Capernwray** **Farmhouse** **Capernwray** **Carnforth LA6 1AD** **Tel: (01524) 734284** **Fax 01524 734284** **Open: ALL YEAR** **Map Ref No. 06**	Nearest Road: A.6, M.6 Ex. 35 Ideal stop London-Scotland, 3 miles from Exit 35, M.6. Set in beautiful countryside, close to Lake District & James Herriot country. High-quality accommodation in 17th-century former farmhouse. Renowned for warm hospitality, peace, comfort & excellent candle-lit dinners. Delightful, fully equipped no-smoking bedrooms, with private & en-suite facilities. Personally conducted tours to Lake District, Herriot country & Hadrian's Wall & personalised itineraries. N.W. Regional winner Best B&B Award for Excellence.	£26.00 *see PHOTO over* CREDIT CARD VISA M'CARD	Y	Y	Y

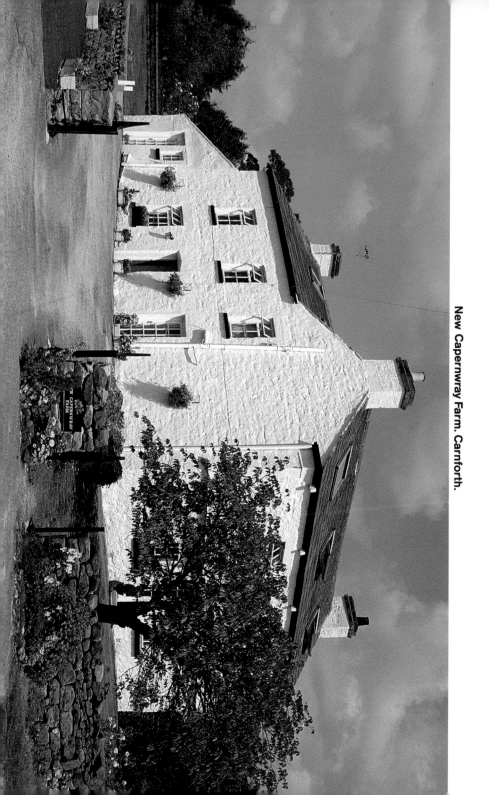

New Capernwray Farm. Carnforth.

Lancashire

		rate from £ per person	children taken	evening meals	animals taken
Gordon & Jean Smith Peter Barn Country House Cross Lane Waddington Clitheroe BB7 3JH Tel: (01200) 28585 Open: ALL YEAR Map Ref No. 07	Nearest Road: A.59 Nestling in the Forest of Bowland, Peter Barn was a Tithe Barn that has been lovingly converted by the Smith family, & is surrounded by an abundance of wildlife on a lane known locally as Rabbit Lane. Furnished with antiques & family 'bric a brac', the first-floor sitting room has panoramic views, a stone fireplace & a pitched roof made of old church rafters. There are 3 very attractive en-suite/private bedrooms.	£17.50	Y	N	N

All the establishments mentioned in this guide

are members of

The Worldwide Bed & Breakfast Association

When booking your accommodation please mention
The Best Bed & Breakfast

Leicester & Notts

Leicestershire
(East Midlands)

Rural Leicestershire is rich in grazing land, a peaceful, undramatic landscape broken up by the waterways that flow through in the south of the county.

The River Avon passes on its way to Stratford, running by 17th century Stanford Hall & its motorcycle museum. The Leicester section of the Grand Union Canal was once very important for the transportation of goods from the factories of the Midlands to London Docks. It passes through a fascinating series of multiple locks at Foxton. The decorative barges, the 'narrow boats' are pleasure craft these days rather than the life-blood of the closed community of boat people who lived & worked out their lives on the canals.

Rutland was formerly England's smallest county, but was absorbed into East Leicestershire in the 1970's. Its name lives on in Rutland Water, one of Europe's largest reservoirs & an attractive setting for sailing, fishing or enjoying a trip on the pleasure cruiser. There is also the Rutland Theatre at Tolethorpe Hall, where a summer season of Shakespeare's plays is presented in the open air.

Melton Mowbray is famous for its pork pies & it is also the centre of Stilton cheese country. The "King of Cheeses" is made mainly in the Vale of Belvoir where Leicestershire meets Nottinghamshire, & the battlements & turrets of Belvoir Castle overlook the scene from its hill-top.

To the north-west the Charnwood Forest area is pleasantly wooded & the deer park at Bradgate surrounding the ruined home of Lady Jane Grey, England's nine-day queen, is a popular attraction.

Nottinghamshire
(East Midlands)

Nottinghamshire has a diversity of landscape from forest to farmland, from coal mines to industrial areas.

The north of the county is dominated by the expanse of Sherwood Forest, smaller now than in the time of legendary Robin Hood & his Merry Men, but still a lovely old woodland of Oak & Birch.

The Dukeries are so called because of the numerous ducal houses built in the area & there is beautiful parkland on these great estates that can be visited. Clumber Park, for instance has a huge lake & a double avenue of Limes.

Newstead Abbey was a mediaeval priory converted into the Byron family home in the 16th century. It houses the poet Byron's manuscripts & possessions & is set in wonderful gardens.

More modest is the terraced house in Eastwood, where D.H. Lawrence was born into the mining community on which his novels are based.

Nottingham was recorded in the Domesday Book as a thriving community & that tradition continues. It was here that Arkwright perfected his cotton-spinning machinery & went on to develop steam as a power source for industry.

Textiles, shoes, bicycles & tobacco are all famous Nottingham products, & the story of Nottingham Lace can be discovered at the Lace Hall, housed in a former church.

Nottingham Castle, high on Castle Rock, was built & destroyed & rebuilt many times during its history. It now houses the city's Art Gallery & Museum. The Castle towers over the ancient 'Trip to Jerusalem' Inn, said to be so named because crusaders stopped there for a drink on their way to fight in the Holy Land.

Leicester & Notts

Leicestershire Gazeteer
Areas of outstanding natural beauty.
Charnwood Forest, Rutland Water.

Historic Houses & Castles
Belvoir Castle - Nr. Grantham
Overlooking the Vale of Belvoir, castle
rebuilt in 1816, with many special events
including jousting tournaments. Home of
the Duke of Rutland since Henry VIII.
Paintings, furniture, historic armoury,
military museums, magnificent stateroom

Belvoir Castle

Belgrave Hall - Leicester
18th century Queen Anne house -
furnishing of 18th & 19th centuries.
Langton Hall - Nr. Market Harborough
Privately occupied - perfect English
country house from mediaeval times -
drawing rooms have 18th century
Venetian lace.

Oakham Castle - Oakham
Norman banqueting hall of late 12th
century
Stanford Hall - Nr Lutterworth
17th century William & Mary house -
collection of Stuart relics & pictures,
antiques & costumes of family from
Elizabeth I onward. Motor cycle museum.
Stapleford Park - Nr. Melton Mowbray
Old wing dated 1500, restored 1663.
Extended to mansion in 1670. Collection
of pictures, tapestries, furniture &
Balston's Staffordshire portrait figures of
Victorian age.

Cathedrals & Churches
Breedon-on-the-Hill (St. Mary & St.
Hardulph)
Norman & 13th century. Jacobean
canopied pew, 18th century carvings.
Empingham (St. Peter)
14th century west tower, front & crocketed
spire. Early English interior -
double piscina, triple sedilla.
Lyddington (St. Andrew)
Perpendicular in the main - mediaeval wall
paintings & brasses.
Staunton Harol (Holy Trinity)
17th century - quite unique Cromwellian
church - painted ceilings.

Museums & Galleries
Bosworth Battlefield Visitor Centre - Nr
Market Bosworth
Exhibitions, models, battlefield trails at site
of 1485 Battle of Bosworth where Richard
III lost his life & crown to Henry.
Leicestershire Museum of Technology -
Leicester
Beam engines, steam shovel, knitting
machinery & other aspects of the county's
industrial past.
Leicester Museum & Art Gallery -
Leicester
Painting collection.
18th & 19th century, watercolours &
drawings, 20th century French paintings,
Old Master & modern prints.
English silver & ceramics, special
exhibitions.
Jewry Wall Museum & Site - Leicester
Roman wall & baths site adjoining
museum of archaeology.

Leicester & Notts

Melton Carnegie Museum-Melton Mowbray
Displays on Stilton cheese, pork pies &
other aspects of the past & present life of
the area.
Rutland County Museum - Oakham
Domestic & agricultural life of Rutland,
formerly England's smallest county.
**Donnington Collection of Single-Seater
Racing Cars** - Castle Donington
Large collection of grand prix racing cars
& racing motorcycles, adjoining Donington
Park racing circuit..
Wygson's House Museum of Costume -
Leicestershire
Costume, accessories & shop settings in
late mediaeval buildings.
The Bellfoundry Museum -
Loughborough
Moulding, casting, tuning & fitting of bells,
with conducted tours of bellfoundry.

Historic Monuments
The Castle - Ashby-de-la-Zouch
14th century with tower added in 15th
century.
Kirby Muxloe Castle - Kirby Muxloe
15th century fortified manor house with
moat ruins.

Other things to see & do
Rutland Farm Park - Oakham
Rare & commercial breeds of livestock in
18 acres of park & woodland, with early
19th century farm buildings.
Stoughton Farm Park - Nr. Leicester
Shire horses, rare breeds, small animals &
modern 140 dairy herd. Milking
demonstrations, farm museum, woodland
walks. Adventure playground.
Twycross Zoo - Nr. Atherstone
Gorillas, orang-utans, chimpanzees,
gibbons, elephants, giraffes, lions & many
other animals.
The Battlefield Line Nr. Market Bosworth
Steam railway & collection of railway
relics, adjoining Bosworth Battlefield.
Great Central Railway - Loughborough
Steam railway over 5-mile route in
Charnwood Forest area, with steam &
diesel museum.
Rutland Railway Museum - Nr. Oakham
Industrial steam & diesel locomotives &
wagons from quarries, mines & factories.

Nottinghamshire Gazeteer
Historic Houses & Castles
Holme Pierrepont Hall - Nr. Nottingham
Outstanding red brick Tudor manor, in
continuous family ownership, with 19th
century courtyard garden.
Newark Castle - Newark
Dramatic castle ruins on riverside site,
once one of the most important castles of
the north.
Newstead Abbey - Nr. Mansfield
Priory converted to country mansion,
home of poet Lord Byron with many of his
possessions & manuscripts on display.
Beautiful parkland, lakes & gardens.
Nottingham Castle - Nottingham
17th century residence on site of
mediaeval castle.
Fine collections of ceramics, silver,
Nottingham alabaster carvings, local
historical displays. Art gallery. Special
exhibitions & events.
Wollaton Hall - Nottingham
Elizabethan mansion now housing natural
history exhibits. Stands in deer park, with
Industrial Museum in former stables,
illustrating the city's bicycle, hosiery, lace,
pharmaceutical & other industries.

Cathedrals & Churches
Egmanton (St. Mary)
Magnificent interior by Comper. Norman
doorway & font. Canopied rood screen,
17th century altar.
Newark (St. Mary Magdalene)
15th century. 2 painted panels of "Dance
of Death". Reredos by Comper.
Southwell Cathedral
Norman nave, unvaulted, fine early
English choir. Decorated pulpitum, 6
canopied stalls, fine misericords.
Octagonal chapter house..
Terseval (St. Catherine)
12th century - interior 17th century
unrestored

Museums & Galleries
Castlegate Museum - Nottingham
Row of Georgian terraced houses showing
costume & textile collection.
Lace making equipment & lace collection.

Leicester & Notts

Nottingham Castle Museum - Nottingham
Collections of ceramics, glass & silver. Alabaster carvings.

D.H. Lawrence Birthplace - Eastwood
Home of the novelist & poet, as it would have been at time of his birth, 1885.

Millgate Museum of Social & Folk Life - Newark
Local social & folk life, with craft workshops.

Brewhouse Yard Museum - Nottingham
Daily life in Nottingham, displayed in 17th century cottages & rock-cut cellars.

The Lace Hall - Nottingham
The story of Nottingham Lace audio-visual display & exhibition with lace shops, in fine converted church.

Museum of Costume & Textiles - Nottingham
Costumes, lace & textiles on display in fine Georgian buildings.

Bassetlaw Museum - Retford
Local history of north Nottinghamshire.

Canal Museum - Nottinghamshire
History of the River Trent & canal history, in former canal warehouse.

Ruddington Framework Knitters' Museum - Ruddington
Unique complex of early 19th-century framework knitters' buildings with over 20 hand frames in restored workshop.

Other things to see & do

The Tales of Robin Hood - Nottingham
A 'flight to adventure' from mediaeval Nottingham to Sherwood Forest through the tales of the world's most famous outlaw.

Clumber Park - Nr. Worksop
Landscaped parkland, with double avenue of limes, lake, chapel. One of the Dukeries' estates, though the house no longer remains.

Rufford - Nr. Ollerton
Parkland, lake & gallery with fine crafts, around ruin of Cistercian abbey.

Sherwood Forest Visitor Centre - Nr. Edwinstowe
Robin Hood exhibition.
450 acres of ancient oak woodland associated with the outlaw & his merry men.

Sherwood Forest Farm Park - Nr. Edwinstowe
Rare breeds of cattle, sheep, pigs & goats. Lake with wildfowl.

White Post Farm Centre - Farnsfield, Nr Newark
Working modern farm with crops & many animals, including cows, sheep, pigs, hens, geese, ducks, llamas, horses. Indoor displays & exhibits.

Newark Castle.

LEICESTERSHIRE & NOTTINGHAMSHIRE

Map reference

0 White
1 Goodwin
2 Gibson
4 Hitchen
4 Hackney
5 Smithers
6 Hinchley
7 Ibbotson
8 Shipside
9 Need
10 Brammer
11 Spratt

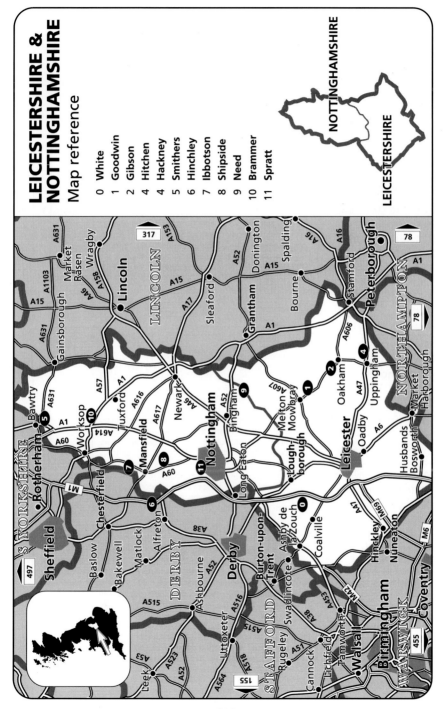

Leicestershire

		rate from £ per person	children taken	evening meals	animals taken
Bill & Audrey White **Abbots Oak Country** **House** **Warren Hills Road** **Greenhill** **Coalville LE67 4UY** **Tel/Fax: (01530) 832328** **Open: ALL YEAR (Excl. Xmas)** **Map Ref No. 00**	Nearest Road: A.50, M.1 A Grade II listed building with a wealth of oak panelling, & including the staircase reputedly from Nell Gynn's town house. Set in mature gardens & woodland, with natural granite outcrops. 4 delightful rooms, all with en-suite/private bathroom. Open fires create a warm & welcoming atmosphere, & Carolyn's superb dinners are served in the candlelit dining room. Stratford, Belvoir Castle & Rutland Water can all be reached within the hour. Tennis court, billiard room.	£32.50	N	Y	Y
Mrs Sue Goodwin **Hillside House** **27 Melton Road** **Burton Lazars** **Melton Mowbray LE14 2UR** **Tel: (01664) 66312** **Mobile 0585 068956** **Open: ALL YEAR (Excl. Xmas)** **Map Ref No. 01**	Nearest Road: A.606 A charmingly converted farmhouse with superb views over open countryside, in the small village of Burton Lazars. Comfortable accommodation is offered in 3 double bedrooms, one of which is en-suite. All have tea/coffee-making facilities & colour T.V.. A pleasant garden, on sunny days. Close to Melton Mowbray, famous for its pork pies & Stilton cheese, & with Belvoir Castle & Rutland Water within easy reach. Children over 10 years welcome.	£16.50	Y	N	N
Mrs Fiona Gibson **Manor House** **Barleythorpe** **Oakham LE15 7EE** **Tel: (01572) 757384** **Fax 01572 755712** **Open: ALL YEAR** **Map Ref No. 02**	Nearest Road: A.606 Home of the renowned Barleythorpe Stud, this beautiful listed family house, dating from 1055, lies in the heart of Rutland. An atmosphere of warmth & comfort greets you under exposed beams. 2 elegantly furnished bedrooms, with en-suite/private facilities, tea/coffee trays & colour T.V.. A swimming pool in the garden. Perfectly situated for Rutland Water, Burghley House & Belvoir Castle. Children over 6 years welcome. Pets by arrangement.	£30.00	Y	N	Y
Mrs Jenny Hitchen **Rutland House** **61 High Street East** **Uppingham LE15 9PY** **Tel/Fax: (01572) 822497** **Open: ALL YEAR** **Map Ref No. 04**	Nearest Road: A.47 Rutland House offers excellent accommodation in 5 delightful guest rooms. All rooms are en-suite, with central heating, colour T.V., radio/alarms & tea/coffee facilities. Being a small establishment, the rooms are quiet & homely. Full English or Continental breakfast served. Close to Rutland Water & Burghley House. Children over 5 yrs. A lovely home, well-placed for touring.	£19.50 CREDIT CARD VISA M'CARD	Y	N	Y
Christine & Ian Hackney **Garden Hotel** **High Street West** **Uppingham LE15 9QD** **Tel: (01572) 822352** **Fax 01572 821156** **Open: ALL YEAR** **Map Ref No. 04**	Nearest Road: A.47 Regarded as Uppingham's best kept secret, this historic hotel has a reputation for friendly, homely service. All rooms en-suite, with colour T.V., telephone, radio and tea/coffee facilities. Comfortable lounge and separate bar, together with large, well-tended garden, provide country-home comforts. The restaurant is renowned for traditional British home cooking. Good wine list. Candlelit French Bistro also available Tues-Sat. Summer barbecues in the garden.	£30.00 CREDIT CARD VISA M'CARD AMEX	Y	Y	Y

Nottinghamshire

		rate from £ per person	children taken	evening meals	animals taken
Mrs Ann Shipside **Holly Lodge** **Ricket Lane** **Ravenshead** **Blidworth NG21 0NQ** **Tel: (01623) 793853** **Open: ALL YEAR** **Map Ref No. 08**	Nearest Road: A.60, M.1 Holly Lodge is situated just off the A.60, 9 miles north of Nottingham. This attractive former hunting lodge stands in 15 acres of grounds. The 4 comfortable, en-suite guest rooms are housed within the converted stables. There are panoramic countryside views on all sides, with woodland walks, tennis, golf & riding nearby. Ideally situated for a peaceful, rural holiday base with a relaxed & friendly atmosphere.	£19.50 🚭 *see PHOTO over* CREDIT CARD VISA M'CARD AMEX	Y	N	N
John & Georgina Smithers **The Old George Dragon** **Scrooby** **Doncaster** **DN10 6AU** **Tel: (01302) 711840** **Open: ALL YEAR** **Map Ref No. 05**	Nearest Road: A.638, A.1 M A warm welcome awaits you at this 18th-century cottage. Situated in the picturesque & historic village of Scrooby. Internationally known for its links with the Pilgrim Fathers, & within easy reach of Robin Hood country. Accommodation is tastefully furnished, retaining many original features, & offers 2 double rooms & 1 twin room, all with en-suite/private facilities, colour T.V. & tea/coffee making. 2 miles from A.1 M.	£19.00	Y	N	N
Mrs B. Hinchley **Titchfield Guest House** **300/302 Chesterfield Rd** **North** **Mansfield NG19 7QU** **Tel: (01623) 810356** **Open: ALL YEAR** **Map Ref No. 06**	Nearest Road: A.617 This is 2 houses converted into 1 family-run guest house, offering 8 comfortable rooms, a lounge with T.V., a kitchen for guests' use, a bathroom & showers. It also has an adjoining garage. Near to Mansfield, which is a busy market town. Sherwood Forest & the Peak District easily accessible. Very handy for touring this lovely area, & for onward travel. A warm & friendly welcome is assured here.	£16.00	Y	Y	Y
June M. Ibbotson **Blue Barn Farm** **Langwith** **Mansfield** **NG20 9JD** **Tel: (01623) 742248** **Open: ALL YEAR (Excl. Xmas & New Year)** **Map Ref No. 07**	Nearest Road: A.616, A.1 M An enjoyable visit is guaranteed at this family-run, 250-acre farm, set in tranquil countryside on the edge of Sherwood Forest (Robin Hood country). 3 guest bedrooms, each with modern amenities including h&c, tea/coffee-making facilities & a guest bathroom with shower. 1 bedroom is en-suite. A colour-T.V. lounge & garden are also available. Guests are very welcome to walk around the farm. Many interesting places, catering for all tastes, only a short journey away.	£16.00	Y	N	Y
Sheila & Michael Spratt **Greenwood Lodge** **Guest House** **Third Avenue** **Sherwood Rise** **Nottingham NG7 6JH** **Tel/Fax: (0115) 9621206** **Open: ALL YEAR** **Map Ref No. 11**	Nearest Road: A.60 A warm, welcoming Victorian house situated in a quiet cul-de-sac, 1 mile from the city centre. The home of Sheila & Michael Spratt, The Lodge is furnished mainly with antiques, & boasts a fine 4-poster bed. All rooms are en-suite & individually decorated & furnished to a high standard, with T.V., hairdryer, trouser press & hospitality tray. Evening meals are by prior arrangement. An ideal base from which to explore Nottingham & its many places of interest.	£20.00 CREDIT CARD VISA M'CARD	Y	Y	Y

Holly Lodge. Blidworth.

Nottinghamshire

		rate from £ per person	children taken	evening meals	animals taken
Peter, Marjorie & Nicky Need **Peacock Farm Guest House & Restaurant** Redmile NG13 0GQ Tel: (01949) 842475 Fax 01949 843127 **Open: ALL YEAR** Map Ref No. 09	Nearest Road: A.1, A.52 Situated within sight of Belvoir Castle, Peacock Farm is a 280-year-old farmhouse with all modern conveniences. Most rooms have unbroken views of the nearby village, & of Belvoir Castle set on wooded hills. A warm welcome is extended to house guests, who are offered a first-class service with old-fashioned English hospitality. The restaurant offers home cooking with local fresh produce. A delightful home, ideal for a relaxing break or for exploring many places of interest.	£19.00 CREDIT CARD VISA M'CARD AMEX	Y	Y	Y
Rosalie Brammer **'The Barns '** **Morton Farm, Babworth** Retford DN22 8HA Tel: (01777) 706336 Fax 01777 709773 **Open: ALL YEAR** Map Ref No. 10	Nearest Road: A.1, B.6420 A delightfully warm welcome & a pleasant, relaxed atmosphere await you at 'The Barns'. This beautifully converted 18th-century barn boasts open fires & many oak beams, & offers guests a choice of 6 comfortable rooms, all with en-suite facilities, radio, T.V. & tea/coffee makers. An interesting base for touring. It is located at Babworth - home of the Pilgrim Fathers - only 2 miles from Robin Hood country.	£20.00 CREDIT CARD VISA M'CARD AMEX	Y	N	N

All the establishments mentioned in this guide are members of
The Worldwide Bed & Breakfast Association

When booking your accommodation please mention
The Best Bed & Breakfast

Lincolnshire

Lincolnshire
(East Midlands)

Lincolnshire is an intriguing mixture of coast & country, of flat fens & gently rising wolds.

There are the popular resorts of Skegness & Mablethorpe as well as quieter coastal regions where flocks of wild birds take food & shelter in the dunes. Gibraltar Point & Saltfleetby are large nature reserves.

Fresh vegetables for much of Britain are produced in the rich soil of the Lincolnshire fens, & windmills punctuate the skyline. There is a unique 8-sailed windmill at Heckington. In spring the fields are ablaze with the red & yellow of tulips. The bulb industry flourishes around Spalding & Holbeach, & in early May tulip flowers in abundance decorate the huge floats of the Spalding Flower Parade.

The city of Lincoln has cobbled streets & ancient buildings & a very beautiful triple-towered Cathedral which shares its hill-top site with the Castle, both dating from the 11th century. There is a 17th century library by Wren in the Cathedral, which has amongst its treasures one of the four original copies of Magna Carta.

Boston has a huge parish church with a distincive octagonal tower which can be seen for miles across the surrounding fenland, & is commonly known as the 'Boston Stump'. The Guildhall Museum displays many aspects of the town's history, including the cells where the early Pilgrim Fathers were imprisioned after their attempt to flee to the Netherlands to find religious freedom. They eventually made the journey & hence to America.

One of England's most outstanding towns is Stamford. It has lovely churches, ancient inns & other fine buildings in a mellow stone.

Sir Isaac Newton was born at Woolsthorpe Manor & educated at nearby Grantham where there is a museum which illustrates his life & work.

The poet Tennyson was born in the village of Somersby, where his father was Rector.

Lincoln Cathedral.

Lincolnshire

Lincolnshire Gazeteer

Areas of outstanding natural beauty.
Lincolnshire Wolds.

Historic Houses & Castles

Auborn House - Nr. Lincoln
16th century house with imposing carved staircase & panelled rooms.

Belton House - Grantham
House built 1684-88 - said to be by Christopher Wren - work by Grinling Gibbons & Wyatt also. Paintings, furniture, porcelain, tapestries, Duke of Windsor mementoes. A great English house with formal gardens & extensive grounds with orangery.

Doddington Hall - Doddington, Nr. Lincoln
16th century Elizabethan mansion with elegant Georgian rooms & gabled Tudor gatehouse. Fine furniture, paintings, porcelain, etc. Formal walled knot gardens, roses & wild gardens.

Burghley House - Stamford
Elizabethan - England's largest & grandest house of the era. Famous for its beautiful painted ceilings, silver fireplaces & art treasures.

Gumby Hall - Burgh-le-Marsh
17th century manor house. Ancient gardens.

Harrington Hall - Spilsby
Mentioned in the Domesday Book - has mediaeval stone base - Carolinean manor house in red brick. Some alterations in 1678 to mullioned windows. Panelling, furnishings of 17th & 18th century.

Marston Hall - Grantham
16th century manor house. Ancient gardens.

The Old Hall - Gainsborough
Fine mediaeval manor house built in 1480's with original kitchen, rebuilt after original hall destroyed during Wars of the Roses. Tower & wings, Great Hall. It was the first meeting place of the "Dissenters", later known as the Pilgrim Fathers.

Woolsthorpe Manor - Grantham
17th century house. Birthplace of Sir Isaac Newton.

Fydell House - Boston
18th century house, now Pilgrim College.

Lincoln Castle - Lincoln
William the Conqueror castle, with complete curtain wall & Norman shell keep. Towers & wall walk. Unique prisoners' chapel.

Tattershall Castle - Tattershall
100 foot high brick keep of 15th century moated castle, with fine views over surrounding country.

Cathedrals & Churches

Addlethorpe (St. Nicholas)
15th century - mediaeval stained glass - original woodwork.

Boston (St. Botolph)
14th century decorated - very large parish church. Beautiful south porch, carved stalls.

Brant Broughton (St. Helens)
13th century arcades - decorated tower & spire - perpendicular clerestory. Exterior decoration.

Ewerby (St. Andrew)
Decorated - splendid example of period - very fine spire. 14th century effigy.

Fleet (St. Mary Magdalene)
14th century - early English arcades - perpendicular windows - detached tower & spire.

Folkingham (St. Andrew)
14th century arcades - 15th century windows - perpendicular tower - early English chancel.

Gedney (St. Mary Magdalene)
Perpendicular spire (unfinished). Early English tower. 13th-14th century monuments, 14th-15th century stained glass.

Grantham (St. Wulfram)
14th century tower & spire - Norman pillars - perpendicular chantry - 14th century vaulted crypt.

Lincoln Cathedral - Lincoln
Magnificent triple-towered Gothic building on fine hill-top site.
Norman west front,
13th century - some 14th century additions. Norman work from 1072. Angel choir - carved & decorated pulpitum - 13th century chapter house - 17th century library by Wren (containing one of the four original copies of Magna Carta).

Lincolnshire

St. Botolph's Church - Boston
Fine parish church, one of the largest in the country, with 272 foot octagonal tower dominating the surrounding fens.
Long Sutton (St. Mary)
15th century south porch, mediaeval brass lectern, very fine early English spire.
Louth (St. James)
Early 16th century - mediaeval Gothic - wonderful spire.
Scotter (St. Peter)
Saxon to perpendicular - early English nave - 15th century rood screen.
Stow (St. Mary)
Norman - very fine example, particularly west door. Wall painting.
Silk Willoughby (St. Denis)
14th century - tower with spire & flying buttresses. 15th-17th century pulpit.
Stainfield (St. Andrew)
Queen Anne - mediaeval armour & early needlework.
Theddlethorpe (All Saints)
14th century - 15th century & reredos of 15th century, 16th century parcloses, 15th century brasses - some mediaeval glass.
Wrangle (St. Mary the Virgin & St. Nicholas)
Early English - decorated - perpendicular - Elizabethan pulpit. 14th century east window & glass.

Museums & Galleries

Alford Manor House - Alford
Tudor manor house - thatched - folk museum. Nearby windmill.
Boston Guildhall Museum - Boston
15th century building with mayor's parlour, court room & cells where Pilgrim Fathers were imprisoned in 1607. Local exhibits.
Lincoln Cathedral Library - Lincoln
Built by Wren housing early printed books & mediaeval manuscripts.
Lincoln Cathedral Treasury - Lincoln
Diocesan gold & silver plate.
Lincoln City & Country Museum - Lincoln
Prehistoric, Roman & mediaeval antiquities with local associations. Armour & local history.
Museum of Lincolnshire Life - Lincoln
Domestic, agricultural, industrial & social history of the county. Edwardian room settings, shop settings, agricultural machinery.

Usher Gallery - Lincoln
Paintings, watches, miniatures, porcelain, silver, coins & medals. Temporary exhibitions. Tennyson collection. Works of English watercolourist Peter de Wint.
Grantham Museum - Grantham
Archeology, prehistoric, Saxon & Roman. Local history with special display about Sir Isaac Newton, born nearby & educated in Grantham.
Church Farm Museum - Skegness
Farmhouse & buildings with local agricultural collections & temporary exhibitions & special events.
Stamford Museum - Stamford
Local history museum, with temporary special exhibitions.
Battle of Britain Memorial Flight - Coningsby
Lancaster bomber, five Spitfires & two Hurricanes with other Battle of Britain memorabilia.
National Cycle Museum - Lincoln
Development of the cycle.
Stamford Steam Brewery Museum - Stamford
Complete Victorian steam brewery with 19th century equipment.

Other things to see & do

Springfield - Spalding
Show gardens of the British bulb industry, & home of the Spalding Flower Parade each May. Summer bedding plants & roses.
Butlins Funcoast World - Skegness
Funsplash Water World with amusements & entertainments
Castle Leisure Park - Tattershall
Windsurfing, water-skiing, sailing, fishing & other sports & leisure facilities.
Long Sutton Butterfly Park - Long Sutton
Walk-through tropical butterfly house with outdoor wildflower meadows & pets corner.
Skegness Natureland Marine Zoo - Skegness
Seal sanctuary with aquaria, tropical house, pets corner & butterfly house.
Windmills - at Lincoln (Ellis Mill - 4 sails), Boston (Maud Foster - 5 sails), Burgh-le-Marsh (5 sails), Alford (5 sails), Sibsey (6 sails), Heckington (8 sails).

LINCOLNSHIRE
Map reference

4 Payne
4 Pritchard
4 Brown
6 Painter
8 Honnor
9 Acton

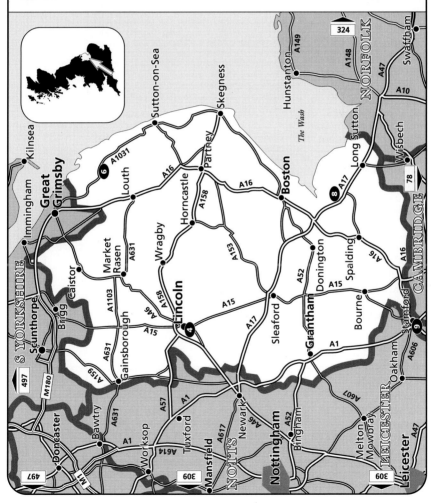

Lincolnshire

		rate from £ per person	children taken	evening meals	animals taken
Gillian & John Pritchard **Carline Guest House** **1 & 3 Carline Road** **Lincoln LN1 1HL** **Tel: (01522) 530422** **Open: ALL YEAR (Excl.** **Xmas & New Year)** **Map Ref No. 04**	Nearest Road: A.57, A.46, A.15 Gill & John Pritchard extend a warm welcome. Excellent accommodation, in 12 attractively furnished bedrooms, 10 with en-suite facilities. Each room has T.V., radio, beverage facilities, hair dryers & trouser press. The Carline is a short, pleasant stroll from the Lawns Tourism & Conference Centre, & from the historic Uphill area of Lincoln. There are several restaurants & public houses nearby for your lunch or evening meal. Ask for recommendations. Children over 2 yrs.	£20.00	Y	N	N
Mr Raymond H. Brown **Minster Lodge Hotel** **3 Church Lane** **Lincoln LN2 1QJ** **Tel: (01522) 513220** **Fax 01522 513220** **Open: ALL YEAR** **Map Ref No. 04**	Nearest Road: A.15, A.46 Minster Lodge is a delightful small hotel refurbished to a high standard. Offering 6 en-suite bedrooms with radio, colour T.V. & beverage facilities. Ideally situated within 50 yards of Newport Arch - the only remaining Roman Arch still in use - & 5 mins' walk from Lincoln's major tourist attractions of Lincoln Cathedral & Castle, as well as a colourful mixture of antique shops, gift shops & boutiques, which are situated in the mediaeval area surrounding the cathedral & castle.	£25.00 CREDIT CARD VISA M'CARD	Y	N	Y
David & Judy Payne **D'Isney Place Hotel** **Eastgate** **Lincoln LN2 4AA** **Tel: (01522) 538881** **Fax 01522 511321** **Open: ALL YEAR** **Map Ref No. 04**	Nearest Road: A.15 D'Isney Place is a very special hotel in the heart of the old city of Lincoln. Its atmosphere is one of elegant luxury & quiet discretion, more private house than hotel. It is the personal touches that make your stay here so special, from the fluffy white towelling robes in every bathroom to the fresh milk in your room every day. There are 17 attractive en-suite bedrooms. This is an ideal centre from which to explore Lincoln.	£32.00 CREDIT CARD VISA M'CARD AMEX	Y	N	Y
Ann & Bill Painter **Wickham House** **Church Lane** **Conisholme** **Louth LN11 7LX** **Tel: (01507) 358465** **Open: ALL YEAR (Excl. Xmas)** **Map Ref No. 06**	Nearest Road: A.1031 Wickham House is a white-washed 18th-century cottage sheltered by trees in a quiet lane. A sitting room, a dining room (with separate tables; both rooms with beamed ceilings) & a cosy library are all available to guests. Attractive, spacious bedrooms, 1 on the ground floor; all with en-suite facilities, colour T.V. & hospitality tray. Children over 8 years welcome. Wickham House is within easy reach of the Lincolnshire Wolds & coast.	£18.50	Y	N	N
Mrs Lesley Honnor **Pipwell Manor** **Washway Road,** **Saracens Head** **Holbeach** **Spalding PE12 8AL** **Tel: (01406) 423119** **Open: ALL YEAR** **Map Ref No. 08**	Nearest Road: A.17 Pipwell Manor is a Grade II listed Georgian Manor house, built in around 1740, set in paddocks & gardens in a small quiet village in the Lincolnshire Fens, just off the A.17. Beautifully restored & decorated in English-country style, but retaining many original features, Pipwell Manor is a delightful place to stay. There are 4 comfortably furnished & attractive bedrooms with tea/coffee-making facilities. Guests are welcomed with tea & home-made cake. Evening meals available with prior notice. Parking available.	£18.00	Y	Y	N

Lincolnshire

		rate from £ per person	children taken	evening meals	animals taken
John & Moya Acton **The Priory** **Church Road, Ketton** **Stamford PE9 3RD** **Tel: (01780) 720215** **Fax 01780 721881** **Open: ALL YEAR (Excl. Xmas)** **Map Ref No. 09**	Nearest Road: A.1, A.6121 Historic country house & family home in quiet village setting near Stamford. England's finest stone town, & setting for 'Middlemarch'. Large en-suite bedrooms, imaginatively & individually decorated. Views over splendid gardens & countryside beyond. Hospitality tray, colour T.V. & 'phone in all rooms. Large conservatory, dining room & 2 lounges. Licensed. Private parking. Close to A.1 & Rutland Water.	£19.00 *see PHOTO over* CREDIT CARD VISA M'CARD	Y	Y	N

All the establishments mentioned in this guide

are members of

The Worldwide Bed & Breakfast Association

When booking your accommodation please
mention
The Best Bed & Breakfast

The Priory. Ketton.

Norfolk

Norfolk
(East Anglia)

One of the largest of the old counties, Norfolk is divided by rivers from neighbouring counties & pushes out into the sea on the north & east sides. This is old East Anglia.

Inland there is great concentration on agriculture where fields are hedged with hawthorn which blossoms like snow in summer. A great deal of land drainage is required & the area is crisscrossed by dykes & ditches - some of them dating back to Roman times.

Holkham Hall.

The Norfolk Broads were formed by the flooding of mediaeval peat diggings to form miles & miles of inland waterways, navigable & safe. On a bright summer's day, on a peaceful backwater bounded by reed & sedge, the Broads seem like paradise. Here are hidden treasures like the Bittern, that shyest of birds, the Swallowtail butterfly & the rare Marsh orchid.

Contrasting with the still inland waters is a lively coastline which takes in a host of towns & villages as it arcs around The Wash. Here are the joys of the seaside at its best, miles of safe & sandy golden beaches to delight children, dunes & salt marshes where birdlife flourishes, & busy ports & fishing villages with pink-washed cottages.

Cromer is a little seaside town with a pier & a prom, cream teas & candy floss, where red, white & blue fishing boats are drawn up on the beach.

Hunstanton is more decorous, with a broad green sweeping down to the cliffs. Great Yarmouth is a boisterous resort. It has a beach that runs for miles, with pony rides & almost every amusement imaginable.

It is possible to take a boat into the heart of Norwich, past warehouses, factories & new penthouses, & under stone & iron bridges. Walking along the riverbank you reach Pulls Ferry where a perfectly proportioned grey flint gateway arcs over what was once a canal dug to transport stone to the cathedral site. Norwich Cathedral is magnificent, with a sharply soaring spire, beautiful cloisters & fine 15th century carving preserved in the choir stalls. Cathedral Close is perfectly preserved, as is Elm Hill, a cobbled street from mediaeval times. There are many little shops & narrow alleys going down to the river.

Norfolk is a county much loved by the Royal family & the Queen has a home at Sandringham. It is no castle, but a solid, comfortable family home with red brick turrets & French windows opening onto the terrace.

Norfolk

Areas of outstanding beauty.
Norfolk coast (part)

Historic Houses & Castles

Anna Sewell House - Great Yarmouth
17th century Tudor frontage. Birthplace of writer Anna Sewell.

Blicking Hall - Aylsham
Great Jacobean house. Fine Russian tapestry, long gallery with exceptional ceiling. Formal garden.

Felbrigg Hall - Nr. Cromer
17th century, good Georgian interior. Set in wooded parklands.

Holkham Hall - Wells
Fine Palladian mansion of 1734. Paintings, statuary, tapestries, furnishings & formal garden by Berry.

Houghton Hall - Wells
18th century mansion. Pictures, china & staterooms.

Oxburgh Hall - Swafftham
Late 15th century moated house. Fine gatehouse tower. Needlework by Mary Queen of Scots.

Wolterton Hall - Nr. Norwich
Built in 1741 contains tapestries, porcelain, furniture.

Trinity Hospital - Castle Rising
17th century, nine brick & tile almshouses, court chapel & treasury.

Cathedrals & Churches

Attleborough (St. Mary)
Norman with late 14th century. Fine rood screen & frescoes.

Barton Turf (St. Michael & All Angles)
Magnificent screen with painting of the Nine Orders of Angles.

Beeston-next-Mileham (St. Mary)
14th century. Perpendicular clerestory tower & spire. Hammer Beam roof, parclose screens, benches, front cover. Tracery in nave & chancel windows.

Cawston (St. Agnes)
Tower faced with freestone. Painted screens, wall paintings, tower, screen & gallery. 15th century angel roof.

East Harding (St. Peter & St. Paul)
14th century, some 15th century alterations. Monuments of 15th-17th century. Splendid mediaeval glass.

Erpingham (St. Mary)
14th century military brass to John de Erpingham, 16th century Rhenish glass. Fine tower.

Gunton (St. Andrew)
18th century. Robert Adam - classical interior in dark wood - gilded.

King's Lynn (St. Margaret)
Norman foundation. Two fine 14th century Flemish brasses, 14th century screens, reredos by Bodley, interesting Georgian pulpit with sounding board.

Norwich Cathedral
Romanesque & late Gothic with 15th century spire. Perpendicular lierne vaults in nave, transeptsand presbytery.

Ranworth (St. Helens)
15th century screen, very fine example. Sarum Antiphoner, 14th century illuminated manuscript - East Anglian work.

Salle (St. Peter & St. Paul)
15th century. Highly decorated west tower & porches. Mediaeval glass, pulpit with 15th century panels & Jacobean tester. Stalls, misericords, brasses & monuments, sacrament font.

Terrington (St. Clement)
Detached perpendicular tower. Western front has fire-light window & canopied niches. Georgian panelling west of nave. 17th century painted font cover. Jacobean commandment boards.

Trunch (St. Botolph)
15th century screen with painted panels, mediaeval glass, famous font canopy with fine carving & painting, ringer's gallery, Elizabethan monument.

Wiggenhall (St. Germans)
17th century pulpit, table, clerk's desk & chair, bench ends 15th century.

Wymondham (St. Mary & St. Thomas of Canterbury)
Norman origins including arcades & triforium windows, 13th century font fragments, complete 15th century font. 15th century clerestory & roof. Comper reredos, famous Corporas Case, rare example of 13th century Opus Anglicanum.

Museums & Galleries

Norwich Castle Museum
Art collection, local & natural history,

Norfolk

Strangers Hall - Norwich
Mediaeval mansion furnished as museum of urban domestic life in 16th-19th centuries.

St. Peter Hungate Church Museum - Norwich
15th century church for the exhibition of ecclesiastical art & East Anglican antiquities.

Sainsbury Centre for Visual Arts - University, Norwich
Collection of modern art, ancient, classical & mediaeval art, Art Nouveau, 20th century constructivist art.

Bridewell Museum of Local Industries - Norwich
Crafts, industries & aspects of city life.

Museum of Social History - King's Lynn
Exhibition of domestic life & dress, etc., noted glass collection.

Bishop Bonner's Cottages
Restored cottages with coloured East Anglia pargetting, c. 1502, museum of archaeological discoveries, exhibition of rural crafts.

The Guildhall - Thetford
Duleep Singh Collection of Norfolk & Suffolk portraits.

Shirehall Museum - Walsingham
18th century court room having original fittings, illustrating Walsingham life.

Historic Monuments

Binham Priory & Cross - Binham
12th century ruins of Benedictine foundation.

Caister Castle - Great Yarmouth
15th century moated castle - ruins. Now motor museum.

The Castle - Burgh Castle
3rd century Saxon fort - walls - ruin.

Mannington Hall - Saxthorpe
Saxon church ruin in gardens of 15th century moated house.

Castle Rising - Castle Rising
Splendid Norman keep & earthworks.

Castle Acre Priory & Castle Gate - Swaffham

Other things to see & do

African Violet Centre - Terrington St. Clements.
60 varieties of African Violets. Talks & Tours.

Norfolk Lavender Centre - Heacham
Open to the public in July & August. Demonstrations of harvesting & distilling the oil.

Thetford Forest
Forest walks, rides & picnic places amongst conifers, oak, beech & birch.

The Broads.

NORFOLK
Map reference

1	Sharples	17	Wright
2	Bartlett	17	Howard
4	Croft	18	Parker
5	Webb	19	Pusey
6	Atkins	23	Lovatt
7	Gillam	24	Rowling
9	Wells	25	Garnier
11	Tweedy	26	Carr
	Smith	27	Ford
11	Porter	28	Whittley
14	Hickey	29	Lock
15	Duthie	30	Collins
16	Tofts		

Bartles Lodge. Elsing.

		rate from £ per person	children taken	evening meals	animals taken

Mr & Mrs John Sharples **Sherbourne Country** **House Hotel, Norwich Rd** **Attleborough NR17 2JX** **Tel: (01953) 454363** **Fax 01953 453509** **Open: ALL YEAR** **Map Ref No. 01**	Nearest Road: A.11 A former rectory, built in 1700, the Sherbourne is now an hotel, & a delightful home, offering 8 charming bedrooms, including 6 en-suite, a 4-poster & 2 spa baths. Sample the award-winning restaurant, & enjoy music at the grand piano whilst taking coffee & drinks in the bar lounge. The gardens are newly landscaped, & there is ample secure parking. Your hosts look forward to welcoming you to their home.	£24.00 CREDIT CARD VISA M'CARD	Y	Y	Y
David & Annie Bartlett **Bartles Lodge** **Church Street, Elsing** **Dereham NR20 3EA** **Tel: (01362) 637177** **Open: ALL YEAR** **Map Ref No. 02**	Nearest Road: A.47, A.1067 Bartles Lodge is in the peaceful, unspoilt village of Elsing, set in 12 acres of landscaped meadows inhabited by plenty of wildlife. The rooms, centred around the patio, pond & fountain, are beautifully furnished in country style, & most overlook the Bartletts' own lakes. All rooms are en-suite with colour T.V.'s, etc. Although Ennis Lodge is licensed, the local village inn is nearby.	£20.00 *see PHOTO over* CREDIT CARD VISA M'CARD	Y	Y	Y
Mr & Mrs M. B. Croft **The Old Bakery** **Church Walk** **Pulham Market** **Diss IP21 4SJ** **Tel/Fax: (01379) 676492** **Open: ALL YEAR (Excl.** **Xmas & New Year)** **Map Ref No. 04**	Nearest Road: A.140 The Old Bakery is a 16th-century oak-framed house standing on a private road in the centre of an award-winning village among thatched period houses. All 3 double rooms are fully en-suite, have colour T.V., clock/radio & hospitality tray. The Old Bakery is licensed, & offers excellent traditional meals prepared by Martin, a Master Chef. These are served in the beamed & log-fired dining room, which glows with warmth & history. Situated near Bressingham, Norwich, the Broads & the Heritage Coast.	£18.00 🚭 *see PHOTO over*	Y	Y	N
Ken & Brenda Webb **The Strenneth** **Airfield Road** **Fersfield** **Diss IP22 2BP** **Tel: (01379) 688182** **Fax 01379 688260** **Open: ALL YEAR** **Map Ref No. 05**	Nearest Road: A.1066 Ken & Brenda Webb invite you to their 17th-century home, where good food & comfortable accommodation is provided. All rooms have en-suite facilities & colour T.V., beverage-making facilities & radio/alarms. 3-course dinner by arrangement (special diets can be catered for). Enjoy a quiet drink in either of the executive lounges, 1 for non-smokers. Super 4-poster & 'Executive' room for special occasions. Log fires in winter. Ample parking. Situated off the A.1066 near South Lopham, 4 miles west of Diss.	£22.00 CREDIT CARD VISA M'CARD AMEX	Y	Y	Y
Connie & Doug Atkins **Ingleneuk Lodge** **Hopton Road** **Garboldisham** **Diss IP22 2RQ** **Tel: (01953) 681541** **Open: ALL YEAR** **Map Ref No. 06**	Nearest Road: A.11, A.1066 A warm welcome is extended to visitors at Ingleneuk Lodge, a large, modern, family-run, single-storey guest house standing in 10 acres of quiet, wooded countryside, with riverside walks. A variety of rooms, most en-suite, all centrally heated, double-glazed, with colour T.V., telephone, electric blankets & hot-drink facilities. Children well provided for. Residents' lounge, licensed bar & evening meals (book by 1 p.m.). Wheelchair-disabled welcome.	£18.75 CREDIT CARD VISA M'CARD AMEX	Y	Y	Y

The Old Bakery. Pulham Market.

Norfolk

	Nearest Road	rate from £ per person	children taken	evening meals	animals taken
Jill & Ian Gillam **The Old Rectory** **Gissing** **Diss** **IP22 3XB** **Tel: (01379) 677575** **Fax 01379 674427** **Open: ALL YEAR** **Map Ref No. 07**	Nearest Road: A.140 This delightful Victorian house stands in grounds of mature gardens & woodland, & is a haven of peace, comfort & elegance. Bedrooms are spacious, with private or en-suite facilities. Every effort has been made to ensure a memorable stay: tea/coffee-making facilities, colour T.V., notepaper, fresh flowers & an extensive range of toiletries. Breakfast is copious, & beautifully presented. Candlelit dinner by prior arrangement. Amenities: croquet, indoor swimming pool. Smoking restrictions. Children over 8.	£24.00 🚭 *see PHOTO over*	Y	Y	N
Mrs Barbara Wells **Spindrift Private Hotel** **36 Wellesley Road** **Great Yarmouth** **NR30 1EU** **Tel/Fax: (01493) 858674** **Open: ALL YEAR** **Map Ref No. 09**	Nearest Road: A.47, A.12 Good food & comfortable accommodation are the by-words at 'Spindrift'. Attractively situated adjacent to the sea front, the Golden Mile, bowling greens, tennis courts & the water ways. Easy-going atmosphere, with keys provided for access at all times. 8 bedrooms, some with excellent sea views, & 5 bedrooms with en-suite facilities. All with modern amenities, colour T.V. & tea/coffee-making facilities. Good on road parking; public car park at rear, if space allows. Children over 3.	£14.00 CREDIT CARD VISA M'CARD AMEX	Y	N	N
Sheila Tweedy Smith **Fieldsend House** **26 Homefields Road** **Hunstanton** **PE36 5HL** **Tel: (01485) 532593** **Open: ALL YEAR** **Map Ref No. 11**	Nearest Road: A.149 Fieldsend is a large Carrstone house, built at the turn of the century & enjoying lovely sea views. There are canopied beds, plus 1 en-suite bedroom with 4-poster. Colour T.V., tea/coffee makers & an oak-panelled sitting room. Guests will enjoy a leisurely stay at this country-house-style home, which is only 4 mins from the centre of town. Delicious breakfasts served by a Cordon Bleu cook. Parking available.	£17.50	Y	N	N
Mrs Susan Morison **Pinewood House** **26 Northgate** **Hunstanton PE36 6AP** **Tel: (01485) 533068** **Open: ALL YEAR (Excl. Xmas & New Year)** **Map Ref No. 11**	Nearest Road: A.149 Enjoy comfort & hospitality in this charming Victorian house with a natural pine look, interesting pictures & antiques, 8 delightfully decorated bedrooms, 1 with a Victorian bedstead & Laura Ashley decor & some with sea views. 4 are en-suite & all have T.V. & tea/coffee-making facilities. A licensed bar & log fires in winter. A choice of breakfast, freshly brewed coffee & homemade marmalade. Ideal base for Sandringham (7 miles), Lavender Fields or the wonderful coastline.	£17.50 CREDIT CARD VISA M'CARD AMEX	Y	N	Y
Gordon & Margaret Burgin **The Limes** **Wretton Road** **Stoke Ferry** **King's Lynn PE33 9QJ** **Tel: (01366) 500340** **Open: ALL YEAR** **Map Ref No. 15**	Nearest Road: A.10, A.134 The Limes is a charming 200-year-old farmhouse set in beautiful secluded gardens. Oak-beamed ceilings & an inglenook fireplace give the dining room great 'olde worlde' charm. Offering attractive bedrooms with tea/coffee-making facilities, T.V.s & private bathrooms. Every effort is made to ensure the comfort of guests & to provide excellent breakfasts, comfortable beds & a warm welcome. Individual tastes catered for when preparing meals. Swimming pool & bicycles for guests' use.	£16.50	Y	Y	Y

The Old Rectory. Gissing.

Norfolk

	rate from £ per person	children taken	evening meals	animals taken

Annette & Peter Tofts **The Toll Barn** **Norwich Road** **North Walsham** **NR28 0JB** **Tel: (01692) 403063** **Fax 01692 406582** **Open: ALL YEAR** **Map Ref No. 16**	Nearest Road: B.1150 Toll Barn offers outstanding comfort & privacy. Delightful guest lodges are set in attractive courtyard gardens, next to an 18th-century converted barn, & guests can enjoy a farmhouse breakfast in the exposed brick & beamed dining room. Each en-suite room is decorated in English-country-house style & has T.V., fridge, hairdryer, tea/coffee-making facilities, & a dining area for guests who prefer a private breakfast. Ideal for the Broads, coast, Norwich & N. Norfolk. Children over 8 years welcome.	£19.00	Y	N	Y
W. R. & A. E. Parker **Elm Farm Chalet Hotel** **St. Faith** **Norwich NR10 3HH** **Tel: (01603) 898366** **Fax 01603 897129** **Open: ALL YEAR** **Map Ref No. 18**	Nearest Road: A.140 Situated in attractive village, 4 miles from city of Norwich, 5 miles from Norfolk Broads & within easy reach of Norfolk & Suffolk coasts. Rooms completely modernised, with en-suite bathrooms, showers & toilets. Also, tea/coffee-making facilities, radio, colour T.V., 'phone, hairdryers, etc. Dining room, & some bedrooms, are non-smoking. Reduced prices for stays of 2 or more nights. Residential & restaurant licence.	£27.00 CREDIT CARD VISA M'CARD AMEX	Y	Y	N
Mrs Katherine Pusey **The Old Rectory** **Norwich Road** **Caistor St. Edmund** **Norwich NR14 8QS** **Tel: (01508) 492490** **Open: ALL YEAR** **Map Ref No. 19**	Nearest Road: A.140 This spacious & elegant listed former rectory & residence of the Bishops of Thetford stands in 11 acres of grounds by the ancient remains of the Roman town of Venta Icenorum. Surrounded by fields & set in the protected Tas Valley to the east of the A.140, Caistor St. Edmund is ideally situated to offer idyllic rural peace, & yet it is within 5 mins' drive of the city of Norwich. 3 attractive guest rooms with an en-suite or private bathroom.	£25.00	Y	Y	Y
Mrs Marion Howard **Steeple Court** **211 Unthank Road** **Norwich NR2 2PH** **Tel: (01603) 502206** **Fax 01603 505278** **Open: ALL YEAR** **Map Ref No. 17**	Nearest Road: A.11, A.140 Steeple Court is an elegant, turreted Victorian residence with an impressive mahogany hall & staircase. 2 attractive & tastefully furnished guest rooms, each with an en-suite bathroom, colour T.V. & radio & tea/coffee-making facilities. Excellent Full English or Continental breakfast served. Ideally placed for exploring this beautiful city & its many churches, & within easy easy reach of the Broads & Constable Country.	£22.50 *see PHOTO over*	Y	N	N
Eddie & Margaret Lovatt **Edmar Lodge** **64 Earlham Road** **Norwich NR2 3DF** **Tel: (01603) 615599** **Fax 01603 632977** **Open: ALL YEAR** **Map Ref No. 23**	Nearest Road: A.47 A large corner house, with parking for 6 cars, situated in a quiet area only 10 mins' walk from the city centre. There are 4 very attractive, comfortable rooms with every modern amenity, including tea/coffee makers & colour T.V.. 2 rooms have en-suite facilities. Mrs Lovatt makes all her guests very welcome, & serves wonderful breakfasts in a pretty dining room. Help is readily given on tour planning, as well as advice on Norwich City & its many gourmet restaurants.	£16.00	N	N	N

Steeple Court. Norwich.

Norfolk

	rate from £ per person	children taken	evening meals	animals taken
Susan & Derek Wright **Earlham Guest House** **147 Earlham Road** **Norwich NR2 3RG** **Tel/Fax: (01603) 454169** **Open: ALL YEAR (Excl. Xmas & New Year)** **Map Ref No. 17**	Nearest Road: A.47 A delightful Victorian residence on the major road from the city centre to the University (B.1108). All of the comfortable rooms have modern amenities, including colour T.V. & a hot-drinks tray, & some have private facilities. Keys are provided for freedom of access. Vegetarian foods are offered as an alternative to a generous Full English breakfast, if preferred. An ideal base from which to explore Norfolk. **£18.00** CREDIT CARD VISA M'CARD	Y	N	N
Jennie & Alex Lock **Greenbanks Country** **Hotel & Restaurant** **Swaffham Rd, Wendling** **Swaffham NR19 2AB** **Tel: (01362) 687742** **Open: ALL YEAR** **Map Ref No. 29**	Nearest Road: A.47 A charming, small, 18th-century hotel, with delightful country restaurant, situated in 9 acres of meadows & lakes. Spectacular gardens. Elegant en-suite rooms, offering peace & comfort. Superb cuisine, with excellent choice from varied menu: special diets catered for. Greenbanks is 15 mins from Norwich, & within easy reach of the coast, the Broads & many stately homes. Walking, fishing & golfing breaks available. **£25.00** CREDIT CARD VISA M'CARD	Y	Y	Y
Linda & Martin Hickey **Corfield House** **Sporle** **Swaffham** **PE32 2EA** **Tel: (01760) 723636** **Open: APR - DEC** **Map Ref No. 14**	Nearest Road: A.47 Corfield House is an attractive brick-built house standing in 1/2 an acre of lawned gardens in the peaceful village of Sporle near Swaffham, an ideal base for touring Norfolk. Some of the 5 very comfortable en-suite bedrooms (1 ground-floor) have fine views across open fields, & all have T.V., clock/radio & a fact-file on places to visit. Good home-cooked food using excellent local produce. Licensed. **£21.50** CREDIT CARD VISA M'CARD	Y	Y	N
Lavender Garnier **College Farm** **Thompson** **Thetford** **IP24 1QG** **Tel: (01953) 483318** **Open: ALL YEAR** **Map Ref No. 25**	Nearest Road: A.1075 Built 600 years ago as a College of Priests, & became a manor house when Henry VIII dissolved the monasteries. College Farm has been modernised to provide 3 comfortable rooms, 2 en-suite & all with T.V. & superb views over farmland & mature trees. Delicious breakfasts served in the panelled dining room. A thatched pub in the village offers tasty meals. Norfolk coast, Norwich, Cambridge & Sandringham within easy reach by car. Children over 7. **£18.00**	Y	N	N
Mrs S. Carr **White Hall** **Carbrooke** **Watton** **Thetford IP25 6SG** **Tel/Fax: (01953) 885950** **Open: ALL YEAR** **Map Ref No. 26**	Nearest Road: B.1108, A.1075 Elegant Georgian country house in delightful grounds of 3 acres, with large natural pond. 3 attractive, comfortable bedrooms (1 en-suite) & spacious, sunny drawing room with colour T.V.. Traditional breakfast served in fine dining room. Early morning tea, evening drinks, full central heating, log fires, etc., ensure that your stay is enjoyable and relaxing. Ideal touring centre, lots of local interest. Good food, golf, swimming nearby. **£18.00** *see PHOTO over*	Y	N	N

White Hall, Carbrooke.

		rate from £ per person	children taken	evening meals	animals taken
Angela & Nigel Rowling **Broom Hall** **Richmond Road** **Saham Toney** **Thetford IP25 7EX** Tel: (01953) 882125 Open: JAN - NOV Map Ref No. 24	Nearest Road: A.1075 A family-run Victorian country house, set in 15 acres of parkland, providing a peaceful haven to the discerning visitor. Broom Hall offers 8 en-suite bedrooms, exclusive use of a large lounge with open fire, a full-size snooker table & an indoor swimming pool. Situated close to Thetford Forest & within easy reach of the coast, the Broads, historic country houses, nature reserves & an 18-hole golf course. A delightful home.	£25.00	Y	Y	N
Mrs Christine Collins **Cedar Lodge** **West Tofts** **Thetford** **IP26 5DB** Tel: (01842) 878281 Open: ALL YEAR Map Ref No. 30	Nearest Road: A.134 Guests receive a true country welcome at this cedar colt house. Standing in a well-kept garden, it is located in the heart of Thetford Forest. Traditionally furnished & offering comfortable guests rooms, 2 with private bathroom, & all with tea/coffee-making facilities. Christine is Cordon Bleu trained, loves entertaining her guests & is pleased to provide packed lunches. The North Norfolk coast, Cambridge, Norwich & Newmarket are within 45 mins' drive. Children over 12 yrs.	£17.50	Y	Y	N
Mrs Marion Ford **Old Bottle House** **Cranwich** **Mundford** **Thetford IP26 5JL** Tel: (01842) 878012 Open: ALL YEAR Map Ref No. 27	Nearest Road: A.134 Old Bottle House is a 275-year-old former coaching inn, on the edge of Thetford Forest. Guests have a choice of 3 spacious, colour-co-ordinated bedrooms with tea/coffee-making facilities & colour T.V.. Delicious meals are served in the dining room, which has an inglenook fireplace. A charming house with every comfort, and a warm, friendly welcome. Children over 5 please. An excellent base from which to explore Norfolk.	£16.50	Y	Y	N
Mr & Mrs M. Whittley **The Grange** **Northwold** **Thetford IP26 5NF** Tel: (01366) 728240 Open: ALL YEAR Map Ref No. 28	Nearest Road: A.134 Do come & see the spring flowers, swim in the pool in the summer or sit & dine by log fires in winter. The bedrooms are all warmly decorated. 2 are en-suite, 3 have private bathroom & all have tea trays & colour T.V.. Local & home-grown produce is freshly cooked, & dinner is served by candlelight. An excellent centre for Norfolk, Suffolk & Cambridgeshire. Children welcome.	£17.00 *see PHOTO over*	Y	Y	Y

When booking your accommodation please mention
The Best Bed & Breakfast

The Grange.   Northwold.

Northumbria

Northumbria

Mountains & moors, hills & fells, coast & country are all to be found in this Northern region which embraces four counties - Northumberland, Durham, Cleveland & Tyne & Wear.

Saxons, Celts, Vikings, Romans & Scots all fought to control what was then a great wasteland between the Humber & Scotland.

Northumberland

Northumberland is England's Border country, a land of history, heritage & breathtaking countryside. Hadrian's Wall, stretching across the county from the mouth of the Tyne in the west to the Solway Firth, was built as the Northern frontier of the Roman Empire in 122 AD. Excavations along the Wall have brought many archaeological treasures to light. To walk along the wall is to discover the genius of Roman building & engineering skill. They left a network of roads, used to transport men & equipment in their attempts to maintain discipline among the wild tribes.

Through the following centuries the Border wars with the Scots led to famous battles such as Otterburn in 1388 & Flodden in 1513, & the construction of great castles including Bamburgh & Lindisfarne. Berwick-on-Tweed, the most northerly town, changed hands between England & Scotland 13 times.

Northumberland's superb countryside includes the Cheviot Hills in the Northumberland National Park, the unforgettable heather moorlands of the Northern Pennines to the west, Kielder Water (Western Europe's largest man-made lake), & 40 miles of glorious coastline.

Holy Island, or Lindisfarne, is reached by a narrow causeway that is covered at every incoming tide. Here St. Aidan of Iona founded a monastery in the 7th century, & with St. Cuthbert set out to Christianise the pagan tribes. The site was destroyed by the Danes, but Lindisfarne Priory was built by the monks of Durham in the 11th century to house a Benedictine community. The ruins are hauntingly beautiful.

Durham

County Durham is the land of the Prince Bishops, who with their armies, nobility, courts & coinage controlled the area for centuries. They ruled as a virtually independent State, holding the first line of defence against the Scots.

In Durham City, the impressive Norman Castle standing proudly over the narrow mediaeval streets was the home of the Prince Bishops for 800 years.

Durham Cathedral, on a wooded peninsula high above the River Wear, was built in the early 12th century & is undoubtably one of the world's finest buildings, long a place of Christian pilgrimage.

The region's turbulent history led to the building of forts & castles. Some like Bowes & Barnard Castle are picturesque ruins whilst others, including Raby, Durham & Lumley still stand complete.

The Durham Dales of Weardale, Teesdale & the Derwent Valley cover about one third of the county & are endowed with some of the highest & wildest scenery. Here are High Force, England's highest waterfall, & the Upper Teesdale National Nature Reserve.

The Bowes Museum at Barnard Castle is a magnificent French-style chateau & houses an important art collection.

In contrast is the award-winning museum at Beamish which imaginatively recreates Northern life at the turn of the century.

Northumbria

Cleveland

Cleveland, the smallest 'shire' in England, has long been famous for its steel, chemical & shipbuilding industries but it is also an area of great beauty. The North Yorkshire National Park lies in the south, & includes the cone-shaped summit of Roseberry Topping, "Cleveland's Matterhorn".

Cleveland means 'land of cliffs', & in places along the magnificent coastline, cliffs tower more than 600 feet above the sea, providing important habitat for wild plants & sea-birds.

Pretty villages such as Hart, Elwick & Staithes are full of steep, narrow alleys. Marton was the birthplace of Captain James Cook & the museum there traces the explorer's early life & forms the start of the 'Cook Heritage Trail'.

The Tees estuary is a paradise for birdwatchers, whilst walkers can follow the Cleveland Way or the 38 miles of the Langbaurgh Loop. There is surfing, windsurfing & sailing at Saltburn, & for the less energetic, the scenic Esk Valley Railway runs from Middlesbrough to Whitby.

Tyne & Wear

Tyne & Wear takes its name from the two rivers running through the area, & includes the large & lively city of Newcastle-on-Tyne.

Weardale lies in a beautiful valley surrounded by wild & bleak fells. Peaceful now, it was the setting for a thriving industry mining coal & silver, zinc & lead. Nature trails & recreation areas have been created among the old village & market towns.

The county was the birthplace of George Stephenson, railway engineer, who pioneered the world's first passenger railway on the Stockton to Darlington Line in 1825.

Durham Cathedral.

Northumbria

Northumbria Gazeeter

Areas of Outstanding Natural Beauty
The Heritage Coast, the Cheviot Hills, the North Pennine chain.

Historic Houses & Castles

Alnwick Castle - Alnwick
A superb mediaeval castle of the 12th century.
Bamburgh Castle-Bamburgh
A restored 12th century castle with Norman keep.
Callaly Castle - Whittingham
A 13th century Pele tower with 17th century mansion. Georgian additions.
Durham Castle - Durham
Part of the University of Durham - a Norman castle.
Lindisfarne Castle - Holy Island
An interesting 14th century castle.
Ormesby Hall - Nr. Middlesbrough
A mid 18th century house.
Raby Castle - Staindrop, Darlington
14th century with some later alteration . Fine art & furniture. Large gardens.
Wallington Hall -Combo
A 17th century house with much alteration & addition.
Washington Old Hall-Washington
Jacobean manor house, parts of which date back to 12th century.

Cathedrals & Churches

Brancepeth (St. Brandon)
12th century with superb 17th century woodwork. Part of 2 mediaeval screens. Flemish carved chest.
Durham Cathedral
A superb Norman cathedral. A unique Galilee chapel & early 12th century vaults.
Escombe
An interesting Saxon Church with sundial.
Hartlepool (St. Hilda)
Early English with fine tower & buttresses.
Hexham (St. Andrews)
Remains of a 17th century church with Roman dressing. A unique night staircase & very early stool. Painted screens.
Jarrow (St. Pauls)
Bede worshipped here. Strange in that it was originally 2 churches until 11th century. Mediaeval chair.

Newcastle (St. Nicholas)
14th century with an interesting lantern tower.
Heraldic font. Roundel of 14th century glass.
Morpeth (St. Mary the Virgin)
Fine mediaeval glass in east window - 14th century.
Pittington (St. Lawrence)
Late Norman nave with wall paintings. Carved tombstone - 13th century.
Skelton (St. Giles)
Early 13th century with notable font, gable crosses, bell-cote & buttresses.
Staindrop (St. Mary)
A fine Saxon window.
Priests dwelling.
Neville tombs & effigies.

Museums & Galleries

Aribea Roman Fort Museum - South Shields
Interesting objects found on site.
Berwick-on-Tweed Museum - Berwick
Special exhibition of interesting local finds.
Bowes Museum - Bernard Castle
European art from mediaeval to 19th century.
Captain Cook Birthplace Museum - Middlesbrough
Cook's life & natural history relating to his travels.
Clayton Collection - Chollerford
A collection of Roman sculpture, weapons & tools from forts.
Corbridge Roman Station - Corbridge
Roman pottery & sculpture.
Dormitory Musuem - Durham Cathedral
Relics of St. Cuthbert.
Mediaeval seats & manuscripts.
Gray Art Gallery - Hartlepool
19th-20th century art & oriental antiquities.
Gulbenkian Museum of Oriental Art - University of Durham
Chinese pottery & porcelain, Chinese jade & stone carvings, Chinese ivories, Chinese textiles, Japenese & Tibetan art. Egyptian & Mesopotamian antiquities.
Jarrow Hall - Jarrow
Excavation finds of Saxon & mediaeval monastery.
Fascinating information room dealing with early Christian sites in England.

Northumbria

Keep Museum - Newcastle-upon-Tyne
Mediaeval collection.
Laing Art Gallery - Newcastle-upon-Tyne
17th-19th century British arts, porcelain,
glass & silver.
National Music Hall Museum -
Sunderland
19th-20th century costume & artefacts
associated with the halls.
Preston Hall Museum - Stockton-on-Tees
Armour & arms, toys, ivory period room
University - New Castle -Upon -Tyne
The Hatton Gallery - housing a fine
collection of Italian paintings.
Museum of Antiquities
Prehistoric, Roman & Saxon collection
with an interesting reconstruction of a
temple.
**Beamish North of England Open Air
Museum** - European Museum of the Year
Chantry Bagpipe Museum - Morpeth
Darlington Museum & Railway Centre.

Historic Monuments

Ariiea Roman Fort - South Shields
Remains which include the gateways &
headquarters.
Barnard Castle - Barnard Castle
17th century ruin with interesting keep.
Bowes Castle - Bowes
Roman Fort with Norman keep.
The Castle & Town Walls - Berwick-on-
Tweed
12th century remains, reconstructed later.
Dunstanburgh Castle - Alnwick
14th century remains.
Egglestone Abbey - Barnard Castle
Remains of a Poor House.
Finchdale Priory - Durham
13 th century church with much
remaining.
Hadrian's Wall - Housesteads
Several miles of the wall including castles
& site museum.
Mithramic Temple - Carrawbrough
Mithraic temple dating back to the 3rd
century.
Norham Castle - Norham
The partial remains of a 12th century
castle.
Prudhoe Castle - Prudhoe
Dating from the 12th century with
additions. Bailey & gatehouse well
preserved.

The Roman Fort - Chesters
Extensive remains of a Roman bath
house.
Tynemouth Priory & Castle - Tynemouth
11th century priory - ruin - with 16th
century towers & keep.
Vindolanda - Barton Mill
Roman fort dating from 3rd century.
Warkworth Castle - Warkworth
Dating from the 11th century with
additions.
A great keep & gatehouse.
Warkworth Hermitage - Warkworth
An interesting 14th century Hermitage.
Lindisfarne Priory - Holy Island
(Lindisfarne)
11th century monastery. Island accessible
only at low tide.

Other things to see & do

Botanical Gardens - Durham University
Bird & Seal Colonies - Farne Islands
Conducted tours by boat
Marine Life Centre & Fishing Museum -
Seahouses
Museum of sealife, & boat trips to the
Farne Islands.
Tower Knowe Visitor Centre - Keilder
Water

Saltburn Victorian Festival.

NORTHUMBERLAND, DURHAM & TYNE & WEAR

Map reference

1	Finn	13	Gay
2	Jackson	14	Reed
3	Inkster	15	Close
4	Laverack	16	Alexander
5	Staff	17	Hagerty
6	Hogg	18	Peel
7	Elliott	19	Whitley
7	Graham-Tomlinson	20	Weightman
8	Carr	21	Harrison
9	Taylor		
10	Lee		
11	Courage		
12	Loyd		
12	Minchin		

Marine House. Alnmouth.

Northumbria
Northumberland

		rate from £ per person	children taken	evening meals	animals taken
Eileen Finn **Thornley House** **Allendale** **NE47 9NH** **Tel: (01434) 683255** **Open: ALL YEAR** **Map Ref No. 01**	Nearest Road: A.69 Large country house in spacious & peaceful grounds, surrounded by fields & woods 1 mile out of Allendale village. Relaxed & comfortable accommodation here; 3 roomy & light bedrooms (2 en-suite, 1 with private bathroom), each with tea/coffee makers. 2 lounges, 1 with colour T.V., 1 with Steinway Grand. Many well-stocked bookshelves. Good food & home baking; unlicensed, but guests are welcome to bring their own wine. Marvellous walking country. Hadrian's Wall, Keilder Forest & stately houses nearby.	£17.50	Y	Y	Y
Gordon & Sheila Inkster **Marine House Hotel** **1 Marine Road** **Alnmouth** **NE66 2RW** **Tel: (01665) 830349** **Open: FEB - DEC** **Map Ref No. 03**	Nearest Road: A.1 A 200-year-old listed building of considerable charm, situated on the edge of the village golf links with magnificent views of the sea. 10 individually appointed bedrooms, some with tester & crown drapes. All en-suite, with colour T.V. & hot beverage tray. Delicious, imaginative home cooking by a dedicated & creative resident chef, with menus changing daily. The prevailing atmosphere of comfort is further enhanced by open log fires. Children over 5 yrs.	£36.00 *see PHOTO over* CREDIT CARD VISA M'CARD	Y	Y	Y
Mrs Dorothy Jackson **Bilton Barns Farmhouse** **Bilton Barns** **Alnmouth** **Alnwick NE66 2TB** **Tel: (01665) 830427** **Open: EASTER - Mid OCT** **Map Ref No. 02**	Nearest Road: A.1 This spacious & well furnished farmhouse has beautiful, panoramic views over Alnmouth & Warkworth Bay, only 1 1/2 miles away. Set in lovely countryside, & well situated for many magnificent beaches, castles, walks & recreational activities. All rooms have c/h & tea bedrooms have their own washbasin, T.V. & tea/coffee, 3 with private bathroom. Dorothy makes many dishes with a distinctly local flavour. Brian is pleased to show any interested visitors the farm.	£18.50	Y	Y	N
Anita & Peter Laverack **Waren House Hotel** **Waren Mill** **Bamburgh NE70 7EE** **Tel: (01668) 214581** **Fax 01668 214484** **Open: ALL YEAR** **Map Ref No. 04**	Nearest Road: A.1 Lovingly restored traditional country house set in 6 acres of wooded grounds on the edge of Budle Bay, overlooking the Holy Island of Lindisfarne. Beautiful bedrooms, some with 4-poster, all with both spacious bathrooms & all the facilities you would expect from one of Northumbria's premier award-winning hostelries. Magnificent dining room offering excellent food. No smoking except in library. Bamburgh Castle 2 miles. Children over 14. (Rates shown are for Dinner, Bed & Breakfast.)	£52.00 *see PHOTO over* CREDIT CARD VISA M'CARD AMEX	Y	Y	Y
Brian & Pauline Staff **'Holmhead' Licensed** **Guest House** **Hadrian's Wall, Greenhead** **Carlisle CA6 7HY** **Tel/Fax: (016977) 47402** **Open: ALL YEAR** **Map Ref No. 05**	Nearest Road: A.69, B.6318 Standing in 300 acres of grounds, with Hadrian's Wall below, Holmhead, a 150-year-old traditional farmhouse, is perfect for visiting an area full of Roman history. 4 charming en-suite bedrooms. Longest breakfast menu in the world. All meals prepared with fresh produce. Guests dine together at a candlelit table. Birdswald, the highest remains of the Wall & the Roman Army Museum are close by. Host is a qualified tour guide & expert on Hadrian's Wall. Licensed. See photo page 131.	£22.50 🚭 CREDIT CARD VISA M'CARD	Y	Y	N

Waren House. Waren Mill.

The Courtyard. Sandhoe.

Northumberland

		rate from £ per person	children taken	evening meals	animals taken
Margaret & Bill Weightman **The Courtyard** **Mount Pleasant** **Sandhoe** **Corbridge NE46 4LX** **Tel: (01434) 606850** **Fax 01434 606632** **Open: ALL YEAR** **Map Ref No. 20**	Nearest Road: A.69, A.68 A warm family welcome greets visitors to this lovingly restored & beautifully furnished country house, dating from 1730. Surrounded by open countryside, with wonderful panoramic views over Corbridge & Corstopitum Roman Fort, both 1 1/2 miles away, & the lovely Tyne Valley. All rooms have exposed oak beams, en-suite bath/shower rooms, colour T.V., central heating & tea/coffee facilities; 1 has an antique 4-poster bed. Evening meals are offered at prior notice. No smoking except in the sitting room.	£22.50 *see PHOTO over*	Y	Y	N
David & Sheila Munro **Hogg** **Wark Farm House** **Wark** **Cornhill-on-Tweed** **TD12 4RE** **Tel: (01890) 883570** **Open: ALL YEAR** **Map Ref No. 06**	Nearest Road: A.697 This traditional stone farmhouse stands a mere 200 yards from the picturesque south bank of the River Tweed. You will be made to feel at home in spacious, comfortable accommodation, which is tastefully furnished & includes 4 super guest bedrooms. 1 is en-suite, & each has beverage facilities. In the dining room, sample fresh local fare, imaginatively cooked & prepared in the farmhouse kitchen. An ideal base for touring, & situated on the border between England & Scotland, with many places of interest & beauty spots close at hand. Children over 5. Licensed.	£23.00 *see PHOTO over* CREDIT CARD VISA M'CARD AMEX	Y	Y	Y
Patricia Graham-Tomlinson **West Close House** **Hextol Terrace** **Hexham** **NE46 2AD** **Tel: (01434) 603307** **Open: ALL YEAR** **Map Ref No. 07**	Nearest Road: B.6305 Surrounded by lovely secluded gardens, this charming & immaculately maintained detached 1920s Villa is situated in a peaceful, leafy cul-de-sac with private parking. Accommodation is in 4 delightful bedrooms, 1 a superb double en-suite, with wash basins, radio/alarms, hairdryers & beverage trays. There is an elegant drawing room & a cosy dining/T.V. room. Wholefood Continental or Full English breakfasts are varied, generous & wholesome. A warm, friendly & relaxing ambience ensure a memorable stay.	£18.00	Y	N	N
Mrs Eileen Elliott **Middlemarch** **Hencotes** **Hexham** **NE46 2EB** **Tel: (01434) 605003** **Open: ALL YEAR** **Map Ref No. 07**	Nearest Road: A.68, A.69 A beautifully restored, award-winning, listed Georgian presbytery perfectly placed in the mediaeval market town. A good stop for exploring Northumberland & the Roman Wall, or for going to & from Scotland. The well-appointed, spacious bedrooms comprise 1 4-poster en-suite, 1 family, 1 double & 1 twin. 2 are en-suite, & all have w.b., tea/coffee facilities, r/c colour T.V., radio/alarms & hairdryers. Private parking. Children over 10.	£20.00	Y	N	Y

When booking your accommodation please mention
The Best Bed & Breakfast

Wark Farm House. Wark.

Northumberland

		rate from £ per person	children taken	evening meals	animals taken
Mrs Susan Carr **East Peterelfield Farm** **Hexham** **NE46 2JT** **Tel: (01434) 607209** **Fax 01434 601753** **Open: ALL YEAR** **Map Ref No. 08**	Nearest Road: A.69 An attractive, listed farmhouse offering super accommodation in 3 well-proportioned guest rooms. Each is well equipped with modern-day comforts, including colour T.V., radio & tea/coffee-making facilities. 2 have en-suite bathrooms. Hearty breakfasts & delicious evening meals are served, & special diets can be catered for. Riding holidays are easily arranged, & 2 golf courses are within easy reach. Children very welcome. Ample parking. An ideal touring centre, & within easy reach of Hadrian's Wall.	£21.00	Y	Y	N
Mrs Margaret Taylor **Croft House** **Main Street** **Slaley** **Hexham NE47 0AA** **Tel: (01434) 673322** **Open: ALL YEAR** **Map Ref No. 09**	Nearest Road: A.68, A.69 Lovely stone Northumbrian house (1820), large garden, wonderful views. Fully modernised, each bedroom providing en-suite or private facilities, radio, tea/coffee tray. Guests' lounge with colour T.V.. 5 miles south of Hexham in unspoilt village providing quiet country base with ideal access to Roman wall, rural & coastal Northumberland, Durham, Newcastle & Gateshead Metro Centre. Village pub & restaurant 100 yards. Children over 12. Come & be spoilt!	£20.00	Y	N	N
Mrs Isobel Lee **Manor House Farm** **Ninebanks** **Allendale** **Hexham** **NE47 8DA** **Tel: (01434) 345236** **Open: ALL YEAR (Excl. Xmas)** **Map Ref No. 10**	Nearest Road: A.686 A listed Georgian farmhouse nestling in the beautiful West Allen Valley, a designated Area of Outstanding Natural Beauty. Accommodation is in 3 attractive bedrooms with modern amenities including tea/coffee makers, radios & hairdryers. A pleasant guests' lounge is also available, in which you may wish to relax after a tiring day. Situated on the Cumbrian-Durham border, Manor House Farm is in a lovely spot, close to Hadrian's Wall. An ideal overnight stop en-route to Scotland. No smoking in bedrooms.	£17.00	Y	N	Y
Elizabeth Courage **Rye Hill Farm** **Slaley** **Hexham NE47 OAH** **Tel: (01434) 673259** **Fax 01434 673608** **Open: ALL YEAR** **Map Ref No. 11**	Nearest Road: A.68, A.69 Rye Hill Farm dates back some 300 years & is a traditional livestock unit in beautiful countryside just 5 miles south of Hexham. Recently, some of the stone barns adjoining the farmhouse have been converted into superb modern guest accommodation. There are 6 bedrooms, all with private facilities, & all have radio, colour T.V. & tea/coffee-making facilities. Delicious home-cooked meals. The perfect place for a get-away-from-it-all holiday.	£18.00	Y	Y	Y

When booking your accommodation please mention
The Best Bed & Breakfast

Westfield. Bellingham.

Northumberland

	rate from £ per person	children taken	evening meals	animals taken
David & June Minchin **Westfield House** **Bellingham** **Hexham NE48 2DP** **Tel/Fax: (01434) 220340** **Open: ALL YEAR** **Map Ref No. 12**	Nearest Road: A.68 Westfield is a truly hospitable home. Built as an elegant, but cosy Victorian gentleman's residence, with nearly an acre of gardens. The 5 bedrooms, including 2 en-suite & a 4-poster, are all totally comfortable, with more than a touch of luxury. Breakfast & dinner are superb, with traditional cooking at its best. Wonderful countryside - ideal touring spot - Roman Wall, castles & N.T. properties, so come & bide-awhile & be spoilt. *see PHOTO over* CREDIT CARD VISA M'CARD	£18.00	Y	Y	Y
Peter & Charlotte Loyd **Mantle Hill** **Hesleyside** **Bellingham** **Hexham** **NE48 2LB** **Tel: (01434) 220428** **Fax 01434 220113** **Open: ALL YEAR** **Map Ref No. 12**	Nearest Road: A.68, A.69 Mantle Hill is a delightful home in a stunning location. The 18th-century Dower House to historic Hensleyside Hall, it is situated 2 miles from Bellingham in the beautiful & peaceful Northumbrian National Park. Guests have their own sitting room, with open fire & T.V.. The lovely bedrooms, each with tea/coffee-making facilities, are very tastefully furnished. En-suite available. Delicious home produce includes fresh vegetables, eggs, beef & lamb. Fishing available on North Tyne, England's premier salmon river. Excellent base for Kielder Water & Hadrian's Wall. Licensed. Children over 3 yrs.	£20.00	Y	Y	N
Stephen & Celia Gay **Shieldhall** **Wallington** **Morpeth NE61 4AQ** **Tel: (01830) 40387** **Fax 01830 40387** **Open: MAR - NOV** **Map Ref No. 13**	Nearest Road: A.696, B.6342 Within acres of well-kept gardens, offering unimpeded views & overlooking the National Trust's Wallington estate, this meticulously restored 18th-century farmhouse is built around a pretty courtyard. All bedrooms are beautifully furnished & have en-suite facilities. There are very comfortable lounges & an extremely charming inglenooked dining room where home produce is often used for delicious meals which are especially prepared when booked in advance. CREDIT CARD VISA M'CARD	£17.00	N	Y	N
Kenneth J. Harrison **Glen View** **6 Meadowfield Road** **Stocksfield NE43 7QX** **Tel: (01661) 843674** **Open: ALL YEAR** **Map Ref No. 21**	Nearest Road: A.68, A.695 This charming family home, dating from 1886, is set in 3 acres of garden, including a woodland area in which deer, foxes & badgers are regularly seen. 3 generous bedrooms have colour T.V., washbasins & tea-making facilities. 1 en-suite with an antique 4-poster. Guests have the use of the heated indoor swimming pool & games room. Delicious candlelit dinners & traditional English breakfasts will ensure a memorable stay. *see PHOTO over* CREDIT CARD VISA	£25.00	Y	Y	N
Mrs Sally Peel **Low Stead** **Wark on Tyne** **NE48 3DP** **Tel: (01434) 230352** **Open: ALL YEAR** **Map Ref No. 18**	Nearest Road: A.69, B.6320 The unspoilt countryside of Northumberland's National Park surrounds Low Stead. A 16th-century 'bastle house' built to repel border reivers, its present tranquility & solitude provide a haven for walkers, wildlife enthusiasts & country lovers. 2 delightful en-suite bedrooms. Imaginatively presented meals using local produce are served in the log-fired oak-beamed dining room. Peace, history & total comfort combine to make Low Stead's unique atmosphere. Children over 9.	£22.50	Y	Y	N

Glen View. Stocksfield.

Durham

		rate from £ per person	children taken	evening meals	animals taken
Mrs B. Reed **Lands Farm** **Westgate-in-Weardale** **Bishop Auckland** **DL13 1SN** **Tel: (01388) 517210** **Open: APR - OCT** **Map Ref No. 14**	Nearest Road: A.689 You will be warmly welcomed to Lands Farm, an old stone-built farmhouse within walking distance of Westgate village. A walled garden with stream meandering by. Accommodation is in centrally heated double & family rooms with luxury en-suite facilities, T.V., tea/coffee making. Full English breakfast or Continental alternative served in an attractive dining room. This is an ideal base for touring (Durham, Hadrian's Wall, Beamish Museum, etc.) & for walking.	£18.00	Y	N	N
Helene P. Close **Grove House** **Hamsterley Forest** **Bishop Auckland** **DL13 3NL** **Tel: (01388) 488203** **Fax 0191 3780836** **Open: ALL YEAR** **Map Ref No. 15**	Nearest Road: A.68 Grove House, once an aristocrat's shooting lodge, is tastefully furnished throughout, & is situated in an idyllic setting in the middle of Hamsterley Forest. A spacious lounge with log fire gives a warm & comfortable country-house atmosphere. The grandeur & fineness of the dining room reminds one of an age gone by. (Take note of the door handles!) 3 bedrooms, all with en-suite/private bathrooms, which are well-appointed. Helene does all the cooking herself to ensure freshness & quality to her evening meals. A wonderful base from which to explore this region.	£19.50 🚭	Y	Y	N
Mrs Rhona Whitley **The Bracken Guest House** **Shincliffe** **Durham** **DH1 2PD** **Tel: (0191) 3862966** **Open: ALL YEAR** **Map Ref No. 19**	Nearest Road: A.177 The Bracken Guest House is situated on the outskirts of Durham City in the nearby village of Shincliffe. The property stands in 2 acres of wood grounds, with safe parking in front of the house. Just 2 mins' drive from the city centre on the A.177 which links up with the A.1/M. All of the attractive bedrooms are en-suite, & 1 is situated on the ground floor & has wheelchair access. There is a residents' lounge/bar in which to relax. An ideal centre from which to explore this lovely region & its many attractions.	£25.00 🚭 *see PHOTO over* CREDIT CARD VISA M'CARD	Y	Y	Y
Belinda & Hamish Alexander **Partridge Close** **Lanchester** **DH7 0SZ** **Tel: (01207) 520896** **Fax 01207 520066** **Open: ALL YEAR** **Map Ref No. 16**	Nearest Road: A.68 Partridge Close is a large country house on a thoroughbred stud farm. The house is beautifully appointed, with many antiques & paintings. Guest accommodation comprises 2 very attractive double bedrooms, each with private bathroom, tea/coffee facilities, radios & superb views. Guests may use the large drawing room, & meals are served in the elegant dining room. Special diets are available. A delightful base from which to explore Northumberland.	£25.00	Y	Y	N

When booking your accommodation please mention
The Best Bed & Breakfast

Bracken Guest House. Shincliffe.

Tyne & Wear

		rate from £ per person	children taken	evening meals	animals taken
Capt. Keith J. Hagerty **Chirton House Hotel** **46 Clifton Road** **Newcastle-upon-Tyne** **NE4 6XH** **Tel: (0191) 2730407** **Open: ALL YEAR** **Map Ref No. 17**	Nearest Road: A.1, A.186 An imposing, elegant house, standing in its own pleasant grounds, offering 11 very comfortable rooms, 5 with en-suite facilities, each with colour T.V. & tea/coffee-making facilities available. A T.V. lounge & cocktail bar with friendly, country-house atmosphere. Situated within a few minutes of the city centre, it is a good base for touring the countryside, including Hadrian's Wall. The beaches are not far away, & there are many places of great interest close by.	£17.00 CREDIT CARD VISA M'CARD	Y	Y	Y

All the establishments mentioned in this guide

are members of

The Worldwide Bed & Breakfast Association

When booking your accommodation please mention
The Best Bed & Breakfast

Oxfordshire

Oxfordshire
(Thames & Chilterns)

Oxfordshire is a county rich in history & delightful countryside. It has prehistoric sites, early Norman churches, 15th century coaching inns, Regency residences, distinctive cottages of black & white chalk flints & lovely Oxford, the city of dreaming spires.

The countryside ranges from lush meadows with willow-edged river banks scattered with small villages of thatched cottages, to the hills of the Oxfordshire Cotswolds in the west, the wooded Chilterns in the east & the distinctive ridge of the Berkshire Downs in the south. "Old Father Thames" meanders gently across the county to Henley, home of the famous regatta.

The ancient track known as the Great Ridgeway runs across the shire, & a walk along its length reveals barrows, hill forts & stone circles. The 2,000 year old Uffington Horse cut into the chalk of the hillside below an ancient hill fort site, is some 360 feet in length & 160 feet high.

The Romans built villas in the county & the remains of one, including a magnificent mosaic can be seen at North Leigh. In later centuries lovely houses were built. Minster Lovell stands beside the Windrush; Rousham house with its William Kent gardens is situated near Steeple Aston & beside the Thames lies Elizabethan Mapledurham House with its working watermill.

At Woodstock is Blenheim Palace, the largest private house in Britain & birthplace of Sir Winston Churchill. King Alfred's statue stands at Wantage, commemorating his birth there, & Banbury has its cross, made famous in the old nursery rhyme.

Oxford is a town of immense atmosphere with fine college buildings around quiet cloisters, & narrow cobbled lanes. It was during the 12th century that Oxford became a meeting place for scholars & grew into the first established centre of learning, outside the monasteries, in England.

The earliest colleges to be founded were University College, Balliol & Merton. Further colleges were added during the reign of the Tudors, as Oxford became a power in the kingdom. There are now 35 university colleges & many other outstanding historic buildings in the city . Christ Church Chapel is now the Cathedral of Oxford, a magnificent building with a deservedly famous choir.

St. Mary's Church.

Oxfordshire

Oxfordshire Gazeteer

Areas of Oustanding Natural Beauty
The North Wessex Downs. The Chiltern Hills. The Cotswolds.

Historic Houses & Castles

Ashdown House - Nr. Lambourn
17th century, built for Elizabeth of Bohemia, now contains portraits associated with her. Mansard roof has cupola with golden ball.
Blenheim Palace - Woodstock
Sir John Vanbrugh's classical masterpiece. Garden designed by Vanbrugh & Henry Wise. Further work done by Capability Brown who created the lake. Collection of pictures & tapestries.
Broughton Castle- Banbury.
14th century mansion with moat - interesting plaster work fine panelling & fire places
Chasleton House-Morton in Marsh
17th century,fine examples of plaster work & panelling.Still has original furniture & tapestries. topiary garden from1700.
Grey Court - Henly-on-Thames
16th century house containing 18th century plasterwork & furniture. Mediaeval ruins. Tudor donkey-wheel for raising water from well.
Mapledurham House - Mapledurham
16th century Elizabethan house. Oak staircase, private chapel, paintings, original moulded ceilings. Watermill nearby.
Milton Manor House - Nr. Abingdon
17th century house designed by Inigo Jones - Georgian wings, walled garden, pleasure grounds.
Rousham House - Steeple Ashton
17th century - contains portraits & miniatures.

University of Oxford Colleges

College	Date
University college,	1249
Balliol,	1263
Merton,	1264
Hertford,	1284
Oriel,	1326
New,	1379
All Souls,	1438
Brasenose,	1509
Christ Church,	1546
St. John's,	1555
Pembroke,	1624
Worcester,	1714
Nuffield,	1937
St. Edmund Hall,	1270
Exeter,	1314
The Queen's,	1340
Lincoln,	1427
Magdalen,	1458
Corpus Christi,	1516
Trinity,	1554
Jesus,	1571
Wadham,	1610
Keble,	1868

Cathedrals & Churches

Abingdon (St. Helen)
14th-16th century perpendicular. Painted roof. Georgian stained & enamelled glass.
Burford (St. John the Baptist)
15th century. Sculptured table tombs in churchyard.
Chislehampton (St. Katherine)
18th century. Unspoilt interior of Georgian period. Bellcote.
Dorchester (St. Peter & St. Paul)
13th century knight in stone effigy. Jesse window.
East Hagbourne (St. Andrew)
14th -15th century. Early glass, wooden roofs, 18th century tombs.
North Moreton (All Saints)
13th century with splendid 14th century chantry chapel - tracery.
Oxford Cathedral
Smallest of our English cathedrals. Stone spire form 1230. Norman arcade has double arches, choir vault.
Ryecote (St. Michael & All Angels)
14th century benches & screen base. 17th century altar-piece & communion rails, old clear glass, good ceiling.
Stanton Harcourt (St. Michael)
Early English - old stone & marble floor. Early screen with painting, monuments of 17th -19th century.
Yarnton (St. Bartholomew)
13th century - late perpendicular additions. Jacobean screen. 15th century alabaster reredos.

Oxfordshire

Museums & Galleries

The Ashmolean Museum of Art & Archaeology - Oxford
British ,European ,Mediterranean, Egyptian & Near Eastern archaeology. Oil paintings of Italian, Dutch, Flemish, French & English schools. Old Master watercolours, prints, drawings, ceramics, silver, bronzes & sculptures. Chinese & Japanese porcelain, lacquer & painting, Tibetan, Islamic & Indian art.

Christ Church Picture Gallery - Oxford
Old Master drawings & paintings.

Museum of Modern Art - Oxford
Exhibitiors of contemporary art.

Museum of Oxford
Many exhibits depicting the history of Oxford & its University.

The Rotunda - Oxford
Privately owned collection of dolls' houses 1700-1900, with contents such as furniture, china, silver, dolls, etc.

Oxford University Museum
Entomological, zoological, geological & mineralogical collections.

Pendon Museum of Miniature Landscape & Transport - Abingdon.
Showing in miniature the countryside & its means of transport in the thirties, with trains & thatched village. Railway relics.

Town Museum - Abingdon
17th century building exhibiting fossil, archaeological items & collection of charters & documents.

T olsey Museum - Burford
Seals, maces, charters & bygones - replica of Regency room with period furnishings & clothing.

Historic Monuments

Uffington Castle & White Horse - Uffington
White horse cut into the chalk - iron age hill fort.

Rollright Stones - Nr. Chipping Norton
77 stones placed in circle - an isolated King's stone & nearby an ancient burial chamber.

Minster Lovell House - Minster Lovell
15th century mediaeval house - ruins.

Deddington Castle - Deddington

Other things to see & do

Didcot railway centre -a large collection of locomotives etc., from Brunel's Great Western Railway.

Filkins -a working wool mill where rugs & garments are woven in traditional way.

Blenheim Palace. Woodstock.

OXFORDSHIRE

Map reference

0	Lloyd	17	Morris
1	Rouse	17	Barrett
2	Ritter	17	Tong
3	Nunneley	17	Trafford
3	Hainsworth	17	Welham
4	Wills	17	Edwards
5	Grove-White	17	Price
6	Allday	17	Tompkins
7	Scavuzzo	18	Savage
8	Wallace	19	Peterson
9	Storch	19	French
10	Ovey	20	Aitken
11	Fulford-Dobson	21	Wadsworth
12	Oxford	22	Spencer-Thomas
13	Naylor	23	Simpson
14	Jones	24	Jones
15	Sykes	25	Shaw
16	Ellis	26	Crofts
		27	Talfourd-Cook

Fulford House.   Banbury.

Oxfordshire

		rate from £ per person	children taken	evening meals	animals taken
Mrs Mary Rouse **The Farmhouse Hotel** **University Farm, Lew** **Bampton OX18 2AU** **Tel: (01993) 850297** **Fax 01993 850965** **Open: ALL YEAR (Excl. Xmas)** **Map Ref No. 01**	Nearest Road: A.4095 A charming 17th-century farmhouse standing in 216 acres. Heavily beamed throughout, with a huge inglenook fireplace in the lounge. 6 prettily decorated bedrooms, all with bath or shower en-suite. Honeymoon suite. A superb timbered dining room & a most attractive lounge with T.V.. A large sun terrace for guests' use. Situated in a small peaceful village, 3 miles from Witney, it is an ideal base for touring. Children over 5.	£25.00 CREDIT CARD VISA M'CARD	Y	Y	N
Patti Ritter **La Madonette Country** **Guest House** **North Newington** **Banbury OX15 6AA** **Tel: (01295) 730212** **Fax 01295 730363** **Open: ALL YEAR** **Map Ref No. 02**	Nearest Road: B.4035, M.40 A peacefully situated 17th-century millhouse set in rural surroundings, where Patti & Michael offer a warm welcome to their guests. The 5 large double en-suite bedrooms are comfortably furnished with full facilities. Well located for the Cotswolds, Stratford-upon-Avon, Oxford & Blenheim. Good local pubs & restaurants offering evening meals nearby. A lounge, gardens & swimming pool for guests' use. Licensed. Evening meals by arrangement in winter only.	£22.50 CREDIT CARD VISA M'CARD	Y	Y	N
Rosemary Nunneley **Sugarswell Farm** **Shenington** **Banbury OX15 6HW** **Tel/Fax: (01295) 680512** **Open: ALL YEAR** **Map Ref No. 03**	Nearest Road: A.422 Situated in an elevated position overlooking fields & woodlands, Sugarswell Farm is an ideal spot from which to tour, or just relax & unwind. Incorporating modern conveniences with gracious style. After a day's exploring, return to the comforts of home, together with the appointments expected of a country-house hotel. As your hostess is a Cordon Bleu cook, fine food is always on the menu.	£25.00	N	Y	N
Stephen & Mary Pen Wills **Fulford House** **The Green, Culworth** **Banbury** **OX17 2BB** **Tel: (01295) 760355** **Fax 01295 768304** **Open: Mid FEB - Mid DEC** **Map Ref No. 04**	Nearest Road: B.4525 Peace, quiet & comfort is assured in this charming 17th-century home. Whether wandering in the old tranquil gardens, watching horses training or chatting with other guests & hosts, there is a great ambience. Just 3 delightfully furnished bedrooms have en-suite/private facilities with T.V.. A drawing room is for guests' use. 1 hour from Heathrow, Fulford House is in rolling Northamptonshire countryside, near Warwick, Stratford & Oxford. A central stop-over for travellers. Some dinners by special arrangement. Licensed. Children over 5.	£22.50 *see PHOTO over*	Y	N	Y
Col. & Mrs Grove-White **Home Farmhouse** **Charlton** **Banbury OX17 3DR** **Tel: (01295) 811683** **Fax 01295 811683** **Open: ALL YEAR** **Map Ref No. 05**	Nearest Road: A.43, A.41 This charming, listed stone house dating from 1637, with its attractive, colourful, paved courtyard, provides an excellent base for visiting Oxford, Blenheim, Stratford-upon-Avon, Warwick & the beautiful Cotswold villages. Mrs Grove-White has used her expertise as a professional interior designer to ensure that the 3 double/twin bedded rooms, with en-suite bathroom & colour T.V., are comfortable & elegantly furnished. Evening meals by arrangement only. Children over 10 yrs.	£23.00 *see PHOTO over* CREDIT CARD VISA M'CARD	Y	Y	Y

Home Farmhouse. Charlton.

College Farmhouse. King Sutton.

Oxfordshire

	rate from £ per person	children taken	evening meals	animals taken
Stephen & Sara Allday **College Farmhouse** **Kings Sutton** **Banbury OX17 3PS** **Tel: (01295) 811473** Fax 01295 812505 **Open: ALL YEAR** **Map Ref No. 06**	Nearest Road: B.4100, A.4260 Fine period farmhouse, with lovely views, set in its own secluded grounds, which include a lake, tennis court & organic vegetable garden. Ideally located for visits to Oxford, Warwick, Stratford-upon-Avon & the Cotswolds. Excellent home-produced food - special diets catered for. Stephen & Sara have considerable local knowledge. They enjoy gardening, bridge & racing. You will be sure of a very comfortable & peaceful stay.	£22.00 *see PHOTO over*	Y	Y	Y
Mr & Mrs P. J. Oxford **Chadlington House Hotel** **Chapel Road** **Chadlington OX7 3LZ** **Tel: (01608) 676437** Fax 01608 676503 **Open: ALL YEAR** **Map Ref No. 12**	Nearest Road: A.361, A.44 Located in the delightful Oxfordshire Cotswold village from which it derives its name, Chadlington House is a lovely gabled residence standing in its own spacious grounds with spectacular views over the glorious Evenlode Valley through which the River Evenlode wends its way to join the River Thames at Newbridge, east of Oxford. A small family hotel, Chadington House retains a restful atmosphere whilst offering personal service.	£20.00 CREDIT CARD VISA M'CARD	Y	Y	N
Mrs Wendy Jones **Hillborough House** **The Green** **Milton-under-Wychwood** **Chipping Norton OX7 6JH** **Tel: (01993) 830501** Fax 01993 832005 **Open: ALL YEAR** **Map Ref No. 14**	Nearest Road: A.361 An early-Victorian house facing the village green in this delightful Cotswold village nestling deep in the Evenlode Valley. The bedrooms are warm, cheerful & spacious, with colour T.V., 'phone & complimentary tea tray. All are en-suite, & some are annexed across the courtyard from the main house. A leafy conservatory with comfy sofas overlooking pretty walled gardens. A cosy licensed bar with open fire. Ideal for touring Oxford, Stratford, the Cotswolds & the Heart of England. Dinner by arrangement.	£24.00 CREDIT CARD VISA M'CARD AMEX	Y	Y	Y
Mrs Audrey Scavuzzo **The Forge House** **Churchill** **Chipping Norton** **OX7 6NJ** **Tel: (01608) 658173** **Open: ALL YEAR** **Map Ref No. 07**	Nearest Road: A.44, A.361 The Forge House is a 150-year-old, traditional Cotswold stone cottage, with inglenook log fires & exposed beams, combining the charm of tradition with the comfort of contemporary living. 4 tastefully furnished en-suite rooms, 2 with 4-poster beds & 1 with jacuzzi. All have radio, T.V. & tea/coffee. A lounge & garden for guests' use. Personal service & advice on touring the area. Convenient for Oxford, Stratford, Warwick Castle, Blenheim Palace & the Cotswolds.	£23.00 *see PHOTO over*	Y	N	N
Wynyard & Julia Wallace **Little Parmoor** **Parmoor Lane, Frieth** **Henley on Thames** **RG9 6NL** **Tel: (01494) 881447** Fax 01494 883012 **Open: ALL YEAR** **Map Ref No. 08**	Nearest Road: M.40, M.4 A pretty Georgian country house surrounded by farmland, situated in the beautiful Chiltern Hills between Henley & Marlow. Within easy reach of Oxford & Windsor, & 40 mins from Heathrow - a perfect & peaceful spot to begin or end a holiday. The spacious & attractively furnished bedrooms have washbasins, colour T.V. & tea-making facilities. A pretty, panelled drawing room. Ample parking. Evening meals served if ordered in advance. Children over 5 yrs.	£18.00 🚭	Y	Y	N

The Forge House. Chipping Norton.

Oxfordshire

		rate from £ per person	children taken	evening meals	animals taken
Mrs Jenny Storch **The Elms** **Gallowstree Road** **Peppard** **Henley RG9 5HT** **Tel: (01734) 723164** **Open: ALL YEAR** **Map Ref No. 09**	Nearest Road: B.481, A.4074 The Elms is a William house built in 1834. The large garden backs onto the Chilterns, an Area of Outstanding Natural Beauty. Only 40 mins from Heathrow, The Elms offers a rural environment, with badminton & swimming in the garden, & a pub that supplies excellent food at the end of the drive. There are 3 rooms in all. 2 are en-suite, & each has T.V., beverage facilities, fruit, flowers, etc. Ample parking. Children over 6 yrs.	£17.50	Y	N	Y
Mr & Mrs Talfourd-Cook **Holmwood, Shiplake Row** **Binfield Heath** **Henley-on-Thames** **RG9 4DP** **Tel: (01734) 478747** **Fax 01734 478637** **Open: ALL YEAR** **Map Ref No. 27**	Nearest Road: A.4155 Holmwood is a large elegant Georgian country house, Grade II listed, furnished with antique, period furniture. There is a galleried hall, coved mahogany doors & marble fireplaces (wood fires in winter). All bedrooms are spacious, attractively furnished & have en-suite facilities. The beautiful gardens extend to 3 1/2 acres & have extensive views over the Thames Valley. This charming home is an ideal base from which to explore London & the South East. Heathrow Airport 30 mins, Reading 4 miles, Henley 2 1/2 miles.	£22.50	Y	N	N
Richard & Gillian Ovey **Hernes** **Henley-on-Thames** **RG9 4NT** **Tel: (01491) 573245** **Fax 01491 574645** **Open: Mid JAN - Mid DEC** **Map Ref No. 10**	Nearest Road: A.423, A.4130 Large, warm, comfortable rooms, full of the history of a family whose roots lie deep in Oxfordshire, & a welcome traditional to Hernes for generations, await guests who visit this part-16th-century house. Gardens, with a pool & croquet lawn, overlook acres of farm & parkland. Ideal for a relaxing rest or for visiting London, Windsor, Eton, Oxford, Cotswolds, Chilterns & Heathrow. Bedrooms (incl. a 4-poster), have private/en-suite bathrooms & tea/coffee. Dinner by arrangement.	£30.00	N	N	N
Mrs Susan Fulford-Dobson **Shepherds** **Rotherfield Greys** **Henley-on-Thames** **RG9 4QL** **Tel: (01491) 628413** **Open: ALL YEAR (Excl. Xmas)** **Map Ref No. 11**	Nearest Road: A.4130 An attractive, part-18th-century house, standing on a peaceful village green in its own gardens & paddocks, covered in roses, wisteria, clematis & jasmine. The pretty guest bedrooms have en-suite or private facilities. Some have T.V., all have clock/radios & tea/coffee. Delightful drawing room for guests, with antiques & open fire. An ideal centre for exploring Chilterns, Windsor & Oxford. Accessible to Heathrow. Children over 12. Evening meals by prior arrangement only.	£20.00	Y	N	N
Brian Sykes **Conygree Gate Hotel** **Church Street** **Kingham** **OX7 6YA** **Tel: (01608) 658389** **Open: ALL YEAR** **Map Ref No. 15**	Nearest Road: A.436, A.361 A small family-run country house in Kingham village, set in the heart of glorious Cotswold countryside. Converted from a farmhouse, this is a 16th-century building with leaded windows, oak beams and inglenook fireplaces. A large rear garden for sitting out in. 10 guest bedrooms, mostly en-suite, with colour T.V., tea/coffee facilities. 2 sitting rooms, a dining room and a licensed bar. Central heating and log fires throughout. Ample parking.	£27.00 CREDIT CARD VISA M'CARD	Y	Y	Y

Oxfordshire

		rate from £ per person	children taken	evening meals	animals taken
Tom & Carol Ellis **Wynford House** **79 Main Road** **Long Hanborough** **OX8 8JX** **Tel: (01993) 881402** **Open: ALL YEAR** **Map Ref No. 16**	Nearest Road: A.4095 Wynford House is situated in the charming village of Long Hanborough. Accommodation is in 3 guest rooms, 1 with en-suite facilities. All have modern amenities, including colour T.V. & tea/coffee makers, & are comfortably furnished. Delicious breakfasts are served, with local pubs & restaurants offering tasty evening meals. Conveniently located on the doorstep of the Cotswolds, with Bladon 1 mile, Woodstock & Blenheim Palace 3 miles & Oxford 12 miles.	£19.00	Y	Y	Y
Anthony & Peta Lloyd **Fallowfields** **Faringdon Road** **Southmoor** **Oxford OX13 5BH** **Tel: (01865) 820416** **Fax 01865 821275** **Open: ALL YEAR** **Map Ref No. 00**	Nearest Road: A.420 Fallowfields, the former home of Begum Aga Khan, is an absolutely delightful 300-year-old Gothic-style manor house. Beautifully furnished, with the emphasis on gracious elegance. The 2 lounges are spacious & comfortable. The pleasant bedrooms have pretty linens, tea/coffee-making facilities, hairdryer, radio, 'phone & valet press. The elegant dining room befits the super cuisine served. Guests are also encouraged to use the tennis court, croquet lawn & the outdoor swimming pool. Children over 10 years.	£29.50 *see PHOTO over* CREDIT CARD VISA M'CARD AMEX	Y	Y	Y
Mr & Mrs P. Welham **Norham Guest House** **16 Norham Road** **Oxford** **OX2 6SF** **Tel: (01865) 515352** **Open: ALL YEAR** **Map Ref No. 17**	Nearest Road: A.423, A.4165 A delightful Victorian house situated in a conservation area yet convenient for the many attractions of Oxford. Accommodation is in 8 tastefully furnished guest rooms, including 7 en-suite & 1 family room with modern amenities. All rooms have T.V. & tea/coffee-making facilities. Delicious breakfasts are served. Vegetarian diets by arrangement. Children over 5 years welcome. Convenient for the city centre. Ideal for visiting the Cotswolds & Stratford-upon-Avon.	£24.00	Y	N	N
Mr & Mrs G. Price **Arden Lodge** **34 Sunderland Avenue** **Woodstock Road** **Oxford OX2 8DX** **Tel: (01865) 52076** **Open: ALL YEAR** **Map Ref No. 17**	Nearest Road: A.40 A modern detached house set, in a tree-lined avenue, in one of Oxford's most select areas. Offering attractively furnished bedrooms, with private facilities, colour T.V. & beverage tray. An excellent base for touring: within easy reach of London, the Cotswolds, Stratford & Warwick. Convenient for the city centre, parks, river, meadows, golf course & country inns, including the world famous 'Trout Inn'.	£20.00	Y	N	N

When booking your accommodation please mention
The Best Bed & Breakfast

Fallowfields.   Abingdon.

Oxfordshire

	Nearest Road	rate from £ per person	children taken	evening meals	animals taken
Sally & Tony Tompkins **Gables Guest House** **6 Cumnor Hill** **Oxford OX2 9HA** Tel: (01865) 862153 Fax 01865 864054 Open: ALL YEAR Map Ref No. 17	Nearest Road: A.34, A.420 Gables is an attractive detached house with a homely atmosphere. 5 rooms are en-suite & 1 has a private bathroom. All are tastefully furnished & have satellite T.V., radio, 'phone & tea/coffee facilities. Ideally situated in a perfect, quiet, residential area close to the A.34 ring road & only 5 mins' drive into the city centre. The railway & bus stations are within a short distance, & Gables is on a regular bus route. A large private car park.	£20.00 CREDIT CARD VISA M'CARD	Y	N	N
Mr & Mrs E. Trafford **Tilbury Lodge Hotel** **5 Tilbury Lane** **Eynsham Rd, Botley** **Oxford OX2 9NB** Tel: (01865) 862138 Fax 01865 863700 Open: ALL YEAR Map Ref No. 17	Nearest Road: A.34, B.4044 Tilbury Lodge is a pleasant, family-run private hotel situated in a quiet residential area. Accommodation is in 9 en-suite rooms with radio, T.V., 'phone, hairdryer & tea/coffee-making facilities. 1 four-poster & 2 ground-floor rooms. A pleasant jacuzzi bath is also available. Ample parking. Residents' lounge & garden in which guests may choose to relax. Located 2 miles west of the city centre, with good pubs & restaurants a few minutes' walk away. Good bus service.	£27.50 CREDIT CARD VISA M'CARD	Y	N	N
Tina & Robin Barrett **Highfield West** **188 Cumnor Hill** **Oxford** **OX2 9PJ** Tel: (01865) 863007 Open: ALL YEAR Map Ref No. 17	Nearest Road: A.420, A.34 Tina & Robin invite guests to enjoy Bed & Breakfast in the comfort of their home, set in a quiet residential area of Oxford, within walking distance of Cumnor village where 2 inns both serve food. Guest rooms have excellent facilities - 1 double, 1 twin, 1 family, all en-suite, & 2 singles sharing a separate bathroom. There is a lounge, dining room & garden with swimming pool, heated in season. Fire certificate & car parking.	£19.50	Y	N	Y
Mr & Mrs P. Morris **Pine Castle Hotel** **290/292 Iffley Road** **Oxford OX4 4AE** Tel: (01865) 241497/728887 Fax 01865 727230 Open: ALL YEAR (Excl. Xmas) Map Ref No. 17	Nearest Road: A.423, A.4158 A warm welcome awaits you at this Edwardian guest house which still retains many of its period features. It is conveniently situated on a main bus route into the city centre. An alternative route is a short walk along the tow path beside the Thames which is both convenient & picturesque. Cots are provided, T.V. & tea/coffee facilities in all rooms. Breakfasts vary from the healthy to the positively indulgent. Evening meals with prior notice.	£20.00 CREDIT CARD VISA M'CARD	Y	N	N
Catherine Tong **Courtfield Private Hotel** **367 Iffley Road** **Oxford OX4 4DP** Tel: (01865) 242991 Fax 01865 242991 Open: ALL YEAR Map Ref No. 17	Nearest Road: A.4158 Courtfield Guest House has been recently refurbished to provide accommodation for guests in 6 comfortable rooms, most with en-suite facilities. A lounge & the garden are also available for visitors to relax in. Ample parking in a mews-style forecourt. Situated on a good bus route 1 1/2 miles from the centre of Oxford. Children over 3 years. No single available. An ideal base from which to explore Oxford.	£20.00 CREDIT CARD VISA M'CARD AMEX	Y	N	N

Oxfordshire

		rate from £ per person	children taken	evening meals	animals taken
Bertram & Doreen Edwards **Highfield House** **91 Rose Hill** **Oxford OX4 4HT** **Tel: (01865) 774083/718524** **Open: ALL YEAR** **Map Ref No. 17**	Nearest Road: A.4158 A pleasing & friendly house, with good access to the city centre & ring road. Accommodation is in 7 spacious bedrooms, all attractively decorated with matching decor. 5 with en-suite bathroom. All have colour T.V. & tea/coffee-making facilities. A short walk brings you to the old attractive village of Iffley. An excellent base for exploring the historic delights of Oxford.	£18.00 CREDIT CARD VISA M'CARD	Y	N	N
Stephen & Anthea Savage **The Manor** **Stadhampton** **Oxford OX44 7UL** **Tel: (01865) 891999** **Fax 01865 891640** **Open: ALL YEAR (Excl. Xmas)** **Map Ref No. 18**	Nearest Road: A.329 On the village green, this peaceful 17th-century stone manor house, with its mullioned windows, oak floors & antique furniture, is only 7 miles from Magdalen Bridge, the colleges & Oxford. The large drawing room, with log fires in winter, & a spacious dining room welcome you. The 2 comfortable en-suite bedrooms overlook the garden. Blenheim Palace, Stratford, the Cotswolds & Bath are all within easy reach.	£30.00 🚭	Y	Y	N
Keith & Eve Naylor **Bowood House Hotel** **238 Oxford Road** **Kidlington** **Oxford OX5 1EB** **Tel: (01865) 842288** **Fax 01865 841858** **Open: ALL YEAR (Excl. Xmas & New Year)** **Map Ref No. 13**	Nearest Road: A.4260 Situated on the A.4260, only 4 miles from Oxford city centre. Bowood House offers accommodation of a high standard in a warm, friendly atmosphere. There is a licensed bar & 'a la carte' restaurant open to residents & their friends. Accommodation is in 20 en-suite rooms, each with colour satellite T.V., 'phone, hairdryers & tea/coffee makers. An ideal centre for a relaxing break, convenient for touring the Cotswolds, Stratford, Warwick, Blenheim Palace, Bladon & of course Oxford's numerous attractions. Heathrow 60 mins away.	£28.00 CREDIT CARD VISA M'CARD	Y	Y	N
Mrs A. Spencer-Thomas **Shipton Grange House** **Shipton-under-Wychwood** **OX7 6DG** **Tel: (01993) 831298** **Fax 01993 832082** **Open: ALL YEAR (Excl. Xmas & New Year)** **Map Ref No. 22**	Nearest Road: A.361 A unique conversion of a Georgian coach house & stabling situated in the former grounds of Shipton Court. Secluded in its own walled garden, & approached by a gated archway. There are 3 elegantly furnished guest rooms, 2 with private bathroom & colour T.V., & all with beverage facilities. Delicious breakfasts served in the attractive dining room. Shipton Grange is a delightful house, & ideal for visiting the Cotswolds, Oxford, Blenheim, etc. Children over 12 years.	£24.00 *see PHOTO over*	Y	N	N
Mrs Susan Peterson **Hawthorn Cottage** **The Downs** **Standlake** **OX8 7SH** **Tel: (01865) 300588** **Open: Mid JAN - Mid DEC** **Map Ref No. 19**	Nearest Road: A.40, A.415 A detached house standing in 1 third of an acre. Private, on the edge of a delightful Oxfordshire village noted for its leisure area. 3 spacious rooms, elegantly furnished with en-suite/private facilities, 1 on the ground floor. T.V. & tea/coffee making in all rooms. A large dining room with lounge area. Standlake is close to Oxford, the Cotswolds & Blenheim Palace, & is therefore an ideal base for touring. Children over 2 yrs.	£19.00 🚭	Y	N	N

Shipton Grange House. Shipton–under–Wychwood.

Upper Green Farm. Towersey.

Oxfordshire

		rate from £ per person	children taken	evening meals	animals taken
Marjorie & Euan Aitken **Upper Green Farm** **Manor Road** **Towersey** **Thame OX9 3QR** **Tel: (01844) 212496** **Fax 01844 260399** **Open: ALL YEAR** **Map Ref No. 20**	Nearest Road: A.4129 A long immaculate drive leads to this 15th-century thatched farmhouse & 18th-century barn, surrounding a lawned farmyard with flower tubs & borders in profusion. Guests may choose to stay in the farmhouse or Paradise Barn where breakfast is served in the old stables. All bedrooms have private/en-suite facilities & lovely views, & are furnished with country antiques, lace & patchwork. 2 rooms suitable for the disabled. A charming base from which to explore this lovely region.	£20.00 🚭 *see PHOTO over*	N	N	N
Mrs Carol Wadsworth **The Craven** **Fernham Road** **Uffington SN7 7RD** **Tel: (01367) 820449** **Open: ALL YEAR** **Map Ref No. 21**	Nearest Road: A.420 An extremely attractive 17th-century thatched farmhouse with exposed beams & open log-burning fire. Accommodation is very comfortable, & comprises 7 bedrooms, 1 with 4-poster bed & private bathroom. Good home cooking with fresh local produce. The Craven offers a friendly, relaxed atmosphere. The perfect base for touring this fascinating area.	£20.00 🚭 *see PHOTO over* CREDIT CARD VISA M'CARD	Y	Y	N
Elizabeth Shaw **Shotover House** **Uffington** **SN7 7RH** **Tel: (01367) 820351** **Open: ALL YEAR** **Map Ref No. 25**	Nearest Road: A.420 Many original paintings adorn the walls of this warm & welcoming home, with views of the famous Uffington White Horse. 3 romantically styled bedrooms, with private/en-suite bathrooms, enjoy crisp white cotton bed linen, fluffy white towels, tea-making facilities & colour T.V.. Breakfasts include home-baked bread, freshly squeezed orange juice, homemade preserves & eggs from the hens in the garden.	£25.00 🚭	Y	Y	Y
Liz & John Simpson **Field View** **Wood Green** **Witney** **OX8 6DE** **Tel: (01993) 705485** **Open: ALL YEAR (Excl. Xmas)** **Map Ref No. 23**	Nearest Road: A.40, A.4095 An attractive Cotswold stone house set in 2 acres, situated on picturesque Wood Green, midway between Oxford University & the Cotswolds. It is an ideal centre for touring, yet only 8 minutes' walk from the centre of this lively Oxfordshire market town. A peaceful setting & a warm, friendly atmosphere await you. Accommodation is in 3 comfortable en-suite rooms with modern amenities & tea/coffee-making facilities.	£20.00 🚭	N	N	N
Jean & Peter Crofts **Crofters Guest House** **29 Oxford Hill** **Witney OX8 6JU** **Tel: (01993) 778165** **Fax 01993 778165** **Open: ALL YEAR** **Map Ref No. 26**	Nearest Road: A.40 Crofters is situated in a lively market town, 10 miles from Oxford, on the edge of the Cotswolds, Blenheim Palace & Burford, & within easy reach of Stratford. Guests are accommodated in comfortable family, double & twin rooms, all with excellent facilities. En-suite & ground-floor rooms available. Your hosts Jean & Peter will make your stay a memorable experience. Arrive as a guest, leave as a friend.	£22.00	Y	N	N

The Craven.   Uffington.

Oxfordshire

		rate from £ per person	children taken	evening meals	animals taken
Sue & Jim French **Yew Tree House** **Abingdon Road** **Standlake** **Witney OX8 7QH** **Tel/Fax: (01865) 300529** **Open: FEB - Mid DEC** **Map Ref No. 19**	Nearest Road: A.415, A.420 A charming former farmhouse (c.1745) set in its own parkland on the edge of the Cotswolds. Superior rooms, all en-suite, with colour T.V., clock radio, 'phone & tea/coffee facilities. Exclusive guests' lounge with inglenook fireplace. Also, a separate room with colour T.V. & satellite receiver. In the village, there are 2 excellent pubs with bar food & a restaurant. Private trout fishing & watersport facilities. Ideal for visiting Blenheim Palace, Oxford, Stratford & the Cotswolds.	**£25.00** 🚭 *see PHOTO over* CREDIT CARD VISA M'CARD AMEX	N	N	N
Mrs Barbara Newcombe-Jones **Gorselands Farmhouse** **Auberge** **Boddington Lane** **Long Hanborough** **Woodstock OX8 6PU** **Tel: (01993) 881895** **Fax 01993 882799** **Open: ALL YEAR** **Map Ref No. 24**	Nearest Road: A.4095 A beautiful, Cotswold-stone, period farmhouse, set in an acre of grounds in idyllic countryside. Retaining much character, with exposed beams, flagstone floors & log fires in winter, it offers 5 comfortable & tastefully furnished guest bedrooms, all en-suite, some with 4-posters. Optional French-style evening meals are served in the conservatory (a table licence). A billiards room & grass tennis court available for guests' use. Situated near Woodstock & Oxford. The perfect base for visiting Blenheim Palace, the Oxford colleges, North Leigh Roman Villa & many Cotswold villages.	**£17.00** 🚭 CREDIT CARD VISA M'CARD AMEX	Y	Y	Y

All the establishments mentioned in this guide are members of
The Worldwide Bed & Breakfast Association

When booking your accommodation please mention
The Best Bed & Breakfast

Yew Tree House. Standlake.

Shropshire

Shropshire
(Heart of England)

Shropshire is a borderland with a very turbulent history. Physically it straddles highlands & lowlands with border mountains to the west, glacial plains, upland, moorlands & fertile valleys & the River Severn cutting through. It has been quarrelled & fought over by rulers & kings from earliest times. The English, the Romans & the Welsh all wanted to hold Shropshire because of its unique situation. The ruined castles & fortifications dotted across the county are all reminders of its troubled life. The most impressive of these defences is Offa's Dyke, an enormous undertaking intended to be a permanent frontier between England & Wales.

Shropshire has great natural beauty, countryside where little has changed with the years. Wenlock Edge & Clun Forest, Carding Mill Valley, the Long Mynd, Caer Caradoc, Stiperstones & the trail along Offa's Dyke itself, are lovely walking areas with magnificent scenery.

Shrewsbury was & is a virtual island, almost completely encircled by the Severn River. The castle was built at the only gap, sealing off the town. In this way all comings & goings were strictly controlled. In the 18th century two bridges, the English bridge & the Welsh bridge, were built to carry the increasing traffic to the town but Shrewsbury still remains England's finest Tudor city.

Massive Ludlow Castle was a Royal residence, home of Kings & Queens through the ages, whilst the town is also noted for its Georgian houses.

As order came out of chaos, the county settled to improving itself & became the cradle of the Industrial Revolution. Here Abraham Darby discovered how to use coke (from the locally mined coal) to smelt iron. There was more iron produced here in the 18th century than in any other county. A variety of great industries sprang up as the county's wealth & ingenuity increased. In 1781 the world's first iron bridge opened to traffic.

There are many fine gardens in the county. At Hodnet Hall near Market Drayton, the grounds cover 60 acres & the landscaping includes lakes & pools, trees, shrubs & flowers in profusion. Weston Park has 1,000 acres of parkland, woodland gardens & lakes landscaped by Capability Brown.

The house is Restoration period & has a splendid collection of pictures, furniture, china & tapestries.

Shrewsbury hosts an annual poetry festival & one of England's best flower shows whilst a Festival of Art, Music & Drama is held each year in Ludlow with Shakespeare performed against the castle ruins.

Coalbrookedale Museum.

Shropshire

Shropshire Gazeteer

Areas of Outstanding Natural Beauty
The Shropshire Hills.

Historic Houses & Castles

Stokesay Castle - Craven Arms
13th century fortified manor house. Still occupied - wonderful setting - extremely well preserved. Fine timbered gatehouse.
Weston Park - Nr. Shifnal
17th century - fine example of Restoration period - landscaping by Capability Brown. Superb collection of pictures.
Shrewsbury Castle - Shrewsbury
Built in Norman era - interior decorations - painted boudoir.
Benthall Hall - Much Wenlock
16th century. Stone House - mullioned windows. Fine wooden staircase - splendid plaster ceilings.
Shipton Hall - Much Wenlock
Elizabethan. Manor House - walled garden - mediaeval dovecote.
Upton Cressett Hall - Bridgnorth
Elizabethan. Manor House & Gatehouse. Excellent plaster work. . 14th century great hall.

Cathedrals & Churches

Ludlow (St. Lawrence)
14th century nave & transepts. 15th century pinnacled tower. Restored extensively in 19th century. Carved choir stalls, perpendicular chancel - original glass. Monuments.
Shrewsbury (St. Mary)
14th, 15th, 16th century glass. Norman origins.
Stottesdon (St. Mary)
12th century carvings.Norman font. Fine decorations with columns & tracery.
Lydbury North (St. Michael)
14th century transept, 15th century nave roof, 17th century box pews and altar rails. Norman font.
Longor (St. Mary the Virgin)
13th century having an outer staircase to West gallery.
Cheswardine (St. Swithun)
13th century chapel - largely early English. 19th century glass and old brasses. Fine sculpture.

Tong (St. Mary the Virgin with St. Bartholomew)
15th century. Golden chapel of 1515, stencilled walls, remains of paintings on screens, gilt fan vaulted ceiling. Effigies, fine monuments

Museums & Galleries

Clive House - Shrewsbury
Fine Georgian House - collection of Shropshire ceramics. Regimental museum of 1st Queen's Dragoon Guards.
Rowley's House Museum - Shrewsbury
Roman material from Viroconium and prehistoric collection.
Coleham Pumping Station - Old Coleham
Preserved beam engines
Acton Scott Working Farm Museum - Nr. Church Stretton
Site showing agricultural practice before the advent of mechanization.
Ironbridge Gorge Museum - Telford
Series of industrial sites in the Severn Gorge.
CoalBrookdale Museum & Furnace Site
Showing Abraham Darby's blast furnace history. Ironbridge information centre is next to the world's first iron bridge.
Mortimer Forest Museum - Nr. Ludlow
Forest industries of today and yesterday. Ecology of the forest.
Whitehouse Museum of Buildings & Country life - Aston Munslow
4 houses together in one, drawing from every century 13th to 18th, together with utensils and implements of the time.
The Buttercross Museum - Ludlow
Geology, natural & local history of area.
Reader`s House-Ludlow
Splendid example of a 16th century town house. 3 storied porch.
Much Wenlock Museum.-Much Wenlock
Geology, natural & local history.
Clun Town Museum - Clun
Pre-history earthworks, rights of way, commons & photographs.

Historic Monuments

Acton Burnell Castle - Shrewsbury
13th century fortified manor house - ruins only.

Shropshire

Boscobel House - Shifnal
17th century house.
Bear Steps - Shrewsbury
Half timbered buildings. Mediaeval.
Abbot's House - Shrewsbury
15th century half-timbered.
Buildwas Abbey - Nr. Telford
12th century - Savignac Abbey - ruins.
The church is nearly complete with 14
Norman arches.
Haughmond Abbey - Shrewsbury
12th century - remains of house of
Augustinian canons.
Wenlock Priory - Much Wenlock
13th century abbey - ruins.
Roman Town - Wroxeter
2nd century - remains of town of
Viroconium including public baths and
colonnade.
Moreton Corbet Castle - Moreton Corbet
13th century keep, Elizabethan features -

gatehouse altered 1519.
Lilleshall Abbey
12th century - completed 13th century,
West front has notable doorway.
Bridgnorth Castle - Bridgnorth
Ruins of Norman castle whose angle of
incline is greater than Pisa.
Whiteladies Priory - Boscobel
12th century cruciform church - ruins.
Old Oswestry - Oswestry
Iron age hill fort covering 68 acres; five
ramparts and having an elaborate western
portal.

Other things to see & do
Ludlow Festival of Art and Drama -
annual event
Shrewsbury Flower Show - every August
Severn Valley Railway - the longest full
guage steam railway in the country

Kings Head Inn. Shrewsbury.

SHROPSHIRE
Map reference

2 Rowlands
3 Davies
4 Love
5 Lloyd
6 Villar
7 Wrigley
8 Wilson-Clarke
9 Hanningan
10 Ross
11 Sanders
12 Thomas
13 Williamson
14 Hunter
16 Harris
16 Stening-Rees
17 Bovill
18 Mitchell
19 Savage

Rectory Farm. Woolstaston.

Upper Buckton Farm. Leintwardine.

Shropshire

		rate from £ per person	children taken	evening meals	animals taken
Mary Rowlands **Middleton Lodge** **Middleton Priors** **Bridgnorth WV16 6UR** **Tel: (01746) 712228** **Open: ALL YEAR** **Map Ref No. 02**	Nearest Road: B.4268 Middleton Lodge is set in 20 acres of beautiful rural Shropshire countryside overlooking Brown Clee Hill. Offering 3 extremely attractive en-suite bedrooms, 1 with a 4-poster. There are many places of interest within easy reach of Middleton: the scenic Severn Valley Railway, Ironbridge, Stokesay Castle, the breathtaking beauty of the Long Mynd & the picturesque Carding Mill Valley.	£20.00 (non-smoking)	N	N	N
Mrs Jeanette Davies **Rectory Farm** **Woolstaston** **Leebotwood** **Church Stretton SY6 6NN** **Tel: (01694) 751306** **Open: FEB - Mid DEC** **Map Ref No. 03**	Nearest Road: A.49 An extremely attractive half-timbered farmhouse dating back to 1620, offering 3 charming rooms, all with bath en-suite. Situated on the edge of the N.T. Long Mynd Hills, it has marvellous views & superb walking right from the door. There is much for the sportsman here: golf, riding, fishing & gliding. Many historic houses & wonderful beauty spots are a short drive away. Children over 12. Restricted smoking. Best B&B Award Winner.	£20.00 *see PHOTO over*	Y	N	N
Derek & Eileen Love **Sayang House** **Hope Bowdler** **Church Stretton** **SY6 7DD** **Tel: (01694) 723981** **Open: JAN - NOV** **Map Ref No. 04**	Nearest Road: A.49 A friendly welcome awaits all guests at Sayang House. Beautifully situated in the peaceful hamlet of Hope Bowdler. Delightful residents' lounge, with inglenook fireplace, oak beams & antique furniture, leading onto a patio & overlooking the garden & surrounding countryside. 3 en-suite bedrooms with tea/coffee & T.V.. Superb walks from the village across the Shropshire hills. Golf, riding, gliding nearby. Midway between the mediaeval towns of Shrewsbury & Ludlow. Many places of historic interest to visit. Good local pub.	£21.00 (non-smoking)	N	N	N
Hayden & Yvonne Lloyd **Upper Buckton** **Leintwardine** **Craven Arms** **SY7 0JU** **Tel: (01547) 540634** **Open: ALL YEAR** **Map Ref No. 05**	Nearest Road: A.4113, A.4110 Set amidst the beautiful unspoilt Teme Valley, a delightful riverside farm situated in the secluded hamlet of Buckton. The Georgian house is surrounded by an attractive garden, millstream & a 12th century motte. The well-appointed rooms with antiques & paintings make this a lovely home with every comfort. Log fires. 3 elegant bedrooms with private bathrooms. Superb traditional & Cordon Bleu Dinners. Guests' own wine welcome. There is much of scenic & historic interest. Ludlow, Offa's Dyke, N.T. properties & gardens.	£20.00 (non-smoking) *see PHOTO over*	Y	Y	N
Michael & Roma Villar **The Old Rectory** **Hopesay** **Craven Arms** **SY7 8HD** **Tel: (01588) 660245** **Open: ALL YEAR (Excl. Xmas)** **Map Ref No. 06**	Nearest Road: A.49 The Old Rectory, dating from the 17th century, is set in beautiful grounds of almost 2 acres. All bedrooms are en-suite, 2 with large double beds & 1 twin bedded room with a small sitting room. All have radio, T.V. & tea/coffee trays. A comfortable drawing room, with a log fire & French windows to a garden, & a splendid dining room with attractive Gothic window. Furnished with antiques & many period pieces. Superb home cooking using fresh garden/local produce. Licensed. Ideal for the Welsh Marches, Ludlow, Shrewsbury & Ironbridge.	£32.00 (non-smoking) *see PHOTO over*	N	Y	N

Old Rectory. Hopesay.

Shropshire

	rate from £ per person	children taken	evening meals	animals taken
Patrick & Lucinda Wrigley **Delbury Hall** **Diddlebury** **Craven Arms SY7 9DH** Tel: **(01584) 841267** Fax 01584 841441 Open: ALL YEAR (Excl. Xmas) Map Ref No. 07	Nearest Road: A.49, B.4368 A beautiful Georgian house (1753), in a stately & tranquil setting in the Corvedale, near Ludlow. Flower-filled gardens, an ornamental lake, trout fishing & a hard tennis court. Home-produced vegetables, milk, eggs, hand-churned Jersey butter, smoked salmon & prosciutto. Beautifully furnished, spacious bedrooms, 1 4-poster, 1 half-tester, with T.V., 'phone, coffee & tea. A guests' sitting room, dining room &, by arrangement, delicious food prepared by your host.	£35.00 *see PHOTO over* CREDIT CARD VISA M'CARD	Y	Y	N
Mr & Mrs Wilson-Clarke **Greenbanks** **Coptiviney** **Ellesmere SY12 0ND** Tel/Fax: **(01691) 623420** Open: ALL YEAR Map Ref No. 08	Nearest Road: A.528 An attractive & comfortable red-brick Victorian house set within its own 20 acres. It is peacefully situated in the tranquility of this totally rural area, yet well placed for Shrewsbury, Oswestry, Wrexham, Chester & Llangollen. Spacious bedrooms with en-suite or private bathrooms, T.V. & tea/coffee-making facilities. Imaginative 4-course dinners by prior arrangement. An extensive garden. A tennis court. Children over 12.	£28.00 CREDIT CARD VISA	Y	Y	Y
Jim & Pauline Hannigan **The Severn Trow** **Church Road** **Jackfield** **Ironbridge TF8 7ND** Tel: **(01952) 883551** Open: JAN - OCT Map Ref No. 09	Nearest Road: M.54, A.442 The Severn Trow is a wonderful place which has seen the hand of hospitality extended by successive occupants for many centuries. It stands on the riverbank where originally travellers would berth their trows before retiring to recuperate. It has been renovated & yet retains many original features which enhance its character, such as an inglenook & a Jackfield mosaic tile floor. Rooms are delightful, en-suite & well-appointed. A choice of eating houses nearby.	£19.00	N	N	N
Patricia Elms Ross **Number Twenty Eight** **28 Lower Broad Street** **Ludlow SY8 1PQ** Tel: **(01584) 876996** Fax 01584 876996 Open: ALL YEAR Map Ref No. 10	Nearest Road: A.49, B.4361 A listed, half-timbered house, centrally situated by the old town walls & close to River Teme. Bedrooms are en-suite, & have tea/coffee facilities, T.V. & many thoughtful extras. Dinner provides a wide-choice, a la carte menu & a range of fine wines. Walled garden for after-dinner coffee, or the snug sitting room with an open fire for relaxation. Riverside & hill walks, castles & lots of book & antique shops to explore in this Tudor & Georgian market town, near the Welsh border.	£23.00 CREDIT CARD VISA M'CARD AMEX	Y	Y	Y
Mrs Judith Sanders **Middleton Court** **Ludlow** **SY8 2DZ** Tel: **(01584) 872842** Open: MAR - NOV Map Ref No. 11	Nearest Road: A.4117 Middleton Court is a fine country house on a working farm, situated 2 1/2 miles from the centre of Ludlow. 1 master en-suite bedroom, with a double & single bed, & 1 double with a private bathroom. Both are comfortably furnished with antiques, & have beautiful views over the terraced gardens & woods beyond. Guests own sitting room, with T.V. & log fires. Excellent Full English breakfasts & traditional 4-course evening meals served in the attractive dining room. Ideal for exploring Shropshire & the Welsh border country.	£18.00	N	Y	N

Delbury Hall. Diddlebury.

Shropshire

	rate from £ per person	children taken	evening meals	animals taken

Mike & Julia Thomas
Stoke Manor
Stoke-on-Tern
Market Drayton TF9 2DU
Tel: (01630) 685222
Fax 01630 685666
Open: JAN - NOV
Map Ref No. 12

Nearest Road: A.41, A.53
A warm welcome awaits guests at Stoke Manor, a 250-acre arable farm with farm trail & vintage-tractor collection. Ironbridge & Cosford Aerospace Museums, Wedgwood Potteries, ancient towns of Shrewsbury & Chester are only a few of the many places to visit locally. Each bedroom has a bathroom, colour T.V., tea/coffee trays. An abundance of good eating places nearby. Residents' licence. Children over 5 years.

£20.00 | Y | N | N

Mrs Pauline Williamson
Mickley House
Faulsgreen
Tern Hill
Market Drayton
TF9 3QW
Tel: (01630) 638505
Open: ALL YEAR (Excl. Xmas)
Map Ref No. 13

Nearest Road: A.41, A.53
When visiting Ironbridge, Shrewsbury, Chester or Hawkstone Park, you can be sure of a warm welcome on this 125-acre working farm in unspoilt Shropshire countryside. Enjoy the comfort of this Victorian farmhouse with its oak doors, beams & inglenook fireplace. Stroll in the tranquil garden, down paths, through pergolas to pools with a trickling waterfall. Tastefully decorated en-suite bedrooms have colour T.V. & hospitality trays. Master bedroom with Louis XIV king-size bed. Ground-floor bedrooms available.

£19.00 | Y | N | N

Miles & Audrey Hunter
Pen-Y-Dyffryn Country Hotel
Rhydycroesau
Oswestry SY10 7DT
Tel/Fax: (01691) 653700
Open: ALL YEAR
Map Ref No. 14

Nearest Road: A.5
Peace, comfort & a warm welcome await you in this former Georgian rectory, splendidly situated in the Shropshire/Welsh hills just 3 miles west of Oswestry. An ideal base for exploring Chester, Shrewsbury & North Wales. Delicious home-cooked evening meals using English & Welsh local produce. Fully licensed. Log fires in the lounge & restaurant. All bedrooms beautifully furnished, en-suite, colour T.V.. 5 acres of grounds, with panoramic views all around.

£29.00 | Y | Y | Y

see PHOTO over

CREDIT CARD
VISA
M'CARD
AMEX

Mrs Mair Harris
Tudor House
2 Fish Street
Shrewsbury SY1 1UR
Tel: (01743) 351735
Open: ALL YEAR
Map Ref No. 16

Nearest Road: A.5, A.49
This Grade II listed building is centrally situated in a quiet mediaeval street in picturesque & historic Shrewsbury (Brother Cadfael country). Dating from 1460, it has a wealth of oak beams, & has been tastefully redecorated & refurbished. Some rooms have en-suite facilities; all have washbasins, colour T.V. & central heating. Special diets available in non-smoking dining room. Drinks are served in residents' licensed lounge.

£19.00 | Y | N | N

Carol & Norman Stening-Rees
Roseville
12 Berwick Road
Shrewsbury SY1 2LN
Tel: (01743) 236470
Open: FEB - DEC
Map Ref No. 16

Nearest Road: A.528, B.5067
Roseville, a late-Victorian, detached town house with own parking. 10 minutes' easy walk to the town centre, rail/bus stations. Offering comfortable, centrally heated & tastefully furnished accommodation (en-suite available) in a no-smoking environment. Relaxed atmosphere encouraged. Tea, coffee, non-alcoholic drinks served on request at all reasonable times in guests' lounge. Wide choice of excellent food. Children over 12.

£20.00 | Y | Y | N

Pen–Y–Dyffryn Hall. Rhydycroesau.

Mytton Hall. Montford Bridge.

Shropshire

	rate from £ per person	children taken	evening meals	animals taken

John & Hermione Bovill **Mytton Hall** **Montford Bridge** **Shrewsbury** **SY4 1EU** **Tel: (01743) 850264** **Open: ALL YEAR** **Map Ref No. 17**	Nearest Road: A.5 An elegant, white, listed Georgian house built in 1790, & with spectacular views. There are 3 attractive & tastefully furnished bedrooms, all en-suite, & a sitting room with T.V. & log fire. Full central heating. Lovely gardens adjoining the River Perry. Private fishing. A tennis court. The welcoming atmosphere of a fine old English country house, located 6 miles from Shrewsbury & in easy reach of Ironbridge & many other attractions. Children over 12 yrs.	£20.00 🚭 *see PHOTO over*	N	N	N
Mike & Gill Mitchell **The White House** **Hanwood** **Shrewsbury** **SY5 8LP** **Tel: (01743) 860414** **Open: ALL YEAR** **Map Ref No. 18**	Nearest Road: A.488, A.5 A lovely, 16th-century, black-and-white, half-timbered guest house with nearly 2 acres of gardens & river, 3 miles south-west of mediaeval Shrewsbury. Ironbridge, Mid-Wales & the Long Mynd within a half-hour drive. 6 guest rooms, some en-suite, each with full c/h & tea/coffee facilities. 2 sitting rooms, 1 with T.V.. Easy car parking. The dining room offers a fresh, varied menu supplemented by seasonal vegetables & herbs from the garden, & the house hens provide your breakfast eggs! Children over 12.	£20.00 🚭 *see PHOTO over*	Y	Y	N
Mrs Jo Savage **Church Farm** **Wrockwardine** **Wellington** **Telford TF6 5DG** **Tel: (01952) 244917** **Open: ALL YEAR** **Map Ref No. 19**	Nearest Road: A.5, M.54 Sit back & relax in this Georgian village farmhouse with beams & inglenook fireplace. The sandstone foundations of the mediaeval manor are revealed in the attractive gardens.There are ovely bedrooms, some en-suite & ground-floor, with colour T.V.s & tea/coffee/hot-chocolate trays. Delicious breakfasts, traditional dinners & puds! Conveniently situated near Shrewsbury, Ironbridge & Telford. 1 mile A.5 & M.54.	£19.00 CREDIT CARD VISA M'CARD	N	Y	Y

When booking your accommodation please mention
The Best Bed & Breakfast

The White House. Hanwood.

Somerset

Somerset
(West Country)

Fabulous legends, ancient customs, charming villages, beautiful churches, breathtaking scenery & a glorious cathedral, Somerset has them all, along with a distinctively rich local dialect. The essence of Somerset lies in its history & myth & particularly in the unfolding of the Arthurian tale.

Legend grows from the bringing of the Holy Grail to Glastonbury by Joseph of Arimathea, to King Arthur's castle at Camelot, held by many to be sited at Cadbury, to the image of the dead King's barge moving silently through the mists over the lake to the Isle of Avalon. Archaeological fact lends support to the conjecture that Glastonbury, with its famous Tor, was an island in an ancient lake. Another island story surrounds King Alfred, reputedly sheltering from the Danes on the Isle of Athelney & there burning his cakes.

Historically, Somerset saw the last battle fought on English soil, at Sedgemoor in 1685. The defeat of the Monmouth rebellion resulted in the wrath of James II falling on the West Country in the form of Judge Jeffreys & his "Bloody Assize".

To the west of the county lies part of the Exmoor National Park, with high moorland where deer roam & buzzards soar & a wonderful stretch of cliffs from Minehead to Devon. Dunster is a popular village with its octagonal Yarn market, & its old world cottages, dominated at one end by the castle & at the other by the tower on Conygar Hill.

To the east the woods & moors of the Quantocks are protected as an area of outstanding natural beauty. The Vale of Taunton is famous for its apple orchards & for the golden cider produced from them.

The south of the county is a land of rolling countryside & charming little towns, Chard, Crewkerne, Ilchester & Ilminster amongst others.

To the north the limestone hills of Mendip are honeycombed with spectacular caves & gorges, some with neolithic remains, as at Wookey Hole & Cheddar Gorge.

Wells is nearby, so named because of the multitude of natural springs. Hardly a city, Wells boasts a magnificent cathedral set amongst spacious lawns & trees. The west front is one of the glories of English architecture with its sculptured figures & soaring arches. A spectacular feature is the astronomical clock, the work of 14th century monk Peter Lightfoot. The intricate face tells the hours, minutes, days & phases of the moon. On the hour, four mounted knights charge forth & knock one another from their horses.

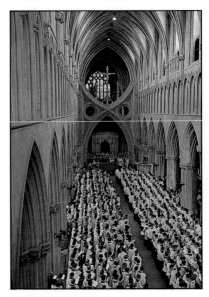

Wells Cathedral Choir.

Somerset

Somerset Gazeteer

Areas of Outstanding Natural Beauty
Mendip Hills. Quantock Hills. National Park - Exmoor.

Historic Houses & Castles

Abbot's Fish House - Meare
14th century house.

Barrington Court - Illminster
16th century house & gardens.

Brympton D'Evercy - Nr. Yeovil
Mansion with 17th century front & Tudor west front. Adjacent is 13th century priest's house & church. Formal gardens & vineyard.

Dodington Hall - Nether Stowey
14th & 15th century hall with minstrels' gallery.

Dunster Castle - Dunster
13th century castle with fine 17th century staircase & ceilings.

East Lambrook Manor - South Petherton
15th century house with good panelling.

Gaulden Manor - Tolland
12th century manor. Great Hall having unique plaster ceiling & oak screen. Antique furniture.

Halsway Manor - Crowcombe
14th century house with fine panelling.

Hatch Court - Hatch Beauchamp
Georgian house in the Palladian style with China room.

King John's Hunting Lodge - Axbridge
Early Tudor merchant's house.

Lytes Carry - Somerton
14th & 15th century manor house with a chapel & formal garden.

Montacute House - Yeovil
Elizabethan house with fine examples of Heraldic Glass, tapestries, panelling & furniture. Portrait gallery of Elizabethan & Jacobean paintings.

Tintinhull House - Yeovil
17th century house with beautiful gardens.

Cathedrals & Churches

Axbridge (St. John)
1636 plaster ceiling & panelled roofs.

Bishop's Lydeard (St. Mary)
15th century Notable tower, rood screen & glass.

Bruton (St. Mary)
Fine 2 towered 15th century church. Georgian chancel, tie beam roof, Georgian reredos. Jacobean screen. 15th century embroidery.

Chewton Mendip (St. Mary Magdalene)
12th century with later additions. 12th century doorway, 15th century bench ends, magnificent 16th century tower & 17th century lecturn.

Crewkerne (St. Bartholomew)
Magnificent west front & roofs, 15th & 16th century. South doorway dating from 13th century, wonderful 15th century painted glass & 18th century chandeliers.

East Brent (St. Mary)
Mainly 15th century. Plaster ceiling, painted glass & carved bench ends.

Glastonbury (St. John)
One of the finest examples of perpendicular towers. Tie beam roof, late mediaeval painted glass, mediaeval vestment & early 16th century altar tomb.

High Ham (St. Andrew)
Sumptuous roofs & vaulted rood screen. Carved bench ends. Jacobean lecturn, mediaeval painted glass. Norman font.

Kingsbury Episcopi (St. Martin)
14th-15th century. Good tower with fan vaulting. Late mediaeval painted glass.

Long Sutton (Holy Trinity)
15th century with noble tower & magnificent tie beam roof. 15th century pulpit & rood screen, tower vaulting.

Martock (All Saints)
13th century chancel. Nave with tie beam roof, outstanding of its kind. 17th century paintings of Apostles.

North Cadbury (St. Michael)
Fine chancel. 15th century roofs, parclose & portion of cope, fragments of mediaeval painted glass.

Pilton (St. John)
12th century with arcades. 15th century roofs.

Taunton (St. Mary Magdalene)
Highest towers in the county. Five nave roof, fragments of mediaeval painted glass.

Trull (All Saints)
15th century with many mediaeval art treasures & 15th century glass.

Somerset

Wells Cathedral-Wells
Magnificent west front with carved figures. Splendid tower. Early English arcade of nave & transepts. 60 fine misericords c.1330. Lady chapel with glass & star vault. Chapter House & Bishop's Palace.
Weston Zoyland (St. Mary)
15th century bench ends. 16th century heraldic glass. Jacobean pulpit.

Museums & Galleries

Admiral Blake Museum - Bridgewater
Exhibits relating to Battle of Sedgemoor, archaeology.
Burdon Manor - Washford
14th century manor house with Saxon fireplace & cockpit.
Borough Museum - Hendford Manor Hall, Yeovil
Archaeology, firearms collections & Bailward Costume Collection.
Glastonbury Lake Village Museum - Glastonbury
Late prehistoric antiquities.
Gough's Cave Museum - Cheddar
Upper Paleolithic remains, skeleton, flints, amber & engraved stones.
Wookey Hole Cave Museum - Wookey Hole
Remains from Pliocene period. Relics of Celtic & Roman civilization. Exhibition of handmade paper-making.

Historic Monuments

Cleeve Abbey - Cleeve
Ruined 13th century house, with timber roof & wall paintings.
Farleigh Castle - Farleigh Hungerford
14th century remains - museums in chapel.
Glastonbury Abbey - Glastonbury
12th & 13th century ruins of St. Joseph's chapel & Abbot's kitchen.
Muchelney Abbey - Muchelney
15th century ruins of Benedictine abbey.

Other things to see & do

Black Rock Nature Reserve - Cheddar
Circular walk through plantation woodland, downland grazing.
Cheddar Caves
Show caves at the foot of beautiful Cheddar Gorge.
Cricket St. Thomas Wildlife Park - Nr. Chard
Wildlife park, heavy horse centre, countryside museum, etc.
West Somerset Railway
Minehead to Bishop's Lydeard preserved steam railway.
Wookey Hole Caves - Wookey Hole, Nr. Wells.

Montacute House. Yeovil.

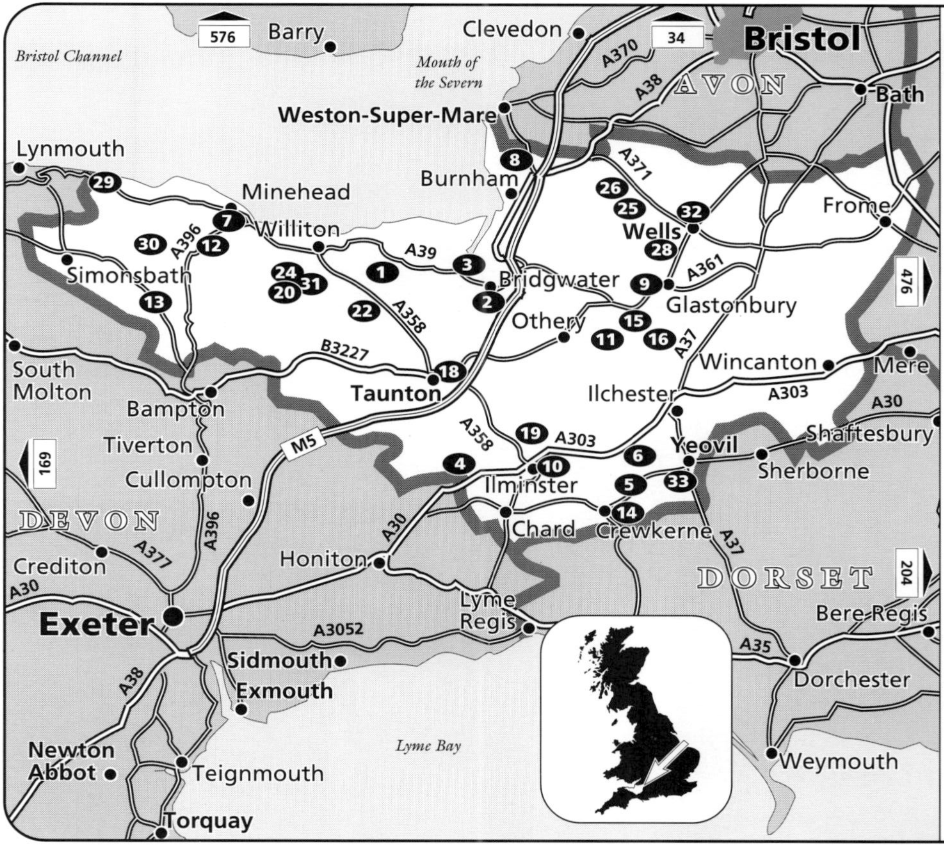

SOMERSET

Map reference

1 Laidler
2 Martin
3 Dyer
4 Newman-Coburn
5 Swann
6 Smith
7 Bradshaw
7 Forshaw
8 Collins
9 Tynan
10 O'Grady
11 Morlock
12 Watson
13 Vicary
13 Alderton
14 Gregory
15 Middle
16 Copeland
18 Clark
19 Mitchem
20 Muers-Raby

22 Eyre
24 Brewer
25 White
26 Thompson
28 Frost
29 Blue
30 Durbin
31 Criddle
32 Nowell
33 Somerville

Quantock House. Holford.

Somerset

			rate from £ per person	children taken	evening meals	animals taken
Mrs Pam Laidler **Quantock House** **Holford** **Bridgwater TA5 1RY** Tel: (01278) 741439 Open: ALL YEAR Map Ref No. 01	Nearest Road: A.39 Quantock House is in the small picturesque village of Holford, historically connected with Wordsworth & Coleridge. Relax in this 400-year-old thatched home with cottage garden. The spacious rooms have en-suite bathrooms, T.V. & tea/coffee. Sample the home cooking on offer, or enjoy nearby homely hostelries. Set near hills & the sea, a perfect centre for exploring by car or on foot.	£19.00 *see PHOTO over*	Y	Y	Y
Elizabeth Martin **West Bower Manor** **West Bower Lane** **Durleigh** **Bridgwater TA5 2AT** Tel: (01278) 422895 Open: ALL YEAR (Excl. Xmas) Map Ref No. 02	Nearest Road: M.5, A.38, A.39 Hidden away down a rough track, disguised as an ordinary farm, this is one of the loveliest surviving small mediaeval houses in England, set amid lawns & apple trees & beside a lake. 3 charming bedrooms, with en-suite/private bathroom, T.V., fresh flowers & fruit. A timbered sitting room, with mediaeval stained glass, is a super room in which to relax. Hearty breakfasts with organic/free-range produce when possible & home-made breads. Vegetarians welcome. Children over 12.	£15.00	N	N	N
Mrs Ann Dyer **Blackmore Farm** **Blackmore Lane** **Cannington** **Bridgwater TA5 2NE** Tel: (01278) 653442 Fax 01278 653442 Open: ALL YEAR Map Ref No. 03	Nearest Road: A.39 Blackmore Farm is a Grade I listed, 14th-century manor house, set in pleasant rural surroundings with views to the Quantock Hills. The house retains many of its period features, including stone archways, garderobes & oak beams. Accommodation includes a 4-poster bedroom & 'The Gallery', with a private sitting room. Breakfast is taken in the Great Hall around the 16ft carved oak table. There are a range of excellent local restaurant facilities. Within easy reach of the Quantock Hills, west Somerset coast & Exmoor.	£20.00	Y	N	N
Sarah & Roger Newman-Coburn **Hawthorne House** **Bishopswood** **Chard TA20 3RS** Tel: (01460) 234482 Open: ALL YEAR Map Ref No. 04	Nearest Road: A.303, B.3170 Hawthorne House is a cosy 19th-century stone house set in the Blackdown Hills, an Area of Outstanding Natural Beauty. It is ideally situated for an overnight stop en-route to Cornwall, & for visiting N.T. properties & the many other attractions in Somerset & Devon. All of the comfortable bedrooms have an en-suite/private bathroom & tea/coffee-making facilities. The attractive dining room has panoramic views over the extensive gardens & surrounding hills. Children over 12.	£17.50	Y	Y	Y
Gillian & Robert Swann **Broadview** **43 East Street** **Crewkerne** **TA18 7AG** Tel: (01460) 73424 Open: ALL YEAR Map Ref No. 05	Nearest Road: A.30 Friendly, informal atmosphere & extremely comfortable & relaxing in an unusual Colonial ambience. The sun porch, dining hall & sitting room are of a unique design & there is a nice collection of porcelain, antiques & rugs. Carefully furnished & decorated en-suite rooms with easy chairs, T.V., tea/coffee, c/h, & particularly well-equipped, achieving top-quality awards. Surrounded by secluded feature gardens, a real gardener's delight. Quality traditional English home-cooking. Dorset border.	£23.00 *see PHOTO over*	Y	Y	Y

Broadview. Crewkerne.

Somerset

	rate from £ per person	children taken	evening meals	animals taken
Guy & Charmian Smith **Chinnock House** **Middle Chinnock** **Crewkerne** **TA18 7PN** **Tel: (01935) 881229** **Open: ALL YEAR** **Map Ref No. 06**	Nearest Road: A.30, A.303 A beautiful Ham stone Georgian house set in a walled garden with glorious views in a quiet Somerset hamlet. 3 twin-bedded rooms, 2 with private bathrooms, 1 en-suite & 1 en-suite double. Ideal for visiting Bath, Stonehenge, Wells, Glastonbury, Sherborne, Dorchester & Hardy Country. Evening meals by prior arrangement, with fresh salmon, home-grown vegetables & raspberries & cream a speciality. Swimming pool & laundry service. Self-catering cottage available.	£25.00	Y	Y	N
John & Sally Gregory **Dryclose** **Newbery Lane** **Misterton** **Crewkerne TA18 8NE** **Tel: (01460) 73161** **Open: ALL YEAR (Excl. Xmas & New Year)** **Map Ref No. 14**	Nearest Road: A.30, A.303 Dryclose is an attractive, 16th-century, listed, beamed & panelled former farmhouse, set in 2 acres of lovely garden, with an outdoor swimming pool. Accommodation is in 3 charming bedrooms, 1 twin, 1 single & 1 twin en-suite. All have hot-drinks facilities. There are 2 sitting rooms, each with T.V., for guests. The area abounds with beautiful gardens & historic houses, & the coast is only 15 miles away. An ideal spot for a relaxing break & for exploring Somerset.	£16.50 🚭	Y	Y	N
Jane Forshaw **The Old Priory** **Dunster** **TA24 6RY** **Tel: (01643) 821540** **Open: ALL YEAR** **Map Ref No. 07**	Nearest Road: A.39 The Old Priory is a small mediaeval house, located in old-fashioned, walled gardens in a peaceful setting opposite a dovecote. 3 tastefully furnished bedrooms, including 1 4-poster. Each has an en-suite or private bathroom & tea/coffee-making facilities. Super wholefood/farmhouse breakfasts served. An interesting home, combining high standards with an informal atmosphere. Ideal for exploring Somerset.	£18.00	N	N	N
Major & Mrs G. Bradshaw **Dollons House** **10 Church Street** **Dunster TA24 6SH** **Tel: (01643) 821880** **Open: ALL YEAR** **Map Ref No. 07**	Nearest Road: A.39 17th-century Dollons House nestles beneath the castle in this delightful mediaeval village in the Exmoor National Park. Dunster is ideal for touring Exmoor & the North Devon Coast. There are 3 en-suite rooms, each with its own character & special decor. 100 years ago, the local pharmacist had his shop in Dollons, & in the back he made marmalade for the Houses of Parliament.	£23.00 🚭 **see PHOTO over** CREDIT CARD VISA M'CARD	N	N	N
Jaqui & Tony Collins **Knoll Lodge** **Church Road** **East Brent** **TA9 4HZ** **Tel: (01278) 760294** **Open: ALL YEAR** **Map Ref No. 08**	Nearest Road: M.5, A.38 Knoll Lodge is a 19th-century, listed Somerset house in an acre of orchard, where you are offered comfortable accommodation & quality food in friendly & peaceful rural surroundings. 3 spacious bedrooms - 2 double en-suite, 1 twin with private bathroom. Centrally heated, & attractively decorated with antique pine furniture & hand-made American patchwork quilts. Colour T.V.s & tea/coffee facilities. Dinner by arrangement. Children over 12.	£20.00 🚭	Y	Y	N

Dollons House. Dunster.

Somerset

		rate from £ per person	children taken	evening meals	animals taken
John & Ann Tynan **Number 3** **3 Magdalene Street** **Glastonbury** **BA6 9EW** **Tel: (01458) 832129** **Open: FEB - NOV** **Map Ref No. 09**	Nearest Road: M.5 Ex. 23, A.39 An attractive Grade II listed Georgian house adjoining the ruin of the once-powerful Abbey. The tomb of King Arthur & Guinevere is claimed to have been discovered here in the 13th century. 6 very attractive rooms, with private facilities, telephone, radio, T.V. & tea/coffee makers. Sports massage therapy & aromatherapy by a highly trained & licensed practitioner available. Excellent base for touring: Cheddar Gorge, Wookey Hole, Wells Cathedral & Bath are within easy reach.	£32.50 CREDIT CARD VISA M'CARD	Y	N	N
Mrs E. M. O'Grady **The Tithe Barn** **Kingstone** **Ilminster** **TA19 0NS** **Tel: (01460) 55447** **Open: ALL YEAR** **Map Ref No. 10**	Nearest Road: A.303, A.30 The O'Gradys have recently converted the Tithe Barn, which dates back to the early 14th century, into a gracious & comfortable home. Sitting high on Kingstone Hill, the property enjoys peace & rural surroundings & yet is only 1 mile from the A.303. Bedrooms have their own private bath/shower room, & an elegant drawing room is available in the evenings. A charming home where a warm welcome is assured.	£22.00	N	Y	N
Mrs S. Morlock **Beer Farm** **Bere Aller** **Langport TA10 0QX** **Tel: (01458) 250285** **Open: ALL YEAR (Excl.** **Xmas & New Year)** **Map Ref No. 11**	Nearest Road: A.372, A.303 This small, predominantly Georgian stone farmhouse is situated in quiet, rural surroundings overlooking Sedgemoor to the Polden & Quantock Hills. The attractive bedrooms have private bathrooms & tea/coffee-making facilities. Guests are welcome to use the sitting room, with colour T.V., & the pretty sheltered garden. It is ideal for bird-watching & for visiting the various N.T. properties, gardens & specialist nurseries. Children over 10 yrs.	£22.00	Y	Y	Y
Mr & Mrs Robin Watson **Old Stowey Farm** **Wheddon Cross** **Minehead** **TA24 7BT** **Tel: (01643) 841268** **Fax 01643 841268** **Open: ALL YEAR** **Map Ref No. 12**	Nearest Road: A.396 Old Stowey is a 16th-century farmhouse set in 80 acres in a sheltered wooded valley within the Exmoor National Park. There are 4 rooms, all with shower or bath en-suite. The rooms are charming & most comfortable, with lovely views. The house has log fires & a woodburning stove. The food here is excellent, with fresh vegetables & game in season. The owners offer super accommodation for horses, with hunting 6 days a week. Also, rough shooting, a croquet lawn & a hard tennis court. Fishing is close by.	£20.00	Y	Y	Y
Mrs V. A. Vicary **Larcombe Foot** **Winsford** **Minehead** **TA24 7HS** **Tel: (01643) 851306** **Open: APR - DEC** **Map Ref No. 13**	Nearest Road: A.396 Larcombe Foot, a comfortable old country house set in the beautiful & tranquil Upper Exe Valley, is an ideal base for walking, riding, fishing & touring Exmoor. Guests' comfort is paramount. There are 3 attractive bedrooms, 2 with private bathroom, & tea/coffee makers in all rooms. A comfortable sitting room with log fire & T.V., plus a pretty garden to relax in. Evening meals by prior arrangement. Winsford is considered one of the prettiest villages on the moor.	£17.50	Y	Y	Y

Somerset

		rate from £ per person	children taken	evening meals	animals taken
Fred Alderton & Jane Young **Karslake House Hotel** **Winsford** **Minehead TA24 7JE** **Tel: (01643) 851242** **Open: EASTER - OCT** **Map Ref No. 13**	Nearest Road: A.396, M.5 This lovely 15th-century former malt house, with low beams & twisting scarlet-carpeted passageways leading to 7 individual pretty bedrooms with modern comforts, welcomes a small number of guests at a time, enabling the hosts to enjoy your company & personally prepare gastronomic delights complemented by a good wine list. The very pretty village of Winsford is in a delightful spot & offers excellent walking & riding in centre of the National Park.	£25.50	Y	Y	Y
Mr & Mrs B. H. Middle **Church Farm Guest House** **Compton Dundon** **Somerton TA11 6PE** **Tel: (01458) 272927** **Open: ALL YEAR (Excl. Xmas)** **Map Ref No. 15**	Nearest Road: B.3151, A.39 A superb thatched cottage, over 400 years old, offering 6 delightful en-suite rooms with T.V. & tea/coffee. Most rooms in a converted barn. Imaginative home cooking from fresh produce, residents' licence with choice of wines. Nestling below St. Andrew's Church in a lovely village, with marvellous views, in the heart of the Vale of Avalon. Walking & wildlife on the doorstep. Ideal for coast & countryside, historic houses & towns. Pretty garden & guests' car park. Children over 5.	£18.50	Y	Y	N
Roy Copeland **The Lynch Country House** **4 Behind Berry** **Somerton TA11 7PD** **Tel: (01458) 272316** **Fax 01458 272590** **Open: ALL YEAR** **Map Ref No. 16**	Nearest Road: A.303 A charming small hotel, standing in acres of carefully tended, wonderfully mature grounds. Beautifully refurbished & decorated to retain all its Georgian style & elegance, it now offers 5 attractively presented rooms, some with 4-posters, others with Victorian bedsteads, all with thoughtful extras including bathrobes & magazines. Each room has en-suite facilities, 'phone, radio, T.V. & tea/coffee. The elegant dining room overlooks the lawns & lake. Single occupancy supplement.	£22.50 *see PHOTO over* CREDIT CARD VISA M'CARD AMEX	Y	N	Y
Mrs C. Clark **Meryan House Hotel** **Bishops Hull** **Taunton TA1 5EG** **Tel: (01823) 337445** **Fax 01823 322355** **Open: ALL YEAR** **Map Ref No. 18**	Nearest Road: A.38 A delightful, 17th-century, listed building of architectural & historical interest. It is set in its own grounds, yet only 1 1/4 miles from Taunton. All bedrooms are elegantly furnished with antiques, & have en-suite, colour T.V. (satellite & video channels) & tea/coffee-making facilities. A delightful house, with a wealth of beams & inglenook fireplaces. Excellent cuisine prepared from home-grown produce.	£26.00 CREDIT CARD VISA M'CARD	Y	Y	Y
Mrs Claire Mitchem **Whittles Farm** **Beercrocombe** **Taunton** **TA3 6AH** **Tel: (01823) 480301** **Open: FEB - NOV** **Map Ref No. 19**	Nearest Road: A.358 Guests at Whittles Farm can be sure of a high standard of accommodation & service. A superior 16th-century farmhouse set in 200 acres of pastureland, it is luxuriously carpeted & furnished in traditional style. Inglenook fireplaces & log-burners. 3 en-suite bedrooms, individually furnished & with T.V. & tea/coffee. Excellent farmhouse food, using own meat, eggs & vegetables, & local Cheddar cheese & butter. Evening meals by prior arrangement. Table licence. Children over 12.	£22.00	Y	Y	N

The Lynch Country House Hotel.   Somerton.

Higher House. West Bagborough.

Somerset

		rate from £ per person	children taken	evening meals	animals taken
Mr & Mrs Martin Eyre **Higher House** **West Bagborough** **Taunton TA4 3EF** **Tel: (01823) 432996** **Fax 01823 433568** **Open: ALL YEAR** **Map Ref No. 22**	Nearest Road: A.358 Higher House is set 650 feet up on the southern slopes of the Quantock Hills. The views from the house & gardens are exceptional. The principal part of the house is 17th-century, built around 2 courtyards, 1 with a heated pool. Each bedroom has its own bathroom, telephone, colour T.V., tea-making facilities, books, magazines. There is a beautifully presented drawing room. There is also an all-weather tennis court available.	£19.50 🚭 *see PHOTO over*	Y	Y	N
Nigel & Finny Muers-Raby **Higher Vexford House** **Higher Vexford** **Lydeard St. Lawrence** **Taunton TA4 3QF** **Tel: (01984) 656267** **Fax 01984 656756** **Open: ALL YEAR** **Map Ref No. 20**	Nearest Road: A.358 This beautiful large Quantock stone country house is located in stunning countryside between The Quantocks, Brendons & Exmoor. A spacious sitting room & dining room all furnished with antiques, log fires & flagstone floors. Lovely bedrooms decorated in traditional country-house style. Books, magazines, tea/coffee facilities. A pretty walled garden with views down this hidden valley. A warm & friendly welcome awaits you. A great place to come & relax & unwind.	£25.00 🚭 *see PHOTO over*	Y	N	Y
Mrs Diana Brewer **Wood Advent Farm** **Roadwater** **Watchet TA23 0RR** **Tel: (01984) 640920** **Fax 01984 640920** **Open: ALL YEAR** **Map Ref No. 24**	Nearest Road: A.39 Set in the Exmoor National Park, Wood Advent Farm is a 340-acre, working sheep farm, with beautiful views & breathtaking parks. 5 relaxing en-suite bedrooms, with tea/coffee facilities. A chintz lounge, with log fire, is always available, & an inglenook woodburner heats the dining room, where country dishes are served, most of the produce being home-produced on the farm, or locally. A grass tennis court & outdoor, heated pool. A wonderful base for the West Country.	£18.50	Y	Y	N
Doug & Carolyn White **Box Tree House** **Westbury-sub-Mendip** **Wells** **BA5 1HA** **Tel: (01749) 870777** **Open: ALL YEAR** **Map Ref No. 25**	Nearest Road: A.371 A warm welcome is assured at this delightful, converted, 17th-century farmhouse located in the heart of the village with an excellent local inn for evening meals. 3 comfortable en-suite bedrooms with tea/coffee-making facilities. A charming T.V. lounge is also available. Box Tree House is renowned for its English breakfasts with local preserves, croissants & home-made muffins. Also, workshops for stained glass & picture framing, with many unique items for sale.	£18.00	Y	N	N
Mrs Wendy Thompson **Stoneleigh House** **Westbury-sub-Mendip** **Wells** **BA5 1HF** **Tel: (01749) 870668** **Open: ALL YEAR (Excl. Xmas)** **Map Ref No. 26**	Nearest Road: A.371 This 18th-century family home is set in beautiful countryside with wonderful views, & surrounded by its own gardens. Stoneleigh House has long enjoyed a reputation for its comfort & congenial atmosphere. It has been carefully modernised so that the wealth of historical features complement the present-day comforts, which include en-suite bathrooms, T.V. & beverage-making facilities. Delicious breakfasts are prepared using local produce & free-range eggs. Evening meals by arrangement. Children over 10.	£19.00 🚭	Y	Y	N

Higher Vexford House. Lydeard St. Lawrence.

Cutthorne. Luckwell Bridge.

Somerset

		rate from £ per person	children taken	evening meals	animals taken
Anita & Chris Frost **Southway Farm** **Polsham** **Wells BA5 1RW** **Tel: (01749) 673396** **Fax 01749 670373** **Open: FEB - NOV** **Map Ref No. 28**	Nearest Road: A.39 Southway Farm is a Grade II listed Georgian farmhouse situated halfway between Glastonbury & Wells. Accommodation is in 3 comfortable & attractively furnished bedrooms, 1 en-suite & 2 with a private bathroom. A delicious Full English breakfast is served, although vegetarians are also catered for. Guests may relax in the cosy lounge, with colour T.V., or in the pretty, tranquil garden. An ideal location for a restful holiday, or for touring the glorious West Country.	£17.50	Y	N	N
Eddie & Holly Nowell **Beryl** **Wells BA5 3JP** **Tel: (01749) 678738** **Fax 01749 670508** **Open: ALL YEAR (Excl. Xmas)** **Map Ref No. 32**	Nearest Road: A.39, B.3139 Beryl is a precious gem in a perfect setting, situated 1 mile from the cathedral city of Wells. This striking 19th-century Gothic mansion has beautifully furnished en-suite bedrooms, interesting views & all the accoutrements of luxury living. Dinner is available by arrangement & is served in the exquisite dining room. Eddie & Holly are charming hosts, & your stay at their home is sure to be memorable.	£32.50 CREDIT CARD VISA M'CARD	Y	Y	Y
Stephen Blue & Peter Clover **Bales Mead** **West Porlock** **TA24 8NX** **Tel: (01643) 862565** **Open: ALL YEAR** **Map Ref No. 29**	Nearest Road: A.39 A small, elegant Edwardian country house offering superb accommodation. An outstanding, peaceful setting, with panoramic views towards both the sea & the rolling countryside of Exmoor. All 3 double bedrooms are exquisitely furnished, offering colour T.V., clock/radio, hairdryer & hot-beverage tray. Breakfast is served in the elegant dining room, or 'al fresco' in the Summer (weather permitting). An excellent base for walking/touring Exmoor & the North Devon Coast.	£22.00	N	N	N
Ann & Philip Durbin **Cutthorne** **Luckwell Bridge** **Wheddon Cross** **TA24 7EW** **Tel: (01643) 831255** **Open: FEB - DEC** **Map Ref No. 30**	Nearest Road: B.3224, A.396 An 18th-century Yeoman's farmhouse, totally secluded in the heart of Exmoor National Park. Spacious & comfortable accommodation, with log fires & central heating. 3 bedrooms with luxury, en-suite bathrooms. Lovely views of the countryside, & the master bedroom boasts a 4-poster bed. Candlelit dinners & delicious home cooking. For extra privacy, there are beautifully appointed medieval stone cottages on the side of the farmhouse, overlooking a pond & a cobbled yard. Ideal base for touring.	£22.00 *see PHOTO over*	Y	Y	Y
Richard & Daphne Criddle **Curdon Mill** **Vellow** **Williton TA4 4LS** **Tel: (01984) 656522** **Fax 01984 656192** **Open: ALL YEAR** **Map Ref No. 31**	Nearest Road: A.358 Curdon Mill is a lovely working water mill situated on 200 acres of farmland at the foot of the beautiful Quantock Hills. 6 pretty, en-suite bedrooms with T.V. & tea/coffee-making facilities. A lounge available for guests' use. Meals are delicious. Real country cuisine using local or home-produced meat & fish, with fresh fruit, vegetables & herbs from the garden. A lovely base for touring the region. A heated outdoor pool in a spacious relaxing garden. Stabling for horses also available.	£25.00 *see PHOTO over* CREDIT CARD VISA M'CARD	N	Y	Y

Curdon Mill. Williton.

Somerset

		rate from £ per person	children taken	evening meals	animals taken
Jackie Somerville Holywell House Holywell, East Coker Yeovil BA22 9NQ Tel: (01935) 862612 Fax 01935 863035 Open: ALL YEAR (Excl. Xmas & New Year) Map Ref No. 33	Nearest Road: A.30 Holywell House has been lovingly restored, tastefully decorated & furnished with many fine antiques. Guests' every need seems to have been anticipated, even down to the hot water bottle for chilly nights! Jackie enjoys cosseting her guests, which is why she wins top awards. Standing in 3 acres of glorious grounds, with tennis court & croquet lawn, Holywell House has literary connections with Thomas Hardy & T. S. Eliot. A delightful home.	£35.00 *see PHOTO over*	Y	Y	N

All the establishments mentioned in this guide

are members of

The Worldwide Bed & Breakfast Association

When booking your accommodation please mention
The Best Bed & Breakfast

Holywell House. Holywell.

Suffolk

Suffolk
(East Anglia)

In July, the lower reaches of the River Orwell hold the essence of Suffolk. Broad fields of green and gold with wooded horizons sweep down to the quiet water. Orwell Bridge spans the wide river where yachts and tan-sailed barges share the water with ocean-going container ships out of Ipswich. Downstream the saltmarshes echo to the cry of the Curlew. The small towns and villages of Suffolk are typical of an area with long seafairing traditions. This is the county of men of vision; like Constable and Gainsborough, Admiral Lord Nelson and Benjamin Britten.

The land is green and fertile and highly productive. The hedgerows shelter some of our prettiest wild flowers, & the narrow country lanes are a pure delight. Most memorable is the ever-changing sky, appearing higher and wider here than elsewhere in England. There is a great deal of heathland, probably the best known being Newmarket where horses have been trained and raced for some hundreds of years. Gorse-covered heath meets sandy cliffs on Suffolks Heritage Coast. Here are bird reserves and the remains of the great mediaeval city of Dunwich, sliding into the sea.

West Suffolk was famous for its wool trade in the Middle Ages, & the merchants gave thanks for their good fortune by building magnificent "Wool Churches". Much-photographed Lavenham has the most perfect black & white timbered houses in Britain, built by the merchants of Tudor times. Ipswich was granted the first charter by King John in 1200, but had long been a trading community of seafarers. Its history can be read from the names of the streets - Buttermarket, Friars Street, Cornhill, Dial Lane & Tavern Street. The latter holds the Great White Horse Hotel mentioned by Charles Dickens in Pickwick Papers. Sadly not many ancient buildings remain, but the mediaeval street pattern and the churches make an interesting trail to follow. The Market town of Bury St. Edmunds is charming, with much of its architectural heritage still surviving, from the Norman Cornhill to a fine Queen Anne House. The great Abbey, now in ruins, was the meeting place of the Barons of England for the creation of the Magna Carta, enshrining the principals of individual freedom, parliamentary democracy and the supremacy of the law. Suffolk has some very fine churches, notably at Mildenhall, Lakenheath, Framlingham, Lavenham & Stoke-by-Nayland, & also a large number of wonderful houses & great halls, evidence of the county's prosperity.

Lavenham.

Suffolk

Suffolk Gazeteer

Areas of Outstanding Natural Beauty
Suffolk Coast. Heathlands. Dedham Vale.

Historic Houses & Castles

Euston Hall - Thetford
18th century house with fine collection of pictures. Gardens & 17th century Parish Church nearby.

Christchurch Mansion - Ipswich
16th century mansion built on site of 12th century Augustinian Priory. Gables & dormers added in 17th century & other alteration & additions made in 17th & 18th centuries.

Gainsborough's House - Sudbury
Birthplace of Gainsborough, well furnished, collection of paintings.

The Guildhall - Hadleigh
15th century.

Glemham Hall - Nr Woodbridge
Elizabethan house of red brick - 18th century alterations. Fine stair, panelled rooms with Queen Anne furniture.

Haughley Park - Nr. Stowmarket
Jacobean manor house.

Heveningham Hall - Nr. Halesworth
Georgian mansion - English Palladian - Interior in Neo-Classical style. Garden by Capability Brown.

Ickworth - Nr. Bury St. Edmunds
Mixed architectural styles - late Regency & 18th century. French furniture, pictures & superb silver. Gardens with orangery.

Kentwell Hall - Long Melford
Elizabethan mansion in red brick, built in E plan, surrounded by moat.

Little Hall - Lavenham
15th century hall house, collection of furniture, pictures, china, etc.

Melford Hall - Nr. Sudbury
16th century - fine pictures, Chinese porcelain, furniture. Garden with gazebo.

Somerleyton Hall - Nr. Lowestoft
Dating from 16th century - additional work in 19th century. Carving by Grinling Gibbons. Tapestries, library, pictures.

Cathedrals & Churches

Bury St. Edmunds (St. Mary)
15th century. Hammer Beam roof in nave, wagon roof in chancel. Boret monument 1467.

Bramfield (St. Andrew)
Early circular tower. Fine screen & vaulting. Renaissance effigy.

Bacton (St. Mary)
15th century timbered roof. East Anglian stone & flintwork.

Dennington (St. Mary)
15th century alabaster monuments & bench ends. Aisle & Parclose screens with lofts & parapets.

Earl Stonhay (St. Mary)
14th century - rebuilt with fine hammer roof & 17th century pulpit with four hour-glasses.

Euston (St. Genevieve)
17th century. Fine panelling, reredos may be Grinling Gibbons.

Framlingham (St. Michael)
15th century nave & west tower, hammer beam roof in false vaulting. Chancel was rebuilt in 16th century for the tombs of the Howard family, monumental art treasures. Thamar organ. 1674.

Fressingfield (St. Peter & St. Paul)
15th century woodwork - very fine.

Lavenham (St. Peter & St. Paul)
15th century. Perpendicular. Fine towers. 14th century chancel screen. 17th century monument in alabaster.

Long Melford (Holy Trinity)
15th century Lady Chapel, splendid brasses. 15th century glass of note. Chantry chapel with fine roof. Like cathedral in proportions.

Stoke-by-Nayland (St. Mary)
16th-17th century library, great tower. Fine nave & arcades. Good brasses & monuments.

Ufford (St. Mary)
Mediaeval font cover - glorious.

Museums & Galleries

Christchurch Mansion - Ipswich
Country house, collection of furniture, pictures, bygones, ceramics of 18th century. Paintings by Gainsborough, Constable & modern artists.

Ipswich Museum - Ipswich
Natural History; prehistory, geology & archaeology to mediaeval period.

Suffolk

Moyse's Hall Musuem - Bury St. Edmunds
12th century dwelling house with local antiquities & natural history.
Abbot's Hall Museum of Rural Life - Stowmarket
Collections describing agriculture, crafts & domestic utensils.
Gershom-Parkington Collection - Bury St. Edmunds
Queen Anne House containing collection of watches & clocks.
Dunwich Musuem - Dunwich
Flora & fauna; local history.

Historic Monuments

The Abbey - Bury St. Edmunds
Only west end now standing.

Framlingham Castle
12th & 13th centuries - Tudor almshouses.
Bungay Castle - Bungay
12th century. Restored 13th century drawbridge & gatehouse.
Burgh Castle Roman Fort - Burgh
Coastal defences - 3rd century.
Herringfleet Priory - Herringfleet
13th century - remains of small Augustinian priory.
Leiston Abbey - Leiston
14th century - remains of cloisters, choir & trancepts.
Orford Castle - Orford
12th century - 18-sided keep - three towers.

The House in the Clouds. Thorpeness.

SUFFOLK
Map reference

1 Roberts
2 Dakin
3 Watchorn
4 Watkins
5 Rolfe
6 Middleton-Stewart
7 Sheppard
8 Hackett-Jones
9 Debenham
10 Hilton
10 Hoepli
11 Bowden
12 Ridsdale
13 Morse
14 Bagnall
15 Hickson
16 Currie
17 Chetwynd

Suffolk

	Nearest Road	rate from £ per person	children taken	evening meals	animals taken
Mrs Bobbie Watchorn **Earsham Park Farm** **Harleston Road** **Earsham** **Bungay NR35 2AG** **Tel/Fax: (01986) 892180** **Open: ALL YEAR** **Map Ref No. 03**	Nearest Road: A.143 A Victorian farmhouse set on a hill overlooking the Waveney Valley, with superb views. Park Farm offers 3 really delightful guest rooms, all furnished to a high standard. Each is en-suite, & well-equipped with T.V., radio/alarm & tea/coffee facilities. 1 4-poster. Breakfast is served in the lovely dining room. Within easy reach of Norwich, Lowestoft & Southwold. A wonderful home, where comfort & a relaxed atmosphere prevail.	£19.00	Y	Y	N
Paul & Sylvia Roberts **Butlers** **Colne Road** **Bures Hamlet** **Bures CO8 5DN** **Tel: (01787) 227243** **Open: ALL YEAR** **Map Ref No. 01**	Nearest Road: A.604 Peace & tranquility away from the bustle of everyday life is found here in this 17th-century timber-framed farmhouse, set in 90 acres of private grounds. Guests keep returning for the comfort & warmth of the 2 rooms with private bathroom & 1 room with adjacent bathroom, the guests' dining room & the lounge. With 24 hours' notice, meals can be willingly arranged. An ideal base from which to explore Suffolk & Constable country. Children over 5 yrs.	£19.00	Y	N	N
Ann & Roy Dakin **Dunston Guest House/ Hotel** **8 Springfield Road** **Bury St. Edmunds** **IP33 3AN** **Tel: (01284) 767981** **Open: ALL YEAR** **Map Ref No. 02**	Nearest Road: A.14 A 19th-century house, full of character, with a warm, friendly atmosphere. Accommodation is in 16 rooms, many with en-suite facilities, all very comfortable, each with colour T.V., tea/coffee & ironing facilities. A T.V. lounge, sun lounge & garden for guests' use. A ground-floor room is also available for handicapped guests. Licensed. Situated in the centre of East Anglia, it is an ideal base for touring this interesting region, with many lovely towns & villages plus a coastline.	£18.00	Y	N	N
Nowell & Penny Watkins **The Bauble** **Higham** **Colchester CO7 6LA** **Tel: (01206) 337254** **Fax 01206 337263** **Open: ALL YEAR** **Map Ref No. 04**	Nearest Road: A.12 The Bauble is a delightful house offering accommodation in 3 attractively furnished bedrooms, with modern amenities including T.V. & tea/coffee-making facilities. A full English breakfast is served. Lounge, garden, heated pool & tennis court available for guests' use. Higham lies in the heart of Constable country & is within easy reach of many wool villages, with their churches, antiques shops & National Trust properties. Children over 12 years welcome.	£20.00	Y	N	N
Angela & Rodney Rolfe **Edgehill Hotel** **2 High Street** **Hadleigh** **IP7 5AP** **Tel: (01473) 822458** **Open: ALL YEAR (Excl. Xmas)** **Map Ref No. 05**	Nearest Road: A.12, A.14 Edgehill is a family-run Georgian house in central Hadleigh. Beautifully restored & tastefully modernised, the hotel offers the ultimate in accommodation. Particular attention is paid to friendly service & traditional home cooking with organic vegetables. Situated in the most picturesque part of Suffolk, it is a good base from which to visit the surrounding beautiful towns & villages of East Anglia.	£22.50 *see PHOTO over*	Y	Y	Y

Edgehill Hotel. Hadleigh.

St. Peters House. Spexhall.

Suffolk

	rate from £ per person	children taken	evening meals	animals taken
Mrs J. Middleton-Stewart St. Peter's House Spexhall Halesworth IP19 0RQ Tel: (01986) 873329/874567 Fax 01986 875275 Open: ALL YEAR Map Ref No. 06	Nearest Road: A.12, A.144 Old-fashioned roses & resident ducks share with visitors the peaceful gardens of this converted 17th-century tithe barn. The unique accommodation, in rolling Suffolk farmland, provides 2 double & 1 twin bedrooms, all en-suite/private, & abundantly equipped. Robust breakfasts, including Suffolk fish & local fare. Dinner only to order. Well placed for Southwold, Aldeburgh & the Heritage Coast & memorable mediaeval monuments.	£20.00 *see PHOTO over*	N	Y	N
Mrs Jane Sheppard The Old Vicarage Great Thurlow Haverhill CB9 7LE Tel: (01440) 783209 Open: ALL YEAR Map Ref No. 07	Nearest Road: A.604 Set in mature grounds & woodlands, this delightful old vicarage has a friendly family atmosphere. Complete peace & comfort are assured. Wonderful views of the Suffolk countryside. Open log fires welcome you in winter. Perfectly situated for Newmarket, Cambridge, Long Melford & Constable country, the attractively furnished bedrooms have en-suite or private facilities, & tea & coffee trays. (No smoking in bedrooms.) Evening meals are available at prior notice. Children over 7 welcome, & pets by arrangement.	£20.00	Y	Y	Y
Raewyn Hackett-Jones Pipps Ford Norwich Road Needham Market Ipswich IP6 8LJ Tel: (01449) 760208 Fax 01449 760561 Open: Mid JAN - Mid DEC Map Ref No. 08	Nearest Road: A.14, A.140 A beautiful, Tudor, beamed guest house in a pretty, old-fashioned garden by the Gipping river. 7 very attractive bedrooms, with private bathrooms & tea/coffee-making facilities. A very extensive breakfast menu & delicious 4-course evening meals, served in the delightful conservatory. Licensed. Colour T.V., tennis court & swimming pool. Winner of The Best Bed & Breakfast award for East Anglia. A good central position for touring all of East Anglia.	£17.50 *see PHOTO over*	Y	Y	N
Mrs Penny Debenham Mulberry Hall Burstall Ipswich IP8 3DP Tel: (01473) 652348 Open: ALL YEAR Map Ref No. 09	Nearest Road: A.12, A.1071 A lovely 16th-century timber-framed farmhouse, once owned by Cardinal Wolsey, standing in one & a half acres of garden. A choice of 3 bedrooms with modern amenities, hair dryer & ironing facilities is available. The house is comfortably & prettily furnished, & guests may use the lounge, with log-burning, inglenook fireplace. Plenty of games & reading matter, plus information on local events. Tennis, badminton & croquet available.	£17.00	Y	Y	N
Tess & Rupert Chetwynd The Old Rectory Nedging Lavenham (Nr) IP7 7HQ Tel/Fax: (01449) 740745 Open: ALL YEAR Map Ref No. 17	Nearest Road: B.1115 The Old Rectory is an elegant Georgian house set in 2 acres of garden near Lavenham. It has been carefully restored, & now offers delightful accommodation in 3 comfortable bedrooms, each with its own bathroom. Excellent dinner available. Nedging is a rural hamlet, & is well placed for visiting many mediaeval villages, historic houses &, of course, 'Constable Country'. A charming home. Children over 12 welcome.	£27.50 (no smoking symbol) CREDIT CARD VISA M'CARD	Y	Y	N

417

Pipps Ford.   Needham Market.

Suffolk

rate per person from £ / children taken / evening meals / animals taken

		rate per person from £	children taken	evening meals	animals taken
Lise & Michael Hilton **Bower Field House** **Helmingham Road** **Otley** **IP6 9NR** **Tel: (01473) 890742** **Fax 01473 890059** **Open: MAR - OCT** **Map Ref No. 10**	Nearest Road: A.12, A.140 A large, handsome, 17th-century, listed stable & barn conversion, set in mature grounds with terraces & a croquet lawn. Beautifully furnished en-suite rooms with antiques, T.V., radio & tea/coffee. Billiard room & drawing room with log fires & grand piano for guests' use. Full English or Scandinavian breakfast served. Evening meals by arrangement only. Lise is the winner of several B & B awards. Within easy reach of Woodbridge, Ipswich, Aldeburgh, Minsemere, Snape Concert Hall & Constable Country . Children over 12.	£21.00	Y	Y	Y
Thomas & Colette Hoepli **Otley House** **Helmingham Road** **Otley** **IP6 9NR** **Tel: (01473) 890253** **Fax 01473 890009** **Open: MAR - NOV** **Map Ref No. 10**	Nearest Road: A.12, A.140 A magnificent 17th-century house standing in its own spacious grounds, surrounded by mature trees with 2 small lakes, a croquet lawn & a putting green. Offering 4 luxuriously furnished en-suite bedrooms, some with colour T.V.. Evening meals are a delight, & are served in the Regency dining room. A billiard room, T.V. & drawing room for guests' use. Ideally located for visiting Woodbridge, Oxford, Southwold & the fine cities of Norfolk & Cambridge. No smoking in the bedrooms. Children over 12.	£26.00	Y	Y	N
Mrs P. J. Bowden **The Old Rectory** **Wetherden** **Stowmarket IP14 3LS** **Tel: (01359) 240144** **Open: MAR - DEC** **Map Ref No. 11**	Nearest Road: A.14 Situated on a hill overlooking the village of Wetherden, just off the A.45 between Bury St. Edmunds & Stowmarket, this beautiful Georgian house is set in 13 acres. Accommodation is in 3 bedrooms, 2 with private/en-suite bathroom. An attractive sitting room with log fire & colour T.V. is available. Large garden, with croquet lawn. Ideally placed for touring East Anglia.	£20.00	N	N	N
Mrs Patricia Currie **The Old Rectory** **Stonham Road** **Mickfield** **Stowmarket IP14 5LR** **Tel: (01449) 711283** **Open: ALL YEAR (Excl.** **Xmas & New Year)** **Map Ref No. 16**	Nearest Road: A.140, A.1120 The Old Rectory has grown from mediaeval origins. It is a timber-framed house, which is quiet & peaceful, surrounded by its own lovely garden, orchard & meadow. It is situated right in the middle of Suffolk, secluded yet within easy reach of main roads. A good base for exploring the whole of East Anglia. There are 2 attractive guest bedrooms, each with en-suite facilities. Also, a single is available for another member of the party. No-smoking in bedrooms. Children over 8. Also, closed during Easter.	£26.00 CREDIT CARD VISA	Y	Y	N
Martin & Diana Ridsdale **Cherry Tree Farm** **Mendlesham Green** **Stowmarket IP14 5RQ** **Tel: (01449) 766376** **Open: ALL YEAR (Excl.** **Xmas & New Year)** **Map Ref No. 12**	Nearest Road: A.140 Traditional timber-framed farmhouse, standing in three quarters of an acre of garden, with orchard & duck ponds, in a peaceful Suffolk village. 3 bedrooms, each with en-suite facilities. A spacious & comfortable lounge, inglenook fireplaces with log fire. Hearty English breakfast served in the oak-beamed dining room. Home-baked bread, own preserves & honey. Imaginative evening meals, with garden & local produce, good cheeses & fine English wines.	£20.00	N	Y	N

Suffolk

		rate from £ per person	children taken	evening meals	animals taken
Catherine & David Morse **St. Mary Hall** **Belchamp Walter** **Sudbury** **CO10 7BB** **Tel: (01787) 237202** **Open: ALL YEAR** **Map Ref No. 13**	Nearest Road: A.604, A.134 Fine example of a mediaeval Suffolk manor house in lovely 4-acre garden, 1 mile south of the village of Belchamp Walter (guests advised to obtain directions in advance). On arrival, you will be warmly welcomed. Two twin/double and one single room, each with private bathroom. Book-lined library with T.V.. Pretty dining room. Large outdoor pool, tennis court, croquet. Catherine, a keen cook, will provide dinner with 24 hr's notice.	£25.00 CREDIT CARD VISA M'CARD	Y	Y	Y
Sue Bagnall **Abbey House** **Monk Soham** **Woodbridge** **IP13 7EN** **Tel: (01728) 685225** **Open: FEB - OCT** **Map Ref No. 14**	Nearest Road: A.1120 Abbey House is a Victorian rectory set in 10 acres of peaceful Suffolk countryside. The house is surrounded by secluded gardens, with mature trees & several large ponds. The remainder of the grounds are occupied by Jersey cows. Also, a flock of sheep, & an assorted collection of chickens & waterfowl. 3 attractive double bedrooms. Private bathrooms, tea-making facilities, & imaginative evening meals made using home-produced meat & vegetables. Outdoor swimming pool.	£18.00	N	Y	N
Elizabeth Hickson **Grange Farm** **Dennington** **Woodbridge IP13 8BT** **Tel: (01986) 798388** **Open: ALL YEAR (Excl.** **Xmas & New Year)** **Map Ref No. 15**	Nearest Road: A.12 This is a charming house in a superb spot, with a lovely garden & an all-weather tennis court. Comprising 4 attractive guest rooms, all overlooking the garden. The beamed guests' dining room & sitting room are beautifully furnished, & very comfortable. Evening meals by arrangement. Vegetables & fresh fruit come straight from the garden whenever possible. Only 25 mins' drive from Minsmere, Snape Maltings & the coast. The perfect spot for a relaxing break.	£18.00	Y	Y	N

When booking your accommodation please mention
The Best Bed & Breakfast

Surrey

Surrey
(South East)

One of the Home Counties, Surrey includes a large area of London, south of the Thames. Communications are good in all directions so it is easy to stay in Surrey & travel either into central London or out to enjoy the lovely countryside which, despite urban development, survives thanks to the 'Green Belt' policy. The county is also very accessible from Gatwick Airport.

The land geographically, is chalk sandwiched in clay, & probably the lack of handy building material was responsible for the area remaining largely uninhabited for centuries. The North Downs were a considerable barrier to cross, but gradually settlements grew along the rivers which were the main routes through. The Romans used the gap created by the River Mole to build Stane Street between London & Chichester, this encouraged the development of small towns. The gap cut by the passage of the River Wey allows the Pilgrims Way to cross the foot of the Downs. Dorking, Reigate & Farnham are small towns along this route, all with attracitve main streets & interesting shops & buildings.

Surrey has very little mention in the Domesday Book, &, although the patronage of the church & of wealthy families established manors which developed over the years, little happened to disturb the rural tranquility of the region. As a county it made little history but rather reflected passing times, although Magna Carta was signed at Egham in 1215.

The heathlands of Surrey were a Royal playground for centuries. The Norman Kings hunted here & horses became part of the landscape & life of the people, as they are today on Epsom Downs.

Nearness to London & Royal patronage began to influence the area, & the buildings of the Tudor period reflect this. Royal palaces were built at Hampton Court & Richmond, & great houses such as Loseley near Guildford often using stone from the monasteries emptied during the Reformation. Huge deer parks were enclosed & stocked. Richmond, described as the "finest village in the British Dominions", is now beset by 20th century traffic but still has a wonderful park with deer, lakes & woodland that was enclosed by Charles I. The terraces & gardens of such buildings as Trumpeters House & Asgill House on the slopes of Richmond overlooking the Thames, have an air of spaciousness & elegance & there are lovely & interesting riverside walks at Richmond.

Polesden Lacey.

Surrey

Surrey Gazeteer

Historic Houses & Castles

Albury Park - Albury, Nr. Guildford
A delightful country mansion designed by Pugin.

Clandon Park - Guildford
A fine house in the Palladian style by Leoni. A good collection of furniture & pictures. The house boasts some fine plasterwork.

Claremont - Esher
A superb Palladian house with interesting interior.

Detillens - Limpsfield
A fine 15th century house with inglenook fireplaces & mediaeval furniture. A large, pleasant garden.

Greathed Manor- Lingfield
An imposing Victorian manor house.

Hatchlands - East Clandon
A National Trust property of the 18th century with a fine Adam interior

Loseley House - Guildford
A very fine Elizabethan mansion with superb panelling, furniture & paintings.

Polesden Lacy - Dorking
A Regency villa housing the Grevill collection of tapestries, pictures & furnishings. Extensive gardens.

Cathedrals & Churches

Compton (St. Nicholas)
The only surviving 2-storey sanctuary in the country. A fine 17th century pulpit.

Esher (St. George)
A fine altar-piece & marble monument.

Hascombe (St. Peter)
A rich interior with much gilding & painted reredos & roofs.

Lingfield (St. Peter & St. Paul)
15th century. Holding a chained bible.

Ockham (St. Mary & All Saints)
Early church with 13th century east window.

Stoke D'Abernon (St. Mary)
Dating back to Pre-conquest time with additions from the 12th-15th centuries. A fine 13th century painting. Early brasses.

Museums & Galleries

Charterhouse School Museum - Godalming
Peruvian pottery, Greek pottery, archaeology & natural history.

Chertsey Museum - Chertsey
18th-19th century costume & furnishing displayed & local history.

Guildford House - Guildford
The house is 17th century & of architectural interest housing monthly exhibitions.

Guildford Museum - Guildford
A fine needlework collection & plenty on local history.

Old Kiln Agricultural - Tilford
A very interesting collection of old farm implements.

Watermill Museum - Haxted
A restored 17th century mill with working water wheels & machinery.

Weybridge Museum - Weybridge
Good archaeological exhibition plus costume & local history.

The Gardens. Wisley

SURREY

Map reference

1 McCarthy
2 Prideaux
3 Hill
4 Franklin-Adams
5 Carmichael
6 Blok
6 Lees
7 Stocks
7 Shortland
9 Bussandri
10 Lowe
11 Leeper
12 Rowse
13 Wolf
14 Higgs
15 Conrad-Pickles

Surrey

	rate from £ per person	children taken	evening meals	animals taken
Tommy & Ann McCarthy **Pineleigh** **10 Castle Road** **Off Waverley Drive** **Camberley GU15 2DS** **Tel/Fax: (01276) 64787** **Open: ALL YEAR** **Map Ref No. 01**	Nearest Road: M.3, A.325 Pineleigh is a spacious Edwardian house, built in 1906 & set in half an acre of mature garden in a very quiet area. Accommodation is in 3 comfortable guest rooms, all en-suite with telephone, T.V. & hospitality tray. Attractively furnished in Victorian style with many old prints & pictures. A full English breakfast is served, evening meals by arrangement. Conveniently located for Heathrow Airport & London.	£22.50 CREDIT CARD AMEX	N	Y	N
Mrs D. Prideaux **Mark Ash** **Abinger Common** **Dorking** **RH5 6JA** **Tel: (01306) 731326** **Open: MAR - NOV** **Map Ref No. 02**	Nearest Road: A.25 A pleasant Victorian house standing in its own delightful garden, & located in An Area of Outstanding Natural Beauty. 3 comfortable rooms, each with private facilities. 2 have modern amenities, including a radio & T.V., & all have tea/coffee-making facilities. A residents' drawing room is also available. Full English or Continental breakfast. Packed lunches can be provided at prior notice. There is also a heated outdoor swimming pool & tennis court. 35 mins to Gatwick & Heathrow. London under 1 hour's drive.	£20.00	Y	N	N
Mrs Gill Hill **Bulmer Farm** **Holmbury St. Mary** **Dorking** **RH5 6LG** **Tel: (01306) 730210** **Open: ALL YEAR** **Map Ref No. 03**	Nearest Road: A.25, B.2126 Enjoy a warm welcome at this delightful 17th-century farmhouse, complete with many beams & an inglenook fireplace. Offering 3 charming rooms, all with h/c & tea/coffee-making facilities. Adjoining the house around a courtyard are 5 attractive barn-conversion en-suite bedrooms for non-smokers. Farm produce & home-made preserves are provided. Situated in a picturesque village, it is convenient for London airports.	£18.00	N	N	Y
Mrs Carol Franklin-Adams **High Edser** **Shere Road** **Ewhurst GU6 7PQ** **Tel: (01483) 278214** **Fax 01483 278200** **Open: ALL YEAR** **Map Ref No. 04**	Nearest Road: A.25 A large, handsome Grade II listed home, the earliest part built in the 14th century, situated in an Area of Outstanding Natural Beauty. There are three rooms available: two doubles and one twin with private facilities. Residents' lounge and T.V.. Tennis court in grounds, and golf nearby. 35 minutes to Gatwick and London Airports. Approximately an hour's drive to London. A delightful home, ideal for a relaxing break.	£20.00	Y	N	Y
Mrs Pam Conrad-Pickles **Liscombe** **Hamlash Lane** **Frensham** **Farnham GU10 3AT** **Tel: (01252) 794409** **Fax 01252 795313** **Open: ALL YEAR** **Map Ref No. 15**	Nearest Road: A.287 A delightful family country house set in beautiful grounds in an Area of Outstanding Natural Beauty, close to Frensham Ponds. A heated swimming pool, & tennis court. 3 attractively decorated bedrooms, 1 double, 1 twin & 1 single, all with en-suite facilities. Dinner by prior arrangement. Approx 1 hr to London, Heathrow & Gatwick. An excellent touring base for Windsor, Hampton Court, Portsmouth, Brighton, Stonehenge. Excellent local theatres, often with pre-West-End productions. Children over 10 yrs.	£25.00	Y	Y	N

Deerfell. Haslemere.

Surrey

		rate from £ per person	children taken	evening meals	animals taken
Mrs Elizabeth Carmichael **Deerfell** **Blackdown Park** **Fernden Lane** **Haslemere** **GU27 3LA** **Tel: (01428) 653409** **Open: Mid JAN - Mid DEC** **Map Ref No. 05**	Nearest Road: A.286 A warm welcome at a spacious & comfortable family home set in downland countryside, with breathtaking views to the hills & valleys of Sussex. Stone-built, at the turn of the century, on a sunny, gorse-clad slope, it was once the coach house to Blackdown House. Offering 2 comfortable, en-suite rooms. Evening meals by prior arrangement. Close by, Haslemere station (4 miles), London (45 mins), Midhurst, Petworth, Goodwood & Chichester. Walking & riding. Children & pets welcome. Gatwick/Heathrow: 1 hour.	£19.00 (no smoking) *see PHOTO over*	Y	Y	N
Mrs Jean Lees **Latchetts Cottage** **Ricketts Wood Road** **Norwood Hill** **Horley RH6 0ET** **Tel: (01293) 862831** **Open: ALL YEAR** **Map Ref No. 06**	Nearest Road: A.217, A.23 Latchetts Cottage is situated in the small hamlet of Norwood Hill, yet is less than 10 mins from Gatwick Airport & the station. This cosy cottage has comfortable accommodation, with a warm welcome & a homely atmosphere. All bedrooms have fine views over uninterrupted countryside. The village pub offers a varied menu, & is within walking distance. N.T. properties & walks nearby. Parking & courtesy transport available.	£18.50	Y	N	N
Gill & Tony Blok **Crutchfield Farm** **Crutchfield Lane** **Hookwood** **Horley RH6 0HT** **Tel: (01293) 863110** **Fax 01293 863233** **Open: ALL YEAR** **Map Ref No. 06**	Nearest Road: A.217 Crutchfield Farm is a Grade II listed, 15th-century timber-framed farmhouse, with 16th-, 17th- & 18th-century additions. There are many massive exposed oak beams & an inglenook fireplace. The lovely bedrooms are tastefully furnished, & all have colour T.V.s & tea/coffee-making facilities. 3 miles from Gatwick. London & south coast 30 mins. Set in 10 acres of beautiful gardens with swimming pool, tennis court & croquet. A delightful home & an ideal base for a relaxing break.	£20.00	Y	N	Y
Janet & Ken Stocks **The Lawn Guest House** **30 Massetts Road** **Horley RH6 7DE** **Tel: (01293) 775751** **Fax 01293 821803** **Open: ALL YEAR** **Map Ref No. 07**	Nearest Road: A.23, M.23 A well-appointed Victorian house 4 minutes from Gatwick & 25 miles to London or Brighton. Very useful as a base for travelling, it is close to the rail station & town centre. There are 7 bedrooms, 3 with en-suite facilities, all very comfortable & well decorated, with colour T.V. & tea/coffee-making facilities. Also, a pleasant breakfast room & a garden for guests' use. There is a supplement payable for single use of rooms.	£17.50 (no smoking) CREDIT CARD VISA M'CARD AMEX	N	N	Y
Mrs Daphne Shortland **Chalet Guest House** **77 Massetts Road** **Horley RH6 7EB** **Tel: (01293) 821666** **Fax 01293 821619** **Open: ALL YEAR** **Map Ref No. 07**	Nearest Road: A.23, M.23 A family-run guest house offering accommodation with modern facilities in a bright and friendly atmosphere. There are 7 bedrooms, mostly en-suite, with T.V., tea/coffee trays. Single availability. Garden and ample parking. Local interests include the Six Bells Pub, circa 827. Lovely Sussex countryside adjacent. Gatwick Airport 5 minutes. London or the South Coast 30 minutes by train. An ideal base from which to explore this region.	£21.00 (no smoking) CREDIT CARD VISA M'CARD	Y	N	N

Knaphill Manor. Knaphill.

Surrey

Name & Address	Description	rate from £ per person	children taken	evening meals	animals taken
Mr & Mrs P. M. J. Wolf **The Old Farmhouse** **Wasp Green Lane** **Outwood** **Redhill RH1 5QE** **Tel: (01342) 842313** **Fax 01342 844744** **Open:** ALL YEAR (Excl. Xmas) **Map Ref No. 13**	Nearest Road: A.25 An early-15th-century mediaeval 4-bay hall house, which is little altered & retains many original features, including the diamond mullions for the hall window & fine panelling. It also has one of the longest unsupported crossing beams in Surrey. 2 of the attractively furnished bedrooms have brass bedsteads, & 1 has an original oak 4-poster bed. A delightful home. The Old Farmhouse is perfect for exploring the south east of England & many places of historic interest.	£23.00	N	Y	N
Mrs Rosemary Higgs **Little Mynthurst** **Smalls Hill Road** **Leigh** **Reigate** **RH2 8QA** **Tel: (01293) 862441** **Open: ALL YEAR** **Map Ref No. 14**	Nearest Road: A.217 Little Mynthurst is an Edwardian country house set in 5 acres, with views over open countryside. Guests can enjoy a peaceful location, whilst being only a few miles from Gatwick Airport. The house has been tastefully renovated to offer modern facilities, & each bedroom has a colour T.V. & tea/coffee facilities. All rooms have either hand basins or full en-suite bathrooms. Little Mynthurst is a family home, & as a result it is both relaxed & flexible in meeting your particular needs. Good pubs close by. Parking & courtesy transport.	£20.00	Y	N	N
Mr & Mrs G. Bussandri **Cranleigh Hotel** **41 West Street** **Reigate RH2 9BL** **Tel: (01737) 223417** **Fax 01737 223734** **Open: ALL YEAR** **Map Ref No. 09**	Nearest Road: A.25, M.25 The Cranleigh Hotel has a reputation for comfort, cleanliness & hospitality. Its modern facilities include hairdryers, T.V. & a pleasant bar & lounge, etc. Comfortable accommodation in pleasant rooms. 45 mins. from London, & a few minutes from Gatwick Airport, the hotel stands in lovely gardens, which provide flowers & fresh food for the table. Very convenient for travellers to the South-West. Ideal for first or last night of travel. CREDIT CARD VISA M'CARD AMEX	£30.00	Y	Y	N
Kevin & Teresa Leeper **Knaphill Manor** **Carthouse Lane** **Woking GU21 4XT** **Tel: (01276) 857962** **Fax 01276 855503** **Open: ALL YEAR** **Map Ref No. 11**	Nearest Road: M.25 Jt. 11 A delightful, large family home, dating back to the 1700s, set in 6 acres of grounds, with a tennis court & croquet lawn. Located in a farming area, the house is quiet & secluded, yet Heathrow & Gatwick are only a 35-min. drive away. Bedrooms are very comfortable, with en-suite/private facilities plus T.V. & tea/coffee makers. A T.V. lounge is also available. Early morning arrivals are welcome. London 25 mins. Ascot, Windsor & Oxford are also easily reached. Children over 8yrs. *see PHOTO over* CREDIT CARD VISA M'CARD	£30.00	Y	N	N
Tony & Susie Rowse **Pankhurst** **Bagshot Road** **West End** **Woking GU24 9QR** **Tel/Fax: (01276) 858149** **Open:** ALL YEAR (Excl. Xmas) **Map Ref No. 12**	Nearest Road: A.319 Pankhurst is an attractive & historic Grade II listed country house, set in a walled garden amid 8 acres of gardens & woods. Situated close to the picturesque village of Chobham, it has 3 beautiful guest rooms, each equipped with T.V., radio & tea/coffee, etc. There is also a tennis court & heated outdoor swimming pool. Close to Heathrow & Gatwick Airports, Ascot, Windsor, Sunningdale & Wentworth. 3 miles M.3. 7 miles M.25.	£25.00	Y	N	N

**All the establishments mentioned in this guide
are members of the
Worldwide Bed & Breakfast Association.**

**If you have any comments regarding your
accommodation please send them to us
using the form at the back of the book.
We value your comments.**

Sussex

Sussex
(South East)

The South Downs of Sussex stretch along the coast, reflecting the expanse of the North Downs of Kent, over the vast stretches of the Weald.

The South Downs extend from dramatic Beachy Head along the coast to Chichester & like the North Downs, they are crossed by an ancient trackway. There is much evidence of prehistoric settlement on the Downs. Mount Caburn, near Lewes, is crowned by an iron age fort, & Cissbury Ring is one of the most important archaeological sites in England. This large earthwork covers 80 acres & must have held a strategic defensive position. Hollingbury Fort carved into the hillside above Brighton, & the Trundle (meaning circle) date from 300-250 B.C., & were constructed on an existing neolithic settlement. The Long Man of Wilmington stands 226 feet high & is believed to be Nordic, possibly representing Woden, the God of War.

Only two towns are located on the Downs but both are of considerable interest. Lewes retains much of its mediaeval past & there is a folk museum in Ann of Cleves' house, which itself is partly 16th century. Arundel has a fascinating mixture of architectural styles, a castle & a superb park with a lake, magnificent beech trees & an unrivalled view of the Arun valley.

The landscape of the inland Weald ranges from bracken-covered heathlands where deer roam, to the deep woodland stretches of the Ashdown Forest, eventually giving way to soft undulating hills & valleys, patterned with hop-fields, meadows, oast houses, windmills & fruit orchards. Originally the whole Weald was dense with forest. Villages like Midhurst & Wadhurst hold the Saxon suffix "hurst" which means wood. As the forests were cleared for agriculture the names of the villages changed & we find Bosham & Stedham whose suffix "ham" means homestead or farm.

Battle, above Hastings, is the site of the famous Norman victory & 16th century Bodiam Castle, built as defence against the French in later times, has a beautiful setting encircled by a lily-covered moat.

Sussex has an extensive coastline, with cliffs near Eastbourne at Beachy Head, & at Hastings. Further east, the great flat Romney Marshes stretch out to sea, & there is considerable variety in the coastal towns.

Chichester has a magnificent cathedral & a harbour reaching deep into the coastal plain that is rich in archaeological remains. The creeks & mudflats make it an excellent place for bird watching.

Brighton is the most famous of the Sussex resorts with its Pier, the Promenade above the beaches, the oriental folly of George IV's Royal Pavilion & its Regency architecture. "The Lanes" are a maze of alleys & small squares full of fascinating shops, a thriving antique trade, & many good pubs & eating places. Hastings to the east preserves its "Old Town" where timbered houses nestle beneath the cliffs & the fishing boats are drawn up on the shingle whilst the nets are hung up to dry in curious tall, thin net stores. Winchelsea stands on a hill where it was rebuilt in the 13th century by Edward I when the original town was engulfed by the sea. It is a beautiful town with a fine Norman church, an excellent museum in the Town Hall, & many pretty houses. Across the Romney Marshes on the next hill stands Rye, its profile dominated by its church. It is a fascinating town with timbered houses & cobbled streets.

Sussex

Sussex Gazeteer

Areas of Outstanding Natural Beauty
The Sussex Downs. Chichester Harbour.

Historic Houses & Castles

Arundel Castle - Arundel
18th century rebuilding of ancient castle, fine portraits, 15th century furniture.
Cuckfield Park - Cuckfield
Elizabethan manor house, gatehouse. Very fine panelling & ceilings.
Danny - Hurstpierpoint
16th century - Elizabethan .
Goodwood House - Chichester
18th century - Jacobean house - Fine Sussex flintwork, paintings by Van Dyck, Canaletto & Stubbs, English & French furniture, tapestries & porcelain.
Newtimber Place - Newtimber
Moated house - Etruscan style wall paintings.
Purham - Pulborough
Elizabethan house containing important collection of Elizabethan, Jacobean & Georgian portraits, also fine furniture.
Petworth House - Petworth
17th century - landscaped by Capability Brown - important paintings - 14th century chapel.
St. Mary's - Bramber
15th century timber framed house - rare panelling.
Tanyard - Sharpthorne
Mediaeval tannery - 16th & 17th century additions.
The Thatched Cottage - Lindfield
Close-studded weald house - reputedly Henry VII hunting lodge.
Uppark - Petersfield
17th century - 18th century interior decorations remain unaltered.
Alfriston Clergy House - Nr. Seaford
14th century parish priest's house - pre-reformation.
Battle Abbey - Battle
Founded by William the Conqueror.
Charleston Manor - Westdean
Norman, Tudor & Georgian architectural styles - Romanesque window in the Norman wing.
Bull House - Lewes
15th century half-timbered house - was home of Tom Paine.

Bateman's - Burwash
17th century - watermill - home of Rudyard Kipling.
Bodiam Castle - Nr. Hawkshurst
14th century - noted example of mediaeval moated military architecture.
Great Dixter - Northiam
15th century half-timbered manor house - great hall - Lutyens gardens
Glynde Place - Nr. Lewes
16th century flint & brick - built around courtyard-collection of paintings by Rubens, Hoppner, Kneller, Lely, Zoffany.
Michelham Priory - Upper Dicker, Nr. Hailsham
13th century Augustinian Priory - became Tudor farmhouse - working watermill, ancient stained glass, etc., enclosed by moat.
Royal Pavilion - Brighton
Built for Prince Regent by Nash upon classical villa by Holland. Exotic Building - has superb original works of art lent by H.M. The Queen. Collections of Regency furniture also Art Nouveau & Art Deco in the Art Gallery & Museum.
Sheffield Park - Nr. Uckfield
Beautiful Tudor House - 18th century alterations - splendid staircase.

Cathedrals & Churches

Alfriston (St. Andrew)
14th century - transition from decorated style to perpendicular, Easter sepulchre.
Boxgrove (St. Mary & St. Blaise)
13th century choir with 16th century painted decoration on vaulting. Relic of Benedictine priory. 16th century chantry. Much decoration.
Chichester Cathedral
Norman & earliest Gothic. Large Romanesque relief sculptures in south choir aisle.
Etchingham (St. Mary & St. Nicholas)
14th century. Old glass, brasses, screen, carved stalls.
Hardham (St. Botolph)
11th century - 12th century wall paintings.
Rotherfield (St. Denys)
16th century font cover, 17th century canopied pulpit, glass by Burne-Jones, wall paintings, Georgian Royal Arms.

Sussex

Sompting (St. Mary)
11th century Saxon tower - Rhenish Helm Spire - quite unique.
Worth (St. Nicholas)
10th century - chancel arch is the largest Saxon arch in England. German carved pulpit c.1500 together with altar rails.
Winchelsea (St. Thomas the Apostle)
14th century - choir & aisles only. Canopied sedilia & piscina.

Museums & Galleries

Barbican House Museum - Lewes
Collection relating to pre-historic, Romano-British & , mediaeval antiquities of the area. Prints & water colours of the area.
Battle Museum-Battle
Remains from archeological sites in area. Diorama of Battle of Hastings.
Bignor Roman Villa Collection - Bignor
4th century mosaics, Samian pottery, hypocaust, etc.
Brighton Museum & Art Gallery - Brighton
Old Master Paintings, watercolours, ceramics, furniture. Surrealist paintings, Art Nouveau & Art Deco applied art, musical instruments & many other exhibits.

Marlipins Museum - Shoreham
12th century building housing collections of ship models, photographs, old maps, geological specimens, etc.
Royal National Lifeboat Institution Museum - Eastbourne
Lifeboats of all types used from earliest times to present.
Tower 73 - Eastbourne
Martello tower restored to display the history of these forts. Exhibition of equipment, uniforms & weapons of the times.
The Toy Museum - Rottingdean, Brighton
Toys & playthings from many countries - children's delight.

Other things to see & do

Bewl Water - Nr. Wadhurst
Boat trips, walks, adventure playground
Chichester Festival Theatre - Chichester
Summer season of plays from May to September.
Goodwood Racecourse

The Royal Pavilion. Brighton.

SUSSEX
Map reference

1	Fuente	23	Chick
2	Howard	24	Simpson
3	Birchell	25	Ticktum
4	Earlam	25	Cox
5	Hansell	26	Skinner
5	Buxton	27	Gough
6	Gregory	28	Pontifex
7	Grocott	29	Mulcare
8	Bruford	30	Field
9	Waller	31	Francis
9	Trotman	32	Steele
10	Blencowe	33	Hadfield
11	Dridge	33	Brinkhurst
12	Wilson	33	Luck
13	Dimopoulos	33	Foster
15	Day	34	Woodhams
17	Lloyd	35	Jempson
18	Cooper	36	Taylor
19	Kent	36	Carver
20	Wilkin	37	Salmon
21	Fowler	38	Hynes
22	Page	39	Evans

Sussex

		rate from £ per person	children taken	evening meals	animals taken
Drew & Lesley Wilson **Crouchers Bottom** **Country Hotel** **Birdham Road** **Apuldram PO20 7EH** Tel: **(01243) 784995** Fax 01243 539797 Open: **ALL YEAR** Map Ref No. 12	Nearest Road: A.27 'Crouchers Bottom' is a converted 1920s farmhouse standing in its own grounds. Offering 6 delightful, en-suite rooms, each with colour T.V., clock radio, tea-making facilities, hair dryer, direct-dial phones, etc. Good wheelchair access. A brick-laid patio overlooks a 'sunken' lawn & small pond with waterfowl. Set in lovely countryside, with views of Chichester Cathedral. Also, Halnaker Mill, with the South Downs. Delicious evening meals available.	£31.50 CREDIT CARD VISA M'CARD AMEX	Y	Y	Y
Peter & Sarah Fuente **Mill Lane House** **Slindon** **Arundel** **BN18 0RP** Tel: **(01243) 814440** Open: **ALL YEAR** Map Ref No. 01	Nearest Road: A.27, A.29 Magnificent views to the coast. Situated in a beautiful downland village with many miles of footpaths. Superb bird-watching locally. All of the 7 comfortable rooms are en-suite & have T.V.s. Within easy reach are Pagham & Chichester Harbour, Arundel Castle, Fishbourne Roman Palace, Goodwood, Chichester, the cathedral & the Festival Theatre. Beaches 6 miles. Excellent pubs within easy walking distance.	£18.50	Y	Y	Y
Mrs Benedetta Howard **Platnix Farm Oast** **Harts Green** **Sedlescombe** **Battle TN33 0RT** Tel: **(01424) 870214** Open: **ALL YEAR** Map Ref No. 02	Nearest Road: A.21 A delightful listed oast house, with a heavily beamed interior. Situated in beautiful countryside on a working sheep farm with a fishing lake; off the beaten track. Accommodation is in 2 double bedrooms, en-suite, & 1 delightful, round, twin-bedded room, each with T.V. & tea/coffee-making facilities. Within easy reach of Bodiam & Sissinghurst Castle. You can be sure of a warm & friendly welcome here.	£20.00 *see PHOTO over*	Y	N	Y
Sally & Geoffrey Earlam **Timbers Edge** **Spronketts Lane** **Warninglid** **Bolney RH17 5TE** Tel: **(01444) 461456** Open: **ALL YEAR** Map Ref No. 04	Nearest Road: A.23, A.272 Beautiful Sussex country house set in over 2 acres of formal garden (with swimming pool) & surrounded by woodlands. There are 4 very attractive bedrooms, each with colour T.V. & beverage-making facilities; some have private bathroom. Located within easy reach of Gatwick Airport (20 mins), Hickstead (10 mins), Ardingly (25 mins), Nymans & Leonardslee Gardens (10 mins), & Brighton (30 mins).	£20.00	Y	N	N
Ruth & Clive Buxton **Adelaide Hotel** **51 Regency Square** **Brighton BN1 2FF** Tel: **(01273) 205286** Fax 01273 220904 Open: **ALL YEAR** Map Ref No. 05	Nearest Road: A.259 A warm welcome, friendly service, comfort & delicious food are the hallmarks of this elegant Grade II listed Regency town-house hotel, modernised but retaining the charm of yesteryear. Centrally situated in Brighton's premier sea-front square, with parking beneath. There are 12 peaceful en-suite bedrooms, tastefully furnished & equipped with 'phone, colour T.V., etc. A beautiful 4-poster bedroom available. Easy access to A.23, 30 mins Gatwick.	£32.50 CREDIT CARD VISA M'CARD AMEX	Y	Y	N

Platnix Farm Oast. Sedlescombe.

Sussex

		rate from £ per person	children taken	evening meals	animals taken
John & Daphne Hansell **Trouville Hotel** **11 New Steine** **Brighton** **BN2 1PB** **Tel: (01273) 697384** **Open: FEB - DEC** **Map Ref No. 05**	Nearest Road: A.23, A.259 The Trouville is a Regency, Grade II listed townhouse, tastefully restored & furnished. Accommodation is in 9 attractive rooms, each with colour T.V. & tea/coffee-making facilities. En-suite & 4-poster rooms available. Situated in a charming sea-front square, the Trouville is convenient for shopping, the Pavilion, the Lanes, Marina & Conference Centre & the many restaurants which are all within walking distance.	£18.00 CREDIT CARD VISA M'CARD AMEX	Y	N	N
Mrs C. B. Gregory **Braemar Guest House** **Steyning Road** **Rottingdean** **Brighton BN2 7GA** **Tel: (01273) 304263** **Open: ALL YEAR** **Map Ref No. 06**	Nearest Road: A.259 A charming house, family-run, offering 14 pleasant, comfortable rooms with modern facilities. The proprietors really go out of their way to make their guests' stay a memorable one. From here, Rudyard Kipling's house is only 2 minutes' walk. The town is a famous smuggling place, with many ancient buildings & a Saxon church. There are a multitude of places to discover in the area, making this an ideal base for touring.	£15.00	Y	N	Y
Mrs D. A. Birchell **Holly House** **Beaconsfield Road** **Chelwood Gate** **RH17 7LF** **Tel: (01825) 740484** **Open: ALL YEAR** **Map Ref No. 03**	Nearest Road: A.275 Holly House, an early-Victorian forest farmhouse with character, offers a warm, friendly welcome to visitors. A 1-acre garden with long views. Situated in an Ashdown Forest village & ideal for touring Sussex, with many N.T. properties nearby. A comfortable lounge is available, & breakfast is taken in the conservatory overlooking the garden. The pleasant rooms have tea-making facilities & T.V.. A small swimming pool heated during the summer. Animals welcome.	£18.50	Y	Y	Y
Mr Allan Bruford **66 The Street** **Boxgrove** **Chichester** **PO18 0EE** **Tel: (01243) 774085** **Open: ALL YEAR** **Map Ref No. 08**	Nearest Road: A.27 Opposite Boxgrove Priory (c. 1105 A.D.) & 1 mile from Goodwood. This turn-of-the-century village house, with rear annex accommodation, offers en-suite twin & 4-poster bedrooms, both with r/c colour T.V., radio/alarm & tea/coffee-making facilities. Trouser press in 4-poster bedroom. Approached through the quiet garden, & with its own private breakfast room, this accommodation is renowned for its sumptuous English breakfasts, & features beamed & flint walls.	£20.00	N	N	N
Robert Grocott **The Old Store Guest House** **Stane Street** **Halnaker** **Chichester PO18 0QL** **Tel: (01243) 531977** **Open: ALL YEAR** **Map Ref No. 07**	Nearest Road: A.27, A.285 An impressive 18th-century Grade II listed house, adjoining the Goodwood Estate. All of the 7 comfortable rooms at The Old Store have en-suite shower rooms, tea/coffee-making facilities, colour T.V.s, hairdryer & trouser press. A full English breakfast is served in a most charming breakfast room. Car park. There is an excellent pub/restaurant within walking distance. The Old Store is ideally situated for Chichester, Bosham, Portsmouth, Petworth, Arundel & Brighton.	£26.00 CREDIT CARD VISA M'CARD	Y	N	N

Hatpins. Old Bosham.

Sussex

		rate from £ per person	children taken	evening meals	animals taken
Mrs Mary Waller **Hatpins** **Bosham Lane** **Old Bosham** **Chichester PO18 8HG** **Tel: (01243) 572644** **Open: ALL YEAR** **Map Ref No. 09**	Nearest Road: A.259 Situated in the charming, picturesque harbour village of Old Bosham, 3 miles west of Chichester, & near to Goodwood House, H.M.S. Victory & the Mary Rose, this elegant property offers luxurious & inviting interior-designed decor & antiques, including a half-tester & Victorian brass beds, & a sauna. Suitable, & welcoming, for honeymoon couples. All rooms have private/en-suite bathrooms. A delightful home.	£22.50 *see PHOTO over*	N	N	N
Susan & Antony Trotman **White Barn** **Crede Lane** **Bosham** **Chichester** **PO18 8NX** **Tel: (01243) 573113** **Open: ALL YEAR** **Map Ref No. 09**	Nearest Road: A.259 An outstanding modern, open-plan house with heavily timbered interior. Located in the attractive Saxon harbour village of Bosham. Accommodation is in 3 delightful en-suite bedrooms with tea/coffee-making facilities & radio. A charming sitting room, with colour T.V. & log fire on chilly evenings. Breakfast is served overlooking the pleasant, colourful garden. Memorable meals, using only the freshest ingredients whenever possible. Every care is taken to ensure your comfort. Children over 10 yrs.	£25.00 *see PHOTO over* CREDIT CARD VISA M'CARD	Y	Y	N
Peter & Anna Blencowe **The Old Rectory** **Cot Lane** **Chidham** **Chichester PO18 8TA** **Tel: (01243) 572088** **Open: ALL YEAR** **Map Ref No. 10**	Nearest Road: A.259 The Old Rectory is a large, comfortable period house, set in a country lane in the quiet village of Chidham. 5 charming bedrooms, 3 with private facilities, a colour T.V., tea-making facilities, a radio & electric underblankets. There is a delightful lounge, with a colour T.V. & grand piano, & a large garden with a swimming pool. Opposite the Saxon church, & close to the village pub serving excellent meals. Chichester Harbour is nearby.	£20.00	Y	N	Y
Mrs Jeannette Dridge **Chichester Lodge** **Oakwood School Drive** **East Ashling** **Chichester PO18 9AL** **Tel: (01243) 786560** **Open: ALL YEAR** **Map Ref No. 11**	Nearest Road: B.2178 A picturesque, Grade II listed 1840s Gothic Lodge set in very quiet country surroundings, yet only 4 minutes' drive from the city centre and the Festival Theatre. Accommodation is in 3 tastefully furnished bedrooms with 4-poster beds & en-suite bathrooms. An adjoining garden room has tea-making facilities and a cosy log-burning fire. You are assured of a warm and friendly welcome at this charming home.	£20.00	N	N	N
Michael & Rosemary Page **Suffolk House Hotel &** **Restaurant** **3 East Row** **Chichester PO19 1PD** **Tel: (01243) 778899** **Fax 01243 787282** **Open: ALL YEAR** **Map Ref No. 22**	Nearest Road: A.27, M.27 Suffolk House is an elegantly refurbished hotel which retains many of its beautiful features. A tranquil atmosphere prevails, & the hotel offers 10 tastefully furnished & well-equipped guest rooms, each with private facilities. Some have splendid views of the gardens & Priory Park. The restaurant offers excellent Cordon Bleu cuisine. Suffolk House is conveniently situated in the heart of the city, & is the ideal base from which to explore this delightful county.	£36.00 CREDIT CARD VISA M'CARD AMEX	Y	Y	Y

White Barn. Bosham.

Sussex

		rate from £ per person	children taken	evening meals	animals taken
Ann & Nick Dimopoulos **Laurel Cottage** **Snow Hill** **Crawley Down** **Crawley RH10 3EB** **Tel: (01342) 718984** **Fax 01342 718985** **Open: ALL YEAR** **Map Ref No. 13**	Nearest Road: M.23, A.264 A charming 17th-century cottage set in a large garden. All bedrooms are beautifully decorated & have colour T.V., satellite, radio/alarm clock & tea/coffee facilities. 1 en-suite. An elegant dining room where a full English breakfast is served. The cosy T.V. lounge, garden & indoor heated swimming pool are available for guests' relaxation. The famous Dukes Head pub & golf course are 5 mins' walk away. 10 mins from Gatwick Airport, Crawley & East Grinstead & trains 30 mins from London. Children welcome.	£25.00 CREDIT CARD VISA M'CARD AMEX	Y	N	N
Mrs Ann Hynes **Lye Green House** **Lye Green** **Crowborough TN6 1UU** **Tel: (01892) 652018** **Open: ALL YEAR** **Map Ref No. 38**	Nearest Road: A.26 A comfortable country house set in 6 acres of beautiful gardens with water. The rooms, with en-suite or private bathrooms, are large & very attractive & have T.V., tea/coffee-making facilities & hairdryers. A full English breakfast is served in the elegant dining room. Private fishing rights. The perfect base for visiting the many castles & gardens in the area. Gatwick 45 mins.	£17.50	N	N	N
Mrs Jill Day **Coneybury** **Hook Lane** **West Hoathly** **East Grinstead RH19 4PX** **Tel: (01342) 810200** **Fax 01342 810887** **Open: ALL YEAR (Excl. Xmas)** **Map Ref No. 15**	Nearest Road: B.2028 Situated in glorious countryside, this unique country house stands in its own grounds with breathtaking views towards the south coast over adjacent farmland & woodland. Accommodation is in a spacious twin & double-bedded room with tea/coffee-making facilities, T.V. & alarm radio. Private bathroom. Ideal centre, castles, gardens, coast, showground, country walks, village pubs, Sussex/Kent/Surrey borders. Easy access M.23, M.25, 10 miles Gatwick. Children over 10 yrs. Animals by arrangement.	£19.00	Y	N	Y
Denis & Jean Lloyd **Racehorse Cottage** **18 Nepcote** **Findon** **BN14 0SN** **Tel: (01903) 873783** **Open: ALL YEAR (Excl. Xmas)** **Map Ref No. 17**	Nearest Road: A.24 A comfortable cottage in a historic & peaceful downland village sheltering under Cissbury Ring. An excellent base for exploring. 4 miles from the South Coast & easily accessible by car, train or bus from Gatwick, Brighton, Arundel, Chichester & London. 2 twin-bedded rooms with downland views, tea/coffee-making facilities & a guests' own bathroom. Visitors have full use of the house, sun room, garden & T.V.. Evening meals with home baking & garden produce by arrangement. Children over 5 years welcome.	£15.00	Y	N	Y

When booking your accommodation please mention
The Best Bed & Breakfast

Bolebroke Watermill. Hartfield.

Sussex

		rate from £ per person	children taken	evening meals	animals taken

Christine & David Cooper
Bolebroke Watermill
Edenbridge Road
Hartfield
TN7 4JP
Tel: (01892) 770425
Fax 01892 770425
Open: MAR - NOV
Map Ref No. 18

Nearest Road: A.264

A magical watermill, first recorded in 1086 A.D., & an Elizabethan miller's barn offer 5 en-suite rooms of genuine, unspoilt rustic charm, set amid woodland, water & pasture, & used as the idyllic setting for the film 'Carrington'. The mill is complete with machinery, trap doors & very steep stairs. The barn has low doors & beamed ceilings, & includes the enchanting honeymooners' hayloft with a 4-poster bed. Light supper trays are available, & award-winning breakfasts are served in the adjoining mill-house. Children over 7.

£26.50 | Y | N | N
see PHOTO over
CREDIT CARD
VISA
M'CARD
AMEX

Mr Brian W. Kent
Parkside House
59 Lower Park Road
Hastings TN34 2LD
Tel: (01424) 433096
Fax 01424 421431
Open: ALL YEAR
Map Ref No. 19

Nearest Road: A.21, A.259

Located in a quiet residential conservation area, & set in an elevated position opposite a beautiful park. This elegant Victorian house retains all its original features, but with every modern facility. High standards of hospitality, comfort & good home-cooking are provided, creating an informal, friendly & welcoming atmosphere. Bedrooms are en-suite, & offer every luxury. The 'Apricot' room has an antique French bed. A quiet location only 15 mins' walk from the town centre & sea front.

£22.00 | Y | N | N
CREDIT CARD
VISA
M'CARD

Mr & Mrs M. Wilkin
Great Wapses Farm
Wineham, Albourne
Henfield BN5 9BJ
Tel: (01273) 492544
Open: ALL YEAR
Map Ref No. 20

Nearest Road: A.23, B.2118

An attractive Tudor/Georgian farmhouse set in rural & peaceful surroundings, with horses, calves, chickens, etc. Offering 3 rooms, all en-suite, with T.V. & tea/coffee-making facilities; 1 with 4-poster bed. Locally, there are plenty of nice pubs & restaurants serving good food. Within easy reach of Brighton, Gatwick, Goodwood & Hickstead. Tennis court available.

£17.00 | Y | N | Y
CREDIT CARD
AMEX

Mrs Sylvia Fowler
Frylands
Frylands Lane
Henfield BN5 9BP
Tel: (01403) 710214
Fax 01403 711449
Open: ALL YEAR (Excl. Xmas)
Map Ref No. 21

Nearest Road: A.272, A.23

Frylands is a timber-framed Tudor farmhouse in a quiet setting of farmland, woods & river. There are 3 lovely bedrooms, 1 with private facilities, all with colour T.V., radio & tea/coffee tray with home-made biscuits. Traditional breakfast cooked to order, with a selection of home-made preserves & local honey. Large garden with heated swimming pool. Good pubs & food nearby. 20 mins Gatwick Airport & Brighton.

£17.50 | Y | N | N

Michael & Mary Chick
The Tithe Barn
Brighton Road
Woodmancote
Henfield BN5 9ST
Tel: (01273) 492267
Fax 01273 833202
Open: ALL YEAR
Map Ref No. 23

Nearest Road: A.281, A.23

The Tithe Barn is a lovely old house converted from a flint barn, set in 2 acres of gardens & enjoying panoramic views to the South Downs. The cottage-style bedrooms are newly decorated in an appropriate style, & are extremely comfortable & well-equipped. Breakfast is served in the spacious conservatory in summer, & in the beamed, log-fired dining room in winter. The Tithe Barn is conveniently situated for the coast, N.T. properties, the Downs & Gatwick Airport.

£16.00 | Y | N | N

Sussex

		rate from £ per person	children taken	evening meals	animals taken
Douglas & Sally Simpson **Cleavers Lyng Hotel** **Church Road** **Herstmonceux BN27 1QJ** **Tel: (01323) 833131** **Fax 01323 833617** **Open: ALL YEAR** **Map Ref No. 24**	Nearest Road: A.271 A delightful 16th-century country hotel offering 7 pleasant, comfortable, en-suite rooms for visitors. Here, one finds age-blackened beams, inglenook fireplaces & a warm welcome. Situated adjacent to Herstmonceux Castle, it is an ideal base for touring the country as there are many historic sites & houses, museums & galleries, plus superb villages within a short drive. Cleavers Lyng is the perfect spot for a relaxing break.	£22.50 CREDIT CARD VISA M'CARD AMEX	Y	Y	Y
Mrs Elizabeth Cox **Glebe End** **Church Street** **Warnham** **Horsham RH12 3QW** **Tel: (01403) 261711** **Fax 01403 271741** **Open: ALL YEAR** **Map Ref No. 25**	Nearest Road: A.24 Glebe End is a fascinating mediaeval house, with a secluded, sunny, walled garden, set in the heart of Warnham village. It retains many original features, including heavy flagstones, curving ships' timbers & an inglenook fireplace. 4 comfortable single, twin or king-sized rooms are charmingly furnished with antiques. All are en-suite, with T.V. & hot-drink trays. Mrs Cox is an excellent cook, & meals are delicious. They include home-grown produce. Tennis & golf nearby. 20 mins to Gatwick Airport.	£18.00	Y	Y	Y
Mrs K. M. Ticktum **Westlands** **Brighton Road** **Monks Gate** **Horsham RH13 6JD** **Tel: (01403) 891383** **Fax 01403 891132** **Open: ALL YEAR** **Map Ref No. 25**	Nearest Road: A.281 Westlands is an elegant Victorian country house offering superb accommodation. It is set in an acre of beautifully tended garden, with terrace & fish pond (floodlit at night). The bedrooms are large & tastefully decorated, with private facilities & T.V.. A comfortable guest lounge, also, with T.V., where you can relax with tea or coffee. Village pubs/restaurants, a golf course & public gardens are nearby. Gatwick 20 mins, the coast 30 mins. An excellent Full English or Continental breakfast is served to order.	£20.00	Y	N	N
Mike & Susie Skinner **Clayton Wickham** **Farmhouse** **Belmont Lane** **Hurstpierpoint BN6 9EP** **Tel: (01273) 845698** **Fax 01273 846546** **Open: ALL YEAR** **Map Ref No. 26**	Nearest Road: A.23 A delightful, secluded 16th-century farmhouse with lovely views, set amidst the beautiful Sussex countryside. The friendly hosts have refurbished their home to a high standard, yet have retained many original features, hence there are a wealth of beams & a huge inglenook fireplace in the drawing room. There are also a variety of tastefully furnished & well-appointed bedrooms, including a super 4-poster en-suite. Excellent 4-course candlelit dinner by arrangement, & lovely 3-acre grounds with tennis court. Ample parking.	£20.00	Y	Y	Y

When booking your accommodation please mention
The Best Bed & Breakfast

Huggetts Furnace Farm. Five Ashes.

Sussex

		rate from £ per person	children taken	evening meals	animals taken
Carol Pontifex **Fairseat House** **Newick** **Lewes** **BN8 4PJ** **Tel: (01825) 722263** **Open: ALL YEAR** **Map Ref No. 28**	Nearest Road: A.272, A.275 Comfortable, elegant Edwardian house with 4 acres of garden & pasture, heated covered swimming pool, period furniture & interesting historical & family artifacts. 3 spacious, prettily decorated rooms with en-suite bathroom, including the Edwardian 4-poster bedroom. Warm, relaxed atmosphere. Excellent food with choice of kippers, fresh fruit salad or traditional English breakfasts, & delicious home-cooked dinners & light suppers. Convenient Gatwick & Glyndbourne.	£19.00 CREDIT CARD VISA M'CARD	Y	Y	Y
Gillian & John Mulcare **Huggetts Furnace Farm** **Stonehurst Lane** **Five Ashes** **Mayfield TN20 6LL** **Tel: (01825) 830220** **Fax 01435 866610** **Open: ALL YEAR** **Map Ref No. 29**	Nearest Road: A.272 A beautiful mediaeval farmhouse (Grade II listed) set well off the beaten track in tranquil countryside. 3 attractive bedrooms, all with en-suite/private facilities, radio & tea/coffee trays. The oak-beamed guests' room has an inglenook fireplace (with log fires on chilly evenings) & a T.V.. Excellent & creatively cooked dinners & breakfasts use the best home-grown & local produce. Heated outdoor swimming pool, & 120 acres of grounds. Gatwick 45 mins, & 30 mins to the coast. Nearby, also, N.T. properties. Children over 5.	£22.50 *see PHOTO over*	Y	Y	N
Mr & Mrs John Field **Mill Farm** **Trotton** **Petersfield GU31 5EL** **Tel: (01730) 813080** **Open: ALL YEAR** **Map Ref No. 30**	Nearest Road: A.272 A Sussex country house set in 15 acres of pasture. A large garden, with a grass tennis court. Delightful accommodation in 4 pleasant rooms, 1 en-suite, each with superb views over the South Downs. Colour T.V.s & tea-making facilities. Log fires in the hall & drawing room. Lovely walks & excellent pubs. Chichester, Goodwood & Petworth Houses, Arundel Castle, Heathrow, Gatwick & the coast within easy reach. Ideal as a holiday base.	£15.00	Y	N	N
Mr & Mrs J. C. Francis **Mizzards Farm** **Rogate** **Petersfield GU31 5HS** **Tel: (01730) 821656** **Fax 01730 821655** **Open: ALL YEAR (Excl. Xmas)** **Map Ref No. 31**	Nearest Road: A.3, A.272 This beautifully modernised farmhouse is set in gardens & farmland by the River Rother. All rooms have en-suite facilities & colour T.V.. There is an elegant drawing room, & breakfast is served in a magnificent vaulted hall dating from the 16th century. There is a covered swimming pool, for guests' use, & beautiful gardens. Situated close to the South Downs, the coast & several National Trust houses. Children over 7 years welcome.	£23.00 *see PHOTO over*	Y	N	N
Alma Steele **New House Farm** **Broadford Bridge Road** **West Chiltington** **Pulborough** **RH20 2LA** **Tel: (01798) 812215** **Open: ALL YEAR** **Map Ref No. 32**	Nearest Road: A.29 A lovely 15th-century house with oak beams & inglenook fireplaces. Situated in a village with a 12th-century church. 3 delightful rooms, 2 with en-suite facilities. T.V. & tea/coffee makers. A pleasant lounge with T.V. & a lovely garden. Gatwick Airport is easily reached. Parham Gardens, W. Sussex golf course, Amberley Wild Brooks, Arundel Castle, Petworth House. Polo at Cowdray Park. Children over 10 years accepted. Good evening meals available at local inns nearby. W. Chiltington golf course also, closeby.	£20.00	Y	N	N

Mizzards Farm. Rogate.

Sussex

		rate from £ per person	children taken	evening meals	animals taken
Sara Brinkhurst **Little Orchard House** **West Street** **Rye** **TN31 7ES** **Tel: (01797) 223831** **Open: ALL YEAR** **Map Ref No. 33**	Nearest Road: A.259, A.268 This charming Georgian townhouse, with traditional walled garden & Smuggler's Watchtower, is a delightful surprise at the heart of ancient Rye. Whilst a perfect base for touring, the house retains many original features. Open fires, antique furnishings & books ensure a peaceful, relaxed atmosphere. Generous country breakfasts feature organic & free-range local products. 3 lovely en-suite bedrooms - 1 with 4-poster - have colour T.V. & hot drinks tray. A romantic suite in the detached Tower offers real seclusion. Children over 12 welcome.	£30.00 CREDIT CARD VISA M'CARD	Y	N	N
Francis & Jenny Hadfield **Jeake's House** **Mermaid Street** **Rye TN31 7ET** **Tel: (01797) 222828** **Fax 01797 222623** **Open: ALL YEAR** **Map Ref No. 33**	Nearest Road: A.259, A.268 Jeakes House is an outstanding 17th-century listed building. Retaining original features, including oak beams & wood panelling, & decorated throughout with antiques. 12 comfortable rooms overlook the peaceful gardens, with either en-suite or private facilities, T.V. & tea/coffee facilities. 4-poster available. Dine in the galleried former Baptist chapel, where a choice of full English, wholefood vegetarian or Continental breakfast is served. Located in one of Britain's most picturesque mediaeval streets.	£20.50 *see PHOTO over* CREDIT CARD VISA M'CARD AMEX	Y	N	Y
Mrs Sarah Foster **The Old Vicarage Hotel** **15 East Street** **Rye TN31 7JY** **Tel: (01797) 225131** **Fax 01797 225131** **Open: FEB - DEC** **Map Ref No. 33**	Nearest Road: A.259 A family-run town-house hotel in a gracious Queen Anne building dating from 1706, offering 4 comfortable bedrooms, all individually furnished in period style, 2 of them having tester beds with fully closing curtains. The elegant restaurant, which serves French/international food with both a fixed-price & a la carte menus, has extensive views over the river & Romney Marsh. A charming hotel, ideal for a relaxing break in Rye.	£28.00 CREDIT CARD VISA M'CARD AMEX	Y	Y	Y
John & Sheila Luck **Green Hedges** **Hillyfields** **Rye Hill** **Rye** **TN31 7NH** **Tel: (01797) 222185** **Open: ALL YEAR (Excl. Xmas)** **Map Ref No. 33**	Nearest Road: A.268 Green Hedges is a large Edwardian house within an easy 10-minute walk of the beautiful mediaeval town of Rye. Set in 1 1/2 acres of lovely gardens with a heated outdoor pool (May to Sept., weather permitting). 3 delightful en-suite rooms, each with colour T.V. & tea/coffee-making facilities. Breakfast prepared from best local produce. Home-made preserves, fruit from garden, (seasonal) local fish, home-made waffles & free-range eggs. Wonderful countryside for touring. Childen over 12 yrs.	£23.50 CREDIT CARD VISA M'CARD	Y	N	N

When booking your accommodation please mention
The Best Bed & Breakfast

Jeake's House.   Rye.

The Old Parsonage. West Dean.

Sussex

		rate from £ per person	children taken	evening meals	animals taken
Woodhams sonage West Dea... Alfriston Seaford BN25 4AL Tel: (01323) 870432 Open: ALL YEAR Map Ref No. 34	Nearest Road: A.259 The Old Parsonage, built in 1280 & reputed to be the oldest continually inhabited small house in England, is situated in a hamlet in the Friston Forest, 1 mile from the Seven Sisters coastline. With chalk & flint walls 2 1/2 feet thick, massive oak beams, stone spiral staircases, log fires & extensive gardens, the house beautifully combines an antique setting with modern comforts. Eastbourne, Brighton & Glyndebourne nearby. Children over 12 yrs.	£25.00 see PHOTO over	Y	N	N
Jean & David Salmon Sliders Farm Sliders Lane Furners Green Uckfield TN22 3RT Tel: (01825) 790258 Fax 01825 790125 Open: ALL YEAR Map Ref No. 37	Nearest Road: A.275 A listed 16th-century farmhouse, with a wealth of oak beams & inglenook fireplaces, in a secluded setting on the Sussex Weald. All rooms are en-suite, with T.V. & tea/coffee facilities. Home-grown produce & home-cooking. A guests' dining room & lounge with inglenooks & billiard table. A heated outdoor pool, all-weather tennis court & own private trout fishing. Convenient for Ardingly Showground, Sheffield Park Gardens, the Bluebell Railway & many N.T. properties & gardens. Coast & Gatwick 30 mins (car). London 45 mins (train).	£17.00 see PHOTO over	Y	Y	N
Mrs M. Ruth Evans Dale Hamme Piltdown Uckfield TN22 3XY Tel: (01825) 712422 Open: ALL YEAR Map Ref No. 39	Nearest Road: A.272 Set in its own grounds of 10 acres in idyllic countryside, Dale Hamme is a 15th-century yeoman's hall house of classical oak-framed construction; it is a 'black & white' period gem. Internally, it has inglenook fireplaces & a wealth of oak beams. There are 4 attractive & well-equipped bedrooms, 2 with en-suite/private bathrooms. Conveniently situated for Glyndebourne, Gatwick Airport, Ashdown Forest, Brighton, Bluebell Railway & the Sussex Downs.	£15.00	Y	N	Y
Mrs Sarah Jempson Cleveland House Rookery Lane Winchelsea TN36 4EE Tel: (01797) 226256 Open: ALL YEAR Map Ref No. 35	Nearest Road: A.259 Cleveland House is a beautiful 18th-century listed house situated in the centre of the historic Cinque Port town of Winchelsea. Its magnificent 1 1/2 acre walled garden, with heated swimming pool & games room, has superb views to the sea. 1 double room with private bathroom, overlooking the sea, & 1 twin room with en-suite shower & toilet, overlooking the rose garden. Both rooms have colour T.V. & hot-drinks tray. Only 2 miles from Rye, it is ideally situated for visiting the many local castles, gardens & places of interest.	£25.00 CREDIT CARD VISA M'CARD	Y	N	N
Dorene & John Taylor Aspen House 13 Winchester Road Worthing BN11 4DJ Tel: (01903) 230584 Open: ALL YEAR Map Ref No. 36	Nearest Road: A.259 Situated in a quiet location, yet close to the sea front & town centre, this elegant Edwardian house offers a caring & relaxed atmosphere. There is 1 single room with shower, 2 doubles & a twin with full en-suite facilities. All rooms are tastefully furnished, with colour T.V., hairdryer, radio alarm & hospitality trays. Traditional full English or Continental breakfast is served in the attractive period dining room.	£22.00	N	N	N

Sliders Farm. Furners Green.

Sussex

		rate from £ per person	children taken	evening meals	animals taken
John & Doreen Carver **Bonchurch House** **1 Winchester Road** **Worthing** **BN11 4DJ** **Tel: (01903) 202492** **Open: ALL YEAR** **Map Ref No. 36**	Nearest Road: A.259 Bonchurch is a home-from-home guest house where a warm welcome is extended to all guests. There are 6 bedrooms, all with shaver points & en-suite shower/bathroom, T.V. & tea/coffee-making facilities. There is, for the convenience of guests, a comfortable lounge with colour T.V.. Home cooking is a speciality. Ideally situated in a picturesque setting, yet close to the sea front, shops & entertainment.	£18.00	Y	Y	N

All the establishments mentioned in this guide

are members of

The Worldwide Bed & Breakfast Association

When booking your accommodation please mention
The Best Bed & Breakfast

Warwickshire

Warwickshire
(Heart of England)

Warwickshire contains much that is thought of as traditional rural England, but it is a county of contradictions. Rural tranquillity surrounds industrial towns, working canals run along with meandering rivers, the mediaeval splendour of Warwick Castle vies with the handsome Regency grace of Leamington Spa.

Of course, Warwickshire is Shakespeare's county, with his birthplace, Stratford-upon-Avon standing at the northern edge of the Cotswolds. You can visit any of half a dozen houses with Shakespearian associations, see his tomb in the lovely Parish church or enjoy a performance by the world famous Royal Shakespeare Company in their theatre on the banks of the River Avon.

Warwickshire was created as the Kingdom of Mercia after the departure of the Romans. King Offa of Mercia left us his own particular mark - a coin which bore the imprint of his likeness known as his "pen" & this became our penny. Lady Godiva was the wife of an Earl of Mercia who pleaded with her husband to lessen the taxation burden on his people. He challenged her to ride naked through the streets of Coventry as the price of her request. She did this knowing that her long hair would cover her nakedness, & the people, who loved her, stayed indoors out of respect. Only Peeping Tom found the temptation irresistible.

The 15th, 16th, & 17th centuries were the heyday of fine building in the county, when many gracious homes were built. Exceptional Compton Wynyates has rosy pink bricks, twisted chimney stacks, battlements & moats & presents an unforgettably romantic picture of a perfect Tudor House.

Coventry has long enjoyed the reputation of a thriving city, noted for its weaving of silks and ribbons, learned from the refugee Huguenots. When progress brought industry, watches, bicycles & cars became the mainstay of the city. Coventry suffered grievously from aerial bombardment in the war & innumerable ancient & treasured buildings were lost.

A magnificent new Cathedral stands besides the shell of the old. Mystery plays enacting the life of Christ are performed in the haunting ruin.

Warwick Castle.

Warwickshire

Warwickshire
Gazeteer

Areas of Outstanding Natural Beauty
The Edge Hills

Historic Houses & Castles

Arbury Hall - Nuneaton
18th century Gothic mansion - made famous by George Elliot as Cheverel Manor - paintings, period furnishings, etc.

Compton Wynyates
15th century - famous Tudor house - pink brick, twisted chimneys, battlemented walls. Interior almost untouched - period furnishing.

Coughton Court - Alcester
15th century - Elizabethan half-timbered wings. Holds Jacobite relics.

Harvard House - Stratford-upon-Avon
16th century - home of mother of John Harvard, University founder.

Homington Hall - Shipston-on-Stour
17th century with fine 18th century plasterwork.

Packwood House - Hockley Heath
Tudor timber framed house - with 17th century additions. Famous yew garden.

Ragley Hall - Alcester
17th century Palladian - magnificent house with fine collection of porcelain, paintings, furniture, etc. & a valuable library.

Shakespeare's Birthplace Trust Properties - Stratford-upon-Avon

Anne Hathaway's Cottage - Shottery
The thatched cottage home of Anne Hathaway.

Hall's Croft - Old Town
Tudor house where Shakespeare's daughter Susanna lived.

Mary Arden's House - Wilmcote
Tudor farmhouse with dovecote. Home of Shakespeare's mother.

New Place - Chapel Street
Shakespeare's last home - the foundations of his house are preserved in Elizabethan garden.

Birthplace of Shakespeare - Henley Street
Many rare Shakespeare relics exhibited in this half-timbered house.

Lord Leycester Hospital - Warwick
16th century timber framed group around courtyard - hospital for poor persons in the mediaeval guilds.

Upton House - Edge Hill
Dating from James II reign - contains Brussels tapestries, Sevres porcelain, Chelsea figurines, 18th century furniture & other works of art, including Old Masters.

Warwick Castle - Warwick
Splendid mediaeval castle - site was originally fortified more than a thousand years ago. Present castle 14th century. Armoury.

Cathedrals & Churches

Astley (St. Mary the Virgin)
17th century - has remains of 14th century collegiate church. 15th century painted stalls.

Beaudesert (St. Nicholas)
Norman with fine arches in chancel.

Brailes (St. George)
15th century - decorated nave & aisles - 14th century carved oak chest.

Crompton Wynyates
Church of Restoration period having painted ceiling.

Lapworth (St. Mary)
13th & 14th century - steeple & north aisle connected by passage.

Preston-on-Stour (The Blessed Virgin Mary)
18th century. Gilded ceiling, 17th century glass

Tredington (St. Gregory)
Saxon walls in nave - largely14th century, 17th century pulpit. Fine spire.

Warwick (St. Mary)
15th century Beauchamp Chapel, vaulted choir, some 17th century Gothic.

Wooten Wawen (St. Peter)
Saxon, with remnants of mediaeval wall painting, 15th century screens & pulpit: small 17th century chained library.

Museums & Galleries

The Royal Shakespeare Theatre Picture Gallery - Stratford-upon-Avon
Original designs & paintings, portraits of famous actors, etc.

Motor Museum - Stratford-upon-Avon
Collection of cars, racing, vintage, exotic, replica of 1930 garage. Fashions, etc. of 1920's era.

WARWICKSHIRE
Map reference

1	Waterworth	13	Hallworth
2	Wilson	13	Mander
3	Howard	13	Workman
4	Boucher	13	Everitt
5	Lawson	13	R. Evans
6	Lea	14	Draisey
7	Walliker	15	Trought
8	Hutsby	16	Greenwood
9	Mills	17	Lyon
11	Mawle	18	Stanton
12	Vernon Miller		
12	Smith		
13	Evans		
13	Andrews		
13	P. Evans		
13	Wootton		
13	Castelli		
13	Pettitt		
13	Wotton		
13	Walters		
13	Tozer		
13	Short		

Sandbarn Farm. Hampton Lucy.

Warwickshire

		rate from £ per person	children taken	evening meals	animals taken
Mrs H. P. Waterworth **Sandbarn Farm** **Hampton Lucy** **CV35 8AU** **Tel: (01789) 842280** **Open: ALL YEAR (Excl. Xmas)** **Map Ref No. 01**	Nearest Road: M.40, A.439 17th-century farmhouse in charming village, offering luxury bed and breakfast accommodation. Tranquil setting with lovely views, only 3 miles from Stratford-upon-Avon. Warwick and Kenilworth Castles are nearby; also, many National Trust houses and parks. Of the 5 guest bedrooms, 4 are en-suite and 1 private. Single availability. Residents' lounge and T.V.. Children over 5 please. Easy access to N.E.C. & N.A.C..	£25.00 *see PHOTO over*	Y	N	N
Mrs Joan Wilson **Ferndale Guest House** **45 Priory Road** **Kenilworth CV8 1LL** **Tel: (01926) 53214** **Fax 01926 58336** **Open: ALL YEAR (Excl. Xmas & New Year)** **Map Ref No. 02**	Nearest Road: A.46 You are assured of a warm welcome in this family-run, spacious Victorian house situated in a quiet tree-lined avenue only 5 mins' walk from the town centre. All of the 8 comfortable bedrooms are en-suite & tastefully decorated & include colour T.V. & coffee/tea-making facilities. A guests' T.V. lounge is available throughout the day. Ideally located for touring & within easy reach of Warwick, Coventry, Leamington Spa, the N.E.C., Stoneleigh Agricultural Centre & Warwick University.	£18.00	Y	N	Y
Carolyn Howard **Willowbrook Farmhouse** **Lighthorne Road** **Kineton** **CV35 0JL** **Tel: (01926) 640475** **Fax 01926 641747** **Open: ALL YEAR (Excl. Xmas)** **Map Ref No. 03**	Nearest Road: B.4100, M.40 Willowbrook is a very comfortable house in gardens & paddocks in rolling countryside, handy for Stratford-upon-Avon, Warwick & the Cotswolds, the N.A.C., the N.E.C. & the Motor Heritage Centre. Twin & double rooms, 1 en-suite, all with tea trays, T.V.s & lovely views. Guests' sitting room, a dining room, winter log fires, c/h & antiques. Enjoy watching lambs & rare breeds of poultry, or sit on the terrace by the garden pond on summer evenings. Friendly, attentive service. M.40 (Ex.12) only 3 1/2 miles.	£15.50 🚭	Y	N	Y
Mrs Dawn Boucher **Lapworth Lodge** **Country Guest House** **Bushwood Lane** **Lapworth B94 5PJ** **Tel: (01564) 783038** **Fax 01564 783635** **Open: ALL YEAR** **Map Ref No. 04**	Nearest Road: A.3400 This imposing Georgian house enjoys outstanding views over the glorious Warwickshire countryside. All of the 7 lovely bedrooms are exceptionally large, with good en-suite facilities, co-ordinated decor, colour T.V., tea/coffee makers & central heating. The excellent 4-course breakfast is renowned. This is a guest house for those who prefer superior comforts combined with the warmest of welcomes. A beautiful home which is conveniently situated for Stratford-upon-Avon, Warwick & the N.E.C..	£22.50 CREDIT CARD VISA M'CARD	Y	N	N
Christine & David Lawson **8 Clarendon Crescent** **Leamington Spa** **CV32 5NR** **Tel: (01926) 429840** **Open: ALL YEAR (Excl. Xmas & New Year)** **Map Ref No. 05**	Nearest Road: A.452 A Grade II listed Regency house overlooking a private dell. Situated in a quiet backwater of Leamington. Elegantly furnished with antiques, & offering 6 tastefully furnished bedrooms, 5 en-suite. A delicious Full English breakfast is served. Located only 5 minutes from the town centre. Very convenient for Warwick, Stratford, Stoneleigh Agricultural Centre, Warwick University & the National Exhibition Centre. Children over 3 yrs.	£25.00 *see PHOTO over*	Y	N	N

8 Clarendon Crescent. Leamington Spa.

Ambion Court Hotel.   Dadlington.

Warwickshire

		rate from £ per person	children taken	evening meals	animals taken
Deborah Lea **Crandon House** **Avon Dassett** **Leamington Spa** **CV33 0AA** **Tel: (01295) 770652** **Fax 01295 770652** **Open: ALL YEAR (Excl. Xmas)** **Map Ref No. 06**	Nearest Road: B.4100, M.40 Crandon House offers an especially warm welcome & exceptionally high standard of accommodation & comfort. Set in 20 acres of beautiful countryside. 3 pretty bedrooms with en-suite/private bathroom, T.V. & tea/coffee. Log fire. Excellent food & an extensive breakfast menu. A large garden. A tranquil rural retreat, yet within easy reach of Stratford, Warwick, Oxford & the Cotswolds. Located between the M.40 Jts 11 & 12 (4 miles). Evening meals & animals by arrangement. Children over 8 years.	£18.00 CREDIT CARD VISA M'CARD	Y	Y	Y
John & Wendy Walliker **Ambion Court Hotel** **The Green, Dadlington** **Nuneaton CV13 6JB** **Tel: (01455) 212292** **Fax 01455 213141** **Open: ALL YEAR** **Map Ref No. 07**	Nearest Road: A.5, M.69. A charming, modernised Victorian farmhouse, overlooking Dadlington's village green, set in rolling countryside 2 miles north of Hinckley. Rustic character abounds, & each room is well-appointed with en-suite bathroom, T.V., radio, 'phone & hospitality tray. The Pine Room is particularly imposing. A lounge, cocktail bar & excellent restaurant. Comfort, hospitality & exceptional tranquility for those seeking complete relaxation. No smoking in restaurant or bedrooms.	£25.00 *see PHOTO over* CREDIT CARD VISA M'CARD AMEX	Y	Y	Y
Sue Hutsby **Nolands Farm &** **Country Restaurant** **Oxhill** **CV35 0RJ** **Tel: (01926) 640309** **Fax 01926 641662** **Open: JAN - NOV** **Map Ref No. 08**	Nearest Road: A.422 Nolands Farm is situated in a tranquil valley surrounded by fields, woods & a lake for fishing. The 9 en-suite bedrooms are annexed to the house in converted stables, with some ground-floor bedrooms, some with a romantic 4-poster. Each has c/h, tea/coffee makers & T.V.. Dine in the beautiful granary-style restaurant, which is licensed & serves the freshest produce & fine cuisine. Everything for the discerning country lover. Clay-pigeon shooting, bicycles for hire & riding nearby. Children over 7.	£15.00 *see PHOTO over* CREDIT CARD VISA M'CARD	Y	Y	N
Alison Mills **Tibbits Farm** **Nethercote** **Flecknoe** **Rugby CV23 8AS** **Tel: (01788) 890239** **Open: ALL YEAR** **Map Ref No. 09**	Nearest Road: A.425, A.45 Retreat along pretty country lanes on the border of Warwickshire & Northants to the haven of this totally secluded 17th-century house, beautifully furnished with antiques, where superb accommodation is offered. The spacious & pretty bedrooms have books, magazines, tea/coffee, T.V., radio & en-suite bathroom. Idyllically situated within acres of rolling countryside, providing an ideal base for exploring an area rich in places of historical, scenic & cultural interest.	£19.00	Y	N	Y
Ken & Jackie Smith **Lower Farm** **Darlingscott** **Shipston-on-Stour** **CV36 4PN** **Tel: (01608) 682750** **Open: ALL YEAR** **Map Ref No. 12**	Nearest Road: A.429 On the edge of the Cotswolds, just off the Fosse Way in the pretty, unspoilt hamlet of Darlingscott stands this fine, 18th-century, listed farmhouse. 3 attractive double rooms, each with en-suite bathroom, colour T.V. & tea-making facilities. This is the perfect location from which to visit Chipping Campden. The magnificent gardens of Hidcote & Kiftsgate are 5 miles away, & Stratford-upon-Avon only 9 miles. Children over 8.	£20.00	Y	N	N

Nolands Farm & Country Restaurant.   Oxhill.

Warwickshire

		rate from £ per person	children taken	evening meals	animals taken
Rebecca Mawle **Lower Farm Barn** **Great Wolford** **Shipston-on-Stour** **CV36 5NQ** **Tel: (01608) 674435** **Open: ALL YEAR** **Map Ref No. 11**	Nearest Road: A.44, A.3400 This lovely, 100-year-old, converted barn stands in the small, peaceful Warwickshire village of Great Wolford. The property retains much of its original form, including exposed beams & ancient stone work. Now tastefully modernised, it makes a very comfortable home. The accommodation is in 2 beautifully furnished double rooms with en-suite facilities. A delightful base from which to explore this fascinating area, within easy reach of Stratford-upon-Avon.	£14.00	Y	N	Y
Mrs Liz Vernon Miller **Blackwell Grange Farm** **Blackwell** **Shipston-on-Stour** **Stratford-upon-Avon** **CV36 4PF** **Tel/Fax: (01608) 682357** **Open: ALL YEAR** **Map Ref No. 12**	Nearest Road: A.3400, A.429 Blackwell Grange is a Grade II listed farmhouse, part of which dates from 1603. Situated on the edge of a peaceful village, with fine views of the Ilmington Hills & surrounding countryside. Good food, log fires & comfortable rooms makes this a great place for relaxation. It includes 2 ground-floor en-suite bedrooms, suitable for disabled, & situated in converted stables. Ideal for touring the Cotswolds, Shakespeare Country & N.T. properties & gardens. 7 miles from Stratford, 8 miles Moreton-in-Marsh. Children over 7.	£22.50 *see PHOTO over* CREDIT CARD VISA M'CARD AMEX	Y	Y	N
Richard & Susan Evans **Oxstalls Farm Stud** **Warwick Road** **Stratford-upon-Avon** **CV37 0NS** **Tel: (01789) 205277** **Open: ALL YEAR** **Map Ref No. 13**	Nearest Road: A.439, M.40 This charming, thoroughbred stud farm overlooks the beautiful Welcombe Hill & golf course. It provides excellent accommodation for touring or relaxing in peaceful surroundings. 25 tastefully furnished bedrooms, many with en-suite facilities, T.V. & tea/coffee makers. For the keen fisherman there is also a well-stocked trout pond. A guided tour of the farm to see the animals is also available. 1 mile from Stratford town centre & the Royal Shakespeare Theatre. Children over 5.	£16.00	Y	N	N
Jo & Roger Pettitt **Parkfield** **3 Broad Walk** **Stratford-upon-Avon** **CV37 6HS** **Tel: (01789) 293313** **Open: ALL YEAR** **Map Ref No. 13**	Nearest Road: B.439 A delightful Victorian house, in a quiet location in Old Town just 5 minutes' walk to the town centre & the Royal Shakespeare Theatre. Ideally situated for touring the Cotswolds, Warwick Castle, etc.. 7 spacious & comfortable rooms, 5 en-suite, all with full central heating, colour T.V. & tea/coffee-making facilities. Excellent breakfasts. Private parking. Lots of tourist information available. Guests can be collected from the station. Children over 3 yrs welcome.	£18.00 (no smoking) CREDIT CARD VISA M'CARD	Y	N	N
Richard Workman **Ravenhurst** **2 Broad Walk** **Stratford-upon-Avon** **CV37 6HS** **Tel: (01789) 292515** **Open: ALL YEAR (Excl. Xmas)** **Map Ref No. 13**	Nearest Road: B.439, A.4390 A Victorian town house with a warm & friendly atmosphere. Ideally situated on the edge of the old town & only a few minutes' walk from the Shakespeare Theatre, town centre & places of historical interest. Enjoy the comfort & quiet of this family-run guest house, where all bedrooms have T.V. & tea/coffee-making facilities. Special double en-suite rooms available with 4-poster beds. The Workmans are Stratfordians, therefore local knowledge is a speciality. Children over 5.	£19.00 (no smoking) CREDIT CARD VISA M'CARD AMEX	Y	N	N

Blackwell Grange. Shipston-on-Stour.

Warwickshire

		rate from £ per person	children taken	evening meals	animals taken
Mr & Mrs I. Castelli **Minola Guest House** **25 Evesham Place** **Stratford-upon-Avon** **CV37 6HT** **Tel: (01789) 293573** **Open: ALL YEAR** **Map Ref No. 13**	Nearest Road: A.439 A comfortable house with a relaxed atmosphere, offering good accommodation in 5 rooms, 2 with private shower, 2 en-suite; all have colour T.V. & tea/coffee makers. Stratford offers a myriad of delights for the visitor, including the Royal Shakespeare Theatre. Set by the River Avon, this makes a lovely place for a picnic lunch or early evening meal before the performance. Cots are provided. Italian & French spoken.	£17.00	Y	N	N
Pat & Peter Short **Nando's** **18 - 20 Evesham Place** **Stratford-upon-Avon** **CV37 6HT** **Tel/Fax: (01789) 204907** **Open: ALL YEAR** **Map Ref No. 13**	Nearest Road: A.34, A.439 Pat & Peter extend the warmest of welcomes to their guests. We pride ourselves on our quality of food & high standard of hygiene. Nando's is conveniently located only minutes away from the Royal Shakespeare Theatre. 21 rooms, 9 with en-suite facilities, all with colour T.V.. A residents' T.V. lounge is also available. Nando's makes the perfect base for visiting the many places of interest in the town and surrounding area. CREDIT CARD VISA M'CARD AMEX	£17.00	Y	N	Y
Mrs Mavis Evans **Kawartha House** **39 Grove Road** **Stratford-upon-Avon** **CV37 6PB** **Tel: (01789) 204469** **Fax 01789 292837** **Open: ALL YEAR** **Map Ref No. 13**	Nearest Road: A.439 Kawartha House is a well-appointed town house with a friendly atmosphere, overlooking the 'old town' park. It is located just a few minutes' walk from the town centre & is ideal for visiting the places of historic interest. Private parking is available. With pretty en-suite bedrooms & quality food, these are the ingredients for a memorable stay. This is a delightful base from which to explore Warwickshire, & is within easy reach of the Cotswolds with its many attractive villages. *see PHOTO over* CREDIT CARD VISA M'CARD	£13.00	Y	N	Y
Drenagh & Simon Wootton **Hardwick House** **1 Avenue Road** **Stratford-upon-Avon** **CV37 6UY** **Tel: (01789) 204307** **Fax 01789 296760** **Open: ALL YEAR** **Map Ref No. 13**	Nearest Road: A.439 You will be welcomed to 'Hardwick House', an impressive Victorian home in a quiet area, yet just 5 mins' walk to the town centre & the theatre. A choice of 14 clean & comfortable bedrooms, many with private facilities, all with T.V. & tea/coffee-making facilities. A residents' lounge, & parking space. Enjoy the friendly atmosphere & home-cooked breakfasts. An ideal base from which to explore Shakespeare country & the many places of historic interest. CREDIT CARD VISA M'CARD AMEX	£19.00	Y	N	N
Kevin & Jeanne Hallworth **The Croft** **49 Shipston Road** **Stratford-upon-Avon** **CV37 7LN** **Tel/Fax: (01789) 293419** **Open: ALL YEAR** **Map Ref No. 13**	Nearest Road: A.3400 The Croft is a friendly, family-run Victorian guest house only 200 yards from the River Avon. Accommodation is in 9 pleasant rooms, 4 with en-suite facilities, all with colour T.V. & tea/coffee-making facilities. Also, an attractive residents' lounge & garden are available. 5 minutes from the theatre, river boats & town. An ideal base for touring the Cotswolds, Warwick & many local places of interest. CREDIT CARD VISA M'CARD AMEX	£17.00	Y	Y	Y

Kawartha House. Stratford-upon-Avon.

Warwickshire

	rate from £ per person	children taken	evening meals	animals taken

Patricia Anne Andrews **Melita Private Hotel** **37 Shipston Road** **Stratford-upon-Avon** **CV37 7LN** **Tel: (01789) 292432** **Fax 01789 204867** **Open: ALL YEAR (Excl. Xmas)** **Map Ref No. 13**	Nearest Road: A.3400 An extremely friendly family-run hotel. Offering pleasant service, good food & accommodation in 12 excellent bedrooms, all with private facilities, colour T.V., tea/coffee & direct-dial telephones. A comfortable lounge/bar & pretty, award-winning garden for guests' use. Ample car parking. A pleasant 5-minute walk to Shakespearian properties/theatres, shopping centre & beautiful riverside gardens. Superbly situated for Warwick Castle, Coventry & the Cotswolds.	£22.50 *see PHOTO over* CREDIT CARD VISA M'CARD AMEX	Y	N	Y
Philip & Jean Evans **Sequoia House Hotel** **51/53 Shipston Road** **Stratford-upon-Avon** **CV37 7LN** **Tel: (01789) 268852** **Fax 01789 414559** **Open: ALL YEAR** **Map Ref No. 13**	Nearest Road: A.3400 A beautifully appointed private hotel situated across the River Avon from the Royal Shakespeare Theatre. 24 bedrooms (mostly en-suite), a cocktail bar, a cottage annex & a garden restaurant. The hotel is comfortably furnished, & decorated in a warm & restful style, with many extra thoughtful touches. The garden overlooks the town cricket ground & the old tramway. Pleasant walks along the banks of the River Avon opposite the Theatre & Holy Trinity Church. Children over 5.	£19.50 CREDIT CARD VISA M'CARD AMEX	Y	N	N
Mrs Margaret Everitt **Eastnor House Hotel** **33 Shipston Road** **Stratford-upon-Avon** **CV37 7LN** **Tel: (01789) 268115** **Fax 01789 266516** **Open: ALL YEAR** **Map Ref No. 13**	Nearest Road: A.3400 By the River Avon, 125 metres from Clopton Bridge, with private parking & just a stroll from theatres & Shakespeares' birthplace. This large Victorian townhouse, built for a wealthy draper, offers excellent accommodation, with oak panelling, central, open staircases, a pleasant breakfast room & elegant lounge. The spacious & tastefully furnished bedrooms have private bathrooms, a T.V. & a welcome tray. Breakfast is individually prepared, completing a comfortable & restful stay.	£21.00 CREDIT CARD VISA M'CARD AMEX	Y	N	N
Mrs Marian J. Walters **Church Farm, Dorsington** **Stratford-upon-Avon** **CV37 8AX** **Tel: (01789) 720471** **Mobile (0831) 504194** **Open: ALL YEAR** **Map Ref No. 13**	Nearest Road: B.439 A warm welcome awaits you at this mixed working farm with lakes, equestrian course & woodlands to explore. Situated on the edge of a quiet, pretty village, yet close to Stratford, Warwick, the Cotswolds & the N.E.C.. Accommodation is in 7 delightful rooms, some with en-suite facilities. Stabling & fishing available. An excellent base from which to explore the region. Mrs Walters can be contacted by fax on 01789 720830.	£14.00	Y	N	Y

When booking your accommodation please mention
The Best Bed & Breakfast

Melita Hotel. Stratford-upon-Avon.

Victoria Spa Lodge. Stratford-upon-Avon.

Warwickshire

		rate from £ per person	children taken	evening meals	animals taken
Mrs G. Lyon **Winton House, The Green** **Upper Quinton** **Stratford-upon-Avon** **CV37 8SX** **Tel: (01789) 720500** **Mobile 0831 485483** **Open: ALL YEAR (Excl. Xmas)** **Map Ref No. 17**	Nearest Road: B.4632 Built in 1856, this creeper-clad, Victorian farmhouse is situated in an Area of Outstanding Natural Beauty only 6 miles from Stratford. En-suite bedrooms feature an antique, wrought-iron half-tester, 4-poster pine box beds & old lace & hand-made quilts. A delicious choice at breakfast, with homemade jam & the 'Winton House Special' which changes daily. Colour T.V. & log fires in the guests' lounge. A lovely home set in an ideal position for touring, walking & cycling.	£21.00	Y	N	N
Paul & Dreen Tozer **Victoria Spa Lodge** **Bishopton Lane** **Stratford-upon-Avon** **CV37 9QY** **Tel: (01789) 267985** **Fax 01789 204728** **Open: ALL YEAR** **Map Ref No. 13**	Nearest Road: A.3400, A.46 Large 19th-century house in country setting, overlooking Stratford canal, with ample parking. A royal coat of arms was built into the gables (with the permission of Queen Victoria) of this Grade II listed building. There are 7 very attractive & comfortable en-suite bedrooms, each has a hostess tray, colour T.V., radio/alarm & hairdryer. (Non-smoking.) 1 1/2 miles from the centre of town. Excellent base for the Cotswolds & Shakespearian properties. Pleasant walks along the tow path to Stratford & Wilmcote.	£19.50 🚭 *see PHOTO over* CREDIT CARD VISA M'CARD	Y	N	N
Mrs Margaret Mander **Pear Tree Cottage** **7 Church Road, Wilmcote** **Stratford-upon-Avon** **CV37 9UX** **Tel: (01789) 205889** **Fax 01789 262862** **Open: ALL YEAR (Excl. Xmas)** **Map Ref No. 13**	Nearest Road: A.46, A.3400 A delightful half-timbered 16th-century house located in the Shakespeare village of Wilmcote. It retains all its original charm & character, with oak beams, flagstone floors, inglenook fireplaces, thick stone walls with deep-set windows, & antiques. Offering 7 very comfortable en-suite rooms, all with tea/coffee-making facilities & colour T.V.. A delicious breakfast is served each morning in the dining room. A comfortable lounge is also provided. Children over 2 yrs. A lovely base from which to tour the whole region.	£20.00 *see PHOTO over*	Y	N	N
Mrs Elizabeth Draisey **Forth House** **44 High Street** **Warwick** **CV34 4AX** **Tel: (01926) 401512** **Open: ALL YEAR** **Map Ref No. 14**	Nearest Road: A.429 This rambling Georgian family home in the centre of Warwick provides 2 peaceful guest suites hidden away at the back. 1 family-sized ground-floor suite with private bathroom, sitting room (with T.V.), fridge & drink facilities opens onto the garden, whilst the other room, also en-suite, overlooks the garden. Ideally situated for holidays or business. Junction 15 (M.40), 2 miles away, brings Oxford, Birmingham (Airport & N.E.C.), Stratford & the Cotswolds within easy reach.	£20.00 🚭	Y	Y	Y
Mrs Judith Stanton **Redlands Farm** **Banbury Rd, Lighthorne** **Warwick CV35 0AH** **Tel: (01926) 651241** **Open: APR - OCT** **Map Ref No. 18**	Nearest Road: M.40, B.4100 A lovely 16th-century farmhouse in 2 acres of garden, with swimming pool. A quiet location, with delightful views over open countryside. Large, beamed bedrooms are tastefully decorated, 1 en-suite with Victorian brass bed. All centrally heated, with tea/coffee facilities. A comfortable guests' lounge with T.V., log fires & homely atmosphere. Ideal for Warwick, Stratford, Cotswolds & Motor Heritage Museum. Parking.	£16.50	Y	N	N

Pear Tree Cottage. Wilmcote.

Warwickshire

		rate from £ per person	children taken	evening meals	animals taken
Mrs Topsy Trought **Brookland** **Peacock Lane** **Tysoe** **Warwick** **CV35 0SG** **Tel: (01295) 680202** **Open: ALL YEAR** **Map Ref No. 15**	Nearest Road: A.422 Dating from 1634, Brookland is beautifully situated in the pretty village of Tysoe, resting in the Vale of the Red Horse. 3 prettily furnished bedrooms. A comfortable lounge with an open fire & T.V.. Topsy provides excellent cuisine, using fresh home-grown produce, served in a 17th-century dining room that includes an inglenook fireplace & wooden beams. Tysoe, a conservation area, is well placed for visiting Shakespeare's country, the Cotswolds & the South Midlands. Only 20 mins from Stratford-upon-Avon.	£16.00	Y	Y	N
Mr & Mrs Greenwood **The Old Rectory** **Vicarage Lane** **Sherbourne** **Warwick CV35 8AB** **Tel/Fax: (01926) 624562** **Open: ALL YEAR (Excl.** **Xmas & New Year)** **Map Ref No. 16**	Nearest Road: A.46, M.40 Jt.15 A licensed Georgian country house rich in beams, flagstones & inglenooks. Situated in a gem of an English village, 1/3 mile from M.40, junction 15. Accommodation is in 14 elegantly appointed en-suite bedrooms which thoughtfully provide all possible comforts, many antique brass beds & some wonderful, Victorian-style bathrooms. Hearty breakfasts served amid antique oak. A delightful home & an ideal base from which to the tour the area & its many attractions.	£22.00 *see PHOTO over* CREDIT CARD VISA M'CARD	Y	Y	Y

All the establishments mentioned in this guide are members of
The Worldwide Bed & Breakfast Association

When booking your accommodation please mention
The Best Bed & Breakfast

471

The Old Rectory. Sherbourne.

Wiltshire

Wiltshire
(West Country)

Wiltshire is a county of rolling chalk downs, small towns, delightful villages, fine churches & great country houses. The expanse of Salisbury Plain is divided by the beautiful valleys of Nadder, Wylye, Ebble & Avon. In a county of open landscapes, Savernake Forest, with its stately avenues of trees strikes a note of contrast. In the north west the Cotswolds spill over into Wiltshire from neighbouring Gloucestershire.

No other county is so rich in archaeological sites. Long barrows and ancient hill forts stand on the skylines as evidence of the early habitation of the chalk uplands. Many of these prehistoric sites are at once magnificent and mysterious. The massive stone arches and monoliths of Stonehenge were built over a period of 500 years with stones transported over great distances. At Avebury the small village is completely encircled by standing stones and a massive bank and ditch earthwork. Silbury Hill is a huge, enigmatic man-made mound. England's largest chambered tomb is West Kennet Long Barrow and at Bush Barrow, finds have included fine bronze and gold daggers and a stone sceptre-head similar to one found at Mycenae in Greece.

Some of England's greatest historic houses are in Wiltshire. Longleat is an Elizabethan mansion with priceless collections of paintings, books & furniture. The surrounding park was landscaped by Capability Brown and its great fame in recent years has been its Safari Park, particularly the lions which roam freely around the visiting cars. Stourhead has celebrated 18th century landscaped gardens which are exceptional in spring when rhododendrons bloom.

Two delightful villages are Castle Combe, nestling in a Cotswold valley, & Lacock where the twisting streets hold examples of buildings ranging from mediaeval half-timbered, to Tudor & Georgian. 13th century Lacock Abbey, converted to a house in the 16th century, was the home of Fox Talbot, pioneer of photography.

There are many notable churches in Wiltshire. In Bradford-on-Avon, a fascinating old town, is the church of St. Lawrence, a rare example of an almost perfect Saxon church from around 900. Farley has an unusual brick church thought to have been designed by Sir Christopher Wren, & there is stained glass by William Morris in the church at Rodbourne.

Devizes Castle

Salisbury stands where three rivers join, on a plain of luxuriant watermeadows, where the focal point of the landscape is the soaring spire of the Cathedral; at 404 feet, it is the tallest in England. The 13th century cathedral has a marvellous & rare visual unity. The body of the building was completed in just 38 years, although the spire was added in the next century. Salisbury, or "New Sarum" was founded in 1220 when the Bishop abandoned the original cathedral at Old Sarum, to start the present edifice two miles to the south. At Old Sarum you can see the foundation of the old city including the outline of the first cathedral.

Wiltshire

Wiltshire Gazeteer

Area of Outstanding Natural Beauty
The Costwolds & the North Wessex Downs.

Historic Houses & Castles

Corsham Court - Chippenham
16th & 17th centuries from Elizabethan & Georgian periods. 18th century furniture, British, Flemish & Italian Old Masters. Gardens by Capability Brown.

Great Chalfield Manor - Melksham
15th century manor house - moated.

Church House - Salisbury
15th century house.

Chalcot House - Westbury
17th century small house in Palladian manner.

Lacock Abbey - Nr. Chippenham
13th century abbey. In 1540 converted into house - 18th century alterations. Mediaeval cloisters & brewery.

Longleat House - Warminster
16th century - early Renaissance, alterations in early 1800's. Italian Renaissance decorations. Splendid state rooms, pictures, books, furniture. Victorian kitchens. Game reserve.

Littlecote - Nr. Hungerford
15th century Tudor manor. Panelled rooms, moulded plaster ceilings.

Luckington Court - Luckington
Queen Anne for the most part - fine ancient buildings.

Malmesbury House - Salisbury
Queen Anne house - part 14th century. Rococo plasterwork.

Newhouse - Redlynch
17th century brick Jacobean trinity house - two Georgian wings,

Philips House - Dinton
1816 Classical house.

Sheldon Manor - Chippenham
13th century porch & 15th century chapel in this Plantagenet manor.

Stourhead - Stourton
18th century Palladian house with framed landscape gardens.

Westwood Manor - Bradford-on-Avon
15th century manor house - alterations in 16th & 17th centuries.

Wardour Castle - Tisbury
18th century house in Palladian manner.

Wilton House - Salisbury
17th century - work of Inigo Jones & later of James Wyatt in 1810. Paintings, Kent & Chippendale furniture.

Avebury Manor - Nr Malborough
Elizabethan manor house - beautiful plasterwork, panelling & furniture. Gardens with topiary.

Bowood - Calne
18th century - work of several famous architects. Gardens by Capability Brown - famous beechwoods.

Mompesson House - Salisbury
Queen Anne town house - Georgian plasterwork.

Cathedrals & Churches

Salisbury Cathedral
13th century - decorated tower with stone spire. Part of original stone pulpitum is preserved. Beautiful large decorated cloister. Exterior mostly early English.

Salisbury (St. Thomas of Canterbury)
15th century rebuilding - 12th century font, 14th & 15th century glass, 17th century monuments. 'Doom' painting over chancel & murals in south chapel

Amesbury (St. Mary & St. Melor)
13th century - refashioned 15th & restored in 19th century. Splendid timber roofs, stone vaulting over chapel of north transept, mediaeval painted glass, 15th century screen, Norman font.

Bishops Cannings (St. Mary the Virgin)
13th-15th centuries. Fine arcading in transept - fine porch doorway.
17th century almsbox, Jacobean Holy table.

Bradford-on-Avon (St. Lawrence)
Best known of all Saxon churches in England.

Cricklade (St. Sampson)
12th -16th century. Tudor central tower vault, 15th century chapel.

Inglesham (St. John the Baptist)
Mediaeval wall paintings, high pews, clear glass, remains of painted screens.

Malmesbury (St. Mary)
Norman - 12th century arcades, refashioning in 14th century with clerestory, 15th century stone pulpitum added. Fine sculpture.

Wiltshire

Tisbury (St. John the Baptist)
14th-15th centuries. 15th-17th century roofing to nave & aisles. Two storeyed porch & chancel.
Potterne (St. Mary)
13th,14th,15th centuries. Inscribed Norman tub font. Wooden pulpit.

Museums & Galleries

Salisbury & South Wiltshire Museum - Salisbury
Collections showing history of the area in all periods. Models of Stonehenge & Old Sarum - archaeologically important collection.
Devizes Museum - Devizes
Unique archaeological & geological collections, including Sir Richard Colt-Hoare's Stourhead collection of prehistoric material.
Alexander Keiller Museum - Avebury
Collection of items from the Neolithic & Bronze ages & from excavations in district.
Athelstan Museum - Malmesbury
Collection of articles referring to the town - household, coin, etc.
Bedwyn Stone Museum - Great Bedwyn
Open-air museum showing where Stonehenge was carved.
Lydiard Park - Lydiard Tregoze
Parish church of St. Mary & a splendid Georgian mansion standing in park & also permanent & travelling exhibitions.

Borough of Thamesdown Museum & Art Gallery - Swindon
Natural History & Geology of Wiltshire, Bygones, coins, etc. 20th century British art & ceramic collection.
Great Western Railway Museum - Swindon
Historic locomotives.

Historic Monuments

Stonehenge - Nr. Amesbury
Prehistoric monument - encircling bank & ditch & Augrey holes are Neolithic. Stone circles possibly early Bronze age.
Avebury
Relics of enormous circular gathering place B.C. 2700-1700.
Old Sarum - Nr. Salisbury
Possibly first Iron Age camp, later Roman area, then Norman castle.
Silbury Hill - Nr. Avebury
Mound - conical in shape - probably a memorial c.3000-2000 B.C.
Windmill Hill - Nr. Avebury
Causewayed camp c.3000-2300 B.C.
Bratton Camp & White Horse - Bratton
Hill fort standing above White Horse.
West Kennet Long Barrow
Burial place c.4000-2500 B.C.
Ludgershall Castle - Lugershall
Motte & bailey of Norman castle, earthworks, also flint walling from later castle.

Castle Combe.

WILTSHIRE
Map reference

1	Hartland	21	Ross
1	Threlfall	22	Arthey
2	Roberts	22	Tucker
2	Price	22	Bone
2	Chapman	22	Rodwell
3	Denning	24	Sykes
4	Sexton	25	Hunt
5	Lippiatt	26	Johnson
6	Steed	27	Bruges
7	Addison	28	Corp
8	Stafford	29	Singer
9	Walker	30	Orman
10	Hawley	31	Thompson
11	Fletcher	32	Humphreys
13	Eavis		
14	Edwards		
15	Francis		
16	Davies		
17	Cornelius		
18	Orssich		
19	Couzens		
20	Lanham		

Widbrook Grange. Widbrook.

Wiltshire

		rate from £ per person	children taken	evening meals taken	animals taken

Mrs Valerie Threlfall
1 Cove House
Park Place
Ashton Keynes SN6 6NS
Tel: (01285) 861226
Open: ALL YEAR
Map Ref No. 01

Nearest Road: A.419
Southern half of a beautiful 17th-century manor house in a pretty Cotswold village. 2 double & 1 twin-bedded room, all elegantly decorated, 2 with en-suite/private facilities. The guests' sitting room is located in the beamed attic, whose interior reflects the hosts' joint hobbies of vintage-car & costume collection. A walled garden/garden room is reached via a recently renovated ballroom. 3 hostelries offering meals within walking distance.

£22.00 · Y · N · Y · (non-smoking)

Peter & Elizabeth Hartland
Two Cove House
Ashton Keynes
SN6 6NS
Tel: (01285) 861221
Fax 01285 861221
Open: ALL YEAR (Excl. Xmas)
Map Ref No. 01

Nearest Road: A.419
Peter & Elizabeth will welcome you warmly to their historic Cotswold manor house, containing many antiques & interesting paintings. This charming old house stands in a large secluded garden, & offers 3 spacious en-suite bedrooms. Dinner 'en famille' (& by arrangement) is ideal for planning the next day's excursions, & guests will enjoy good home cooking, using garden produce (when in season). Bath, Oxford, Avebury & the delightful Cotswold villages are within easy reach.

£23.00 · Y · Y · N

Elizabeth & John Denning
Burghope Manor
Winsley
Bradford-on-Avon BA15 2LA
Tel: (01225) 723557
Fax 01225 723113
Open: ALL YEAR (Excl. Xmas & New Year)
Map Ref No. 03

Nearest Road: A.36
This historic 13th-century family home is set in beautiful countryside on the edge of the village of Winsley - overlooking the Avon Valley - 5 miles from the centre of Bath & 1 1/2 miles from Bradford-on-Avon. Although steeped in history, it is first & foremost a living family home, which has been carefully modernised so that the wealth of historical features may complement the present-day comforts, which include en-suite bathrooms. Village pub & restaurant within walking distance. Evening meals for groups only. Children over 10.

£32.50 · Y · Y · N

see PHOTO over

CREDIT CARD
VISA
M'CARD
AMEX

Priscilla & Peter Roberts
Bradford Old Windmill
4 Masons Lane
Bradford-on-Avon BA15 1QN
Tel: (01225) 866842
Fax 01225 866648
Open: ALL YEAR
Map Ref No. 02

Nearest Road: M.4, A.363
A cosy, relaxed atmosphere greets you at this converted windmill high on the hill above the town. The old stone tower overflows with character, & with the many finds picked up by Peter & Priscilla on their backpacking trips around the world. Most of the unusually shaped bedrooms have their own distinctive en-suite bathrooms. Imaginative breakfasts are served beneath the massive grain weighing scales. 5 minutes' walk from the town centre.

£22.50 · Y · Y · N · (non-smoking)

CREDIT CARD
VISA
M'CARD
AMEX

John & Pauline Price
Widbrook Grange
Trowbridge Rd, Widbrook
Bradford-on-Avon
BA15 1UH
Tel: (01225) 864750/863173
Fax 01225 862890
Open: ALL YEAR
Map Ref No. 02

Nearest Road: A.363
Widbrook Grange is a Georgian, Grade II listed house set in 11 acres & only 8 miles from the fascinating Georgian city of Bath. The house has been lovingly restored by John & Pauline, with elegant rooms offering en-suite facilities (& some 4-poster beds) in both the house & the courtyard 'cottages'. Peaceful comfort & a warm welcome await you. Evening meals served Mon-Thurs. Beautiful indoor swimming pool & gym area. An ideal base from which to explore the West Country.

£35.00 · Y · Y · N

see PHOTO over

CREDIT CARD
VISA
M'CARD
AMEX

Burghope Manor. Bradford-upon-Avon.

**All the establishments mentioned in this guide
are members of the
Worldwide Bed & Breakfast Association.**

**If you have any comments regarding your
accommodation please send them to us
using the form at the back of the book.
We value your comments.**

Wiltshire

		rate from £ per person	children taken	evening meals	animals taken
Carey & Diana Chapman **Priory Steps** **Newtown** **Bradford-on-Avon** **BA15 1NQ** **Tel: (01225) 862230** **Fax 01225 866248** **Open: ALL YEAR** **Map Ref No. 02**	Nearest Road: A.363 A warm & friendly welcome awaits you at this delightful, mellow, stone-built, 17th-century, former clothier's house. Tastefully renovated & furnished with antiques, Priory Steps offers guests a choice of 5 individually decorated en-suite bedrooms with tea/coffee-making facilities & colour T.V.. All rooms have super views over the town towards Westbury Hills. A wide choice of delicious breakfasts is available - these are served in the elegant dining room - & Diana's delicious evening meals are not to be missed.	£30.00 CREDIT CARD VISA M'CARD	Y	Y	N
Mr & Mrs J. Lippiatt **Manor Farm** **Alderton** **Chippenham** **SN14 6NL** **Tel: (01666) 840271** **Open: ALL YEAR** **Map Ref No. 05**	Nearest Road: A.46 Nestling in the picturesque village of Alderton, yet within an easy drive of Bath, you are invited to enjoy warm hospitality in this beautiful 17th-century home. Furnished to a high standard, the 3 lovely bedrooms, with en-suite facilities, are warm & comfortable. Nearby is an excellent choice of country pubs & restaurants. Guests are welcome to enjoy the garden & the interest of this working farm. Children over 10.	£23.00 *see PHOTO over*	Y	N	N
Mrs R. E. Sexton **Elm Farmhouse** **The Green** **Biddestone** **Chippenham SN14 7DG** **Tel: (01249) 713354** **Open: ALL YEAR** **Map Ref No. 04**	Nearest Road: A.420, A.4, M.4 Elm Farmhouse is located in the centre of beautiful Biddestone & is a fine Grade II listed building retaining many original features. 2 large double bedrooms are offered with private facilities, tea/ coffee & T.V.. Built in 1778, the house is situated opposite the pond & is close to 2 village pubs. The charming rooms have views overlooking the pond & walled garden. Biddestone is between Lacock & Castle Combe & is only 9 miles from Bath.	£16.00	Y	N	Y
Richard & Gloria Steed **The Cottage** **Westbrook** **Bromham** **Chippenham** **SN15 2EE** **Tel: (01380) 850255** **Open: ALL YEAR** **Map Ref No. 06**	Nearest Road: A.342, A.3102, This delightful cottage is reputed to have been a coaching inn, & dates back to 1450. There are 3 charming bedrooms, all with private shower, T.V. & tea/coffee makers, in a beautifully converted barn. Also, many exposed beams that were once ships' timbers. Breakfast is served in the old beamed dining room. A lovely garden & paddock for guests' use. An ideal centre for visiting Bath, Bristol, Devizes, Marlborough, Avebury, Stonehenge, Longleat, Castle Combe & Lacock. Self-catering cottage available.	£20.00	Y	N	N

When booking your accommodation please mention
The Best Bed & Breakfast

Manor Farm. Alderton.

Old Rectory. Lacock.

Wiltshire

		rate from £ per person	children taken	evening meals	animals taken
Mrs Margaret Addison **The Old Rectory** **Cantax Hill** **Lacock** **Chippenham SN15 2JZ** **Tel: (01249) 730335** **Open: ALL YEAR** **Map Ref No. 07**	Nearest Road: A.350, A.4 Situated in the mediaeval village of Lacock, the Old Rectory, built in 1866, is a fine example of Victorian Gothic architecture, with creeper-clad walls & mullioned windows. It stands in 12 acres of its own carefully tended grounds, which include a tennis court & croquet lawn. The Old Rectory offers 5 very attractive bedrooms, all with a private bath. An excellent base from which to explore the glorious West Country.	£20.00 *see PHOTO over*	Y	N	N
Mrs Gill Stafford **Pickwick Lodge Farm** **Guyers Lane** **Corsham SN13 0PS** **Tel: (01249) 712207** **Fax 01249 701904** **Open: ALL YEAR (Excl.** **Xmas & New Year)** **Map Ref No. 08**	Nearest Road: M.4 Jt. 17, A.4 A delightful 17th-century Cotswold stone farmhouse, set in peaceful surroundings. Accommodation is in 3 well-appointed & tastefully furnished bedrooms, each with a private bathroom, radio, T.V. & tea/coffee-making facilities. Hearty & delicious breakfasts are served. Ideally situated for visiting many sites of historical interest, such as the Wiltshire White Horses, Avebury & Stonehenge; many stately homes & National Trust properties within easy reach. Ample car parking.	£18.00	Y	N	N
Mr Carton Walker **Latton House** **Latton** **Cricklade** **SN6 6DP** **Tel: (01793) 751982** **Open: ALL YEAR (Excl. Xmas)** **Map Ref No. 09**	Nearest Road: A.419 Latton House is situated between the M.4 motorway & Cirencester. The house is a Georgian manor house, tucked away behind the village church in 2 acres of gardens. The atmosphere is friendly & informal. Antiques & items of interest abound. Bedrooms are attractively furnished & overlook the gardens with open fields beyond. Ideal for exploring the Cotswolds, Blenheim, Bath, Cheltenham, Longleat & Oxford.	£25.00	Y	Y	N
Sir Donald & Lady Hawley **Little Cheverell House** **Little Cheverell** **Devizes** **SN10 4JJ** **Tel: (01380) 813322** **Fax 01380 813322** **Open: ALL YEAR** **Map Ref No. 10**	Nearest Road: A.360 This fine Georgian former rectory set in 4 1/2 acres of charming well-tended gardens offers a warm welcome & comfortable stay. 2 spacious, well-furnished twin-bedded rooms, each with its own bathroom; a guest sitting room with T.V.; & a tennis court. Delicious meals draw on an interesting repetoire of international cuisine, using fresh garden produce. Ideal for Stonehenge, Salisbury, Avebury, Bath, Wells & Glastonbury. Walking, riding & golf nearby. Single supplement.	£24.00 *see PHOTO over*	Y	Y	Y
Peter & Barbara Fletcher **Rathlin Guest House** **Wick Lane** **Devizes** **SN10 5DP** **Tel: (01380) 721999** **Open: ALL YEAR** **Map Ref No. 11**	Nearest Road: A.360 A beautiful detached Edwardian house set in tranquil gardens, with ample car-parking space, situated in a quiet residential area only a short walk from the town centre. Tastefully furnished with antiques, the house has great period charm. An elegant staircase leads to individually furnished en-suite bedrooms, all with T.V.s & hospitality tray. Ideal touring base for Bath, Stonehenge, Avebury, Longleat, Bowood, Salisbury, etc.	£20.00	Y	Y	N

Little Cheverell House. Little Cheverell.

Wiltshire

		rate from £ per person	children taken	evening meals	animals taken
Mrs Ross Eavis **Manor Farm** **Corston** **Malmesbury SN16 0HF** **Tel/Fax: (01666) 822148** **Open: ALL YEAR** **Map Ref No. 13**	Nearest Road: A.429 Relax & unwind in this charming, award-winning, 17th-century listed farmhouse on a working dairy/arable farm. 6 spacious tastefully furnished bedrooms, 3 en-suite, all with tea/coffee-making facilities, radio & T.V.. A beautiful lounge with inglenook fireplace & a secluded garden for guests' use. Meals available in the local pub within walking distance. An ideal base for exploring the Cotswolds, Bath, Stonehenge & stately homes. CREDIT CARD VISA M'CARD	£16.00	Y	N	N
John & Edna Edwards **Stonehill Farm** **Charlton** **Malmesbury** **SN16 9DY** **Tel: (01666) 823310** **Open: ALL YEAR** **Map Ref No. 14**	Nearest Road: B.4040, M.4 Stonehill Farm is a 15th-century Cotswold stone farmhouse situated on a working dairy farm in the lush & rolling countryside on the Wiltshire-Gloucestershire border. 1 of the bedrooms has its own shower room en-suite, & all rooms have tea/coffee-making facilities. Children & dogs are welcome, & a full English breakfast is served in the guests' sitting/dining room. Ideal for 1 night or several days. Oxford, Bath, Stratford, Stonehenge & the delightful Cotswold Hills & villages are all within easy reach by car.	£15.00	Y	N	Y
Adrienne & Graham Francis **Laurel Cottage** **Southend** **Ogbourne St. George** **Marlborough SN8 1SG** **Tel: (01672) 841288** **Open: ALL YEAR** **Map Ref No. 15**	Nearest Road: A.346 Nestling in a fold of the Marlborough Downs, this 16th-century thatched cottage has been fully modernised whilst retaining its unique 'olde worlde' charm. Low, beamed ceilings, an inglenook fireplace & a bread oven are characteristics of this property. 4 attractive bedrooms, 2 en-suite. Situated 30-40 miles from Bath, Oxford & Salisbury. Stonehenge & Avebury close by. An ideal base for touring. High Season min. 2 nights.	£17.00	Y	N	N
Mrs Judy Davies **Marridge Hill** **Ramsbury** **Marlborough SN8 2HG** **Tel: (01672) 520237** **Fax 01672 520053** **Open: ALL YEAR** **Map Ref No. 16**	Nearest Road: M.4, B.4192 A mainly Victorian family home set in glorious countryside, yet only 1 hour's drive from Heathrow Airport. You will be warmly welcomed into a relaxed, informal atmosphere. There are 3 comfortable & attractive rooms (1 with spacious en-suite facilities) & both bathrooms have power showers. Pleasant lounge & dining room, with books galore, & an acre of well-kept garden. Ideal for Neolithic Avebury, Salisbury, Bath, Oxford & the Cotswolds. Good pubs & restaurants nearby. CREDIT CARD VISA M'CARD	£18.00	Y	N	Y
Mrs Jane Cornelius **The Old Vicarage** **Burbage** **Marlborough SN8 3AG** **Tel: (01672) 810495** **Fax 01672 810663** **Open: ALL YEAR (Excl. Xmas & New Year)** **Map Ref No. 17**	Nearest Road: A.338, A.4, M.4 A large Victorian vicarage on the village green, next to the church, surrounded by thatched cottages. This pleasant country house offers guests 3 large, pretty rooms, decorated & furnished to a very high standard, with good en-suite bathrooms. A spacious drawing room, sunny dining room & 2 acres of beautifully maintained gardens complement Jane's superlative cooking. Within easy reach is Stonehenge, Avebury & Savernake Forest. The perfect base from which to visit Bath, Oxford & Salisbury. *see PHOTO over* CREDIT CARD VISA M'CARD	£30.00	N	N	N

The Old Vicarage. Burbage.

Wiltshire

		rate from £ per person	children taken	evening meals	animals taken
Angela Orssich **Mayfield** **West Grafton** **Marlborough SN8 3BY** **Tel: (01672) 810339** **Fax 01672 811158** **Open: ALL YEAR** **Map Ref No. 18**	Nearest Road: A.338, A.346 A delightful 15th-century thatched house set in beautiful, peaceful grounds, with tennis court & heated swimming pool. The property has been carefully extended to provide 3 very pretty en-suite bedrooms. There is a choice of lounges, 1 with an inglenook fireplace, the other more of a family room. All rooms are decorated with style & fine antiques, but the family kitchen is the heart of the house, where Chris & Angie welcome guests with open arms & a relaxed atmosphere.	£20.00	Y	N	Y
Barbara Couzens **Sunrise Farm** **Manton** **Marlborough** **SN8 4HL** **Tel: (01672) 512878** **Fax 01672 512878** **Open: APR - OCT** **Map Ref No. 19**	Nearest Road: A.4 A warm welcome awaits you at Sunrise, peacefully situated on the outskirts of Manton village, 1 mile from the historic town of Marlborough, with panoramic views over the Marlborough Downs. Sunrise has 1 double & 2 twin rooms. 1 twin on the ground floor has a private bathroom. The large guest lounge has T.V. & tea/coffee-making facilities, while the attractive conservatory is a favourite for that final breakfast cup of coffee. An ideal base for Salisbury, Stonehenge, Avebury & Bath. Ample parking available.	£16.00 🚭	N	N	N
Colin & Susan Ross **Chetcombe House Hotel** **Chetcombe Road** **Mere** **BA12 6AZ** **Tel: (01747) 860219** **Open: ALL YEAR** **Map Ref No. 21**	Nearest Road: A.303 Chetcombe is a country-house hotel set in an acre of lovely garden in the picturesque little town of Mere. 5 attractively furnished rooms with en-suite facilities & modern amenities, including T.V. & tea/coffee. Delicious meals are served. Guests may relax in the comfortable lounge or enjoy the pretty garden. Ideal as a stop-over en-route to the West Country, or as a base for exploring the delights of Wiltshire. No smoking in bedrooms.	£25.00 🚭 CREDIT CARD VISA M'CARD AMEX	Y	Y	Y
Mrs Mary Tucker **1 Riverside Close** **Laverstock** **Salisbury SP1 1QW** **Tel/Fax: (01722) 320287** **Open: ALL YEAR** **Map Ref No. 22**	Nearest Road: A.30 An executive's home in a quiet area 1 1/2 miles from Salisbury Cathedral. A tastefully furnished ground-floor suite, with a private shower room, & a double & single room with a patio door opening onto a beautiful flower arranger's garden. A double en-suite bedroom is also available. Guests have their own colour T.V. & tea/coffee facilities. An excellent base for visiting this historic city. Guests will receive every consideration here.	£22.50 🚭	Y	N	N
Ann & Peter Arthey **Byways House** **31 Fowlers Road** **Salisbury SP1 2QP** **Tel: (01722) 328364** **Fax 01722 322146** **Open: ALL YEAR (Excl. Xmas & New Year)** **Map Ref No. 22**	Nearest Road: A.30, A.36 An attractive, family-run Victorian house situated close to the cathedral in a quiet residential area of the city centre. Leaving your car in the car park enables you to walk to Salisbury's magnificent cathedral. Most of the comfortable bedrooms are with en-suite bathroom facilities & colour T.V.s. Traditional English breakfasts, together with vegetarian menus, are included. Byways is the ideal place to stay to visit Salisbury, Stonehenge, Avebury & the New Forest.	£19.50 CREDIT CARD VISA M'CARD	Y	N	Y

All the establishments mentioned in this guide
are members of the
Worldwide Bed & Breakfast Association.

If you have any comments regarding your
accommodation please send them to us
using the form at the back of the book.
We value your comments.

	rate from £ per person	children taken	evening meals	animals taken
Mrs Sandra Bone **Glen Lyn House** **6 Bellamy Lane** **Milford Hill** **Salisbury** **SP1 2SP** **Tel: (01722) 327880** **Open: ALL YEAR** **Map Ref No. 22** Nearest Road: A.36 Situated in a quiet tree-lined lane, 5 mins' walk from the city centre, Glen Lyn is an elegant Victorian house offering 9 individually appointed bedrooms, all with colour T.V.. Enjoy a great English breakfast & superb home-produced dinner, then relax in the lounge or listen to birdsong in the beautiful garden. Glen Lyn House is the ideal tranquil base for visiting the cathedral & Stonehenge, & for exploring the New Forest. Ample parking. Children over 12.	£19.00	Y	Y	N
Mrs Gill Rodwell **Farthings** **9 Swaynes Close** **Salisbury SP1 3AE** **Tel: (01722) 330749** **Open: ALL YEAR** **Map Ref No. 22** Nearest Road: A.30 Farthings is a comfortable old house in a very quiet tree-lined street conveniently close to Salisbury's market square & its many excellent restaurants. There are 4 bedrooms, 2 single & 2 double/twin en-suite, each with tea/coffee makers. Residents' lounge with colour T.V., & an interesting collection of old photos. A delicious choice of breakfast is available. Children over 4 yrs.	£18.00	Y	N	N
Mrs Christine Sykes **Elm Tree Cottage** **Stapleford** **Salisbury** **SP3 4LH** **Tel: (01722) 790507** **Open: APR - OCT** **Map Ref No. 24** Nearest Road: A.303, A.36 Elm Tree Cottage is a 17th-century character cottage with inglenook & beams. The bedrooms are light & airy, are attractively decorated & have T.V. & tea/coffee facilities. The atmosphere is relaxed & warm, & breakfast is served as required. Situated in a picturesque village, there are views across various valleys. Elm Tree Cottage is a good centre for Salisbury, Wilton, Longleat, Stonehenge, Avebury, etc.	£21.00	Y	N	N
Mrs Joy Orman **Swainscombe** **East Knoyle** **Salisbury** **SP3 6BN** **Tel: (01747) 830224** **Open: ALL YEAR (Excl.** **Xmas & New Year)** **Map Ref No. 30** Nearest Road: A.303, A.350 Swainscombe is a charming, thatched, 17th-century period house constructed of local stone & set in a beautiful garden. Offering guests superb accommodation, the house has 5 bedrooms (1 with 4-poster), & retains many of its original features, with beamed ceilings & inglenook fireplaces. Delicious meals are served. The historic village (the birthplace of Sir Christopher Wren) is located in an Area of Outstanding Natural Beauty, & is ideally situated for visiting the many places of historical & archaeological interest.	£18.00	Y	Y	N
Suzi Lanham **Newton Farmhouse** **Southampton Road** **Whiteparish** **Salisbury SP5 2QL** **Tel: (01794) 884416** **Open: ALL YEAR** **Map Ref No. 20** Nearest Road: A.36 A Grade II listed, part 16th-century farmhouse, formerly part of the Trafalgar Estate. Situated 8 miles south of Salisbury on the A.36 Southampton Rd. Convenient for Stonehenge, Winchester, Romsey & the New Forest. 8 attractive en-suite rooms (2 with 4-posters), each with colour T.V., tea/coffee facilities. A super beamed dining room with a flagstone floor. Large grounds, outdoor swimming pool. Evening meals by arrangement.	£17.50	Y	Y	N

Wiltshire

	rate from £ per person	children taken	evening meals	animals taken
Mrs Norma Hunt **Bridge Farm** **Lower Road** **Britford** **Salisbury SP5 4DY** **Tel: (01722) 332376** **Open: ALL YEAR** **Map Ref No. 25** Nearest Road: A.338 A warm welcome & a hearty English breakfast are assured at this charming 18th-century farmhouse on a 120-hectare farm on the southern edge of Salisbury. It is within easy walking distance of the cathedral, & has famous views of the spire along the River Avon that flows alongside the beautiful gardens. Centrally situated for touring the area, with many attractions including Stonehenge, Wilton House & the New Forest.	£18.00	Y	N	N
Jill Johnson **Newcourt Lodge** **Nunton Drive** **Nunton** **Salisbury** **SP5 4HZ** **Tel: (01722) 335877** **Open: ALL YEAR** **Map Ref No. 26** Nearest Road: A.338 An attractive house, with a friendly atmosphere, situated in a quiet village 3 miles from Salisbury. Newcourt Lodge incorporates original old bricks & timber features, & has a large, mature garden giving extensive views over the rolling countryside. Each bedroom is furnished to a high standard & includes a T.V., C.H. & tea/coffee-making facilities. Ideal for visiting Salisbury, Stonehenge, New Forest & the West Country. Nearby are attractive country pubs serving evening meals.	£17.00	Y	N	N
Mrs Michael Bruges **Brook House** **Semington** **Trowbridge** **BA14 6JR** **Tel: (01380) 870232** **Open: FEB - NOV** **Map Ref No. 27** Nearest Road: A.350 This Georgian listed house is set in its own grounds, with tennis & croquet lawns, swimming pool & a brook, bordering the orchard, where kingfishers can be seen. Offering 1 twin-bedded & 1 family room with cot. Both have wash basins & tea/coffee-making facilities. The drawing room & conservatory can be made available for guests' use. Conveniently located for Bath, Longleat, Stourhead & Badminton horse trials.	£18.00 *see PHOTO over*	Y	N	Y
Diane & Barry Humphreys **The Old Manor Hotel** **Trowle** **Trowbridge** **BA14 9BL** **Tel: (01225) 777393** **Fax 01225 765443** **Open: ALL YEAR** **Map Ref No. 32** Nearest Road: A.363 An attractive, Grade II listed, 500-year-old farmhouse, peacefully situated in 4 1/2 acres. Converted barns form a charming ground-floor courtyard complex (traditional lounges in the main house). Many rooms feature antiques, pine & romantic 4-posters. Tastefully furnished, & yet retaining many period features, all have beverage facilities, an en-suite bathroom & satellite T.V.. Parking. A good base for touring the Cotswolds, Stonehenge, Glastonbury & the West Country.	£25.00 CREDIT CARD VISA M'CARD AMEX	Y	Y	N
Mr & Mrs Colin Thompson **The Old House** **Sutton Veny** **Warminster BA12 7AQ** **Tel: (01985) 840344** **Open: ALL YEAR (Excl.** **Xmas & New Year)** **Map Ref No. 31** Nearest Road: A.36, A.303 This thatched, 300-year-old stone house has been thoroughly modernised over the years but retains its charm & tranquility, within 4 acres of grounds which include a tennis court. Offering 2 charming guest rooms with a private bathroom. There are log fires & a delightfully welcoming, relaxed & homely atmosphere. The Old House is centrally placed for Stonehenge, Stourhead, Longleat, Salisbury & Bath.	£30.00 CREDIT CARD VISA M'CARD	N	Y	N

Brook House. Semington.

Wiltshire

		rate from £ per person	children taken	evening meals	animals taken
Mrs Lynn Corp **Sturford Mead Farm** **Corsley** **Warminster** **BA12 7QU** **Tel: (01373) 832213** **Open: ALL YEAR** **Map Ref No. 28**	Nearest Road: A.362 Sturford Mead is conveniently located between Frome & Warminster, opposite Longleat with its Safari Park, lake & grounds. Offering comfortable accommodation in 3 rooms, 1 with private facilities, 2 en-suite, all with radio, tea/coffee makers & T.V.. There is also a T.V. lounge & garden for guests' use. This is an ideal base for visiting the ancient cities of Wells & Bath. Cheddar Gorge & Wookey Hole are close by. Single supplement.	£17.00	Y	N	N
Colin & Rachel Singer **Springfield House** **Crockerton** **Warminster** **BA12 8AU** **Tel: (01985) 213696** **Open: ALL YEAR** **Map Ref No. 29**	Nearest Road: A.350, A.36 Situated in the beautiful Wylye Valley, on the edge of the famous Longleat Estate, Springfield House is a charming village house dating from the 17th century. Rachel & Colin welcome you to their home, with its beams, open fires, fresh flowers & sunny en-suite rooms, overlooking the garden & grass tennis court. Dinner by candlelight in the inglenook dining room is much recommended, & is a wonderful way to end the day. Springfield House is a marvellous base for touring, walking or relaxing. Bath, Salisbury, Wells, Stonehenge, Stourhead are all easily reached.	£22.00	Y	Y	N

All the establishments mentioned in this guide are members of
The Worldwide Bed & Breakfast Association

When booking your accommodation please mention
The Best Bed & Breakfast

Yorkshire

Yorkshire & Humberside

England's largest county is a region of beautiful landscapes, of hills, peaks, fells, dales & forests with many square miles of National Park. It is a vast area taking in big industrial cities, interesting towns & delightful villages. Yorkshire's broad rivers sweep through the countryside & are an angler's paradise. Cascading waterfalls pour down from hillside & moorland.

The North sea coast can be thrilling, with wild seas & cliff-top walks, or just fun, as at the many resorts where the waves break on long beaches & trickle into green rock-pools. Staithes & Robin Hoods Bay are fascinating old fishing villages. Whitby is an attractive port where, Abbey, the small town tumbles in red-roofed tiers down to the busy harbour from which Captain Cook sailed.

The Yorkshire Dales form one of the finest landscapes in England. From windswept moors to wide green valleys the scenery is incomparable. James Herriot tells of of the effect that the broad vista of Swaledale had on him. "I was captivated", he wrote, "completely spell-bound....". A network of dry stone walls covers the land; some are as old as the stone-built villages but those which climb the valley sides to the high moors are the product of the 18th century enclosures, when a good wall builder would cover seven meters a day.

Each of the Dales has a distinctive character; from the remote upper reaches of Swaledale & Wensleydale, where the air sings with the sound of wind, sheep, & curlew, over to Airedale & the spectacular limestone gorges of Malham Cove & Gordale Scar, & down to the soft meadows & woods of Wharfedale where the ruins of Bolton Priory stand beside the river.

To the east towards Hull with its mighty River Humber crossed by the worlds largest single-span suspension bridge, lie the Yorkshire Wolds. This is lovely countryside where villages have unusual names like Fridaythorpe & Wetwang. Beverley is a picture-postcard town with a fine 13th century Minster.

The North Yorks National Park, where the moors are ablaze with purple fire of heather in the late summer, is exhilarating country. There is moorland to the east also, on the Pennine chain; famous Ilkley Moor with its stone circle known as the twelve apostles, & the Haworth Moors around the plain Yorkshire village where the Bronte sisters lived; "the distant dreamy, dim blue chain of mountains circling every side", which Emily Bronte describes in Wuthering Heights.

The Yorkshire Pennines industrial heritage is being celebrated in fascinating museums, often based in the original Woolen Mills & warehouses, which also provide workshop space for skilled craftspeople.

Yorkshires Monastic past is revealed in the ruins of its once great Abbeys. Rievaulx, Jervaux & Fountains, retain their tranquil beauty in their pastoral settings. The wealth of the county is displayed in many historic houses with glorious gardens, from stately 18th Century Castle Howard of 'Brideshead Revisited' fame to Tudor Shibden Hall, portrayed in Wuthering Heights.

York is the finest mediaeval city in England. It is encircled by its limestone city walls with four Great Gates. Within the walls are the jumbled roof line, dog-leg streets & sudden courtyards of a mediaeval town. Half timbered buildings with over-sailing upper storeys jostle with Georgian brick houses along the network of narrow streets around The Shambles & King Edward Square.

Yorkshire

Areas of Outstanding Natural Beauty.
The North Yorkshire Moors & The
Yorkshire Dales.

Historic Houses & Castles.

Carlton Towers
17th century, remodelled in later centuries.
paintings, silver, furniture, pictures.
Carved woodwork, painted decorations,
examples of Victorian craftmanship.
Castle Howard - Nr. York
18th century - celebrated architect, Sir
John Vanbrugh - paintings, costumes,
furniture by Chippendale, Sheraton,
Adam. Not to be missed.
East Riddlesden Hall - Keighley
17th century manor house with fishponds
& historic barns, one of which is regarded
as very fine example of mediaeval tithe
barn.
Newby Hall - Ripon
17th century Wren style extended by
Robert Adam. Gobelins tapestry,
Chippendale furniture, sculpture galleries
with Roman rotunda, statuary. Award-
winning gardens.
Nostell Priory - Wakefield
18th century, Georgian mansion,
Chippendale furniture, paintings.
Burton Constable Hall - Hull
16th century, Elizabethan, remodelled in
Georgian period. Stained glass,
Hepplewhite furniture, gardens by
Capability Brown.   .
Ripley Castle - Harrogate
14th century, parts dating during 16th &
18th centuries. Priest hole, armour &
weapons, beautiful ceilings.
The Treasurer's House - York
17th & 18th centuries, splendid interiors,
furniture, pictures.
Harewood House - Leeds
18th century - Robert Adam design,
Chippendale furniture, Italian & English
paintings. Sevres & Chinese porcelain.
Benningbrough Hall - York
18th century. Highly decorative
woodwork, oak staircase, friezes etc.
Splendid hall.
Markenfield Hall - Ripon
14th to 16th century - fine Manor house
surrounded by moat.
Heath Hall - Wakefield

18th century, palladian. Fine woodwork &
plasterwork, rococo ceilings, excellent
furniture, paintings & porcelain
Bishops House - Sheffield
16th century. Only complete timber
framed yeoman farmhouse surviving.
Vernacular architecture. Superb
Skipton Castle- Skipton
One of the most complete & well
preserved mediaeval castles in
England.

Cathedral & Churches

York Minster
13th century. Greatest Gothic Cathedral
north of the Alps. Imposing grandeur -
superb Chapter house, contains half of the
mediaeval stained glass of England.
Outstandingly beautiful.
York (All Saints, North Street)
15th century roofing in parts - 18th century
pulpit wonderful mediaeval glass.
Ripon Cathedral
12th century - though in some parts Saxon
in origin. Decorated choir stalls - gables
buttresses. Church of 672 preserved in
crypt, , Caxton Book, ecclesiastic
treasures.
Bolton Percy (All Saints)
15th century.
Maintains original glass in east window.
Jacobean font cover. Georgian pulpit.
Interesting monuments.
Rievaulx Abbey
12th century, masterpiece of Early English
architecture.
One of three great Cistercian Abbeys built
in Yorkshire.
Impressive ruins.
Campsall (St. Mary Magdalene)
Fine Norman tower - 15th century rood
screen, carved & painted stone altar.
Fountains Abbey - Ripon
Ruins of England's greatest mediaeval
abbey - surrounded by wonderful
landscaped gardens. Enormous tower,
vaulted cellar 300 feet long.
Whitby (St. Mary)
12th century tower & doorway, 18th
century remodelling - box pews much
interior woodwork painted - galleries. High
pulpit. Table tombs.

Yorkshire

Whitby Abbey - Whitby (St. Hilda)
7th century superb ruin - venue of Synod
of 664. Destroyed by Vikings, restored
1078 - magnificent north transept.
Halifax (St. John the Baptist)
12th century origins, showing work from
each succeeding century - heraldic
ceilings. Cromwell glass.
Beverley Minster - Beverley
14th century. Fine Gothic Minster -
remarkable mediaeval effigies of
musicians playing instruments. Founded
as monastery in 700.
Bolton Priory - Nr. Skipton
Nave of Augustinian Priory, now Bolton's
Parish Church, amidst ruins of choir &
transepts, in beautiful riverside setting.
Selby Abbey - Selby
11th century Benedictine abbey of which
the huge church remains. Roof &
furnishings are modern after a fire of 1906,
but the stonework is intact.

Museums & Galleries

Aldborough Roman Museum -
Boroughbridge
Remnants of Roman period of the town -
coins, glass, pottery, etc.
Great Ayton
Home of Captain Cook, explorer &
seaman. Exhibits of maps, etc.
Art Gallery - City of York
Modern paintings, Old Masters,
watercolours, prints, ceramics.
Lotherton Hall - Nr. Leeds
Museum with furniture, paintings, silver,
works of art from the Leeds collection &
oriental art gallery.
National Railway Museum - York
Devoted to railway engineering & its
development.
York Castle Museum
The Kirk Collection of bygones including
cobbled streets, shops, costumes, toys,
household & farm equipment - fascinating
collection.
Cannon Hall Art Gallery - Barnsley
18th century house with fine furniture &
glass, etc. Flemish & Dutch paintings.
Also houses museum of the 13/18 Royal
Hussars.
Mappin Art Gallery - Sheffield
Works from 18th,19th & 20th century.

Graves Art gallery-Sheffield.
British portraiture. European works, &
examples of Asian & African art. Loan
exhibitions are held there.
Royal Pump Room Museum - Harrogate
Original sulphur well used in the Victorian
Spa. Local history costume & pottery.
Bolling Hall - Bradford
A period house with mixture of styles -
collections of 17th century oak furniture,
domestic utensils, toys & bygones.
Georgian Theatre - Richmond
Oldest theatre in the country - interesting
theatrical memorabilia.
Jorvik Viking Centre - York
Recently excavated site in the centre of
York showing hundreds of artifacts dating
from the Viking period. One of the most
important archaeological discoveries this
century.
Abbey House Museum - Kirkstall, Leeds
Illustrated past 300 years of Yorkshire life.
Shows 3 full streets from 19th century with
houses, shops & workplaces.
Piece Hall - Halifax
Remarkable building - constructed around
huge quadrangle - now Textile Industrial
Museum, Art Gallery & has craft & antique
shops.
**National Museum of Photography, Film
& Television** - Bradford
Displays look at art & science of
photography, film & T.V. Britain's only
IMAX arena.
The Colour Museum - Bradford
Award-winning interactive museum,which
allows visitors to explore the world of
colour & discover the story of dyeing &
textile printing.
Calderdale Industrial Museum - Halifax
Social & industrial Museum of the year
1987
Shibden Hall & Folk Museum of Halifax
Half-timbered house with folk museum,
farmland, miniature train & boating lake.
**Leeds City Art Gallery & Henry Moore
Sculpture Gallery**
Yorkshire Sculpture Park - Wakefield
Yorkshire Museum of Farming - Murton
Award-winning museum of farming & the
countryside.

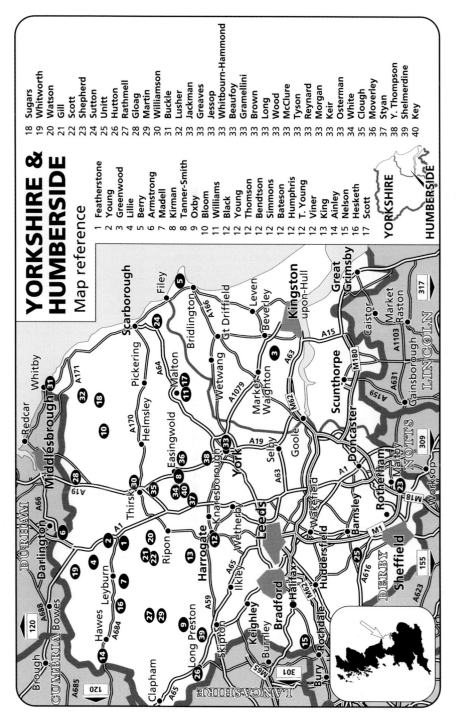

YORKSHIRE & HUMBERSIDE

Map reference

1 Featherstone
2 Young
3 Greenwood
4 Lillie
5 Berry
6 Armstrong
7 Madell
8 Kirman
8 Tanner-Smith
9 Oxby
10 Bloom
11 Williams
12 Black
12 Young
12 Thomson
12 Bendtson
12 Simmons
12 Bateson
12 Humphris
12 T. Young
12 Viner
13 King
14 Ainley
15 Nelson
16 Hesketh
17 Scott

18 Sugars
19 Whitworth
20 Watson
21 Gill
22 Scott
23 Shepherd
24 Sutton
25 Unitt
26 Hutton
27 Rathmell
28 Gloag
29 Martin
30 Williamson
31 Buckle
32 Lusher
33 Jackman
33 Greaves
33 Jessop
33 Whitbourn-Hammond
33 Beaufoy
33 Gramellini
33 Brown
33 Long
33 Wood
33 McClure
33 Tyson
33 Reynard
33 Morgan
33 Keir
33 Osterman
34 White
35 Clough
36 Moverley
37 Styan
38 Y. Thompson
39 Shelmerdine
40 Key

497

Yorkshire

		Rate from £ per person	Children taken	Evening meals	Animals taken
Jane & Peter Young **The Old Vicarage** Crakehall Bedale DL8 1HE Tel: (01677) 422967 Open: ALL YEAR Map Ref No. 02	Nearest Road: A.1, A.684 The Old Vicarage is a charming Georgian house set in a lovely garden of 1 acre, with many unusual plants. Cosy afternoon teas, & evening drinks served in front of a log fire. Hearty breakfasts, including home-cooked ham, fruits from the garden & home-made preserves. 5 spacious bedrooms - some en-suite - with tea/coffee-making facilities, colour T.V. & radio. An ideal base for exploring the Dales & Moors. Local golf club & riding nearby. Children over 7.	£20.00	Y	N	N
Edith & Jim Lillie **Elmfield Country House** Arrathorne Bedale DL8 1NE Tel: (01677) 450558 Fax 01677 450557 Open: ALL YEAR Map Ref No. 04	Nearest Road: A.1/M Located in its own grounds in the country. Enjoy a relaxed, friendly atmosphere in spacious surroundings, with a high standard of furnishings. 9 en-suite bedrooms comprising twin bedded, double & family rooms. 2 rooms have been adapted for disabled guests, & another has a 4-poster bed. All rooms have satellite colour T.V., 'phone, radio/ alarm & tea/coffee makers. A games room & solarium are also available. Excellent farmhouse cooking. Residential licence.	£19.50 CREDIT CARD VISA M'CARD	Y	Y	N
Oriella Featherstone **The Hall** Newton-le-Willows Bedale DL8 1SW Tel: (01677) 450210 Open: ALL YEAR Map Ref No. 01	Nearest Road: A.684 Come stay awhile: enjoy comfort, spaciousness & privacy within this glorious listed Georgian hideaway. A place to collapse, read, listen to music or simply wander out through the French windows into secluded gardens beneath the aged copper beaches. Oriella aims to provide whatever you might need to make your stay a joy. Come see the dales, moors, castles & ruins & make yourselves at home. (Stable facilities - dogs/ horses.) A delightful home.	£35.00 *see PHOTO over*	N	N	Y
Mrs Pauline Greenwood **Rudstone Walk** South Cave Beverley HU15 2AH Tel: (01430) 422230 Fax 01430 424552 Open: ALL YEAR Map Ref No. 03	Nearest Road: A.63 Rudstone Walk is renowned for its hospitality & good food. Accommodation is in the very tastefully converted farm buildings, adjacent to the main farmhouse where meals are served. Each of the attractive bedrooms has excellent en-suite facilities, colour T.V., 'phone, hairdryer & much more. Rudstone provides a peaceful retreat after a tiring day. It is ideal for a relaxing break, & is within easy reach of York & many other attractions.	£25.00 CREDIT CARD VISA M'CARD AMEX	Y	Y	N
Lesley Berry **The Manor House** Flamborough Bridlington YO15 1PD Tel: (01262) 850943 Fax 01262 850943 Open: ALL YEAR (Excl. Xmas) Map Ref No. 05	Nearest Road: A.165, A.166 A manor of Flamborough is recorded in the Domesday Book. The current Georgian house is a handsomely proportioned family home offering spacious & comfortable accommodation in well-appointed rooms. Historic Flamborough Head is designated a Heritage Coast, with many interesting walks & a nearby bird reserve. Ideally placed for exploration of North & East Yorkshire. Dinner, by prior arrangement, features local seafood when available. Children over 8 yrs.	£28.00 CREDIT CARD VISA M'CARD AMEX	Y	Y	N

The Hall. Newton-Le-Willows.

Yorkshire

	rate from £ per person	children taken	evening meals	animals taken

David & Heather Armstrong
Clow Beck House
Croft-on-Tees
Darlington DL2 2SW
Tel: (01325) 721075
Fax 01325 720419
Open: ALL YEAR
Map Ref No. 06

Nearest Road: A.1, A.167
A modern stone farmhouse set in 2 acres of garden with outstanding views over open countryside. Exceptional accommodation, each of the 5 rooms (4 en-suite, 1 with private bathroom) being tastefully furnished in an individual style, including 1 with a tented ceiling. The elegant dining room features hand-crafted furniture, & is the perfect setting for a hearty Yorkshire breakfast. A charming home which is convenient for Herriot country, York, Durham & the east coast.

£21.00   Y   N   N

see PHOTO over

CREDIT CARD
VISA
M'CARD

Christine & John Kirman
The Old Vicarage
Market Place
Easingwold
YO6 3AL
Tel: (01347) 821015
Open: FEB - NOV
Map Ref No. 08

Nearest Road: A.19
A listed property of immense character built in the 18th century & thoughtfully brought up to modern standards, & yet still retaining many delightful features. Now offering 5 en-suite rooms with T.V. & tea/coffee makers. Standing in extensive lawned gardens, overlooking the market square, & with a croquet lawn & a walled rose garden, it is an ideal touring centre for York, the Dales, the Yorkshire Moors & 'Herriot' countryside.

£20.00   Y   N   N

Mrs Daphne Tanner-Smith
Alderside
Thirsk Road
Easingwold
YO6 3HJ
Tel: (01347) 822132
Open: MAR - NOV
Map Ref No. 08

Nearest Road: A.19
Alderside is a comfortable Edwardian former school house set in large private gardens. 2 comfortable double bedrooms, with private bathroom, & 1 twin, each with colour T.V., radio & tea/coffee facilities. A full English breakfast is served using local produce & home-made preserves. A pleasant walk to Easingwold market place, with its variety of shops, pubs, etc. Easy access to York & surrounding countryside.

£16.50   N   N   N

Stephen & Julia Oxby
Greenways Guest House
Wharfeside Avenue
Threshfield
Grassington BD23 5BS
Tel: (01756) 752598
Open: ALL YEAR
Map Ref No. 09

Nearest Road: A.65
Greenways is situated half a mile off the main Skipton-to-Grassington road, & is set overlooking the River Wharfe. The accent is on homely comfort throughout & Julia aims to produce meals, prepared from local produce, which are satisfying & attractive. Greenways is a good centre to explore from: the Bronte Parsonage at Haworth, Fountains Abbey, historic York, the Settle-to-Carlisle railway & the lovely Yorkshire Dales are all within easy access.

£20.00   Y   Y   Y

Dr & Mrs M. Bloom
Manor House Farm
Ingleby Greenhow
Great Ayton
TS9 6RB
Tel: (01642) 722384
Open: ALL YEAR (Excl. Xmas)
Map Ref No. 10

Nearest Road: A.172
A charming old farm in idyllic surroundings at the foot of the Cleveland Hills in the North York Moors National Park. Set in park & woodland, this lovely house, with beams & open fires, has 3 delightful rooms with en-suite/private facilities, a pretty lounge, with T.V. for guests, & a garden. Very friendly, personal service. The hosts are proud of their reputation for fine cooking. Wine & dine by candlelight. Horse riding & golf locally, plus stabling if you can bring your own mount. Children over 12 welcome. Animals by arrangement.

£25.00   Y   Y   Y

500

Clow Beck House. Croft-on-Tees.

Yorkshire

		rate from £ per person	children taken	evening meals	animals taken
Gill & Kristian Bendtson **Ashwood House** **7 Spring Grove** **Harrogate HG1 2HS** **Tel: (01423) 560081** **Fax 01423 527928** **Open: ALL YEAR (Excl. Xmas)** **Map Ref No. 12**	Nearest Road: A.61 An elegant 8-bedroomed Edwardian house, situated in a quiet residential cul-de-sac minutes from the town centre. Charmingly decorated, it offers attractive bedrooms, some with 4-poster beds & all with en-suite bathrooms, tea/coffee-making facilities, hair dryers, radio & colour T.V.. A high standard of service, a warm welcome & an ample & delicious breakfast is assured. Ashwood House is an ideal base for touring Yorkshire.	£23.00	Y	N	N
Mr & Mrs John Black **Alexa House** **26 Ripon Road** **Harrogate HG1 2JJ** **Tel: (01423) 501988** **Fax 01423 504086** **Open: ALL YEAR** **Map Ref No. 12**	Nearest Road: A.61 Built in 1830 for Baron de Ferrier, & now a warm & welcoming small hotel. Offering 13 comfortable en-suite bedrooms, each with 'phone, colour T.V., clock/radio alarms & tea/coffee makers. There is a friendly atmosphere, nurtured by staff who 'belong' & guests who regularly return. The breakfasts are superb. Harrogate's many restaurants are only a stroll away, so you may leave your car in Alexa's car park.	£25.00 CREDIT CARD VISA M'CARD	Y	Y	N
Peter & Dee Bateson **Acacia Lodge** **21 Ripon Road** **Harrogate** **HG1 2JL** **Tel: (01423) 560752** **Open: ALL YEAR** **Map Ref No. 12**	Nearest Road: A.61 A warm, elegant Victorian house set in pretty gardens, & with a car park, in a select central area only a stroll from fashionable shops & restaurants. Full of graceful charm, & retaining all original character, with a liberal sprinkling of antiques. All bedrooms are en-suite, with every comfort & facility. Award-winning breakfasts. A beautiful, relaxing guest lounge/library with open fire. Scenic Oakdale golf club 800 yds away. The personal attention of the owners, Dee & Peter, assures you of a very comfortable stay.	£24.00	N	N	N
Rupert & Marian Viner **Delaine Hotel** **17 Ripon Road** **Harrogate HG1 2JL** **Tel: (01423) 567974** **Fax 01423 561723** **Open: ALL YEAR (Excl. Xmas)** **Map Ref No. 12**	Nearest Road: A.61 The Delaine is a Victorian, family-run hotel set in beautiful award-winning gardens. Offering guests a warm welcome & the personal attention of owners Rupert & Marian Viner. All of the delightful bedrooms have en-suite facilities, are very comfortable & have co-ordinated furnishings, & all the usual amenities & more. Excellent home-cooked meals are available. This is the perfect base for touring the Yorkshire Dales.	£25.00 CREDIT CARD VISA M'CARD AMEX	Y	Y	N
Mrs Julia Humphris **Crescent Lodge** **20 Swan Road** **Harrogate** **HG1 2SA** **Tel: (01423) 503688** **Open: ALL YEAR (Excl. Xmas)** **Map Ref No. 12**	Nearest Road: A.61, A.1 This charming, period, Grade II listed family home, overlooking crescent gardens & only a short walk from the Valley Gardens & Pump Rooms, offers 4 well-appointed rooms, 2 en-suite, each with tea/coffee makers & complimentary toiletries. A hairdryer & laundry facilities available. An elegant guests' drawing room with colour T.V. Ideally placed for the conference centre, exhibition halls, shops & theatre, as well as Yorkshire's finest Dales scenery. French, German & Spanish spoken.	£21.00	N	N	N

Yorkshire

		rate from £ per person	children taken	evening meals	animals taken
John & Maria Simmons **The Ruskin Hotel** **1 Swan Road** **Harrogate** **HG1 2SS** **Tel: (01423) 502045** Fax 01423 506131 **Open: ALL YEAR** **Map Ref No. 12**	Nearest Road: A.61, A.1 A truly outstanding small Victorian hotel, set in lovely lawned grounds (with a car park). In a quiet conservation area only mins' stroll from the town, famous gardens & attractions. Beautiful, antique-furnished, spacious en-suite bedrooms with every facility. Superior beds, including a 4-poster. A charming guest drawing room/library with an open fire. Renowned for superb breakfasts & excellent English/French cuisine served in the delightful Victorian-style restaurant with bar. The Ruskin is rather special. A warm welcome awaits you. CREDIT CARD VISA M'CARD	£27.00	Y	Y	N
Mrs Elizabeth Young **Daryl House Hotel** **42 Dragon Parade** **Harrogate** **HG1 5DA** **Tel: (01423) 502775** **Open: ALL YEAR** **Map Ref No. 12**	Nearest Road: A.59 A small, friendly, family-run house offering excellent accommodation in 6 most pleasant rooms with every modern comfort. Tea/coffee makers & T.V. in all rooms. An attractive lounge with colour T.V. & garden for guests' enjoyment. Home-cooked food & personal attention are the hallmarks of Daryl House. Close to the town centre with its conference facilities. A very warm welcome awaits all visitors.	£15.00	Y	Y	Y
Mike & Tricia Young **Shannon Court Hotel** **65 Dragon Avenue** **Harrogate HG1 5DS** **Tel: (01423) 509858** Fax 01423 530606 **Open: ALL YEAR** **Map Ref No. 12**	Nearest Road: A.59 Charming Victorian house hotel overlooking the 'stray' in High Harrogate. Enjoy real home cooking in this family-run hotel. There are 8 delightful bedrooms, all en-suite, with every modern comfort including radio, colour T.V. & tea/coffee-making facilities. Licensed for residents & their guests. Close to town centre, railway station & conference centre, with easy parking, & direct to main routes for moors & dales. An excellent touring base. CREDIT CARD VISA M'CARD	£17.00	Y	Y	N
Peter & Marion Thomson **Knox Mill House** **Knox Mill Lane** **Harrogate** **HG3 2AE** **Tel: (01423) 560650** **Open: ALL YEAR (Excl.** **Xmas & New Year)** **Map Ref No. 12**	Nearest Road: A.61 Built in 1785, this lovely old millhouse stands on the banks of a stream in a quiet rural setting, & yet is only 1 1/2 miles from the centre of Harrogate. Beautifully renovated, it still retains all its original features: oak beams, an inglenook fireplace & stone arches. There are 3 delightful rooms, attractively & comfortably furnished. 2 are en-suite, & all have tea/coffee makers & views over the stream & fields. A delightful lounge with colour T.V., & a garden for guests' enjoyment.	£19.00	N	N	N
Clive & Gill King **High Winsley Cottage** **Burnt Yates** **Harrogate** **HG3 3EP** **Tel: (01423) 770662** **Open: FEB - DEC** **Map Ref No. 13**	Nearest Road: A.61 Traditional Dales cottage in Nidderdale, situated well off the road in peaceful countryside, with lovely views all around, & ideally placed for both town & country. 3 twin & 2 double rooms, well-appointed & all with en-suite facilities. 2 large sitting rooms, with guide books, games, T.V., etc. Imaginative home cooking using produce from the extensive kitchen garden, complemented by wines from an interesting list. *see PHOTO over*	£20.00	N	Y	N

High Winsley Cottage. Burnt Yates.

Yorkshire

		rate from £ per person	children taken	evening meals	animals taken
Gail Ainley & Ann Macdonald **Brandymires Guest House** **Muker Road** **Hawes DL8 3PR** **Tel: (01969) 667482** **Open: FEB - OCT** **Map Ref No. 14**	Nearest Road: A.684 A warm welcome awaits you in this comfortable mid-19th-century stone house in a tranquil rural setting. Every room has a splendid view over the fells. 4 spacious double bedrooms, 2 with 4-poster beds, full central heating. Good home cooking is an important feature, & dinner is available with prior notice, except on Thursdays. Brandymires is an ideal centre for exploring both the glorious countryside of the Yorkshire Dales & the historic surrounding towns. No T.V.. Ample car-parking space.	£17.00	N	Y	Y
Mrs Nora W. Nelson **'Springfield'** **Cragg Road** **Cragg Vale** **Hebden Bridge HX7 5SR** **Tel: (01422) 882029** **Open: ALL YEAR** **Map Ref No. 15**	Nearest Road: A.646, B.6138 A warm Yorkshire welcome awaits visitors at Springfield. Standing in an acre of garden in a picturesque wooded valley in the South Pennines, with open views of woods & moorland. Guests may choose from 4 comfortably furnished, centrally heated rooms with adjacent bath/shower; 1 with en-suite facilities. All rooms have modern amenities, including T.V., radio & tea/coffee makers. Sauna available. Mrs Nelson's breakfasts have won a Best Yorkshire Breakfast Award.	£16.00	Y	N	N
Mr & Mrs G. E. Hesketh **High Green House** **Thoralby** **Leyburn** **DL8 3SU** **Tel: (01969) 663420** **Open: APR - OCT** **Map Ref No. 16**	Nearest Road: A.684 Pat & Ted Hesketh offer the discerning visitor many comforts, a friendly, relaxed atmosphere & excellent home cooking. All 3 bedrooms have en-suite/private facilities, & there is a ground-floor room designed for visitors with impaired mobility. Situated in the heart of the Yorkshire Dales National Park, on the edge of Thoralby village green, the house is a small Georgian property enjoying wide views across Bishopdale. Excellent for touring & walking. CREDIT CARD VISA M'CARD	£20.50	Y	Y	Y
Everyl & Brian Madell **Waterford House** **Kirkgate, Middleham** **Leyburn DL8 4PG** **Tel: (01969) 622090** **Fax 01969 624020** **Open: ALL YEAR** **Map Ref No. 07**	Nearest Road: A.6108, A.684 A beautiful, traditional stone-built Georgian residence overlooking the market square of Middleham. Once the centre of government in mediaeval England & featuring the ruins of Richard III's castle. 5 spacious en-suite bedrooms, some beamed, including a 4-poster, & exquisitely decorated in keeping with the period atmosphere. The restaurant has an a la carte menu that changes daily & over 700 wines, many from the 50's, 60's & 70's. Ideal base for the Dales & Herriot country. CREDIT CARD VISA M'CARD	£30.00 *see PHOTO over*	Y	Y	Y
Paul & Pat Williams **Newstead Grange** **Beverley Road, Norton** **Malton YO17 9PJ** **Tel: (01653) 692502** **Fax 01653 696951** **Open: FEB - NOV** **Map Ref No. 11**	Nearest Road: A.64 An elegant Georgian country house set in 2 1/2 acres of gardens & grounds with delightful views of the North Yorkshire moors & wolds. The style of the house is tastefully enhanced by antique furniture, open log fires burn in cooler weather & the bedrooms are individually furnished. The proprietors personally prepare the meals to a very high standard from vegetables & fruit in the organic kitchen garden & fresh local produce. Totally non-smoking. Children over 10. CREDIT CARD VISA M'CARD	£26.00	Y	Y	N

Waterford House. Middleham.

Yorkshire

		rate from £ per person	children taken	evening meals	animals taken
Richard & Stella Scott **Red House** **Wharram-le-Street** **Malton** **YO17 9TL** **Tel: (01944) 768455** **Open: ALL YEAR** **Map Ref No. 17**	Nearest Road: A.64, B.1248 Stella & Richard warmly welcome everyone to their elegant 19th-century home. Standing in an acre of garden in the heart of the Yorkshire Wolds, it offers 3 very comfortable bedrooms, with private facilities, T.V. & tea/coffee makers, & a guests' lounge with lovely log fires. Good home cooking, using their own produce. Special diets catered for. Licensed dining rooms. Nearby are Castle Howard, Sledmere House & Nunnington Hall. York 23 miles. Grass tennis facility.	£21.60	Y	Y	Y
Linda Sugars **Sevenford House** **Rosedale Abbey** **Pickering** **YO18 8SE** **Tel: (01751) 417283** **Open: ALL YEAR (Excl. Xmas Day)** **Map Ref No. 18**	Nearest Road: A.170 Originally a vicarage, & built from the stones of Rosedale Abbey, 'Sevenford House' stands in 4 acres of lovely gardens in the heart of the beautiful Yorkshire Moors National Park. 3 tastefully furnished, en-suite bedrooms, with T.V., radio, & tea/coffee, offer wonderful views overlooking valley & moorland. A relaxing guests' lounge/library with open fire. This is an excellent base for exploring the region. Riding & golf locally. Also, ruined abbeys, Roman roads, steam railways, the beautiful coastline & pretty fishing towns. *see PHOTO over*	£17.50	Y	N	N
Ian & Angela Whitworth **The White House** **Arkle Town** **Arkengarthdale** **Richmond DL11 6RB** **Tel: (01748) 884203** **Open: JAN - NOV** **Map Ref No. 19**	Nearest Road: A.6108 An 18th-century former farmhouse, modernised, tastefully decorated and furnished to a high standard. 3 rooms offer modern amenities (2 en-suite). Cosy visitors' lounge with open fire. Only the best ingredients used, in tasty, home-cooked meals. In the heart of Herriot country, and set above the road with superb uninterrupted views, the ideal centre for exploring the Yorkshire Dales. Children over 10 please. Reduced rates for 2 or more nights inc. dinner.	£19.00	N	Y	N
Mrs Elaine M. Watson **Sleningford Grange** **North Stainley** **Ripon HG4 3HX** **Tel/Fax: (01765) 635252** **Open: ALL YEAR (Excl. Xmas & New Year)** **Map Ref No. 20**	Nearest Road: A.1 A delightful listed manor house dating from the 15th century, Sleningford Grange stands in lovely & extensive gardens on the verge of the Yorkshire Dales. The interior is elegant, & furnished with antiques. There are 4 most comfortable & spacious bedrooms with en-suite facilities & views across rolling countryside. An ideal base for exploring the Dales/Moors & the wealth of historic towns & abbeys - or for an overnight break midway between London & Edinburgh. Children over 5 yrs.	£30.00	Y	N	N
Phillip Gill & Anton Van Der Horst **Bank Villa** **The Avenue, Masham** **Ripon HG4 4DB** **Tel: (01765) 689605** **Open: APR - OCT** **Map Ref No. 21**	Nearest Road: A.6108, A.1 A fine Georgian house overlooking the River Ure in large terraced gardens, offering delightful accommodation in 7 comfortable double rooms, some with private showers. It is a super base for visiting the Druids Temple, Jervaulx Abbey, Middleham Castle, Fountains Abbey & the wonderful 'James Herriot Country'. Dutch is spoken. Meals are excellent value. Children under 5 not accommodated.	£18.00	Y	Y	Y

Sevenford House. Rosedale Abbey.

Yorkshire

			rate from £ per person	children taken	evening meals	animals taken

Avril Scott
Pasture House
Healey, Masham
Ripon HG4 4LJ
Tel: (01765) 689149
Fax 01765 689990
Open: ALL YEAR
Map Ref No. 22

Nearest Road: A.6108
Pasture House is a large, comfortable house providing guests with pleasant accommodation in the quiet of the lovely Yorkshire Dales. A perfect centre for walkers & horse-racing enthusiasts, with several courses & Middleham training gallops nearby. 4 comfortable rooms with T.V. & tea/coffee makers, a residents' lounge & large garden are also available. Pony trekking, golf & fishing locally. Children & pets welcome. Facilities for babies. A lovely home.

£14.00   Y   Y   Y

Mr & Mrs M. A. Shepherd
Stonecroft Hotel
Main Street, Bramley
Rotherham S66 0SF
Tel: (01709) 540922
Open: ALL YEAR
Map Ref No. 23

Nearest Road: M.18 Ex. 1
Stonecroft is a Grade II listed building with a homely atmosphere. The main building is 300 years old, with a profusion of oak beams & open fireplaces. 8 tastefully furnished rooms, 7 with en-suite bathroom, all with modern amenities including T.V., radio & tea/coffee-making facilities. A residents' lounge & delightful garden also available for guests to relax in. Ideally situated for visiting the many attractions in Yorkshire & Derbyshire.

£20.56   Y   N   Y

CREDIT CARD
VISA
M'CARD

Mrs Virginia Sutton
Willerby Wold Farm
Staxton
Scarborough
YO12 4TF
Tel/Fax: (01944) 710747
Open: ALL YEAR (Excl. Xmas)
Map Ref No. 24

Nearest Road: A.64
Peacefully situated on an 800-acre farm on the edge of the Yorkshire Wolds, this elegant country house is ideally located for exploring the east coast, the North York Moors & York. The 3 attractive bedrooms have private bathrooms, tea & coffee facilities & colour T.V.. Guests are welcome to use the garden & all-weather tennis court. Stabling available. Evening meals by arrangement. A delightful family home.

£18.00   Y   Y   N

Ann Unitt
Aldermans Head Manor
Hartcliffe Hill Road
Langsett, Stocksbridge
Sheffield S30 5GY
Tel/Fax: (01226) 766209
Open: ALL YEAR (Excl. Xmas & New Year)
Map Ref No. 25

Nearest Road: A.616
Set in 50 acres of dramatic countryside, the Manor enjoys panoramic views across the Peak District moorland. 7 centuries ago, the monks of Kirkstead Abbey are believed to have farmed here. Today, the welcoming atmosphere of peace & tranquility still prevails. Home cooking with fresh local produce, beamed ceilings, log fires & superb views from all bedrooms. An ideal centre for local walking, or for exploring Yorkshire & Derbyshire. Children over 12 yrs.

£22.50   Y   Y   N

Richard & Rosalind
Shelmerdine
Eshton Grange
Gargrave
Skipton
BD23 3QE
Tel: (01756) 749383
Open: ALL YEAR
Map Ref No. 39

Nearest Road: A.65
Farmhouse bed & breakfast is found at this attractive, 18th-century listed house, situated on a 20-acre working stock farm with various animals including Shetland ponies. Located in the Yorkshire Dales National Park, it is close to many beauty spots, with walking, potholing & pony trekking nearby. 3 bedrooms, all with private bathroom, T.V., & tea/coffee-making facilities. A sitting room with open fire in winter. A lovely walled garden with beautiful views. Evening meals available Fri - Sun.

£20.00   Y   Y   N

Yorkshire

		rate from £ per person	children taken	evening meals taken	animals taken
Don & Dorothy Hutton **The Country House Hotel** **Long Preston** **Skipton BD23 4NJ** **Tel: (01729) 840246** **Open: FEB - Mid DEC** **Map Ref No. 26**	Nearest Road: A.65 An elegant Victorian country house, situated in its own grounds in the Yorkshire Dales. 6 en-suite bedrooms, with colour T.V. & tea/coffee facilities. Drawing room with log fire & extensive library. Fine food, but please bring your own wine. A sauna & spa bath are also provided for relaxation. Delightful house, offering a personal service in homely, informal & restful surroundings.	£25.00	Y	Y	N
Tim & Marie Louise Rathmell **Hilltop Country Guest House** **Starbotton** **Skipton BD23 5HY** **Tel: (01756) 760321** **Open: MAR - NOV** **Map Ref No. 27**	Nearest Road: A.59, B.6160 Hilltop Country Guest House is a 17th-century listed house situated in 4 acres of beckside gardens & overlooking an unspoilt village in the heart of the Yorkshire Dales. An excellent centre for fell & riverside walks, or for touring. Spacious & immaculate bedrooms, all en-suite. Fine food & wine served by candlelight in an oak-beamed dining room at weekends & to parties of six or more guests. A delightful home.	£25.00	Y	Y	N
Robin Martin & Tim Earnshaw **High Fold** **Kettlewell** **Skipton** **BD23 5RJ** **Tel: (01756) 760390** **Open: FEB - DEC** **Map Ref No. 29**	Nearest Road: A.59 High Fold is a dales barn, recently converted to a high standard of accommodation, offering elegant yet relaxing surroundings in a quiet & picturesque location. Enhanced by beamed ceilings, stone features & antiques. 4 beautifully furnished & well-equipped en-suite bedrooms. 2 are situated on the ground floor & have been carefully designed for disabled/elderly guests. A large drawing room with log fire, books, etc. Imaginative cuisine using quality produce. An ideal base for the Dales, Skipton, Grassington, Malham & Bolton Abbey.	£25.00	Y	Y	Y
Mrs Anne Gloag **Busby House** **Stokesley** **TS9 5LB** **Tel: (01642) 710425** **Fax 01642 713838** **Open: FEB - NOV** **Map Ref No. 28**	Nearest Road: A.1, A.19, A.172 This is a lovely old farmhouse, with an enclosed cobbled courtyard to the rear, situated 2 1/2 miles south of Stokesley. Delightfully furnished, the principal rooms look south over the large garden & fields to the hills beyond. The atmosphere is peaceful & relaxed & exudes warmth & friendliness. Renowned for comfort, & excellent candlelit dinners can be provided. The perfect base for exploring the Moors, Dales & coast, & within easy reach of York, Durham & many places of historic interest. Only 25 mins from the A.1.	£28.00 *see PHOTO over*	N	Y	N
Mrs Tess Williamson **Thornborough House Farm** **South Kilvington** **Thirsk YO7 2NP** **Tel/Fax: (01845) 522103** **Open: ALL YEAR** **Map Ref No. 30**	Nearest Road: A.19 A warm welcome awaits you at this 200-year-old farmhouse, set in lovely countryside. Only one & a half miles north of Thirsk, this working farm is situated in the town made famous by James Herriot. 3 warm & comfortable rooms, each with en-suite/private bathroom, all with tea/coffee-making facilities. Guests have their own sitting/dining room with colour T.V. & open fire. Good home cooking a speciality. Convenient for York, Ripon, the Pennine Dales & the East Coast.	£14.00 CREDIT CARD VISA M'CARD	Y	Y	Y

Busby House. Stokesley.

Yorkshire

Ann & Robin Clough **Spital Hill** **York Road** **Thirsk** **YO7 3AE** **Tel: (01845) 522273** **Open: ALL YEAR** **Map Ref No. 35**	Nearest Road: A.19 Quiet, peaceful & relaxing, Spital Hill is situated in 1 1/2 acres of secluded garden surrounded by parkland. Originally a Georgian farmhouse, it was extended in 1884, & is now a warm & comfortable home from which to explore York, Harrogate, the Moors, the Dales & Herriot Country. Dinner is en-famille, & the whole meal, including a range of breads, is home-prepared drawing from the kitchen garden. The bedrooms are delightfully furnished, with comfortable beds, & the bathrooms are large, warm & well-provisioned.	£30.00 🚭 CREDIT CARD VISA M'CARD AMEX	Y	Y	N
Ian & Rosalie Buckle **Dunsley Hall** **Dunsley** **Whitby YO21 3TL** **Tel: (01947) 893437** **Fax 01947 893505** **Open: ALL YEAR (Excl.** **Xmas Day & Boxing Day)** **Map Ref No. 31**	Nearest Road: A.171 Peaceful & elegant country hall in 4 acres of secluded grounds, providing a truly relaxed atmosphere. Oak-panelled rooms, including superb carved Billiard Room with stained glass window. 11 delightful en-suite bedrooms, with full facilities & central heating. Within North York Moors National Park, 3 miles outside Whitby (Captain Cook country) & ideal for Heritage Coast, Castle Howard & York. Offering indoor, heated swimming pool, fitness room, sauna, tennis, putting or croquet. Licensed.	£35.00 *see PHOTO over* CREDIT CARD VISA M'CARD	Y	Y	Y
John & Pauline Lusher **Whitfield House Hotel** **Darnholm** **Goathland** **Whitby YO22 5LA** **Tel: (01947) 896215** **Open: FEB - NOV** **Map Ref No. 32**	Nearest Road: A.169 Once a 17th-century farmhouse, Whitfield House has been carefully modernised to provide every comfort whilst retaining its old-world charm. 8 cottage-style en-suite bedrooms (no smoking), with T.V., tea maker, telephone, hairdryer & clock/radio alarm. Quietly situated in the heart of the North Moors National Park. Superb country cooking using fresh produce. Residential licence. The perfect base for touring or just relaxing.	£24.00 CREDIT CARD VISA M'CARD	Y	Y	Y
Elsie & Leonard Osterman **Barbican Hotel** **20 Barbican Road** **York** **YO1 5AA** **Tel/Fax: (01904) 627617** **Open: ALL YEAR** **Map Ref No. 33**	Nearest Road: A.19 Small in size but large in character. Barbican Hotel overlooks the mediaeval city walls. Leave your car in the floodlit car park & walk to all the city-centre attractions. All bedrooms are en-suite & attractively furnished with colour T.V., 'phone, coffee/tea, hairdryer, etc. Traditional or vegetarian breakfasts served in the dining room with a lovely original kitchen range in superb condition. A friendly Northern welcome always assured.	£19.00 🚭 CREDIT CARD VISA M'CARD AMEX	Y	N	N
Mr & Mrs S. Long **Grasmead House Hotel** **1 Scarcroft Hill** **York YO2 1DF** **Tel: (01904) 629996** **Fax 01904 629996** **Open: ALL YEAR** **Map Ref No. 33**	Nearest Road: A.1036 An attractive, small, family-run hotel, situated within easy walking distance of the city centre. The charming bedrooms feature antique furniture, 4-poster beds (1 dating back to 1730), en-suite bathrooms, tea/coffee-making facilities & colour T.V.. Also a comfortable lounge with a small bar where you can relax after spending the day exploring historic York. Delicious breakfasts served in the attractive dining room. An ideal centre for visiting the Dales, Moors & coast.	£25.00 CREDIT CARD VISA M'CARD	Y	N	N

Dunsley Hall. Dunsley.

Easton's. York.

Yorkshire

	rate from £ per person	children taken	evening meals	animals taken

L. M. Keir & M. D. Easton **Easton's** **90 Bishopthorpe Road** **York** **YO2 1JS** **Tel: (01904) 626646** **Open: ALL YEAR** **Map Ref No. 33**	Nearest Road: A.64, A.19 A sympathetically & beautifully restored Victorian wine-merchants residence, centrally situated just 300 yds from the mediaeval city walls. The period furniture, William Morris decor, open fires & fully equipped bedrooms are in accord with the character of the building, & with the standard of excellence that the owners strive for. The Victorian sideboard breakfast menu follows the same theme of quality, & includes a selection of traditional & vegetarian dishes. Children over 4 yrs.	£18.50 🚭 *see PHOTO over* CREDIT CARD VISA M'CARD	Y	N	N
Keith Jackman **Dairy Guest House** **3 Scarcroft Road** **York** **YO2 1ND** **Tel: (01904) 639367** **Open: ALL YEAR (Excl. Xmas)** **Map Ref No. 33**	Nearest Road: A.64 The Dairy is a tastefully renovated Victorian house within walking distance of the city centre & just 200 yards from the mediaeval city walls. Decorated & furnished in the styles of Habitat, Sanderson's & Laura Ashley, with the emphasis on pine & plants. 5 bedrooms, some en-suite (& 4-poster available), & each with modern amenities, colour T.V., hot-drink facilities & extensive information on York & Yorkshire. There is a lovely enclosed courtyard. Breakfast choices are from English to wholefood vegetarian.	£16.00 🚭	Y	N	N
Russell & Cherry **Whitbourn-Hammond** **Nunmill House** **85 Bishopthorpe Road** **York YO2 1NX** **Tel: (01904) 634047** **Open: FEB - NOV** **Map Ref No. 33**	Nearest Road: A.64, A.59 A warm friendly welcome awaits you at Nunmill House, a delightful late-Victorian house, tastefully restored throughout with Laura Ashley furnishings to enhance the original architectural features. Offering a choice of 8 delightful bedrooms, each with en-suite or private facilities. Ideally situated just outside the mediaeval walls, & a 10-minute walk to all the historic attractions of the city. Complimentary tea & coffee are available, & special diets can be catered for by arrangement.	£20.00 🚭	Y	N	N
Malcolm & Liz Greaves **Carlton House Hotel** **134 The Mount** **York YO2 2AS** **Tel: (01904) 622265** **Open: ALL YEAR (Excl.** **Xmas & New Year)** **Map Ref No. 33**	Nearest Road: A.1036, A.64 Each & every guest will receive a warm & friendly welcome from proprietors Liz & Malcolm Greaves. This pleasant, family-run hotel offers guests a choice of 14 rooms, all with colour T.V., radio & tea/coffee makers. Many have en-suite facilities. The spacious lounges are comfortable & pleasantly furnished. A traditional English breakfast is cooked to order. Light refreshments are available at most times throughout the day. Nearby are York race course & the Minster.	£23.00	Y	N	N
Robin & Anne McClure **4 South Parade** **York** **YO2 2BA** **Tel: (01904) 628229** **Fax 01904 628229** **Open: ALL YEAR** **Map Ref No. 33**	Nearest Road: A.1036, A.64 An elegant Grade II listed Georgian townhouse in a private cobbled street. Beautifully decorated and furnished with antiques. 3 lovely guest rooms, each with its own individual character; en-suite facilities in Edwardian style, original fireplaces with working cast-iron hob grates, fresh flowers, bowls of fruit, Teletext remote-control T.V. & direct-dial telephones. Be pampered with old-fashioned hospitality & service, & delicious food.	£34.00 🚭 *see PHOTO over*	N	N	N

4 South Parade. York.

Arndale Hotel. York.

Yorkshire

		rate from £ per person	children taken	evening meals	animals taken

			rate from £ per person	children taken	evening meals	animals taken
Dick & Jean Tyson **Byron House Hotel** **7 Driffield Terrace** **The Mount** **York YO2 2DD** **Tel: (01904) 632525** **Fax 01904 638904** **Open: ALL YEAR (Excl. Xmas)** **Map Ref No. 33**	Nearest Road: A.64, A.1036 A small, elegant hotel, circa 1830. It has lofty & spacious bedrooms, with modern facilities, suitable for business or leisure guests. The hotel is situated in an attractive tree-lined area 10 minutes' walk from the city walls. The airy dining room serves well-cooked English food, & dietary arrangements are catered for. There is a comfortable lounge & bar combined which overlooks the landscaped car park. Byron House is the perfect spot from which to explore York & this very beautiful region.	£24.00 CREDIT CARD VISA M'CARD AMEX	Y	Y	N
David & Gillian Reynard **Arndale Hotel** **290 Tadcaster Road** **York YO2 2ET** **Tel: (01904) 702424** **Open: ALL YEAR (Excl.** **Xmas & New Year)** **Map Ref No. 33**	Nearest Road: A.64, A.1036 A delightful Victorian house, directly overlooking York's famous race course, with beautiful enclosed walled gardens giving a country-house atmosphere within the city. A spacious, elegant lounge, complete with antiques, fresh flowers, paintings & a small bar. 10 outstanding & well-equipped bedrooms, all en-suite. Many bathrooms are Victorian in style, with modern whirlpool baths. Antique half-tester/4-poster beds. A substantial English breakfast is served. Car park.	£23.00 *see PHOTO over*	N	N	N
Richard & Wendy Wood **Curzon Lodge & Stable** **Cottages** **23 Tadcaster Road** **Dringhouses** **York YO2 2QG** **Tel: (01904) 703157** **Open: ALL YEAR** **Map Ref No. 33**	Nearest Road: A.64, A.1036 A charming 17th-century Grade II listed house & delightful stables conversion with original oak beams, in a conservation area overlooking the racecourse. Once a home of the Terry family, the renowned York chocolate makers. Guests are invited to share the unique atmosphere, in 10 comfortably furnished rooms. All have en-suite, colour-T.V., telephone, radio, hairdryer & tea/coffee facilities. Some 4-posters & brass beds. Many antiques, a pretty lounge & a farmhouse kitchen breakfast room. Large, walled car park.	£24.00 *see PHOTO over* CREDIT CARD VISA M'CARD	Y	N	N
Mrs Julie Brown **Four Seasons Hotel** **7 St. Peters Grove** **Bootham** **York YO3 6AQ** **Tel: (01904) 622621** **Fax 01904 430565** **Open: ALL YEAR (Excl. Xmas)** **Map Ref No. 33**	Nearest Road: A.19 An elegant Victorian residence with much character & appeal. Ideally situated in a peaceful cul-de-sac, yet only 7 mins' stroll from the Minster & York's many other historic attractions. Offering 5 beautifully furnished & well-appointed en-suite bedrooms, all fully equipped. Full English breakfast, residential licence & private car parking. A warm & friendly reception awaits you from Julie & Adrian Brown. This is an ideal base from which to explore York with its many attractions & places of historic interest.	£22.00 CREDIT CARD VISA M'CARD	Y	N	Y
Mike & Ann Beaufoy **18 St. Paul's Square** **York** **YO2 4BD** **Tel: (01904) 629884** **Open: ALL YEAR** **Map Ref No. 33**	Nearest Road: A.59 A delightful Victorian house located in a pleasant Victorian garden square in the centre of York. Skilfully restored & furnished with period antiques, it now offers 3 very comfortable en-suite/private bedrooms, a guests' colour T.V. lounge & a garden. Mike & Ann enjoy sharing their home & knowledge of York with their guests, & are happy to give advice on where to go & what to see locally.	£30.00 🚭	Y	N	N

Curzon Lodge. York.

Holmwood House Hotel.   York.

Yorkshire

		rate from £ per person	children taken	evening meals	animals taken
Mr & Mrs R. Gramellini **Holmwood House** **114 Holgate Road** **York YO2 4BB** **Tel: (01904) 626183** **Fax 01904 670899** **Open: FEB - DEC** **Map Ref No. 33**	Nearest Road: A.59, A.1, M.1 The conversion of 2 listed, early-Victorian town houses has created an elegant hotel that offers guests a feeling of home with a touch of luxury. All rooms - which, of course, have en-suite facilities - are different both in size & decoration, & there are 3 honeymoon rooms (2 with 4-poster beds), a suite, on the ground floor, with spa bathroom & a guest sitting room with an open fire. A large proportion of rooms are set aside for non-smokers. *see PHOTO over* CREDIT CARD VISA M'CARD AMEX	£27.50	N	N	N
Mr & Mrs Jessop **Bloomsbury Hotel** **127 Clifton** **York** **YO3 6BL** **Tel: (01904) 634031** **Open: ALL YEAR** **Map Ref No. 33**	Nearest Road: A.19 The Bloomsbury is a beautiful large Victorian town house with adequate car parking. Situated in a conservation area only a 12-minute walk from York Minster in the historic centre of York. Each of the 8 guest rooms in this delightful family-run establishment has been individually designed by the owners for your comfort. The proprietors will gladly give assistance & advice to ensure your stay is enjoyable & successful. CREDIT CARD VISA	£16.00	Y	N	N
Michael & Juliet Morgan **The Bentley** **25 Grosvenor Terrace** **Bootham** **York** **YO3 7AG** **Tel: (01904) 644313** **Open: ALL YEAR (Excl. Xmas)** **Map Ref No. 33**	Nearest Road: A.19 Relax in an elegant Victorian town house, furnished with quality, care & comfort in mind for the really discerning guest. Enjoy the spacious en-suite rooms (with T.V., tea/coffee-making facilities, etc.), most of which have a fine view across parkland to the beautiful York Minster. The Bentley is just a few minutes' stroll from the city centre & its many historical treats, yet in a quiet one-way street, with parking. York is also a unique shopping experience. *see PHOTO over*	£21.00	N	N	N
Tony & Tricia Styan **Primrose Cottage** **Lime Bar Lane, Grafton** **York YO5 9QJ** **Tel: (01423) 322835/322711** **Fax 01423 323985** **Open: ALL YEAR** **Map Ref No. 37**	Nearest Road: A.1 A warm friendly welcome awaits you at Primrose Cottage, in a quiet picturesque village 1 mile east of the A.1. Comfortable bedrooms with washbasins & tea/coffee facilities. 2 bath/shower rooms. Spacious T.V. lounge, & sheltered patio garden with barbecue for guests' use. 2 local inns serving excellent food. Ideally situated 15 mins north of York. Ripon, Harrogate & Yorkshire Dales within easy distance.	£15.00	Y	N	Y
Mrs Yvonne Thompson **Brentwood Cottage** **Main Street** **Shipton-by-Beningbrough** **York YO6 1AB** **Tel: (01904) 470111** **Open: ALL YEAR** **Map Ref No. 38**	Nearest Road: A.19 A warm & friendly welcome awaits all guests at Brentwood Cottage. Located 5 miles outside the historic city of York, it offers guests a choice of 5 pleasant bedrooms, 2 with en-suite/private facilities & amenities, & each with tea/coffee-making facilities. There is also a comfortable residents' lounge & garden available. This makes a good base for touring York & the surrounding countryside. A large car park.	£16.00	Y	N	N

The Bentley. York.

Yorkshire

			rate from £ per person	children taken	evening meals	animals taken

John & Sue White Brafferton Hall Brafferton Helperby York YO6 2NZ Tel/Fax: (01423) 360352 Open: ALL YEAR Map Ref No. 34	Nearest Road: A.1 Brafferton Hall is a comfortable family home set in a quiet village near the River Swale in the heart of North Yorkshire, yet only 4 miles from the A.1. Offering 4 comfortable & attractively furnished bedrooms, each with en-suite or private facilities, T.V., radio & tea/coffee-making facilities. Ideally placed for exploring York, the National Parks & Herriot country all within an easy 30-minute drive. Informality, accompanied by excellent fare, is to be enjoyed at Brafferton Hall.	£30.00 🚭 CREDIT CARD VISA M'CARD AMEX	Y	Y	Y
Annie & Sam Key Laurel Farm Brafferton York YO6 2NZ Tel/Fax: (01423) 360436 Open: ALL YEAR Map Ref No. 40	Nearest Road: A.1, A.19 A large, listed farmhouse, set in 28 acres. Laurel Farm offers tennis, fishing, croquet & farm & river walks all within the grounds. The unspoilt village of Brafferton-Helperby, only 2 mins away, has 4 pubs - 2 do excellent meals. Situated in Herriot country, with the Dales, Moors (steam railway), York, Harrogate, cathedrals & abbeys all within easy reach. Accommodation is in 4 attractive rooms. The hallmark is hospitality.	£20.00 *see PHOTO over*	Y	Y	Y
Geoff Moverley The Hermitage Crayke York YO6 4TB Tel: (01347) 821635 Open: JAN - NOV Map Ref No. 36	Nearest Road: A.19 Set in a large garden on the edge of the picturesque village of Crayke, with panoramic views of the Howardian Hills. The Hermitage, an attractive farmhouse, offers accommodation in 2 comfortable & attractively furnished rooms, 1 en-suite & 1 with private bathroom. Guests may relax in the pleasant sitting room with colour T.V. & log fires in season. Delicious breakfasts served in the conservatory. A good base for York, the Moors & the Dales. A warm & friendly host.	£22.00	Y	N	N

When booking your accommodation please mention
The Best Bed & Breakfast

Laurel Farm. Brafferton.

Scotland

Scotland

Scotland's culture & traditions, history & literature, languages & accents, its landscape & architecture, even its wildlife set it apart from the rest of Britain. Much of Scotland's history is concerned with the struggle to retain independence from England.

The Romans never conquered the Scottish tribes, but preferred to keep them at bay with Hadrian's Wall, stretching across the Border country from Tynemouth to the Solway Firth.

Time lends glamour to events, but from the massacre of Glencoe to the Highland Clearances, much of Scotland's fate has been a harsh one. Robert the Bruce did rout the English enemy at Bannockburn after scaling the heights of Edinburgh Castle to take the city, but in later years Mary, Queen of Scots was to spend much of her life imprisoned by her sister Elizabeth I of England. Bonnie Prince Charlie (Charles Edward Stuart) led the Jacobite rebellion which ended in defeat at Culloden.

These events are recorded in the folklore & songs of Scotland. The Border & Highland Gatherings & the Common Ridings are more than a chance to wear the Tartan, they are reminders of national pride.

Highland Games are held throughout the country where local & national champions compete in events like tossing the caber & in piping contests. There are sword dances & Highland flings, the speciality of young men & boys wearing the full dress tartan of their clan.

Scotland's landscape is rich in variety from the lush green lowlands to the handsome splendour of the mountainous Highlands, from the rounded hills of the Borders to the far-flung islands of the Hebrides, Orkney & Shetland where the sea is ever-present.

There are glens & beautiful lochs deep in the mountains, a spectacular coastline of high cliffs & white sandy beaches, expanses of purple heather moorland where the sparkling water in the burns runs brown with peat, & huge skies bright with cloud & gorgeous sunsets.

Argyll & The Islands

This area has ocean & sea lochs, forests & mountains, 3000 miles of coastline, about 30 inhabited islands, the warming influence of the Gulf Stream & the tallest tree in Britain (in Strone Gardens, near Loch Fyne).

Sites both historic & prehistoric are to be found in plenty. There is a hilltop fort at Dunadd, near Crinan with curious cup-&-ring carvings, & numerous ancient sites surround Kilmartin, from burial cairns to grave slabs.

Kilchurn Castle is a magnificent ruin in contrast to the opulence of Inveraray. Both are associated with the once-powerful Clan Campbell. There are remains of fortresses built by the Lords of the Isles, the proud chieftains who ruled the west after driving out the Norse invaders in the 12th century.

Oban is a small harbour town accessible by road & rail & the point of departure for many of the islands including Mull.

Tobermory. Isle of Mull.

Scotland

Mull is a peaceful island with rugged seascapes, lovely walks & villages, a miniature railway & the famous Mull Little Theatre. It is a short hop from here to the tiny island of Iona & St. Columba's Abbey, cradle of Christianity in Scotland.

Coll & Tiree have lovely beaches & fields of waving barley. The grain grown here was once supplied to the Lords of the Isles but today most goes to Islay & into the whisky. Tiree has superb windsurfing.

Jura is a wilder island famous for its red deer. The Isles of Colonsay & Oronsay are joined at low water.

Gigha, 'God's Isle', is a fertile area of gardens with rare & semitropical plants.The Island of Staffa has Fingal's Cave.

The Borders, Dumfries & Galloway

The borderland with England is a landscape of subtle colours & contours from the round foothills of the Cheviots, purple with heather, to the dark green valley of the Tweed.

The Lammermuir Hills sweep eastwards to a coastline of small harbours & the spectacular cliffs at St. Abbs Head where colonies of seabirds thrive.

The Border towns, set in fine countryside, have distinctive personalities. Hawick, Galashiels, Selkirk & Melrose all played their parts in the various Border skirmishes of this historically turbulent region & then prospered with a textile industry which survives today. They celebrate their traditions in the Common Riding ceremonies.

The years of destructive border warfare have left towers & castles throughout the country. Roxburgh was once a Royal castle & James II was killed here during a siege. Now there are only the shattered remains of the massive stone walls. Hermitage Castle is set amid wild scenery near Hawick & impressive Floors Castle stands above Kelso.

At Jedburgh the Augustine abbey is remarkably complete, & a visitors centre here tells the story of the four great Border Abbeys; Jedburgh itself, Kelso, Dryburgh & Melrose.

The lovely estate of Abbotsford where Sir Walter Scott lived & worked is near Melrose. A prolific poet & novelist, his most famous works are the Waverley novels written around 1800. His house holds many of his possessions, including a collection of armour. Scott's View is one of the best vantage points in the borderlands with a prospect of the silvery Tweed & the three distinctive summits of the Eildon Hills.

Eildon Hills.

There are many gracious stately homes. Manderston is a classical house of great luxury, & Mellerstain is the work of the Adam family. Traquair was originally a Royal hunting lodge. Its main gates were locked in 1745 after a visit from Bonnie Prince Charlie, never to be opened until a Stuart King takes the throne.

Dumfries & Galloway to the southwest is an area of rolling hills with a fine coastline.

Plants flourish in the mild air here & there are palm trees at Ardwell House& the Logan Botanic Garden.

Scotland

The gardens at Castle Kennedy have rhododendrons, azaleas & magnolias & Threave Gardens near Castle Douglas are the National Trust for Scotland's School of gardening.

The Galloway Forest Park covers a vast area of lochs & hills & has views across to offshore Ailsa Craig. At Caerlaveroch Castle, an early Renaissance building near the coast of Dumfries, there is a national nature reserve.

The first church in Scotland was built by St. Ninian at Whithorn in 400 on a site now occupied by the 13th century priory. The spread of Christianity is marked by early memorial stones like the Latinus stone at Whithorn, & the abbeys of Dundrennan, Crossraguel, Glenluce & Sweetheart, named after its founder who carried her husband's heart in a casket & is buried with it in the abbey.

At Dumfries is the poet Burns' house, his mausoleum & the Burns Heritage Centre overlooking the River Nith.

In Upper Nithsdale the Mennock Pass leads to Wanlockhead & Leadhills, once centres of the lead-mining industry. There is a fascinating museum here & the opportunity of an underground trip.

Lothian & Strathclyde

The Firth of Clyde & Glasgow in the west, & the Firth of Forth with Edinburgh in the east are both areas of rich history, tradition & culture.

Edinburgh is the capital of Scotland & amongst the most visually exciting cities in the world. The New Town is a treasure trove of inspired neo-classical architecture, & below Edinburgh Castle high on the Rock, is the Old Town, a network of courts, closes, wynds & gaunt tenements around the Royal Mile.

The Palace of Holyrood House, home of Mary, Queen of Scots for several years overlooks Holyrood Park & nearby Arthur's Seat,is a popular landmark.

The City's varied Art Galleries include The Royal Scottish Academy, The National Gallery, Portrait Gallery, Gallery of Modern Art & many other civic & private collections.

The Royal Museum of Scotland displays superb historical & scientific material. The Royal Botanic Gardens are world famous.

Cultural life in Edinburgh peaks at Festival time in August. The official Festival, the Fringe, the Book Festival, Jazz Festival & Film Festival bring together artistes of international reputation.

The gentle hills around the city

Inverary Castle.

offer many opportunities for walking. The Pentland Hills are easily reached, with the Lammermuir Hills a little further south. There are fine beaches at Gullane, Yellowcraigs, North Berwick & at Dunbar.

Tantallon Castle, a 14th century stronghold, stands on the rocky Firth of Forth, & 17th century Hopetoun House, on the outskirts of the city is only one of a number of great houses in the area.

North of Edinburgh across the Firth of Forth lies the ancient Kingdom

Scotland

of Fife. Here is St. Andrews, a pleasant town on the seafront, an old university town & Scotland's ecclesiastical capital, but famous primarily for golf.

Glasgow is the industrial & business capital of Scotland. John Betjeman called it the 'finest Victorian city in Britain' & many buildings are remarkable examples of Victorian splendour, notably the City Chambers.

Many buildings are associated with the architect Charles Rennie MacKintosh; the Glasgow School of Art is one of them. Glasgow Cathedral is a perfect example of pre-Reformation Gothic architecture.

Glasgow is Scotland's largest city with the greatest number of parks & fine Botanic Garden. It is home to both the Scottish Opera & the Scottish Ballet, & has a strong & diverse cultural tradition from theatre to jazz. Its museums include the matchless Burrell Collection, & the Kelvingrove Museum & Art Gallery, which houses one of the best civic collections of paintings in Britain, as well as reflecting the city's engineering & shipbuilding heritage.

The coastal waters of the Clyde are world famous for cruising & sailing, with many harbours & marinas. The long coastline offers many opportunities for sea-angling from Largs to Troon & Prestwick, & right around to Luce Bay on the Solway.

There are many places for birdwatching on the Estuary, whilst the Clyde Valley is famous for its garden centres & nurseries.

Paisley has a mediaeval abbey, an observatory & a museum with a fine display of the famous 'Paisley' pattern shawls.

Further south, Ayr is a large seaside resort with sandy beach, safe bathing & a racecourse. In the Ayrshire valleys there is traditional weaving & lace & bonnet making, & Sorn, in the rolling countryside boasts its 'Best Kept Village' award.

Culzean Castle is one of the finest Adam houses in Scotland & stands in spacious grounds on the Ayrshire cliffs.

Robert Burns is Scotland's best loved poet, & 'Burns night' is widely celebrated. The region of Strathclyde shares with Dumfries & Galloway the title of 'Burns Country' . The son of a peasant farmer, Burns lived in poverty for much of his life. The simple house where he was born is in the village of Alloway. In the town of Ayr is the Auld Kirk where he was baptised & the footbridge of 'The Brigs of Ayr' is still in use. The Tam O'Shanter Inn is now a Burns museum & retains its thatched roof & simple fittings. The Burns Trail leads on to Mauchline where Possie Nansie's Inn remains. At Tarbolton the National Trust now care for the old house where Burns founded the 'Batchelors Club' debating society.

Perthshire, Loch Lomond & The Trossachs

By a happy accident of geology, the Highland Boundary fault which separates the Highlands from the Lowlands runs through Loch Lomond, close to the Trossachs & on through Perthshire, giving rise to marvellous scenery.

In former times Highlanders & Lowlanders raided & fought here. Great castles like Stirling, Huntingtower & Doune were built to protect the routes between the two different cultures.

Stirling was once the seat of Scotland's monarchs & the great Royal castle is set high on a basalt rock. The Guildhall & the Kirk of the Holy Rude are also interesting buildings in the town, with Cambuskenneth Abbey & the Bannockburn Heritage Centre close by.

Perth 'fair city' on the River Tay,

Scotland

has excellent shops & its own repertory theatre. Close by are the Black Watch Museum at Balhousie Castle, & the Branklyn Gardens, which are superb in May & June.

Scone Palace, to the north of Perth was home to the Stone or Scone of Destiny for nearly 500 years until its removal to Westminster. 40 kings of Scotland were crowned here.

Pitlochry sits amid beautiful Highland scenery with forest & hill walks, two nearby distilleries, the famous Festival theatre, Loch Faskally & the Dam Visitor Centre & Fish Ladder.

In the Pass of Killiecrankie, a short drive away, a simple stone marks the spot where the Highlanders charged barefoot to overwhelm the redcoat soldiers of General MacKay.

Queens View.

Famous Queen's View overlooks Loch Tummel beyond Pitlochry with the graceful peak of Schiehallion completing a perfect picture.

Other lochs are picturesque too; Loch Earn, Loch Katrine & bonnie Loch Lomond itself, & they can be enjoyed from a boat on the water. Ospreys nest at the Loch of the Lowes near Dunkeld.

Mountain trails lead through Ben Lawers & the 'Arrocher Alps' beyond Loch Lomond. The Ochils & the Campsie Fells have grassy slopes for walking. Near Callander are the Bracklinn Falls, the Callander Crags & the Falls of Leny.

Wooded areas include the Queen Elizabeth Forest Park & the Black Wood of Rannoch which is a fragment of an ancient Caledonian forest. There are some very tall old trees around Killiecrankie, & the world's tallest beech hedge - 26 metres high - grows at Meikleour near Blairgowrie.

Creiff & Blairgowrie have excellent golf courses set in magnificent scenery.

The Grampians

This is spacious countryside with glacier-scarred mountains & deep glens cut through by tumbling rivers. The Grampian Highlands make for fine mountaineering & walking.

There is excellent skiing at Glenshee, & a centre at the Lecht for the less experienced, whilst the broad tops of the giant mountains are ideal for cross-country skiing. The chair-lift at Glenshee is worth a visit at any season.

The Dee, The Spey & The Don flow down to the coastal plain from the heights. Some of the world's finest trout & salmon beats are on these rivers.

Speyside is dotted with famous distilleries from Grantown-on-Spey to Aberdeen, & the unique Malt Whisky Trail can be followed.

Royal Deeside & Donside hold a number of notable castles. Balmoral is the present Royal family's holiday home, & Kildrummy is a romantic ruin in a lovely garden. Fyvie Castle has five dramatic towers & stands in peaceful parkland. nearby Haddo House, by contrast, is an elegant Georgian home.

There is a 17th century castle at Braemar, but more famous here is the Royal Highland Gathering. There are wonderful walks in the vicinity - Morrone Hill, Glen Quoich & the Linn O'Dee are just a few.

The city of Aberdeen is famed for its sparkling granite buildings, its

Scotland

university, its harbour & fish market & for North Sea Oil. It also has long sandy beaches & lovely year-round flower displays, of roses in particular.

Around the coast are fishing towns & villages. Crovie & Pennan sit below impressive cliffs. Buckie is a typical small port along the picturesque coastline of the Moray Firth.

The Auld Kirk at Cullen has fine architectural features & elegant Elgin has beautiful cathedral ruins. Pluscarden Abbey, Spynie Palace & Duffus Castle are all nearby.

Nairn has a long stretch of sandy beach & a golf course with an international reputation. Inland are Cawdor Castle & Culloden Battlefield.

Dunnottar Castle.

The Highlands & Islands

The Northern Highlands are divided from the rest of Scotland by the dramatic valley of the Great Glen. From Fort William to Inverness sea lochs, canals & the depths of Loch Ness form a chain of waterways linking both coasts.

Here are some of the wildest & most beautiful landscapes in Britain. Far Western Knoydart, the Glens of Cannich & Affric, the mysterious lochs, including Loch Morar, deeper than the North Sea, & the marvellous coastline, all are exceptional.

The glens were once the home of crofting communities, & of the clansmen who supported the Jacobite cause. The wild scenery of Glencoe is a favourite with walkers & climbers, but it has a tragic history. Its name means 'the glen of weeping' & refers to the massacre of the MacDonald clan in 1692, when the Royal troops who had been received as guests treacherously attacked their hosts at dawn.

The valleys are empty today largely as a result of the infamous Highland Clearances in the 19th century when the landowners turned the tenant crofters off the land in order to introduce the more profitable Cheviot sheep. The emigration of many Scots to the U.S.A. & the British Colonies resulted from these events.

South of Inverness lie the majestic Cairngorms. The Aviemore centre provides both summer & winter sports facilities here.

To the north of Loch Ness are the remains of the ancient Caledonian forest where red deer & stags are a common sight on the hills. Rarer are sightings of the Peregrine Falcon, the osprey, the Golden Eagle & the Scottish wildcat. Kincraig has excellent wildlife parks.

Inverness is the last large town in the north, & a natural gateway to the Highlands & to Moray, the Black Isle & the north-east.

The east coast is characterised by the Firths of Moray, Cromarty & Dornoch & by its changing scenery from gentle pastureland, wooded hillsides to sweeping coastal cliffs.

On the Black Isle, which is not a true island but has a causeway & bridge links with the mainland, Fortrose & Rosemarkie in particular have lovely beaches, caves & coastal walks. There is golf on the headland at Rosemarkie & a 13th century cathedral of rosy pink sandstone stands in Fortrose.

Scotland

Scotland Gazeteer

Areas of outstanding natural beauty

It would be invidious, not to say almost impossible, to choose any particular area of Scotland as having a more beautiful aspect than another - the entire country is a joy to the traveller. The Rugged Highlands, the great glens, tumbling waters, tranquil lochs - the deep countryside or the wild coastline - simply come & choose your own piece of paradise.

Historic Houses & Castles

Bowhill - Nr. Selkirk
18th-19th century - home of the Duke of Bucceleugh & Queensberry. Has an outstanding collection of pictures by Canaletto,Claude, Gainsborough, Reynolds & Leonardo da Vinci. Superb silver, porcelain & furniture.16th & 17th century miniatures. -

Traquair House - Innerleithen
A unique & ancient house being the oldest inhabited home in Scotland. It is rich in associations with every form of political history & after Bonnie Prince Charlie passed through its main gates in 1745 no other visitor has been allowed to use them. There are treasures in the house dating from 12th century, & it has an 18th century library & a priest's room with secret stairs.

Linlithgow Palace - Linlithgow
The birthplace of Mary, Queen of Scots.

Sirling Castle - Stirling
Royal Castle.

Drumlanrigg Castle - Nr. Thornhill
17th century castle of pale pink stone - romantic & historic - wonderful art treasures including a magnificent Rembrandt & a huge silver chandelier. Beautiful garden setting.

Braemar Castle - Braemar
17th century castle of great historic interest. Has round central tower with spiral staircase giving it a fairy-tale appearence.

Drum Castle - Nr. Aberdeen
Dating in part from 13th century, it has a great square tower.

Cawdor Castle - Nairn
14th century fortress - like castle - has always been the home of the Thanes of Cawdor - background to Shakespeare's Macbeth.

Dunvegan Castle - Isle of Skye
13th century - has always been the home of the Chiefs of McLeod.

Hopetoun House - South Queensferry
Very fine example of Adam architecture & has a fine collection of pictures & furniture. Splendid landscaped grounds.

Inverary Castle - Argyll
Home of the Dukes of Argyll. 18th century - Headquarters of Clan Campbell.

Burn's Cottage - Alloway
Birthplace of Robert Burns - 1659 - thatched cottage - museum of Burns' relics.

Bachelors' Club - Tarbolton
17th century house - thatched - where Burns & friends formed their club - 1780.

Blair Castle - Blair Atholl
Home of the Duke of Atholl, 13th century Baronial mansion - collection of Jacobite relics, armour, paintings, china & many other items.

Glamis Castle - Angus
17th century remodelling in Chateau style - home of the Earl of Strathmore & Kinghorne. Very attractive castle - lovely grounds by Capability Brown.

Scone Palace - Perth
has always been associated with seat of Government of Scotland from earliest times. The Stone of Destiny was removed from the Palace in 1296 & taken to Westminster Abbey. Present palace rebuilt in early 1800's still incorporating parts of the old. Lovely gardens.

Edinburgh Castle
Fortress standing high over the town - famous for military tattoo.

Culzean Castle & Country Park - Maybole
Fine Adam house & spacious gardens perched on Ayrshire cliff.

Dunrobin Castle - Golspie
Ancient seat of the Earls & Dukes of Sutherland.

Eilean Donan Castle - Wester Ross
13th century castle, Jacobite relics.

Manderston - Duns
Great classical house with only silver staircase in the world. Stables, marble diary, formal gardens.

Scotland

Cathedrals & Churches

Dunfermline Abbey - Dunfermline
Norman remains of beautiful church.
Modern east end & tower.
Edinburgh (Church of the Holy Rood)
15th century - was divided into two in 17th
century & re-united 1938. Here Mary,
Queen of Scots was crowned.
Glasgow (St. Mungo)
12th-15th century cathedral - 19th century
interior. Central tower with spire.
Kirkwall (St. Magnus)
12th century cathedral with very fine nave.
Falkirk Old Parish Church - Falkirk
The spotted appearance (faw) of the
church (kirk) gave the town its name. The
site of the church has veen used since 7th
century, with succesive churches built
upon it. The present church was much
rebuilt in 19th century. Interesting
historically.
St Columba's Abbey - Iona

Museums & Galleries

Agnus Folk Museum - Glamis
17th century cottages with stone slab
roofs, restored by the National Trust for
Scotland & houses a fine folk collection.
Mary, Queen of Scots' House - Jedburgh
Life & times of the Queen along with
paintings, etc.
Andrew Carnegie Birthplace -
Dunfermline
The cottage where he was born is now
part of a museum showing his life's work.
Aberdeen Art Gallery & Museum -
Aberdeen
Sculpture, paintings, watercolours, prints
& drawings. Applied arts. Maritime
museum exhibits.
Provost Skene's House - Aberdeen
17th century house now exhibiting local
domestic life, etc.
Highland Folk Museum - Kingussie
Examples of craft work & tools - furnished
cottage with mill.
West Highland Museum - Fort William
Natural & local hsitory. Relics of Jacobites
& exhibition of the '45 Rising.
Clan Macpherson House - Newtonmore
Relics of the Clan.

Glasgow Art Gallery & Museum -
Glasgow
Archaeology, technology, local & natural
history. Old Masters, tapestries, porcelain,
glass & silver, etc. Sculpture.
Scottish National Gallery - Edinburgh
20th century collection - paintings &
sculpture - Arp, Leger, Giacometti,
Matisse, Picasso. Modern Scottish
painting.
**National Museum of Antiquities in
Scotland** - Edinburgh
Collection from Stone Age to modern
times - Relics of Celtic Church, Stuart
relics, Highland weapons, etc.
Gladstone Court - Biggar
Small indoor street of shops, a bank,
schoolroom, library, etc.
Burns' Cottage & Museum - Alloway
Relics of Robert Burns - National Poet.
Inverness Museum & Art Gallery -
Inverness
Social history, archaeology & cultural life
of the Highlands. Display of the Life of the
Clans - good Highland silver - crafts, etc.
Kirkintilloch - Nr. Glasgow
Auld Kirk Museum. Local history,
including archaeological specimens from
the Antonine Wall (Roman). Local
industries, exhibitions, etc
Pollock House & Park - Glasgow
18th century house with collection of
paintings, etc. The park is the home of the
award-winning Burrell Collection
The foregoing are but a few of the many
museums & galleries in Scotland - further
information is always freely available from
the Tourist Information

Historic Monuments

Aberdour Castle - Aberdour
14th century fortification - part still roofed.
Balvenie Castle - Duffton
15th century castle ruins.
Cambuskenneth Abbey - Nr. Stirling
12th century abbey - seat of Bruce's
Parliament in 1326. Ruins.
Dryburgh Abbey - Dryburgh
Remains of monastery.
Loch Leven Castle - Port Glasgow
15th century ruined stronghold - once lived
in by Mary, Queen of Scots.

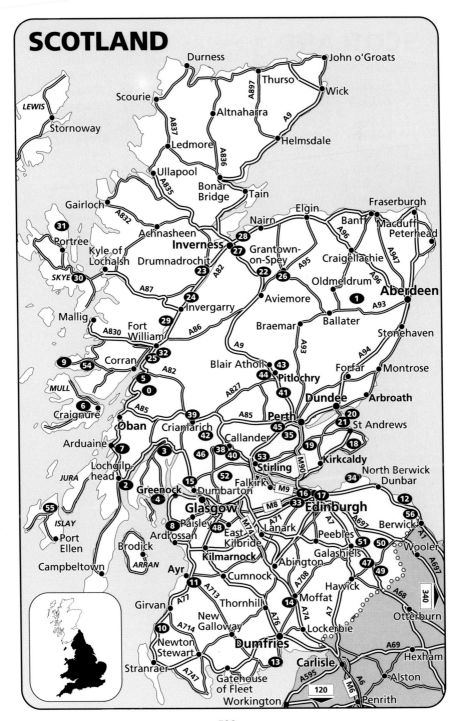

SCOTLAND

SCOTLAND

Map references

WESTERN ISLES
LEWIS
SUTHERLAND
ROSS-SHIRE
HIGHLAND
ABERDEENSHIRE
SKYE
GRAMPIAN
INVERNESS
PERTHSHIRE
MULL
TAYSIDE
ARGYLL
CENTRAL
FIFESHIRE
JURA
DUMBARTON
LOTHIAN
LANARKSHIRE
SELKIRK
AYRESHIRE
PEEBLES
STRATHCLYDE
ROXBURGHSHIRE
BORDER
BERWICKSHIRE
DUMFRIES & GALLOWAY

Abbot's Brae. Dunoon.

		rate from £ per person	children taken	evening meals	animals taken
Anne & Eddie Strachan **Hazlehurst Lodge** **Ballater Road** **Aboyne AB34 5HY** **Tel: (013398) 86921** **Fax 013398 86660** **Open: FEB - DEC** **Map Ref No. 01**	Nearest Road: A.93 Charming Victorian coachman's lodge on the way to Aboyne Castle, set in wooded garden. Reflecting the owners' artistic background, in 5 beautifully designed en-suite bedrooms. Anne is a fine chef, with a growing reputation for imaginative cooking using the best of Scottish produce. Her superb meals are served with friendly informality in the small licensed restaurant. Aboyne is ideal for a relaxing stay on Royal Deeside, an Area of Outstanding Natural Beauty.	£30.00 (no smoking) CREDIT CARD VISA M'CARD AMEX	Y	Y	Y

Argyll

		rate from £ per person	children taken	evening meals	animals taken
Peter & Helen Stockdale **Feorag House** **Glenborrodale** **Acharacle PH36 4JP** **Tel: (01972) 500248** **Open: ALL YEAR** **Map Ref No. 54**	Nearest Road: A.861 Set amongst 13 acres of grounds, with its own private shoreline, Feorag House is a haven of comfort, peace, warmth, good food & good friends; surrounded by wild mountainous beauty & the timeless lap of the waves of Loch Sunart. Each bedroom is tastefully furnished & enjoys a sea view & a bathroom en-suite. The home-baking & varied menus make a stay at Feorag House a sheer delight. Children over 10 yrs.	£25.00 CREDIT CARD VISA M'CARD	Y	Y	Y
Mrs Stella Broadbent **Lochside Cottage** **Fasnacloich** **Appin PA38 4BJ** **Tel/Fax: (01631) 730216** **Open: ALL YEAR** **Map Ref No. 00**	Nearest Road: A.828 Total peace on the shore of Loch Baile Mhic Chailen, in an idyllic glen of outstanding beauty. There are many walks from the cottage garden; or, visit Fort William, Glencoe & Oban, from where you can board a steamer to explore the Western Isles. At the end of the day, a warm welcome awaits you: delicious home-cooked dinner, a log fire & the certainty of a perfect night's sleep in one of 3 en-suite bedrooms.	£18.00 (no smoking)	Y	Y	Y
Margaret & Harvey McKay **'Allt-na-Craig'** **Tarbert Road** **Ardrishaig PA30 8EP** **Tel: (01546) 603245** **Open: ALL YEAR (Excl. Xmas & New Year)** **Map Ref No. 02**	Nearest Road: A.83 The McKays warmly welcome all their guests to 'Allt-na-Craig', a lovely old Victorian mansion set in picturesque grounds overlooking Loch Fyne. 6 comfortable en-suite bedrooms with tea/coffee makers. A guests' lounge with open fire & dining room is also available. This is a perfect base for outdoor activities, like hill-walking, fishing, golf, riding & windsurfing, or for visiting the islands. Delicious evening meals by arrangement.	£25.00	Y	Y	Y
Duncan & Carole Nairn **Abbot's Brae Hotel** **West Bay** **Dunoon PA23 7QJ** **Tel: (01369) 705021** **Fax 01369 705021** **Open: MAR - OCT** **Map Ref No. 04**	Nearest Road: A.815 Friendly, family-run Victorian country house hotel in secluded 2-acre woodland glen, with breathtaking views of the sea & hills. 7 tastefully furnished, spacious bedrooms, all en-suite with colour T.V., radio, 'phone & tea/coffee facilities. Unwind with a drink by the fire in the comfortable lounge, dine in the cosy dining room with delicious a la carte menu & select wine list. The ideal base for exploring Argyll & the Western Highlands. Only 1 hour from Glasgow Airport. Licenced.	£21.50 *see PHOTO over* CREDIT CARD VISA M'CARD	Y	Y	Y

Scotland
Argyll

		rate from £ per person	children taken	evening meals taken	animals taken
Flavia MacArthur **Ardsheal Home Farm** **Kentallen** **Duror in Appin** **PA38 4BZ** **Tel: (01631) 740229** **Open: APR - OCT** **Map Ref No. 05**	Nearest Road: A.828 A charming Scottish hill farm of 1,000 acres, surrounded by breathtaking scenery on the shores of Loch Linnhe, overlooking the Morvern Hills. A warm welcome is assured from the most friendly hosts, who offer 3 attractive bedrooms, comfortable & well-furnished, with tea/coffee-making facilities, electric blankets, etc. Delicious evening meals (no vegetarian) served by prior arrangement. Convenient for touring, sailing to the inner Isles. An idyllic holiday retreat, there is 1 mile of private beach. Riding & tennis nearby.	£15.00	Y	Y	N
Mrs Margaret Rozga **Kilmeny Farmhouse** **Ballygrant** **Isle of Islay** **PA45 7QW** **Tel: (01496) 840668** **Open: ALL YEAR** **Map Ref No. 55**	Nearest Road: A.846 Islay is well-known for its abundant & wonderful wildlife & its many malt-whisky distilleries. Kilmeny Farmhouse, in the heart of a 300-acre beef farm, commands magnificent views of the surrounding hills & glen. This family-run business places emphasis on quality & personal service. The exquisite en-suite bedrooms, with country views, are elegantly furnished. The public rooms are charming, with a country-house influence. A 4-course dinner menu available.	£28.00 🚭	N	Y	Y
John & Eleanor Wagstaff **Red Bay Cottage** **Deargphort, Fionnphort** **Isle of Mull** **PA66 6BP** **Tel: (01681) 700396** **Open: ALL YEAR** **Map Ref No. 06**	Nearest Road: A.849 A really warm welcome awaits the visitor to this charming modern house, offering 3 very comfortable rooms with modern facilities. Situated only 20 metres from the sea, & overlooking Iona Sound & the white sandy beaches on the Isle of Iona, this surely must be the ideal base for a relaxing & peaceful holiday. Mr Wagstaff offers superb food. Eleanor is a qualified, practising silversmith, so why not enjoy a winter break on their residential silversmithing course?	£15.50	Y	Y	Y
Dr & Mrs D. Bannister **Tigh an Lodan** **Ford** **By Lochgilphead** **PA31 8RH** **Tel: (01546) 810287** **Open: APR - OCT** **Map Ref No. 07**	Nearest Road: A.816 In scenic seclusion at the southern end of Loch Awe, Ford is well situated for enjoying the under-appreciated attractions of mid-Argyll, as well as for fishing & walking. The hosts offer an interesting cuisine in a relaxing environment. It has all the comforts you expect, coupled with pampering touches such as an open fire & plentiful books in the elegant sitting room. There is comfortable accommodation for 6 in 3 bedrooms, all en-suite. Children over 13. Pets by arrangement.	£18.00 🚭 CREDIT CARD VISA M'CARD	Y	Y	Y
William Mercer **Arnish Cottage,** **Christian Guest House** **Poll Bay** **St. Catherines PA25 8BA** **Tel: (01499) 302405** **Open: ALL YEAR** **Map Ref No. 03**	Nearest Road: A.815 Situated across the Loch from Inveraray, a truly idyllic setting on a private road 20 feet from the Lochside, & approx. 1 hr's drive from Glasgow Airport. A T.V. lounge & viewing conservatory are provided, & all bedrooms are en-suite. Non-smoking throughout. A variety of home-cooked meals are available, using local produce & seafood from the Loch. Loch fishing, hill & forest walks, pony trekking, etc., are readily organised.	£24.00 🚭	N	Y	N

537

Cosses. Ballantrae.

Scotland
Argyll & Ayrshire

		rate from £ per person	children taken	evening meals	animals taken
Mrs Sandra Cameron **Thistle House** **St. Catherines** **PA25 8AZ** **Tel: (01499) 302209** **Open: APR - OCT** **Map Ref No. 03**	Nearest Road: A.815 Superbly situated Victorian country house retaining many original features. Surrounded by 2 acres of mature garden, with spectacular views of Loch Fyne & sitting directly across the Loch from Inverary & its famous castle. 5 comfortably furnished bedrooms, 3 en-suite, with tea/coffee-making facilities. Guest lounge with open fire. Good eating place in village & other restaurants nearby for evening meals. The Cowal Peninsula is well located for exploring Argyll & the Loch Lomond area. 1 hour's drive from Glasgow Airport.	£19.00 CREDIT CARD VISA M'CARD	Y	N	Y
Roy & Janet Smith **'Meall Mo Chridhe'** **Country House** **Kilchoan** **West Ardnamurchan** **PH36 4LH** **Tel: (01972) 510238** **Fax 01972 510238** **Open: APR - OCT** **Map Ref No. 09**	Nearest Road: B.8007 Meall Mo Chridhe (Little Hill of my Heart) is a Grade II listed former manse (c.1790) situated on the most westerly point of the U.K. mainland. Peace & tranquility, cosy log fires, elegant furnishings & imaginative cooking using local game & seafoods, including venison, quail, king scallops, salmon, & langoustines. Janet makes her own bread, jam preserves & fruit sorbets. Spectacular coastal scenery, excellent walking & wildlife. Car ferry to Tobermory, the ideal location from which to visit Mull, Iona, Coll & Tiree. Children over 12.	£33.00	Y	Y	Y

Ayrshire

		rate from £ per person	children taken	evening meals	animals taken
Susan & Robin Crosthwaite **Cosses Country House** **Ballantrae** **KA26 0LR** **Tel: (01465) 831363** **Fax 01465 831598** **Open: ALL YEAR (Excl. Xmas & New Year)** **Map Ref No. 10**	Nearest Road: A.77 A former shooting lodge (1800s) & home farm (1900s), Cosses is now a country house, set in a secluded valley of garden & woodland. Superb accommodation, en-suite facilities, a colour T.V., hospitality tray & roaring log fire on chilly evenings. A good base from which to explore this delightful part of Scotland. The kitchen & herb garden supplement local produce for you to enjoy the taste of Scotland dinners. Castles (incl. Culzean), gardens, Burns's birthplace, golf courses, fishing, walks & cycling all within easy reach. Irish ferry terminals 30 mins' drive.	£30.00 *see PHOTO over*	Y	Y	Y
Brenda & Bert Taylor **Brenalder Lodge** **39 Dunure Road** **Doonfoot** **KA7 4HR** **Tel: (01292) 443939** **Open: ALL YEAR** **Map Ref No. 11**	Nearest Road: A.77 Brenda & Bert Taylor welcome you to Brenalder Lodge. There are panoramic views of the Carrick Hills & the Firth of Clyde. Easy access to Prestwick airport & the world-famous Turnberry & Royal Troon golf courses. The Lodge is an ideal base for touring the Burns country. All rooms have en-suite facilities, colour T.V. & tea/coffee makers. A delicious 4-course Scottish breakfast is served in the new conservatory-style dining room. All-day access to the Lodge, & ample parking. A 4-course dinner is served at 6 p.m. if 24 hrs' notice is given. Children over 7.	£25.00 *see PHOTO over*	Y	Y	Y

Brenalder Lodge.   Doonfoot.

Scotland
Ayrshire

	rate from £ per person	children taken	evening meals	animals taken

Christine & Jim Ondersma
Spottiswoode
Sandy Road
Seamill
West Kilbride
KA23 9NN
Tel: (01294) 823131
Fax 01294 823179
Open: ALL YEAR
Map Ref No. 08

Nearest Road: A.78
A Victorian shore-side home, with attentive hosts & personal touches, from complimentary afternoon tea, on arrival, to mints by the bedside, & many extras. Breakfast is a special occasion, featuring treats like popovers, crepes, quiches & casseroles, all made with the finest local ingredients. Also, home-made yoghurt, muffins, breads & preserves. From Loch Lomond to Burns Country, golfing to sailing, museums to Glasgow's culture & night life, this is a perfect vacation base. Flowers, lace, island sunsets, walks on the shore, music, books & a wee dram to settle down for the night. Carlisle 2 hrs. Edinburgh 1 1/2 hrs.

£22.00 N Y N

(no smoking symbol)

CREDIT CARD
VISA
M'CARD

Berwickshire

Donald & Leslie Brown
Dunlaverock House
Coldingham Bay
TD14 5PA
Tel: (018907) 71450
Fax 018907 71450
Open: ALL YEAR
Map Ref No. 12

Nearest Road: A.1
This spacious, late-Victorian villa is spectacularly situated on cliffs overlooking Coldingham Sands & the rugged surrounding coastline. Magnificent scenery & beautiful gardens offer true peace & serenity. Large, warm en-suite bedrooms, heated bathrooms & fine Scottish fayre all add to your comfort & enjoyment. Activities include bird watching, walking, golf, fishing, boat cruises & touring the historical Borders region & Edinburgh. A warm welcome awaits. Children over 9.

£25.00 Y Y Y

CREDIT CARD
VISA
M'CARD

Michael & Caroline Thomson
Kirkside House
Bonkyl
Duns TD11 3RJ
Tel: (01361) 882825
Fax 01361 882157
Open: MAY - OCT
Map Ref No. 56

Nearest Road: A.1, A.6112
Kirkside House is an early-Victorian, former manse set in a peaceful, rural location. Charming en-suite/private bedrooms have lovely views to the hills & are thoughtfully equipped. Super breakfasts served using free-range produce. Guests may choose to relax in the delightful walled garden with clematis, honeysuckle & roses. An acclaimed restaurant nearby. An ideal base for local country pursuits, Edinburgh, Berwick & Dunbar. 'Phone for directions.

£20.00 Y N N

(no smoking symbol)

Dumfriesshire

Mr & Mrs F. D. Jeffries
Cavens House
Kirkbean-by-Dumfries
DG2 8AA
Tel: (01387) 880234
Open: ALL YEAR
Map Ref No. 13

Nearest Road: A.710
Formerly an old mansion, this charming guest house offers 6 really comfortable rooms with modern facilities, including a private bath or shower. Tea-making facilities & colour T.V. in each room. Standing in 11 acres of mature gardens & woodland, it makes a perfect base for those wishing to explore the joys of the Solway Coast, with its beautiful scenery & excellent beaches. Sailing, fishing, walking, golfing & riding all local. An excellent cuisine here. A friendly atmosphere & good value.

£22.00 Y Y Y

see PHOTO over

CREDIT CARD
VISA
M'CARD

Cavens House.   Kirkbean-by-Dumfries.

Scotland
Dumfriesshire

		rate from £ per person	children taken	evening meals	animals taken
Alan & Andrea Daniel **Hartfell House** **Hartfell Crescent** **Moffat DG10 9AL** **Tel: (01683) 20153** **Open: MAR - NOV** **Map Ref No. 14**	Nearest Road: A.74 Hartfell House is a splendid Victorian manor house located in a rural setting overlooking the hills, yet only a few mins' walk from the town. A listed building known locally for its fine interior woodwork. Offering 9 spacious bedrooms, 5 with en-suite facilities. Standing in landscaped gardens of approximately 2 acres of lawns & trees, & providing an atmosphere of peaceful relaxation.	£18.00	Y	Y	Y

Dunbartonshire

		rate from £ per person	children taken	evening meals	animals taken
Mr & Mrs S. MacDonald **Kirkton House** **Darleith Road** **Cardross** **G82 5EZ** **Tel: (01389) 841951** **Fax (01389) 841868** **Open: ALL YEAR (Excl.** **Xmas & New Year)** **Map Ref No. 15**	Nearest Road: A.814 Experience a blend of olde worlde charm, modern amenities & superb views at this converted 18/19th-century farmhouse, set in a tranquil location & yet handy for Glasgow Airport (20/25 mins), Loch Lomond, The Trossachs & most West Highland routes. All the spacious bedrooms have full en-suite facilities. The cosy lounge has a roaring fire on chilly evenings. Enjoy home-cooked food, & savour a glass of wine at dinner by oil lamplight. Like the lounge, the convivial dining room has the original stone walls & a rustic fireplace, with the old swee from which the cooking pots were hung.	£27.00 *see PHOTO over* CREDIT CARD VISA M'CARD AMEX	Y	Y	Y

Edinburgh

		rate from £ per person	children taken	evening meals	animals taken
Mrs Helen Baird **Arisaig** **64 Glasgow Road** **Corstorphine EH12 8LN** **Tel: (0131) 3342610** **Open: APR - OCT** **Map Ref No. 16**	Nearest Road: M.8, M.9, A.720 A warm Scottish welcome awaits you here at this very pleasant & comfortable detached bungalow, situated only 3 miles from the city centre. There are 2 lovely bedrooms, all with modern amenities, & all kept to a very high standard. Tea/coffee-making & en-suite facilities available. Parking. Excellent bus service. An ideal base from which to explore Edinburgh.	£19.00	N	N	N
Mrs Jenny Wilson **Camus House** **4 Seaview Terrace** **Joppa** **Edinburgh EH15 2HD** **Tel: (0131) 6572003** **Open: ALL YEAR** **Map Ref No. 16**	Nearest Road: A.1 A Victorian, terraced villa overlooking the Firth of Forth, Camus House enjoys the peace of the seaside, along with an excellent bus service to the city centre, with its cultural, historical and leisure interests. The 4 guest rooms are comfortably furnished, and have washbasins, colour T.V., radio alarms & tea/coffee facilities. A genuine and friendly welcome is assured. A delightful base for a relaxing break.	£16.00 CREDIT CARD VISA M'CARD	Y	N	Y

Kirkton House. Cardross.

Scotland
Edinburgh

		rate from £ per person	children taken	evening meals	animals taken
Vi & Bob Clark **Pearl View** **2 Seaview Terrace** **Edinburgh** **EH15 2HD** **Tel: (0131) 6698516** **Open: ALL YEAR** **Map Ref No. 16**	Nearest Road: A.1 Pearl View is a Victorian terraced villa with panoramic views over the Firth of Forth. Offering guests a choice of 4 attractive bedrooms, 2 en-suite, all with modern amenities, including radio, colour T.V. & tea/coffee-making facilities. Conveniently located, frequent bus service to the city centre & many sporting facilities nearby. Pearl View welcomes all guests with a warm & friendly atmosphere. Free parking.	£15.00	Y	N	N
Mr & Mrs William Wright **The Salisbury** **45 Salisbury Road** **Edinburgh** **EH16 5AA** **Tel/Fax: (0131) 6671264** **Open: ALL YEAR** **Map Ref No. 16**	Nearest Road: A.7, A.68 Enjoy real Scottish hospitality in the comfort of this Georgian house. The Wright family offer you tastefully decorated, comfortable bedrooms, all with private facilities, colour T.V. & tea/coffee makers. Their home has been carefully refurbished during their 12-year ownership. Central heating throughout. Secluded garden to the rear. 10 mins by bus to the city centre, railway station & tourist attractions. Private car park.	£20.00	Y	N	N
Richard & Dorothy Vidler **Kenvie Guest House** **16 Kilmaurs Road** **Edinburgh** **EH16 5DA** **Tel: (0131) 6681964** **Fax 0131 6681964** **Open: ALL YEAR** **Map Ref No. 16**	Nearest Road: A.7, A.68, A.1 Kenvie Guest House is charming, comfortable, warm, friendly & inviting. This small Victorian town house is situated in a quiet residential street, 1 small block from the main road, leading to the city centre (an excellent bus service) & the bypass to all routes. Offering, for your comfort, lots of caring touches, including complimentary tea/coffee, colour T.V. & no-smoking rooms. Private facilities available. You are guaranteed a warm welcome from Richard & Dorothy. CREDIT CARD VISA M'CARD	£16.00	Y	N	N
Wilma, Bill & Sandy Hogg **Kingsley Guest House** **30 Craigmillar Park** **Newington** **Edinburgh** **EH16 5PS** **Tel/Fax: (0131) 6678439** **Open: ALL YEAR** **Map Ref No. 16**	Nearest Road: A.701 You are assured of a warm welcome & personal attention at this family-run guest house. The pleasant Victorian terraced villa offers 6 comfortable rooms, 4 en-suite. All rooms are well-equipped, with colour T.V., tea/coffee-making facilities & central heating. Conveniently situated on the south side of the city centre, in the residential university area. A really good base for everyone, with an excellent bus service from the door & a private car park. Children over 5. CREDIT CARD VISA M'CARD	£16.00	Y	N	N
Norah Alexander **Tiree Guest House** **26 Craigmillar Park** **Edinburgh EH16 5PS** **Tel: (0131) 667 7477** **Fax 0131 662 1608** **Open: ALL YEAR** **Map Ref No. 16**	Nearest Road: A.701 Situated on the south side of Edinburgh, about 1 1/2 miles from the city centre. Offering accommodation in 8 comfortable rooms, 5 with en-suite facilities. All rooms have colour T.V. & tea/coffee makers. Conveniently located for Edinburgh University, Holyrood Palace & the shopping centre. Children are very welcome here, & are given reduced rates. A Full Scottish breakfast is served.	£16.00	Y	N	Y

		rate from £ / per person	children taken	evening meals	animals taken
Annie Deacon **53 Eskside West** **Musselburgh** **Edinburgh** **EH21 6RB** **Tel: (0131) 6652875** **Open: ALL YEAR** **Map Ref No. 16**	Nearest Road: A.1 A warm, friendly & helpful hostess awaits you at this very pleasant stone-built terraced house located right on the banks of the River Esk. Charmingly decorated & furnished throughout to a high standard, it offers 2 delightful bedrooms with fresh flowers, radio, T.V., tea/coffee facilities & luxurious guests' bathrooms. Annie Deacon is a professional cook, & breakfast is excellent; it is beautifully prepared & served with grace & charm. This makes a really super base. 15 mins by car from Holyrood Palace, & 20 mins from Edinburgh.	£15.00	Y	Y	N
Mrs Mairi Dewar **Glenesk** **Delta Place, Smeaton Gr,** **Inveresk, Musselburgh** **Edinburgh EH21 7TP** **Tel: (0131) 6653217** **Open: ALL YEAR** **Map Ref No. 17**	Nearest Road: A.1 Quietly situated in the picturesque village of Inveresk, 'Glenesk' is a spacious, detached villa. It is convenient for all the scenic beauties, beaches & sporting activities of the east coast, while only 7 miles from the centre of Edinburgh & 1 mile from the busy shopping centre of Musselburgh. All 3 bedrooms have en-suite shower rooms or bathrooms, colour T.V. & tea/coffee-making facilities. A comfortable lounge. Parking space. No signs displayed: conservation area.	£17.00	Y	N	N
Gloria Stuart **Twenty London Street** **Edinburgh** **EH3 6NA** **Tel: (0131) 557 0216** **Fax 0131 556 6445** **Open: ALL YEAR** **Map Ref No. 16**	Nearest Road: A.1 This is a handsome house at the heart of Georgian Edinburgh. It is spacious & high-ceilinged, lovingly restored & elegantly decorated. Enter from the street, through a vestibule & hall vibrant with colour. A lovely sitting room where breakfast is served. 2 double bedrooms (king-size beds) & 1 twin bedroom. Each room has en-suite facilities, T.V., 'phone, hospitality tray, & more, & is furnished to create an atmosphere of comfort & elegance. Each room overlooks a secret garden, & you'll enjoy a view of classic Edinburgh splendour. *see PHOTO over*	£35.00	N	N	N
Ian & Rosemary Maitland **Hume** **27A Scotland Street** **Edinburgh EH3 6PY** **Tel: (0131) 556 3024** **Open: ALL YEAR** **Map Ref No. 16**	Nearest Road: A.1 A light garden flat in a listed building, extremely well situated in the Georgian New Town & exceptionally convenient for all city-centre attractions - only 10 mins' walk from Princes St, with a large variety of restaurants in the neighbourhood. A warm & family atmosphere provided by former country-house hosts who have an excellent knowledge of the city & of Scotland & its history.	£20.00	Y	N	N
Cecilia Leishman **Ellesmere House** **11 Glengyle Terrace** **Edinburgh EH3 9LN** **Tel: (0131) 229 4823** **Fax 0131 229 5285** **Open: ALL YEAR** **Map Ref No. 16**	Nearest Road: A.702 A warm welcome is extended to all visitors at this attractive & comfortable Victorian house overlooking the park. The spacious bedrooms are decorated & furnished to a high standard, & well-equipped with every comfort in mind. Delicious breakfasts are served, with special diets provided by arrangement. Good local restaurants. Convenient for the castle, Princes St., The Royal Mile, shops & theatres. Children over 10.	£19.00	Y	N	N

Twenty London Street. Edinburgh.

Scotland
Edinburgh

		rate from £ per person	children taken	evening meals	animals taken
Marny Hill **Elmview** **15 Glengyle Terrace** **Edinburgh** **EH3 9LN** **Tel: (0131) 2281973** **Fax 0131 2281973** **Open: ALL YEAR** **Map Ref No. 16**	Nearest Road: A.702 — Quietly situated in a fine Victorian terrace only 15 mins' (1 km's) walk from Edinburgh Castle & the city centre, Elmview has recently been completely restored & refurbished to a very high standard. Each of the 3, spacious & comfortable, en-suite bedrooms have all the expected amenities, as well as several thoughtful extras. Elmview is delightfully furnished & decorated, & you will find an atmosphere of comfort & relaxation, as well as a friendly & personal service. (non-smoking) CREDIT CARD / VISA / M'CARD	£30.00	N	N	N
Jon Stuart **Meadows Guest House** **17 Glengyle Terrace** **Edinburgh EH3 9LN** **Tel: (0131) 229 9559** **Fax 0131 229 2226** **Open: ALL YEAR (Excl. Xmas)** **Map Ref No. 16**	Nearest Road: A.702 — Quietly situated overlooking a park, Meadows is warm, comfortable & spacious, with a friendly atmosphere. 6 attractive rooms, all with colour T.V. & tea/coffee-making facilities, some with private bathroom. Jon will welcome you, & help you with where to go, what to do & where to eat. Bookings of 3 nights or more taken in advance. Centrally located & within easy reach of the Castle, Princes St., shops, theatres & restaurants. CREDIT CARD / VISA / M'CARD / AMEX	£25.00	Y	N	Y
Sheila & Bob Clark **Galloway** **222 Dean Park Crescent** **Edinburgh** **EH4 1PH** **Tel: (0131) 332 3672** **Open: ALL YEAR** **Map Ref No. 16**	Nearest Road: A.9, A.90 — A warm welcome, delightful atmosphere & superb breakfasts combine to make quality the hallmark of this well-known Victorian town house. Located half a mile from Princes Street, with free street parking. It offers accommodation in 10 comfortable rooms, 6 en-suite, all with colour T.V. & tea/coffee makers. Visitors have the whole of Edinburgh on their doorstep from this central vantage point. 7 nights for the price of 6.	£17.00	Y	N	Y
Mrs Moira Conway **Crannoch But and Ben** **467 Queensferry Road** **Edinburgh EH4 7ND** **Tel: (0131) 3365688** **Open: ALL YEAR** **Map Ref No. 16**	Nearest Road: A.90 — Warm Scottish hospitality at this very pleasant private house. The two ground-floor guest rooms have private facilities & tea/coffee-making. The guest lounge has T.V., and evening tea or coffee is served whilst you digest the available information on all there is to do in Edinburgh. Private parking on site, and an excellent bus service to the heart of the city (just 3 miles to Princes Street). (non-smoking)	£19.00	Y	N	N
Len & Sue Welch **Ravensdown Guest House** **248 Ferry Road** **Edinburgh** **EH5 3AN** **Tel: (0131) 5525438** **Open: ALL YEAR** **Map Ref No. 16**	Nearest Road: A.1, A.199 — Built at the beginning of the 1900s, Ravensdown offers unsurpassed panoramic views of the Edinburgh skyline. Each of the 6 spacious, well-decorated bedrooms have modern amenities, colour T.V. & tea/coffee-making facilities. A warm lounge enables guests to socialise, with bar service on the premises. Your friendly hosts are always available to offer assistance with tours, etc. A delicious breakfast gets you off to a good start each morning. Private parking available. Only 3 kilometres from the city centre. (non-smoking)	£16.00	Y	N	N

Scotland
Edinburgh

		rate from £ per person	children taken	evening meals	animals taken
Mrs Gillian McCowan Hill **2 Bonnington Terrace** **Trinity** **Edinburgh** **EH6 4BP** **Tel: (0131) 5549007** **Open: ALL YEAR** **Map Ref No. 16**	Nearest Road: A.1 A super Georgian town house, situated in Trinity, Edinburgh, only 5 mins from the city centre. This is an elegant & very stylish home which offers superb accommodation. Each guest bedroom is beautifully furnished & has a spacious private bathroom. Breakfast is taken in the kitchen/dining room which is particularly attractive & has pine furnishings. Convenient for all business & shopping amenities. Parking available. A delightful home where a comfortable stay is assured.	**£25.00** CREDIT CARD VISA M'CARD	Y	N	Y
Rosalind Ritchie **Rosebank House** **190 Newhaven Road** **Edinburgh EH6 4QB** **Tel: (0131) 5533223** **Fax 0131 5550308** **Open: ALL YEAR (Excl.** **Xmas & New Year)** **Map Ref No. 16**	Nearest Road: A.1, A.90 Rosebank is a tranquil house of hidden delights. Walled gardens with thyme & camomile lawns surround this early-Georgian home. Bedrooms are elegant & comfortably furnished, & all have excellent private facilities. Situated 2 mins from the sea, Rosebank is only 10 mins from Princes St.. There is unrestricted street parking & frequent buses to the city centre. Your hosts enjoy spoiling their guests & providing delicious breakfasts. A delightful non-smoking house.	**£30.00** CREDIT CARD VISA M'CARD	N	N	Y
Nan Stark **Ben-Cruachan** **17 McDonald Road** **Edinburgh** **EH7 4LX** **Tel: (0131) 5563709** **Open: APR - OCT** **Map Ref No. 16**	Nearest Road: A.1 A warm welcome is extended to all guests at this attractive house situated 1 km from Princes St. & close to most tourist attractions. There is unrestricted street parking, although it is also on a main bus route. A theatre & various restaurants nearby. The comfortable rooms are all en-suite & have colour T.V. & tea/coffee-making facilities. A full Scottish breakfast is served. A friendly & personal service is assured at all times.	**£20.00**	Y	N	N
Jim Houston **Greenside Hotel** **9 Royal Terrace** **Edinburgh EH7 5AB** **Tel: (0131) 5570121** **Tel/Fax 0131 557 0022** **Open: ALL YEAR** **Map Ref No. 16**	Nearest Road: A.1, A.7 Built in 1820, the Greenside Hotel is an elegant Georgian town-house hotel situated in the city centre & surrounded by peaceful garden settings in one of Edinburgh's most prestigious terraces. A few mins' walk from Waverly Station, Princes St., tourist attractions, local restaurants & theatre. 14 tastefully decorated rooms with all facilities. Large family rooms also available. Full Scottish Breakfast is served each morning.	**£22.50** CREDIT CARD VISA M'CARD AMEX	Y	Y	N
Irene & Dennis Robins **Sonas** **3 East Mayfield** **Edinburgh EH9 1SD** **Tel: (0131) 6672781** **Fax 0131 6670454** **Open: ALL YEAR** **Map Ref No. 16**	Nearest Road: A.68, A.7, A.701 Guests are assured of a warm welcome & a memorable stay at Sonas (the old Gaelic word for peace & happiness). Built in 1876, & recently refurbished, it now provides 8 tastefully decorated bedrooms with en-suite facilities, & retains many of its original features, including a lovely sweeping staircase & ornate cornices. A delicious Scottish breakfast is served each morning. Private parking. Excellent bus service.	**£19.00**	Y	N	Y

			rate from £ per person	children taken	evening meals	animals taken
Mr & Mrs A. Gallo **Rosedene Guest House** **4 Queen's Crescent** **Edinburgh EH9 2AZ** **Tel: (0131) 6675806** **Open: MAR - NOV** **Map Ref No. 16**	Nearest Road: A.68, A.7, A.701 A fine, detached Victorian villa with beautiful garden - situated in a select residential area just off the main road. Queen's Crescent lies between the A.7/701 & A.68 main roads coming into the city from the south, & is only 1 1/2 miles from Princes Street. Private parking available. 8 guest bedrooms, 3 with en-suite facilities, & each with tea/coffee makers & T.V..		£16.00	Y	N	N
Mrs A. Helen Telfer **Ard-Thor** **10 Mentone Terrace** **Newington** **Edinburgh EH9 2DG** **Tel: (0131) 6671647** **Open: ALL YEAR** **Map Ref No. 16**	Nearest Road: A.1, A.68, A.7 A charming, 19th-century Victorian guest house situated only 10 mins from the city centre, castle & Princes Street by a good local bus service. The Ard-Thor is quiet & friendly, & your comfort is ensured by the personal attention of your host. Guests are offered a choice of 3 rooms, all with T.V. & tea/coffee-making facilities. Queens Park & Commonwealth Pool are nearby. This is an ideal base from which to explore Edinburgh.	🚭	£16.00	Y	N	N
Alan & Angela Vidler **Rowan Guest House** **13 Glenorchy Terrace** **Newington** **Edinburgh EH9 2DQ** **Tel: (0131) 6672463** **Open: ALL YEAR** **Map Ref No. 16**	Nearest Road: A.701, A.7, A.68 Quietly located in one of Edinburgh's loveliest areas, Rowan House, built in 1880, combines the character of a bygone age with present-day comfort. Bedrooms are tastefully furnished, some with private facilities. Complimentary tea, coffee & biscuits available. Unrestricted parking. City centre only 10 mins by bus. Breakfast includes traditional porridge & freshly baked scones. You will receive a warm welcome & attentive service.	CREDIT CARD VISA M'CARD	£18.00	Y	N	N
Mrs Jane Coville **Teviotdale House** **53 Grange Loan** **Edinburgh** **EH9 2ER** **Tel: (0131) 6674376** **Fax 0131 6674376** **Open: ALL YEAR** **Map Ref No. 16**	Nearest Road: A.7, A.702 Tastefully restored, elegant, Victorian gentleman's town house. Located in a quiet residential conservation area. Lovely original woodwork. All 8 spacious rooms have every modern facility, with private or en-suite bathrooms, colour T.V., radio & tea/coffee makers. Some rooms have a refrigerator. Breakfast is a banquet. Home-baked scones, jams & bread. Guaranteed to delight the most travelled of guests. Parking. 10 mins to town centre. A delightful home.	🚭 CREDIT CARD VISA M'CARD AMEX	£24.00	Y	N	Y
Mrs Maureen Invernizzi **Roselea House** **11 Mayfield Road** **Edinburgh** **EH9 2NG** **Tel: (0131) 6676115** **Fax 0131 6673556** **Open: ALL YEAR** **Map Ref No. 16**	Nearest Road: A.701 Always a warm welcome from Maureen & Adolfo at their elegant Victorian house. They have tastefully restored & refurbished their home to a high standard; whilst still retaining the original features. Each room has colour T.V., tea/coffee facilities &, of course, an en-suite or private bathroom. Whether on business or on holiday, this is an ideal oasis to return to & relax in. A delightful home, offering easy access to the many attractions & places of historic interest that Edinburgh has to offer.	CREDIT CARD VISA M'CARD AMEX	£23.00	Y	N	N

Forgan House. Newport-on-Tay.

Scotland
Fifeshire

		rate from £ per person	children taken	evening meals	animals taken
Mrs Ella MacGeachy **The Dykes** **69 Pittenweem Road** **Anstruther KY10 3DT** **Tel: (01333) 310537** **Open: MAR - SEPT** **Map Ref No. 18**	Nearest Road: A.915 A delightful modern bungalow offering 2 comfortable guest rooms, including 1 family room, with modern facilities. Situated overlooking the golf course & the sea, this is an ideal base for families, & for tourists to this lovely region. There are many historic houses & golf courses locally, & the walking & riding are excellent. Only 9 miles from St. Andrews.	£15.00 (non-smoking)	Y	N	N
Donald & Isobel Steven **Ardchoille Farmhouse** **Dunshalt** **Auchtermuchty** **KY14 7EY** **Tel/Fax: (01337) 828414** **Mobile 0589 988174** **Open: ALL YEAR** **Map Ref No. 19**	Nearest Road: A.91, B.936 Relax & enjoy the warm comfort, delicious Taste of Scotland food & the excellent hospitality at Ardchoille Farmhouse. 3 en-suite twin-bedded rooms, tastefully furnished, with colour T.V. & tea/coffee trays offering home-made butter shortbread. Large comfortable lounge, & elegant dining room with fine china & crystal. Dinner is 4-course. Situated close to the Royal Palace of Falkland, the historic home of Mary Queen of Scots. 20 mins from St. Andrews, & 1 hr from Edinburgh. Ideal base for golfing & touring.	£25.00 CREDIT CARD VISA M'CARD	Y	Y	N
Mrs Patricia Scott **Forgan House** **Newport-on-Tay** **DD6 8RB** **Tel/Fax: (01382) 542760** **Open: ALL YEAR** **Map Ref No. 20**	Nearest Road: A.92 Forgan House, the former manse of the area, is a listed Georgian country house situated in 5 acres of grounds & gardens (incl. a paddock & walled garden) in open countryside 6 miles from St. Andrews. The emphasis is on quality & comfort, & the spacious rooms provide panoramic views & private facilities. World-famous golf courses & 3 miles from one of Scotland's most secret & beautiful sandy beaches. A delightful home.	£25.00 *see PHOTO over* CREDIT CARD VISA M'CARD	Y	Y	N
Mrs Helen Black **Milton Farm** **Milton of Leuchars** **St. Andrews** **KY16 0AB** **Tel: (01334) 839281** **Open: ALL YEAR** **Map Ref No. 21**	Nearest Road: A.919, A.91 A warm & friendly welcome awaits you at Milton Farm. A spacious, tastefully modernised & peaceful Georgian farmhouse. Accommodation is in 3 stylish & elegantly furnished bedrooms with very pretty linen. A full English breakfast is served, including home-made bread, preserves & fresh farm eggs. Packed lunches are provided on request. Guest lounge with colour T.V. & delightful garden. Many excellent golf courses nearby. St. Andrews 5 miles. Children over 10.	£22.50 (non-smoking) *see PHOTO over*	Y	N	N

Inverness-shire

Peter & Penny Rawson **Feith Mhor Country House** **Station Road** **Carrbridge** **PH23 3AP** **Tel: (01479) 841621** **Open: Mid DEC - Mid NOV** **Map Ref No. 22**	Nearest Road: A.9 A warm friendly atmosphere is found at this charming 19th-century house set in 1 1/2 acres of delightful garden, surrounded by peaceful, unspoilt countryside. Tastefully furnished, & full of character. 6 comfortable en-suite bedrooms with tea/coffee & T.V.. Excellent views from each room. A pleasant dining room & spacious, comfortable lounge. Super home-cooking, using fresh produce in season. Vegetarian dishes provided, with prior notice. Children over 10. Special low-season-break prices.	£22.00	Y	Y	Y

552

Milton Farm. St. Andrews.

Borlum Farmhouse. Drumnadrochit.

Scotland
Inverness-shire

		rate from £ per person	children taken	evening meals	animals taken
V. M. MacDonald-Haig **Borlum Farmhouse** **Drumnadrochit** **IV3 6XN** **Tel: (01456) 450358** **Fax (01456) 450358** **Open: ALL YEAR** **Map Ref No. 23**	Nearest Road: A.82 This 180-year-old farmhouse has a unique position overlooking Loch Ness. Each year, visitors worldwide are delighted with the fresh, tastefully furnished rooms, good food & friendly atmosphere. Borlum is an historic working hill farm, dating back to its service to Urquhart Castle in the 16th century. Excellent base for touring. The farm also has its own B.H.S.-approved riding centre, making it the ideal place to spend a riding holiday.	£19.00 *see PHOTO over* CREDIT CARD VISA M'CARD	Y	N	N
Mrs Jenny Mackenzie **Old Pier House** **Fort Augustus** **PH32 4BX** **Tel: (01320) 366418** **Fax 01320 366770** **Open: APR - OCT** **Map Ref No. 24**	Nearest Road: A.82 Warm, friendly, Highland hospitality in this pretty farmhouse on the shores of Loch Ness, half a mile north of historic Fort Augustus & the famous Benedictine Abbey. Panoramic views over Loch Ness & surrounding mountains. 4 attractive en-suite bedrooms. Highland cattle, pony trekking, boats, fishing & a beautiful nature trail. Home-cooked meals with organic local produce used where possible. Log fires. Children over 5.	£20.00	Y	Y	N
Joan & John Campbell **The Grange** **Grange Road** **Fort William** **PH33 6JF** **Tel: (01397) 705516** **Open: MAR - OCT** **Map Ref No. 32**	Nearest Road: A.82 Set in quiet gardens overlooking Loch Linnhe, yet only 10 mins from the town centre. The Grange offers superb accommodation in 3 superb en-suite rooms, each well-equipped & enhanced by a very relaxed atmosphere. The area is charming & the house is well-situated, only 1 1/2 hrs from Oban, Inverness & the Isles. An ideal base for touring the Highlands, & returning to a comfortable lounge log fire for chilly evenings. Vegetarians catered for. Children over 12.	£27.00 *see PHOTO over* CREDIT CARD VISA	Y	N	N
Vera G. Waugh **Cabana House** **Union Road** **Fort William** **PH33 6RB** **Tel: (01397) 705991** **Open: ALL YEAR** **Map Ref No. 25**	Nearest Road: A.82 This elegant Victorian house has been renovated to an exceptional standard. 3 designer-decorated bedrooms, 2 en-suite, all with every modern amenity. T.V. lounge/dining room. Excellent home cooking, tastefully presented with true Scottish hospitality. Situated in a prime position close to the Fort William town centre, with private parking & garden. An ideal holiday base for touring the spectacular Highlands & islands. Open for winter skiing holidays.	£20.00	N	N	N
David & Katherine Elder **Kinross House** **Woodside Avenue** **Grantown-on-Spey** **PH26 3JR** **Tel: (01479) 872042** **Fax 01479 873504** **Open: APR - OCT** **Map Ref No. 26**	Nearest Road: A.9, A.95 Kinross House sits on a quiet & pretty avenue. Lovely, en-suite bedrooms are warm & restful, all with T.V. & welcome trays; 1 is on the ground floor. Drawing/painting holidays available in Spring & Autumn. Delicious meals are served by David dressed in his MacIntosh kilt. Children from 7 yrs. Enjoy Highland hospitality & comfort at its very best with your Scottish hosts. Drawing/painting holidays in Spring/Autumn. Send for a brochure.	£22.00	Y	Y	N

The Grange. Fort William.

Scotland
Inverness-shire

		rate from £ per person	children taken	evening meals	animals taken
Barbara & Jim Casey **Ardconnel House** **Woodlands Terrace** **Grantown-on-Spey** **PH26 3JU** **Tel: (01479) 872104** **Fax 01479 872104** **Open: MAR - NOV** **Map Ref No. 26**	Nearest Road: A.95, A.9 Built in 1890, during the Victorian era of elegance, Ardconnel House stands in its own spacious grounds overlooking a glorious pine forest, Lochan & Cromdale Hills. 6 bedrooms are en-suite, with quality beds, colour T.V., hairdryer & welcome tray, & are charmingly decorated. A superb 4-poster bedroom. Excellent home cooking is complemented by a well-selected, modestly priced wine list. Taste of Scotland selected member. Children over 10 yrs.	£24.00 see PHOTO over CREDIT CARD VISA M'CARD	Y	Y	N
Jim & Geraldine Reid **The Old Royal Guest House** **10 Union Street** **Inverness IV1 1PL** **Tel: (01463) 230551** **Open: FEB - NOV** **Map Ref No. 27**	Nearest Road: A.9 Personally managed by the resident proprietors Jim & Geraldine, The Old Royal is conveniently situated in the centre of town, opposite the railway station. Accommodation is in 14 comfortable guest bedrooms, 5 with en-suite facilities. All have colour T.V. & tea/coffee makers. The Old Royal has a, home from home atmosphere, & provides visitors with a comfortable holiday base from which to tour the locality. Children over 3 yrs.	£18.50 CREDIT CARD VISA M'CARD	Y	N	N
Barbara Kinnear **Glenashdale** **Daviot East** **Inverness** **IV1 2EP** **Tel: (01463) 772221** **Open: ALL YEAR** **Map Ref No. 27**	Nearest Road: A.9 Glenashdale is situated 7 miles south of Inverness in quiet countryside, with lovely views. All the comfortable bedrooms have en-suite facilities, central heating, T.V., radio & tea/coffee tray. Dinner is available by arrangement. Joe & Babs Kinnear invite you to escape the hustle & bustle of everyday living & join them in the beauty of the Scottish Highlands, where making all guests feel welcome is a top priority.	£17.00	Y	Y	N
Mrs Margaret Pottie **Easter Dalziel** **Farmhouse** **Dalcross** **Inverness IV1 2JL** **Tel: (01667) 462213** **Fax 01667 462213** **Open: ALL YEAR** **Map Ref No. 28**	Nearest Road: A.96, B.9039 This Scottish farming family offer the visitor a friendly Highland welcome on their 200-acre stock/arable farm. 3 charming bedrooms are available in the delightful early-Victorian farmhouse. The lounge has log fire & colour T.V.. Delicious home cooking & baking served, including a choice of breakfasts. Ideal base for exploring the scenic Highlands. Local attractions are Cawdor Castle, Culloden, Fort George, Loch Ness & nearby Castle Stuart. A delightful home.	£15.00 CREDIT CARD VISA M'CARD	Y	Y	Y
Mrs Catherine Baillie **Victoria Guest House** **1 Victoria Terrace** **Inverness IV2 3QA** **Tel/Fax: (01463) 237682** **Open: APR - OCT** **Map Ref No. 27**	Nearest Road: A.9 A pleasant Victorian terraced house offering 1 family, 1 double & 1 twin room, each with private showers. Situated near the site of King Duncan's Castle, it is a good base for touring. Clava Stones, a Druid burial ground, is well worth visiting. Cots & highchairs provided for. A delightful home, ideal for a relaxing break or for exploring the many places of interest in the region.	£17.00	Y	N	N

Ardconnel House. Grantown–on–Spey.

Scotland
Inverness-shire

		rate from £ per person	children taken	evening meals	animals taken

Mrs Margaret Cairns
Invergloy House
Spean Bridge
PH34 4DY
Tel: (01397) 712681
Open: ALL YEAR
Map Ref No. 29

Nearest Road: A.82
A really interesting Scottish coach house, dating back 110 years, offering 3 charming, comfortable twin-bedded rooms, with modern facilities, & 2 bathrooms. Situated 5 miles north of the village of Spean Bridge towards Inverness, it is signposted on the left, along a wooded drive. Guests have use of own sitting room, overlooking Loch Lochy in 50 acres of superb woodland of rhododendron & azaleas. Fishing from the private beach & rowing boats, & hard tennis court. Children over 8 welcome. Non-smokers only, please.

£17.00 | Y | Y | N

(non-smoking)

Isle of Skye

Mrs Jane Wilcken
Corry Lodge
Liveras
Broadford
IV49 9AA
Tel: (01471) 822235
Fax 01471 822318
Open: ALL YEAR
Map Ref No. 30

Nearest Road: A.850
Corry Lodge, on the Isle of Skye, is a most attractive period house dating from the late 18th century. It has a fine open outlook over Broadford bay, but with a sheltered location, & approximately 1,150 metres of unspoilt sea frontage. There are 5 comfortable & tastefully furnished bedrooms, each with en-suite bathroom, radio, colour T.V. & tea/coffee-making facilities. Corry Lodge forms an ideal base from which to tour the island either by car or bicycle, or on foot.

£20.00 | Y | Y | Y

Paul & Cathie Booth
Glenview Inn &
Restaurant, Culnacnoc
Staffin
IV51 9JH
Tel: (01470) 562248
Open: MAR - JAN
Map Ref No. 31

Nearest Road: A.855
A traditional island house lying between Trotternish Ridge & the sea & ideally situated for exploring North Skye. Bedrooms are individually decorated, warm & comfortable, with tea/coffee-making facilities. Glenview offers a relaxed & friendly atmosphere & the best of Scotland's varied larder. Only fresh food is used to create a menu including traditional, ethnic & vegetarian specialities. An excellent base for a relaxing break.

£18.00 | Y | Y | Y

CREDIT CARD
VISA
M'CARD

Lothian

Derek & Elizabeth Scott
Ashcroft Farmhouse
East Calder
EH53 0ET
Tel: (01506) 881810
Fax 01506 884327
Open: ALL YEAR
Map Ref No. 33

Nearest Road: A.71
Ashcroft is a new farmhouse, with all rooms on the ground floor. Surrounded by farmland, yet only 10 miles from Edinburgh city centre; 5 miles from the airport, city bypass, M.8/M.9 motorways. Mrs Scott provides morning tea in bed, before tempting guests with a full Scottish breakfast, including home-made sausage, local produce & even Whisky marmalade. Ideal for touring. Tastefully furnished en-suite bedrooms - & 1 4-poster bedroom.

£24.00 | Y | N | N

(non-smoking)

CREDIT CARD
VISA
M'CARD

All the establishments mentioned in this guide
are members of the
Worldwide Bed & Breakfast Association.

If you have any comments regarding your
accommodation please send them to us
using the form at the back of the book.
We value your comments.

Scotland
Lothian

		rate from £ per person	children taken	evening meals	animals taken

Misses E. & L. Stewart & **Mr D. Wimberley** **Point Garry Hotel** **20 West Bay Road** **North Berwick EH39 4AW** **Tel: (01620) 892380** **Fax 01620 892848** **Open: APR - OCT** **Map Ref No. 34**	Nearest Road: A.1 The Royal Burgh of North Berwick is situated between the historic castles of Tantallon & Dirleton. Point Garry, a Victorian listed building, overlooks both the 1st tee of the West Links Championship Golf Course & the sea. There are 15 rooms, all en-suite, with colour T.V., central heating, tea/coffee-making facilities, telephone & parking. 12 golf courses within 10 miles, including the world-famous Muirfield (4 miles). Free golf booking. Edinburgh only 30 mins.	£27.00 CREDIT CARD VISA M'CARD	Y	Y	Y

Perthshire

Mr Iain H. Aitchison **Invertrossachs Country House** **Invertrossachs Road** **By Callander** **FK17 8HG** **Tel: (01877) 331126** **Fax 01877 331229** **Open: ALL YEAR** **Map Ref No. 38**	Nearest Road: A.84, A.81 Escape for some privacy & comfort in the unforgettable setting of this splendid Lochside Edwardian mansion with 33 acres, by the southern shores of Loch Venachar. Choose from the elegant Loch Room, the Victoria Suite or the Menteith Apartment. A king-size double or twin room; or a suite of rooms accommodating up to 4/5 persons. Enjoy fine Loch views, or the adjacent Menteith Hills. All 3 units have T.V., radio, 'phone, hairdryers, video & CD, & tea/coffee facilities. Complete with a 5-course breakfast served in the conservatory overlooking the Loch, it all adds up to the perfect break away from it all. Evening meals by arrangement.	£35.00 *see PHOTO over* CREDIT CARD VISA M'CARD AMEX	Y	Y	Y
Roger McDonald **Allt-Chaorain House** **Crianlarich** **FK20 8RU** **Tel: (01838) 300283** **Fax 01838 300238** **Open: MAR - OCT** **Map Ref No. 39**	Nearest Road: A.82 Allt-Chaorain House is a small family hotel situated in an elevated position, with commanding views of Ben More & Strathfillian from the south-facing sun lounge. There are 8 very comfortable bedrooms, all with private facilities. 'Taste of Scotland' home cooking & packed lunches available on request. The friendly & relaxing atmosphere will unwind you as you sit by the log fire after walking, fishing or touring the central Highlands. Children over 7 years welcome.	£30.00 *see PHOTO over* CREDIT CARD VISA M'CARD	Y	Y	Y
Jean & Jimmy Young **The Lodge House** **Crianlarich** **FK20 8RU** **Tel: (01838) 300276** **Open: MAR - NOV** **Map Ref No. 39**	Nearest Road: A.82 'Every room with a view.' Unwind in the space & fresh air of the mountains & glens surrounding this home. Enjoy a dram in the malt-whisky bar (offering 40 different malts). 6 beautiful en-suite bedrooms all with colour T.V.. Experience real Scottish hospitality, & renowned home cooking. Sample menu: cullen skink soup, haggis vol au vents, grapefruit drambuie, venison chasseur & trout rob roy, & many delicious desserts. No smoking, except in bar.	£26.00 CREDIT CARD VISA M'CARD	Y	Y	N

Invertrossachs. Callender.

Allt-Chaorain House Hotel, Crianlarich.

Scotland
Perthshire

		rate per person from £	children taken	evening meals	animals taken

Janice & Sandy Chisholm	Nearest Road: A.82	£16.00	Y	N	Y
Tigh Na Struith	Alongside the River Fillan, & 200 yds from the main road, this friendly family home guarantees a quiet night's sleep. In the same hands for 15 years, this guest house has earned itself high praise for realistic prices together with clean, smoke-free accommodation. Still the best value for money, as awarded in 1984 by the Guild of Travel Writers. All rooms with h/c, colour T.V., tea/coffee-making, central heating & superb views. Party-goers please note: no licence.				
Riverside Guest House					
Crianlarich					
FK20 8RU					
Tel: (01838) 300235					
Open: MAR - OCT					
Map Ref No. 39					

Colin & Fiona Graham	Nearest Road: A.84, M.9	£22.00	Y	Y	Y
Mackeanston House	Mackeanston is a comfortable, pretty family home, originally dating back to the 17th century, set in 1 acre of beautiful gardens, surrounded by farmland. Fresh flowers, tea/coffee facilities, radios, en-suite/private facilities. Home-made bread, home-grown vegetables & a warm Scottish welcome. Colour T.V.. Picnics & evening meals by arrangement. Excellent base for Trossachs, Stirling. 1 hr to Perth, Glasgow, Edinburgh. Hill walking, golf, riding & historical sites.				
Doune					
FK16 6AX					
Tel: (01786) 850213					
Fax 01786 850414					
Open: ALL YEAR					
Map Ref No. 40					

Mrs Patricia W. Buxton	Nearest Road: A.9	£19.00	N	Y	N
Bheinne Mhor	A warm welcome awaits you at this comfortable, Victorian, detached house, with turret & private garden, ideally situated for lovely walks both in Macbeth's Birnam Woods & alongside the rivers Tay & Braan. Many places of historic interest & beauty nearby, including Dunkeld Cathedral, Scottish N.T.'s 'The Hermitage' & the Loch of Lowes Wildlife Reserve. Boundless opportunities for anglers & golfers. 3 bedrooms, all with en-suite/private facilities, & modern amenities. Evening meals by arrangement.				
Perth Road					
Birnam					
Dunkeld					
PH8 0DH					
Tel: (01350) 727779					
Open: ALL YEAR					
Map Ref No. 41					

Robert & Jean Lewis	Nearest Road: A.84	£25.00	N	Y	N
Monachyle Mhor	Monachyle Mhor is a small, 18th-century, award-winning farmhouse hotel set in its own 2,000 acres, with magnificent views over 2 lochs. The house is furnished with period furniture & fine pictures. All rooms have wonderful outlooks, & all 9 bedrooms are en-suite. The dining room & conservatory restaurant allow you to wine & dine on the very finest of Scottish food, including game from our own estate. Walking & fishing in season.				
Balquhidder					
Lochearnhead FK19 8PQ					
Tel: (01877) 384622					
Fax 01877 384305		CREDIT CARD			
Open: ALL YEAR		VISA			
Map Ref No. 42		M'CARD			

Derek & Angela Straker	Nearest Road: A.9, M.90	£45.00	Y	Y	Y
Dupplin Castle	Dupplin, a rare mid-20th-century Scottish mansion, stands in 30 acres of private parkland with views over the lovely River Earn valley to the hills beyond. All the superb bedrooms are en-suite & individually appointed. Dupplin Castle is a country house of the highest quality, with the sophistication & relaxed informality of an old-fashioned house party. Shooting, fishing & golf within easy reach, & available from Dupplin by prior arrangement. Perth 15 mins' drive. Edinburgh/Glasgow 1 hr. Children over 12.				
By Perth					
PH2 0PY					
Tel: (01738) 623224					
Fax 01738 444140					
Open: ALL YEAR		CREDIT CARD			
Map Ref No. 35		VISA			
		M'CARD			

Gloagburn Farm. Tibbermore.

Scotland
Perthshire

		rate from £ per person	children taken	evening meals	animals taken
Mae & Bob Collier **Dundarave House** **Strathview Terrace** **Pitlochry** **PH16 5AT** **Tel: (01796) 473109** **Open: MAR - NOV** **Map Ref No. 43**	Nearest Road: A.9 A charming Victorian house, specialising in bed & breakfast. Set in formal terraced gardens in a secluded location of approx. half an acre. Quality accommodation, with 7 well-appointed bedrooms (5 en-suite) with T.V. & tea/coffee makers, & a comfortable, period lounge. A hearty Scottish breakfast is served in the tastefully decorated dining room. The owners aim to provide a personal & friendly atmosphere in relaxing surroundings.	£22.00	Y	Y	Y
Elizabeth Goodfellow **Tigh Dornie** **Alo Clune** **Killiecrankie** **Pitlochry PH16 5LR** **Tel: (01796) 473276** **Open: ALL YEAR** **Map Ref No. 44**	Nearest Road: A.9 Tigh Dornie is situated amid beautiful Perthshire scenery, approx. 5 miles north of Pitlochry. Offering attractive accommodation in 3 very comfortable & tastefully furnished guest bedrooms, each with private/en-suite bathroom, T.V. & tea/coffee-making facilities. A warm & friendly welcome is assured from your hosts, who will ensure that your stay is a memorable one. An ideal spot for a relaxing break & for touring Scotland. Ample private car parking.	£18.00	N	N	N
Alison & Ian Niven **Gloagburn Farm** **Tibbermore by Perth** **PH1 1QL** **Tel: (01738) 840228** **Fax 01738 840228** **Open: ALL YEAR** **Map Ref No. 45**	Nearest Road: A.9 A spacious & attractively furnished family farmhouse set on a 450-acre working farm in beautiful open countryside. There is a choice of 3 stylish bedrooms with pretty linens, 2 with excellent private bathrooms. Suppers available by prior arrangement. Full breakfast is served, including home-made preserves & home-produced fresh eggs. Within 3 miles of the A.9, & within easy reach of many golf courses & sites of historic interest. A relaxed & friendly home.	£21.00 *see PHOTO over*	Y	Y	N
Morna Dalziel-Williams **Dundarroch Country** **House** **Brig O'Turk** **Trossachs-by-Callander** **FK17 8HT** **Tel: (01877) 376200** **Fax 01877 376202** **Open: APR - OCT** **Map Ref No. 46**	Nearest Road: A.84 Enjoy award-winning hospitality in this delightful Victorian country house, set in peaceful meadows in the heart of the Trossachs, 'Rob Roy' country. The perfect location for a relaxing break. There are 3 beautifully furnished bedrooms, each with en-suite facilities, drinks refrigerator, 'phone, colour T.V., tea/coffee maker, etc. Also, a residents' lounge & dining room furnished with paintings & fine antiques. Superb views to the river & mountains. Wonderful breakfasts! Dinners served in a separately owned quaint bar/restaurant in the grounds of Dundarroch.	£28.75 *see PHOTO over* CREDIT CARD VISA M'CARD	Y	Y	N

When booking your accommodation please
mention
The Best Bed & Breakfast

Dundarroch Country House. Trossachs-by-Callander.

Scotland
Renfrewshire

		rate from £ per person	children taken	evening meals	animals taken

Mrs Kate Bewick **Six Fathoms** **6 Polnoon Street** **Eaglesham** **Renfrewshire by** **Glasgow G76 0BH** **Tel/Fax: (01355) 302321** **Open: ALL YEAR** **Map Ref No. 48**	Nearest Road: A.77, A.74 Set in the picturesque village of Eaglesham, 10 miles from Glasgow. Guests can be sure of a warm, Scottish welcome at this delightful home, with a choice of 2 twin rooms - 1 with sitting room & private facilities - or 2 single rooms, 1 spacious, 1 cosy. All rooms have T.V. & tea/coffee-making facilities. 3 pubs/restaurants, excellent & varied, within 5 mins' walk. Convenient for Glasgow & Prestwick International Airports, the M.74, Loch Lomond, Burns Country & the Burrell Collection.	£20.00	N	N	N

Roxburghshire

Mrs H. Irvine **'Froylehurst'** **Friars** **Jedburgh TD8 6BN** **Tel/Fax: (01835) 862477** **Open: MAR - NOV** **Map Ref No. 49**	Nearest Road: A.68 An attractive late-Victorian house offering 4 comfortable guest rooms & residents' lounge. H/c, tea/coffee-making facilities & colour T.V. in all bedrooms. Situated in a large garden overlooking the town in a quiet residential area. Edinburgh only 1 hour by car. Golf, pony trekking, fishing & sports centre all local. Children over 5. An ideal base from which to explore this beautiful region.	£16.00	Y	N	N
Mrs P. Jill Hensens **Ancrum Craig** **Ancrum** **Jedburgh** **TD8 6UN** **Tel: (01835) 830280** **Open: APR - OCT** **Map Ref No. 47**	Nearest Road: A.68 This is a comfortable country house with authentic Victorian features. Situated 2 miles from the village of Ancrum, it is surrounded by farmland & enjoys magnificent views to the south. The elegant lounge offers an open fire. The hosts serve their own eggs for breakfast, in the main dining room. The bedrooms are spacious & with modern facilities, & all the rooms situated at the front benefit from the wonderful views.	£19.00	Y	N	Y
Mrs Betty Smith **Whitehill Farm** **Nenthorn** **Kelso TD5 7RZ** **Tel/Fax: (01573) 470203** **Open: ALL YEAR (Excl.** **Xmas & New Year)** **Map Ref No. 50**	Nearest Road: A.6089 A comfortable & peaceful farmhouse with a large garden standing on a 455-acre, mixed farm 4 miles from Kelso. 4 attractive bedrooms - 2 single & 2 twin, 1 with en-suite shower room - have superb views over rolling countryside. All have central heating & washbasins. A pleasant sitting room with log fire is available to guests. An ideal base for touring; maps available. Good home cooking. Dinner by arrangement.	£16.50	Y	Y	Y
Mrs P. M. Schofield **Torwood Lodge** **High Cross Avenue** **Melrose** **TD6 9SU** **Tel: (01896) 822220** **Open: ALL YEAR** **Map Ref No. 51**	Nearest Road: A.7, A.6091 Melrose, famous for its abbey, is located 37 miles south of Edinburgh at the heart of the beautiful border country, with its contrasting scenery & many stately homes. Torwood Lodge is a Victorian family house situated within easy walking distance of the town centre, & with superb views towards the River Tweed & hills beyond. There are 3 attractive bedrooms, each with en-suite bathrooms, tea/coffee-making facilities & colour T.V.. Private parking.	£21.00	Y	N	N

Scotland
Stirlingshire

		rate from £ per person	children taken	evening meals	animals taken
Laird Andrew Haslam **Culcreuch Castle** **Fintry** **Loch Lomond** **Stirling** **G63 0LW** **Tel: (01360) 860555/860228** **Fax 01360 860556** **Open: ALL YEAR** **Map Ref No. 52**	Nearest Road: A.811, A.81 Retreat to 700 years of history at magical Culcreuch, the ancestral fortalice and clan castle of the Galbraiths, home of the Barons of Culcreuch, & now a country house hotel where the Laird and his family extend an hospitable welcome. Set in 1,600 spectacular acres, yet only 19 miles from central Glasgow & 17 miles from Stirling. 8 handsome, well-appointed bedrooms with en-suite or private facilities, 4-poster bedroom supplement of £12 per person per night. Elegant period-style decor and antiques, log fires, the romance of dining by candlelight. Prices £43.00 Apr & Oct, £48.00 May - Sept p.p.p.n..	£35.00 *see PHOTO over* CREDIT CARD VISA M'CARD AMEX	Y	Y	N
Jane & Adrian O'Dell **Westbourne** **10 Dollar Road** **Tillicoultry FK13 6PA** **Tel: (01259) 750314** **Fax 01324 826677** **Open: ALL YEAR** **Map Ref No. 53**	Nearest Road: A.91 A Victorian mill-owner's mansion set in wooded grounds beneath Ochil Hills, surrounded by excellent walking country & numerous golf courses. A warm, friendly atmosphere, & an unusual collection of arts & curios from around the world. Delicious home-cooking, with vegetarian food a speciality. Log fires, T.V. in all rooms (1 on the ground floor). Centrally situated for Edinburgh, Glasgow, Perth & Stirling, & motorways 15 mins. Secure off-street parking.	£18.00	Y	N	Y

All the establishments mentioned in this guide are members of
The Worldwide Bed & Breakfast Association

When booking your accommodation please mention
The Best Bed & Breakfast

Culcreuch Castle.   Fintry.

Wales

Wales

Wales is a small country with landscapes of intense beauty. In the north are the massive mountains of the Snowdonia National Park, split by chasms & narrow passes, & bounded by quiet vales & moorland. The Lleyn peninsula & the Isle of Anglesey have lovely remote coastlines.

Forests, hills & lakeland form the scenery of Mid Wales, with the great arc of Cardigan Bay in the west.

To the south there is fertile farming land in the Vale of Glamorgan, mountains & high plateaux in the Brecon Beacons, & also the industrial valleys. The coastline forms two peninsulas, around Pembroke & the Gower.

Welsh, the oldest living language of Europe is spoken & used, most obviously in the north, & is enjoying a resurgence in the number of its speakers.

From Taliesin, the 6th century Celtic poet, to Dylan Thomas, Wales has inspired poetry & song. Every August, at the Royal National Eisteddfod, thousands gather to compete as singers, musicians & poets, or to listen & learn. In the small town of Llangollen, there is an International Music Eisteddfod for a week every July

North Wales.

North Wales is chiefly renowned for the 850 miles of the Snowdonia National Park. It is a land of mountains & lakes, rivers & waterfalls & deep

The Snowdon Mountain Railway.

glacier valleys. The scenery is justly popular with walkers & pony-trekkers, but the Snowdon Mountain Railway provides easy access to the summit of the highest mountain in the range with views over the "roof of Wales".

Within miles of this wild highland landscape is a coastline of smooth beaches & little fishing villages.

Barmouth has mountain scenery on its doorstep & miles of golden sands & estuary walks. Bangor & Llandudno are popular resort towns.

The Lleyn peninsula reaches west & is an area of great charm. Abersoch is a dinghy & windsurfing centre with safe sandy beaches. In the Middle Ages pilgrims would come to visit Bardsey, the Isle of 20,000 saints, just off Aberdaron, at the tip of the peninsula.

The Isle of Anglesey is linked to the mainland by the handsome Menai Straits Suspension Bridge. Beaumaris has a 13th century castle & many other fine buildings in its historic town centre.

Historically North Wales is a fiercely independent land where powerful local lords resisted first the Romans & later the armies of the English Kings.

The coastline is studded with 13th century castles. Dramatically sited Harlech Castle, famed in fable & song, commands the town, & wide sweep of the coastline.

The great citadel of Edward I at Caernarfon comprises the castle & the encircling town walls. In 1969 it was the scene of the investiture of His Royal Highness Prince Charles as Prince of Wales.

There are elegant stately homes like Plas Newydd in Anglesey & Eriddig House near Wrexham, but it is the variety of domestic architecture that is most charming. The timber-frame buildings of the Border country are seen at their best in historic Ruthin set in the

Wales

beautiful Vale of Clwyd. Further west, the stone cottages of Snowdonia are built of large stones & roofed with the distinctive blue & green local slate. The low, snow-white cottages of Anglesey & the Lleyn Peninsula are typical of the "Atlantic Coast" architecture that can be found on all the western coasts of Europe. The houses are constructed of huge boulders with tiny windows & doors.

By contrast there is the marvellous fantasy of Portmeirion village. On a wooded peninsula between Harlech & Porthmadog, Sir Clough Williams Ellis created a perfect Italianate village with pastel coloured buildings, a town hall & luxury hotel.

Mid Wales

Mid Wales is farming country where people are outnumbered three to one by sheep. A flock of ewes, a lone shepherd & a Border Collie are a common sight on these green hills. Country towns like Old Radnor, Knighton & Montgomery with its castle ruin, have a timeless quality. The market towns of Rhyader, Lampeter & Dolgellau have their weekly livestock sales & annual agricultural festivals, the largest of which is the Royal Welsh Show at Builth Wells in July.

This is the background to the craft of weaving practised here for centuries. In the valley of the River Tefi & on an upper tributary of the Wye & the Irfon, there are tiny riverbank mills which produce the colourful Welsh plaid cloth.

Towards the Snowdonia National Park in the North, the land rises to the scale of true mountains. Mighty Cader Idris & the expanses of Plynlimon, once inaccessible to all but the shepherd & the mountaineer, are now popular centres for walking & pony trekking with well-signposted trails.

The line of the border with England is followed by a huge earth work of bank & ditch. This is Offa's Dyke, built by the King of Mercia around 750 A.D. to deter the Welsh from their incessant raids into his kingdom. Later the border was guarded by the castles at Hay-on-Wye, Builth Wells, Welshpool, & Chirk which date from mediaeval times.

North from Rhayader, lies the Dovey estuary & the historic town of Machynlleth. This is where Owain Glyndwr's parliament is thought to have met in 1404, & there is an exhibition about the Welsh leader in the building, believed to have been Parliament House.

Wales lost many fine religious houses during the Dissolution of the Monasteries under Henry VIII. The ruins at Cymer near Dolgellau & at Strata Florida were abbeys of the Cistercian order. However, many remote Parish Churches show evidence of the skills of mediaeval craftsmen with soaring columns & fine rood screens.

The Cambrian Coast (Cardigan Bay) has sand dunes to the north & cliffs to the south with sandy coves & miles of cliff walks.

Llangrannog Headland.

Aberystwyth is the main town of the region with two beaches & a yachting harbour, a Camera Obscura on the cliff top & some fine walks in the area. Water-skiing, windsurfing &

572

Wales

sailing are popular at Aberdovey, Aberaeron, New Quay, Tywyn & Barmouth & there are delightful little beaches further south at Aberporth, Tresaith or Llangrannog.

South Wales

South Wales is a region of scenic variety. The Pembrokeshire coastline has sheer cliffs, little coves & lovely beaches. Most of the area is National Park with an 80 mile foot path running along its length, passing pretty harbour villages like Solva & Broad Haven.

A great circle of Norman Castles stands guard over South Pembrokeshire, Roch, Haverfordwest, Tenby, Carew, Pembroke & Manorbier.

The northern headland of Saint

Tenby.

Brides Bay is the most westerly point in the country & at the centre of a tiny village stands the Cathedral of Saint David, the Patron Saint of Wales. At Bosherton near Saint Govans Head, there is a tiny chapel hidden in a cleft in the massive limestone cliffs.

The Preseli Hills hold the vast prehistoric burial chambers of Pentre Ifan, & the same mountains provided the great blue stones used at faraway Stonehenge.

Laugharne is the village where Dylan Thomas lived & worked in what was a boat-house & is now a museum.

In the valleys, towns like Merthyr

Tydfil, Ebbw Vale & Treorchy were in the forefront of the boom years of the Industrial Revolution. Now the heavy industries are fast declining & the ravages of the indiscriminate mining & belching smoke of the blast furnaces are disappearing. The famous Male Voice Choirs & the love of rugby football survives.

The Vale of Glamorgan is a rural area with pretty villages. Beyond here the land rises steeply to the high wild moorlands & hill farms of the Brecon Beacons National Park & the Black Mountains, lovely areas for walking & pony trekking.

The Wye Valley leads down to Chepstow & here set amidst the beautiful woodlands is the ruin of the Great Abbey of Tintern, founded in 1131 by the Cistercian Order.

Swansea has a strong sea-faring tradition maintained by its new Marine Quarter - marina, waterfront village, restaurants, art gallery & theatre.

Cardiff, the capital of Wales, is a pleasant city with acres of parkland, the lovely River Taff, & a great castle, as well as a new civic centre, two theatres & the ultra-modern St. David's Concert Hall. It is the home of the Welsh National Opera & here also is the National Stadium where the singing of the rugby crowd on a Saturday afternoon is a treat.

Pony Trekking

Wales

Wales
Gazeteer

Areas of Outstanding Natural Beauty
The Pembrokeshire Coast. The Brecon Beacons. Snowdonia. Gower.'

Historic Houses & Castles

Cardiff Castle - Cardiff
Built on a Roman site in the 11th century.
Caerphilly Castle - Caerphilly
13th century fortress.
Chirk Castle - Nr. Wrexham
14th century Border Castle. Lovely gardens.
Coity Castle - Coity
Mediaeval stronghold - three storied round tower.
Gwydir Castle - Nr. Lanrwst
Royal residence in past days - wonderful Tudor furnishings. Gardens with peacocks.
Penrhyn Castle - Bangor
Neo-Norman architecture 19th century - large grounds with museum & exhibitions. Victorian garden.
Picton Castle - Haverfordwest
12th century - lived in by the same family continuously. Fine gardens.
Caernarfon Castle - Caernarfon
13th century - castle of great importance to Edward I.
Conway Castle - Conwy
13th century - one of Edward I's chain of castles.
Powis Castle - Welshpool
14th century - reconstruction work in 17th century.
Murals, furnishings, tapestries & paintings, terraced gardens.
Pembroke Castle - Pembroke
12th century Norman castle with huge keep & immense walls.
Birthplace of Henry VII.
Plas Newydd - Isle of Anglesey
18th century Gothic style house.
Home of the Marquis of Anglesey.
Stands on the edge of the Menai Strait looking across to the Snowdonia Range. Famous for the Rex Whistler murals.
The Tudor Merchant's House - Tenby
Built in 15th century.
Tretower Court & Castle - Crickhowell
Mediaeval - finest example in Wales.

Cathedrals & Churches

St. Asaph Cathedral
13th century - 19th century restoration. Smallest of Cathedrals in England & Wales.
Holywell (St. Winifred)
15th century well chapel & chamber - fine example.
St. Davids (St. David)
12th century Cathedral - splendid tower - oak roof to nave.
Gwent (St. Woolos)
Norman Cathedral - Gothic additions - 19th century restoration.
Abergavenny (St. Mary)
14th century church of 12th century Benedictine priory.
Llanengan (St. Engan)
Mediaeval church - very large with original roof & stalls 16th century tower.
Esyronen
17th century chapel, much original interior remaining.
Llangdegley (St. Tegla)
18th century Quaker meeting house - thatched roof - simple structure divided into schoolroom & meeting room.
Llandaff Cathedral (St. Peter & St. Paul)
Founded in 6th century - present building began in 12th century. Great damage suffered in bombing during war, restored with Epstein's famous figure of Christ.

Museums & Galleries

National Museum of Wales - Cardiff (also Turner House)
Geology, archaeology, zoology, botany, industry, & art exhibitions.
Welsh Folk Museum - St. Fagans Castle - Cardiff
13th century walls curtaining a 16th century house - now a most interesting & comprehensive folk museum.
County Museum - Carmarthen
Roman jewellery, gold, etc. Romano-British & Stone Age relics.
National Library of Wales - Aberystwyth
Records of Wales & Celtic areas. Great historical interest.
University College of Wales Gallery - AberystwythTravelling exhibitions of painting & sculpture.

Wales

Museum & Art Gallery - Newport
Specialist collection of English
watercolours - natural history, Roman
remains, etc.
Legionary Museum - Caerleon
Roman relics found on the site of
legionary fortress at Risca.
Nelson Museum - Monmouth
Interesting relics of Admiral Lord Nelson &
Lady Hamilton.
Bangor Art Gallery - Bangor
Exhibitions of contemporary paintings &
sculpture.
Bangor Museum of Welsh Antiquities -
Bangor
History of North Wales is shown. Splendid
exhibits of furniture, clothing, domestic
objects, etc. Also Roman antiquities.
Narrow Gauge Railway Museum - Tywyn
Rolling stock & exhibitions of narrow
gauge railways of U.K.
Museum of Childhood - Menai Bridge
Charming museum of dolls & toys &
children's things.

Brecknock Museum - Brecon
Natural history, archaeology, agriculture,
local history, etc.
Glynn Vivian Art Gallery & Museum -
Swansea
Ceramics, old & contemporary, British
paintings & drawings, sculpture, loan
exhibitions.
Stone Museum - Margam
Carved stones & crosses from pre-
historic times.
Plas Mawr - Conwy
A beautiful Elizabethan town mansion
house in its original condition. Now holds
the Royal Cambrain Academy of Art.

Historic Monuments

Rhuddlan Castle - Rhuddlan
13th century castle - interesting diamond
plan.
Valle Crucis Abbey - Llangollen
13th century Cistercian Abbey Church.

Cader Idris.

575

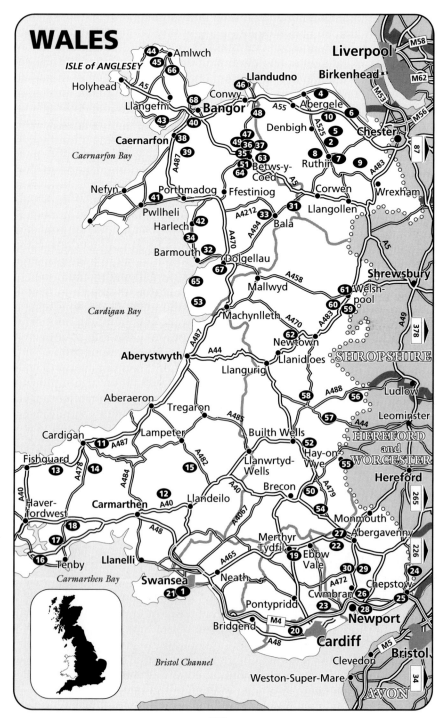

WALES

ISLE of ANGLESEY

Amlwch

Holyhead

Llangefni

Caernarfon

Caernarfon Bay

Nefyn

Pwllheli

Harlech

Barmouth

Cardigan Bay

Aberystwyth

Aberaeron

Cardigan

Fishguard

Haver-fordwest

Carmarthen

Tenby

Carmarthen Bay

Swansea

Bristol Channel

Llandudno

Conwy

Bangor

Denbigh

Betws-y-Coed

Ffestiniog

Porthmadog

Bala

Dolgellau

Mallwyd

Machynlleth

Newtown

Llangurig

Tregaron

Lampeter

Llandeilo

Neath

Bridgend

Birkenhead

Abergele

Chester

Ruthin

Corwen

Llangollen

Wrexham

Shrewsbury

Welshpool

SHROPSHIRE

Llanidloes

Ludlow

Leominster

Builth Wells

Hay-on-Wye

HEREFORD and WORCESTER

Hereford

Llanwrtyd-Wells

Brecon

Monmouth

Merthyr Tydfil

Ebbw Vale

Abergavenny

Cwmbran

Pontypridd

Chepstow

Newport

Cardiff

Clevedon

Bristol

Weston-Super-Mare

AVON

Liverpool

576

WALES
Map references

1	Maybery	36	Gibson	52	N. Jones
2	Carrington-Sykes	37	Pitman	53	Tregarthen
4	Steele-Mortimer	38	Bayles	54	Cracroft
5	Evans	39	Pinnock	55	P. Roberts
6	M. Jones	40	Kettle	56	Hood
7	Spencer	41	Murray	57	Knott
7	Mitchell	41	Clayton	58	Millan
8	Jones	42	Newton Davies	59	Bright
9	Parry	43	Roberts	60	Marriott
10	A, Roberts	44	Hirst	61	S. Jones
11	Humphreys	45	Hughes	62	C. Davies
12	Dent	46	Rigby	63	Bower
13	Heard	47	Aplin	64	Cutler
14	Vaughton	48	Marrow	65	Smyth
15	D. Davies	49	Barker	66	Brown
16	McHugh	50	Cole	67	D. Jones
17	Fielder	51	Betteney	68	Abas
18	Gilder				
19	Hurley				
20	Renwick				
21	Wearing				
22	Weatherill				
23	Price				
24	Stubbs				
25	Hunter				
26	Watkins				
27	Harris				
28	Park				
29	Bradley				
30	Hayman-Joyce				
31	Fullard				
32	Michael				
33	Cunningham				
34	Thompson				
35	Valadini				
35	Muskus				
35	Howard				
35	Whittingham				
35	Roobottom				

		rate from £ per person	children taken	evening meals	animals taken

Mrs Marie Carrington-Sykes
Pentre Bach
Llandyrnog
Denbigh LL16 4LA
Tel/Fax: (01824) 790725
Open: ALL YEAR
Map Ref No. 02

Nearest Road: A.525
Pentre Bach is situated near the village of Llandyrnog in the beautiful Vale of Clwyd. Built in 1745, of Dutch red brick, it is a peaceful setting for the country lover, with good walks & access onto the famous 'Offa's Dyke' trail which is close by. 2 charming bedrooms, each with private/en-suite bathroom & beverage facilities. Ideally situated a few miles from the market towns of Ruthin & Denbigh, & a short drive from the North Wales coast, Snowdonia National Park & Chester.

£17.00 | Y | N | Y

Mrs Mary Jones
Greenhill Farm
Bryn Celyn
Holywell
CH8 7QF
Tel: (01352) 713270
Open: MAR - OCT
Map Ref No. 06

Nearest Road: A.55
A 16th-century working dairy farm, overlooking the Dee Estuary, which retains its old-world charm, with a beamed & panelled interior. Bedrooms are tastefully furnished, some having bathroom/shower en-suite. Relax & enjoy typical farmhouse food in the attractive dining room. Children's play area & utility/games room also available. A lovely home, within easy reach of both the coastal & mountain areas of North Wales.

£16.00 | Y | Y | N

N. & M. Steele-Mortimer
Golden Grove
Llanasa
Holywell CH8 9NE
Tel: (01745) 854452
Fax 01745 854547
Open: ALL YEAR (Excl. Xmas & New Year)
Map Ref No. 04

Nearest Road: A.55, A.5151
Beautiful Elizabethan manor house set in 1,000 acres, close to Chester, Bodnant Gardens & Snowdonia, & en route to Holyhead. The Steele-Mortimer brothers & wives, having returned to the family home from Canada & Ireland, provide a warm welcome for their guests. The menu features home produce, including lamb & pheasant, together with interesting wines & home baking. The atmosphere is friendly & informal. No smoking in bedrooms. Children over 8 yrs. Licensed.

£32.00 | Y | Y | N

see PHOTO over

CREDIT CARD
VISA
M'CARD

Neil & Susan Evans
The Old Mill Private Hotel
Melin-Y-Wern
Denbigh Road, Nannerch
Mold CH7 5RH
Tel: (01352) 741542
Fax 01352 740254
Open: FEB - DEC
Map Ref No. 05

Nearest Road: A.541, A.55
This small & friendly comfortable hotel has been created by owners Neil & Susan Evans by the careful conversion of 19th-century stone-built stables. Now forming part of a watermill conservation area together with an adjacent wine bar, restaurant, gallery & traditional British pub. The 6 fully equipped en-suite rooms are complemented by a residents' lounge in which to relax & read about 'places to visit & things to do'. Enjoy your first-class British breakfast in the spacious pine-furnished dining room.

£25.50 | Y | Y | Y

CREDIT CARD
VISA
M'CARD
AMEX

Judith Mitchell
The Castle Hotel
St. Peters Square
Ruthin LL15 1AA
Tel: (01824) 702479
Fax 01824 704924
Open: ALL YEAR
Map Ref No. 07

Nearest Road: A.494
A happy hotel, with a friendly, informal atmosphere. Originally a 17th-century coaching inn - & latterly a favourite meeting place for King Eward VII & one of his paramours! Overlooking the market square of this pretty mediaeval town in the beautiful Vale of Clwyd. Freshly prepared local food, a comfortable bar & a lovely restaurant. En-suite bedrooms, colour T.V. & tea/coffee-making facilities. A short scenic drive to Llangollen. 5 mins' walk to a mediaeval banquet.

£21.00 | Y | Y | Y

CREDIT CARD
VISA
M'CARD
AMEX

Golden Grove. Llanasa.

Wales
Clwyd

		rate from £ per person	children taken	evening meals	animals taken
Beryl J. Jones **Bryn Awel** **Bontuchel** **Ruthin LL15 2DE** **Tel: (01824) 702481** **Open: ALL YEAR (Excl.** **Xmas & New Year)** **Map Ref No. 08**	Nearest Road: B.5105 This 35-acre working farm is situated in the beautiful hamlet of Bontuchel, where you can relax in perfect peace & tranquility & enjoy a wealth of wonderful walks, wild flowers & wildlife. Beryl has many cooking awards to her credit, & can oblige most requests for special diets. 1 room is en-suite, the other has private bathroom. Each has colour T.V. & tea-making facilities. Heating throughout. A warm welcome & good food is top priority at this farmhouse.	£16.00	Y	Y	N
Jen & Bert Spencer **Eyarth Station** **Llanfair D. C.** **Ruthin** **LL15 2EE** **Tel: (01824) 703643** **Fax 01824 707464** **Open: ALL YEAR** **Map Ref No. 07**	Nearest Road: A.525 A warm & friendly reception awaits the visitor to Eyarth Station. A super, converted, former railway station located in the beautiful countryside of the Vale of Clwyd. 6 bedrooms, all en-suite. A comfortable colour-T.V. lounge, & guests are welcome to use the garden, sun patio & outdoor heated pool. Conveniently located for the many historic towns in the region including Conwy, Caernarfon & Ruthin & their castles, with mediaeval banquet 2 minutes' drive away. The Roman town of Chester is within driving distance. 1987 winner of Best Bed & Breakfast Award.	£20.00 *see PHOTO over* CREDIT CARD VISA M'CARD	Y	Y	Y
Mrs E. A. Parry **Llainwen Ucha** **Pentre Celyn** **Ruthin LL15 2HL** **Tel: (01978) 790253** **Open: ALL YEAR (Excl.** **Xmas & New Year)** **Map Ref No. 09**	Nearest Road: A.525 A working farm set in 130 acres overlooking the very beautiful Vale of Clwyd. Offering 3 pleasantly decorated rooms with modern amenities, & accommodating up to 5 persons. All rooms are centrally heated. Good home cooking made with fresh local produce; vegetarian meals on request. Conveniently situated for visiting Chester, Llangollen, Snowdonia & the coast. Offa's Dyke & fishing nearby. Mediaeval banquets are held at Ruthin Castle throughout the year.	£14.00	Y	Y	N
Anwen Roberts **Bach-Y-Graig** **Tremeirchion** **St. Asaph** **LL17 0UH** **Tel: (01745) 730627** **Open: ALL YEAR** **Map Ref No. 10**	Nearest Road: A.541, A.55 A super 16th-century farmhouse nestling at the foot of the Clwydian range, with undisturbed views of the surrounding countryside. Walk a 40-acre mediaeval woodland trail on the farm where the royal Black Prince once hunted, & enjoy the wealth of rare plants & flowers. All rooms are en-suite/private, with tea/coffee, radio/alarms & colour T.V.. A large lounge with colour T.V., an inglenook with roaring log fires (during the colder part of the season) & central heating. Central for Chester, Snowdonia & coastal resorts.	£19.00	Y	N	N

When booking your accommodation please mention
The Best Bed & Breakfast

Eyarth Station.   Llanfair D.C.

Wales
Dyfed

		rate from £ per person	children taken	evening meals	animals taken
Mrs C. M. Vaughton **Awel-Y-Grug** **Boncath** **SA37 0JP** Tel: (01239) 841260 Open: APR - OCT Map Ref No. 14	Nearest Road: A.478 A small, family-run guest house with a relaxed homely atmosphere. Good & plentiful home-cooked food is served, including vegetarian meals. Licensed. There are 4 charming bedrooms, 2 en-suite, 1 with a private bathroom & 1 with a shower. An attractive dining room. A cosy lounge with T.V.. Laundry facilities, a games room, a lounge & a large & pleasant garden are available to guests. Children are welcome (cots & high chairs). Please place dinner orders by 6 p.m.	£17.00	Y	Y	Y
G. B. & M. M. Humphreys **Penbontbren Farm Hotel** **Glynarthen** **Cardigan SA44 6PE** Tel: (01239) 810248 Fax 01239 811129 Open: ALL YEAR Map Ref No. 11	Nearest Road: A.487 Penbontbren is a rare kind of place: a hotel which offers a genuine taste of Wales accompanied by modern comforts. Barrie & Nan Humphreys are your welcoming hosts - & you stay quite literally at their home. A row of converted farmyard barns have been transformed into rooms finished to extremely high standards, with the full range of facilities. Perfect for a relaxing holiday, tucked away down a country lane & only a few miles from the sandy coves & headlands of Cardigan Bay.	£31.00 *see PHOTO over* CREDIT CARD VISA M'CARD AMEX	Y	Y	Y
Mrs Charlotte Dent **Plas Alltyferin** **Pontargothi, Nantgaredig** **Carmarthen SA32 7PF** Tel/Fax: (01267) 290662 Open: ALL YEAR (Excl. Xmas & Easter) Map Ref No. 12	Nearest Road: A.40 A classic Georgian country house lying in a bowl of hills above the beautiful Towy Valley, overlooking a Norman hillfort & the River Cothi - famous for salmon & seatrout. 2 spacious, comfortable, twin-bedded rooms. Guests welcomed as part of the family on this working farm. Excellent local pubs & restaurants. Totally peaceful, & marvellous touring country for castles, beaches & rural Wales. Children over 10.	£20.00	Y	N	Y
Peter & Jane Heard **Tregynon Country** **Farmhouse Hotel** **Gwaun Valley** **Fishguard SA65 9TU** Tel: (01239) 820531 Fax 01239 820808 Open: ALL YEAR Map Ref No. 13	Nearest Road: B.4313, B.4329 This is a traditional, beamed, award-winning, 16th-century, family-run farmhouse, standing in acres of grounds next to ancient oak woodlands & overlooking the glorious Gwaun Valley in the Pembrokeshire Coast National Park. It is unique, of great natural beauty & still quite unspoilt. 8 en-suite, ground floor rooms. Traditional & special diets, wholefood & vegetarian specialities, using fresh local produce when possible. A good range of wine is also available. Own trout ponds, 200ft waterfall & Iron Age fort, abundant wildlife.	£23.00 CREDIT CARD VISA M'CARD	Y	Y	N
David & Bronwen Davies **Glanrannell Park Country** **House Hotel, Crugybar** **Llanwrda SA19 8SA** Tel: (01558) 685230 Fax 01558 685784 Open: APR - OCT Map Ref No. 15	Nearest Road: A.482 In the lovely secluded Cothi Valley, this peaceful country house is 10 miles from the 3 Welsh market towns, Lampeter, Llandovery & Llandeilo. Within easy reach of the west coast & Brecon Beacons, it is a superb centre. Family-run by the Davieses for over 25 years, it has a reputation for excellent service, good food & fine wine. There are 8 attractive bedrooms, many en-suite. The colour brochure is a call away.	£28.00 CREDIT CARD VISA M'CARD	Y	Y	Y

Penbontbren Farm Hotel. Glynarthen.

Wales
Dyfed & Glamorgan

		rate from £ per person	children taken	evening meals	animals taken
Mrs Jill McHugh **The Old Vicarage** **Manorbier** **SA70 7TN** **Tel: (01834) 871452** **Mobile 0421 595858** **Open: ALL YEAR** **Map Ref No. 16**	Nearest Road: A.4139 Overlooking the coastal village of Manorbier with its 11th-century castle & beautiful beaches, & offering 2 spacious bedrooms with views across Barafundle Bay. Set in mature grounds of 2 1/2 acres, it features log fires & is furnished with antiques & period pieces. The Pembrokeshire Coastal Path passes through the village & offers the perfect stepping-off point for exploring the glorious coastline. Beaches 5 mins walk. Irish ferries, Pembroke 20 mins, Fishguard 45 mins.	£18.50	Y	N	N
L. E. & J. M. Fielder **Old Stable Cottage** **Carew** **Tenby** **SA70 8SL** **Tel: (01646) 651889** **Open: APR - OCT** **Map Ref No. 17**	Nearest Road: A.477 The Cottage (Grade II listed), with inglenook fireplace & original bread oven, was once a stable & carthouse to 13th-century Carew Castle situated near the entrance & the creek of Carew River with its Tidal Mill. A spiral staircase leads to 3 charming, oak-beamed en-suite bedrooms with colour T.V., home-baked Welsh cakes & tea/coffee. Delicious food is prepared in the farmhouse kitchen on the Aga. Dinners by arrangement. A conservatory overlooks the garden.	£22.50	Y	Y	N
Peter & Margaret Gilder **Llangwm House** **Whitland** **SA34 0RB** **Tel: (01994) 240621** **Fax 01994 240621** **Open: ALL YEAR** **Map Ref No. 18**	Nearest Road: A.40 Llangwm House is a large, fully modernised farmhouse with panoramic views, ideally situated for the Pembrokeshire Coast, with its beautiful beaches, walks & abundant wildlife. The spacious bedrooms, with private facilities, are tastefully furnished with comfort in mind. All have T.V. & tea/coffee-making facilities. Guests are assured of a warm welcome, & may find it interesting to watch Peter train his sheepdogs. Children over 5. Evening meals by prior arrangement.	£19.50	Y	Y	Y

Glamorgan

Michael & Kathleen Hurley **Tregenna Hotel** **Park Terrace** **Merthyr Tydfil CF47 8RF** **Tel: (01685) 723627** **Fax 01685 721951** **Open: ALL YEAR** **Map Ref No. 19**	Nearest Road: A.470, M.4 Family-run hotel with high level of comfort & class. 24 bedrooms with bathroom, 7 of which are designated for tourists & family use at special rates (50% reduction for children sharing). Telephone, tea/coffee service tray, colour T.V. in all rooms. Lunch, afternoon tea & dinner served 7 days a week. Brecon Beacons National Park 8 minutes' drive. 45 minutes Cardiff/Wales Airport, 2 1/4 hours London Heathrow Airport.	£25.00 CREDIT CARD VISA M'CARD AMEX	Y	Y	Y
Paul & Monica Renwick **Sant-Y-Nyll House** **St. Brides-Super-Ely** **CF5 6EZ** **Tel: (01446) 760209** **Open: ALL YEAR** **Map Ref No. 20**	Nearest Road: M.4 You can be assured of a friendly welcome to Sant-Y-Nyll, a charming Georgian country residence set in its own extensive grounds, with spectacular views over the Vale of Glamorgan. There are 6 guest rooms with modern facilities, T.V. & tea/coffee-making. Comfortable, warm & relaxing. Licensed. Children welcome. Cardiff just 7 miles. St. Fagans Welsh Folk Museum 2 miles. Paul & Monica look forward to meeting you.	£17.50 CREDIT CARD AMEX	Y	N	Y

The Wenallt. Gilwern.

Wales
Glamorgan & Gwent

	Nearest Road	rate from £ per person	children taken	evening meals	animals taken
Bruce & Heather Wearing **Parkway Hotel** **253 Gower Road, Sketty** **Swansea SA2 9JL** **Tel: (01792) 201632** **Fax 01792 201839** **Open: ALL YEAR** **Map Ref No. 21**	Nearest Road: A.4118 A small, mansion-style house set in its own grounds offering 13 pleasant, comfortable, en-suite rooms with tea-making facilities, T.V. etc. This is an ideal base for touring the lovely Gower Peninsula & Swansea Bay. The city centre is easily accessible, & is full of interest, as are the many historic sites which are found in this region. Personal service & a warm welcome await all visitors, in a friendly & relaxed atmosphere.	£24.50 CREDIT CARD VISA M'CARD AMEX	Y	Y	Y
Jan Maybery **Tides Reach** **388 Mumbles Rd, Mumbles** **Swansea SA3 5TN** **Tel: (01792) 404877** **Open: ALL YEAR** **Map Ref No. 01**	Nearest Road: A.4067 The warmest of welcomes & an excellent standard of accommodation await you at Tides Reach, which is tastefully decorated & beautifully furnished with antiques. Offering 8 attractive bedrooms, 5 with either en-suite or private bathroom. Well-situated on the seafront in the delightful village of Mumbles (the gateway to Gower), yet only 4 miles from Swansea; ideal for business or pleasure. Children over 7 yrs welcome.	£15.50	Y	N	Y

Gwent

	Nearest Road	rate from £ per person	children taken	evening meals	animals taken
Mr & Mrs B. L. Harris **The Wenallt** **Abergavenny** **NP7 0HP** **Tel: (01873) 830694** **Open: ALL YEAR** **Map Ref No. 27**	Nearest Road: A.465 A 16th-century Welsh longhouse set in 50 acres of farmland in the Brecon Beacons National Park & commanding magnificent views over the Usk Valley. Retaining all its old charm, with oak beams & inglenook fireplace, yet offering a high standard of accommodation, with en-suite bedrooms, good food & a warm welcome. An ideal base from which to see Wales & the surrounding areas. Licensed.	£18.00 *see PHOTO over*	Y	Y	Y
Mr & Mrs B. Weatherill **Llanwenarth House** **Govilon** **Abergavenny NP7 9SF** **Tel: (01873) 830289** **Fax 01873 832199** **Open: MAR - Mid JAN** **Map Ref No. 22**	Nearest Road: A.465 A truly delightful 16th-century manor house, standing in its own beautiful grounds & surrounded by the tranquil scenic hills of the Brecon Beacons National Park. Elegantly furnished, tastefully decorated & with superb views, this house is a real pleasure to visit. Dinner, prepared by Amanda, a Cordon Bleu cook, is a delight. It is served by candlelight in the lovely dining room. 4 rooms, all with en-suite facilities. Fishing, golf, climbing, walking & shooting nearby. Children over 10 yrs.	£34.00	Y	Y	Y
Dinah Price **'Great House'** **Isca Road** **Old Village** **Caerleon** **NP6 1QG** **Tel: (01633) 420216/420312** **Open: ALL YEAR** **Map Ref No. 23**	Nearest Road: M.4, B.4596 'Great House' is an attractive 16th-century house located on the banks of the River Usk. Retaining much of its original character (including beams & inglenook fireplaces) 3 pretty bedrooms with T.V. & tea/coffee facilities. Charming drawing room with T.V. & woodburner. Garden to rear leads to the riverbank. Within easy reach of superb golf course, fishing & forest trails. The ancient village of Caerleon is near with its ampitheatre, museums & Roman Baths. Good pubs. Ideal stop-over on the way through Wales or onto Ireland.	£18.00	Y	N	N

Parva Farmhouse and Restaurant. Tintern.

Wales
Gwent

		rate from £ per person	children taken	evening meals	animals taken

Dereck & Vickie Stubbs **Parva Farmhouse Hotel** **& Restaurant** **Tintern** **Chepstow NP6 6SQ** **Tel: (01291) 689411** **Fax 01291 689557** **Open: ALL YEAR** **Map Ref No. 24**	Nearest Road: A.466, M.4, M.5 A delightful 17th-century stone farmhouse situated 50 yards from the River Wye. The quaint en-suite bedrooms, with their designer fabrics, are gorgeous, & some offer breathtaking views over the River Wye & woodland. The beamed lounge, with log fires, leather Chesterfields & 'Honesty Bar', is a tranquil haven in which to unwind. Mouth-watering dishes, served in the intimate, candlelit Inglenook Restaurant, reflect the owner's love of cooking. A super home, perfect for a relaxing break or for exploring beautiful Wales.	£27.00 *see PHOTO over* CREDIT CARD VISA M'CARD	Y	Y	Y
Mrs Julia Hunter **Spring Farm** **Brockweir** **Chepstow** **NP6 7NU** **Tel/Fax: (01291) 689439** **Open: MAR - NOV** **Map Ref No. 25**	Nearest Road: A.466 Spring Farm is located in an area of outstanding beauty with breathtaking views across the Wye Valley. This lovely old stone farmhouse stands in an idyllic, peaceful setting, nestled into the hillside overlooking the River Wye. Beautifully furnished, with 3 lovely en-suite bedrooms. Deep in the country, yet only 15 mins from the M.4. The only noise to be heard is the bleating of the sheep. Close to Tintern Abbey & Welsh border castles. Riding, fishing, pony trekking & golf nearby.	£28.00 *see PHOTO over* CREDIT CARD VISA M'CARD	N	Y	N
Mrs Beryl Watkins **The Glebe** **Crematiourm Road** **Croes-Y-Ceiliog** **Cwmbran NP44 2DE** **Tel: (01633450) 251/242** **Open: ALL YEAR** **Map Ref No. 26**	Nearest Road: A.4042, M.4 A friendly & helpful host awaits you at Glebe Farm, a spacious, modern farmhouse overlooking a lovely corner of rural Wales where the family have farmed for generations. Offering 4 attractive & comfortable rooms, with modern amenities. A substantial breakfast is served in the morning, & in the evening, good pub fare can be found a pleasant walk away. Ideal for a relaxing break. Convenient for the M.4/M.5.	£16.00	Y	N	N
Mrs C. T. Park **Brick House Country** **Guest House, Redwick** **Newport NP6 3DX** **Tel: (01633) 880230** **Fax 01633 882441** **Open: ALL YEAR** **Map Ref No. 28**	Nearest Road: M.4 Jt. 23 Brick House Farm is a listed Grade II Georgian farmhouse dating from about 1765, but with up-to-date conveniences. All double bedrooms have an en-suite bathroom. A pleasant T.V. lounge, dining room & bar. Full central heating. There is also a delightful garden where guests may take cream teas, weather permitting. Brick House is ideally placed for touring South Wales & the Wye Valley, or as a stopping-off point just over the Severn Bridge. Single room supplement.	£20.00 🚭	Y	Y	N
Ann Bradley **Pentwyn Farm** **Little Mill** **Pontypool NP4 0HQ** **Tel: (01495) 785249** **Fax 01495 785249** **Open: FEB - NOV** **Map Ref No. 29**	Nearest Road: A.472 Pentwyn is a 120-acre farm situated on the edge of the Brecon Beacons National Park. Good food and hospitality are of prime importance. The 16th-century, pink-washed longhouse has all the comforts of the 20th century without losing its charm. A large garden, with swimming pool. There are 4 pretty bedrooms (2 en-suite), with tea-making facilities. An attractive sitting room with open fire, piano & books. A restaurant licence. Rough shooting available.	£15.00	Y	Y	N

Spring Farm. Brockweir.

Abercelyn. Llanycil.

Wales
Gwent & Gwynedd

		rate from £ per person	children taken	evening meals	animals taken
Mrs Diana Hayman-Joyce **Ty Isha** **Mamhilad** **Pontypool NP4 0JE** **Tel: (01495) 785573** **Open: ALL YEAR** **Map Ref No. 30**	Nearest Road: A.4042 This attractive house is set amongst the green fields of Gwent, not far from the Monmouth Brecon Canal. The lovely views & peaceful surroundings give an atmosphere of tranquility which, combined both with comfortable accommodation in 2 well-equipped rooms (with private facilities) & with a sumptuous breakfast, make it a place well worth visiting.	£18.00	Y	N	Y
	## Gwynedd				
Richard Fullard & **Beryl Gunn** **Melin Meloch** **Bala LL23 7DP** **Tel: (01678) 520101** **Open: FEB - DEC (Excl.** **Xmas & Jan.)** **Map Ref No. 31**	Nearest Road: A.494, B.4401 Just outside Bala, on the B.4401, close to the River Dee, stands this historic Water Mill, its stone walls draped in Virginia creeper. Set in lovely water gardens with a river running through the Victorian turbine. 5-ft wide doors lead into a galleried interior, with period furniture & bygones. Here, breakfast & dinner are served. Pretty en-suite rooms in Mill cottage & granary offer comfort & privacy, with T.V. & hot-drinks trays. A lodge is available. Animals taken by prior arrangement	£17.00	Y	Y	Y
Mrs Judy Cunningham **Abercelyn Country House** **Llanycil** **Bala LL23 7YF** **Tel: (01678) 521109** **Fax 01678 520556** **Open: ALL YEAR** **Map Ref No. 33**	Nearest Road: A.494 Set in landscaped gardens with its own mountain stream running alongside, this former rectory dates back to before 1721. Situated in the Snowdonia National Park, it is ideally located for walking or touring amongst the spectacular scenery. Bright & spacious en-suite bedrooms with views over Bala Lake, evenings relaxing before open log fires, & informal conversation over traditional breakfasts with hot home-baked bread, preserves & fresh coffee.	£18.50 *see PHOTO over* CREDIT CARD VISA M'CARD	Y	N	N
Paula & Peter Thompson **Llwyndu Farmhouse** **Llwyndu** **Llanaber** **Barmouth LL42 1RR** **Tel/Fax: (01341) 280144** **Open: ALL YEAR** **Map Ref No. 34**	Nearest Road: A.496 Enjoy a relaxed, friendly stay in this 17th-century farmhouse & converted granary. Wonderfully situated over Cardigan Bay. All 7 bedrooms have great charm, & are en-suite - with T.V.. Savour imaginative dishes, including vegetarian ones, in a superb setting, with oak beams & inglenooks. Dinner by candlelight. Licensed. Log fires in Winter. Children very welcome. Beaches nearby. Peacefully secluded, yet convenient for Barmouth. A beautiful region to explore.	£24.00 *see PHOTO over*	Y	Y	Y
Mrs Hazel Michael **Plas Bach** **Glandwr** **Bontddu** **Barmouth LL42 1TG** **Tel: (01341) 281234** **Open: MAR - DEC** **Map Ref No. 32**	Nearest Road: A.496 Plas Bach is a small, comfortable Victorian country house ideally situated for exploring southern Snowdonia, & offering a rare combination of exceptional value & genuine hospitality in an outstanding setting, with magnificent views of the Mawddach estuary & Cader Idris. The bedrooms are cosy & thoughtfully furnished, with en-suite bath/shower rooms, hospitality tray & T.V.. Breakfast is a feast - definitely worth a brisk walk after - & dinner is offered most evenings.	£27.50 *see PHOTO over*	N	Y	Y

Llwyndu Farmhouse. Llanaber.

Plas Bach. Bontddu.

Tan Dinas. Betws–Y–Coed

Wales
Gwynedd

		rate from £ per person	children taken	evening meals taken	animals taken
Teresa & Keith Roobottom **The Ferns Guest House** **Holyhead Road** **Betws-Y-Coed** **LL24 0AN** **Tel/Fax: (01690) 710587** **Open: ALL YEAR** **Map Ref No. 35**	Nearest Road: A.5, A.470 The Ferns Guest House is conveniently situated in the village of Betws-Y-Coed in the beautiful Snowdonia National Park. 9 attractively furnished bedrooms, many en-suite, all with T.V. & tea/coffee-making facilities. Betws-Y-Coed is an ideal base for exploring this spectacular region, & is within easy reach of Llanrwst, Conwy, Caernarfon, Blaenau Ffestiniog & Portmeirion. Keith & Teresa will make every effort to ensure that your stay is a pleasantly memorable one.	£17.00	Y	N	N
Marion & Bill Betteney **Bryn Afon Guest House** **Pentre Felin** **Betws-Y-Coed** **LL24 0BB** **Tel: (01690) 710403** **Open: ALL YEAR** **Map Ref No. 51**	Nearest Road: A.5, A.470 A Victorian stone-built house situated on the banks of the River Llugwy overlooking the Pont-Y-Pair Bridge & waterfall. Well-appointed bedrooms with comfortable beds ensure a good night's sleep. Central for all tourist attractions & many local walks through the forests. Drying facilities available. Parking for all guests on the premises & a good choice of restaurants within 5-10 mins' walking distance.	£14.00	Y	N	N
Jean & Peter Whittingham **Fron Heulog Country House** **Betws-Y-Coed** **LL24 0BL** **Tel: (01690) 710736** **Open: ALL YEAR** **Map Ref No. 35**	Nearest Road: A.5, A.470 The Country House in the Village! Enjoy the warmest welcome, a friendly atmosphere & real hospitality in this elegant Victorian stone-built house, located in quiet, peaceful, wooded, riverside scenery. Superb accommodation: comfortable bedrooms, full-facility en-suite bathrooms, spacious lounges & a pleasant dining room. Private parking. The heart of wonderfully picturesque Snowdonia - so much to see & do. More home than hotel! Croeso! - Welcome!	£18.00	N	Y	N
Ann Howard **Tan Dinas** **Coed Cynhelier Road** **Betws-Y-Coed** **LL24 0BL** **Tel: (01690) 710635** **Open: ALL YEAR** **Map Ref No. 35**	Nearest Road: A.5 A warm welcome awaits you at this lovely Victorian country home, situated in 3 acres of woodland gardens, offering peace & seclusion, & yet only 500 yds from the village centre. Guests may choose from 8 spacious, centrally heated rooms with lovely views. All rooms have h&c & tea/coffee facilities. 4 rooms are en-suite. Log fires in winter. Forest walks from house. Golf & fishing nearby. Ideal touring centre. Ample parking. Evening meals available. Licensed. Video library.	£18.00 *see PHOTO over*	Y	Y	N
Ann & Clive Muskus **Aberconwy House** **Llanrwst Road** **Betws-Y-Coed** **LL24 0HD** **Tel: (01690) 710202** **Fax 01690 710800** **Open: ALL YEAR** **Map Ref No. 35**	Nearest Road: A.5, A.470 A high standard of comfort & friendly, helpful hosts await you at Aberconwy. This large Victorian home, located in a lovely position above the picturesque village of Betws-Y-Coed, has panoramic views of the Llugney Valley, mountains & the River Conway. Accommodation is in a choice of 8 very comfortable en-suite bedrooms, with T.V. & tea/coffee makers. Most, also, have wonderful views. A residents' T.V. lounge & garden are also available. This is an ideal centre for touring, walking, fishing & golf.	£20.00 *see PHOTO over*	Y	N	Y

Aberconwy House. Betws-Y-Coed.

Tan-y-Foel Country House. Capel Garmon.

Wales
Gwynedd

		rate from £ per person	children taken	evening meals	animals taken
Modwena & Ian Cutler **Penmachno Hall** **Penmachno** **Betws-Y-Coed** **LL24 0PU** **Tel: (01690) 760207** **Open: ALL YEAR** **Map Ref No. 64**	Nearest Road: A.5 Penmachno Hall was built as a rectory in 1862. Situated on the edge of the village in grounds of 2 1/2 acres, it is ideally located, being peaceful & secluded but enjoying easy access to all the various attractions of North Wales. The aim is to provide an informal, cosy atmosphere, with the very best of home cooking. Accommodation is in 4 delightful en-suite bedrooms. This is the perfect spot for a relaxing break.	£25.00 CREDIT CARD VISA M'CARD	Y	Y	N
Ray & Barbara Valadini **Henllys (Old Court) Hotel** **Old Church Road** **Betws-Y-Coed** **LL24 OAL** **Tel: (01690) 710534** **Open: FEB - NOV** **Map Ref No. 35**	Nearest Road: A.5 No wonder our guests return time after time to this beautifully converted Victorian magistrates court, set in peaceful riverside gardens. Choose from judges chambers to the convicted felon's single cell. Each individually designed bedroom is fully equipped for your comfort. The police station houses our cosy fireside bar, & the magistrates court our dining room, where superb food is imaginatively prepared from freshly grown produce. Non-smoking throughout.	£20.00 🚭 CREDIT CARD VISA M'CARD	Y	Y	N
Anne Gibson **Bron Eirian Guest House** **Town Hill** **Llanrwst** **Betws-Y-Coed** **LL26 0NF** **Tel: (01492) 641741** **Open: ALL YEAR** **Map Ref No. 36**	Nearest Road: A.5, A.55 A lovely Victorian house in a peaceful spot set on an hill overlooking the market town of Llanrwst, the Conway Valley & the mountains of Snowdonia. 3 en-suite guest rooms, with colour T.V., tea trays, hairdryers & central heating, all very tastefully furnished. A pretty lounge for relaxing & a dining room where guests can enjoy a hearty breakfast. An ideal base from which to explore Snowdonia, walk, fish or pony-trek. Whatever your choice, a warm welcome is assured. Children over 10 yrs.	£16.00	Y	Y	Y
Peter & Janet Pitman **Tan-Y-Foel Country House** **Capel Garmon** **Betws-Y-Coed** **LL26 0RE** **Tel: (01690) 710507** **Fax 01690 710681** **Open: JAN - NOV** **Map Ref No. 37**	Nearest Road: A.470 Tan-y-Foel is a country house, set in the Snowdonia National Park with wonderful views across the Conwy Valley. The characterful stone-built house, dating from the 16th century, has been tastefully refurbished, & hosts Peter & Janet go out of their way to provide a personal style of service which many would find hard to emulate. The 9 en-suite bedrooms (some with 4-posters) are individually decorated, & fresh flowers are in abundance. Superb cuisine. Children over 7 years.	£38.00 🚭 *see PHOTO over* CREDIT CARD VISA M'CARD	Y	Y	N
Roger & Megan Bower **The White Horse Inn** **Capel Garmon** **Betws-Y-Coed LL26 0RW** **Tel: (01690) 710271** **Fax 01690 710271** **Open: ALL YEAR** **Map Ref No. 63**	Nearest Road: A.5, A.470 A 16th-century country inn set in the heart of the Snowdonia National Park with breathtaking views. The Inn has 7 en-suite bedrooms & a charming cottage restaurant, cocktail bar & lounge where, in the winter, log fires blaze & in summer fresh flowers fill the old windowsills. A delicious farmhouse breakfast is served. Taste of Wales home-cooking. A warm welcome & best ales & fine wines await you.	£24.00 *see PHOTO over* CREDIT CARD VISA M'CARD	Y	Y	Y

The White Horse Inn. Capel Garmon.

Wales
Gwynedd

		rate from £ per person	children taken	evening meals	animals taken
Beverley & Richard Bayles **The White House** **Llanfaglan** **Caernarfon** **LL54 5RA** **Tel: (01286) 673003** **Open: ALL YEAR** **Map Ref No. 38**	Nearest Road: A.487 The White House is a large detached house set in its own grounds, overlooking Foryd Bay, & with the Snowdonia mountains behind. There are 4 tastefully decorated bedrooms, all with bath or shower, tea/coffee-making facilities & colour T.V.. Guests are welcome to use the residents' lounge, outdoor pool & gardens. Ideally situated for birdwatching, walking, windsurfing, golf & visiting the historic Welsh castles.	£17.00	Y	N	Y
Mr & Mrs J. Pinnock **Cae Cyd** **Groeslon** **Caernarfon LL54 7DP** **Tel: (01286) 880253** **Open: Late MAR - OCT** **Map Ref No. 39**	Nearest Road: A.487 For a peaceful bed and breakfast, stay in Cae Cyd, a small Welsh stone cottage with character, set in 3 acres of garden on the edge of Snowdonia National Park. Delight in the views of Caernarfon Bay and Anglesey, walk in the fields, watch the sunsets over the sea. Accommodation is in 2 guest bedrooms: a double room & a twin-bedded room. Evening meals by prior arrangement.	£18.50	N	Y	N
Nigel & Lynda Kettle **Tyn Rhos Country House** **Seion** **Llanddeiniolen** **Caernarfon** **LL55 3AE** **Tel: (01248) 670489** **Fax 01248 670079** **Open: ALL YEAR (Excl. Xmas)** **Map Ref No. 40**	Nearest Road: A.487, A.5 Tyn Rhos is a special place, set in a splendid location on the wide-open plain between Snowdonia & the sea. Once a working farmhouse, it has now been transformed into a country house of great charm & comfort. Each individually designed bedroom has been furnished to the highest of standards. 2 delightful rooms, situated on the ground floor, have patio doors opening onto the garden. Lynda is an award-winning cook who prepares wonderful dishes using own & fresh local produce. Quality allied to exceptional value are the keynotes at Tyn Rhos. Children over 6.	£28.00 *see PHOTO over* CREDIT CARD VISA M'CARD AMEX	Y	Y	N
Patricia Clayton **Trefaes Guest House** **Y Maes** **Criccieth LL52 0AE** **Tel: (01766) 523204** **Fax 01766 523013** **Open: ALL YEAR (Excl. Xmas)** **Map Ref No. 41**	Nearest Road: A.497 An elegant Edwardian house on the edge of Criccieth Green, with views of the sea and Castle. The 3 comfortable bedrooms have en-suite facilities, T.V., tea/coffee tray & central heating. Quiet lounge for reading, writing & cards, & secluded garden. Great Welsh breakfasts & 'Taste of Wales' evening meals with fish & vegetarian specialities. Parking in grounds. Excellent base for historic sites, sea and walking holidays. Children over 12 please.	£20.00	Y	Y	Y
Mrs Rita Murray **Min-Y-Gaer Hotel** **Porthmadog Road** **Criccieth LL52 OHP** **Tel: (01766) 522151** **Fax 01766 522151** **Open: MAR - OCT** **Map Ref No. 41**	Nearest Road: A.497 A pleasant, licensed house in a quiet residential area, offering very good accommodation in 10 comfortable rooms, of which most have a bathroom en-suite. All have colour T.V. & tea/coffee-making facilities. The hotel enjoys commanding views of Criccieth Castle & the scenic Cardigan Bay coastline, & is only 2 mins' walk from the safe, sandy beach. Car parking on the premises. An ideal base for touring Snowdonia.	£18.00 CREDIT CARD VISA M'CARD AMEX	Y	N	N

Tyn Rhos Country House. Llanddeiniolen.

		rate from £ per person	children taken	evening meals	animals taken

Nick & Margaret Smyth **Pentre Bach** **Llwyngwril** **Dolgellau LL37 2JU** **Tel: (01341) 250294** **Fax 01341 250885** Open: **ALL YEAR (Excl. Xmas)** **Map Ref No. 65**	Nearest Road: A.493 Large, warm, peaceful farmhouse in pretty coastal village, with BR station. Delicious food prepared by Mid-Wales Cook of the Year 1994, including free-range eggs, organic produce & herbs. There are 3 attractive en-suite guest rooms. In Snowdonia National Park, the adjacent mountains offer walks through history from Stone Age to present day. Also, sea, forests, rivers, steam railways, castles, pony trekking or relaxing on uncrowded beaches.	£20.00 🚭 *see PHOTO over* CREDIT CARD VISA M'CARD	Y	Y	N
Mr & Mrs Dewi Jones **Fronoleu Farm** **Tabor** **Dolgellau LL40 2PS** **Tel: (01341) 422361** Open: **ALL YEAR** **Map Ref No. 67**	Nearest Road: A.470 Secretly secluded, yet overlooking the magnificent Mawddach Estuary, stands Fronoleu. This tranquil family-run hotel combines traditional warmth with modern comfort. Log-fired, welcoming lounges, an award-winning restaurant & 10 superbly facilitated bedrooms all ensure a pleasant & memorable experience. A delightful hotel & the perfect location for a relaxing break.	£14.50	Y	Y	Y
Gillian & Eric Newton **Davies** **Noddfa Hotel** **Lower Road** **Harlech LL46 2UB** **Tel: (01766) 780043** **Fax 01766 781105** Open: **ALL YEAR** **Map Ref No. 42**	Nearest Road: A.496 A Victorian country house situated within the National Park, with superb views of Snowdon, Tremadog Bay & Harlech Castle. 4 comfortable rooms (2 en-suite, T.V.). Extensive menu, licensed. Gillian & Eric will be delighted to talk about both the medieval weaponry, displayed in the bar, & the history of Harlech Castle, & to give archery lessons in the hotel grounds. Very close to the Castle, beach, indoor swimming pool & theatre. An ideal touring base.	£18.00 CREDIT CARD VISA M'CARD	Y	Y	N
Ms. Rosemary Abas **Bwthyn** **Brynafon** **Menai Bridge** **Isle of Anglesey** **LL59 5HA** **Tel: (01248) 713119** Open: **ALL YEAR** **Map Ref No. 68**	Nearest Road: A.5, A.55 Bwthyn ('dear little house' in Welsh) is in a charming Victorian terrace, 1/2 a minute from the beautiful Menai Strait, close by Telford's famous Suspension Bridge. 2 warm, welcoming, tastefully fitted en-suite double bedrooms & a cosy lounge to relax in (with colour T.V. & well-stocked bookshelves), offering character, comfort & a degree of hospitality rarely experienced in such a modestly priced guest house. Scrumptious home-cooking. An excellent touring base for the coast, castles & Snowdonia's mountains.	£12.00 🚭	N	Y	N
Marian Roberts **Plas Trefarthen** **Brynsiencyn** **Isle of Anglesey** **LL61 6SZ** **Tel: (01248) 430379** Open: **ALL YEAR** **Map Ref No. 43**	Nearest Road: A.4080 Plas Trefarthen is a large Georgian house standing in 200 acres of land on the shores of the Menai Straits, with uninterrupted views of Caernarfon Castle & the Snowdonia mountain range. An ideal touring base, close to Plas Newydd, Penrhyn Castle National Trust & the Sea Zoo. Elegant rooms with en-suite bathrooms, colour T.V. & tea/coffee facilities. A warm Welsh welcome awaits you from Marian Roberts. Excellent self-catering accommodation available.	£20.00 CREDIT CARD VISA M'CARD	Y	N	N

Pentre Bach. Llwyngwril.

Llwydiarth Fawr Farm. Anglesey.

Wales
Gwynedd

		rate from £ per person	children taken	evening meals	animals taken
Tony & Gina Hirst **Hafod Country House** **Cemaes Bay** **Isle of Anglesey** **LL67 0DS** **Tel: (01407) 710500** **Open: MAR - NOV** **Map Ref No. 44**	Nearest Road: A.5025 A spacious Edwardian house standing in an acre of garden. Set in peaceful surroundings, with superb sea & mountain views. Only a 10-min. walk to the village, with its picturesque harbour & sandy beach. 3 delightful, en-suite bedrooms, with panoramic views, T.V. & tea/coffee facilities. Large, elegant lounge & separate dining room. Garden with tennis & croquet. Renowned for excellent food. Licensed. Nearby is golf, bird sanctuary, lake & sea fishing.	£18.50	Y	Y	N
Mrs Jane Bown **Drws Y Coed** **Llannerch-Y-Medd** **Isle of Anglesey** **LL71 8AD** **Tel: (01248) 470473** **Open: JAN - NOV** **Map Ref No. 66**	Nearest Road: A.5025, A.5 With wonderful panoramic views of Snowdonia, this beautifully appointed farmhouse, on a 550-acre working beef, sheep, arable farm, is situated in peaceful wooded countryside in the centre of Anglesey. Beautifully decorated & furnished en-suite bedrooms, with T.V., clock/ radio, hairdryer & tea tray. Central heating, & log fires. Delicious breakfasts served. Games room available. Lovely private walks. Visitors return year after year to enjoy the warm hospitality.	£18.00	Y	N	N
Mrs Margaret Hughes **Llwydiarth Fawr Farm** **Llanerchymedd** **Isle of Anglesey** **LL71 8DF** **Tel:(01248) 470321/470540** **Open: ALL YEAR** **Map Ref No. 45**	Nearest Road: A.5 Secluded Georgian mansion set in 800 acres of woodland & farmland, with lovely open views. Ideal touring base for the island's coastline, Snowdonia & North Wales coast. 5 delightfully furnished bedrooms with en-suite facilities & T.V.. Full central heating, log fires. Enjoy a taste of Wales with delicious country cooking using farm & local produce. Personal attention & a warm Welsh welcome to guests, who will enjoy the scenic walks & private fishing. Convenient for Holyhead-to-Ireland crossings.	£22.50 *see PHOTO over* CREDIT CARD VISA M'CARD	Y	Y	N
Eileen & Peter Rigby **White Lodge Hotel** **9 Neville Crescent** **Central Promenade** **Llandudno LL30 1AT** **Tel: (01492) 877713** **Open: MAR - NOV** **Map Ref No. 46**	Nearest Road: A.55, A.470 Situated on the promenade of this beautiful Victorian holiday resort. All of the attractive bedrooms have en-suite bathrooms & tea/coffee-making facilities & colour T.V.s. There is a small bar & a pleasant lounge, facing the sea, for guests' use. 'White Lodge' offers an ideal touring centre for those day trips to Conway Castle, Caernarfon Castle, Chester or the mountains & valleys of Snowdonia.	£21.50 CREDIT CARD AMEX	Y	Y	N
Kate Aplin **Cae'r Berllan** **Betws Road** **Nr. Betws-Y-Coed** **Llanrwst LL26 0PP** **Tel: (01492) 640027** **Open: MAR - OCT (& Dec)** **Map Ref No. 47**	Nearest Road: A.5, A.470 Tranquility reigns in this magnificent 16th-century country house with massive oak beams and family antiques, set in beautiful private gardens in the Conwy Valley near Betws-Y-Coed. An ideal base for Snowdonia and North Wales. Luxurious beamed bedrooms, private facilities, T.V., etc. Wonderful views from every window. Renowned for high standards of international cuisine, served in the relaxed atmosphere of the inglenook dining room. The warmest of welcomes awaits you.	£25.00 *see PHOTO over* CREDIT CARD VISA M'CARD	Y	Y	Y

Cae'r Berllan. Betws-y-Coed.

Hafod House, Trefriw.

Wales
Gwynedd & Powys

	rate from £ per person	children taken	evening meals	animals taken

Jack & Mary Marrow **Firs Cottage** **Maenan** **Llanrwst LL26 0YR** **Tel: (01492) 660244** **Open: ALL YEAR (Excl. Xmas)** **Map Ref No. 48**	Nearest Road: A.470 A 17th-century Welsh cottage & comfortable family home, situated in the beautiful Conway Valley, with excellent views to the hills. Firs Cottage offers 3 attractively furnished rooms, as well as a lovely garden in which to relax & plan visits to the many North Wales attractions, which are all within easy reach. Good food & a warm Welsh welcome will make for a memorable holiday.	£14.50	Y	N	Y
Norman T. Barker **Hafod House** **Trefriw** **LL27 0RQ** **Tel: (01492) 640029** **Fax 01492 641351** **Open: ALL YEAR** **Map Ref No. 49**	Nearest Road: A.5, A.55 Sympathetically restored to a high standard, this 17th-century farmhouse, located in a peaceful, edge-of-village setting in the heart of the spectacular Conway Valley near Betws-Y-Coed, offers guests 7 fully equipped, warm, comfortable bedrooms, all with en-suite bathrooms. A superb restaurant & award-winning cuisine from the chef/proprietor. Tour the whole of North Wales from this central location in Snowdonia National Park. A special all-year-round price, for Best Bed & Breakfast clients, of £24.50 p.p..	£24.50 *see PHOTO over* CREDIT CARD VISA M'CARD AMEX	N	Y	N
Lizzie & Richard Tregarthen **Ty Mawr** **Llanegryn** **Tywyn** **LL36 9SY** **Tel: (01654) 710507** **Open: ALL YEAR** **Map Ref No. 53**	Nearest Road: A.493 With mountains to the east & sea to the west, Ty Mawr snugs into the south-facing slope of the Dysnni Valley. Total peace & quiet. There are private entrances to each ground-floor, en-suite bedroom, which also have tea/coffee-making facilities. Enjoy meals in the conservatory overlooking the garden & valley. Evening meals by arrangement. Numerous venues of interest, & local heritage. Links golf at Aberdovey.	£20.00 🚭 *see PHOTO over*	N	Y	N

Powys

Mrs Mary Cole **'Dolycoed'** **Talyllyn** **Brecon LD3 7SY** **Tel: (01874) 658666** **Open: ALL YEAR** **Map Ref No. 50**	Nearest Road: A.40 Dolycoed, built at the turn of the century, retains many of its interesting original features. Standing in a sheltered position in Brecon Beacons National Park, it offers a warm, friendly, homely welcome to all. 3 comfortable guest bedrooms, with radio & tea/coffee makers, & a guests' lounge with colour T.V.. Many outdoor activities nearby: pony trekking, riding, fishing, watersports & walking.	£15.00	Y	N	Y
Nancy M. Jones **Ty-Isaf Farm** **Erwood** **Builth Wells LD2 3SZ** **Tel: (01982) 560607** **Open: ALL YEAR** **Map Ref No. 52**	Nearest Road: A.470 Ty-Isaf Farm, situated in the attractive village of Erwood, offers accommodation in 3 comfortably furnished rooms with modern amenities & tea/coffee-making facilities. Plentiful English or Continental breakfasts are served. Special diets, & packed lunches provided by arrangement. Guests may relax in the cosy lounge, with T.V. throughout the day. An ideal base for touring.	£13.00	Y	Y	Y

Ty Mawr. Llanegryn.

Wales
Powys

	Nearest Road	rate from £ per person	children taken	evening meals	animals taken
Mr & Mrs P. K. Cracroft **Tretower House** **Tretower** **Crickhowell NP8 1RF** Tel: (01874) 730225 Open: ALL YEAR Map Ref No. 54	Nearest Road: A.40 Charming old family house set in the beautiful Usk Valley, with views of the Black Mountains. A warm welcome awaits at Tretower House, where there are 2 comfortable rooms, 1 en-suite & 1 with private bathroom. Each has tea/coffee-making facilities. Beautiful garden & plenty of walks, pony trekking, fishing & golf locally. Ideal first stop as you enter Wales.	£18.00 🚭	Y	N	N
Peter & Olwen Roberts **York House** **Hardwicke Road** **Cusop** **Hay-on-Wye HR3 5QX** Tel: (01497) 820705 Open: ALL YEAR Map Ref No. 55	Nearest Road: A.438 Peter and Olwen Roberts welcome you to their traditional Victorian guest house quietly situated in beautiful gardens on the edge of Hay. Sunny mountain views are enjoyed by the well-appointed rooms, mostly en-suite. Ideal for a relaxing holiday spent browsing in the world-famous bookshops, exploring the National Park and Kilvert country, or just enjoying the freshly prepared home cooking. Private parking. Children over 8 please.	£20.00 🚭 CREDIT CARD VISA M'CARD AMEX	Y	Y	Y
Mrs Heather Hood **Pilleth Court** **Whitton** **Knighton** **LD7 1NP** Tel: (01547) 560272 Open: ALL YEAR (Excl. Xmas) Map Ref No. 56	Nearest Road: A.488 An Elizabethan house, with all its character & atmosphere retained. 3 delightful guest rooms, 1 en-suite, with radio & tea/coffee-making facilities. Set in 600 acres, it is surrounded by marvellous, unspoilt countryside. The site of the Battle of Pilleth & a 12th-century church are close by. A wonderful base for walking or touring. Evening meals, cooked with 'flair', are available by arrangement. Children over 9 welcome.	£16.00	Y	Y	N
Mrs Ceinwen Davies **Trewythen Farm** **Llandinam** **SY17 5BQ** Tel: (01686) 688444 Fax 01686 688444 Open: APR - NOV Map Ref No. 62	Nearest Road: A.470 A warm Welsh welcome awaits at Trewythen, this mixed working farm which stands in quiet scenic surroundings, where an abundance of wildlife can be seen. The farmhouse offers superb bedrooms, with en-suite/private bathroom & tea-making facilities. A separate guests' dining room. The lounge (with its beams) has a log fire for the cooler evening as well as a colour T.V.. Evening meals & animals by arrangement. Golf, fishing, pony trekking & lakes nearby.	£18.00 *see PHOTO over*	Y	Y	N
Leslie & Sylvia Knott **The Ffaldau Country** **House** **Llandegley** **Llandrindod Wells** **LD1 5UD** Tel: (01597) 851421 Open: ALL YEAR Map Ref No. 57	Nearest Road: A.44 A picturesque, listed, c.1500 cruck house set in 1 1/2 acres of pretty garden. Country-cottage bedrooms with en-suite/private facilities & thoughtful extra touches. Relax in the sitting room, cosy smoker's bar, with a log fire, or non-smoking room with books, T.V. & board games. Superb breakfasts, with unequalled selection, & evening meals served in the oak-beamed dining room full of romantic charm & family history. Meals are prepared from quality produce & home-grown vegetables. Irresistible desserts may tempt you. Selection of quality wines. Children over 10.	£20.00 CREDIT CARD VISA M'CARD	Y	Y	N

Trewythen. Llandinam.

Guidfa House. Llandrindod Wells.

Wales
Powys

		rate from £ per person	children taken	evening meals	animals taken
Anne & Tony Millan **Guidfa House** **Crossgates** **Llandrindod Wells LD1 6RF** **Tel: (01597) 851241** **Fax 01597 851875** **Open: ALL YEAR** **Map Ref No. 58**	Nearest Road: A.483, A.44 Licensed Georgian guest house, situated in an ideal location for touring lakes, mountains, national parks & the coast. The bedrooms are all comfortable & spacious, most en-suite, all with colour T.V. & tea/coffee-making facilities. A ground-floor room is also available. Meals are prepared by Anne, who is Cordon-Bleu-trained. Dinner is a set menu, but special diets/requests can always be catered for with a little prior notice. *see PHOTO over* CREDIT CARD VISA M'CARD	£21.00	N	Y	N
Mrs Gaynor Bright **Little Brompton Farm** **Montgomery** **SY15 6HY** **Tel: (01686) 668371** **Open: ALL YEAR** **Map Ref No. 59**	Nearest Road: B.4385, A.489 Robert & Gaynor welcome you to this charming 17th-century farmhouse, situated on this working farm. The house has much original character, with beautiful old oak beams. Furnished with traditional antiques. Pretty bedrooms, with en-suite or private bathrooms, enhanced by quality antiques. T.V. on request. Home-cooking is a speciality (meals by arrangement). Offa's Dyke runs through the farm. On the B.4385, 2 miles east of the Georgian town of Montgomery. Come & relax in peaceful, stress-free countryside.	£18.00	Y	Y	Y
Paul & Maureen Marriott **A Country Manor** **Dysserth Hall** **Powis Castle** **Welshpool** **SY21 8RQ** **Tel: (01938) 552153** **Open: MAR - NOV** **Map Ref No. 60**	Nearest Road: A.483, A.490 Dysserth Hall is a delightful Georgian manor house standing in the peaceful countryside of Mid-Wales, & a short walk from Powis Castle (N.T.). The accommodation is very comfortable, with antique furnishings. 4 bedrooms are individually decorated, 1 with 5' antique mahogany & 1 twin with Victorian brass beds. All have magnificent views, electric blankets, bathrobes & trays. A 3-course dinner by arrangement. Paul & Maureen are most helpful hosts, & can arrange golf, fishing, riding, shooting. A grass tennis court. Children over 8.	£17.00	Y	Y	N
Mrs Sue Jones **Lower Trelydan** **Farmhouse** **Guilsfield** **Welshpool** **SY21 9PH** **Tel: (01938) 553105** **Fax 01938 553105** **Open: ALL YEAR** **Map Ref No. 61**	Nearest Road: A.483, A.490 Graham & Sue welcome you to their wonderful, award-winning black-&-white farmhouse, set on their working farm & listed for its history & beauty. The bedrooms are tastefully furnished, with en-suite facilities & colour T.V. (on request). An oak-beamed lounge, & a dining room where home cooking is a speciality. Also, a licensed bar. Powis Castle & many beauty spots are nearby, as well as leisure activities & walks. Relax in this lovely home, & capture the atmosphere of 4 centuries of history in this outstanding house. Self-catering available in a new barn conversion. *see PHOTO over*	£18.00	Y	Y	N

When booking your accommodation please mention
The Best Bed & Breakfast

Lower Trelydan Farm. Guilsfield.

Towns & Counties Index

615

Towns & Counties Index

Towns & Counties Index

Town	County	Country
Lincoln	Lincolnshire	England
Little Shelford	Cambridgeshire	England
Liverpool	Merseyside	England
Lizard	Cornwall	England
Llandinam	Powys	Wales
Llandrindod Wells	Powys	Wales
Llandudno	Gwynedd	Wales
Llanrwst	Gwynedd	Wales
Llanwrda	Dyfed	Wales
Lochearnhead	Perthshire	Scotland
Lochgilphead	Argyll	Scotland
Long Hanborough	Oxfordshire	England
Longhope	Gloucestershire	England
Looe	Cornwall	England
Louth	Lincolnshire	England
Ludlow	Shropshire	England
Lydney	Gloucestershire	England
Lyme Regis	Dorset	England
Lymington	Hampshire	England
Lyndhurst	Hampshire	England
Lynton	Devon	England
Macclesfield	Cheshire	England
Maidenhead	Berkshire	England
Malmesbury	Wiltshire	England
Malpas	Cheshire	England
Malton	Yorkshire	England
Malvern	Worcestershire	England
Manningtree	Essex	England
Manorbier	Dyfed	Wales
Mansfield	Nottinghamshire	England
Margate	Kent	England
Market Drayton	Shropshire	England
Marlborough	Wiltshire	England
Marlow	Buckinghamshire	England
Mayfield	Sussex	England
Melrose	Roxburghshire	Scotland
Melton Mowbray	Leicestershire	England
Mere	Wiltshire	England
Merthyr Tydfil	Glamorgan	Wales
Mevagissey	Cornwall	England
Minchinhampton	Gloucestershire	England
Minehead	Somerset	England
Mitcheldean	Gloucestershire	England
Moffat	Dumfriesshire	Scotland
Mold	Clwyd	Wales
Montgomery	Powys	Wales
Morchard Bishop	Devon	England
Moreton-in-Marsh	Gloucestershire	England
Moretonhampstead	Devon	England
Morpeth	Northumberland	England
Nantwich	Cheshire	England
New Milton	Hampshire	England
Newbury	Berkshire	England
Newcastle-upon-Tyne	Tyne & Wear	England
Newent	Gloucestershire	England
Newport	Gwent	Wales
Newport-on-Tay	Fifeshire	Scotland
Newquay	Cornwall	England
Newton Abbot	Devon	England
North Berwick	Lothian	Scotland
North Walsham	Norfolk	England
Northwich	Cheshire	England
Norwich	Norfolk	England
Nottingham	Nottinghamshire	England
Nuneaton	Warwickshire	England
Oakham	Leicestershire	England
Osmington	Dorset	England
Oswestry	Shropshire	England
Otley	Suffolk	England
Oundle	Northamptonshire	England
Oxford	Oxfordshire	England
Oxhill	Warwickshire	England
Padstow	Cornwall	England
Painswick	Gloucestershire	England
Par	Cornwall	England
Penrith	Cumbria	England
Penryn	Cornwall	England
Penshurst	Kent	England
Penzance	Cornwall	England
Perth	Perthshire	Scotland
Petersfield	Hampshire	England
Pickering	Yorkshire	England
Pitlochry	Perthshire	Scotland
Plymouth	Devon	England
Polperro	Cornwall	England
Pontypool	Gwent	Wales
Portsmouth	Hampshire	England
Pulborough	Sussex	England
Reading	Berkshire	England
Redditch	Worcestershire	England
Redhill	Surrey	England
Redmile	Nottinghamshire	England
Redruth	Cornwall	England
Reigate	Surrey	England
Renfrewshire/Glasgow	Renfrewshire	Scotland
Retford	Nottinghamshire	England
Richmond	Yorkshire	England
Ringwood	Hampshire	England
Ripon	Yorkshire	England
Romsey	Hampshire	England
Ropley	Hampshire	England
Ross-on-Wye	Herefordshire	England
Rotherham	Yorkshire	England
Roxton	Bedfordshire	England
Royston	Cambridgeshire	England
Rugby	Warwickshire	England
Ruthin	Clwyd	Wales
Rye	Sussex	England
Saffron Walden	Essex	England
Salcombe	Devon	England
Salisbury	Wiltshire	England
Sandy	Bedfordshire	England
Sandy	Cambridgeshire	England
Scarborough	Yorkshire	England
Seaford	Sussex	England
Sedbergh	Cumbria	England
Sevenoaks	Kent	England
Shaftesbury	Dorset	England

617

Towns & Counties Index

Recommendations / Complaints

Thank you for taking the trouble to supply this information .
We value your comments & will take appropriate action where necessary.
We regret that we are unable to reply to you individually.

Proprietors _____

House Name _____

Address _____

_____

_____

General information about your
stay, the house & hosts etc.

_____

_____

_____

_____

_____

_____

_____

Your Name _____

Address _____

_____

Reply to: W.W.B.B.A. P.O. Box 2070.
London. W12 8QW

Recommendations / Complaints

*Thank you for taking the trouble to supply this information .
We value your comments & will take appropriate action where necessary.
We regret that we are unable to reply to you individually.*

Proprietors_____

House Name_____

Address_____

_____

_____

**General Information about your
stay, the house & hosts etc.**

_____

_____

_____

_____

_____

_____

_____

Your Name_____

Address_____

_____

_____

**Reply to: W.W.B.B.A. P.O. Box 2070,
London. W12 8QW**

Recommendations / Complaints

Thank you for taking the trouble to supply this information .
We value your comments & will take appropriate action where necessary.
We regret that we are unable to reply to you individually.

Proprietors _____

House Name _____

Address _____

_____

_____

**General information about your
stay, the house & hosts etc.**

_____

_____

_____

_____

_____

_____

_____

Your Name _____

Address _____

_____

**Reply to:W.W.B.B.A. P.O. Box 2070,
London. W12 8QW**

Recommendations / Complaints

Thank you for taking the trouble to supply this information .
We value your comments & will take appropriate action where necessary.
We regret that we are unable to reply to you individually.

Proprietors _____

House Name _____

Address _____

_____

_____

General information about your
stay, the house & hosts etc.

_____

_____

_____

_____

_____

_____

_____

Your Name _____

Address _____

_____

Reply to: W.W.B.B.A. P.O. Box 2070.
London. W12 8QW

Recommendations / Complaints

Thank you for taking the trouble to supply this information .
We value your comments & will take appropriate action where necessary.
We regret that we are unable to reply to you individually.

Proprietors _____

House Name _____

Address _____

_____

_____

General information about your
stay, the house & hosts etc.

_____

_____

_____

_____

_____

_____

_____

Your Name _____

Address _____

_____

Reply to: W.W.B.B.A. P.O. Box 2070.
London. W12 8QW